Developmental/Adapted Physical Education

Making Ability Count

Fourth Edition

Related Benjamin Cummings Kinesiology Titles

Anshel, *Sport Psychology: from Theory to Practice*, Fourth Edition (2003)

Bishop, *Fitness through Aerobics*, Fifth Edition (2002)

Darst/Pangrazi, *Dynamic Physical Education for Secondary School Students*, Fourth Edition (2002)

Darst/Pangrazi, *Lesson Plans for Dynamic Physical Education for Secondary School Students*, Fourth Edition (2002)

Freeman, *Physical Education and Sport in a Changing Society*, Sixth Edition (2001)

Fronske, *Teaching Cues for Sport Skills*, Second Edition (2001)

Fronske/Wilson, *Teaching Cues for Basic Sports Skills for Elementary and Middle School Children* (2002)

Harris/Pittman/Waller/Dark, *Social Dance from Dance a While*, Second Edition (2003)

Housh/Housh/Johnson, *Introduction to Exercise Science*, Second Edition (2003)

Lacy/Hastad, *Measurement and Evaluation in Physical Education and Exercise Science*, Fourth Edition (2003)

Mosston/Ashworth, *Teaching Physical Education*, Fifth Edition (2002)

Pangrazi, *Dynamic Physical Education for Elementary School Children*, Thirteenth Edition (2001)

Pangrazi, *Lesson Plans for Dynamic Physical Education for Elementary School Children*, Thirteenth Edition (2001)

Plowman/Smith, *Exercise Physiology for Health, Fitness, and Performance*, Second Edition (2003)

Powers/Dodd, *Total Fitness and Wellness*, Third Edition (2003)

Powers/Dodd, *Total Fitness and Wellness*, Brief Edition (2003)

Schmottlach/McManama, *Physical Education Activity Handbook*, Tenth Edition (2002)

Silva/Stevens, *Psychological Foundations of Sport* (2002)

Check out these and other Benjamin Cummings kinesiology titles at: www.aw.com/bc.

Developmental/Adapted Physical Education

Making Ability Count

Fourth Edition

Michael Horvat Ed.D. University of Georgia

Carl Eichstaedt Ph.D. Emeritus, Illinois State University

Leonard Kalakian Ph.D. Emeritus, Minnesota State University–Mankato

Ron Croce Ph.D. University of New Hampshire

Benjamin Cummings

San Francisco   Boston   New York
Cape Town   Hong Kong   London   Madrid   Mexico City
Montreal   Munich   Paris   Singapore   Sydney   Tokyo   Toronto

Publisher: Daryl Fox
Acquisitions Editor: Deirdre McGill
Publishing Assistant: Michelle Cadden
Managing Editor: Wendy Earl
Production Editor: Michele Mangelli
Copyeditor: Sally Peyrefitte
Cover and Text design: Brad Greene
Manufacturing Buyer: Stacey Weinberger
Marketing Manager: Sandra Lindelof

Cover photography courtesy of OSSUR, USA.

Library of Congress Cataloging-in-Publication Data

Developmental/adapted physical education : making ability count /
Michael Horvat ... [et al.].
     p. cm.
Prev. ed. main entry under Carl B. Eichstaedt.
Includes bibliographical references and index.
    ISBN 0-205-31391-4 (alk. paper)
  1. Physical education for people with disabilities--United States. 2.
Mainstreaming in education--United States. I. Horvat, Michael A., 1947-

    GV445 .E34 2002
    796.04'56--dc21   2002067678

ISBN 0-205-31391-4
1 2 3 4 5 6 7 8 9 10—DVA—06 05 04 03 02
www.aw.com/bc

This book is dedicated to my wife Glada and wonderful children Ian, Kala, and Michael who light up my life.

MH

I would like to dedicate my part in this book to the "kids next door"—my two youngest grandchildren, Jackson and Lanie Whelpley.

CE

To my mom (in memory) and dad, who taught me the importance of self-respect and the imperative of hard work and doing what is right; and to all my colleagues and students—past, present, and future—who have shown me the way.

RC

TABLE OF CONTENTS

*D*evelopmental/Adapted Physical Education: Making Ability Count serves not only as the title of this book but also as its underlying statement of philosophy. The fourth edition was undertaken to provide a reliable and updated source of detailed information regarding the ever-expanding focus on physical activity for individuals with disabilities. Since 1986, extensive changes have occurred in methodology, teaching techniques, and legal requirements for individuals with disabilities. These educational changes have evolved from both empirical and experimental research as well as the impact of federal and state legislation. We are convinced that all physical education curricula and all children will benefit from using a developmental approach.

We realize that the term *developmental* is characterized by an orderly, sequential achievement of milestones that may be affected by genetic inducement as well as experiences and exposure to learning. The universality of human development is founded in the fact that relative ability or disability does *not* have a material impact on the sequence of developmental achievements. Relative ability or disability may, however, affect both the rate of developmental achievement and the potential for ultimate achievement.

Teachers must understand human development as a basis for understanding differences in meeting developmental milestones. When circumstances impede development, the teacher must seek alternative approaches that accommodate the learner's unique needs to facilitate development, restore functioning, or develop functional capabilities. The development of fitness, perception, and motor skills are all essential to developing a sound physical education program.

Throughout the text, we stress that adaptations should be made only to the extent necessary to accommodate the learner's unique developmental needs. Too often, the task of teaching an individual with a disability is perceived in the negative context of what *cannot* be done. The individual is perceived more as a "handicapped" person than as a person who *happens* to have a disability. In contrast, the idea of "making ability count" places the person *before* the disability and shifts the emphasis to what the individual *can* accomplish and accentuates the capabilities of the individual.

As authors and teachers, we receive questions continually from physical education, special education, and elementary classroom teachers on how certain activities should be taught and which activities should be taught to children with disabilities.

We also often hear questions like these:

What can I do to help, and what is contraindicated for these children?

What is acceptable, and what is dangerous?

What are the limitations?

How can activities be modified for children with disabilities in physical education classes?

Today's physical educator must be able to teach all children, including those with disabilities. In addition, the teacher must know how to perform and use assessment information, write appropriate motor and fitness programs, suggest proper placement, and how to implement various teaching methods.

We continually emphasize using the team approach, incorporating special educators, physicians, administrators, therapists, parents, and children into a smoothly functioning unit. The physical educator must be able to use the vocabulary of the other professionals on the team. Without a thorough background in and understanding of various conditions, the physical educator risks being excluded (overtly or covertly) from the important opportunity to make decisions concerning placement.

Finally, physical educators must never lose sight of the overall role they play in the total development of each child who comes under their guidance. The physical, emotional, social, and cognitive benefits that accrue from positive experiences of physical activity should never be underestimated. No child should ever be excluded from participation in physical education and sport. The fourth edition of *Developmental/Adapted Physical Education: Making Ability Count* was written with these basic tenets continually in mind.

Our years as public school physical education teachers, adapted physical education teachers, and coaches, in addition to our experience in higher education, has prepared us to write a text that is knowledge based and field tested. In addition, we have all taught adapted physical education courses, have supervised clinical and practicum experiences, and have an understanding of what the teacher needs to be successful in teaching or coaching individuals with disabilities.

Acknowledgement

This textbook could not have been written without the insight and assistance of many individuals. We are especially grateful to colleagues who provided editorial comments throughout the project and encouraged us to continue. We are also indebted to the coaches, students, and athletes with disabilities who have taught us about individual differences and reaching for new heights.

We also wish to acknowledge all the reviewers who forced us to think and explain things more clearly. We extend special thanks to Peter Aufsesser and Paul Bishop for their comments and suggestions, to Dr. Larry Verity for his input on the diabetes chapter, and to Vince Ramsey and Bruce Blasch for their suggestions on the chapter covering visual impairments. The contributions of these professionals were essential to the project. In addition, we thank the agencies and individuals who provided photos, especially Joni Schneider of OSSUR and the parents and children of the Pediatric Exercise and Motor Development Clinic at the University of Georgia. Their support is greatly appreciated.

We also want to thank Melanie Blakeman for the hours of typing and patience in the revision of this project. We appreciate her assistance and that of Wei Bien and Karen Smail in developing the instructor's manual.

Finally, we thank the publishing team at Benjamin Cummings and Wendy Earl Productions, especially Michele Mangelli and Michelle Cadden for their patience in completing this project.

Michael Horvat
Carl Eichstaedt
Leonard Kalakian
Ron Croce

Section I

Introduction: Physical Education for Children with Disabilities

The preliminary chapters of this book provide basic information concerning legal mandates and placement of children with disabilities into physical education. The initial steps in providing services for children with disabilities are described in chapters that address the collaborative programming team; the parent-teacher team; assessment and evaluation; cognitive and perceptual development; and development of physical fitness. With this information, you should be able to

1. understand the basis for physical education services at the federal, state, and local level

2. understand how to develop an individualized education plan (IEP) and what it means to place children with disabilities in the least restrictive environment or most appropriate environment

3. understand the roles of various professionals and parents in the educational process

4. understand the process of evaluation and assessment in program planning and implementation

5. understand and apply the concepts of physical fitness, perceptual development, and motor development to teaching children with disabilities

CHAPTER 1

But First I Have Some Questions, Professor

The professor looked at her watch and put away her notes. The students had picked up their backpacks and stored their course outlines and notes from today's lecture. The first day was over. She felt this was going to be a good group. Several students had volunteered. Others had asked insightful questions. One young man told of his experience as a volunteer for a local Special Olympics team. Another shared that she had a brother who had died from Duchenne muscular dystrophy. One young woman expressed concern about the impact of teaching physical education in a full inclusion setting and wondered whether she would really be able to effectively teach children with disabilities. The class wasn't at all hesitant about asking questions such as these:

- You mean children with disabilities haven't always been in school? Why and when did this come about?
- How do I know whether a condition qualifies as a disability? Who decides?
- If I'm teaching regular physical education, what kinds of disabilities might some of my children have?
- What are some causes of disabilities?
- Is physical education really required for ALL children with ALL types of disabilities?
- Who decides whether a child with a disability is going to be in my physical education class?
- How will I know children with disabilities' physical education needs?
- What if one of my children is blind? Can I say things like, "See you later?"
- Sometimes kids (and adults) can be insensitive, even cruel. Will children in my regular class (and my colleagues) be accepting of children they perceive as "different"? What can I do?
- What do all these terms mean?

After returning to the office, the professor thought that, yes, there were many questions to answer regarding individuals with disabilities and their ability to participate in physical activity, sports, and recreation. When these students graduate, they may be faced with the challenge to provide exciting and demanding physical activity opportunities for individuals with disabilities in a variety of settings. From there, the professor's thoughts turned to fine-tuning the next day's lecture and discussion for the Adapted Physical Education class.

This chapter focuses on questions that you may want to ask, or at least are thinking about, as you start your experience in adapted physical education. When confronted by new and challenging situations, you need to know where any given new situation might lead.

We all tend to be more inclined to want to ask questions when we face new situations that seem relatively removed from our previous experiences. However, the more we need to know, the more fearful we may be about exposing our perceived inadequacies. As a physical education teacher, you may be particularly concerned about your responsibility to develop and implement programs for children with disabilities.

At the outset of this book, let us consider some important initial questions. As concerns arise in the course of your class experience, we anticipate that your questions will be encouraged and welcomed. Be assured there is far less risk in asking a question than in allowing a possible harmful situation to develop because your question went unasked.

■ You mean children with disabilities haven't always been in school? Why and when did all this come about?

Until relatively recently, many children with disabilities were not merely isolated from regular school programs—in many cases, they were excluded from school entirely. Parents of children with disabilities became accustomed to "Sorry, but" excuses for their child's ineligibility for public education: "Sorry, but . . . your child has too serious a behavior problem . . . we are not able to provide special services for children with severe mental retardation . . . our school buildings are not designed to accommodate children who use wheelchairs." Until recently, parents had little alternative but to accept explanations without recourse. Whereas well-to-do parents were able to provide their children with private education at personal expense, parents who were unable to afford private education often were forced to let their children go without needed services.

In situations where children with disabilities were afforded public learning opportunities, they often were grouped categorically (i.e., segregated) according to disability labels. Such attempts at education, though often well intentioned, typically denied the individuality of children with disabilities. Often, the child's individuality was overshadowed by preconceived notions and stereotypes about the child's disability label. In categorical approaches of this nature, it is the preconceived notions and stereotypes about disability labels, not the individual children's needs, that tend to drive curriculum development. Often, however, children who have the same disability label may well have nothing in common except their shared disability label.

Categorical approaches often are burdened by yet another significant drawback. They tend to focus on the negative—on the disability—which, in turn, focuses on what the child cannot do. Questions about children's needs tend to be formulated around the label, for example, "What are the educational needs of children with cerebral palsy?" The nature of such questions obscures the individuality of the child, who first and foremost is a child and only secondarily, who happens to have the condition cerebral palsy. A better question, one less burdened by labels and stereotypes, might be: "Here is a child who happens to have cerebral palsy. What are the unique, individual educational needs of this child?" (Figure 1.1).

In the 1960s through the 1970s, professional, parental, public, and political dissatisfaction with categorical approaches to special education became a significant catalyst for change. As public opinion from many sectors mounted, new special education laws were proposed and passed, and profound, positive changes began to occur in the educational lives of students with disabilities.

On November 29, 1975, Congress enacted Public Law 94-142, the Education for All Handicapped Children Act. In 1990, a new law was passed changing the name and number of PL 94-142 to PL 101-476, the Individuals with Disabilities Education Act (IDEA). Additionally, PL 101-476 encompassed another law passed by Congress in 1986 (Education of All Handicapped Children Act, PL 99-457) to ensure consistent, nationwide attention to special education in early childhood (birth through 4 years of age). All parts of the original 1975 law remained intact with passage of IDEA (i.e., guarantee of a free, appropriate public education in the least restrictive environment, designation of priority children, and guarantees of due process).

In 1997, Congress revisited and refined IDEA. Refinements include more explicit rights for parents and a provision that all educational rights pass from

Figure 1.1 Focus on ability, not disability.

parent to child upon the child's reaching age 18, provided that the child is deemed mentally competent. The most recent revision is known variously as IDEA 97 and New IDEA. Full significance of the IDEA 97, with a specific view to physical education of children with disabilities, is addressed in Chapter 2.[1]

Through guarantees ensured by IDEA 97, children with disabilities are granted a "free, appropriate public education in the least restrictive environment." *Free* means than a local education agency is obligated by federal law to accept and educate a child with a disability, providing all education at no cost (beyond common taxes paid to support public education) to the parent or guardian. *Appropriate* means that, through valid assessment, the child's education will be individualized to meet her or his unique educational needs. *Least restrictive environment* means that the child cannot be removed arbitrarily from the regular education setting and placed in a segregated environment.

"To the maximum extent appropriate, children with disabilities . . . are educated with children who do not have disabilities; and . . . special classes, separate schooling, or removal of children with disabilities from the regular educational environment occurs only when the nature and severity of the disability is such that education in regular classes cannot be achieved satisfactorily" (p. 135, citing 134 CFR 300.550 [a] and [b]). Today, to be in compliance with the law, schools can place children with dis-

---

[1] The individuals with Disabilities Education Act (IDEA) is scheduled for reauthorization in 2002. As of press time, changes to the existing legislation had not yet been determined.

abilities in modified settings only when the results of individualized assessment justify such placement. Above all, federal legislation, most recently IDEA 97, requires that the child's individual educational need, not a categorical disability grouping, provide the basis for determining educational placement of the child.

■ How do I know whether a condition qualifies as a disability? Who decides?

IDEA 97 lists conditions that the law recognizes as disabilities. Although a child must be recognized as having one of the conditions to become a candidate for special education, the conditions by themselves do not determine specific educational programming for the child. Once the child is deemed eligible for special education services by virtue of disability, the disability, for educational programming purposes, becomes subordinate to the child's assessment-determined individual needs.

The law identifies the following conditions as disabilities:

- autism
- deaf-blindness
- deafness
- hearing impairment
- mental retardation
- multiple disabilities
- orthopedic impairment

- other health impairment
- serious emotional disturbance
- specific learning disability
- speech or language impairment
- traumatic brain injury
- visual impairment, including blindness

Having one of these disabilities serves only to determine that a child qualifies for consideration for special education services; it does not automatically mean a child will receive special education. That determination is to be based solely on need, not on label. Determination of a child's need for special education services, including adapted physical education, typically is made at the local level with direction or assistance from state and federal laws and guidelines.

■ If I'm teaching regular physical education, what kinds of disabilities will I have in my class?

Refer to the above list of disability categories. You may expect to see children from any category in a regular physical education class. Two decades ago, Julien Stein (1979) stated, "The success and effectiveness of programs, activities, and efforts should be based upon numbers of children screened out of—not into—special programs". He suggested that there is a potential to successfully integrate 90–95% of children with disabilities into regular physical education programs. His prediction has largely come to fruition. Over the years, more and more children with disabilities have been placed safely and successfully in regular physical education settings and served by regular physical education teachers. Increasingly, adapted physical education specialists primarily serve children whose disabilities prohibit them from participating in regular physical education classes as well as serving as consultants to physical education teachers in inclusion settings.

■ WHAT ARE SOME CAUSES OF DISABILITIES?

Disabilities may be congenital or acquired. A congenital disability is one that comes with and is apparent at birth. An acquired disability is one that can occur anytime in life following birth. Certain disabilities may not clinically manifest themselves or be diagnosed until sometime after birth, such as muscular dystrophy. Nonetheless, such conditions are considered congenital.

Congenital disabilities can be caused by genetic abnormalities. Down syndrome, a condition that among other manifestations causes mental retardation, is one familiar example. Congenital disabilities can be caused by certain maternal infections during pregnancy. Rubella (German measles) during the first trimester is known to cause cerebral palsy. Ingesting certain intoxicants during pregnancy, including drugs (both legal and illicit), tobacco, and alcohol, can result in birth defects. These are only a few examples. More complete listings and descriptions of congenital disabilities and their causes are found throughout this text.

Acquired disabilities can result from reasons ranging from obvious (e.g., illness or injury) to unknown. Someone might acquire a heart condition from rheumatic fever (disease) or sustain spinal cord damage in a fall (injury). Yet another might develop asthma (unknown cause).

■ IS PHYSICAL EDUCATION REALLY REQUIRED FOR ALL CHILDREN WITH ALL TYPES OF DISABILITIES?

The answer is a qualified yes. IDEA 97 specifies conditions that qualify as disabilities. A child who has a qualifying disability is entitled, at the federal level, to a free, appropriate education (individually designed, if necessary) in the least restrictive environment. IDEA defines special education as "specially designed instruction, at no cost to parents or guardians, to meet the unique needs of a child with a disability, including—(A) instruction conducted in the classroom, in the home, in hospitals and institutions, and in other settings; and (B) instruction in physical education."

The IDEA definition of special education explicitly includes physical education within the definition of special education. Thus, IDEA specifies that physical education is, indeed, special education. Because special education services are the legal right of every qualifying child with a disability, and because physical education is integral to special education, all qualifying children with disabilities are therefore fully entitled to be considered for physical education services. Such services must be provided within the context of the regular curriculum or be individually designed, as needed, and delivered in segregated settings. This is not only a moral and professional obligation; it is the law.

Children who have conditions that do not qualify as disabilities under IDEA may qualify for individualized programming under Section 504 of the Rehabilitation Act of 1973. Section 504 specifies that no person by reason of disability alone "shall . . . be excluded from participation in, denied the benefits of, or be subjected to discrimination under any program receiving Federal financial assistance." Section 504, unlike IDEA, does not rely on disability labels to determine eligibility for special services. Instead, Section 504 specifies that anyone with significant limitations in one or more major life activities is eligible to be considered for special services. Therefore, for example, a person with obesity that is not associated with any legally recognized disability could be eligible for individualized education (including physical education) under Section 504 if the obesity significantly limited the person in any recognized major life activity (e.g., mobility, education, work).

■ WHO DECIDES WHETHER A CHILD WITH A DISABILITY IS GOING TO BE IN MY PHYSICAL EDUCATION CLASS?

Virtually anyone in any given educational setting can make a referral to initiate an inquiry as to whether a child with a disability should receive physical education. You, as a physical education teacher, whether you teach regular or adapted physical education, may be a part of this decision-making process.

Once a child is referred and assessed to identify his or her unique educational needs, IDEA designates who shall be part of the needs assessment and placement determination process. Designees include the following:

- someone representing regular education
- someone representing special education
- someone representing school administration
- parent or guardian
- child (when appropriate)
- any additional person mutually agreed on by the above parties (e.g., school nurse, school psychologist, physical therapist)

Although IDEA does not specify that someone representing physical education, regular or adapted, must be a member of the above team, the law clearly intends that persons with special expertise in educational areas being assessed are to be integral to the decision-making process. Even though the intent of the law is clear, however, parents and teachers need to be vigilant to ensure that physical education is represented whenever the child's physical education is being considered.

■ HOW WILL I KNOW WHAT A CHILD NEEDS IN PHYSICAL EDUCATION?

If you are a regular physical education teacher, keep in mind that children with disabilities are children who first and foremost are children but who happen to have disabilities. Quite generally, children and youth with disabilities and those without disabilities tend to be more alike than different. The vast majority of what good teachers know about educating children and youth without disabilities is directly applicable to children with disabilities. Whenever one allows disability to inordinately stand at the forefront of relationships with the persons who have disabilities, it is easy to lose sight of the reality that people typically are much more alike than different.

If you are an adapted physical education teacher, you will have specialized in the education of persons who have disabilities, and you will be knowledgeable across a spectrum of situations and conditions that may affect a person's physical education attitudes, aptitudes, and experience. You may well be the person to whom the regular physical education teacher comes for consultation about a question concerning a child. When you, as an adapted physical education specialist, have questions, you might consult with a college or university colleague specializing in adapted physical education. Additionally, you will be able to access recent research available on the Internet and in printed publications.

Finally, whenever a child with a disability has physical education needs that are different from those met within the context of the regular curriculum, an individualized education plan (IEP) will be developed. The IEP, where it addresses physical education, will give the physical education teacher direction in meeting the child's unique physical education needs.

■ WHAT IF ONE OF MY CHILDREN IS BLIND? CAN I SAY THINGS LIKE, "SEE YOU LATER?"

Generally, yes. "See you later" quite typically is construed as nothing more than an acknowledgment that two or more people are temporarily parting company. Likewise, generally it is fine to go out for a "run" with a friend who trains in a wheelchair or to say to your friend who is deaf, "I hear you're having a good football season this year." Whenever you are in doubt about something that a person with a disability might be sensitive about, just ask. Most persons with disabilities will respond readily and frankly and empathize with your need to know.

■ SOMETIMES KIDS (AND ADULTS) CAN BE INSENSITIVE, EVEN CRUEL. WILL MY CHILDREN WITHOUT DISABILITIES (AND MY COLLEAGUES) BE ACCEPTING OF CHILDREN THEY PERCEIVE AS "DIFFERENT?" WHAT CAN I DO?

Be the best example possible, avoiding any inclination toward self-righteousness. People would likely, and rightly, perceive such an attitude as condescension.

Be positive in efforts to promote an environment that is fair for all. Try not to look the other way when your intervention might make a positive difference. Try to avoid laughing at remarks or jokes made at another's expense. Indeed, try thoughtfully to intervene. It can be particularly trying when colleagues are the source of questionable remarks and jokes. When you hear remarks and behaviors directed at others, ask yourself, "Is this the way I would want to be thought of, spoken about, or treated?"

Try to avoid refering to children with disabilities as "special." Many persons with disabilities do not want or appreciate the "special" designation. "Special" has a habit of pushing to the forefront that one part of the person's being which sets her or him apart, obscuring the many more things the person may have in common with others.

Further, do not be overly indulgent toward or accepting of behaviors among children who have disabilities that, were it not for disability, you might find irritating or unacceptable. Such a double standard is not helpful to the person in question and serves only to perpetuate the objectionable behavior. The presence of disability, by itself, is not grounds for expecting less from your child.

■ WHAT DO ALL THESE TERMS MEAN?

Such terms as *adapted, developmental, rehabilitation* or *functional* can be confusing. In this book, we use the term *adapted* when there is a need to change or modify the setting, equipment, or an instructional technique. But not all children require adaptations to be successful in physical education. Some may not possess the motor capabilities or strength to complete a task; these children require a *developmental* approach that addresses their needs at their level of functioning and brings them to age-expected standards. Other children may lose function through accident, illness, or injury; for these children, physical education can be a means to restore or *rehabilitate* their functioning. Lastly, *functional* skills describe skills that the child can use in home and community settings. Examples of functional skills include walking and play skills.

CHAPTER SUMMARY

1. Students who are new to adapted physical education often ask questions like those addressed in this chapter. Many people, including some teachers, apply labels and stereotypes to people with disabilities, allowing the disability to obscure the person's individuality and unique needs.

2. Physical education teachers must become familiar with the origin, duration, and severity of many disabling conditions, but even more important, they must learn to look beyond the disability and to develop challenging and exciting physical education experiences that help students maximize their learning and performance potential. One reason for the unnecessary, continuing exclusion of youngsters with disabilities from regular physical education is the failure to recognize that children with disabilities and those without typically are more alike than different.

3. IDEA is federal legislation that calls for children with disabilities to be afforded a free, appropriate education in the least restrictive environment. This law includes physical education in its definition of special education and designates physical education as a requirement for all students with disabilities. IDEA is explicit in its definition of conditions that render a child eligible for special education services. Section 504 of the Rehabilitation Act of 1973 may be invoked to provide specially designed educational services, including physical education, for children who are unable to participate safely or successfully in regular physical education, but who do not have an IDEA-identified condition. A child may qualify for special services under Section 504 if she or he is determined to have limitations in one or more major life activities, regardless of label.

4. IDEA and, to a lesser extent, Section 504 are acknowledged as the driving forces behind improvements in the quality of education for persons who have disabilities. These mandates reinforce our moral and professional obligation to ensure that persons with disabilities fully benefit from what physical education has to offer to better the human condition.

REFERENCES

Individuals with Disabilities Education Act of 1997 (IDEA 97), Pub. L. No. 105-17. (1997, June 4).

Rehabilitation Act of 1973, Pub. L. No. 93-112. § 504, Title V.

Stein, J. U. (1979, June). The mission and the mandate: Physical education, the not so sleeping giant. *Education Limited*, 27–29.

CHAPTER 2

Legal Mandates

During the 19th century, federal laws concerning individuals with disabilities were designed primarily to meet the needs of specific groups, such as people who were deaf and those who were blind. Not until the 1920s were laws enacted to provide services for all people with disabilities. This change came about through vocational rehabilitation legislation that was drafted to assist people who had been disabled during World War I or had been injured in the rapidly growing industrial workplace. Over the next 35 years, legislation for individuals with disabilities focused mainly, although not exclusively, on services and programs for persons who where blind. These early laws did little for children with disabilities in public schools.

Education of Individuals with Disabilities—1954 to 1973: A Precedent Is Set

Increasing national concern for the needs of children with disabilities is of relatively recent origin. The initial impetus for establishing equal education rights for children with disabilities came in the historic 1954 Supreme Court desegregation case, *Brown v. Board of Education* in Topeka, KS. The Court's rationale for this decision was stated as follows: "In these days it is doubtful that any child may reasonably be expected to succeed in life if he is denied the opportunity for an education. Such an opportunity, where the state has undertaken to provide it, is a right which must be made available to all on equal terms."

Relying on legal principles of the Brown decision and, later, the Civil Rights Act of 1964 (which explicitly outlawed discrimination based on race), parents of children with disabilities began to demand equal Constitutional rights for their children. Parents of children with disabilities and their advocates alleged that persons with disabilities, like persons of color (both groups had been historically disenfranchised from the mainstream of the American experience), were entitled to equal protection under the laws. Parents of children with disabilities and their advocates asserted that equal protection under the law called for education for children with disabilities that must be both free and appropriate.

The first major breakthrough resulting from such advocacy came in 1965 with Title IV of the Elementary and Secondary Education Act (Public Law 89-750). This law, signed by President Lyndon Johnson, authorized grants to states to initiate, expand, and improve educational programs for children with disabilities and created a Bureau of Education for the Handicapped.[1]

Although PL 89-750 was designed to provide educational opportunities for children with disabilities, many schools circumvented its directives. At that point, the courts began to exert even more pressure. What was to become a national phenomenon began in 1971 when the Pennsylvania Association for Retarded Children filed suit *(PARC v. Commonwealth of Pennsylvania)* on behalf of 13 citizens in that state with mental retardation. Citing the U.S. Constitution's guarantees of equal protection under the law, the suit argued that these children's access to public education should be equal to that afforded children without disabilities. In a consent agreement, the court ruled in favor of PARC.

One year later (1972), the federal court in the District of Columbia made a similar ruling involving not only children with mental retardation, but also those with the full range of conditions causing disability. All children, said U.S. District Judge Joseph Waddy *(Mills v. Board of Education),* have a right to suitable publicly supported education, regardless of the degree of the child's mental, physical, or emotional disability. In response to arguments that this position would impose an intolerable financial burden on the community, Judge Waddy added the following: "If sufficient funds are not available to finance all of the services and programs needed and desirable in the system, then the available funds must be expended equitably in such a manner that no child is entirely excluded from a publicly supported education" (p. 1728).

Section 504 Of The Rehabilitation Act Of 1973 (PL 93-112)

In September 1973 Congress passed a law prohibiting agencies receiving federal funding from discriminating on the basis of disability. Section 504 of the Rehabilitation Act of 1973 (PL 93-112) states: "No otherwise qualified handicapped individual in the United States . . . shall, solely by reason of his handicap, be excluded from the participation in, be denied the benefits of, or be subjected to discrimination under any program or activity receiving Federal financial assistance."

In April 1977 the U.S. Department of Health, Education, and Welfare (HEW) issued the final Section 504 rules and regulations governing all recipients of federal funds, which included all elementary and secondary public schools. This law affects many facets of life in the United States and has a direct bearing on all individuals with disabilities. Joseph A. Califano, Jr., then Secretary of HEW, is quoted in the *Federal Register* (April 23, 1977) as saying:

> *Today I am issuing a regulation, pursuant to Section 504 of the Rehabilitation Act of 1973, that will open a new world of equal opportunity for more than 35 million handicapped*

---

[1]The term *handicap* appeared in federal language as a descriptor of federal choice until passage of Public Law 101-476 (Individuals with Disabilities Education Act [IDEA], 1990). Passage of this law marked the end of *handicap* as a descriptor in federal language. With passage of Public Law 101-476, the word *disability* in all federal language has replaced *handicap*. Rationale for this change appears elsewhere in this text. Within the remainder of this chapter, where the term *handicap* or other terms or phrases no longer considered current continue to be used, the authors' purpose is to remain true to the text of language as written at the time.

Americans—the blind, the deaf, persons confined to wheelchairs, the mentally ill, or retarded, and those with other handicaps . . . . The 504 Regulation attacks the discrimination, the demeaning practices and the injustices that have afflicted the nation's handicapped citizens. It reflects the recognition of Congress that most handicapped persons can lead proud and productive lives. It will usher in a new era of equality for handicapped individuals in which unfair barriers . . , will begin to fall before the force of law. (p. 32, 101).

This law provides that programs must be accessible to people with disabilities. It does not require that every building or part of a building be accessible, but the whole program must be directly available. Structural changes in buildings must be undertaken, but only if alternatives, such as reassignment of classes or rooms, are not reasonably possible.

All buildings for which construction clearance was given after June 3, 1977, must have been designed and constructed to be accessible to persons with disabilities. Design standards of the American National Standards Institute determine minimal requirements for accessibility.

Implications of Section 504 for physical education become exceedingly clear. Section 504 emphasizes that no individual shall be excluded from, denied benefits of, or discriminated against in any program sponsored by recipients of federal funds, and public schools universally are recipients of federal funds. Guarantees of protection against discrimination are afforded in all aspects of school offerings, and this includes, if not explicitly then clearly implicitly, opportunities for physical education, intramural sports, and interscholastic sports (Horvat, 1990).

Section 504 also emphasizes that activities and learning experiences for all people must be conducted in the least restrictive and most integrated setting feasible. It imposes two kinds of restrictions in conducting programs: An agency (1) must not categorically separate individuals with disabling conditions from individuals without such conditions, and (2) must not indiscriminately place individuals with disabling conditions in special or segregated programs and/or activities.

Compliance with the above is reinforced by law. When a child with a disability is denied opportunity to participate pursuant to law, that individual has the legal right to sue for discrimination. If any public agency does not comply with Section 504, that agency jeopardizes its federal funds.

Education for All Handicapped Children Act Of 1975 (PL 94-142)

Public Law 94-142 clearly was a law of blockbuster proportions. This law, perhaps more than any other, has been singularly responsible for the kind and quality of education for children with disabilities that we see, and sometimes take for granted, today. Although PL 94-142 has since undergone two significant revisions (PL 101-476, Individuals with Disabilities Education Act [IDEA], 1990 and Individuals with Disabilities Education Act Amendments, 1997 [IDEA, 97]), it is widely recognized as a major turning point in education, including physical education, for persons with disabilities in the United States.

Unlike previous federal initiatives in special education, PL 94-142 had no expiration date and was regarded as a permanent instrument. The law addressed special education needs of children with disabilities of chronological ages 3 through 21. This law did not simply mark another expression of federal interest in special education. Rather, it provided a specific educational commitment to all children with disabilities. Public Law 94-142 clearly set forth as national policy the proposition that meaningful education must be extended as a fundamental right to individuals with disabilities. Public Law 94-142 became a lightning rod for both positive and negative reaction from all branches of education. Regardless of individual perceptions of the propriety of this law, its provisions since passage have had far-reaching affects on the education of virtually every child with a disability.

Though not a new term in federal language, PL 94-142 made clear reference to *child find*. The child find provision of PL 94-142 required that all children in a state who need special education, regardless of severity of disability, must be located, identified, and evaluated. This mandate was born of the premise that all children have value and can learn if given appropriate educational opportunity and that society can no longer excuse its failure to provide that opportunity by claiming lack of funds and/or unawareness of the existence of children with disabilities. Youngsters with disabilities were now to be brought out of the educational shadows and accounted for by local school districts. Public Law 94-142 called for education in the *least restrictive environment* (LRE). LRE, in the original law and subsequent revisions, refers to the place in school where the child is to be assigned educationally; it must be the most beneficial teaching and learning environment for the child. To the maximum extent possible, children with disabilities are to be educated alongside and along with children without disabilities. Although there is nothing in the mandate requiring that children with disabilities be educated alongside and along with children without disabilities, clearly the mandate is that such educational placements occur to the maximum extent whenever reasonably possible.

LRE emphasizes identification of the individual child's unique educational needs. Recognizing such needs before considering the most appropriate (i.e., LRE) placement or placements is of utmost importance. These placements (note the plural, because often the child benefits most from more than a single placement) can be in different groupings and/or at different sites, but all must be identified and justified as necessary to adequately address the child's individual needs.

To ensure that the education of a child with a disability was indeed appropriate, each child whose educational needs could not be met within the context of the regular curriculum became entitled to an individualized education plan (IEP). The IEP in its inception and as it exists today is a written document developed cooperatively by parents and the school (and the child, when appropriate). This document specifies what unique or special programs and/or services will be provided to meet the child's unique educational needs. Not all children with disabilities necessarily have IEPs. However, any child with a disability is entitled to an IEP (and by law, one must be in place) whenever any special program or service is provided specifically to meet the child's unique educational needs.

Public Law 94-142 mandated that all expenses incurred by the school to educate a child with a disability occur at no cost to the parent. The district within which the child with disability resides must either provide a free, appropriate education in the least restrict environment or contract for and stand the cost of educating the child in some alternative setting. Regardless of where the education transpires and costs incurred, parents incur no educational costs for educating their child with a disability beyond paying taxes earmarked to support public education.

Explicit Inclusion of Physical Education

Public Law 94-142 and its subsequent two major revisions (IDEA 1990 and IDEA 1997) specifically require that all children with disabilities be provided with a physical education program designed to meet individual and specific motor needs. The law clearly identifies the importance of physical education in the total education of the child with a disability, as stated in the *Federal Register*: "Physical education services, specially designed if necessary, must be made available to every handicapped child receiving a free, appropriate public education" (1977, p. 42, 489). Further, the law explicitly includes *physical education* within the definition of *special education*. This definition reads: "The term special education means specifically designed instruction, at no cost to the parent, to meet the unique needs of a handicapped child including . . . instruction in physical education" (1977, p. 42, 480).

It is worthy of note that through the entire language of this legislation, physical education is the only subject area specifically and explicitly mentioned by name. Perhaps even more significant, physical education's mention is specifically within and integral to the law's definition of special education.

Physical education's prominence within the law is no mere accident or coincidence. Support for physical education and for its explicit mention in the law, particularly within the law's definition of special education, was steadfast within the congressional committee that authored the bill. The committee's position, which became part of the law's final language, read as follows:

> *Special education as set forth in the Committee bill includes instruction in physical education, which is provided as a matter of course to all nonhandicapped children enrolled in public elementary and secondary schools. The Committee is concerned that although these services are available to and required of all children in our schools, they are often viewed as a luxury for handicapped children. The Committee expects the Commissioner of Education to take whatever action is necessary to assure that physical education services are available to all handicapped children and has specifically included physical education within the definition of special education to make clear that the Committee expects such service, specially designed when necessary, to be provided as an integral part of the educational program of every handicapped child. (1977, p. 42, 489)*

Education for All Handicapped Children Act Amendments of 1986 (PL 99-457)

Although PL 94-142 addressed educating children with disabilities ages 3 through 21, the language of the law contained a loophole that resulted in the law's failure to be applied evenly across all 50 states. Specifically, in some states, children ages 3 and 4 were not covered. This circumstance was remedied with passage of PL 99-457, wherein education of children with disabilities ages 3 and 4 became an across-the-board requirement throughout the United States. This component of the law was termed *mandatory*. Additionally, this law included a *discretionary component* calling on states to address the early intervention needs of infants and toddlers with disabilities ages 0–2. *Discretionary* meant that provision of such services was not required. However, with passage of PL 99-457, the federal government offered attractive financial incentives to states willing to mount and undertake early intervention initiatives for children with disabilities ages 0–2.

Serving a purpose similar in intent to the IEP, PL 99-457 called for development of an individualized family service plan (IFSP) for each child and family being served pursuant to the law. The purpose of the plan is to give parents insights and guidance regarding their child's education-related needs and how such needs might be met. The IFSP specifies services designed to meet the young child's unique needs. Further, the IFSP development process is one that actively solicits family involvement in both the development and implementation of the IFSP (Hallahan & Kauffman, 1997).

Americans with Disabilities Act (ADA) Of 1990 (PL 101-336)

The Americans with Disabilities Act (ADA), passed in 1990, became operational on June 26, 1992. The law states in essence that individuals with disabilities *must* be provided equal opportunities in all aspects of life. In practice this act prohibits the private sector and agencies that do not receive financial assistance from discriminating against individuals with disabilities. (Section 504 of the Rehabilitation Act of 1973 had limited this prohibition to agencies that received federal financial assistance.) Communities, schools, and employers are now required to comply with mandates of ADA. For example, more stringent regulations are in effect regarding physical changes in buildings (e.g., restrooms, drinking fountains, ramps, elevators, telephones), parking lots, parks, swimming pools (including health spas), and schools.

Title I of this law pertains to employment policies affecting individuals with disabilities. Business owners must meet the following requirements:

- Existing facilities used by employees must be made readily accessible and usable by persons with disabilities.

- Job restructuring, modification of work schedules, and reassignment to a vacant position must be utilized.

- Equipment, devices, examinations, training materials, and policies must be acquired or modified, and qualified readers or interpreters must be provided.

For children with disabilities who are moving into their transition phase from public schools into adult life, many new opportunities have become available. The role of physical education has thus become even more important in the individual's development.

Although the ADA does not specifically identify public school physical education, individuals with disabilities can no longer be denied access to classes or activities solely on the basis of disability. School administrators, teachers, or coaches cannot prevent persons with disabilities from participating in an activity simply because the person may not be able to participate in *all* activities. When the person is able to participate in any part of a given activity, reasonable accommodations and adaptations must be made to enable the individual to participate meaningfully in the activity. For example, a person who does not walk may wish to bowl. An ADA case can be made to require a school or bowling establishment to provide a ramp from which the person can deliver the ball while sitting.

Violations of ADA may result in litigation and fines. Public entities, including schools, that continue to be in violation of ADA requirements risk loss of funds emanating from both state and federal government.

Individuals with Disabilities Education Act (IDEA) Of 1990 (PL 101-476)

The Individuals with Disabilities Education Act of 1990 (IDEA) became federal law on October 30, 1990. However, much of what became law with IDEA's passage already had been mandated by Congress with two previously passed federal laws, PL 94-142 (Education for All Handicapped Children Act, 1975) and PL 99-457 (Education for All Handicapped Children Act Amendments, 1986). Passage of PL 101-476

- combined Public Laws 94-142 and 99-457 under one umbrella law.

- marked the beginning of removal of the word *handicap* from federal language in favor of *disability*. The term *disability* is believed to be less judgmental, subjective, and devaluing than is *handicap*. The rationale is that a disability may or may not be handicapping, depending on how one relates to one's disability. To label a disability as handicapping tends to promote the notion that all disabilities in general may be handicapping and that a given individual's disability is, indeed, handicapping to that individual. Words or phrases that promote preconceived notions about disability, particularly words and phrases that might be arbitrarily or unfairly judgmental or devaluing, need be avoided, hence the impetus for the language change.

- provided that at age 16 (lowered to 14 with passage of IDEA 97), individualized education of children with a disability includes an individualized transition plan (ITP) designed to better enable the child to make the transition from life in school to life in the community.

- somewhat modified disability categories from their original appearance in PL 94-142. These modifications, as they appeared in IDEA 1990, have remained intact with passage of the Individuals with Disabilities Education Act Amendments of 1997 (PL 105-17), commonly referred to as New IDEA or IDEA 97.

Disabilities as they appeared in IDEA 1990 and as they continue to appear in IDEA 97 are as follows:

- mental retardation
- hearing impairments (including deafness)
- speech or language impairments
- visual impairments (including blindness)
- serious emotional disturbance
- orthopedic impairments
- autism

- traumatic brain injury
- other health impairments
- specific learning disabilities

By law, a person is considered as having one or more of the above disabilities if "by reason thereof, (she/he) needs special education and related services."

Individuals with Disabilities Education Act Amendments Of 1997 (PL 105-17)

Public Law 105-17 (IDEA 97) marks a significant review and revision of PL 94-142. Several motivations prompted Congress to review this vital law. Certain discretionary programs under the original IDEA had expired and were in need of reconsideration and reauthorization. During the ensuing years, school discipline and safety had increasingly become issues that needed to be addressed. Parents, teachers, and administrators had often been critical of the lack of achievement by children with disabilities under the original IDEA, and strategies have been adopted in the new law to address these concerns. Special education funding, in the view of special education advocates, had reached crisis proportions because of increasing costs and, in part, because of backlash from some advocates of children without disabilities. Advocates for the latter argued that special education funding was increasingly taking a toll on the total education budget, and education of children without disabilities had long since begun to suffer.

Significant revisions to the law represent the nation's attempt to deal with these concerns. Numerous questions have been raised about specifics of the new law with answers, both factual and opinion, emanating from varied sources. Among the most factual and authoritative sources for answers is perhaps the United States Department of Education, Office of Special Education and Rehabilitative Services (OSERS). The OSERS general information website regarding IDEA 97 provides the following questions and answers (Q&As). While these Q&As are not specific to adapted physical education, each Q&A is related to adapted physical education, precisely because physical education remains integral to the definition of special education in IDEA 97. OSERS Q&As are as follows:

1. **How will the new law help children with disabilities reach higher levels of achievement?**

   The 1997 Individuals With Disabilities Education Act which [was] signed into law by President Clinton aims to strengthen academic expectations and accountability for the nation's 5.4 million children with disabilities, and bridge the gap that has too often existed between what those children learn and the regular curriculum. From now on, the Individualized Education Program (IEP)—the plan that spells out the educational goals for each child and the services he will receive for his education—must relate more clearly to the general curriculum that children in regular classrooms receive. The law will also require regular progress reports to parents, include children with disabilities in state and district assessments and in setting and reporting on performance goals as they do for non-disabled children. Teachers will benefit from advancements in research through professional development initiatives.

2. **What about parents? How are parents involved in decisions about their child's education?**

Parental involvement will increase under the new law. In all states, parents will now be included in groups making eligibility and placement decisions about children with disabilities. Previously, in some states, parents only had a right to be included in IEP meetings. Parents also have a right to consent to periodic reevaluations of their children's program, in addition to initial evaluations. Currently, parents of children with disabilities rarely get regular reports from schools on their child's progress in achieving academic goals set forth in the IEP. The new law aims to increase parental involvement by requiring regular progress reports that are commonly made for other children.

3. **Will more children with disabilities be placed in regular classroom settings under the law?**

The new law is designed to remove financial incentives for placing children in more separate settings when they could be served in a regular classroom, and it will include regular classroom teachers in the meetings at which the academic goals of children with disabilities are set. The new law also eases some of the restrictions on how IDEA funding can be used for children served in regular classrooms. Specifically, such funds can be used for providing services to children with disabilities in regular classroom settings even if non-disabled children benefit as well.

4. **How does the new law change the roles and responsibilities of regular classroom teachers?**

A critically important feature of the new law specifies that regular teachers will be part of the team that develops each child's IEP. That is especially important since the law removes barriers to placing children with disabilities in regular classroom settings and ties the education of children with disabilities more closely to the regular education curriculum. The law requires that IEPs include the program modifications and supports for the child and teacher to enable the child to succeed in the classroom. The law also provides continued federal support to improve teacher training nationwide and adds support of teacher training programs in geographic areas with acute teacher shortages.

5. **How will IDEA 97 prevent inappropriate placements for minority children?**

Whether the child is a minority or not, IDEA 97 emphasizes that for most children with disabilities, special education is not a place. Rather, special education is a set of services to support the needs of children with disabilities to succeed in general education classrooms. For the first time, states will be required to gather data to ensure that school districts are not disproportionately identifying and placing children with disabilities from minority or limited English proficiency backgrounds in separate educational settings, and that such children are not being disproportionately suspended or expelled. In addition, in determining their education services, schools will be required to address the language needs of children who have limited English proficiency. Teachers will be provided training and research based knowledge to meet the special needs of these children.

6. **How will this law help school districts meet the costs of special education?**

The new law directs more federal dollars to school districts and allows them greater flexibility to meet the needs of children with disabilities in their schools. States and other public agencies will continue their level of support to school districts. Unnecessary assessments will be eliminated, saving school districts an estimated $765 million per year.

7. **How does IDEA promote safe, well-disciplined schools?**

All children deserve safe and well-disciplined schools. For the first time, the new law sets out and clarifies how school disciplinary rules and the obligation to provide a Free Appropriate Public Education to children with disabilities fit together. The law explicitly requires that children who need it receive instruction and services to help them follow the rules and get along in school. However, the law also recognizes that if children bring a weapon or illegal drugs to school, schools have the right to remove children with disabilities to an alternative educational setting for up to 45 days. The new law permits schools to go to a hearing officer for an injunction to remove a child for up to 45 days if the child is considered substantially likely to injure himself or others. Previously, only a court had that authority. And the law also recognizes the right of schools to report crimes to law enforcement or judicial authorities. At the same time, the law guarantees that children under suspension or expulsion would still receive special education services elsewhere.

8. **How does the law affect infants, toddlers, and preschoolers with disabilities?**

The law allows federal funding to rise to $400 million for infants and toddlers programs from current appropriations of $315 million. For preschoolers allowable funding is up to $500 million up from current spending of $360 million. It clarifies that infants and toddlers should receive services in the home or in other natural settings where possible. It also improves the coordination and transition for children from infant and toddler programs to preschool programs.

9. **Will these changes and new requirements affect the number of lawsuits and due process hearings by parents and legal bills for school districts?**

When parents and schools districts collaborate on children's education, conflict is minimized. IDEA 97 recognizes and encourages these positive relationships and non-adversarial methods of resolving disputes. The new law includes parents in placement decisions and requires schools to report regularly to parents on their child's progress.

Problems and Solutions—The Law and Physical Education

The American Alliance for Health, Physical Education, Recreation, and Dance (AAHPERD) originally developed information regarding the implementation of federal legislation specific to physical education. The following Q&As were developed from AAHPERD but have been modified by these authors to reflect current laws and language. The questions remain enduringly relevant and answers continue to be correct (Eichstaedt & Kalakian, 1993).

QUESTION: Some state agencies and state boards of education have asserted that physical education is not required for children with disabling conditions if it is not required for children [without disabilities]. Does this conflict with other interpretations of IDEA 97?

RESPONSE: All children with disabilities must be assessed to determine whether the individual has special physical or motor needs or both. Specific physical education areas defined in the rules and regulations of [IDEA 97] include development of physical and motor fitness, fundamental motor skills and patterns, and skills in aquatics, dance, individual and group games, and sports, including lifetime sports. The child with no special physical or motor needs is governed by the same requirements as those used for other children at the same grade level. If, after appropriate assessment procedures, an individual is identified as having special physical or motor needs, then that child must be given an individualized program, regardless of whether or not [children without disabilities] are required to take physical education. This is consistent with the provisions of the law, intent of Congress, and further interpretations regarding needed services. Whether those services are currently available or not, or whether such services are provided to [children with disabilities] does not affect the individualized program content.

QUESTION: Must children be placed in regular classes if their needs can be more effectively met in a separated setting such as adapted physical education class?

RESPONSE: The fact that children are not [included] in the regular program indicates that they have certain physical or motor needs or both that require a specially designed adapted physical education physical education program. Placement decisions are based on previous physical fitness and on [overall] motor ability assessment. Scheduling flexibility is of extreme importance in such situations. Learning opportunities are maximized when children are placed in different classes to meet [unique] weekly or daily needs. For example, a child with asthma who is allergic to swimming pool chemicals could be transferred temporarily to another activity that has similar basic strength and fitness components (arm, shoulder, and leg strength and cardiorespiratory endurance). . . . Individuals with low motor skill ability often need short-term placement in a separate adapted physical education class where they can receive intensive and exacting instruction. The child's needs dictate placement. The adapted class is *less* restrictive in [the swimming pool case] than the regular class would be. Both the setting and the time involved must be considered when applying the least restrictive environment mandate. Children identified as [having disabilities] who have been receiving special education services do not automatically need an adapted physical education program. As with any specially designed program, adapted physical education must be prescribed in the child's IEP. Before PL 94-142, a child with special needs was often labeled, placed, and *then* programmed. Now the process moves from assessment, to programming, and then to appropriate placement. No longer can placement be a function of organizational pattern or administrative inflexibility of the school system or the teacher. If a child cannot learn in one way, then the teacher must teach in another way that enables the child to learn.

QUESTION: Should a special education class consisting entirely of children grouped homogeneously according to specific disabling conditions (e.g., all [children with mental retardation]) be sent as a group to physical education class?

RESPONSE: Emphatically no! One of the main reasons for PL 94-142 [through IDEA 97 has been] to stop such indiscriminate placement and to force educators to look specifically at each child's unique needs. Each child must be placed according to individual, not group, needs. Grouping children categorically by disabling condition is not appropriate in terms of either the intent or letter of the law. Once a child has been assessed and found to possess physical and motor abilities consistent with those of children with no disabilities, then the school district should follow the same processes and procedures that govern all children [without disabilities] in its jurisdiction. A child [with low vision], for example, should not be placed automatically in an adapted physical education swimming class if his or her potential to learn swimming techniques is similar to that of children without disabilities. Decisions regarding program placement must be based on present ability level (i.e., beginning swimmer, intermediate swimmer). Teachers and leaders must strive to identify children with special physical and motor needs that require attention, determine specific goals and objectives, and alter teaching methods to include appropriate activities, adaptations, and modifications. For example, a teaching technique modified for a child [with low vision] might involve moving the youngster's arms, rather than saying, "Watch me do this."

QUESTION: What type of adapted physical education program can be provided without a special facility?

RESPONSE: When the needs of a child with a disability cannot be met in the regular class setting, the adapted physical education placement becomes the least restrictive environment. Special program needs must be justified on the basis of IEP planning. Legal, legislative, philosophical, and programmatic trends are away from segregated facilities and special programs, except in cases in which a productive educational experience is not possible in the regular classroom. For example, a 16-year-old youngster with spastic cerebral palsy might have great difficulty trying to participate in regular class units in volleyball and basketball. Extreme rule modifications of either game would so restrict the participation of the [teenagers without disabilities] that the game would not fulfill their needs. That would be a violation of the goals of IDEA 97 and Section 504. Assuming that playing volleyball and basketball is essential for the motor development (i.e., agility, balance, explosive leg power, and hand-eye coordination) of all individuals, then these sports should be offered also to the child with a disability in a form commensurate with individual ability. The adapted physical educator will have to modify specific activities to allow for improvement and success for the individual with a disability. In this example, it is questionable if the regular program would span such extreme ability differences.

Placement in the adapted physical education class must ensure that the new program is as good or better than the regular class. In the past, too many children with disabilities were given nonchallenging, irrelevant, and inappropriate activities. The adapted physical education program must *not* consist of handing out towels, keeping score, or maintaining equipment, nor will a watered-down activity program of checkers, chess, ping-pong, shuffleboard, or table tennis satisfy the mandates of IDEA 97.

QUESTION: If a child is so disruptive that he makes it difficult for others to learn or function effectively, must he be kept in a given educational setting?

RESPONSE: No. The laws emphasize that when a child with a disability impairs the learning opportunity of another child, then placement is not considered appropriate and additional assessment is necessary. Assignment must be made to an alternative least restrictive setting (e.g., adapted physical education class could afford a lower teacher-pupil ratio and thus provide a more individualized program).

QUESTION: My 13-year-old daughter with autism is not getting physical education which I requested during the IEP conference. I was told that gross motor activities are part of the classroom program. I asked for physical education in the gym or outdoors, not in the regular classroom. Doesn't my child have the right to participate in a program defined specifically as "physical education"?

RESPONSE: Physical education is the only curricular area in the definition of special education in [IDEA 97]. As such, physical and motor needs must be considered by every IEP planning committee. If, based on appropriate assessment, a child is found to have no special physical or motor needs, then nothing more need be done at the committee meeting. Ideally, the IEP form should indicate this and specify that the child is therefore subject to the same rules, regulations, and requirements as other students. A child with special physical or motor needs must be IEP-processed and programmed. It is important to distinguish between children with special needs who have specific goals and those who require adaptive devices, curricular adjustments and method adaptations. In the latter case, a modification of rules may be all that is necessary to allow a child to remain in the regular class.

The purpose of activity must be considered. IDEA 97, its rules and regulations, and official interpretions all state clearly that physical education must be included. Physical and motor activities used for social or emotional purposes [alone] do not meet the intent or letter of the law, which insists on provision of physical education [according to the IDEA 97 definition of physical education]. Indeed, physical activities should be encouraged for many reasons, including academic and social, but these activities must be in addition to and not in place of activities designed to meet physical and motor needs.

A local education agency is therefore not fulfilling the mandates of either IDEA 97 or Section 504 if (1) no consideration is given to a child's physical and motor needs during the IEP committee meeting and in the IEP itself, or if (2) the child is being denied categorically the participation in physical education programs or activities comparable to those provided to [children without disabilities].

QUESTION: If a regular or special education classroom teacher uses motor, physical, or recreational activities that reach certain children, has the physical education requirement been satisfied?

RESPONSE: No. To satisfy the requirements of [IDEA 97], a certified physical education instructor must make a clear-cut effort to meet the child's motor needs. Although classroom teachers should be encouraged to provide additional physical and developmental activities, these opportunities are in addition to, and not in place of, instruction by a professional physical educator. Free play, recess, or recreational activities do not meet the intent of physical education for the IEP. Having trained physical educators is just as important as having trained driver education teachers. Although almost everyone can learn to drive a car without the aid of a trained educator, the child's safety and meaningful progression are left to chance.

QUESTION: Do these same provisions that apply to children with disabilities also apply to children who are obese or malnourished, or who possess low levels of physical ability or have poor motor performance?

RESPONSE: Children not legally identified as having disabilities may may also need an adapted physical education program to meet their needs effectively. Despite the need, however, there are no legal or binding statements requiring development of an IEP for these children. Additional [IDEA 97] money is not available to support programs for such students. The rationale for hiring an adapted physical education specialist can be supported strongly when children [both those with and those without disabilities] require highly individualized instruction. Children who are obese may exhibit needs that cannot be met if they are always included in regular physical education programs. The structured activities of specific units (e.g., gymnastics and tumbling) will not provide proper exertion to stimulate the cardiovascular system. A flexible physical education curriculum can result in a program that is better for all children. The assumption that a regular curriculum will meet the individual needs of all children is outdated. Physical education programs should include regular and adapted classes to provide a range of activities to meet the fluctuating and individual motor needs of all children.

QUESTION: What can be done for children with disabilities who are excused completely from physical education because no adapted physical education program exists?

RESPONSE: According to both [IDEA 97[and Section 504, which mandate a free appropriate education for every child with a disability, no child should be excused from physical education. Both laws require that a child's special needs be met through individualized programs. [IDEA 97] requires that this be done through a written IEP, which must include annual goals, short-term instructional objectives, a statement of specific special education and related services to be provided, dates for initiation of services and anticipated duration of services, and criteria and procedures by which achievement can be evaluated. Congressional intent is to provide every child with a disability with an appropriate physical education program. Interpretations of both laws indicate clearly that no justification exists for not meeting the identified needs of any child. The fact that a local education agency or school does not have a particular service is not an acceptable justification. Needed services are to be provided whether they are currently available or not; this is the responsibility of the local education agency. The interpretation includes adapted physical education if necessary.

Amateur Sports Act Of 1978

The Amateur Sports Act of 1978 was initiated to renew the United States Olympic Committee's (USOC) commitment to amateur athletics. Reauthorized in 1998 as the Olympic and Amateur Sports Act, the Stevens Amendments to this act strengthened the original legislation and provided updates to the previous legislation to help strengthen the original act. For example, the recent legislation incorporates Paralympics and projects an equal status for athletes with disabilities. The legislation also continues the focus of integrating sports for athletes with disabilities with the national governing bodies (NGBs) of organizations for athletes without disabilities and allows the USOC to recognize problems that do not serve the best interests of sports for the disabled.

The primary mission of the USOC is to develop and prepare elite athletes, including those with disabilities. This commitment demonstrates a long-term investment aimed at providing services and training that are comparable to those accessible to the athletes without disabilities as well as advancing the status and integration of elite athletes with disabilities in open competition. The Committee on Sports for the Disabled (COSD) represents athletes with disabilities as one of the standing committees that provide recommendations to the USOC board of directors. The COSD is also the liaison between Disabled Sports Organizations (DSOs) and the USOC and attempts to promote a smooth working relationship between the national governing bodies, the USOC, and the DSOs.

Disabled Sports Organizations

There are seven Disabled Sports Organizations (DSOs) recognized as USOC member organizations:

Paralympic Affiliated Sport Organizations

1. United States Association of Blind Athletes (USABA)
2. Dwarf Athletic Association of America (DAAA)
3. National Disability Sports Alliance (NDSA)
4. Wheelchair Sports USA (WSUSA)
5. Disabled Sports USA (DS/USA)
6. Special Olympics International (SOI)

Non-Paralympic Disabled Sports Organization

7. USA Deaf Sports Federation (USADSF)

The Paralympic DSOs support a total of approximately 20,000 elite athletes (not including the 438,000 SOI athletes and recreational participants). Currently, there are 25 Paralympic sports, 19 summer and 6 winter sports. The USOC provides direct financial support to the Paralympic Games (winter and summer) as well as fostering the development of elite disabled athletes with disabilities and their Olympic equivalent events.

United States athletes participating in the Paralympics are members of one of the above-named organizations and represent five international federations of disability groups under the jurisdiction of the International Paralympic Committee:

1. ISMWSF (wheelchair athletes)—International Stroke Mandeville Wheelchair Sports Federation
2. ISOD (amputee/dwarf/Les Autres athletes)—International Sports Organization for the Disabled
3. CP-ISRA (cerebral palsy athletes)—Cerebral Palsy International Sports and Recreation Association
4. IBSA (blind athletes)—International Blind Sports Association
5. INAS-FMH (cognitively impaired athletes)—International Association for Mentally Handicapped

It is important to note that all athletes selected to compete for their country are elite athletes and must qualify for competition along similar guidelines set for Olympic athletes. All athletes must adhere to grueling training regimens and meet strict qualifying standards to be eligible for participation.

The interaction and support of the COSD and the USOC are important steps in providing opportunities and increasing the capabilities of all athletes. Children with disabilities who possess a sound movement background should be encouraged to participate and train in order to achieve their potential. Teachers may also contribute to their development by encouraging participation in local recreational and sports competitions. Participation in sports not only increases overall physical development, but also may contribute to a positive self-concept and successful inclusion in community settings.

CHAPTER SUMMARY

1. Special education legislation is complex and continues to evolve. Federal legislation centered on special education and civil rights has made a significant impact on instruction in physical education.

2. IDEA 97 is the latest revision of blockbuster federal legislation on special education that was first passed by Congress as PL 94-142 (Education for All Handicapped Children Act, 1975). Physical education continues to occupy a prominent place within this legislation. Special education within the context of IDEA 97 is deemed primary service. PL 94-142 and each of its subsequent revisions have included physical education explicitly within the law's very definition of special education. Given physical education's explicit inclusion within the law's definition of special education (i.e., the primary service), physical education, individually designed when necessary, is primary-service special education.

3. Physical education also is mandated, although perhaps less explicitly than in IDEA 97, in Section 504 of the Rehabilitation Act of 1973 (PL 93-112) and the Americans with Disabilities Act of 1990 (PL 101-336). These civil rights laws specifically mandate that no person, solely by virtue of disability, can be denied access to programs or services available to persons without disabilities. These laws further provide that when regular programs and services are not suitable, appropriately modified programs and services must be offered *and* be of comparable quality.

4. It remains incumbent on teachers of physical education, both regular and adapted, to know the law. Laws addressed in this chapter provide the very context within which physical education services are provided to students who have disabilities. Further, the laws provide strong and convincing legal arguments to support the moral argument that school-aged children with disabilities throughout the United States are fully entitled to a free, appropriate education (explicitly including physical education) in the least restrictive environment.

5. The Amateur Sport Act was reauthorized in 1998 to strengthen the United States Olympic Committee's commitment to athletes with disabilities. The USOC commitment is designed to foster cooperation between national governing bodies and Disabled Sport Organizations and to provide training services and foster competition for elite athletes with disabilities.

REFERENCES

Americans with Disabilities Act of 1990, Pub. L. No. 101-336. (1990, July 26).

Brown v. Board of Educ., 347 U.S. 483, 74 Ct. 686, 98L. Ed. 873 (1954).

Department of Health, Education, and Welfare, Office of Education. (1977, April 23). Final regulations of education of handicapped children, implementation of Part B of the Education of the Handicapped Act. 42(163) Fed. Reg. Part II, § 121a302, Residential Placement, 42,488. § 121a301(b), Free appropriate public education-methods and payments, 42,488. § 121a307, Physical education. § 121a14, Special education, p. 42,489.

Department of Health, Education, and Welfare, Office of Education. (1977, April). Rules and regulations—§ 504. 42(65) Fed. Reg. § 84.34, Participation of Students, p. 22,682.

Education Amendments of 1974, Pub. L. No. 93-380. (1974, August 21).

Education for All Handicapped Children Act of 1975, Pub. L. No. 94-142, S.6 20 U.S.C. §1401, (1975, November 29).

Education of the Handicapped Act of 1986, Pub. L. No. 99-457. (1986, October 6).

Education of the Handicapped Act Amendments of 1983, Pub. L. No. 98-199. (1983, December 2).

Eichstaedt, C., & Kalakian, L. (1993). *Developmental/adapted physical education: Making ability count,* (3rd ed.). New York: Macmillian.

Hallahan, D. P., & Kauffman, J. M. (1997). *Exceptional learners: Introduction to special education* (7th ed.). Boston: Allyn & Bacon.

Horvat, M. (1990). *Physical education and sport for exceptional students.* Dubuque, IA: Wm. C. Brown.

Individuals with Disabilities Education Act, Pub. L. No. 101-476. (1990, October 30).

Individuals with Disabilities Education Act of 1997, Pub. L. No. 105-17. (1997, June 4).

Mills v. Board of Education of the District of Columbia, 348 F. Supp. 866, (D.D.C., 1972).

PARC v. Commonwealth of Pennsylvania, 334 F. Supp. 1257 (E.D. Pa. 1971) and F. Supp. 279 (E.D. Pa. 1972).

Rehabilitation Act of 1973, Pub. L. No. 93-112, § 504, Title V. (1977, April 23).

CHAPTER 3

Continuum of Placements and Program Planning

The enactment of legislation and the public's commitment to education have brought about a variety of placement options for individuals with disabilities. Commonly, such terms as *integration, normalization,* and *mainstreaming* have been used to describe the process of placement in such an environment. More recently, *inclusion* has been mandated as the proper placement for children with disabilities.

Based on the legal mandates, placement options must be available to all children with disabilities. Seldom has an issue caused so much controversy among teachers, parents, and administrators as the effort to determine the most effective vehicle for meeting the mandates of federal and state legislation. In our view, proper placement of children should depend on their background, motor ability, cognitive level, self-concept, emotional stability, and specific educational needs. For most children, placement in a regular physical education class is appropriate. This placement should be implemented when the child's needs can be met in the regular class and the child's functioning is appropriate for meeting regular class goals and objectives. For some children, placement in regular physical education may not be appropriate, realistic, or safe. These children may have physical or educational needs that require extensive special services that should be met in an alternative setting.

From the historical perspective, formal instruction based on disability and carried out in a segregated class setting has evolved to inclusion and education of children with disabilities into regular education classes. Much of this impetus for change was initially a direct result of federal and state mandates, supported by program gains and increases in the functional ability of children with disabilities, and the realization that all children may benefit from some form of mainstreaming or inclusion experiences.

Before we can discuss the proper placement options, we must clarify terminology. In order of their usage, common terms used to describe placement options include *mainstreaming,* the *least restrictive environment* (LRE), and *inclusion.*

Mainstreaming initially denoted the placement of individuals with disabilities in regular classes with nondisabled individuals (Reynolds, 1962). Mainstreaming supported the notion that children with disabilities should be provided the opportunity to be educated in the regular school environment. Philosophically, this placement provided opportunities for children but suggested that the child must fit into the existing environment or system without placing an undue burden on the teacher (Aufsesser, 1991). Because this concept did not provide a support system for general and special educators to ensure success, the term generally fell out of favor and was construed to mean "dumping" children with disabilities (Hardman, Drew & Egan, 1999). The term as used today describes educating children with disabilities in general education settings; with the passage of PL 94-142 in 1975, the term was replaced by *least restrictive environment.*

The *least restrictive environment* (LRE) was an initial attempt to place individuals with disabilities into regular class environments (Aufsesser, 1991). The purpose of placement in the LRE was to educate children with disabilities and their peers to the maximum extent possible. If placement in a regular class was not appropriate, placement close to the regular setting was favored (Aufsesser, 1991; Hardman, et al., 1999). It was also suggested that for children to be successful, appropriate placement in regular settings might require supplemental aids or supports (Block, 1994; Block & Krebs, 1992).

Mainstreaming and the LRE are not synonymous. The LRE may consist of a continuum of alternative placements that include the regular education setting and/or a more restricted setting based on the needs of the child. Opponents of the LRE indicate that although it emphasizes placement with nondisabled children, the LRE supports restricted settings and fosters inappropriate attitudes toward children. It may also create a "pull-out" program, wherein the child with disabilities travels to the intended services rather than making services available in the regular educational environment (Block, 1994; Hardman, et al., 1999).

Based on some of these objections, the concept of inclusion has been advanced as the desirable placement option for all children with disabilities. By most definitions, inclusion denotes the practice of educating a child with a disability in age-appropriate education classes with the child's home school community, with the proper supports and personnel to provide a successful and meaningful educational experience for all children within that regular classroom setting (Block, 1994). Therefore, children with various types of disabilities at all levels of severity, can be served in an inclusion setting: children with sensory impairments, learning or behavior disorders, traumatic brain injury, health or orthopedic impairments, or autism. Depending on the recommendation of the collaborative team, this placement can be *full inclusion*, with all instruction in a general education setting, or *partial inclusion*, wherein some components of the instruction are provided in alternative settings. The support system can include teachers and aides as well as instructional materials and assistive technology that facilitate the instructional process.

As professionals in the field, we philosophically support the premise of inclusion but believe the LRE not only allows for individuals with disabilities to be educated in the regular education environment if it is appropriate, but also provides alternative placements for children who require significant support to accomplish their program goals and objectives. Whatever one's professional views, however, one must remain aware of the concerns for placement and how children will receive services and in what environment.

Conceptually, we see inclusion as a placement option and one of the emerging trends in education. We also feel that the following emerging trends and disability model must be emphasized to promote the most advantageous placement for children with disabilities (Aufsesser, 1991; Nagi, 1991; Rikli & Jones 1997):

Emerging Trends

Currently, the following trends are emerging in placements and program planning for children with disabilities:

- Utilize a collaborative team approach for assessment, program planning, and instruction.
- Incorporate family life profiles, and focus on transition from home to school to work to community integration.
- Utilize school-based decision making for placement, collaborative consultation, services, program planning, and implementation.
- Apply a functionally based curriculum across all subjects.
- Provide placements in inclusion settings, including unified sports and recreational programs.
- Focus on independence and vocational training, which requires improves fitness and motor control.
- Utilize community-based instruction (CBI) with all types and severities of disabilities.
- Capitalize on technological advances, including communication devices, computers, assistive devices, equipment, and Internet capabilities.
- Utilize innovative teaching methods, including cooperative teaching, cooperative learning, peer and cross-aged tutoring, and curriculum materials designed to facilitate positive attitudes.

Disability Model

The disability model was initially developed to delay the onset of physical frailty and disability in older adults. We favor using the disability model to develop intervention programs and placement options (Nagi, 1991; Rikli & Jones, 1997). This model includes four progressive stages: pathology (the disease, injury, or developmental disorder), impairment, functional limitation, and disability. We have expanded on this model, (Figure 3.1) and believe that the overall capabilities of children with disabilities should be assessed against it.

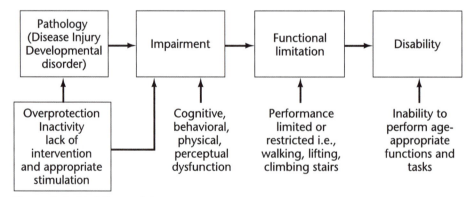

Figure 3.1 Disability model.

In the disability model, the stages are progressive in nature. Disability is the final stage and is defined as the child's inability to perform age-appropriate tasks. It is essential that educators plan and implement programs that are aggressive and help children be as functional and independent as possible. We want to enable children to perform according to their capabilities and not accept disability as a rationale for inactivity.

Program Planning

Major provisions of IDEA 97 include the development of an individualized family service plan (IFSP), individualized education plan (IEP), and individualized transition plan (ITP). We also include leisure services in conjunction with the IEP through the recreational services plan (RSP) to emphasize community integration. Each of these plans is aimed at providing the services that children need at that stage in their development.

The IFSP evolved from earlier revisions of IDEA that required states to provide a free and appropriate education for children 3–5 years of age with disabilities. Part C of IDEA 97 was amended to provide early intervention services for children from birth to 2 years of age. Services such as special instruction, diagnostic testing and services, assistive technology, and health services are to be provided to infants and toddlers based on the provisions set forth in the IFSP. The components of the ISFP plan include the following (Hallahan & Kauffman, 1997):

- the child's present level of development
- family concerns, priorities, and resources for the child's development
- expected outcomes to be achieved by the child and family and the criteria, procedures, and time frame for progress
- specific intervention services required
- projected dates for initiation of services
- service coordinator who will implement the plan
- procedures for transition from early intervention into a preschool program.

Although the IFSP is similar to the IEP, it is the intent of IDEA 97 to provide both developmental and therapeutic approaches that actively address program areas at a stage in development that is advantageous to development. The early years are critical to the physical, motor, social, and cognitive development, and the IFSP should be designed to facilitate transition to the school years and the development of the IEP.

The Individualized Education Plan

A major provision of IDEA 97 is the individualized education plan (IEP). An IEP is a written document delineating the comprehensive education plan or program of each child. It is developed in a meeting with teachers, parents, local administrators, other individuals who have knowledge about the child, including related services if appropriate. This written plan is a means of translating the federal legislation into an educational experience. An IEP then becomes a flexible agreement, rather than a binding contract, to ensure that children receive an appropriate educational experience in the least restrictive environment.

Because physical education is a direct service, it should be an integral part of the IEP. Every child should be allowed the opportunity to participate in physical education and to achieve the same program goals as his or her peers. The component parts of the IEP as defined by IDEA 97 include the following (California Department of Education, 1997):

1. present levels of educational performance, including
   - how the child's disability affects involvement and progress in the general curriculum, or
   - for preschoolers, how the disability affects participation in appropriate activities

2. measurable annual goals, including benchmarks or short-term objectives related to
   - meeting the child's needs that result from the child's disability so that the child can be involved in and progress in the general curriculum, and
   - meeting each of the child's other educational needs that result from the child's disability

3. special education, related services, and supplementary aids and services to be provided and program modifications or supports provided for school personnel that will be provided for the child
   - to advance appropriately toward attaining annual goals
   - to be involved and progress in the general curriculum and to participate in extracurricular and other nonacademic activities
   - to be educated and participate with other children with and without disabilities

4. explanation of extent, if any, to which the child will not participate in the regular class and the activities described above

5. any individual modifications needed for the child to participate in state or districtwide assessments and, if the child will not participate in general assessments, why the assessment is not appropriate and how the child will be assessed

6. projected date for the beginning of services and modifications, and the anticipated frequency, location, and duration of those services and modifications

7. beginning at age 14 and updated annually, transition service needs focusing on the child's course of study; beginning at age 16 (or younger if determined appropriate by the IEP team) needed transition services, including, when appropriate, the interagency responsibilities or needed linkages; and, beginning at least one year before child reaches age of majority, information regarding rights transferred on reaching age of majority

8. how the child's progress toward annual goals will be measured and how parents will be regularly informed of progress

When children are identified with special needs, the local education agency (LEA) assumes the responsibility to determine the level of performance within 30 calendar days in order to develop an appropriate plan. Information on the child's performance is gathered from a variety of professionals who make up the collaborative team and are involved in the educational process.

Input on performance is generated from formal assessments; medical, educational, and psychological records; and observations of teachers and parents. During the formal development of the IEP, members of the collaborative team report on the assessment or observational data concerning child aid in determining the functional level, or the child's present level of functioning, at the time of testing. Based on the documented reports and input from other related service personnel or parents, an appropriate placement is developed. This placement should allow the child to achieve success and include any additional services, special equipment, or modifications required to ensure an appropriate educational experience.

Physical education should always be included on the IEP. However, the kind and amount of information to be included on the IEP depends on the physical and motor needs of the child. Following is a description of IEP formulation for children in various physical education placements:

1. *Regular physical education (ability to meet program goals).* When children are enrolled in the regular physical education class and no specific modifications or adaptations are necessary to meet the instructional and program goals, only a minimal amount of information is required on the IEP concerning physical education. It will be sufficient to indicate that children are participating in the regular physical education program. Children who are mildly involved, physically disabled, or have a learning disorder are commonly enrolled in regular physical education with adaptations.

2. *Regular physical education (supports to meet program goals).* Some children are able to participate in the regular physical education but may require special adaptations or supports, such as equipment or instructional modifications, to achieve program goals. For example, children may require a wheelchair to participate effectively or a modified handgrip to manipulate a racket effectively. For these children, the IEP should include a statement of the present level of physical or motor performance and a description of special adaptations or supports that are necessary to implement instruction.

3. *Specially designed physical education.* Sometimes children may require a specially designed program that may differ from the kind of physical education provided to other children. Children might participate in a special body conditioning or resistance-training program designed to overcome a lack of muscular strength or a muscular imbalance, while others may participate in some type of individual sport skill depending on their needs and interests. For these children, the regular physical education program, even with adaptations, is not an appropriate setting. In this program all parts of the IEP (e.g., present levels of educational performance, goals and objectives, and specific services to be provided) should be included, as well as the opportunities to participate in the regular program.

4. *Physical education in special settings.* Under certain circumstances, some children may require services in a special setting. Primarily we think of services being provided in a remedial school or hospital. For some children this may be appropriate if their medical condition does not allow them to function in the regular education setting. In addition, services must be available to children in community-based settings in order to generalize to the vocational environment. When children in a special setting receive instruction with other children and no individual adaptations are needed, only minimal information is required in the IEP. For example, it would be enough to indicate that children are participating in the program and to mention specific activities. However, if children have extensive physical and motor needs, physical education should be addressed in all component parts of the IEP.

Physical Education in the IEP

The role of physical education teachers revolves around developing and monitoring the physical education portion of the child's IEP. The physical education teacher should

1. ensure that physical education is an integral part of the child's IEP

2. prepare information about the child's behavior, fitness, sports skill, and motor ability for review by the collaborative team

3. volunteer to be a member of the IEP team

4. ensure that the child can safely and successfully participate in the program without compromising safety or program goals

Physical Education Portion of the IEP Form

The following example is the physical education portion of the IEP for a 12-year-old child with an orthopedic disorder who uses a wheelchair. Although all parts of the IEP are addressed, only a minimal amount of information would be required because the child participates in the regular physical education program with adaptations and supports.

This written statement will provide direction for the delivery of education services in meeting program goals. Variations of the plan should be based on the student's functional ability to meet these goals, and the plan should be revised as appropriate. The collaborative programming team, including the physical educator, should plan and monitor the IEP to evaluate the student's progress toward projected goals. (Figure 3.2)

Individualized Transition Plan (ITP)

As a basic premise of IDEA 97, the individualized transition plan (ITP) is a component of the IEP that describes services required for transition into the community or work environment. The ITP should be based on the child's functional levels, on the previous experiences of the child, the services needed to facilitate access to adult programs, and any necessary timelines that are required to complete the requested services. The ITP should gradually build on a functionally based curriculum and the IEP to ensure that at the designated age the child is identified and prepared for transitional services. Wehman (1996) recommended seven steps in the process: (1) organizing ITP teams, (2) organizing a circle of support, (3) identifying key activities, (4) holding ITP meetings in conjunction with IEP meetings, (5) implementing the ITP, (6) updating the ITP annually during IEP meetings and providing quarterly progress reports, and (7) ensuring that employment, recreational integration, and community integration is provided via an exit meeting. In each case, services are provided, support systems are identified, and progress is tracked to ensure that the individual is ready for employment and interaction in his or her own community setting. The ITP will then establish a working relationship between the school, parent, child and appropriate services that are required to be successful (Hardman et al., 1999). For some children, the ITP may focus on developing muscular strength and endurance in a supported work environment; for others, participation in outdoor recreation or sports or, in some cases, accessing community facilities and supported living (Figure 3.3).

Child's Name:	Ron
Birth Date:	September 6, 19XX
Chronological Age:	12 years, 6 months
Classification:	Orthopedically impaired

Present Level of Performance

Ron's overall level of physical and motor fitness is below average for boys at 12 years of age. Ron demonstrated deficiencies in range of motion in the shoulder and elbow and weakness in his arms and trunk. He scored below the 40th percentile on the long-distance run and isometric strength items.

Annual Goals
1. Develop and maintain a functional level of cardiorespiratory endurance.
2. Increase and maintain a functional level of upper body strength and conditioning.
3. Increase flexibility of his upper body.

Short-Term Objectives (Fall)

Goal 1: Ron will demonstrate
1. the ability to propel his wheelchair for 100 yds. in one minute
2. the ability to run continuously for 20 minutes

Goal 2: Ron will
1. perform the flexed arm hang for 2 seconds
2. increase his isometric strength to 17 kg with each hand; 30 kg in shoulder, flexion and extension
3. complete a 6-station circuit training program
4. increase his ROM in the shoulder areas to 30°

Evaluation Criteria (Criteria, Procedures, Scheduling)

Criteria: Levels of performance as specified in the short-term objectives

Procedures: Use of dynamometers, resistance equipment (Dumbbells, surgical tubing)

Scheduling: Fitness testing will be administered during class time at the end of the semester. Corresponding teacher observations and checklists of performance will be required.

Services Provided, Initiation, and Duration
1. instruction in the regular physical education program
2. consultant services with the educational service unit's special physical education teacher
3. services to be initiated September 12, 20XX, with instruction in regular physical education 4 days per week, 30 minutes per day for the calendar year

Participation in the Regular Program

The child will be integrated into regular physical education resistance training and body-conditioning classes. He will have the use of the wheelchair for running activities.

YOUR SCHOOL NAME
YOUR SCHOOL ADDRESS
Individualized Education Program (IEP)

Notification of Meeting

Student _____   Date _____

Dear Parent or Guardian:

We invite and urge you to attend an Individualized Education Program (IEP) Team meeting regarding your child. You may invite individuals with knowledge of your child or special expertise to the meeting. Please inform us as to whom these people will be.

The meeting will be at _____

on _____ at _____

The purpose of this meeting :

[ ] Annual Review

[ ] Review Current Educational Programs and/or Placement

[ ] Discuss Initial Evaluation Results and Determine Eligibility for Placement

[ ] Discuss Reevaluation Data/Information and Eligibility

[ ] Review Behavior

[ ] Discuss Extended School Year

[ ] Develop Transition Plan

The following persons have been invited to attend this meeting:

Name	Title	Name	Title
	Parent(s)		General Education Teacher
	Student		Speech Language Pathologist
	Principal / Assistant Principal		School Psychologist
	Director / Assistant Director		
	Special Education Teacher		
	Special Education Teacher		

Please indicate below if you plan to attend this meeting and return this letter to your child's teacher. If you have any questions, please contact your child's teacher.

Sincerely,
Special Education Department

[ ] YES,   I plan to attend the meeting.

[ ] NO,   I do not plan to be present, but the IEP Team may proceed. Please send me a copy of the Team's recommendations.

[ ] NO,   I cannot be present. I would like to reschedule the meeting. A better time for me is _____

_____   _____
Parent / Guardian Signature   *Date*

ATTACHMENTS: *Your Rights As Parents Regarding Special Education*   *White - Central Office   Canary - School   Pink - Parent   1999 -00r*

Figure 3.2 Individualized education plan (IEP) worksheet.

YOUR SCHOOL NAME
YOUR SCHOOL ADDRESS
Individualized Education Program (IEP)

Date _____

Signature Page
Page ____ of ____

Student _____ DOB _____

School _____ Grade _____ SS# _____

Parent/Guardian _____ Phone - Home _____

Address _____ Work _____

I.   Type of Meeting

☐ Initial Plan   ☐ Amendment ★*Date* _____   ☐ Interim Placement

☐ Annual Review   ☐ Continuation of meeting dated _____   ☐ Behavior Plan

☐ Reevaluation   ☐ Review current educational programs and / or placement   ☐ Transition Plan
                                                                                                        ☐ Extended School Year

II   Participants of IEP Team

Name	Title	Name	Title
1.	Parent	6.	
2.	LEA	7.	
3.	Special Ed Teacher	8.	
4.	General Ed Teacher	9.	
5.		10.	

III.   Programs For Which Student Is Eligible *(Current eligibility is on file)*

☐ None   ☐ Hearing Impairment   ☐ Orthopedic Impairment
☐ Autism   ☐ Intellectual Disability - Mild   ☐ Other Health Impairment
☐ Deaf / Blind   ☐ Intellectual Disability - Moderate   ☐ Significant Developmental Delay
☐ Emotional / Behavior Disorder   ☐ Intellectual Disability - Severe   ☐ Speech/Language Impairment
☐ Emotional / Behavior Disorder - Severe ☐ Intellectual Disability - Profound ☐ Traumatic Brain Injury
                                    ☐ Specific Learning Disability   ☐ Visual Impairment

IV.   Present Level of Performance - Consideration of Special Factors

A.   Does the student exhibit behavior which impedes his/her learning or the learning of others?   ☐ Yes   ☐ No
If yes, consider, if appropriate, strategies including positive behavioral interventions, and supports to address the behavior.
☐ **Check if a behavior intervention plan is developed and attached.**   *(See Behavior Intervention Plan)*

B.   Does the student have limited English proficiency?   ☐ Yes   ☐ No
If yes, consider the language needs as related to the IEP and describe in present level of performance narrative.

C.   Is the student blind or visually impaired?   ☐ Yes   ☐ No
If yes, provide instruction in Braille and the use of Braille, unless the IEP team determines that instruction in Braille or the use of Braille is not appropriate for the student (after an evaluation of the student's reading and writing skills, needs, and appropriate reading and writing media, including evaluation of future needs for instruction in Braille or the use of Braille.) Document decisions in the present level of performance.

D.   Does the student have communication needs?   ☐ Yes   ☐ No
If yes, consider the communication needs and describe them in the present level of performance narrative.

E.   Is the student deaf or hard of hearing?   ☐ Yes   ☐ No
If yes, consider and describe below the student's language and communication needs, opportunities for direct communication with peers and professional personnel in the student's language and communication mode, academic level, and full range of needs, including opportunities for direct instruction in the student's language and communication mode.

F.   Does the student need assistive technology devices or services?   ☐ Yes   ☐ No   ☐ **Check if report is included**
                                                                                                  ☐ **Check if evaluation recommended.**

Continues.

YOUR SCHOOL NAME
YOUR SCHOOL ADDRESS
Individualized Education Program (IEP)

Date _____

Student _____ DOB _____

VII.   Placement / Options Considered

- ☐ 1. Regular Education with no Special Education Support
- ☐ 2. Regular Education with Supplemental Aids and Services
- ☐ 3. Regular Education with Special Education Consultation
- ☐ 4. Regular Education with Collaborative Instruction
- ☐ 5. Regular Education with Special Education Resource
- ☐ 6. Special Education Self-Contained Program

- ☐ 7. Community / Homebased Instruction
- ☐ 8. Hospital / Homebound Instruction
- ☐ 9. Additional evaluative data is not necessary to determine eligibility
- ☐ 10. A complete Psychological Reevaluation is recommended to determine continued eligibility
- ☐ 11. Other _____

VIII.   Related Services   ☐ Not Applicable

- ☐ Adapted P.E. *(Goals & Objectives must be included)*
- ☐ Audiology
- ☐ Occupational Therapy
- ☐ Orientation & Mobility

- ☐ Physical Therapy
- ☐ Speech / Language Therapy
- ☐ Special Transportation

- ☐ Related Vocational Instruction
- ☐ Supplementary Aids / Assistance
  _____

IX.   Placement / Options Rejected and Rationale *(Referenced to VII) (Example # 1, # 4)*

_____
_____
_____
_____
_____
_____
_____
_____
_____
_____

X.   Placement / Options Accepted and Rationale *(Referenced to VII) (Example # 2, # 5)*
(Include an explanation of the extent, if any, to which the student will not participate in the regular class.)

_____
_____
_____
_____
_____
_____
_____
_____
_____
_____
_____
_____

ATTACHMENTS: ☐ ESY IEP Addendum #01   ☐ Transition IEP Addendum #02

1998 -99r   *White - Central Office*   *Canary - School*   *Pink - Parent*   **Reminder: Complete Documentation of Parent Participation**

YOUR SCHOOL NAME
YOUR SCHOOL ADDRESS
Individualized Education Program (IEP)

Services
Page _____ of _____

Date _____

Student _____   DOB _____

XI.   **Recommended Special Education and Related Services**   _____ minutes = 1 segment

High School: Report frequency as blocks per year   _____ minutes = 1 block   _____ blocks per school year

Program/Service	Delivery Model	Frequency*	Start / End Date**	Setting of Services
Specific Learning Disability			/	
Emotional / Behavior Disorder			/	
_____ Intellectual			/	
Speech / Language Impairment			/	
			/	
			/	
			/	

* Indicate for each program/service whether frequency is minutes, segments, blocks per day, week, month or year.

** If parent does not attend, implementation date shall be at least one week after meeting date to provide opportunity for parental input.

Physical Education   ☐ Regular P.E.   ☐ Adapted P.E.   ☐ Not required for this school year
(Objectives must be included)   (preschool and high school only)

Transportation   ☐ Regular   ☐ Special | For your child's safety and the safety of others on the bus, the school district reserves the right to use safety devices. |

Modifications - Classroom   ☐ Not Applicable   ☐ See Classroom Modifications - *attached*

Behavior Intervention Plan   ☐ Not Applicable   ☐ See Behavior Intervention Plan - *attached*

Extended School Year   ☐ **Not considered during this meeting.** *(will meet to consider at a later date)*
☐ **Not recommended** *(Complete ESY Checklist)*
☐ **Recommended** *(Complete ESY Checklist and attach ESY IEP Addendum #01)*

XII.

Summary of Services	Elementary	Middle School and High School
Total segments / blocks in general education		
Total segments / blocks in special education		
Total segments / blocks in other related services		
Total Segments / Blocks Per Week or Year		

XIII.   **Annual Goals and Short Term Objectives / Benchmarks**

☐ **Developed and Accepted** - *attached*

☐ **Reviewed and Continued from IEP dated** _____

☐ **Reviewed and Modified from IEP dated** _____

☐ **Other** _____

1999 -00r   *White - Central Office*   *Canary - School*   *Pink - Parent*   **Reminder: Complete Documentation of Parent Participation**

Continues.

YOUR SCHOOL NAME
YOUR SCHOOL ADDRESS
Individualized Education Program (IEP)

Date _____

Testing / Diploma Options

Page ____ of ____

Student _____ DOB _____

XIV.   Student Progress - Method of Reporting *(Progress toward annual goals will be reported at least as often as parents of nondisabled students.)* *(How will the parents be informed of the student's progress toward the annual goals and the extent to which that progress is sufficient to enable the student to achieve the goals by the end of the year?)*

☐ IEP Progress Reports   ☐ Report Cards   ☐ Parent Conferences   ☐ Other _____

XV.   Participation in Mandated Testing
(Check all appropriate choices below and specify Norm. Referenced Test - ITBS, etc., CRCT, BLT, Writing Assessment.)
(Consult manual of each specific test for standard modifications which may used.)

It is recommended by the IEP committee that this student participates in:
☐ Testing with Standardized Format with no modifications (specify) _____
☐ Testing with Standardized Format with modification(s) indicated below (specify) _____
☐ Testing with Non-standardized Format with modification(s) indicated below (specify) _____
☐ Georgia Alternate Assessment *(Complete GAA Student Reporting Form)* (specify) _____
_____

Testing Modifications *(System-wide)*

Setting:
☐ Individually
☐ In a small group
☐ In a carrel
☐ In the special education room or other setting (specify)
_____
☐ With test administrator facing student
☐ Using a manual communication interpreter during oral instructions
☐ With special lighting or acoustics (specify) _____

Recording:
☐ Mark answers in test booklets
☐ Have answers recorded, recopied or verified by proctor or assistant
    (Does not apply to the writing test)
☐ Mark answers by machine (word processor, typewriter, etc.)
☐ Provide written responses in Braille
☐ Provide written responses on special paper
☐ Other _____

Format and Equipment:
☐ Test will be read to student
☐ Large print materials
☐ Braille materials
☐ Magnifying equipment
☐ Amplification equipment
☐ Noise buffers
☐ Place markers, templates, graph paper, etc.
☐ Out of level test
☐ Optical to tactile transformation device
☐ Communication device (specify) _____
☐ Partial test administered (specify) _____
_____

Scheduling:
☐ At time of day most beneficial to student (specify) _____
☐ At several sessions up to _____ minutes with rest breaks between
☐ Until, in the administrator's judgement, the session should be terminated. Additional sessions may be scheduled provided the test is completed by the final test date.
☐ With extended time limits as needed
☐ Other _____

XVI.   High School Considerations - Diploma Options *(To be addressed with rising 9th grade and older students)*

☐ High School Diploma
   Program of Study _____

☐ High School Certificate

☐ Special Education Diploma

☐ All classes will earn Carnegie units
☐ No classes will earn Carnegie units
☐ Classes not earning Carnegie units
_____
_____

Reminder: Complete Documentation of Parent Participation

Individualized Transition Plan

Student: _____   Meeting Date: _____
School:_____   School Principal: _____
Parent/Guardian: _____   Special Education Teacher: _____
Teacher: _____   Adapted Physical Education Teacher: _____
ITP Coordinator: _____   Vocational Trainer: _____

Assessment: Manual Testing; 1 repetition maximum on weight machines; flexibility. Job
analysis in community setting.

Transition Goal: To develop a sufficient level of muscular strength and endurance to improve
work productivity on the following tasks:

stacking boxes
carrying weighted objects
propelling a weighted dolly

Desired Outcomes:
1. Improve overall level of muscular strength and endurance in a community based
weight training program.
2. Improve ability to perform job related tasks for a duration of 4 hours.

Support Activities	Personnel	Date
Analyze skills needed for work experience	Vocational Trainer	3/14/2002
Determine physical functioning skills needed to perform tasks	Adapted Physical Education Teacher	4/1/2002
Identify community facility for exercise program	Adapted Physical Education Teacher	4/15/2002
Schedule and implement exercise program	Adapted Physical Education and Special Education Teacher	8/17/2002
Complete work application	Child and Parents	9/1/2002
Select appropriate work experience	Special Education and Vocational Trainer	9/15/2002
Begin work program	Special Education Teacher; Job Supervisor	10/15/2002
Evaluate Progress	Collaborative Program Team	Ongoing

Figure 3.3 Sample individualized transition plan (ITP).

CHAPTER SUMMARY

1. Placement of children in physical education centers on providing services based on the needs of the child. Children may be placed in a range of services from regular physical education with no adaptations to physical education with adaptations.

2. Placement of children in sports and recreation should also be encouraged and based on the individual's needs.

3. An individualized education plan (IEP) is a written document specifying the child's present level of functioning, goals and objectives, specific educational services to be provided, the extent of participation in regular education programs, dates of service initiation and duration, and evaluation criteria. The IEP should be reviewed annually to reflect changes in a child's functional ability.

4. Physical education must be an integral part of the IEP. In cases where no adaptations are needed, it is enough to indicate on the IEP that the child is participating in the regular physical education program.

5. The individualized family service plan (IFSP) and individualized transition plan (ITP) should be designed to identify the needs of the child at his or her age level. The IFSP and ITP must be consistent with a functionally based curriculum.

6. Current and future trends include technological advances, inclusion placement, community-based instruction, and transitional services.

REFERENCES

Aufsesser, P. (1991). Manufacturing and the least restrictive environment: How do they differ? *Palaestra, 7,* 31–35.

Block, M. E. (1994). A teacher's guide to including students with disabilities in regular physical education. Baltimore: Paul Brooks Publishing Co.

Block, M. E., & Krebs, P. (1992). An alternative to the least restrictive environment: A continuum of support to regular physical education. *Adapted Physical Activity Quarterly, 9,* 97–113.

California Department of Education. (1997). The new Individuals With Disabilities Education Act. *The Special Edge,* Sacramento, CA: Author.

Hallahan, D. P., & Kaufman, J. M. (1997). *Exceptional learners: Introduction to special education* (7th ed.). Boston: Allyn and Bacon.

Hardman, M. L., Drew, C. L., and Egan, M. W. (1999). *Human exceptionality: Society, schools and family* (6th ed.). Boston: Allyn and Bacon.

Nagi, S. Z. (1991). Disability concepts revisited: Implications for prevention. In A. M. Pope & A. R. Tarlov (Eds.), *Disability in America: Toward a national agenda for prevention* (pp. 309–327). Washington, DC: National Academy Press.

Reynolds, M. (1962). A framework for considering some issues in special education. *Exceptional Children, 28,* 367–370.

Rikli, R. E., & Jones, C. J. (1997). Assessing physical performance in independent older adults: Issues and guidelines. *Journal of Aging and Physical Activity, 5,* 244–261.

Wehman, P. (1996). *Life beyond the classroom: Transitions strategies for young people with disabilities,* (2nd ed.). Baltimore: Paul Brooks Publishing Co.

Psychosocial Aspects of Disability

I am America's child, a spastic slogging on demented limbs
drooling I'll trade my PhD for a telephone voice.

Bart Lanier Safford III, *An Obscured Radiance*

T his chapter investigates psychosocial variables influencing the adjustment of
individuals with disabilities. Sometimes greater degrees of disability are associated with greater adjustment challenges, but this generalization is an oversimplification. Any study of psychosocial variables must be tempered by respect for the person's
individuality and the disability's significance to that person. As Levine (1959) states:

> *The extent of the [disability's] impact experienced by each individual is related to the sig-*
> *nificance which the disability possesses for him. This, in turn, will depend on the pattern of*
> *events in his life that have contributed to the values he holds, the way he perceives himself*
> *in relation to the rest of the world, and the form which his reactions to stress take. (p. 1)*

Self-Concept

Self-concept is an important psychosocial variable that influences disability's impact
on the individual. Just as each person formulates attitudes about others, so each person also formulates attitudes about the self. Research in social psychology indicates
consistently that arousal levels, motivation to achieve, and quality of interpersonal
relationships are closely related to strength of self-concept. Researchers further assert
that the strength of one's self-concept is governed by one's understanding of how one
is perceived by others. This implies that if an individual's feeling of self-worth is not
shared by important others, it is of little positive value to the individual. Simply stated,
"What I think about me depends largely on what I think you think about me."

Self-concept is a dynamic phenomenon. Among adults, self-concept is relatively
stable; among young people, it is often in a state of flux. A self-concept that is not
improving may well be diminishing.

Self-concept is also a psychophysical phenomenon. No dichotomy exists between
the mind and the body in a person's evaluation of self-worth. The individual with a
disability who perceives the entire person negatively may be unable to formulate a
valid concept of self-worth. As Best, Carpignano, Sirvis, and Bigge (1991) state:

A disabled person who grows up in a family with fixed attitudes toward disability, and living in a society which treats persons with disability as a disfavored minority, the person with the disabling condition is faced with preconceived, distorted perceptions of his state. . . . The fact that a disabled person may be different in appearance, behavior, or habits often suggests to others (and eventually to the person) that there is something deviant about him. (p. 111)

For some people with disabilities, distorted perceptions of self-worth and of deviance become the basis for a distorted, negative self-concept.

Best et al. state further that "if a disabled person can be perceived as 'a person with a disability' rather than as 'a disabled person,' there will be greater emphasis placed upon the person than upon the disability" (p. 111). When we focus primarily on the person and secondarily on the disability as only one of the person's numerous traits, we realize that many persons with disabilities are not disabled in all contexts or settings. Important others who perceive the individual's disability in a holistic context can play a significant role in facilitating the development of the individual's realistic, positive self-concept.

Dealing with the individual first and with the disability second does not avoid or ignore the disability. Avoidance or denial of disability is nonproductive. Treating the disability as though it were nonexistent does not allow the individual to accept limitations, to make an accurate appraisal of strengths and abilities, or to apply concerted effort toward achievable ends (Best et al., 1991) (Figure 4.1).

Figure 4.1 Child achieving success.

Defense Mechanisms

Everyone relies on defense mechanisms at one time or another to deal with stress. When a person relies consistently on defense mechanisms as an escape, however, the individual is perhaps unconsciously avoiding the source of stress. The following defense mechanisms are among the most common:

- *Regression*—confronted by a threatening situation, the person returns to an earlier level of maturity or adjustment.
- *Repression*—the person purposefully, but unconsciously, forgets (obliterates from memory) events with which he or she is unable to cope.
- *Denial*—the person refuses to acknowledge the existence of real situations and circumstances. In repression, the person obliterates stressful situations and circumstances from his or her thoughts. In denial, the person may acknowledge stressful situations and circumstances but denies they have consequence or significance.
- *Rationalization*—the person creates "acceptable" reasons for events or circumstances because the true reasons are emotionally unacceptable.
- *Resignation*—the person gives up when confronted by seemingly insurmountable circumstances.
- *Becoming dependent, or demanding*—the person requires unnecessary assistance to ensure they get attention, affection, and care from important others.

An overreliance on defense mechanisms is incompatible with healthy, adaptive attitudes toward sources of stress. Developing realistic attitudes about one's disability can help avoid self-defeating behaviors and inordinate reliance on defense mechanisms. Fostering healthy, adaptive attitudes facilitates one's ability to progress toward achievable ends. Remember the adage that developing new habits is less difficult than breaking old ones.

Body Image

The image of one's own body and the value one places on that image are significant in formulating self-concept. The body is the hub of one's identity. The individual's somatic limitations and strengths have the potential either to bond the individual with or to alienate the individual from the environment. Individuals with physical disabilities may have difficulty positively integrating their disability into a healthy self-concept. Best, Bigge, and Sirvis (1990) confirm that social adjustment correlates negatively with self-concept when the disability is visible. The more visible the disability, often the greater the difficulty in adjusting socially and developing a positive self-concept.

Striving for Acceptance and the Price It Extracts

Virtually everyone strives to be accepted by others and to count positively in another's life. Both people with disabilities and those without can become trapped in the effort to develop false fronts that might be more acceptable to others. This behavior can be self-defeating for the person with a disability, particularly if a false front is used to cover up certain traits. As Wright (1960) states:

The price of trying above all to hide and forget is high. It is high because the effort is futile. A person cannot forget when reality requires him to take his disability into account time and again. The vigilance required for covering up leads to strain, not only physically but also in interpersonal relations, for one must maintain a certain distance (social as well as physical) in order to fend off the frightening topic of the disability. . . . Trying to forget is the best way of remembering. (p. 24)

Wright (1960, pp. 36–37) points out that "acting like a normal person" is not the same as "feeling like a normal person" (i.e., a worthy human being). She concludes that "all too often, one pays a price for the apparent success when the motivation (to act like a normal person) is to prove that one is 'as good as anybody else.'" Any attempt to hide, forget, or cover up traits considered unacceptable likely will have a negative impact on a person's self-concept. Homey (1937) believes that a person wishing to obscure a disability often ends up without associates. On the one hand, the person may resist associating with other people with similar disabilities for fear of drawing attention to the disability. On the other hand, the person may avoid association with persons who do not have disabilities for fear of having the differences become even more obvious. The person threatened by contact will avoid contact with either group. Given the need to feel "at home" with oneself, such a person is virtually homeless.

Severity Of Disability, Adjustment, and Self-Concept

Empirical evidence suggests that severe disability does not necessarily go hand in hand with maladjustment. Conversely, mild disability offers no guarantee of positive adjustment. Some persons with mild disability, because they are relatively normal, may recognize greater potential for hiding their disability. The hiding process can prompt denial and thwart adjustment, because the person hiding a trait judged to be undesirable has engaged in self-devaluation. Self-devaluation, in turn, negatively affects the self-concept. Persons with severe undeniable disabilities may have little recourse but to accept themselves as persons with a disability. In either case, the person who does adjust may need to cling temporarily to the "normal ideal." It may be necessary to embrace that ideal before one can truly give it up and find satisfaction in being oneself.

The foregoing discussion is not intended to deny the significance of adjustment challenges confronting the person with severe disabilities. Persons with severe *congenital* disabilities often experience the least status in the social community. Persons with severe *acquired* disabilities often experience a higher social status. It is hypothesized that a severe congenital disability, because it is present from birth, greatly limits experiences that ensure status in the community.

The degree and type of disability confronting the individual thus play a significant role in adjustment and self-concept development. Each person's unique individuality is, however, also significant in the process of adjustment and self-concept development.

Empathy Versus Sympathy

Empathy and sympathy are similar in sound only. Recognizing the difference in the meaning of these words and the different concepts they embody is critical for people who teach or otherwise function in a professional or personal relationship with people who have disabilities.

Empathy is the mature, genuine understanding of another's situation and circumstances. A saying in Native American lore speaks eloquently to the issue of empathy when the speaker admonishes, "Make no judgments about me until you have walked a mile in my moccasins." Empathy is the ability to understand another's thoughts or state of mind without actually having experienced the person's circumstances. Inability to empathize with another diminishes the teacher's potential to influence positively the learner's development. The ability to empathize goes beyond establishing rapport; it fosters insight, which in turn helps an effective working relationship.

Sympathy is feeling sorry for another. It connotes, "Oh, you poor unfortunate fellow!" Sympathy is synonymous with pity; pity devalues worth, and devalued worth causes additional suffering. People tend to want understanding, not pity.

Stories about outstanding achievements by persons with disabilities often unwittingly provoke sympathy and pity. The story of Pete Gray provides a case in point. Gray, who at age 6 lost an arm in a truck accident, became a major league baseball player. One newspaper account (cited in Rusk and Taylor, 1946) of Gray's achievement read as follows:

> *Gray is an inspiration. . . . The mere fact that a one-armed ball player has crashed the big league opens up new and electrifying vistas for each of them [similarly handicapped persons]. If one can overcome his handicap in such fashion, there is hope for them all. (p. 140)*

Reference to "them" effectively, though unwittingly, promotes the we-they dichotomy, which, based on disability alone, sets the individual with a disability apart from persons without disabilities. The last phrase, "there is hope for them all," drives home the stigma: "Poor fellow. But don't worry. Even for people like you there is hope." Inspirational messages should not be eliminated, but they should be tempered with empathy and an understanding that undertones can devalue the self-worth of the persons for whom the message is intended.

Handling Of Death In Our Society

Life's ultimate reality is death, yet death remains a reality with which many persons are unable to cope. Anxieties surrounding the imminent death of a terminally ill child are perplexing for everyone. People accept the death of older persons, but a child's death assaults reason. Human beings need to search philosophically for some purpose surrounding a child's death, yet an obsessive search disallows dealing with death's reality.

Some decades ago, most people in the United States were born and died at home. Three generations (children, parents, and grandparents) often lived together in a single dwelling, and the entire family was witness to birth, life, and death. Today, birth and death have been effectively obscured from human experience, because people are born and die in hospitals. Once, death was part of life's experiences; today, death has become taboo because of its physical remoteness. Although death in the home was not a welcome event, those who witnessed death were somewhat better prepared to accept its consequences as life's natural culmination.

Terminal Illness in Children

The dying child, if he or she is mature enough to grasp death's significance, and those affected by the child's death experience change in attitude as death approaches. If there has been enough time to adjust, people can accept death as imminent and inevitable. The dying person often takes comfort in the closeness and presence of loved ones.

Changes in attitude that lead to acceptance include anger, denial, bargaining (often with God), and depression. Kübler-Ross (1969) believes that each stage, given sufficient time, is "worked through," with the person ultimately accepting death's arrival and reality. Both the dying person and those affected progress through the stages.

Kübler-Ross says that the dying child often will single out one adult with whom to communicate feelings about death. That person is often not a parent but a teacher or therapist. The child tends to chose someone else because the child, sensitive to the parents' grief, does not wish to compound that grief. The selected person must be willing to accept the child's feelings, or the child will experience profound loneliness.

The Teacher's Roles

The teacher's roles are complex, for the teacher must communicate personally and sensitively with the child, the child's parents, and the child's friends. The teacher must recognize that his or her primary role is that of teacher to the dying child and teacher to the child's classmates. The teacher bears a responsibility not only to the terminally ill child but also to the children who remain.

In coping with this situation, teachers must first work through their own thoughts and concepts about death. Best, Carpignano, Sirvis, and Bigge's work (1991) on the psychological aspects of physical disability, particularly implications of terminal illness, is a valuable resource. They suggest strategies and attitudes helpful to parents and professionals who work with terminally ill children:

- Treat all children the same. If children with cerebral palsy are disciplined, also discipline those with terminal illness.
- Be objective in goal setting, building toward attainable goals.
- Maintain mental health. Be available to those who are dying and to those who remain after the classmate's death.
- Develop an understanding of the Kübler-Ross stages of coping with death and how children, parents, and professionals may use them. Recognize that everyone does not progress at the same pace, and allow for individual differences in coping.
- Define your role as an educator, remembering that your role is to teach. Included in that role is a responsibility as a human being to meet the personal needs of children. Your primary role, however, remains that of teacher.
- Respond to, and accept, your own feelings of anxiety, anger, guilt, and sorrow, and share these, when appropriate, with the children.
- Recognize that as a teacher you may be a catalyst for hope, but do not be foolishly optimistic.
- Prepare to answer the child's questions, such as, "Am I going to die?" Such questions must be answered carefully and honestly in response to individual needs.

- Prepare yourself to deal with the behavior of youngsters who cannot act out physically, and thus may rebel verbally against the world.
- Establish rapport with professionals in medicine and mental health who can be valuable resources.
- Deal with yourself.

Teachers will find that the psychological challenges manifested in children with terminal illnesses are more difficult to deal with. The affected youngsters and their peers, families, and teachers all need the insights that can be gained from death education programs. Wolery and Haring (1990) state the following:

These programs [death education] can be incorporated into the curriculum so that younger children can learn from stories about the life cycle of plants and animals, and eventually, of people. Curricula must reflect age-related conceptualizations of death, because the child's knowledge of change, disappearance, and finality must be established before death is fully understood. . . . The teacher's task is to help the student with a terminal illness develop a concept of quality in a limited life-span. . . . Thus, curricula for students with muscular dystrophy, cystic fibrosis, and terminal cancer should stress development and achievement of attainable short-term goals. Overindulgence should be avoided at all costs. (pp. 310–311)

The Helping Relationship

In a helping relationship, the person being helped is often assumed to be unable to help himself or herself. The act of helping another can be easily interpreted as helplessness on the part of the person receiving assistance. Determination that the person is helpless can be made by the helper, by the person being helped, or by persons observing the assistance. Because helping suggests a one-sided relationship, value judgments often are made about the person receiving aid. The person who receives help consistently may be judged inferior to others who seem self-reliant and independent.

Virtually everyone needs help sometimes, and one's sensitivity to receiving help is highly individual. Most people respond positively to assistance if it is genuinely needed and is not offered primarily to satisfy the helper's ego.

A person with a disability usually desires minimum assistance and only when necessary. Before helping, always obtain the consent of the person involved. Do not assume that help is needed or wanted. Assistance, particularly unsolicited assistance, may be interpreted as denial of the person's independence. If a person desires help but the helper is uncertain about what exactly is needed, the helper should simply ask. The helper should focus assistance on the task, not on the relationship. Fuss and emotional display by the helper suggest ego feeding at the expense of the person receiving assistance.

Helping has psychological as well as physical impact on the recipient. Helpers who understand clearly their own motivations will probably offer specific assistance only when needed. This kind of approach acknowledges the recipient's self-respect and is one that the recipient appreciates.

This chapter opened with a line of poetry by Bart Lanier Safford III. We close this chapter with another of Safford's poems. Safford, who has cerebral palsy, has earned three degrees in higher education. In the opening excerpt, however, he placed his academic achievements in perspective in fewer than 20 words. For Safford and those for whom he speaks, the psychosocial aspect of disability is not pristine, abstract theory but an enduring fact of life. Safford, whose gift with words enables him to say more in a few words than some say in volumes, has written the following poem, which might well have been directed to physical education teachers or to those who coach persons with disabilities. His poem is titled, "The Baseball Manager and the Warm-up Jacket":

> In high school in Brooklyn
> I was the baseball manager,
> proud as I could be
> I chased baseballs,
> gathered thrown bats,
> handed out the towels
> It was very important work
> for a small spastic kid,
> but I was a team member
> When the team got
> their warm-up jackets
> I didn't get one
> Only the regular team
> got these jackets, and
> surely not a manager
> Eventually, I bought my own
> but it was dark blue while
> the official ones were green
> Nobody ever said anything
> to me about my blue jacket;
> the guys were my friends
> Yet it hurt me all year
> to wear that blue jacket
> among all those green ones
> Even now, forty years after,
> I still recall that jacket
> and the memory goes on hurting.
>
> Bart Lanier Safford III

CHAPTER SUMMARY

1. The psychosocial implications of disability can extend further than the direct impact of the disability itself. Disabilities of great proportion do not, however, always precipitate greater problems of psychosocial adjustment. The impact that any disability has on psychosocial well-being is largely an individual phenomenon.

2. When difficulties in adjustment are apparent, the person with a disability may turn to defense mechanisms. These include regression, repression, denial, rationalization, resignation, and becoming dependent or demanding.

3. Teachers should strive to empathize with the person with disabilities. Sympathy denies the self-worth of the individual at whom it is directed and has a devaluing effect on the recipient's self-esteem. The person whose level of self-esteem wavers will find pity particularly devastating. Conversely, empathy reflects a mature effort to understand the circumstances and challenges confronting an individual. Sympathy is synonymous with pity, empathy with understanding.

4. The teacher may encounter children with terminal illness. In these circumstances, the teacher should be prepared to provide support to the dying child and to the child's peers. Both the dying child and the child's peers may rely heavily on the teacher. The educator must understand her or his own responses to death and must be prepared to deal with the children's responses.

5. In the adapted physical education setting, the teacher becomes involved in helping relationships. These relationships must preserve the recipient's self-esteem. Help should be offered only when needed and desired. Offering help too quickly in specific situations may deny the recipient the opportunity to achieve independence. In many instances, the teacher, uncertain of how much help is needed, should simply ask the child.

6. All people, irrespective of disability or nondisability, have psychosocial needs. Whether these needs are met determines the individual's adjustment to personal circumstances. Just as not all persons without disabilities manifest positive psychosocial adjustment, neither do all persons with disabilities exhibit difficulty in adjusting. In facilitating all psychosocial adjustments, the teacher must preserve the individual's integrity.

REFERENCES

Best, S., Bigge, J., & Sirvis, B. (1990). Physical and health impairments. In N. G. Haring & L. McCormick (Eds.), *Exceptional children and youth*, 5th ed. (pp. 283–324). New York: Merrill/Macmillan.

Best, S. J., Carpignano, J. L., Sirvis, B., & Bigge, J. L. (1991). Psychosocial aspects of disability. In J. L. Bigge, *Teaching individuals with physical and multiple disabilities*, 3rd ed. (pp. 110–137). New York: Merrill/Macmillan.

Homey, K. (1937). *The neurotic personality of our time*. New York: W. W. Norton.

Kübler-Ross, E. (1969). *On death and dying*. New York: Macmillan.

Levine, L. (1959, October). *The impact of disability*. Address to Oklahoma Rehabilitation Association Convention, Oklahoma City. (As cited by Best, Carpignano, Sirvis, & Bigge, 1991.)

Rusk, H. A., & Taylor, E. J. (1946). *New hope for the handicapped*. New York: Harper & Row.

Safford, B. L. III. (1978). The baseball manager and the warm~up jacket. *Disabled USA* 2(2).

Safford, B. L. III. (n.d.). *An obscured radiance*. El Paso, TX: Endeavors of Humanity Press.

Wolery, M., & Haring, T.G. (1990). Moderate, severe, and profound handicaps. In N. G. Haring & L. McCormick (Eds.), *Exceptional children and youth*, 5th ed. (pp. 239–280). New York: Merrill/Macmillan.

Wright, B. A. (1960). *Physical disability—A psychological approach*. New York: Harper & Row.

CHAPTER 5

Parents and The Collaborative Team Approach

To develop appropriate educational and service plans that will achieve educational objectives, teachers, physicians, therapists, and families need to work together. This necessitates cooperation among the home, community, and school to make informed decisions on the child's educational and physical needs.

The legal background and justification for a collaborative team is contained in the Individuals with Disabilities Education Act (IDEA). In accordance with the mandates of IDEA, evaluation, placement, and program planning for children with disabilities are carried out by a group of individuals, or collaborative team, drawing on expertise from a variety of sources. In the school setting, this team may consist of teachers, administrators, and consultants who bring their skills to bear in developing an approximate educational program for the child. This group is sometimes referred to as an educational multidisciplinary, transdisciplinary, interdisciplinary, or cross-disciplinary team (Jansma & French, 1994). Table 5.1 includes a brief description of the different types of teams and their roles. In practice, the integration of children into regular physical education classes requires input from a variety of services or team professionals to ensure that a proper educational program is developed based on each individual's needs.

Table 5.1 Types of Roles for Collaborative Teams

Team	Role
Multidisciplinary team	Initial assessment Program development Surfacing medical, physiological, psychological, and educational concerns Recommendations to classroom teacher concerning instructional programming No ongoing feedback
Interdisciplinary team	Direct contact with classroom teacher Initial assessment Program recommendations Establishing goals that are consistent within each professional area No ongoing feedback
Cross-disciplinary team	Direct delivery of services by several professionals (e.g., physical therapist and physical educator both contribute to improving a child's range of motion) Initial assessment Program recommendations and implementation Consultation between professionals

le 5.1 Types of Roles for Collaborative Teams *(continued)*

am	Role
ransdisiciplinary team	Ongoing dialogue and feedback Assessment and screening Program recommendations Program planning Consultation
Educational programming team	Assessment and evaluation Ongoing dialogue and feedback Program implementation and recommendations Consultation among professionals Direct service delivery by several professionals

The makeup of the team and interaction of professionals will be dictated by the needs of the child. Services may be intermittent, periodic, or continual, contingent on special or unique needs. For example, children with diabetes may require ongoing medical consultation to maintain effectively the proper balance of insulin, dietary intake, and physical activity, whereas children with mild respiratory disorders may require only periodic evaluations from a medical professional.

The nature of the team may therefore vary according to both the extent of involvement and the services required. In many smaller school districts, some professional services may not be available. In that case, alternative professionals may at times contribute their expertise to provide a portion of the needed information.

This unit should on an ongoing basis communicate among various professionals and supply current assessment data and information needed to plan, implement, and evaluate the child's progress and instructional program. The team will also provide clarification regarding proper placement, educational alternatives, unique styles of learning, and instructional continuity from the school to the home.

Potential Team Members and Services

The team members on the collaborative team generally fill a number of different professional roles. Some of those roles include the following (Table 5.2).

Regular Physical Education Teacher

Although the regular physical education teacher is not specifically trained to teach children with disabilities, this teacher will have direct contact with children on a daily basis and is responsible not only for including individuals with disabilities into the regular physical education program, but also for implementing the educational program. The physical education teacher often provides screening or diagnostic information concerning the individual's functional ability through observation or assessment in the regular instructional setting. Once the input from the programming team is gathered and assessed, the regular physical education teacher is responsible for planning and implementing the physical activity program with or without supportive services or equipment. The teacher is also charged with implementing the instructional objectives for all children in regular classes to ensure that program goals and objectives are

Table 5.2 Collaborative Educational Programming Team Members and Services

Team Members	Role / Services
Regular physical educator	Provides screening or diagnostic information Provides referral for exceptional services Engages in planning and implementation of instructional program Ensures that all children meet program objectives Consults with programming team Records progress and achievement Interacts with parents Offers social-emotional interaction Fosters fitness and motor skill development Provides behavior management
Adapted physical educator	Fosters fitness and motor skill development Provides behavior management Fosters sports skill development Assesses nutritional status and provides dietary consultation Provides screening and assessment of physical functioning Provides program development and implementation Consults with parents Develops after-school program Fosters social-emotional development Consults with regular physical education teacher
Special educator	Provides educational diagnosis Observes and screens for learning problems Records functional ability and progress Designs appropriate instructional program materials Aids regular education teacher in determining special needs, including attention programs, behavior management Provides ongoing consultation with team members Provides additional physical activity opportunities
Physical therapist	Aids in planning, conducting, and evaluating program Consults with programming team Provides muscle testing and posture evaluation Provides gait analysis Provides information on primitive reflexes and reactions Provides ambulation training Carries out sports classification
Occupational therapist	Restores daily living skills Implements self-help skills Helps develop vocational skills Helps with sensory integration Evaluates reflex behavior and postural reactions, play, muscle tone Consults with programming team members
Recreational therapy specialist	Promotes social, emotional, and physical development Assesses play and recreation skills Aids in integration between school and community Provides after-school program

Table 5.2 Collaborative Educational Programming Team Members *(continued)*

Team Members	Role / Services
Administrators	Provide budgetary control Assign staff and class schedules Aid in securing equipment and make decisions on accessibility of environment Develop programming team Establish class times and facilitate program implementation Serve as liaison between school and community
Physicians	Provide primary care of child with disability Provide data concerning functional ability Evaluate levels of performance Reassess and consult on an ongoing basis with programming team Provide information on medical history and changes in condition Provide information on medication Provide specialized information needed to implement program
School nurse	Collects and interprets medical information Provides postural, vision, and auditory screening Provides record keeping and treatment information Provides in-service training Interprets effects of medication Provides temporary health care
Parents	Particapate in initial referral and planning of IEP Provide medical and developmental history Report changes in condition or medication Advocate for child Communicate with other members of the team
School psychologist	Assesses and interprets educational, psychological, and behavioral instruments Evaluates suspected area of deficit Consults with the classroom teacher Provides information on medication and exceptionality Interprets assessment information to parents Aids in program planning and implementation between home and school Aids in behavior and environmental management Aids in developing social-emotional interaction
Nutritionist	Recommends dietary program Provides consultation on allergies, additives, and their effects on functioning Provides in-service training and counseling on dietary intake and exercise for specific exceptionalities Provides nutritional guidance and counseling
Athletic coach	Encourages active participation Supervises training and extent of participation Provides opportunities to participate with peers Promotes social and psychological interaction

achieved. A physical education teacher who is teaching more children with disabilities in regular education settings should consult on an intermittent or continual basis with other team members.

Adapted Physical Educator

Traditionally, the adapted physical educator has been trained to provide special, developmental, or adapted physical education services consistent with the definition of physical education in the IDEA. This professional usually is a full-time specialist or may serve a school district as a consultant or on an itinerant basis. The adapted physical educator should provide the primary assessment of physical and motor functional that leads to subsequent program planning. Recently, the adapted physical education teacher's role has evolved from providing direct services to consulting with regular physical education teachers to implement a more diversified program based on the unique needs of children and to provide in-service training on specific program needs.

Additionally, the adapted physical educator will be knowledgeable in appropriate evaluation instruments to assess the functional level performance in physical fitness, motor development, perceptual motor functioning, posture, and gait analysis. For school districts that do not have direct access to adapted physical educators, these services may be provided by state departments of education, regional resource centers, or universities on a consultant basis for both regular and special education teachers who have the responsibility of implementing the physical education activity program.

Special Educator

The special education teacher is commonly located in a self-contained classroom or resource room to accommodate children with physical or learning disorders (Hallahan & Kauffman, 1997). Services that this professional can contribute to regular classes include educational diagnosis, determination of learning and attention problems, behavior and environmental management, and perceptual motor functioning. Each of these services can aid in developing instructional units. For example, children who experience problems in visual-motor perception may have difficulty catching a ball, but children who respond visually to color contrasts may be successful in tracking and catching an appropriately colored ball. The interaction of both professionals through ongoing consultation, communication, and record keeping can contribute immensely to improving the physical and motor development of children with disabilities. Furthermore, if special education teachers provide a portion of the physical activity program, children benefit from the added practice, individual attention, and additional expertise that are available in the regular school setting.

Physical Therapist

The physical therapist (PT) is an individual responsible for planning, conducting, and evaluating an individualized program for medically referred children. Services provided by this professional are designed to increase the functional ability of children with neurological, musculoskeletal, and physical impairments. Although physical therapy is *not* an alternative to physical education, this professional is critical to enabling the physical education teacher to adequately address specific needs.

The physical therapist can help the teacher evaluate the functioning and strength of muscles; provide screening to evaluate postural deficiency and/or weakened muscles; conduct gait analysis to determine improper body or foot placements or inappropriate postural compensations as well as movement potential; assess range of motion to determine the flexibility of joints and muscles or the effect of contractures; and assess neuromotor coordination to determine functional ability of muscle groups and muscle tone. Physical therapists may also provide information on the presence of primitive reflexes and their influence in motor development as well as sensorimotor and/or perceptual motor functioning. Physical therapists are frequently responsible for ambulation training and the fitting and/or modification of ambulatory aids, such as crutches.

Physical therapists may also provide information on the sports classification of children through an evaluation of their remaining functional ability. The information from physical therapists can be helpful in planning the program and providing appropriate services through a cooperative effort with other teachers. For example, the use of range-of-motion exercises in a therapeutic setting can easily be implemented by physical education teachers in a resistance training program. In this manner the cooperative effort of two or more professionals can provide a more extensive physical activity program for the child. Another important role of the therapist is to encourage parents to provide more opportunities for developing motor skills or increasing strength. Although the services of a physical therapist may be sporadic or nonexistent in some school districts, even ongoing consultation on a limited basis can effectively enable parents, teachers, and therapists to accomplish common goals.

Occupational Therapist

The occupational therapist (OT) is another professional who may be available to the school on a part-time basis. An occupational therapist is an individual who formulates and administers activity programs designed to restore or develop skills of daily living. As part of the restoration of functional ability, the OT will base therapeutic interventions on fine motor muscle activity that can aid children in managing implements or eating utensils.

The occupational therapist may also contribute to enhancing sensory and vestibular functioning and developing higher neural functioning based on the work and training in sensory motor integration pioneered by Dr. Jean Ayres. These services should be coordinated by the physical education teacher and conducted in cooperation with a developmental physical education program consisting of balance and coordination skills to provide children a sound movement base that will aid in developing functional self-help skills.

Other responsibilities of the occupational therapist may include evaluating reflex behavior, postural adjustment reactions, muscle tone, play, and social interaction skills. The OT should also provide ongoing consultation with other teachers, therapists, and parents to increase the child's ability to initiate movement and develop self-care and vocational skills.

Recreational Therapist

The recreational therapist (RT) is a professional who is not generally available in the school setting. However, the services of the recreational therapist in a community-based recreational setting can contribute to increasing social, emotional, and physical functioning. The recreational therapist can provide experiences that are nonexistent in the school setting, such as camping, hiking, or skiing, which aid in integrating children within the community and peer group. A recreational therapist can also provide services such as leisure assessments for play or recreation and the selection of recreation activities to achieve program objectives. More important, community-based recreational organizations provide additional opportunities to develop and practice skills learned in the school instructional program. The more success children experience, the more adaptable they become to their home, community, and school environments. Although recreational therapy is not a direct service, nor should it replace physical education, an ongoing dialogue with recreational professionals should be encouraged.

Administrators

The administrative makeup of the educational programming team can include a variety of professionals. The school principal or vice principal, superintendent, and director of special education all contribute to the delivery of services. Administrators will coordinate the school instructional program and assign staff and supportive services to the programming unit. These professionals act as liaison between school and home by coordinating meetings, interpreting test results, and securing services that are requested by team members.

Each of these professionals must interact with other team members to adequately channel appropriate funding and equipment needed for children with disabilities. A primary responsibility of the administrative unit is to arrange flexible schedules to accommodate special needs. For example, children with diabetes may function more appropriately if their physical activity program is scheduled after lunch to ensure the proper balance of food and insulin prior to activity.

Administrators also make decisions regarding the accessibility of the building and classrooms as well as the interpretation and evaluation of the overall program. A thoroughly informed administrator can often generate funds and alternative services to offset the lack of facilities, equipment, or other professionals needed to provide the best available instructional program.

Physicians

The physician often provides an essential component of the integration process. For many physical disabilities, the physician provides the primary care and is responsible for information concerning the student's functional ability. Rather than confining children to inactivity, physicians can evaluate levels of performance that are within a medical margin of safety.

As children improve in functional ability, physicians can reassess and collaborate with teachers on recommended changes or appropriate levels of activity. For example, children with respiratory disorders may be under the care of a pulmonary physician who recommends periodic rest intervals during periods of physical activity to prevent exercise-induced bronchospasm.

Other physicians may provide information on the medical history and changes in the child's condition. If medication is indicated, physicians will prescribe the medication and provide information related to usage as well as potential side effects. Furthermore, teachers should be aware of the types of medication prescribed, their use, and any changes in dosage or type used by children.

If a specialist is available, such as a neurologist, this professional may provide the specialized information needed for placement or for determining the level of functioning. Recently, a physician provided specific information on a child with a head injury to assist the IEP team in developing the most appropriate placement. When physicians are not associated with the school district, the family physician or specialist may also provide the information on the child's functioning required to develop the individual program.

School Nurse

The school nurse may be housed in the school and serves as a health care professional who collects and interprets relevant medical information for the programming team. This information may include postural, visual, and auditory screening. The school nurse may also maintain medical records and update the treatment information for children.

In addition, the school nurse may provide in-service training on the onset of disease, dietary concerns and/or nutritional disorders, and on the referral process for specific services. When children experience respiratory distress or seizures, the school nurse provides intervening health care until the children recover or more extensive medical supervision is provided. In other instances, school nurses will dispense or interpret the effects of medication and consult with teachers when children are excused from physical activity for problems associated with their condition.

Parents

The cooperation of parents or guardians is essential for effective programming. Parents will be involved in the initial referral and planning stages of the IEP. They can also provide the medical and developmental history as well as any recent changes in the child's condition or medication. Parents are also the primary advocates for children and ensure that a proper placement and instructional program is provided. Parents should be viewed not as adversaries but as professionals who provide useful input when other team members formulate an appropriate instructional program. Parents then conduct a structured home learning program to supplement the school instructional program.

School Psychologist

The school psychologist can provide additional information that is outside the realm of the physical education teacher or special educator. The psychologist may assess, diagnose, and design appropriate interaction techniques in areas where physical education teachers require assistance. Through intensive evaluations, school psychologists may determine the area of deficit or suspected cause of the deficiency. This will enable physical education teachers to plan more appropriately for the child's special needs. They can also provide continuous monitoring and follow-up observations to rule out intervening causes of learning or behavior problems. For example, they can substantiate suspected soft neurological signs and sensory or perceptual problems. School psychologists may also interpret much of the assessment information for parents, may coordinate efforts to determine the appropriate educational placement, and may assist in planning and implementing the program in the home and school.

Nutritionist

The nutritionist is not a common addition to the programming team but can provide essential information for successful integration. Children with nutritional disorders, for example, require a sound dietary program as well as an appropriate exercise regimen to control weight gain or loss. Additionally, children with learning deficiencies may be required to plan a diet exclusive of sugar or food additives that may contribute to learning or attention disorders. Other children requiring insulin or dietary supplements will benefit from counseling on proper dietary intake and exercise. Finally, some children fast unduly or partake in eating binges and then regurgitate the food to lose weight. Nutritional guidance and counseling may be essential for these individuals with eating disorders.

Coach

The coach of an athletic team or the intramural sports director may have a significant impact on the successful integration. Rather than confining children to the sidelines away from active participation, allowing them to participate in sports under proper supervision can strengthen them physiologically and psychologically. Children with disabilities can particapate in sports and in the training that is required for sports competition at a level equal to that of their peers without disabilities. The increased physical fitness and motor performance can only benefit their overall performance. After-school training programs not only provide the skills necessary for sports participation, but also have contributed to positive psychological adjustments for many children with disabilities (Horvat, Henschen & French, 1986).

Putting Theory Into Practice

In the ideal setting, cooperation and interaction between all these professional groups would ultimately aid in developing the best educational program available for children with disabilities. However, in many school districts little information is shared among professionals for a variety of reasons, including conflict over who should assume what role. Ideally all team members will recognize the roles of other team members and function within their assignments. As indicated earlier, therapists and educators can cooperate to achieve the same goal, such as improving range of motion, by incorporating certain elements or activities into their own discipline.

Part of the conflict of roles comes from the inclusion of physical education as a primary service and therapy as a related service under the IDEA. This practice does not need to be detrimental to effective programming if lines of communication remain open and there is mutual respect among professionals.

Another reason for a lack of appropriate services is the attitude of some school districts toward compliance. Minimal compliance means providing the fewest services required under the law. Even though such school districts satisfy the letter of the law, they do not address the intent of the law: to provide the best educational atmosphere. Many school districts are faced with budgetary problems that prohibit buying equipment or providing appropriate accessibility. However, lack of funds should not affect the commitment of those school districts to develop a sound educational program based on individual needs.

The school district or local educational system may also be hindered by a lack of trained professionals in one or more areas. This state of affairs is more the rule than the exception. The lack of professional expertise can severely detract from the planning of an appropriate program; however, the support of the administration and existing professionals sometimes can overcome this deficiency. Requested assistance may take several years of planning and negotiation before appropriate services are rendered. This is especially true in the training of personnel in physical education who may not have expertise to teach children with disabilities. The teaching load in many school districts may preclude the hiring of a full-time specialist except on an itinerant or consulting basis. However, with the help of additional funds, in-service education or consultant physical education services can be made available to the school districts.

Time factors can also present a problem. Staff conferences, professional meetings, planning, and teaching time can burden even the most well-meaning teacher. For teachers in regular physical education, staffing meetings may be most important, but the placement and programming needs of children with disabilities also require significant teacher input. If not, the school's unique blend of talents is not being used to the greatest extent possible.

Finally, all members of the team should be treated as professionals who can contribute equally to the physical activity program. For the most part, physicians and administrators are regarded with professional esteem because of their professional status or experience. Regular and special physical education teachers, however, as well as therapists and school nurses, are also professionally trained and can contribute immensely to the programming team. Finally parents, although they may possess no formal educational background or training, are truly professionals: The valuable insights they can contribute from their intimate knowledge of, and love for, the child render them professionals in their own field.

In spite of the potential conflicts and lack of adequate resources in some situations, the programming team can be a viable aid in developing and planning the educational program. Although not all elements of the team may be included, or different terminology may be used to describe different roles, the nature of the interaction among professionals will ultimately determine the effectiveness of the program.

Developing the Parent-Teacher Team

Parents are generally active in supporting and promoting legislation for children with disabilities as well as making up a functional unit of the individuaizedl education plan (IEP) or individualized family service plan (IFSP). Additionally, because they function as the child's first teacher, parents exert a great deal of influence on overall development. Unfortunately, many teachers view parents as a threat to their educational domain. Instead of considering parents as partners in the education of children with disabilities, they view parents as combatants who are often blamed for the lack of educational progress.

The partnership between teachers and parents does not just happen. It must be developed, encouraged, and nurtured. Parents and teachers should work together to ensure the achievement of program goals and objectives. A major consideration for determining educational success is the communication and teamwork established between the educator and the parent (Wagonseller, 1981). Because teachers have personal contact with children only for a small segment of the school day and/or portion of the year, the parents' contribution to the educational process should not be discounted.

By developing such a partnership, the teacher can inform parents about goals and expectations in the educational process. In this manner, parents may supplement the contact hours by providing additional opportunities for needed practice or developing fitness (Hopper, Gruber, Munoz & Herb, 1992). Instead of blaming parents for shortcomings, behavior problems, and learning deficiencies, teachers can systematically involve parents in the education process. Teachers must be aware that the parent can often contribute pertinent information about the functioning of a child that may substantially aid the teacher in planning an appropriate program. When parents are informed about educational goals, and when they provide input to the teaching process, the consistency of learning between home and school is increased (Lillie, 1976).

Conversely, because parents usually do not possess the knowledge or skill to develop appropriate strategies and techniques for teaching, teachers can provide the expertise necessary for implementing a successful home instructional program. By sharing the educational strategies and teaching techniques acquired from their professional training, teachers can increase the effectiveness of parents as teachers.

The Individuals with Disabilities Education Act (IDEA) includes provisions for parents to serve as members of the collaborative team and share in the educational decisions of their children. For the teacher to effectively incorporate parents in the learning process and satisfy the requirements of the IDEA, educators should emphasize the positive aspects of a partnership and develop an effective parent-teacher relationship.

Benefits of Parent-Teacher Interaction

Communication and interaction with parents can be helpful to the overall educational process. Teachers should recognize that parents can periodically update background information on children that may be more useful than a formal assessment for determining strength and weaknesses. Teachers can also provide guidance on specific needs to the parents and communicate the achievement of program goals. By creating a positive home-school relationship and establishing parents as partners, the following benefits will accrue for the teachers (Horvat, 1991; Kalish, 1996; Sallis & Nader, 1990):

1. additional information related to child's physical fitness, sport, and motor functioning

2. positive interaction and involvement for both parents and children in fitness and community activities

3. more opportunities to learn new skills and practice learned skills

4. enhanced development of fitness, motor skills and play

5. increased opportunity for individualized instruction based on individual needs and rate of learning

6. increased opportunity to reinforce appropriate fitness, skill, and/or behavior concepts

7. reaching educational goals more quickly and effectively by promoting continuity between home and school

Establishing Communication Between Home and School

There are many ways to develop communication between home and school. Most teachers recognize the importance of ongoing communication with other teachers or support staff, yet they may neglect to develop effective communication with parents. An important thing to remember in the communication process is that the attitudes, trust, and confidence of parents are directly affected by the teacher's ability to communicate program goals and objectives (Beale & Beers, 1982; de Beltencourt, 1997). In order to establish these lines of communication, several methods, including the following, may be employed:

1. communication by letter or newsletters

2. home and/or school visitations or meetings

3. parent education or training sessions

4. regular telephone or electronic mail conversations

5. coordinated community activities outside the school that provide opportunities to learn and practice skills

6. specific home programs conducted by trained parents or school programs conducted with parents as aides

Parent Education

Parent education involves more than providing information in the traditional parent-teacher conference. These conferences are just the starting point in parent education. In parent-teacher conferences, teachers can provide more specific information to parents about developmental deficiencies, behavior disorders, or learning or processing problems. Parent education meetings are then implemented to promote understanding and knowledge of deficiencies that affect physical fitness and recreational or motor skill development. These meetings can be conducted periodically throughout the school year to cover topics of interest, or several meetings can be held to provide greater depth in one area. Teachers may also arrange for other speakers or for demonstrations on a particular topic. For example, one session could involve the use of motor training for individuals deficient in balance skills; or another might address more general areas, such as recreational activities, programs, or camps that may be available for children.

Wagonseller (1981) has suggested compiling a menu of topics for parents to rank in order of preference. By analyzing these and other parent concerns through conferences and IEP meetings, the school and/or school district can select meaningful parent education topics for programs. Additionally, it is important to conduct parent education meetings with a knowledgeable professional who is capable of interacting with parents and selecting the program goals that are appropriate to parent concerns. For example, school psychologists may speak on motivational techniques, or physical therapists on inhibiting reflex movements.

By matching the program goals with parent concerns, teachers can impart to parents a more thorough knowledge of physical activity programs. Common areas of concern can be addressed, and parents can gain a better understanding of the role of physical activity. Constructive communication can evolve as parents make known their needs and teachers respond in a professional manner, taking the first step to effectively develop the parent-teacher team.

Parent Training

Parent training extends the education of parents a step beyond the information or understanding phase of the parent-teacher relationship. The primary reasons for conducting parent-teacher sessions are to inform parents about specific teaching or behavior management techniques and to develop home-based activity programs designed to improve functional ability.

Training sessions can be conducted at schools, at parent-teacher association (PTA) meetings, at mental health centers, or in informal group settings. Generally the training sessions should concentrate on intervention and prevention programs that address more serious developmental or functional problems. To conduct a parent-training session, teachers should adhere to the following guidelines (de Beltencourt, 1997; Wagonseller, 1981):

1. Be positive in your communication and respect for parents.

2. Be direct and to the point with your questions. Do not give a double message and expect a direct answer.

3. Be a good listener and sensitive to parental concerns.

4. Be assertive and not passive or aggressive. For example, a parent might say, "Is there any long-range effect of this type of medication that I should be aware of before we make this decision?" The teacher should respond directly and forthrightly with the benefits and side effects of the medication and address any additional concerns of the parent.

The length of the parent-training session may vary according to parental interest. Most sessions will require follow-up communication, specifically with at least one parent in the home. Because most parents are not able to develop their own teaching materials or strategies even with the parent-training sessions, teachers play an essential role in this process.

Teachers can also direct parents to commercial products that have been developed for implementing home programs. Many products include guides, instructional manuals, and sequenced tasks that require only a minimum amount of training. Table 5.3 lists several examples of these resources.

Table 5.3 Resources for Developing Home Learning Programs

- Horvat, M. (1991). *Home learning program for developing gross motor skills.* Kearney, NE: Educational Systems Associates. (Text)
- Kalish, S. (1996). *Your child's fitness: Practical advice for parents.* Champaign, IL: Human Kinetics. (Text)
- Kennedy Foundation, Special Olympics. (1978). *Let's play to grow.* Washington, DC: Kennedy Foundation. (Packaged program).
- Seaman, J., & DePaun, K. P. (1995). *Sensory-motor experiences for the home: A manual for parents.* (2nd ed.). Reston, VA: AAEP.
- Werder, J., & Bruiniks, R. (1988). *A motor development program for children.* Circle Pines, MN: American Guidance Systems. (Packaged program).
- Wessel, J. (1980). *I Can: Fundamental skills; health and fitness; body management.* Northbrook, IL: Hubbard Scientific. (Packaged program).
- Wessel, J. (1986). *I Can: Sports skills.* Northbrook, IL: Hubbard Scientific. (Packaged program).

Home Programs

Initially, designing home programs may appear burdensome and time consuming for teachers. However, the extra practice at home may alleviate a child's motor deficiency and enhance the teaching process. Physical education teachers may be limited by time, number of children, and/or space requirements that hamper their ability to provide individualized instruction. Therefore, children who require additional instruction may lag behind their peers in developing physical fitness and motor skills. A home learning program can be implemented in such instances to provide extra practice and enhance the school program (Bishop & Horvat, 1984; Horvat, 1991). Home programs can be completed outside of class on an individual or family basis and range from developing task cards or long-term learning programs.

A task card is a developmentally sequenced set of skills prepared on an individual basis. Each card should contain a clear explanation of the task, the amount of time to spend on the task, safety precautions, and an evaluation procedure. Task cards can be used to accomplish short-term objectives, or they can be incorporated into a comprehensive home learning program to satisfy long-term goals. A home learning program is a developmentally sequenced set of skills prepared for an individual, family, or group (Horvat, 1982). All of the information contained in the task card is included in a developmentally sequenced series of activities that parents implement to accomplish long-term goals. Because more time, equipment, and knowledge are needed to implement long-term assignments, the parent and teacher require a complete understanding of the home learning program. Included in this chapter is an example of a home learning program that was used to enhance the balance performance of elementary-school-aged children with learning disabilities.

Developing Homework Materials

The key to providing a positive learning experience is to devise a structured home program based on needs and/or interests. To be successful, any home learning program should include the following components: (a) a clear explanation of the task; (b) specific teaching directions, including modeling and prompting procedures; (c) equipment needed; (d) safety factors; (e) time for each teaching session; (f) recording procedures; and (g) a specific amount of time needed to complete the assignment. By including all these program components, the teacher leaves nothing to chance and ensures that each task is divided into segments that are appropriate for the child's individual needs and can be easily understood by the parents. While implementing a home program, parents can acquire additional clarification of teaching skills through visits or phone contacts from the teacher.

In many cases, a short-term assignment will enable children to learn a motor task. However, long-term assignments are sometimes necessary for the child to attain goals over a period of time. For such occasions, teachers should design comprehensive developmental progressions of motor skills or physical fitness activities. The following sample includes one segment of a balance program—the locomotor balance skill of hopping. The same procedure can be used to teach additional physical fitness or motor tasks.

How To Use the Home Learning Program

This program is designed to provide children with opportunities to develop balance and gross motor ability. The teacher demonstrates the use of all materials in a parent-training session before the beginning of the program.

Teaching Directions

Length   Sessions should last approximately 30 minutes three times weekly. Skills may be taught anytime during playtime but should be limited to one session per day.

Place   Sessions may be conducted inside or outdoors. A level area is needed for balance activities.

Preparation   An effective way to become familiar with this parent program is to administer it to another person outside of the parent-training session. Instruct the person acting as the child to make mistakes so that you can practice the prompting procedures.

Pace   Additional skill assignments will be sent home each week, depending on the student's rate of improvement. A student who has difficulty completing a skill may need several sessions to learn or master the skill. Also, if the child becomes bored, utilize the games included in each section to renew interest and supplement the instructional technique.

Proceeding to the Next Level   Because each skill level is based on the preceding skill, each skill is to be completed before progressing to the next skill level. If children have difficulty, utilize another skill in the progression. Utilize only the skills that children have not mastered. Mastery consists of children performing at the "What to Say" level for each skill. Send new activities home weekly that depend on the child's ability to accomplish each task and can be inserted into the parent's program.

Program Segment

The following is an example of a home program segment.

Timing

Use a wristwatch with a second hand to time children on activities that require a time sequence, or count 1001, 1002, 1003, keeping pace constant.

Dynamic Balance—Hopping

Skill Level 1: Hop on preferred and then the nonpreferred foot (Figure 5.1).

What to Say

Parent: "Hop on your preferred [or nonpreferred] foot, landing on the same foot at least three times."

Child: Hops on preferred/nonpreferred foot three times.

Parent: "Wow! That was really good."

What to Do If the child has difficulty with the skill, show (model) the correct method, emphasizing bending the nonsupported leg at the knee and taking off and landing on the same foot.

Prompt If the child still has difficulty, place the child in the proper position, bending the nonsupported leg at the knee. If the child still has difficulty, support the child by the hand. Then allow the child to attempt the skill, and remember to praise.

Praise Remember to praise the child for any improvement or accomplishment.

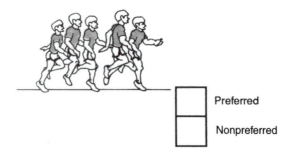

Preferred

Nonpreferred

Figure 5.1 Skill level 1: Hop on preferred/nonpreferred foot.

Skill Level 2: Hop for distance. (Figure 5.2).

What to Say

Parent: "Hop forward, taking off and landing on the same foot as far as you can."

Child: Hops forward on the preferred/nonpreferred foot ___ feet.

Parent: "Good hopping."

What to Do If the child has difficulty, show (model) the correct method. Then let the child try the skill, and give praise for any accomplishment.

Prompt If the child still has difficulty, return to Skill Level 1 and try again.

Praise Remember to praise the child for any improvement or accomplishment.

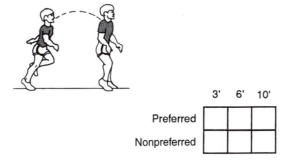

Figure 5.2 Skill level 2: Hop for distance.

Skill Level 3: Hop forward/backward/sideways over a line (Figure 5.3).

What to Say

Parent: "Hop forward/backward/sideways over the line, taking off and landing on the same foot." (Give just one command.)

Child: Hops on preferred/nonpreferred foot forward/backward/sideways over a line.

What to Do   If the child has difficulty, show (model) the correct method of hopping. (Remember to give only one command at a time.) Then let the child try the skill, and give praise for any accomplishment.

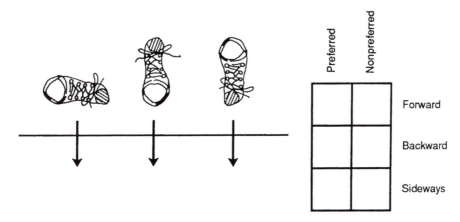

Figure 5.3 Skill level 3: Hop forward/backward/sideways over a line.

Skill Level 4: Hop forward/backward in succession over lines (Figure 5.4).

What to Say

Parent: "Hop on your preferred or [nonpreferred] foot, taking off and landing on the same foot forward/backward over these lines."

Child: Hops forward/backward over four lines in succession on the preferred/non-preferred foot.

Parent: "That was really hard! Good job."

What to Do If the child has difficulty with the skill, show (model) the correct procedure. Then let the child try the skill, and give praise for any accomplishment.

Prompt If the child still has difficulty, return to Skill Level 1 and Skill Level 2 for more practice.

Praise Remember to praise the child for any improvement or accomplishment.

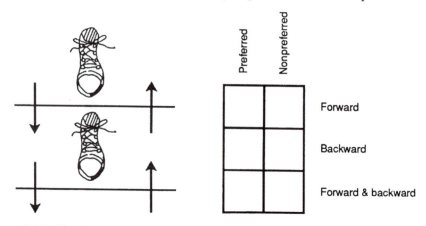

Figure 5.4 Skill level 4: Hop forward/backward in succession over lines.

In addition to basic motor skills, other skills and physical activities (such as sports skills and recreational activities) can be included in a home program to solidify the parent-teacher team (Taggart, Taggart & Siedentop, 1986). Several teachers have also incorporated sport and learning concepts, such as academic games, that can generalize to classroom activities and to behavior management strategies. A structured home program can benefit everyone and foster a positive relationship between the teachers and parents. Children can develop the skills that are common to their age group, parents can assume a larger role in the educational process, and teachers can provide individualized instruction outside the classroom and reinforce learning by increasing the opportunities to practice the task. Additional opportunities can then be afforded on a short-term or long-term basis, depending on the responsiveness of children and/or parent(s) and used after school, on weekends, or during vacations. Most important, a home learning program can initiate and foster communication between parents and teachers, serving as a means by which the parents can become a vital resource in the educational process.

CHAPTER SUMMARY

1. The purpose of the collaborative team is to help children achieve established educational objectives. The team is responsible for making informed decisions on evaluation, placement, and program planning.

2. The makeup of the team is dictated by individual needs and the services required. Information should be gathered from as many different sources as possible, including the student, to develop an appropriate program.

3. Communication and cooperation are essential in developing the most appropriate education for the child. All team members, including parents, should be treated as professionals who can contribute equally to the process.

4. Lack of interaction and cooperation among team members can result from a number of problems, including conflict over professional roles, the prevailing attitude of school district on compliance, a lack of trained professionals in one or more areas, time factors related to scheduling team conferences, and unequal regard for the professional role of each team member.

5. Many educators view parents as a threat to their educational domain. However, because parents are the child's first teachers, a relationship between parents and teacher should be developed and fostered to ensure the most appropriate educational program.

6. When parents are part of a partnership in the educational process, the goals, expectations, and progress of children are more easily communicated. Parents can take an active part in the educational process by continuing many of the concepts and objectives of the school program in the home environment.

7. Interaction and communication between educators and parents can be helpful to the overall educational process and the total development of the child. Parents can provide additional background information that contributes to formal assessments. The child can attain many benefits when there is a close working relationship between teachers and parents: learning new skills, opportunities for additional practice, individualized instruction, positive interaction, and opportunities to reinforce skills or certain types of behavior.

8. Parent education should go further than the traditional parent-teacher conference. Parent education meetings promote the parents' understanding and knowledge of deficiencies that affect the child's physical or motor skill development.

9. Parent training goes beyond the information-gathering and understanding phase of the parent-teacher relationship. Through parent training, the teacher informs parents about specific teaching or behavior management techniques and works with them to develop a home learning program based on individual needs.

10. Homework is an often neglected strategy in physical education. Task cards and home learning programs are two examples of strategies that provide further practice for children who require additional assistance.

11. Home learning programs not only provide additional opportunities for practice but also allow parents to become actively involved in the educational process. Through home learning programs, educators can utilize parents as a vital resource in the educational program and bridge the gap between home and school.

REFERENCES

Beale, A., & Beers, C. S. (1982). What do you say to parents after you say hello? *Teaching Exceptional Children, 15,* 34–38.

Bishop, P., & Horvat, M. A. (1984). Effects of home instruction on the physical and motor performance of a clumsy child. *American Corrective Therapy Journal, 38,* 6–10.

de Beltencourt, L. U. (1997). How to develop parent relationships. *Teaching Exceptional Children, 19,* 26–27.

Hallahan, D. P., & Kauffman, J. M. (1997). *Exceptional learners: Introduction to special education*, 4th ed. Boston: Allyn and Bacon.

Hopper, C. A., Gruber, M. B., Munoz, K. D., & Herb, R. A. (1992). Effect of including parents in a school-based exercise and nutrition program for children. *Research Quarterly for Exercise and Sports, 63,* 315–321.

Horvat, M. A. (1982). Effect of a home learning program on learning-disabled children's balance. *Perceptual and Motor Skills, 55,* 1158.

Horvat, M. (1989). *A manual of activities to improve perceptual motor skills.* Kearney, NE: Educational Systems Associates.

Horvat, M. (1991). *Home learning program for developing gross motor skills.* Kearney, NE: Educational Systems Associates.

Horvat, M., Henschen, K., & French, R. (1986). A comparison of the psychological characteristics of male and female able-bodied and wheelchair athletes. *Paraplegia, 24,* 115–22.

Jansma, P., & French, R. (1994). *Special physical education.* Englewood Cliffs, NJ: Prentice-Hall.

Kalish, S. (1996). *Your child's fitness: Practical advice for parents.* Champaign, IL: Human Kinetics.

Lillie, D. A. (1976). An overview to parent programs. In E. L. Lillie & P. L. Trohanis (Eds.), *Teaching parents to teach: A guide for working with the special child.* New York: Walker.

Sallis, J. F. & Nader, P. R. (1990). Family exercise: Designing a program to fit everyone. *The Physician and Sports Medicine, 18,* 130–136.

Seaman, J., & DePawn, K. P. (1995). *Sensory-motor experiences for the home: A manual for Parents,* 2nd ed. Reston, VA: AAEP.

Taggart, A. C., Taggart, J., & Siedentop, D. (1986). Effects of a home based activity program: A study with low fitness elementary children. *Behavior Modification, 10,* 487–507.

Wagonseller, B. A. (1981). The parent/professional team. In M. L. Hardman, M. W. Egan, & E. D. Landau (Eds.), *What will we do in the morning: The exceptional student in the regular classroom.* Dubuque, IA: Wm. C. Brown.

Werder, J., & Bruiniks, R. (1988). *A motor development for children.* Circle Pines, MN: American Guidance Sytems.

Wessel, J. (1980). I can. Northbrook, IL: Hubbard Scientific Co.

Wessel, J. (1986). I can: Sports skills. Northbrook, IL: Hubbard Scientific Co.

CHAPTER *6*

Assessment and Evaluation

The evaluation of children's capabilities and appropriate placement require information and data from all members of the educational team. In order to develop an instructional program and rehabilitation plan to document change, complete and ongoing data are required to determine the level of educational functioning and physical capabilities of children. These data are translated into program planning that commonly includes the child's short-term objectives and annual goals. Reevaluation of these goals and objectives is used to determine the progress and the effectiveness of the instructional program.

The evaluation process includes observations, screenings, and assessments in formal and informal settings. For teachers, the resulting data are used to make accurate judgments about the child's physical or motor functioning. Two types of evaluations are available: formative and summative. Formative evaluations are conducted throughout the teaching process or learning activity. For example, a formative evaluation of tennis would include the swing, various shots, and ball placement during every class. A summative evaluation occurs at the end of a program unit to determine the results of instruction or practice. For example, a summative evaluation in tennis would rate the child's ability to accurately serve or hit a specific shot at the end of the teaching unit. The environment itself should also be considered in assessments. Such factors as temperature, humidity, ventilation, and illumination all affect the instructional environment and the child's ability to learn. In addition, if space is inadequate, attention problems may develop that hinder effective teaching. Other environmental factors that should be considered include the child's accessibility to the program or ability to use equipment in the instructional setting.

The learner comes into the class with a variety of strengths and/or limitations. Some children who ambulate in a wheelchair may be athletes capable of outperforming others in a class or recreational setting. In contrast, some children may be lacking in physical development because of their disabilities and may require an extensive evaluation of their performance level. In each case, a specific awareness of the physical and motor performance capabilities is appropriate for developing instructional or clinical programs.

The process of learning is also critical for evaluating children. It is obvious that not all individuals learn at the same rate or retain all the information presented during a teaching session. To evaluate the annual goals and objectives requires that the instructional program be implemented in a manner most advantageous to facilitate learning. Some children may learn a skill more efficiently when they are placed in the proper position (haptic instruction) than when they hear the skill explained verbally; others may learn more efficiently when the stimulus is presented visually; and some children may need more time or trials to process the information.

Each type of evaluation should contribute to determining present levels of performance and whether or not the child has achieved program goals after the instructional plan is implemented. In most instances, assessments are usually conducted prior to planning the IEP and the instructional program. However, we should not discount the benefit of ongoing and continuous evaluation techniques that allow for teaching modifications or task analyses that coincide with the child's functional level.

Primarily, assessment should be used for the following purposes:

1. screening
2. placement
3. instructional planning
4. functional skill development
5. reviewing progress

Purpose of Assessment

The existing legislation for children with disabilities provides for evaluation of those who receive special services or are integrated into regular classrooms. This provision was intended to ensure that children are evaluated to determine their initial performance level, to aid in developing the program, and to determine the effectiveness of the instructional program and the potential for changing the behavior or condition. Although specific legal mandates cover children with disabilities, there are some children whose needs are not effectively addressed. Many children may be low in physical functioning, clumsy, or overweight. Although these children do not qualify for services, effective assessment and evaluation procedures are required to develop specific performance goals for their functional ability.

The process of assessment is also used to determine the effectiveness of the instructional program. Program evaluations should be concerned with the learning environment, the learner, teaching materials, and teaching styles in order to ensure that skills are being presented in a manner that is conducive to achieving program goals and objectives.

Components for Evaluation

The collaborative team will use a variety of measurement instruments, tests, screenings, and observations to determine appropriate placement, instruction, and program evaluation. For regular educators, effective teaching requires an understanding of the data generated from these techniques. This available information can be translated into effective programming by providing teachers with a more comprehensive picture of a child's functional ability. The areas that are tested or assessed by various team members include medical history, reflex behavior, perceptual and sensory functioning, motor development, physical fitness development, and sports skills and motor control.

Medical History

A thorough medical history and evaluation should be performed by physicians to determine the individual's level of functioning and complicating factors. This information can be used as a basis for initiating the program. Essential information for teachers/clinicians include the following (Horvat & Kalakian, 1996):

- chronic or acute illness, such as diabetes or asthma
- physical impairments, such as spinal cord injury, amputation, or muscular or neurological impairment
- sensory impairments, such as loss of vision or hearing, or vestibular dysfunction
- evidence of developmental delays, such as problems with coordination, balance, or muscle tone
- medications used, including dosage, side effects, and influence on functional ability

Reflex Behavior

In the early school years, reflex behaviors that are persistent or uneven will interfere with the development of motor skills. Teachers should be aware of existing reflexes that may be elicited with movement and the common effects of reflex movements on motor control. The evaluation of reflex behavior is initiated by physical or occupational therapists and is essential for developing postural control and a sound movement base prior to learning skilled movements. In addition, the reevaluation of reflexes or reactions may determine whether the instructional program is effective in inhibiting reflexes and developing more appropriate movement responses.

Perceptual and Sensory Functioning

The primary senses of visual acuity and auditory functioning are evaluated by selected professionals or by the school nurse. In addition, the auditory, visual, and haptic (tactile-kinesthetic) senses should be assessed by physical education teachers to determine areas of strength or potential problems in motor development. If more extensive testing is required, school psychologists or special education teachers may provide additional assessment information to detect the suspected causes of perceptual deficiency. These assessments are common for children who receive information properly but have difficulty integrating the information to make a decision prior to the motor output or action (Horvat & Kalakian, 1996).

Motor Development

The patterns and control of movements can be directly assessed by physical educators to determine functional locomotor patterns (running, jumping) and object control patterns (throwing, catching). If assistance is required to detect deviant patterns, teachers, therapists, or other health personnel can provide additional information on gait analysis or postural evaluation to supplement the evaluation. In this manner, the teacher can assess the developmental components of a movement and receive input from other personnel on the presence of reflexes or muscle imbalances that may contribute to delayed motor skill development.

Physical Fitness Development

The physical development and functional ability of children need to be accurately determined by teachers and/or appropriate support personnel. Commonly, muscular strength, endurance, flexibility, cardiorespiratory endurance, and body composition

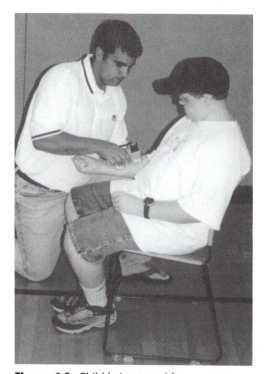

are directly assessed by teachers in the context of fitness (Figure 6.1). A more comprehensive assessment should relate to how these parameters affect functional skill development. For example, what is the level of strength that is necessary for walking or throwing? We should also evaluate physical functioning through gait analysis, muscle testing, and sports classification to determine how self-sufficient the child can be in home and community settings. Additional information may be required from physicians to provide information on metabolic levels of work (METS) desired, pulmonary function, duration, or extent of activity.

Sports Skills and Motor Control

When motor skills are learned, developed, and refined through instruction, they need to be continually assessed to determine whether children achieve typical developmental milestones and acquire the appropriate skills needed for the activity. Children with movement control may lag behind in motor development or require further evaluation to determine whether other sensory or perceptual factors may be interfering with learning.

Figure 6.1 Child being tested for muscular strength.

The assessment of sports skills or the ability to process and retain information may provide information regarding the child's learning style or ability to use information to achieve a motor output.

Types of Assessment Procedures

There are several assessment procedures that can be used to gather information concerning physical and motor functioning. When selecting any of these procedures, teachers or clinicians should be cognizant of how they help children attain their program goals. Test selection should be based on the purpose of the assessment, the test's validity and reliability, and its appropriateness for screening, placement, instructional planning, functional skill development, and/or reviewing progress to determine which formal and informal test procedures are best (Horvat & Kalakian, 1996).

In addition, testing procedures should reflect the validity of the test, the background of the tester, precision and reliability of instruction, time, functional ability, and size of the group. Many intricate evaluations are not appropriate for a particular

Table 6.1 Formal and Informal Assessment Methods

Assessment Method	Description	Relationship to Instructional Program
Formal		
Norm-referenced tests	Direct measure of physical fitness and motor development; cognitive development	Determination of present level of performance; documentation of progress
Medical evaluation	Direct measure of physical functioning	Determination of present level of performance; documentation of progress; determination of changes in physical condition
Informal		
Observation	Direct measure of physical fitness, motor development	Determination of present level of performance; documentation of progress
Criterion-referenced tests	Direct measure of performance on a specific task compared to external criteria for success	Determination of present level of performance; documentation of progress
Task analyses	Evaluation of physical fitness to locate appropriate subtasks for instructional progression	Direction for selection of appropriate criterion-referenced or informal tests; direction for selection of annual goals and objectives
Checklists, ratings, scales, questionnaires	Evaluation of performance based on accumulation of information from parents, teachers	Estimation of present level of performance in physical activity

situation and will consume valuable teaching time while adding a minimal amount of information for planning the instructional program. Selection of the most expedient tests available also should be based on the kind and amount of information needed to develop the educational program. Several types of testing procedures that are commonly used by teachers are summarized in Table 6.1. They include norm-referenced tests, criterion-referenced tests, direct observation, task analysis, checklists, rating scales, and interviews and questionaires.

Norm-Referenced Tests

The norm-referenced, or standardized, test is a formal testing procedure that enables educators to make comparisons among individuals with similar characteristics such as age, sex, height, weight, or exceptionality. These tests are useful in the diagnosing an individual's functional ability or relationship to the peer group or norm. Norm-referenced testing procedures include specific instructions and administration procedures to ensure valid and reliable results that can be generalized to a similar group. Common methods of reporting scores include standard scores, age equivalents, or percentiles that are useful to determine cut-off points for placement decisions.

Criterion-Referenced Tests

Criterion-referenced tests are informal assessments that compare an individual's performance to a predetermined criterion rather than to the performance of others.

These tests are usually curriculum based and are conducted to determine which skills have been mastered. Scores are generated on the individual's performance rather than on the average performance of the group. These scores are directly related to the selected task, such as the ability to maintain a balanced position for a recorded period of time.

Direct Observation

Direct observation is an informal technique designed to gather information on specific performance characteristics. Teachers may compile observations related to physical functioning, such as coughing or wheezing after 6 minutes of activity; motor performance, such as falling down or tripping; or behavior, such as fighting. Informal documented observations can indicate the number of times these characteristics occur and their effect on instruction by focusing on the child's performance and can possibly provide grounds for more formalized evaluations. Further, direct observation can determine such factors as interactions or time spent in play-related activities.

Task Analysis

Task analysis is an informal assessment related specifically to instruction. The task that needs to be performed can be assessed by dividing it into teachable units that can be observed and measured. As children meet each objective, they progress in developing the total skill. Conversely, difficulties with the task may indicate the need for further division of the task into smaller instructional units.

Checklists

Checklists are also informal assessments that can be used to accumulate information or to record the performance of children on selected tasks. Most developmental landmarks or profiles are already indicated on a checklist; parents or teachers can thus easily determine whether children meet specific performance indicators. For other skills, such as archery, a checklist format can help to determine whether basic skills can be performed, for example, those skills required to string a bow, notch an arrow, or shoot appropriately. No hard data are generated from checklists other than an indication whether a particular level has been reached. Many teachers also provide a section for comments to record more precise information about the performance on a test item. Checklists also provide an excellent format for gathering information not readily available in the educational or clinical setting by collecting information from parents, physicians, or therapists about the child's developmental history and medical concerns.

Rating Scales

Rating scales are informal techniques that enable teachers to express opinions and judgement as well as rate a performance from "poor" to "excellent." Ratings can be helpful in assessing new skills and monitoring performance.

Interviews and Questionnaires

Interviews and questionnaires are other informal methods used to gather information. Parents can thus provide information on medical and birth history, development, medication, and changes in condition, thereby offering useful insights into program planning. Other questionnaires can determine the child's social interaction, play behavior, self-concept, or attitude toward his or her disability or physical activity.

Teacher-Developed Evaluation Instruments

In some instances, no specific tests are appropriate to accommodate all children and their individual differences. In addition, when tests are available, some portions of the country may not be as adept as others in performance on the test items. A child from the state of Georgia, for example, will probably be more proficient in football than in ice hockey; youngsters in Indiana may be more inclined to develop basketball skills than football skills. Each region may affect the experience and background of the child.

If a situation dictates that an assessment is needed, teachers or clinicians may utilize informal teacher-developed instruments that are situation specific and meet the goals and objectives of the instructional program. Block, Lieberman and Connor-Kurtz (1998) have referred to dissatisfaction regarding how assessments are conducted and used in adapted physical education. They identified four problem areas (Block et al., 1998):

1. Standardized tests are misused for developing the IEP by including items that have no functional relevance for the child's program.

2. Standardized tests do not provide specific information on appropriate instructional techniques or for making decisions concerning placement. Many times, social, emotional, or cognitive abilities that affect performance are evident but are not taken into account by the test.

3. Standardized tests are not sensitive to environment contexts that may change and not generalize to other settings.

4. Letter grades, which are commonly used, do not convey specific information regarding the child's progress or performance.

Authentic assessment is used to measure areas that are specific to performance in naturalistic and generalized settings. This is a specific attempt to provide a more comprehensive assessment that is more functional in nature. For example, individuals with spinal injuries who are integrated into regular weight-training classes may require a specific evaluation of their physical conditioning prior to participation. To meet the goals of the program and to ascertain an entry level for resistance training, the teacher may design a specific assessment to evaluate the child's functional abilities as well as the starting point for a resistance training program. Such components as the amount of force generated, range of motion, and endurance can be assessed that are specific to the child and the environment in which he or she participates. In addition, the assessment can be based on the components of the environment; the child may be asked to perform necessary skills, such as work-specific tasks in the community that are situational and context related (Croce & Horvat, 1992; Zetts, Horvat & Langone, 1995). In addition, assessment can be movement specific, such as the example in Table 6.2 of authentic assessment for selected basketball skills.

Table 6.2 Sample Authentic Assessment for Selected Basketball Skills

	Simple ⟵				⟶ Complex
Environment	Individualized instruction APE class	Combination of skills into patterns	General skills in drills and lead-up activities	Play in recess and after school	Community/recreation participation in competition
Skill performance	Dribbles/passes with prompts and guided assistance	Dribbles/passes but hesitant and slow responses	Dribbles/passes with verbal cue	Dribbles/passes independently and appropriately	Dribbles/passes independently to correct player
Game performance	Dribbles/passes inappropriately	Dribbles/passes but does not look for teammate	Moves independently with dribble and looks for a teammate	Independently dribbles and passes to teammate	Moves with dribble and passes

Recommended Assessment Instruments in Physical Education

The assessment instruments in Table 6.3 include examples of physical fitness, motor development, sports skills acquisition, and attitude assessments. Teachers should use as many of these devices as needed, as well as authentic assessments, to provide the information required for the IEP meeting and to ensure that the educational goals of all children are being met. When other assessment information is required, teachers should supplement the ongoing assessment information needed to develop the most appropriate instructional program.

Table 6.3 Recommended Assessment Instruments

Test	Ages	Components	Test Administrator	Comments
MOTOR BEHAVIOR				
Bayley II Scales of Infant Development (Bayley, 1993)	Birth to 6 years	Mental scale; Motor scale; Behavior rating scale	Teachers	Screening for psychomotor development; Bayley Infant Neurodevelopmental Seven (BINS) measures basic neurological function
Brigance Diagnostic Inventory of Early Development (Brigance, 1978)	Birth to 7 years	Gross and fine motor movements; language and comprehension skills	Teachers	Flexible criterion-referenced instrument based on developmental sequences
Denver II Developmental Screening Test (Frankenburg, Dodds & Archer, 1990)	Birth to 6 years	Gross motor, fine motor, personal language, social development	Teachers	Screening for developmental delays in primary ages

Table 6.3 Recommended Assessment Instruments *(continued)*

Test	Ages	Components	Test Administrator	Comments
MOTOR BEHAVIOR				
Cratty's Category Gross Motor Test (Cratty, 1969)	4–22 years	Body perception, gross and locomotor ability, balance, ball throwing, and talking	Teachers	Screening for motor development and perceptual functioning
Bruininks-Oseretsky Test of Motor Proficiency (Bruininks, 1978)	5–14.5 years	Static balance, dynamic balance, coordination, strength, visual-motor coordination, response speed, visual-motor control, upper limb speed	Teachers	Assess gross and fine motor functioning: 8 subtests and 46 items; long and short forms
I CAN System (Wessel, 1976a, 1976b, 1976c, 1976d)	5–25 years	Aquatics body management, health and fitness, fundamental skills, sports skills	Teachers	Assessment and program curriculum to meet instructional goals
Ohio State University SIGMA (Loovis & Ersing, 1979)	2.5–14 years	Basic locomotor, object control skills plus ladder and stair climbing	Teachers	Criterion-referenced at four levels of SIGMA development with accompanying curriculum
Peabody Developmental Motor Scales (Folio & Fewell, 2000)	Birth to 7 years	Gross 7 fine motor skills including reflexes, balance, locomotor, non-locomotor, manual dexterity, eye-hand coordination	Teachers	Norm-referenced developmental screening on skill development at various ages
Project Active (Vadola, 1975)	3 years and above	Gross body coordination, balance, posture, eye-hand coordination, strength endurance	Teachers	Norm-referenced physical fitness and motor ability assessment and accompanying curriculum
Movement Assessment Battery for Children (Henderson & Sudgen, 1992)	4–12 years	Balance, control, coordination, throwing, kinesthetic awareness	Teachers	Norm-referenced assessed for functional or neurological motor dysfunction
Test of Gross Motor Development (Ulrich, 1999)	3–10 years	12 locomotor skills plus throwing, catching, kicking, striking, bounding	Teachers	Criterion- and norm-referenced assessment of locomotor and object control skills
Fundamental Movement Checklist (McClenaghan & Gallahue, 1978)	2–7 years	Locomotor and object control skills	Teachers	Criterion-referenced checklist of patterns at initial, elementary, and mature level
Fundamental Motor Patterns (Wickstrom, 1983)	2–7 years	Locomotor and object control skills	Teachers	Criterion-referenced checklist of locomotor and object control skills
Special Olympics Sports Skill Manuals (Kennedy Foundation, 1985)	6 years and above	Individual and team sports for winter and summer sports	Teachers	Assessment of various skill levels and accompanying teaching techniques

Continues.

Table 6.3 Recommended Assessment Instruments *(continued)*

Test	Ages	Components	Test Administrator	Comments
POSTURE/GAIT				
New York Posture Screening (New York State Department of Education 1966)	10 years and above	Shoulder girdle, back, foot placement, body alignment	Teachers	Criterion-referenced posture screening on 13 areas of the body
San Diego State University Posture Evaluation (Lasko & Aufsesser, n.d.)	10 years and above	Strength, flexibility, orthopedic evaluation and posture	Teachers	Criterion- referenced screening of orthopedic deviations and improper gait and body mechanics
Rancho Los Amigos Observational Gait Analysis (Gronley & Perry, 1993)	10 years and above	Range of motion in trunk, pelvis, hip, knee, ankle, and toes during gait	Teachers	Range of motion during gait cycle on weight acceptance, single limb support and swing limb advancement
PERCEPTUAL MOTOR				
Southern California Sensory, Motor Integration Test (Ayres, 1976)	4 years and above	Limitation of postures, crossing midline, bilateral coordination, right-left discrimination balance	Licensed testers	Measures sensory integration
Developmental Test of Visual Perception DTVP-2 (Hammill, 1993)	4–9 years	Eye-hand coordination, copying, spatial relations, positions in space, figure ground, visual closure, visual motor speed	Teachers	Based on updated theories of spacial perception
Purdue Perceptual Motor Survey (Godfrey & Kephart, 1969)	6–10 years	Balance and posture, body image and differentiation, ocular control; form perception, perceptual motor match	Teachers	Quantifies perceptual motor abilities of children in early grades
FITNESS				
12 min/1.5 mile test (Cooper, 1978)	13 years and above	Cardiovascular endurance	Teachers	Norm-referenced measure of fitness measured in time and distance
Youth Fitness Tests (AAHPERD 1968, 1974, 1976a, 1976b, 1980, 1988)	6 years and above	Strength, endurance, cardiorespiratory endurance, flexibility, body composition	Teachers	Series of norm-referenced tests on physical fitness of exceptional and regular educational students
Special Olympics Fitness Test Battery (Roswal, 1985)	8 years and above	Grip strength, flexibility, body composition, leg strength, abdominal strength	Teachers	Normed on Special Olympics with mild and moderate classifications
Hand-held dynamometer	6 years and above	Muscular strength	Teachers	Assessment of isometric strength in variety of muscle groups; sides of the body
Isokinetic dynamometer	10 years and above	Muscular strength endurance, work power	Teachers, therapists, clinicians	Assessment of strength and endurance at various speeds, reciprocal muscle functions

Table 6.3 Recommended Assessment Instruments *(continued)*

Test	Ages	Components	Test Administrator	Comments
FITNESS				
Repetition maximum (1RM; 3RM)	13 years and above	Muscular strength	Teachers, coaches	Estimation of maximal strength with free weights
Project transition (Jansma, 1986)	7 years and above	Physical fitness, personal hygiene	Teachers	Criterion-referenced and task-analyzed skills with accompanying scoring system
Project Unique (Winnick & Short, 1985)	10–17 years	Body composition, strength and endurance, agility, static balance, strength, cardiorespiratory function	Teachers	Norm-referenced physical and motor fitness assessment for sensory and orthopedic disabilities
Kansas Adapted/Special Physical Education (Johnson and Lavay, 1988)	5–21 years	Flexibility, upper body strength/endurance, aerobic movement and endurance	Teachers	Adaptations to accommodate most children with special needs in health-related fitness
Fitnessgram (Cooper Institute for Aerobic Research, 1999)	5–25 years	Aerobic capacity, body composition, muscular strength, endurance, flexibility	Teachers	Currently used by 6,000 schools; accompanied by Physical Best and Individuals with Disabilities Education Kit
President's Challenge Youth Physical Education Program (President's Council on Physical Fitness and Sports, 1997)	6–17 years	One-mile run/walk; curl-up; shuttle run; pull-ups; v-sit reach	Teachers	Includes set of guidelines for qualifying children with disabilities
National Youth Physical Fitness Program (United States Marines Youth Fitness Program, 1997)	5–21 years	Push-ups; pull-ups; sit-ups; standing long jump; 300-yard shuttle run	Teachers	Requires a minimum amount of space and allows modification of standards for children with disabilities
Brockport Physical Fitness Test (BPFT) (Winnick & Short, 1999)	10–17 years	Aerobic functioning pacer; target movement test; one-mile run/walk	Teachers	Norm-referenced health-related physical fitness test
		Musculoskeletal functioning; trunk lift; grasp strength; bench press; isometric push-up; dumbell press; reverse curl; pull-up; wheelchair ramp test; body composition skinfold BMI		Flexibility; back saver; shoulder stretch; Apley Test; Thomas Test
SELF CONCEPT-ATTITUDE				
Body Image Screening Test for Blind Children (Cratty, 1971)	8–19 years	Body planes, body parts, body movement, laterality and directionality	Teachers	Body image and screening for awareness for visually impaired and sighted children

Continues.

Table 6.3 Recommended Assessment Instruments *(continued)*

Test	Ages	Components	Test Administrator	Comments
SELF CONCEPT-ATTITUDE				
Self-Concept Scale (Piers & Harris, 1969)	9–18 years	Behavior, intellectual and school status, physical appearance, anxiety, popularity, happiness, and satisfaction	Teachers	Adjective checklist to determine children's feelings about themselves
Perceived Physical Competence Scale for Children (Harter, 1985)	Grades 3–6	Assesses cognitive, social, physical and general self-worth domains	Teachers	28-item scale on child's perception of competences in sports and outdoor games
Psychological Skills Inventory for Sports (Mahoney, Gabriel & Perkins, 1987)	Athletes	Assesses psychological skills consistent with elite performance	Licensed Psychologist	Used with athletes with disabilities
Piers-Harris Children's Self-Concept Scale (Piers & Harris, 1969)	Grades 3–12	Measures behavior; intellectual and school status; physical appearance; anxiety; popularity and happiness	Teachers	80 statements with yes or no responses and children's self concept
Martinek-Zaichkowsky Self-Concept Scale (Martinek & Zaichkowsky, 1977)	Grades 1–8	Measures satisfaction and happiness; home and family relationships; ability in sports, games, behavior, and personality traits	Teachers	Child points to a picture and responds how they feel to 25 pictures
FUNCTIONAL ACTIVITIES				
Sit-to-stand	6 years and above	Level of assistance needed	Teachers	Criterion-referenced based on developmental capabilities

CHAPTER SUMMARY

1. Assessment and evaluation are integral parts of developing the individualized education plan and implementing the instructional process. The process of evaluation is ongoing and includes observations, screening, and assessments in formal and informal settings.

2. There are two types of evaluation: formative and summative. Formative evaluations are conducted throughout the teaching process or educational activity. Summative evaluations occur at the end of a program unit to determine the result of instruction or practice.

3. Evaluation is required to track progress as well as to determine the effectiveness of the instructional process.

4. The educational team will use a variety of assessments to aid in the evaluation process. Teachers should be prepared to address the following areas with the help of other team members: medical evaluations, reflex behavior, perceptual and sen-

sory functioning, motor development, physical fitness development, and sports skills and motor control.

5. Norm-referenced tests enable teachers to make comparisons among individuals with similar characteristics, such as age, height, weight, gender, and exceptionality.

6. Criterion-referenced tests compare an individual's performance to a selected criterion rather than to the performance of others.

7. Direct observation is a useful informal technique that allows teachers to gather information on specific performance characteristics.

8. Task analysis is an informal technique specifically related to instruction. By developmentally sequencing a task, teachers can determine problem areas within a skill.

9. Other informal techniques include checklists, rating scales, and interviews and questionnaires. These enable teachers to accumulate information on individual performance from a variety of settings.

10. Because of the wide variety of functional capabilities, some tests may not be appropriate to use with all individuals. Furthermore, additional information that is task or program specific may not be available. Therefore, authentic assessments or teacher-developed instruments can be developed to generate the necessary information to evaluate the child's functional capabilities and develop the instructional plan.

REFERENCES

American Alliance of Health, Physical Education, Recreation, and Dance (AAHPERD). (1968). *Special fitness manual for mildly retarded persons.* Reston, VA: Author.

American Alliance of Health, Physical Education, Recreation, and Dance (AAHPERD). (1974). Youth fitness test for the blind. In *Physical education and recreation for the visually handicapped.* Reston, VA: Author.

American Alliance of Health, Physical Education, Recreation, and Dance (AAHPERD). (1976a). *AAHPERD youth fitness test.* Reston, VA: Author.

American Alliance of Health, Physical Education, Recreation, and Dance (AAHPERD). (1976b). *Motor fitness testing manual for the moderately retarded.* Reston, VA: Author.

American Alliance of Health, Physical Education, Recreation, and Dance (AAHPERD). (1980). *Health related fitness test.* Reston, VA: Author.

American Alliance of Health, Physical Education, Recreation, and Dance (AAHPERD). (1988). *Physical best: A physical fitness education and assessment program.* Reston, VA: Author.

Ayres, J. (1976). *Southern California sensory integration test.* Los Angeles: Western Psychological Services.

Bayley, N. A. (1993). *Manual for the Bayley Scales of infant development.* New York: Psychological Cooperation.

Block, M. E., Lieberman, L.J., & Connor-Kurtz, F. (1998). Authentic assessment in adapted physical education. *Journal of Physical Education Recreation and Dance, 69,* 48–55.

Brigance, A. H. (1978). *Brigance inventory of early development.* Woburn, MA: Curriculum Associates.

Bruininks, R. (1978). *Bruininks-Oseretsky test of motor proficiency.* Circle Pines, MN: American Guidance Service.

Cooper, K. (1978). *The aerobics way.* New York: M. Evans.

Cooper Institute for Aerobic Research (CIAR). (1999). *Fitnessgram Test administration manual.* Champaign, IL: Human Kinetics.

Cratty, B. J. (1969). *Cratty six category gross motor test.* Springfield, IL: Charles C. Thomas.

Cratty, B. J. (1971). *Movement and spatial awareness in blind children and youth.* Springfield, IL: Charles Thomas.

Croce, R., & Horvat, M. (1992). Effect of reinforcement based exercise on fitness and world productivity in adults with mental retardation, *9*, 148–178.

Folio, M. R., & Fewell, R. (2000). *Peabody developmental motor scales* (2nd ed.). Austin, TX: Pro-Ed.

Frankenburg, W. K., Dodds, J. B., & Archer, P. (1990). *Denver II developmental screening test.* Denver: Denver Developmental Materials.

Godfrey, E., & Kephart, N. (1969). *The Purdue perceptual-motor survey.* Columbus, OH: Charles E. Merrill.

Gronley, J. K., & Perry, J. (1993). *Gait analysis techniques: Observational gait analysis.* Downey, CA: Los Amigos Research and Education Institute.

Hammill, D. V. (1993). *Developmental test of visual perception* (2nd ed.). Austin, TX: Pro Ed.

Harter, S. (1985). *Manual for self-perception for children.* Denver: Author.

Henderson, S., and Sudgen, D. (1992). *Movement assessment: Battery for children.* San Antonio, TX: Psychological Corporation.

Horvat, M., & Kalakian, L. (1996). *Assessment in adapted physical education and therapeutic recreation.* Dubuque, IA: Brown & Benchmark.

Jansma, P. (1986). *Project transition.* Columbus, OH: Ohio State University Press.

Johnson, R. E., & Lavay, B. (1988). *Kansas adapted/special physical education test manual.* Kansas State Department of Education. Topeka, KS.

Kennedy Foundation. (1985). *Sports skill training manuals.* Washington, DC: Author.

Lasko, P., & Aufsesser, P. (n.d.). *San Diego State posture evaluation.* San Diego, CA: Authors.

Loovis, M., & Ersing, W. (1979). *Ohio State scale of intra gross motor assessment (SIGMA).* Laudonville, OH: Mohican Press.

Mahoney, M. J., Gabriel, T. J., and Perkins, T. S. (1987). Psychological skills and exceptional athletic performance. *The Sport Psychologist, 1,* 181–199.

Martinek, T., & Zaichkowsky, L. (1977). *Manual for the Martinek-Zaichkowsky self-concept scale for children.* Jacksonville, FL: Psychologists and Educators.

McClenaghan, B., & Gallahue, D. (1978). *Fundamental movement.* Philadelphia: Saunders.

New York State Department of Education. (1966). *New York posture screening.* Albany, NY: Author.

Piers, E., & Harris, D. (1969). *The Piers-Harris self-concept scale.* Los Angeles: Western Psychological Services.

President's Council on Physical Fitness and Sports. (1997). *President's youth physical education program.* Washington, DC: Author.

Roswal, G. (1985). *Special Olympics fitness battery.* Jacksonville, AL: Alabama Special Olympics.

Ulrich, D. (1999). *Test of gross motor development.* Austin, TX: Pro-Ed.

United States Marines. (1997). *United States Marines youth fitness program,* Washington, DC: Author.

Vadola, T. (1975). *Project active.* Oakhurst, NJ: Township of Ocean Park.

Wessel, J. (1976a). *I CAN: Body management.* Worthbrook. IL: Hubbard Scientific.

Wessel, J. (1976b). *I CAN: Fundamental skills.* Worthbrook, IL: Hubbard Scientific.

Wessel, J. (1976c). *I CAN: Health and fitness.* Worthbrook, IL: Hubbard Scientific.

Wessel, J. (1976d). *I CAN: Sports skills.* Worthbrook, IL: Hubbard Scientific.

Wickstrom, R. (1983). *Fundamental movement patterns* (3rd ed.). Philadelphia: Lea and Febiger.

Winnick, J., & Short, F. (1985). *Physical fitness testing of the disabled: Project unique.* Champaign, IL: Human Kinetics.

Winnick, J., & Short, F. (1999). *The Brockport physical fitness test.* Champaign, IL: Human Kinetics.

Zetts, R., Horvat, M., & Langone, J. (1995). Effect of a community based resistance training program on the work productivity of adolescents with moderate to severe intellectual disabilities. *Education and Training in Mental Retardation and Developmental Disabilities, 30,* 166–178.

CHAPTER 7

Motor Development and Postural Control

Motor skills develop in a predictable sequence from basic skills to more complex movement patterns, beginning at the head and proceeding to the feet, and beginning from the midline of the body and proceeding to the extremities. The head develops initially and has the greatest degree of control in the upper extremities. During the process of maturation, the arms will develop in mass and control before the lower extremities. Similarly, control of the large muscles of the trunk and shoulder girdle develops before control of the hands and fingers.

This sequence of motor development and postural control is orderly, although not all abilities will be mastered at a specific age. On the contrary, innate potential is not a guarantee of appropriate development unless one receives appropriate sensory and environmental stimulation that is necessary to facilitate development (Haywood, & Getchell, 2001). Children will possess a variety of physical characteristics, genetic factors, levels of motivation, and opportunities to practice that will either foster or restrict their developmental progress.

As individuals progress through development, teachers should ascertain individual needs before proceeding to the next level of development. Therefore, programming for special needs must be implemented at the appropriate functioning level, with age providing a general guideline of expected skill development. If children can overcome or compensate for deficiencies, they will attain similar levels of functional ability. For children with movement disorders, the more completely we understand the stages of development and underlying mechanisms of disease or injury, the more likely we can develop an instructional program based on individual needs. With this premise in mind, we will provide an overview of the developmental system of movement, motor control, and physical fitness from anatomical and motor control perspectives.

Random and Reflexive Movement

A newborn infant will move the head, arms, and legs when it is awake and alert, producing some apparently disorganized movement. The movements of kicking the legs, waving the arms, and rocking the body appear to be more spontaneous rather than goal directed or reflexive in the developing infant. Although these movements appear spontaneous and unorganized, they are actually coordinated (Keogh & Sudgen, 1985). From the recordings of infants' muscular activity, we see that supine kicking movements are rhythmic and have a coordinated pattern. Although disorganized, the hip, ankle, and knee move cooperatively rather than independently and may be the infant's first attempts to produce some purposeful movement (Gabbard, 2000; Haywood, & Getchell,. 2001). These movements are considered normal in healthy babies, whereas persistence in older children may be indicative of developmental or motor delay.

The earliest movements of newborns are reflexive. These reflexes are involuntary, subcortical movements that are exhibited as responses to the external environment and provide various functions, such as protection, information gathering, and nourishment. Internally, infants also respond involuntarily to sensory stimulation of touch, pressure, and sound.

These initial involuntary movements are spontaneous and stereotypical but serve as the foundation for future motor development. With the development of the central nervous system, primitive reflexes are relegated to the lower areas of the brain (medulla and spinal cord). Primitive reflexes are innate and generally will persist for a specific number of weeks or until the brain develops sufficiently to achieve control. They will gradually decrease in strength and are inhibited as voluntary control is assumed. Although reflexes are involuntary, they can be used to evaluate the soundness of the neurological system. When a reflex cannot be elicited, is uneven in strength, or persists too long, a dysfunction of the nervous system is suspected.

The earliest reflexes are indicative of the undeveloped nervous system. With maturation, the control of these reflexes extends from the spinal cord to the brain stem and midbrain control. The highest level of nervous system development is achieved when the reflexes become inhibited and voluntary control of movements is initiated (Table 7.1) (Gabbard, 2000; Haywood & Getchell, 2001; O'Sullivan & Schmitz, 1988).

Additional reflexes will also appear at birth and become assimilated into the voluntary response system. Swallowing, blinking, pupillary response, sweating, stretch response, and the pattern jerk function initially as reflexes and will continue to function in the voluntary response system.

In the early stages of development, reflexes under control of the spinal cord are necessary for motor development. These include the stretch reflex, flexion reflex, crossed extension reflex, and extensor thrust reflex. The flexion reflex is a contraction of the flexor muscles while the extensor muscles are inhibited or relaxed. Commonly this is exhibited as withdrawal from a painful or hot stimulus and is achieved through the reciprocal reactions of flexing and extending opposing muscle groups.

The crossed extension reflex will function in conjunction with the flexion reflex, allowing the stimulated limb to extend and push itself away from the source of heat or pain. In a motor pattern, this reflex is used to maintain posture; stimulation of a leg will result in flexion, while the opposite limb provides stability and postural adjustments. In jumping patterns, persistence of the reflex will not allow both legs to extend independently. If only one leg flexes while the other extends because of persistence of the reflex, the individual is restricted in movement ability. Additionally, standing posture is initiated by the extensor thrust reflex, allowing the leg muscles to make necessary postural adjustments for support when the feet are stimulated.

For more sophisticated motor development, reciprocal intervention is required to alternately flex and extend muscles involved in coordinated movement patterns. If reflexes are not inhibited—as often seen in cerebral palsy—stability, muscle tone, and movement ability will obviously be impeded.

Table 7.1 Common Reflexes Used to Identify Motor Problems

Reflex (Reaction)	Stimulus	Response	Persistence
BRAIN STEM REFLEXES			
Asymmetrical tonic neck reflex (ATNR)	Rotation or lateral flexion of the head.	Increased extension on chin side with accompanying flexion of limbs on head side.	Difficulty in rolling because of extended arm; interferes with holding the head in midline, resulting in problems with tracking and fixating on objects. Evident in catching and throwing when one elbow is bent while the other extends because head position rotates or tilts to track a ball.
Symmetrical tonic neck reflex (STNR)	Flexion or extension of the head and neck.	With head flexion, flexes arms and upper extremities with extension of the legs. Backward extension of head results in extension of arms and flexion of legs.	Prevents creeping because head controls position of arms and legs. Retention prohibits infants from flexing and extending legs in creeping patterns. Also interferes with catching, kicking, and throwing because changes in head position affect muscle tone and reciprocation of muscle groups.
Tonic labyrinthine reflex (TLR) (prone and supine)	Stimulation of vestibular apparatus by tilting or changes in head position.	In prone position, increased flexion in the limbs; in supine position, extension occurs in limbs.	Affects muscle tone and ability to move body segments independently into various positions, such as propping the body up in a support position prior to crawling or rolling.
Positive support	Stimulation when the balls of the feet touch a firm surface in an upright position.	Extension of the legs to support individual's weight in a standing position.	Disruption of muscle tone needed to support weight, or adduction and internal rotation of the hips that interfere with standing and locomotion.
SPINAL REFLEXES			
Grasping reflex (palmar and plantar grasping)	Pressure on palm of hand or hypertension of wrist. Plantar grasping: stroking the sole of foot will initiate contraction of toes.	Flexion of fingers to grasp then extension to release. In foot, toes contract around object stroking foot.	In hand causes difficulty in releasing objects, in throwing and striking, and in reception of tactile stimuli. In foot interferes with static and dynamic balance while standing and walking.
Crossed extension reflex	Stimulation to ball of foot.	Flexion followed by extension and adduction of opposite leg.	Coordination of leg movements in creeping and walking impeded by stiffness and lack of reciprocal leg movement.
Extensor thrust reflex	Sudden pressure or prick to sole of foot in sitting or supine position.	Toes extend, foot dorsiflexes with increased extensor tone.	Balance between flexion and extension impeded, often seen as stiffness of body in sitting position.
Moro reflex	Change in head position; drop backward in a sitting position.	Arms and legs extend, fingers spread; then arms flex and adduct across chest.	Interferes with ability to sit unsupported and with locomotor patterns or sports skills involving sudden movements (e.g., abduction of arms and legs during gymnastics interferes with balance).

Reflex (Reaction)	Stimulus	Response	Persistence
SPINAL REFLEXES			
Body righting	Rotate upper or lower trunk.	Body segment that is not rotated allows to align body.	Interferes with ability to right itself when head is held in a lateral position.
Neck righting	Turn head sideways.	Body follows head in rotation.	Cannot align head with neck when body is turned. Impeded segmental rolling.
Labyrinthine righting	Limit vision or tilt body in various directions.	Head will move to maintain upright position.	Unable to reorient head in proper body alignment and position. Interferes with head control in movement.
Optic righting	Tilt body in various directions.	Allows head to achieve upright position.	Unable to reorient head in proper body alignment and body posture. Interferes with head control in movement.
Parachute reactions	Lower infant forward rapidly or tilt forward to prone position.	Legs and arms extend and abduct to protect from fall.	Lack of support to prevent body from falling.
Tilting reactions	Display center of gravity by tilting or moving support surface.	Protective extension and muscle tone on downward side. Upward side has curvature of trunk and extension and abduction of extremities.	Clumsiness and awkwardness resulting in loss of balance, muscle tone, and falling.

Righting Reflexes

The brain stem signals the emergence of the ability to control muscle tone and posture, as well as several equilibrium reactions, including the righting reflexes. The righting reflexes are concerned with maintaining the position of the body through the input of sensory information into the vestibular apparatus. Sensory information is then sent to the brain stem, which controls contraction of the appropriate postural muscles necessary to maintain an upright posture. The brain stem also controls the visual muscles that fixate the eyes while the head is moving. Four righting reflexes that are under brain stem control are the labyrinthine-righting, neck righting, body righting, and the optic-righting reflex. The labyrinthine-righting reflex is concerned with the infant's ability to lift the head and maintain an upright head position when the body is turned. The neck-righting reflex is concerned with the alignment of the neck to the head. While the labyrinthine reflex keeps the head upright when the body is turned, the neck-righting reflex will allow the neck to follow the head to an upright position, leading to segmental rolling. The body-righting reflex is responsible for stimulation of one side of the body and subsequent ability of the infant to right itself even when the head is held in a lateral position. The optic-righting reflex allows the infant to alter and attain positions necessary to achieve an upright posture and head position.

In the horizontal position, head control is achieved through reliance on vision; the righting reflexes in combination allow the infant to assume and maintain an appropriate upright body and head position. When the body is reoriented or a posi-

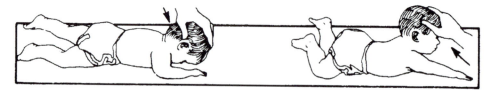

Figure 7.1 Symmetrical tonic neck reflex.

tion is changed, the head assumes control by interacting with the labyrinthine and optic reflexes. The upper body assumes a proper alignment in conjunction with the head by mediating the neck-righting reflexes, while alignment of the lower extremities generally follows alignment of the upper body. Increased control of upright posture is achieved by providing infants with an increasing amount of visual, vestibular, and tactile stimulation from the environment.

If the righting reflexes persist, infants experience difficulty with posture and muscle tone. They will be unable to run, change directions, and maintain body alignment in movements requiring proper head control (Schmidt & Lee, 1999). Without the persistence of these reflexes or any maturational delays, the reflex movements are replaced by equilibrium reactions. Reactions are automatic responses that proceed from reflexes as the individual's central nervous system matures. These reactions allow individuals to maintain body support and to develop posture and balance control. Problems encountered in this stage of development include the inability to establish basic stability, body positioning, and muscle tone necessary for movement.

Other reflexes necessary for postural control are also mediated by the brain stem. The symmetrical tonic neck reflex (STNR) and the asymmetrical tonic neck reflex (ATNR) appear during the first 6 months of life and are elicited by a rotation of the head and stimulation of joint receptors in the neck (Figure 7.1). The STNR is elicited by forward flexion of the neck, resulting in flexion of the arms and upper extremities and extension of the legs. A backward extension of the head results in extension of the arms and upper torso and flexion of the legs and lower extremities. The persistence of the STNR reflex prevents assuming a four-point creeping pattern, because the head position controls the movements of the arms and legs. Retention of the reflex will prohibit infants from appropriately flexing and extending their arms and legs to complete the creeping pattern. This reflex also interferes with catching, kicking, throwing, and tumbling, because the changes in head position may affect muscle tone and reciprocation of muscle groups.

The asymmetrical tonic neck reflex (ATNR) in a supine position is elicited by rotation or lateral flexion (tilt) of the head leading to increased extension of the limbs on the chin side with accompanying flexion of limbs on the head side (Figure 7.2). Persistence of the reflex will cause difficulty in rolling, because the extended arm impedes rolling. Furthermore, the reflex interferes with holding the head in the midline, resulting in visual perceptual problems commonly associated with tracking or fixating on objects. The reflex is also evident in skills such as catching and throwing, where one elbow is bent while the other extends because the head position is rotated or tilted to track a ball. In sports such as tennis or baseball, rotation of the head will interfere with crossing the midline and smooth integration of the movement.

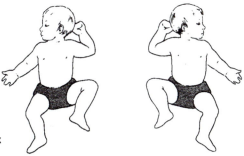

Figure 7.2 Asymmetrical tonic neck reflex
(fencing position).

Another tonic reflex concerned with body position is the tonic labyrinthine reflex (TNR) (Figure 7.3), which is elicited from stimulation of the vestibular apparatus during the first 4 months. In a prone position, the TLR is elicited by changes in head position, causing increased flexion in the limbs, while in the supine position extension occurs in all limbs. Persistence of this reflex affects the infant's muscle tone and ability to move body segments independently into various positions required for purposeful movement. For example, the infant's ability to prop itself into a support position prior to crawling or rolling will be affected.

The blending and inhibition of the tonic reflexes by the righting reflexes can ensure proper head and body positioning, whereas retention of these reflexes will adversely affect overall motor development. In a prone position, difficulties may be evident in raising the head or placing the hands under the body to achieve and maintain support, as in a kneeling position. Infants placed in the supine position may experience difficulties lifting the head and turning from the back to the side or performing a sit-up. Some activities, however, such as archery, baseball, and fencing, actively demonstrate the continued influence of reflexes on movements. For example, during periods of stressful activity and fatigue, sustained muscular contractions and endurance needed to perform the skill may be reinforced by reflexes (Sage, 1984). Furthermore, these reflex patterns are often basic components of skilled motor acts. This phenomenon is evident in the baseball player who jumps and stretches the glove hand overhead to catch a ball, with the head turned to the left, extension on the left

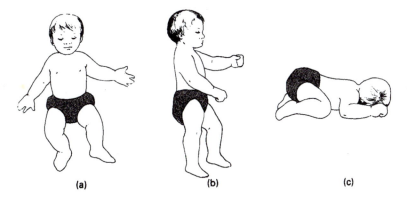

(a)   (b)   (c)

Figure 7.3 Tonic labyrinthine reflex.

side, and flexion on the right side that is similar to the motion elicited by the tonic neck reflex (Schmidt & Lee, 1999).

Grasp Reflex

The grasp reflex is elicited by pressure on the palm of the hand or hyperextension of the wrist, causing infants to grasp and then release. This reflex will become inhibited at approximately the 6th month. Persistence of this reflex causes difficulty in releasing objects used in throwing and striking and interferes with the reception of tactile stimuli.

In the lower extremities, the foot grasp reflex is persistent until 9 months and is elicited by stimulating the sole of the foot, resulting a curling of the toes. Persistence of this reflex results in difficulties achieving both static and dynamic balance, especially while standing and walking.

Moro Reflex

The Moro reflex is elicited by a sudden noise, tapping of the abdomen, or insecure position of support. Infants will first extend the fingers, abduct the arms and legs, and then adduct the limbs and flex the fingers. Persistence of the Moro reflex after 9 months interferes with the ability to sit unsupported, to assume a four-point crawling position, or to stand unsupported in a two-point position. This reflex can also interfere with locomotor patterns and sport skills requiring sudden movement. For example, in gymnastics a fast movement may cause a loss of equilibrium while the individual performs a skill. The influence of the Moro reflexes would be apparent as the arms and legs abduct, causing the loss of balance.

Rudimentary Movement

Rudimentary movements are some of the first voluntary movements demonstrated by infants. They generally occur from birth to 2 years of age in a predictable sequence as the individual matures and receives sensory stimulation from the environment. These movements are often uncoordinated and hesitant because infants are limited in using any external perceptual information for any purposeful movement. At this stage, a primary accomplishment is to maintain an upright posture and control of the head and neck muscles.

Control of later movement is difficult if the infant cannot achieve postural and head control. In addition the initiation and mastery of manipulative tasks, such as reaching, grasping, and releasing, are additional milestones. The infant processes a great deal of information by moving to and exploring objects in the environment that are necessary for social, cognitive, and motor development. Simplistic locomotor patterns, such as creeping, crawling, and walking, also develop, progressing from the position of full contact with the ground, to an upright position on all fours, to an upright kneeling position, and finally to a standing upright posture.

Gallahue and Ozmun (2002) have indicated that rudimentary movements can be divided into two substages to represent an increased amount of motor control as a basis for the further movement development. The first substage includes the inhibition of primitive postural reflexes and the initiation of voluntary control. Voluntary movements are initiated but still lack the refinement necessary for skilled movement patterns. This lack of precision is evident in children who initiate a voluntary movement to grasp an object yet still move the entire hand, wrist, arm, and shoulder while attempting the movement. The second substage incorporates an increasing amount of perceptual awareness of the environment and more precise control of movement. Children need not rely solely on sensory information for movement responses but will begin to make perceptual judgments by integrating sensory and motor information for more precise movement decisions (French & Horvat, 1986), such as incorporating visual sensory information with tactile sensory information when grasping and releasing an object. This process becomes quite evident as children achieve more control of movement sequences.

These rudimentary movements are further refined when reflexes are inhibited and higher neurological control is achieved. The rudimentary skills that are commonly developed during this stage include rolling, sitting, standing, walking, grasping, and releasing (Wickstrom, 1983).

Rolling

In learning how to roll, infants are required to develop control of the head and neck. The skill occurs at approximately 4 months beginning from a back-lying position. Initially infants turn the head to focus on an object, inhibiting the body-righting reflex and allowing the body to turn in the same direction as the head. At times infants roll to the side after turning the head. With maturation, segmental rolling will improve as the hips and shoulders turn while the other body parts follow. The initial attempts at voluntary control of rolling occur from a front-to back-lying position and later from the back to stomach.

Sitting

The achievement of the sitting position generally will follow rolling. Initially, when infants are pulled into a sitting position, the head sags backward and then forward on the chest. At approximately 5 months the ability to hold the head upright is developed; by $6^{1}/_{2}$ months the baby will be sitting without support; and at 9 months the baby voluntarily assumes a sitting position.

Crawling and Creeping

The ability to crawl is demonstrated by dragging the body, using the arms and legs, with the abdomen in contact with a supporting surface. (Creeping uses the arms and legs for propulsion without the chest and abdomen in contact with the floor.) Crawling occurs at approximately 7 months as infants attempt to reach for an object and then, following the reach, move the head and chest forward. Creeping develops after a supporting position on the hands and knees has been achieved. Development of creeping proceeds from moving one arm and then one leg, to homolateral movements, and finally to crossed-extension patterns, which appear at 10–11 months.

Standing and Walking

The ability to maintain a standing position is achieved at approximately 9 months with the assistance of a table or railing. When upright, infants can move around furniture or the play area with assistance. After unsupported standing is developed, walking develops as infants move from one area to another. A variety of individual differences are apparent in walking patterns between 8 and 18 months, depending on stability, strength, and motivation.

The initial patterns of walking are awkward; precise control is achieved with more opportunities to practice. Refinements in the walking pattern are demonstrated by an increase in speed and length of step, a decrease in the base of support, the ability to position the feet forward, and finally the synchronized coordination of the arms and legs. Further maturation and practice refine the walking pattern, while the ability to walk backward occurs at 19 months and ascending stairs at approximately 21 months.

Reaching and Grasping

The manipulative skills of reaching and grasping will appear at approximately 4 months. Grasping develops from palm grabbing at 5 months to a pincher-type movement using the thumb and forefinger at 13 months. Releasing is more difficult for infants because the ability to relax the hand muscles is not usually developed until 18 months. Reaching and grasping skills illustrate that proximodistal development is occurring, with movement sequences uncoordinated and slow until motor development is further advanced.

Fundamental Movement

The fundamental movement stage continues the expansion of motor development and progress from rudimentary movements. In this stage, more voluntary control and active movement within the environment are possible. Movements become more predictable as the ability to move, the combining of movements into patterns, and the modification of movements according to task and environmental demands are achieved. For children this stage reflects the integration of cerebellum, basal ganglia, and motor cortex as the child begins to plan and execute appropriate movements.

From the stable upright position of the rudimentary stage, locomotor patterns such as running, jumping, hopping, galloping, and skipping can be developed. Object control or manipulation patterns such as throwing, catching, and kicking also proceed from the rudimentary skills of grasping and releasing, while stability movements such as static (standing on one foot) and dynamic (beam walking) balance movements develop after achieving an upright stable position. In this stage of development, the child must rely on visual, auditory, and tactile-kinesthetic (haptic) perceptual skills in the environment to incorporate play and movement patterns into sequences, such as combining a locomotor (running) and ball-control (catching) skill. These environmental influences create the need for executing movement patterns in reaction to stimuli in stable and changing environments. For example, the pattern of running must first be developed with a smooth integration of stride and upper body movements. As a mature pattern is developed, the movement is incorporated into games that require children to use and modify movements on situational demand, such as stopping, starting, or running backward. As stated earlier, breakdown in coordinating these stimuli or breakdown in the feedback loops results in a motor dysfunction.

The emphasis in this stage of development should be placed on the individuals' ability to incorporate a wide variety of movements into their learning repertoire. The appearance and sophistication of these skills will develop from the initial appearance of the patterns, to moderate control, and finally to a highly efficient, coordinated, mature pattern that can be used in a variety of movement settings.

Skills in the fundamental movement stage will develop in stages or levels. Substage 1 constitutes the initial attempts to perform the movement pattern. Movement may be poorly coordinated and may include improper sequences or restricted use of the body, a lack of spatial and/or temporal awareness, and a nonfluid integration of the movement. This is evident in the skill of throwing, when the initial attempts may be characterized by a step with the improper foot, a lack of hip rotation and follow-through, and an exaggerated use of the upper body when releasing the ball. At this time the schema or pattern is not fully developed and will require practice and feedback on the appropriate technique.

Substage 2 incorporates more coordination and control of the pattern. When the child throws an object, a proper cross-step, initial follow-through, and less restriction of movement may be apparent. McClenahan and Gallahue (1978) have indicated that with maturation, most individuals will achieve this stage of physical functioning if they have the proper opportunities for practice and instruction. Children with disabilities may be restricted in their opportunities for practice or opportunity for specific instruction or feedback on their performance. Additional practice and instruction are required to reach this level of functioning to enable children to develop their movement schema and adjust to using feedback information.

As children mature and receive instruction and opportunities to practice (substage 3), all the elements of a proficient pattern should be evident as well as increased control of the movement. Throwing will consist of a proper stride, upper rotation of body and hip, overarm release, and follow-through. In order to complete the skill and to be successful at throwing, the learner requires practice, instruction, and an interest in or motivation for the activity. Practice should vary, and learners must adapt to various amounts and situations in order to be flexible in generating their movement sequences. A sound developmental foundation, or schema, in motor development is needed for children to control movements required in complex movement patterns such as sport and recreational activities. A lack of development in this stage restricts future success because fundamental skills are the foundation for more precise control and development. Skills commonly developed in this stage are running, jumping, hopping, galloping and skipping, throwing, catching, and kicking (Gabbard, 2000; McClenahan & Gallahue, 1978; Wickstrom, 1983).

Running

Running originates from the development of a proficient walking pattern. Initially the feet are turned out, while the arms are held away from the body. The first attempts at running are unstable and uncoordinated because children do not have appropriate balance or leg strength to achieve a period of nonsupport. Between 2 and 3 years of age, they gain the ability to attain balance and development of strength, enabling them to leave the ground in a nonsupport position. In general, a mature running pattern is achieved by 6 years of age when the stride and flight phase are lengthened, the trailing foot is swung forward during recovery, arms are used in opposition with a forward lean of the body, and a pronounced period of nonsupport is evident.

Jumping

Jumping develops after proficient walking and running patterns are achieved. Initial jumping occurs at approximately 18 months, beginning with an exaggerated motion such as walking down a step. Although this is not a true jumping pattern, it seems to be a preliminary step to jumping with two feet. Next, children because able to jump up and down in a stationary position while development of leg strength and coordination allows them to elevate the body from the ground. At about 2 years of age, children will be able to push off with two feet and land without losing balance. By 5 years of age, adequate leg strength enables developing children to achieve a mature jumping pattern.

The vertical jump and horizontal jump each have common characteristics, such as a preparatory crouch, a forward and upward swing of the arms to initiate action, a rapid extension of the legs to propel the body, flight time when the body is extended, and flexion of the hips, knees, and ankles to absorb the landing. The extra dimension of the horizontal jump requires a forward and upward movement rather than just an upward movement. This slight variation is more complex because a momentary loss of balance allows the legs to move forward in preparation for the landing.

Hopping

The ability to hop requires more stability and strength than jumping because the takeoff and landing are on one foot. The first attempts at hopping (stationary and moving) involve uncoordinated movements and a minimal amount of flexion and extension of the support leg, with a corresponding lack of height and a flat-footed landing. Children also do not use the arms effectively, while the nonhopping leg is often rigid and may touch the floor. As balance and coordination are developed, the nonsupport leg is more controlled, does not touch the floor, and arm action while hopping is less extraneous.

Initial stages of hopping are prevalent by the age of 4, while proficiency is achieved at the age of 6 with both preferred and nonpreferred legs. Girls are generally more proficient because of their physical maturity and a social and play environment that provides them with more opportunities to practice hopping.

Galloping and Skipping

The skills of galloping and skipping are learned when basic skills in other locomotor movement patterns are developed. Galloping is a combination of walking and leaping that occurs when the transfer of weight from one foot to the other is achieved. Initially, at about 3 years of age, children demonstrate a slight leap coupled with a run. From this initial sequence the gallop is mastered with a transfer of weight to the forward foot on the same side, incorporating a step-leap pattern. By 5 or 6 years of age, a mature pattern will develop by coordinating arm movements and a momentary elevation of the feet.

Galloping seems to be favored by boys, whereas girls prefer skipping. Skipping is a step-hop pattern, with the step longer than the hop before the pattern is repeated on the opposite side of the body. For a mature pattern, precise timing and control is essential because the transfer of weight and the shift to step-hop on the opposite side is intricate. Skipping occurs at 6 or 7 years from a mature hopping pattern. As hopping proficiency increases, the movement adds a step on one side of the body. With the improvement of balance, the step-hop pattern becomes an ingrained movement on the opposite side of the body. Final development of skipping includes the refinement of both the arms and legs as well as elevation and control of the movement.

Throwing

The pattern of throwing can be seen as early as 6 months, when infants are first able to grasp and release an object. At this substage, the action is initiated from a sitting position primarily with the arms because infants are still unable to assume an upright position.

With the development of stability and other locomotor movements, the throwing action will begin to appear. Initially, at approximately 2 years, an object is released with a forearm extension and no body rotation. The feet remain stationary throughout the action except for a slight flexion of the trunk when the ball is released. At approximately 3–5 years, children begin to rotate the hips and spine, although the feet remain in a stationary position. Prior to the throw, the object is brought backward and momentarily held with a cocked wrist before the child initiates a forward horizontal movement. The elementary substage at 6 years is more proficient because a transfer of weight forward is evident on the same side of the body as the throwing arm. Also evident are trunk rotation and overarm movement, with the elbow leading and the beginning of a follow-through. In the mature pattern at 6 to 7 years age, a more complete transfer to the foot opposite the throwing arm, trunk rotation, and follow-through are demonstrated. Children can achieve greater control in both speed and precision when integrating both sides of the body and can achieve a wider base of support.

Catching

Catching is a fundamental skill that requires the ability to control a thrown object. Initial attempts at catching are characterized by avoidance of the thrown object or a tendency to extend the arms and allow the ball to bounce off them. Children also attempt to trap balls against their chest, turn their head, or close their eyes when objects approach.

During the elementary substage at 4 years, children visually track the ball yet may still blink before catching it. At this substage, the arms are outstretched with the palms perpendicular, although the coordination of the movement is poor. The hands unevenly grasp the ball and pull it to the chest. At approximately 6 years, a mature pattern is evident as the individual tracks the released ball until task completion, prepares the arms for catching, and controls the ball with the hands and fingers while "giving" with the arms to absorb the ball's momentum.

Other factors also affect the ability to catch, including the size and velocity of the ball. Although a large ball is easier to catch, more precise control is difficult. A larger ball will result in more elementary catching patterns, such as trapping, because the hands and fingers are needed for precise control. In contrast, a smaller object such as a tennis ball is also difficult to control until the mature catching pattern is achieved. The most appropriate ball size is one that allows children to cup with the hands but does not require precise fine motor control to throw (Gallahue & Ozmun, 2002; Williams, 1983).

Speed and angle of release will also affect catching. Children experience difficulty judging the speed of an object, and performance deteriorates as speed is increased. As they mature perceptually and receive training and experience in catching at different speeds, children will not require as much time to track the ball before making decisions.

Another factor that affects catching patterns is the individual's position. A stationary position, with the ball tossed directly at children, is initially the best position to assume when learning to catch. Moving to catch an object will disrupt performance until students are able to master the catching pattern as well as sideways, forward, or backward movements.

Kicking

Kicking is a fundamental pattern that requires the use of the feet to propel an object. The kicking pattern (directed at a stationary ball) originates at 24 months, beginning with an initial step with a straight leg and little accompanying movement of the arms and upper body. While the kicking leg is swung forward with a minimal amount of force and no follow-through, the opposite foot assumes a position of stability and support.

During the elementary substage of the pattern, the trunk leans slightly forward while the arms are held out at the side for balance. Children take several approach steps and begin to flex the kicking leg at the knee, swinging the leg backward and then forward in a striking motion. The children also initiate extension of the leg on follow-through.

The mature kicking pattern incorporates the arms swinging in opposition while kicking, a forceful leg swing, increased flexion, and extension action at the hip and knee to generate a more pronounced backswing, follow-through, and impact with the ball. The development of strength, stability, and practice in the mature pattern allows more force to be generated in the kick. As with catching, children find control of the ball in games such as soccer or kickball more difficult because it requires coordination of the hands and eyes as well as the extremities.

Sport and Recreational Movement

The final stage of motor development and control occurs at approximately age 7 and is characterized by the attainment of specific goals and changes in the external environment. Games, sports, and recreational activities require children to constantly alter and match their movements with a more skilled pattern. The basic locomotor, manipulation, and stability movements must then be more elaborate and coordinated as the demands of a particular sport or recreational activity require more intricate and combined movements. For example, the sport of softball would involve the execution of overhand and underhand throws; the catching of ground balls and fly balls; striking a ball; running the bases and fielding fly balls; stability movements for batting, pitching, and fielding; and dynamic movements to change levels and directions.

At this stage, more immediate and accurate decisions are needed about movements. Children also need to remember previous experiences and compare new information to what was previously learned. Likewise, children become more adept at modifying movement behaviors according to the changing environment and meeting a variety of movement challenges.

Functional Movement

In addition to movement skills, changes in development contribute to the functional development of children. In this context, functional development relates to the development of those skills that are required to perform many activities of play, daily living, or self-care needed to function in home and community-based settings (Horvat & Croce 1995). These skills may be related to reaching or grasping to play with a toy, eating a meal, or brushing their teeth. In other contexts, functional skill development is related to work-specific tasks.

Movements become more automatic as the demand for more sophistication requires responses to the environment and the development of more complex patterns. Combining cognitive and affective attributes refines these skills.

Within this substage there are three separate but overlapping transitional stages that lead to the development of highly skilled performance. As previously stated, teaching should emphasize cognitive development, physical abilities, and motivation of children rather than conform to specific age guidelines. Furthermore, the ability to reach the pinnacle of motor development and control will depend on how much time is allocated for instruction, practice, and competition.

Most authors combine the sport and recreational skill phase into a series of substages or skill levels. In most instances the child first attempts to refine and combine mature movement patterns into total body movement as he or she adds range and complexity to a previously learned fundamental task. Children are limited in overall skill and proficiency at this stage and usually possess an interest in a wide variety of activities. This provides the first opportunity for competition and testing one's skills against others' (and is commonly integrated into lead-up activities), while the teacher emphasizes accuracy and skill in performing movement patterns to achieve proficiency.

The child attains some proficiency through practice of selected activities and movement experiences. The child may focus on a select number of activities limited by personal preference and physical attributes. An increasing emphasis on form, skill, and accuracy is needed for the child to control intricate movements for sports competition and recreational pursuits. As the perceptual process is developed, the child can incorporate external information into playing strategies that are needed for developing skill and accuracy and that can be repeated consistently. It is also important to emphasize the proper technique and practice opportunities for children to improve. Often a child whose play or movement opportunities are limited will be restricted in skill development.

At the highest level of motor development and control, movements are sophisticated and automatic. Children who reach this level of development practice and continually refine their skills to achieve the highest level of performance. All aspects of development, including genetic endowment, fitness, motivation, and instructional opportunities, must be present to attain this level of functioning. Conscious involvement of movement is minimal, and the cognitive appraisal of information must be sophisticated and precise, because optimal performance depends on prior experience and strategy. Children are more precise and can make distinctions among different kinds of intersensory information, while the control mechanism related to postural stability and body movement is highly developed, thus enabling them to complete the motor action accurately and consistently.

CHAPTER SUMMARY

1. Children enter school with a variety of needs, interests, and ability levels. All children will develop at their own rate. However, all children follow a similar sequential order of motor development. This process can be identified by the stages and patterns apparent in the developmental sequence that is commonly age related.

2. Although using these age-related guidelines for most children is beneficial, their use with exceptional students may be less effective. A knowledge and understanding of basic principles of motor development are necessary to assess functional ability adequately.

3. Motor skills develop in a sequence from basic skills to more complex motor patterns. The sequence is fairly predictable, although not all abilities will be mastered at a specific age.

4. Programming for children with disabilities must be implemented at the appropriate functioning level, with age providing a general guideline of expected skill development. Children with a disability will still progress through similar stages of motor development and control if they can overcome or compensate for the deficiency.

5. Stages of development proceed from primitive reflexive movements to specialized skill development and control.

6. Reflexes are subcortical in nature and present at birth. These serve as the foundation for future motor development. Reflexes usually persist until the brain develops sufficiently to achieve control. At this point, the reflexes do not disappear but rather become inhibited.

7. As neurological development proceeds to the higher areas of the brain, movement control is possible. The cerebral cortex, basal ganglia, cerebellum, and brain stem are important in the control of movements. Each provides a varying influence on motor control, which is reflective of higher neural control.

8. Rudimentary movements are some of the first voluntary movements demonstrated by young children. These usually occur from birth to 2 years of age. These rudimentary movements are refined when reflexes become inhibited and higher neurological control is achieved.

9. Fundamental movements develop after rudimentary movements. Movements at this stage become more predictable, and more complex patterns of movements can be observed. Some examples of fundamental movements include running, hopping, throwing, and kicking.

10. The final stage of motor development and control occurs at approximately age 7 and is characterized by the attainment of specific goals and changes in the external environment. Games, sports, and recreational activities require children to change and match their movements constantly when a more skilled pattern is required.

11. Motor control is analyzed by the study of isolated tasks under specific conditions. The development of motor control is closely aligned to motor development.

12. For children with disabilities, the process of motor control may be adversely affected; that is, they may experience difficulty achieving precise control. Neurological or muscular deficiencies contribute to spatial and temporal awareness problems. Sensory deficits result in a lack of specific cues within the environment, while students with learning problems may be weak in input and decision making, as well as in judgment about changing demands and stimuli.

13. The teacher should strive to provide instruction at the appropriate level of development and control for all children. Each child may have special needs or may possess certain characteristics that influence his or her functional ability. To implement a program, the cooperation of other support personnel may be required to develop the awareness of the student's ability. Additionally, teachers should incorporate the following basic factors into their programs: instruction based on developmental principles and the functional ability of the child; the most appropriate method of learning for the child (e.g., auditory, visual) based on assessment information; individualized instruction and opportunities for the student to practice at school and/or at home; and the attempt to develop form and precision as well as performance measures of distance or height.

14. With the incorporation of these basic principles, the teacher should then select activities to enhance or develop the child's functional ability. Furthermore, a more thorough assessment and evaluation may be indicated before a specific activity program or individualized educational plan is begun. The input from the educational team and specific evaluation information can then be used to develop the child's abilities at his or her functional level.

REFERENCES

French, R., & Horvat, M. A. (1986). The acquisition of perceptual skills by motorically awkward children. *Motor skills: Theory into practice, 8,* 27–38.

Gabbard, C. P. (2000). *Lifelong motor development* (3rd ed.). Boston: Allyn & Bacon.

Gallahue, D. L., & Ozmun, J. C. (2002). *Understanding motor development: Infants, children, adolescents, adults* (5th ed.). Dubuque, IA: McGraw-Hill.

Haywood, K. M., & Getchell, M. (2001). *Life span motor development* (3rd ed.). Champaign, IL: Human Kinetics.

Horvat, M., & Croce, R. (1995). Physical rehabilitation of individuals with mental retardation: Physical fitness and information processing. *Critical Reviews in Physical and Rehabilitation Medicine, 1*(3), 233–252.

Keogh, J., & Sugden, D. (1985). *Movement skill development.* New York: MacMillan.

McClenahan, B. A., & Gallahue, D. L. (1978). *Fundamental movement: A development and remedial approach*. Philadelphia: Saunders.

O'Sullivan, S. B., & Schmitz, T. J. (1988). *Physical rehabilitation: Assessment and treatment* (2nd ed.). Philadelphia: Davis.

Sage, G. H. (1984). *Motor learning and control: A neuropsychological approach*. Dubuque, IA: Wm. C. Brown.

Schmidt, R. A., & Lee, T. D. (1999). *Motor control and learning: A behavioral emphasis* (2nd ed.). Champaign, IL: Human Kinetics.

Wickstrom, R. L. (1983). *Fundamental motor patterns* (3rd ed.). Philadelphia: Lea and Febiger.

Williams, H. G. (1983). *Perceptual and motor development*. Englewood Cliffs, NJ: Prentice-Hall.

CHAPTER 8

Information Processing and Perceptual Development

Motor performance is based on the ability to receive and interpret sensory information prior to executing a movement task or sequence. This sensory information informs the brain of the body's position in space, positions of different body parts in relation to each other, environmental changes, and various movement parameters that will be needed to perform the skill correctly (e.g., force, speed, duration, and direction of the movement in question). Perception is the means by which we receive and interpret sensory information from the environment. The body is constantly bombarded with sensory information (tactile, kinesthetic, auditory, visual) that is gathered by sensory receptors and sent to higher brain areas for analysis and integration before movement execution.

When a child has difficulty learning or performing a new skill, often teachers erroneously look solely at the child's motor output. Rather than focus only on the motor output, teachers should take into account all aspects of information processing and perceptual development. In this context, when teaching a skill the teacher views motor performance as encompassing all aspects of sensory input, decision making, motor output, and feedback as points of emphasis (Figure 8.1). With this in mind, teachers should use the following steps to understand information processing and how children use perceptual skills in the learning process:

1. stimulus reception (input)
2. sensory integration and processing
3. motor output
4. feedback

Step 1—Stimulus Reception (Input) The first step focuses on the ability to gather relevant features of the task, such as the speed, direction, and trajectory of a Frisbee, while positioning the body for stability (kinesthetic) and moving the arms and hands to a position (kinesthetic) to catch (tactile) the object. For children, and especially for those children with cognitive and attention deficits, selecting pertinent information becomes difficult if they cannot detect the relevant features of the task or if they become distracted by irrelevant information. Children also have difficulty retaining sensory information. Williams (1983) indicated that children lose up to 60% of all sensory information within 1–5 seconds after being presented with the stimulus. For children with cognitive and attentional difficulties, this may result in the loss of 80–90% of the stimulus. More importantly, when a sensory stimulus is presented

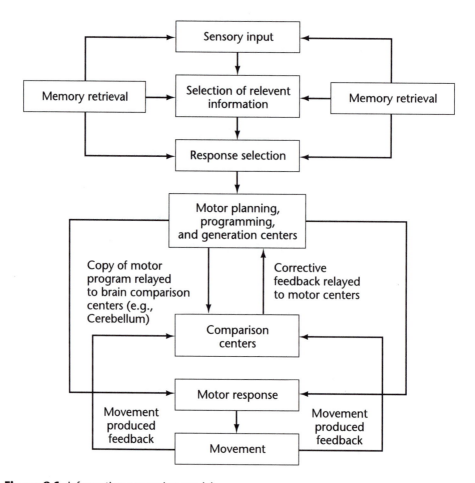

Figure 8.1 Information processing model.

to a child with disability, the child may not be able to select pertinent task-related information and may retain even less in short-term memory (STM) before analysis. In this case inefficient or inadequate use of sensory input will directly impact the child's ability to make a decision when selecting the most appropriate motor output. Developmentally, it appears that STM ability improves markedly up to early adolescence, with the largest changes taking place between 3 and 7 years of age. For some children, the ability to use STM will be effected by disability. For others, the rapid increase in STM during childhood has been attributed to increased speed in identifying stimuli and in search and recall strategies (Gabbard, 2000).

For example, some children frequently have problems receiving information from the environment because of concomitant sensory impairments. As a result, these children do not have sufficient information to adequately develop correct motor responses. It is important for teachers to understand that the movement responses are predicated on large quantities of sensory input from numerous sources located throughout the body. This information is then processed, and an appropriate response is selected, programmed, and executed (Figure 8.1). Each sensory system additionally provides the performer with constantly updated information regarding the quality of the movement (feedback). A loss of input from one sensory system can significantly affect a child's motor performance. To offset this loss of input, teachers can assist these children by maximizing sensory input through those sensory systems which are functioning properly.

In contrast, some children will not cope well with vast amounts of sensory input. When working with these children, teachers should limit the amount of stimuli presented at one time. This allows the children to attend to smaller amounts of information, which they then can process and integrate more efficiently. Teachers must ensure that these "sensory defensive" children are not overwhelmed with sensory information.

Moreover, the inability to attend selectively to relevant information can have serious consequences on the performance of a skill, especially during the early stages of learning. This fact is compounded in children with developmental disorders or attention deficits because they have limitations in information processing. For these children, even selectively attending to small amounts of performance-generated information takes a considerable amount of their total information processing capacity and makes it very doubtful that additional information can be attended to and digested adequately.

Step 2—Sensory Integration and Processing   The next step in the process involves the integration and analysis of sensory information. Processing mechanisms receive sensory stimuli, process and integrate the stimuli, and decide on the most appropriate plan of action. This decision mechanism is important because it can restrict the amount of information processed both before and during performance. Naturally, if more sensory information can be processed, the child can make a more appropriate decision concerning the desired motor output. For children with some prior experience with the task, the ability to use and process sensory information becomes more efficient as they become better able to use previously learned skills and experiences to execute the proper movement. They may also access long-term memory (LTM) to compare present and past experiences related to the task. As with STM, LTM also improves significantly during childhood, enabling children to recall and retrieve information as well as improving decision-making capabilities (Gabbard, 2000). In addition, the child is better able to adjust the motor output to the new situations or changes in the environment because of a greater repository of motor experiences from which to choose an appropriate motor response.

If the learner is able to gather and decipher incoming sensory information, a decision concerning the correct motor output can be selected and executed. If a child has problems deciphering incoming sensory information, then the amount of stimuli must be restricted. For example, if a child cannot track a pitched ball and has difficulty judging when to swing, to practice swinging at pitched balls may be unwise. In this case, the teacher may start with the ball on a tee to eliminate the need to track the speed and direction of the ball and enable the child to concentrate on the swing mechanics and making contact. In essence, the teacher simplifies the task and allows the child to concentrate on a more limited amount of sensory information. As the child becomes more proficient at hitting the stationary ball and develops skill, the teacher can have the child swing at a tossed ball from a close distance, eventually adding a greater distance to the toss. The key here is manipulating the context in which the child must perform. Often, the context must be simplified so that the child can experience success. When the child masters the skill in this simplified context, then the teacher can incorporate increasingly greater complexity to the situation.

Children with cognitive and/or attention difficulties have particular problems with processing information and developing appropriate motor responses. Children may not have sufficient prior sensory and motor experiences, be able to attend to appropriate sensory cues, or be capable of recalling experiences from LTM to aid in the integration and analysis of new sensory information. The more we place these children in situations where they have to focus on and analyze appropriate sensory stimuli, the more proficient they will become in the process and, hence, better at choosing the most appropriate motor response for the environmental context in which they must respond.

Step 3—Motor Output

Once all sensory information is processed and analyzed, the performer selects the most appropriate motor response given the particular environmental constraints. At this point, a certain motor response is desired, and a central processor (motor areas in the brain) is commanded to execute the movement. The brain triggers movement by way of messages to the body's muscles. Motor skills are acquired when an individual practices a new skill. Over time, this repetition creates new "motor memories," or engrams, which essentially produce automatization of the newly learned skill. The ability to learn new skills is based on the ability to perform more simple subskills (often referred to as subroutines). Most children routinely progress through motor development milestones and learn the prerequisite subroutines needed to learn more complex skills. However, children with disabilities may not have the necessary prerequisite skills or motor patterns to learn and perform a new skill. Frequently, children with disabilities have delayed motor development and lack basic motor patterns that are essential to performing complex motor behaviors (see Chapter 7). In order for these children to learn more complex skills, they first must learn basic motor patterns and develop the appropriate level of physical functioning to execute the movement. For children with motor delays, learning begins at a much lower organizational level and needs to be emphasized to promote not only learning but also retention of the movement.

Step 4—Feedback

When the learner executes the movement, some feedback is available while the task is being performed via proprioceptive, tactile, kinesthetic, auditory, and visual information. Often, movement-produced feedback may not be processed appropriately by children with disabilities. However, feedback concerning the movement can also be represented after the movement is completed, when the child is better able to process the information. This type of feedback is called augmented feedback and usually takes the form of verbal or visual instructions after the task is completed. For example, if the child missed a target when throwing a ball, the teacher can use feedback to help the child readjust his or her body position and release so that on the next attempt, the child will throw the ball more accurately. Because feedback provides information, motivation, and reinforcement to the learner, it is extremely important for promoting successful motor skill acquisition. In conjunction with providing ample opportunity to practice the skill, the teacher should offer feedback to enable the child to process the information concerning his or her performance.

As we relate teaching and learning to information processing, we see that if the amount of sensory information is inadequate or not retained, the child will have difficulty making a precise decision concerning the appropriate motor output. Likewise, if the decision-making capabilities or past experiences (LTM) are compromised, the child again is placed at a disadvantage in selecting the appropriate motor output. By determining where in the input–processing–output–feedback sequence the breakdown in skill development occurs, the teacher can devise the most appropriate motor remediation program. Then, the teacher can teach to the specific area of deficit or compensate by providing a more appropriate input modality that may be more efficient for the child. In either case, the ability to process information and the extent of perceptual development is essential for learning to occur. We cannot assume that the child is processing all the information that is being presented and using all of feedback appropriately. Teachers must be aware of the most efficient modality of learning and present information that the child can assimilate to properly execute the intended task.

Perception

As the central nervous system develops and the child comes to rely on sensory information, we see that the child develops an increasing reliance on perceptual information. The ability to integrate sensory information (process whereby the individual collects information) and perceptual information (process whereby the individual associates meaning to this information) is integral for skilled motor behavior. According to Keogh and Sugden (1985), sensory information is paramount for children to understand how the body moves alone or in relation to the environment. As movers, we must have information regarding what our body can do and what it is doing during movement. This allows us to develop a body knowledge system and a means to select, plan, execute, evaluate, and modify our movements. Therefore, it is paramount that teachers (a) understand the preferred sensory modality the child uses to process sensory information and feedback and then (b) use that modality as the conduit for providing sensory input.

The primary sensory systems children use in learning situations include the visual, auditory, and tactile-kinesthetic systems. At birth, the perceptual systems are intact and functioning, although the infant is still relying on primitive reflexes for information, protection, and nourishment. As the child develops, there is a gradual change in the perceptual system as reflexes are inhibited and more information is obtained through sensory modalities to make decisions.

The first major change in sensory-perceptual processing involves a shift in reliance on information from the tactile-kinesthetic system to the visual system. The second major change involves a refinement or improvement in the discriminatory ability of each sensory system. This is often referred to as *intrasensory development*. This leads to an increase in the capacity of each sensory system to handle more information and to a refinement in the discriminatory abilities of each sensory system. This rapid increase in intrasensory development occurs from the ages of 3 to 6 years. As a result, the child is better able to process available sensory information and to control motor processes. The final major change centers around improved *intersensory processing and integration*; that is, the developing child is better able to integrate simultaneously information from multiple sensory systems. This process overlaps intrasensory develop, so that both intrasensory and intersensory development are often occurring simultaneously (Williams, 1983).

Visual-Perceptual Development

By the time a child reaches the age of 2, the ocular apparatus is fully mature (Gallahue & Ozmun, 2002). Although the ocular apparatus is physically mature, visual-perceptual abilities lag behind in development; although children may be able to fixate on objects and track them, refinements in visual-perception still need to occur. For example, a young child has extreme difficulty in intercepting a tossed ball with any appreciable degree of control, because the perception of moving objects, perception of distance, and anticipatory timing skills are not yet developed (Gallahue & Ozmun, 2002).

The relationship between movement and visual-perceptual development has been debated for many years. Many researchers adhere to the hypothesis that movement is integral for visual-perceptual development in children (Gallahue & Ozmun, 2002; Payne & Issacs, 2002). Further, without volitional movements, visual-perceptual adjustments to environmental changes will not occur, or at least will be delayed. Although this hypothesis is an intriguing one, research in this area is speculative at best. According to Gallahue and Ozmun, movement is in all likelihood effective for promoting perceptual abilities in children; whether it is a necessary condition is doubtful. Although volitional movement may not be a necessary condition for developing visual-perceptual abilities, the level of a child's perceptual skills will affect a child's ability to learn and perform a motor skill (Gallahue & Ozmun, 2002).

Visual perception is often broken down into visual acuity, depth and movement perception, figure-ground perception, spatial orientation and perception of spatial relationships, and visual-motor coordination. *Visual acuity* is defined as the ability of the visual system to discern detail in objects and may be measured both statically and dynamically. Static visual acuity encompasses the ability to distinguish detail when both the individual and object are stationary. Dynamic visual acuity encompasses the ability to distinguish detail when the object is moving. Overall, dynamic visual acuity appears to develop somewhat later than does static visual acuity (Gallahue & Ozmun, 2002; Williams, 1983).

Depth perception is defined as the ability to judge how near or far away one or more objects are from a person. Depth perception also allows an individual to see three-dimensionally. *Movement perception* involves the ability to perceive that an object is moving. Together, depth perception and movement perception constitute two of the more important visual-perceptual abilities in children.

Our sense of depth perception is derived from many visual cues, such as the relative sizes of objects, the observed size of objects of known height, shadows and lighting, and movement parallax. *Parallax* refers to the geometrical phenomenon that the direction of a stationary object from an observer changes if the observer changes location and that the direction of an object changes less for a distant than for a near object. Also, as we all well know, objects closer to an observer that are in motion seem to move faster than distant objects (movement parallax).

Stereopsis (seeing in three dimensions) requires that the brain recognize that objects at various distances have images on the two retinas, which do not fall on exactly corresponding locations; that is, the image has disparity. For example, suppose that you are fixating (converging) on an object 1 meter away. Images of an object 2 meters away will lie somewhat nasally on both retinas; the images of an object 0.5 meters away will lie somewhat temporally. Thus, some retinal cells will be responding to near objects, some to far objects, and others to in-between distances—the neural basis for stereopsis. Finally, another visual cue for distance and depth is *optical expansion* (or retraction). This occurs whenever the distance between an individual (the perceiver) and another person or object changes. If an object's retinal size increases, say, by one-half when the object moves toward the individual, then the brain will perceive that the object is one-half the distance closer. Both optical expansion and retraction specify proportional changes from a starting point rather than distance in more absolute terms (Keogh & Sugden, 1985).

Figure-ground perception is the ability to extract relevant detail from contexts (object of visual regard) that contain irrelevant or distracting information (visual surroundings). Often, visually-oriented combinations containing a maximum amount of blending and distraction are the most disruptive when the individual attempts to distinguish a figure from its background. Moreover, according to Gallahue and Ozmun (2002), maturity in this ability also involves elements of attention. In conjunction with visual acuity, visual figure-ground perception enables a performer to clearly distinguish an object and to separate it from its surroundings. Clearly, such a skill is integral not only for performing physical skills, but also for obtaining vital feedback on performance.

Spatial orientation refers to the ability to recognize an object's arrangement in space. *Perception of spatial relationships* involves the relationship between the self and objects in the environment. Many motor tasks are performed in environments in which objects are oriented in specific ways or in environments whereby performance is defined by particular spatial dimensions. Together, spatial orientation and perception of spatial relationships allow us to move freely through our environment safely and proficiently. Very early in life, by about age 4, children can learn and distinguish between directional extremes (e.g., high–low, over–under, front–back, etc.), and can learn and distinguish vertical from horizontal positions; they still have problems with oblique or diagonal orientations. By age 8, most children can differentiate oblique and diagonal orientations but may still confuse left and right (Haywood & Getchell, 2001). Based on this information, teachers should be cognizant of how young children respond to directional orientations and how feedback given in these terms might be misconstrued.

Visual-motor coordination is often defined as the ability to integrate eyes and hands for object tracking, manipulation, and interception (Gallahue & Ozmun, 2002). According to Payne and Issacs (2002), as dynamic visual acuity improves so does the ability to track fast-moving objects. Williams (1983) has stated that accurate perception of movement matures at about 10 to 12 years of age. The ability to accurately intercept objects is often termed *object interception* or, more accurately, as *coincidence-anticipation timing*. This involves the ability to match the final location of a moving object with a specific motor response (e.g., catching or striking the object). This ability improves throughout childhood and, according to Gallahue and Ozmun (2002), it is difficult to establish a concrete developmental model for this behavior. Whatever the age when this skill becomes fully mature, the ability to perform a coincidence-anticipation timing skill is a cornerstone of performance in many sport-oriented skills. Table 8.1 summarizes the basic visual-perceptual abilities and the approximate age equivalences for developing these abilities (Gallahue & Ozmun, 2002; Williams, 1983).

Table 8.1 Intrasensory Development in Young Children

Sensory Modality / Behavior	Age
VISUAL-PERCEPTUAL DEVELOPMENT	
Visual acuity (capacity to distinguish detail in objects in static and dynamic situations)	Improves rapidly between ages 5 and 7 and again between 9 and 10; static visual acuity matures prior to dynamic visual acuity (about age 10 and 11, respectively).
Depth perception (capacity to judge how near or far an object is from oneself)	Improves rapidly between ages 7 and 11; matures by age 12.
Movement perception (capacity to judge movement of an object)	Improves rapidly between ages 8 and 12; by age 9 can make accurate judgments regarding moving objects; by age 12 can make quick and accurate judgments regarding moving objects.
Figure-ground perception (capacity to distinguish an object from its surroundings)	Improves rapidly between ages 4 and 6; matures between ages 8 and 12.
Spatial orientation/relationships	Spatial orientation improves rapidly between ages 5 and 7; by age 4 can learn directional extremes and vertical from horizontal positions; by age 8 may still confuse left and right directions. Success with increasingly more difficult spatial relationships shows a progressive improvement throughout early childhood.
Visual-motor coordination (capacity to integrate eyes and hands for object tracking, manipulation, and interception)	Improves rapidly between ages 3 and 7; matures between ages 10 and 12. Object interception improves significantly throughout childhood.
Processing of visual information	Children process information more slowly than do adults; this ability improves rapidly between ages 6 and 10, maturing shortly thereafter.
AUDITORY-PERCEPTUAL DEVELOPMENT	
Auditory acuity (ability to discern presence or absence of sound)	By 6 months adult-like hearing; one does see improvement throughout childhood, but this may be attributed to improved attention.
Auditory discrimination (capacity to differentiate between two acoustic stimuli)	Improves from 3 to 5 years of age; continued refinement until approximately 13 years of age.
Sound localization (capacity to localize sounds emanating from different spatial locations)	Although the ability to localize sounds is present early in infancy, refinement in the ability to localize the general direction of sound well occurs at about age 3.
Auditory figure-ground (capacity to select relevant auditory stimuli from irrelevant ones)	Many children have difficulty selecting relevant sounds from irrelevant ones. Although an important skill, little is known regarding age changes in ability.

Sensory Modality / Behavior	Age
TACTILE-KINESTHETIC DEVELOPMENT	
One-point touch localization (ability to discern one point of contact on the skin)	Appears to be well developed by age 5.
Multiple-point touch localization (ability to discern two or more points of contact on the skin)	Dramatic improvement between ages 4 and 6, maturing shortly thereafter.
Tactile-kinesthetic recognition (haptic memory-recognition of objects through manipulation)	Haptic memory for forms improves rapidly between ages 6 and 8, with the most dramatic changes occurring between 4 and 5.
Spatial Orientation (knowledge of body in space)	Rapid improvement between ages 6 and 8.

Auditory-Perceptual Development

Although not quite as important as visual-perceptual and tactile-kinesthetic development, auditory-perceptual development is nonetheless exceedingly important for skilled motor behavior in children. In addition to the act of hearing, children must learn to judge the particular characteristics of the sounds heard. Auditory perception is often broken down into auditory acuity, sound localization, and auditory figure-ground (see Table 8.1). *Auditory acuity* is defined as the ability of the auditory system to discern the presence or absence of sound. Auditory acuity improves progressively throughout childhood and even into adolescence, although improvements in late childhood and adolescence may be attributed to improved attention level and the ability to follow directions on auditory tests more closely (Haywood & Getchell, 2001).

Sound localization refers to the ability to recognize the direction from which a sound emanates. Sound localization is important for the child's overall motor development insofar as it allows the child to visually link sounds with their sources and helps the child to establish associations between specific sounds and objects and events within the environment (Williams, 1983). The ability to localize sounds is enhanced by the child's ability to select relevant sounds from irrelevant ones *(auditory figure-ground)*. Children continue to improve in sound localization and by age 3 can localize the general direction of distant sounds. Little is known regarding developmental changes in auditory figure-ground in children (Haywood & Getchell, 2001).

Tactile-Kinesthetic Perceptual Development

Tactile-kinesthetic perception can be considered a combination of the following "subsystems" or "subsenses": (1) cutaneous or touch, which provides information regarding stimulation of the skin and/or deeper tissues; (2) kinesthetic, which provides information regarding joint movement and position and muscle stretch and tension (touch and kinesthetic receptors are often collectively termed proprioceptors); and (3) vestibular, which provides information about linear and angular acceleration and deceleration and/or position of the head relative to the body. Some authors also include the haptic subsystem, which is a unique combination of information from touch and kinesthetic subsystems and from dynamic touch, which integrates information from muscular, kinesthetic, and touch subsystems (Gibson, 1996). Other authors, such as Warren, Yezierski, and Capra (1997a, 1997b), separate the touch-tactile system into the sub-modalities of discriminative touch, vibratory touch, proprioception (position sense), crude nondiscriminitive touch, thermal (hot and cold) sensations, and nociception (pain). Regardless of the number of subsystems used to describe tactile-kinesthetic perception, this system as a whole is important for supplying information about the external environment, such as shape, size, angle, and texture of objects, and about the relative position of the body in space (Williams, 1983).

It is apparent that the tactile-kinesthetic system is not a single sensory system, as are the visual and auditory systems. The tactile-kinesthetic system is made up of quite a number of different sensory receptors that collectively provide vital information about the external environment (exteroceptive sensations) impinging on the body (tactile-touch) and the internal environment (proprioceptive sensations), as well as about the body's position in space (vestibular receptors and proprioceptors). Also, unlike the visual and auditory systems, receptors from this sensory system are found throughout the body, rather than in a more clearly defined area (i.e., eyes for seeing and ears for hearing).

The primary exteroceptors found in the cutaneous and subcutaneous tissues can be broken down into three major groups: mechanoreceptors (touch and pressure receptors), nociceptors (pain receptors), and thermoceptors (hot and cold detectors). Only mechanoreceptors will be discussed here, because these receptors have the most to do with movement and sensory feedback during movement.

Mechanoreceptors are specialized cells that provide information to the central nervous system (CNS) regarding touch, pressure, vibration, and skin tension. They include the following receptors (Table 8.2): Meissner's corpuscles, Pacini's corpuscles, Ruffini's corpuscles, Merkel's disks, and hair follicle receptors. Each of these receptors respond to different types of mechanical stimuli and have both varying threshold levels for activation (either high or low levels of sensitive to stimulation) and varying rates of adaptation to stimuli (i.e., rapidly adapting, so that they respond maximally but their response levels decrease if the stimulus is maintained; or slowly adapting, so that they keep transmitting information for as long as the stimulus is applied). Also, these receptors tend to be found in different places within the skin and deeper tissues (Figure 8.2).

Whereas cutaneous mechanoreceptors provide detailed information about external stimuli impinging on the body proper, there is another major class of receptors providing information about mechanical forces arising from within the body. These are called proprioceptors (meaning "receptors for self"). The primary purpose of proprioceptors is to provide continuous information about position of the limbs in space and forms the basis of our kinesthetic awareness. Kinesthesis is defined as a person's awareness, without the use of vision, of positions and movements of the body and its parts and the person's ability to identify the agent (itself or externally generated) causing the movement. Another type of proprioceptive feedback that is important for motor control is vestibular input. Although vestibular input is considered a proprioceptive source of information and is paramount for controlled movement, information from the vestibular system is not consciously perceived. In total, development of kinesthesis is crucial to movement skill production and feedback analysis.

Table 8.2 Tactile, Kinesthetic, and Vestibular Receptors and Their Stimuli and Locations

Receptor(s)/Location	Stimulus
MECHANORECEPTORS IN SKIN AND DEEPER TISSUES	
Meissner's corpuscles	Detect low-frequency vibration, touch, and pressure on skin
Hair follicle receptors	Motion detection and direction
Pacini's corpuscles	Detect high-frequency vibration and deep pressure
Merkel's cells	Skin displacement—localize touch and pressure over skin
Ruffini's corpuscles (endings)	Skin displacement and stretching
PROPRIOCEPTORS IN MUSCLE, TENDON, AND JOINTS	
Muscle spindles	Detect length (stretch) and rate of change of stretch of muscle tissue
Golgi tendon organs	Detect tension at musculotendinous junction; protect from overstretching or excessive tension
Joint receptors (Ruffini endings, modified Pacini corpuscles, and Golgi-type receptors)	Joint movement and pressure; detect limb position
VESTIBULAR RECEPTORS	
Hair cells in semicircular canals in membranous labyrinth inner ear	Detect angular acceleration motions of the head
Hair cells in saccule and utricle in membranous labyrinth	Detect gravitational forces and linear acceleration motions of the head

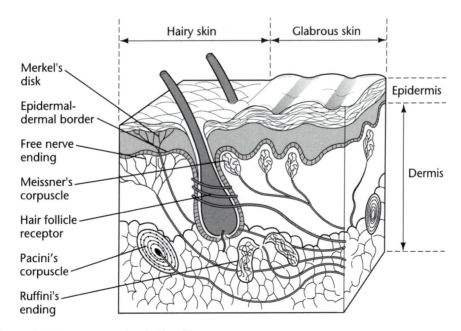

Figure 8.2 Sensory receptors in the skin.
Source: Reprinted by permission from M. F. Bear, B.W. Connors, and M.A. Paradiso, in Neuroscience: Exploring the Brain by T.S. Satterfiled (Ed.). Copyright © 1996 Lippincott, Williams and Wilkins, Balitmore.

There are numerous proprioceptive receptors located in the muscles, joints, and tendons, which when taken together contribute to our sense of kinesthesis. These proprioceptors are involved with coding the parameters of joint movement and position—direction, rate, and duration—and providing information about muscle length (how much and how fast it changes) and tension (Keogh & Sugden, 1985). Although researchers cannot document the developmental progress of these proprioceptors precisely, their importance in providing information about muscle, joint, and tendon position is crucial for an individual's ability to move and process feedback.

Muscle spindles (Figure 8.3) are one type of proprioceptor and are located parallel to the skeletal muscle fibers (cells). The muscle spindle is a morphologically extremely complex sensory receptor and is made up of a number of small muscle fibers enclosed in a connective tissue capsule. These smaller muscle fibers are referred to as intrafusal fibers (within capsule); those muscle fibers outside the muscle spindle are called extrafusal fibers (outside capsule). Sensory axons innervate muscle spindles by encircling the intrafusal fibers (often termed *spindle afferents*). Also, these intrafusal fibers are innervated by a special class of motor neurons called gamma motor neurons (alpha motor neurons are the class of motor neurons that innervate the actual muscle fibers). The function of these gamma motor neurons is to reset the spindle once it has been stretched. They do not function directly in overall muscle contraction (Enoka, 2001).

Because muscle spindles are parallel to the extrafusal fibers (muscle fibers), stretching of the muscle causes a stretch on the intrafusal fibers of the muscle spin-

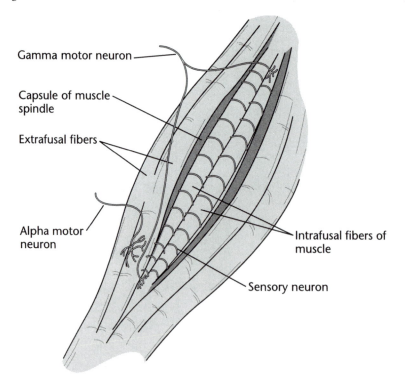

Figure 8.3 Anatomy of the muscle spindle and Golgi tendon organ.
Source: J. H. Wilmore and D. L. Costill, *Physiology of Sport and Exercise*, 2nd ed., Human Kinetics, Champaign, Il, 1999

dle. This action displaces the spindle afferents, producing spindle afferent discharge. This discharge is coded in such a way that the CNS is informed of how much and how quickly the muscle is being stretched. Contraction of the muscle produces the opposite effect: the spindles are silent, and there is no spindle afferent discharge. The muscle spindle is reset by the gamma motor neurons, whereupon the muscle spindle is ready once again to detect stretch in the muscle tissue.

How is information from the muscle spindle used during movement? At the lowest levels, information is involved in the reflexive activation of muscles (stretch reflex). As information ascends the central nervous system, it provides important feedback to the brain regarding muscle position and contributes to our perception of body position in space. Moreover, the muscle spindles are extremely important in maintaining the body in an upright posture.

The muscle spindle is the cornerstone of a very important physiological reflex called the myotatic reflex (Figure 8.4). This reflex is also referred to as the deep tendon reflex (DTR) or stretch reflex. This reflex involves the contraction of a muscle when it is rapidly stretched and relaxation of its antagonist muscles. To elicit this reflex, the muscle spindle is activated by either quickly stretching the muscle or by briskly tapping either the muscle directly or its tendon with a reflex hammer (e.g., knee-jerk reflex). Clinically one may observe a hyperactive stretch reflex in individ-

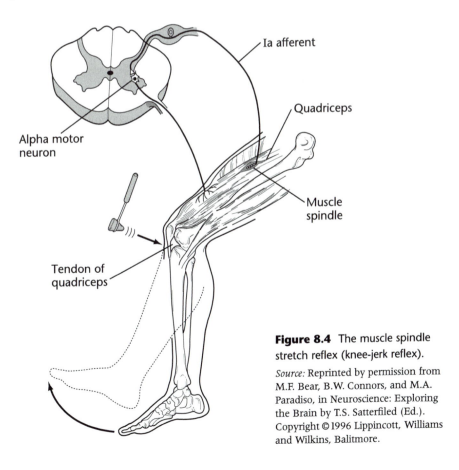

Figure 8.4 The muscle spindle stretch reflex (knee-jerk reflex).

Source: Reprinted by permission from M.F. Bear, B.W. Connors, and M.A. Paradiso, in Neuroscience: Exploring the Brain by T.S. Satterfiled (Ed.). Copyright © 1996 Lippincott, Williams and Wilkins, Balitmore.

uals with various types of brain damage (e.g., cerebral palsy, stroke, or head trauma). This is often referred to as hyperactive or increased muscle tone and is manifested by an increased resistance to passive stretch. It is especially pronounced in the antigravity muscles, that is, flexors of the arm and fingers, and extensors of the leg.

A second type of proprioceptor is the *Golgi tendon organ (GTO)* (Figure 8.3). Unlike the muscle spindle, the GTO is a relatively simple sensory receptor made up of a single afferent (sensory) connection and no efferent (motor) connections. The GTO is arranged in series with the muscle and tendon. Whether a muscle is stretched or contracted, tension is developed within the tissue, and forces are applied to the GTO. Hence, the GTO acts as a tension detector. This is in contrast to the aforementioned parallel muscle spindle, which detects length and rate of length change of the muscle (Enoka, 2001).

The GTOs function in the following way. The GTO is sensitive to tension changes resulting from either stretch or contraction of the muscle. This elicits a reflex called the GTO or inverse myotatic reflex, whose primary function is to protect the muscle tendon from injury that would result from too much tension. The GTO reflex is an inhibitory reflex, inhibiting its own muscle (that is, inhibiting the muscle having the tension) and exciting antagonists.

Teachers may witness an abnormal reaction of the GTO reflex in children who have overly tight or spastic muscles. A characteristic of the increased resistance seen in spastic muscles is the clasp-knife reflex. This response reflects a sudden collapse of all resistance when a spastic muscle is aggressively stretched. The clasp-knife response is due to increased GTO activity, resulting from increased tension levels within the muscle stretched. Motor neurons responsible for the hypertonicity are quickly inhibited, thereby reducing the dangerously high tension levels within the muscle. As a result of this reflex, the muscle relaxes extremely fast, often resembling the quick opening of a pocket knife: hence, the term *clasp-knife reflex* (Figure 8.5). Together, the muscle spindles and GTOs reciprocally control force (GTO) and unit length (muscle spindle) of the muscle.

In conjunction with the muscle spindle and GTO, joint receptors provide information about limb position in space. However, in contrast to the muscle spindle and GTO, joint receptors are not a single, well-defined entity. More readily what one finds are various types of receptors (e.g., Golgi-type endings, pacinian corpuscles, and Ruffini's endings), in various locations surrounding and within the joint proper (e.g., joint capsule, ligaments, and loose connective tissue). These joint receptors provide the CNS with information about joint velocity, acceleration, displacement, and position of limbs during movement (Enoka, 2001).

Finally, the vestibular system (Figure 8.6) is involved in kinesthesis by detecting acceleration movements of the head and using this information to orient the head and eyes during movement and to control posture. Tiny hair cells found within the inner ear detect linear and angular acceleration movements of the head and through an intricate and complex network influence eye and body movements. The primary receptors for the vestibular system are tiny hair cells that are found within the semicircular canals (detecting angular acceleration of the head), and the saccule and utricle (detecting linear acceleration of the head). In total, vestibular receptors are sensitive to (1) head position in space (i.e., whether the head is upright, upside down, or in some other position) and (2) sudden changes in direction of the body.

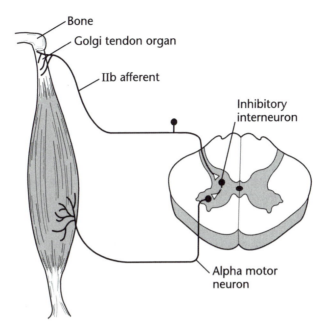

Figure 8.5 Circuitry of the clasp-knife reflex.
Source: Reprinted by permission from M. F. Bear, B. W. Connors, M. A. Paradiso, and M. A. Paradiso, in Neuroscience: Exploring the Brain by T. S. Satterfield (Ed.). Copyright © 1996 Lippincott Williams and Wilkins, Baltimore.

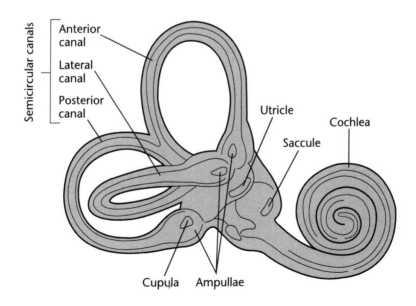

Figure 8.6 Anatomy of the vestibular apparatus in the inner ear.

Tactile-kinesthetic perceptual development is often broken down into the following functional abilities: one-point touch localization, or discrimination, multiple-point touch localization, tactile-kinesthetic recognition, and spatial orientation (Table 8.1). *One-point touch localization or discrimination* involves the ability to discern whether a single stimulus is in contact with the body independent of vision. Based on limited research, perception of a single point of the hands and arms appears to be mature by age 5 (Haywood & Getchell, 2001). In *multiple-point touch localization* testing, the minimal interstimulus distance required to perceive two simultaneously applied skin indentations as distinct is measured. The accuracy with which more than one stimulus can be sensed on the body varies from region to region of the body, such that in the fingertips stimuli can be perceived if they are only 2 mm apart. In contrast, stimuli applied to the forearm are not perceived as distinct until they are minimally 40 mm apart (Warren et al., 1997b). Based on limited data, it appears that this ability is developed by age 7.

Tactile-kinesthetic recognition has to do with the ability to recognize objects and their characteristics by tactile-kinesthetic manipulation alone (Williams, 1983). Finally, *spatial orientation* is a more global or all-inclusive tactile-kinesthetic ability that deals with perception of the body's location and orientation in space independent of vision. Usually, this ability is tested by having the child walk a straight line while blindfolded and measuring the deviation from the straight path (Haywood & Getchell, 2001). One sees significant improvement in the skill between the ages of 6 and 8.

Intrasensory and Intersensory Development

With a general understanding of the major sensory-perceptual systems, we now can investigate what is meant by intersensory and intrasensory integration. *Intrasensory* integration refers to the ability to integrate sensory information within one sensory system, whereas *intersensory* integration refers to the ability to integrate or use multiple sources of information simultaneously to solve problems and/or to adapt to the environment. Intersensory integration involves the transfer of ideas or concepts across different modalities (Williams, 1983).

Intersensory integration has been further distinguished between cross-modal (or intermodal) equivalence (CME) and cross-modal concepts (CMC) (Blank & Bridger, 1974; Keogh & Sugden, 1985). Cross-modal equivalence involves recognizing a particular set of stimulus features as the same or equivalent when they appear in two different sensory modalities. Cross-modal concept encompasses the ability to utilize a concept or principle to solve problems that are associated with distinct yet equivalent information presented through more than one sensory modality (Williams, 1983). As one can see, intersensory integration is a much more complex phenomenon involving widespread areas within the CNS where sensory information from multiple sensory modalities converge (e.g., multimodal areas in frontal, parietal, and temporal lobes). Intersensory development and function thus represent an advanced form of brain development and processing.

The ability to function in a multiple sensory mode is believed to involve the gradual integration of all available stimuli by the child into a more complex sensory picture of the environment. Therefore, the ability to integrate several sources of information simultaneously into one map or picture is not something that is performed discretely at visual, auditory, and tactile-kinesthetic levels, but rather is performed intermodally and multidimensionally (Williams, 1983). According to Williams, there are three levels of intersensory functioning: (1) a low, more automatic level of integration, which is prewired into the nervous system and which appears to be present at birth; (2) a higher level of integration, which involves analyzing perceptual features and which occurs at a more conscious, thinking level; and (3) a cognitive-conceptual level of integration, which involves transferring ideas and concepts across different sensory modalities. As children move up through these levels of intersensory development, they become more efficient at using multiple sources of sensory information. This allows for much more adaptive behaviors and a higher level of neural functioning.

It is important to note that refinement of both intrasensory and intersensory functions occurs simultaneously and that at any given age of development, certain intrasensory abilities may be more advanced than selected intersensory functions. Further, a disruption in the organization and interaction of multiple sensory systems can lead to developmental delays that may have serious deleterious effects on motor functioning. For example, Williams, Temple, and Bateman (1978) found that children (approximately 6 years old and younger) with advanced intersensory integration ability were superior in learning performance than children with less advanced intersensory development. According to these authors, it appears that at younger ages, the level of intersensory integration directly affects a child's ability to perform a gross perceptual-motor task involving the sequencing of a series of simple motor tasks into one, smooth movement chain of greater complexity. As the child increases in age, the ability to use multiple sensory cues appears to have little effect on learning and mastery of such motor skills. Table 8.3 summarizes intersensory abilities and the approximate age equivalences for developing these abilities (Williams, 1983).

When a child embarks on learning a new physical skill or changes the way he or she is already performing a skill, intimate cooperation between body and brain is required. No one knows for sure just how and where memories are stored in the brain, but scientists are learning more about the subject every day. Neuroscientists have found that the frontal lobe—the conscious, verbal, problem-solving, hard-thinking area of the brain—is most active when you learn a skill. This makes intuitive sense, because during skill practice the performer is thinking about the information the teacher is imparting as well as analyzing the feedback being generated by the movement. The performer is analyzing instructions and thinking about where various body parts need to be during every part of the movement.

Also, the brain stays active for several hours after a practice session has ended, actively processing all of this new information and building what is often called an "internal model" of the skill. As the skill is progressively learned, activity shifts to deeper parts of the brain—to areas that handle automatic, nonconscious activity. This shift in processing allows the skill to be recalled and "run" quickly, without much thinking. A novice might have to consciously think through over a dozen distinct steps to get a skill right. For the expert, the skill is automatic, with little thinking required. The degree of practice required to automate a particular skill can range well into the hundreds of thousands of repetitions (Kottke, 1980). Often individuals with cognitive and/or attention deficits have problems developing this internal model and have problems developing appropriate strategies that facilitate skill acqui-

Table 8.3 Timeline for Intersensory Development in Young Children

---

Sensory Modalities/Behaviors

VISUAL-AUDITORY INTEGRATION

Children 5 years and younger have problems performing auditory-visual integration tasks.

Rapid development in performing auditory-visual integration occurs between ages 5 and 7, with 6- and 7-year-olds significantly better than 5-year-olds.

8-year-olds perform at a similar level on auditory-visual, visual-auditory, visual-visual, and auditory-auditory tasks.

Rapid improvement in auditory-visual integration between ages 8 and 10.

Auditory-visual integration improves until approximately age 12.

Intersensory integration of auditory and visual information is more efficient when task is presented visually first.

VISUAL-TACTILE/KINESTHETIC INTEGRATION

3-year-olds perform poorly in tasks involving visual-tactile/kinesthetic integration.

Visual-tactile/kinesthetic integration abilities involving shape recognition are almost mature by age 5.

Significant refinement of visual-tactile/kinesthetic integration abilities occurs between ages 5 and 7, plateauing thereafter.

A second period of improvement in visual-tactile/kinesthetic integration abilities occurs between ages 9 and 11; integration is more effective when presented visually first, which appears not to be the case in younger children.

AUDITORY-TACTILE/KINESTHETIC INTEGRATION

Although not supported by some researchers, it appears that the child's awareness of tactile stimulation is more accurate when accompanied by auditory stimulation.

Auditory-tactile/kinesthetic integration abilities show improvement throughout childhood. Also, there appears to be a more natural connection between these two modalities compared to visual-tactile/kinesthetic integration abilities.

Overall, intersensory integration is extremely important in developing skilled motor behavior. It appears that this is particularly so in the early development of both gross and fine motor skills.

---

sition and attention. It is important for teachers to understand the developmental changes in movement and perception that influence motor skill acquisition and to plan their instructional program to accommodate the learning needs and styles of children with various disabilities. This may entail rethinking how the task is presented or the appropriate practice considerations. At one time or another, we have heard the aphorism "practice makes perfect," and to retain what we have learned, we need practice. However, the conditions under which one practices also have a profound impact on learning. If one practices a skill incorrectly, then one will end up learning that skill perfectly incorrectly. Also, if practice is not efficient and does not incorporate the most appropriate perceptual information, feedback, contextually-related aspects skill retention will suffer significantly. From what has been discussed previously, this means that teachers should provide children with appropriate perceptual information regarding their performance and use the most efficient modality to provide appropriate sensory input.

CHAPTER SUMMARY

1. At birth the perceptual systems are intact and functioning although the infant still relies on primitive reflexes.

2. The first major change in sensory-perceptual processing involves a shift in reliance on the tactile-kinesthetic system to reliance on the visual system for modifying motor behavior.

3. Visual acuity is the ability to discern detail in objects, statically and dynamically; depth perception is the ability to judge how far away or near objects are from a person; and movement perception is the ability to perceive an object while moving.

4. Stereopsis, or three-dimensional vision, requires the brain to recognize objects at various distances.

5. Figure-ground perception is the ability to extract relevant detail from contexts.

6. Spatial orientation refers to the ability to recognize an object's orientation or arrangement.

7. Visual-motor coordination is the ability to integrate the eyes and hands.

8. Auditory acuity is the ability of the auditory system to discern sound; sound localization is the ability to recognize the direction of the sound.

9. The tactile-kinesthetic system is not a single sensory system, as are the visual and auditory systems. This system is made up of sensory receptors that provide information from the environment (exteroceptive sensations), sensations impending on the body (tactile) and the internal environment (proprioceptive), and position in space (vestibular and proprioceptors).

REFERENCES

Blank, M., & Bridger, W. (1974). Cross modal transfer in nursery school children. *Journal of Experimental Psychology, 58,* 277–282.

Enoka, R. M. (2001). *Neuromechanics of Human Movement,* (3rd ed.). Champaign, IL: Human Kinetics.

Gabbard, C. P. (2000). *Lifelong motor development* (3rd ed.). Boston: Allyn & Bacon.

Gallahue, D. L., & Ozmun, J. C. (2002). *Understanding motor development: Infants, children, adolescents, adults* (5th ed.). Dubuque, IA: McGraw-Hill.

Gibson, J. (1996). *The senses considered as perceptual systems.* New York: Houghton Mifflin.

Haywood, K. M., & Getchell, M. (2001). *Life span motor development* (3rd ed.). Champaign, IL: Human Kinetics.

Keogh, J., & Sugden, D. (1985). *Movement skill development.* New York: MacMillan.

Kottke, F. J. (1980). From reflex to skill: The training of coordination. *Archives of Physical Medicine and Rehabilitation, 59,* 551–561.

Payne, V. G., & Issacs, L.D. (2002). *Human motor development: A life span approach* (5th ed.). Mountain View, CA: Mayfield.

Rock, I. (1975). *An introduction to perception.* New York: Macmillan.

Schmidt, R. A. (1988). *Motor control and learning: A behavioral emphasis* (2nd ed.). Champaign, IL: Human Kinetics.

Warren, S., Yezierski, R. P., & Capra, N. F. (1977a). The somatosensory system I: Discriminative touch and position. In D. E. Haines (Ed.), *Fundamental neuroscience* (pp. 219–235). New York: Churchill Livingstone.

Warren, S., Yezierski, R. P., & Capra, N. F. (1977b). The somatosensory system II: Nondiscriminative touch, temperature and nociception. In D. E. Haines (Ed.), *Fundamental neuroscience* (pp. 237–253). New York: Churchill Livingstone.

Williams, H. G. (1983). *Perceptual and motor development*. Englewood Cliffs, NJ: Prentice-Hall.

Williams, H., Temple, I., & Bateman, J. (1978). Perceptual-motor and cognitive learning in young children. In *Psychology of motor behavior and sport*. Champaign, IL: Human Kinetics.

CHAPTER 9

Physical Fitness Development

There are many definitions for the term *physical fitness*, which reflects its multidimensional and hierarchical nature. Physical fitness is defined by most professionals as a set of attributes, which either people have or acquire, relating to their ability to perform physical activity. Additionally, one may view physical fitness as a state of well-being, characterized by a low risk of premature development of hypokinetic disease (conditions related to inactivity, such as obesity and cardiovascular disease) and by having the energy to participate in a variety of activities (Physical Fitness and Sports Research Digest, 2000). Because of the multifaceted nature of physical fitness, professionals often view fitness as being made up of several subcomponents. These most often include the health-related and skill-related components of fitness.

Health-related fitness consists of those components of physical fitness that are most directly related to good health and well being. The health-related components are commonly defined as cardiovascular fitness, body composition, flexibility, and muscular strength and endurance. Skill-related fitness is comprised of those components of physical fitness that are most directly related to enhanced performance in sports and motor skills. The skill-related components are commonly defined as power, speed, agility, balance, coordination, and reaction time. Because this text is concerned more with the ameliorative effects of exercise to counteract the detrimental effects of inactivity and to optimize the child's functional capacity within the physiological limitations of his or her disability, we will be concerned chiefly with the components of health-related fitness.

Much of our survival depends on the development of physical fitness. Independent movement implies ability, to the extent possible, to initiate movement independently to fulfill life's most basic and not-so-basic needs. Persons who, for whatever reason, cannot move to meet requirements (and beyond) of daily living must rely on others for mobility and are rendered relatively dependent on them for survival.

Physical fitness is essential for independence of movement and for maintaining or developing functional skills. Fitness development is also important for play, sports participation, and job-related skills that rely on high levels of physical development (Seaman, 1999). Not all individuals may achieve total independence of movement, but everyone should be afforded the full opportunity to achieve independence in accordance with his or her potential. Likewise, individuals with disabilities and those without disabilities can gain similar benefits from physical activity programs (see Chapter 23).

Fitness Is Fitness, Regardless of Ability or Disability

We believe it difficult to overstate the case that fitness for persons with disabilities is, first and foremost, simply fitness. From this perspective, there is a need to demystify some of the folklore about providing physical education opportunities for persons with disabilities. When one looks at each specific fitness component under the comprehensive fitness umbrella, the label "disability" by itself, does not redefine fitness. All people, as individuals, have individual fitness needs. Some people have labels, and some labels are disability labels (e.g., cerebral palsy, spina bifida, mental retardation). However, any given label does not redefine fitness for the individual, nor does it necessarily redefine that individual's fitness needs or requirements. The individual's unique needs remain the defining factors for developing and maintaining physical functioning.

Prioritizing Fitness Needs

While we need to recognize the uniqueness of each person's fitness needs, there is also a need to recognize that certain kinds of fitness, for most people, likely are more important than others. Instead of focusing on cardiovascular or aerobic fitness, there is a growing consensus that health-related fitness is more essential for children during development (Rowland, 1999). In this context, fitness is related not only to cardiovascular functioning but also to muscular strength/endurance, caloric expenditure and body composition, and flexibility (Rowland, 1999). Rationale for this growing consensus is that health factors are everyone's concern, and, in fact, health-related fitness promotes good health and independent functioning. For example, by successfully engaging in health-related fitness activities, an individual is likely to enjoy benefits of lower cholesterol, lower blood pressure, normal-range blood glucose levels, and an optimal level of lean muscle tissue (i.e., better health). Perhaps the bottom-line rationale for prioritizing health-related fitness is that fitness is essential for independent living and for developing functional skills.

Winnick and Short (2000) emphasize that health entails two constructs: physiological health and functional health. Physiological health is viewed as capacities associated with well-being, such as appropriate levels of body fat and aerobic functioning, whereas functional health is related to physical capability, such as activities of daily living and leisure skill participation. Certainly, as physical educators we would like everyone to share our enthusiasm for an active lifestyle; however, physical educators need to recognize and respect that being athletic, for whatever reason, may not be particularly crucial in some people's constellation of lifestyle choices and one need not be athletic as a prerequisite to being healthy. Likewise, we emphasize the concept of functional skill development in physical fitness. In this context, the term *functional* or *functional skills* is the ability to perform those activities of daily living or self-care activities that are essential for promoting independence required in home and community settings. In addition, *functional* relates to work-specific tasks, sports, or play activities that promote independent functioning (Horvat & Croce, 1995).

The potential health benefits of exercise in children can be summarized as follows: Regular physical training is beneficial in preventing cardiovascular disease, respiratory disease, and certain metabolic disorders (Shephard, 1984). In addition, by controlling those risk factors specific to disease (e.g., coronary artery disease), exercise can protect against developing diseases in the future. Thus, a program of intensified physical activity favors wellness and also promotes overall functioning in children. Regular physical activity is an important factor in regulating and maintaining body weight and generally results in an increase in lean body mass and fat-free mass (FFM), with a corresponding decrease in body fat. Exercise can also help children with disabilities develop motor skills and promote or restore functioning from an acquired disability. Further, fitness can be functional and help individuals with disabilities maintain independent living, perform work-related tasks, and maintain attention.

Challenges to Physical Fitness Development

Seaman (1999) has indicated that people with disabilities face many challenges that impede their progress to become physically active. Horvat and Croce (1995), Seaman (1999), and Winnick and Short (2000) have identified the following challenges to fitness development faced by individuals with disabilities:

- Architectural barriers may require an inordinate amount of energy expenditure and impede independent movement.
- Many people with disabilities are overprotected, fostering an inactive lifestyle and the potential for obesity and other health concerns.
- Inefficient movement patterns and poor body alignment increase energy expenditure required to perform everyday tasks. Fatigue occurs easily, reducing job efficiency and the desire to participate in leisure activities.
- Restricted sensory input, abnormal reflex activity, spasticity, and/or paralysis reduces mechanical efficiency and functioning, which in turn fosters inactivity.
- The use of prosthetic and orthotic devices contributes to a loss of functional muscle mass, reduces neuromuscular efficiency, and contributes to excessive fatigue.
- Depression or anger often results from an accident, disease, or acquired disability, often leading to reduced participation in physical activities.
- Individuals with cognitive or attention deficits require behavior intervention and prompting to sustain a sufficient level of fitness.
- Motivation to complete a task or sustain an effort to induce a training effect is often lacking.
- Children with disabilities often do not develop age-appropriate play skills, which further decreases their physical functioning and social interaction.
- Attitudinal barriers often focus on what the individual cannot do instead of what the individual can accomplish.

Development of Fitness

Basically, physiological responses to exercise during acute (single-bout) or chronic (repeated) exercise sessions are similar in individuals of all ages, and there are no underlying physiological factors that make individuals with disabilities less suitable for prolonged, intense exercise (Bar-Or, 1983). Likewise, individuals with disabilities respond to training interventions in a manner similar to that of their able-bodied counterparts in stereotypical ways (specificity of training). Developmentally, Bar-Or

(1989a) concluded that the research indicates that aerobic power, muscle strength, and anaerobic muscle power are trainable in children, although the degree of trainability of aerobic power is somewhat lower in prepubescents than in older age groups. Likewise, we see that children and adults with disabilities will respond to exercise challenges similarly and will display many of the same physiological adaptations as their nondisabled peers. For instance, individuals with disabilities will respond to both intensity and duration of the training stimulus in a similar manner to that of their nondisabled peers. For the teacher and coach it is essential to understand that exercise interventions that improve aerobic functioning, muscular strength and endurance, flexibility, and body composition all should be emphasized to promote functional health in individuals with disabilities. Winnick and Short (2000) recommend identifying health-related concerns and establishing a fitness profile for children as the first step in the assessment process. Variations from typical development can then be addressed by the teacher to ensure that children can attain the same functional level as their peers.

Aerobic and Anaerobic Capacities

From basic physiology, you will recall that metabolism increases proportionally to increases in workload. However, when faced with increasingly higher energy demands, the body ultimately reaches a limit for oxygen consumption. At this point, oxygen consumption peaks and remains constant even with increasing workloads. This peak value is often referred to as maximal oxygen uptake (VO_2max), maximal aerobic power (capacity), or simply cardiorespiratory endurance capacity. This value is often regarded as the best single measure of cardiorespiratory endurance and aerobic fitness.

When VO_2max is used as a criterion measure, maximal aerobic capacity in children is lower than that found in the adult population during physical activities, such

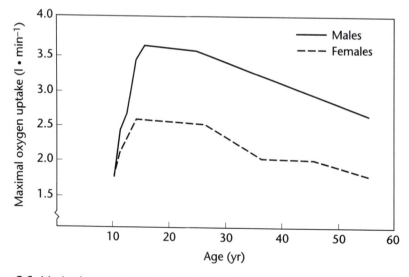

Figure 9.1 Maximal oxygen uptake as a function of age.
Source: Reprinted by permission from Carl P. Gabbard, Lifelong Motor Development, 3rd ed. Copyright © 2000 Allyn & Bacon Publishers, Needham Heights.

as pushing a wheelchair, that require sustained energy utilization (Figure 9.1). As a child grows, there is a concomitant increase in aerobic capacity; aerobic capacity of boys increases until about age 18, whereas in girls it hardly increases beyond age 14 (Bar-Or, 1993; Rowland, 1996). This rise in aerobic capacity is due primarily to increases in the size of the heart, lungs, and skeletal muscle. One must note, however, that an individual's need for energy is related to body size, so aerobic capacity, or VO_2max, is more appropriately expressed relative to body weight in milliliters of oxygen consumed per kilogram of body weight, or by fat-free weight. When one expresses VO_2max in relative rather than absolute terms (e.g., body weight or lean body mass), there is hardly any age-related change in the VO_2max of boys, whereas there is a continual decline in the VO_2max of girls. This decline in VO_2max in girls is most likely due to the increase in body fatness and the decrease in lean body mass that occur in girls during adolescence (Bar-Or, 1993; Rowland, 1996). One must also note that training increases observed in growing children may reflect activity levels as well as growth-related factors. For example, Rowland (1996) indicated that a 6-year-old boy whose activity is sedentary until the age of 12 will improve his VO_2max by over 100 percent.

Therefore, maximal aerobic capacity, when using VO_2max per kilogram of body weight as the criterion, is not deficient in most children. Although the aerobic capacity of children might not be deficient, one must note that the metabolic cost of running and walking (and possibly in other activities) at a given intensity is greater in children (and far greater in some children with disabilities) due to a biomechanically wasteful locomotion style (Bar-Or, 1993; Rowland, 1990). This leaves children with a lower energy reserve, which may be evident if they have to perform a maximal effort. If one considers the fact that many children with disabilities, in particular those children with physical disabilities, are more inefficient than their nondisabled peers, this lower energy reserve may be even more extensive. During growth, improvements in endurance capacity occur primarily from improved gait mechanics, qualitative changes in oxygen delivery, and/or increases in speed and strength (Rowland, 1990). In contrast, children with disabilities generally are less efficient and possess lower levels of strength, which will then affect their overall functioning.

As a rule, children can generally perform endurance tasks reasonably well but fatigue more quickly in high-intensity anaerobic activities. This is not surprising, for if we observe children playing, we seldom see them performing high-intensity activities for extended time periods. Moreover, children with disabilities often demonstrate lower levels of functioning at each age level and consistently underperform when compared to their nondisabled peers. Whether this is due to a lack of activity, overprotection, or lack of motivation, the end result may be a lower level of physical functioning.

A child's anaerobic capacity (ability to perform supramaximal tasks of 1 minute or less in duration), is lower than that of an adult (Bar-Or, 1993). Thus, an 8-year-old boy produces about 45–50% of the mechanical power produced by a 14-year-old boy, and even when adjusted for body weight, this amount is still only about 65–70%. In girls the trend is similar, although performance per kilogram of body weight plateaus at about ages 11 to 12 (Bar-Or, 1993). Compared to adults, children display a lower tolerance for anaerobic activity, yet, through maturation, anaerobic capacity will improve with age (Rowland, 1996). The reasons for this improvement appear to be

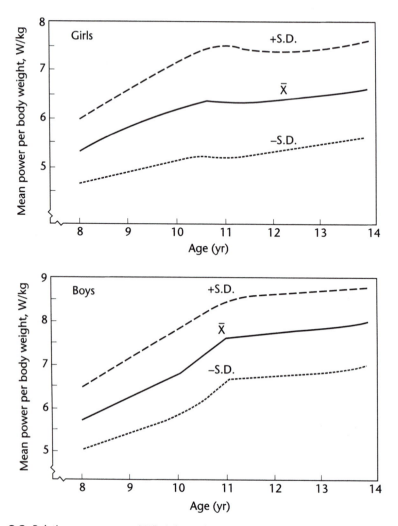

Figure 9.2 Relative mean power (W/kg) from the Wingate Anaerobic Test across age for boys and girls.

Source: Reprinted by permission from Carl P. Gabbard, Lifelong Motor Development, 3rd ed. Copyright © 2000 Allyn & Bacon Publishers, Needham Heights.

related to the concentration and rate of utilization of muscle glycogen (Pfitzinger & Freedson, 1997). Glycogen is the form of carbohydrate stored in muscle tissue, which can be broken down rapidly in the cell and used as an energy source. Without this essential energy server, children cannot sustain high levels of anaerobic activity and will fatigue more easily (Figure 9.2).

In summary, maximal aerobic power does not change (in boys) or even decreases (in girls) with age. This is not found with anaerobic performance, which is lower in children, whether expressed in absolute or relative terms (i.e., whether scaled to body weight or lean body mass). Consequently, children—and, especially, children with disabilities—are at a functional disadvantage when performing activities lasting between 10 and 60 seconds.

Cardiovascular Function

From the beginning of growth as a single tube in utero to the detection of a heartbeat during the fifth prenatal month, the heart undergoes some rather dramatic changes. The size of the heart will increase in a similar manner as body weight, while its weight will double during the first year, quadruple by 5 years, and increase six times by the age of 9. From the ages 9–18, heart growth parallels the general growth curve and functionally has all the mechanisms that are essential to the adult heart. Heart volumes also increase from approximately 40 ml at birth, to 80 ml at 6 months, to 160 ml at 2 years of age.

Basal heart rates or beats per minute (bpm) decrease progressively during childhood. At birth, higher heart rates are present because of the smaller dimensions of the heart but fall approximately 10–20 bpm during the ages of 5–15 (Rowland, 1996). Gender differences are apparent, with females manifesting a rate 5 bpm higher than males. However, maximal heart rate remains constant, independent of age or body dimensions. In terms of efficiency, the preadolescent heart rate is 30–40 bpm higher than a young adult while engaged in the same task (Gabbard, 2000).

Heart rate and stroke volume in children vary because stroke volume is related to heart size; the larger the heart, the more blood can be pumped during each beat. At birth, stroke volume is 3–4 ml, as opposed to 40 ml in the preadolescent and 60 ml in the young adult. As a way of compensating for the smaller stroke volume, children will elicit higher average heart rates: 120–140 bpm in newborns, 100 bpm by age 4, 90 bpm by age 6, and 80 bpm by age 14 (Gabbard, 2000). For children under 10 years of age, no gender differences are present (Malina & Bouchard, 1991). Blood pressure changes are also apparent: Average blood pressure is 70/55 in the newborn, 100/62 by age 10, and 115/65 by age 15 (Rowland, 1996).

Children have particular hemodynamic characteristics, which may be rate limiting under certain exercise conditions (see the *Cardiovascular Terminology* box for definitions of key terms). The primary cardiovascular limitations in children include the following. First, children have a lower concentration of hemoglobin, the oxygen carrying molecules in the blood. These levels increase slowly during childhood for both genders until puberty from 10 g/dl at 6 months to adult levels of 16 g/dl (men) and 14 g/dl

---

Cardiovascular Terminology

- Heart rate (HR)—the number of times the heart beats per minute.
- Stroke volume (SV)—the amount of blood ejected from the left ventricle during contraction of the heart musculature.
- Arteriovenous oxygen difference (AVD-O_2)—the difference in oxygen content found in arterial and mixed-venous blood. This difference reflects the amount of oxygen removed by the tissues and increases with increased workloads.
- Cardiac output—the volume of blood pumped by the heart per minute; represented by the formula:

Cardiac output = heart rate (HR) x stroke volume (SV).

(women) (Malina & Bouchard, 1991). This, in and of itself, can limit exercise capacity in children. At puberty, one sees a significant rise in boys' hemoglobin concentrations due to bone marrow stimulation by testosterone and a plateau in girls' concentrations. Secondly, children have a lower stroke volume (SV) at rest and during submaximal exercise compared to adults, but a higher heart rate (HR) and a greater capacity to extract oxygen from the blood (termed arteriovenous oxygen difference, or AVD-O_2). The end result is that children have a much lower cardiac output (the amount of blood pumped by the heart per minute) than that found in adults at any given level of oxygen consumption (Bar-Or, 1993). Individuals with disabilities will vary from this typical developmental scenario, impacting their ability to engage in strenuous activity. For example, children with Down syndrome may be limited in their cardiac output because of cardiac insufficiency or damage to the heart. Likewise, an individual with a spinal injury will be affected because of differences in autonomic responses from the central nervous system. Further, children with cardiovascular diseases, such as aortic stenosis or pulmonary stenosis, will have reduced stroke volume and cardiac output, thus limiting their capacity to perform aerobically.

Children with disabilities also tend to be at a disadvantage during maximal exercise, when oxygen extraction can no longer keep pace with the exercise workload or when exposed to the combined stresses of intense exercise and extreme heat. Consequently, teachers should use caution when exercising children in hot, humid environments. As a general rule, teachers must be aware that when individuals with disabilities exercise at high intensity levels under hot, humid conditions, they will have greater difficulty trying to maintain their exercise performance. Moreover, if children have poor mechanical efficiency when engaged in physical activity (e.g., children having neuromuscular or orthopedic disabilities), a specific workload will require a greater energy expenditure than in children whose techniques are more biomechanically correct. The combination of a "wasteful" biomechanical style and performing activities under hot, humid conditions makes for a situation that can be quite dangerous for any child, and for children with disabilities even more so.

Muscular Strength

Muscular strength is the ability of the muscle tissue to apply force and refers to a maximal or near-maximal muscular exertion of brief duration. Often we define strength as the maximal force that can be exerted in a single voluntary contraction. An example of muscular strength is lifting oneself from the ground onto a wheelchair or transferring from a wheelchair to the driver's seat of an automobile. In regard to a functional task, strength may, for example, be the ability to lift and carry an object in the home or a work-related setting. Virtually any activity meeting the criteria of brief duration and maximal or near-maximal exertion would require strength to perform.

Strength development is important for all persons, regardless of ability or disability, because a certain amount of strength is required to perform virtually all activities. Even the seemingly simplest activities are strength activities for the person who is strength deficient. Indeed, minimum levels of strength must be achieved before minimal skill levels can be achieved. For example, one cannot become proficient using crutches until minimum levels of grip, arm, and shoulder girdle strength have been developed. Without strength, even the simplest activities are difficult.

Developmentally, the growth of the muscle occurs by hypertrophy (size). The number of muscle fibers is fixed at birth or within the first year of life. Increases in muscle fiber size during the growth process reflect an increase in total muscle mass and increases linearly with age (Beunen & Thomis, 2000).

Muscular strength increases with age in both sexes, reaching a peak at about 29 years of age. Increases for males are much greater than for females (Figures 9.3

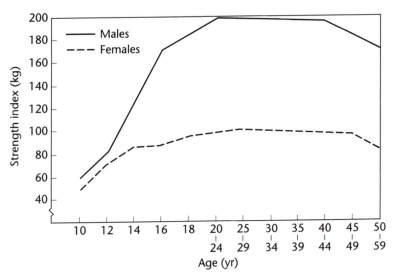

Figure 9.3 Strength index (means) of right and left grip of arm.
Source: Reprinted by permission from Carl P. Gabbard, Lifelong Motor Development, 3rd ed. Copyright © 2000 Allyn & Bacon Publishers, Needham Heights.

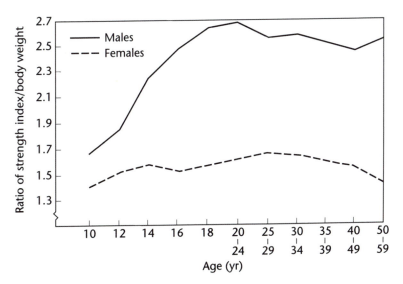

Figure 9.4 Ratio of strength index to body weight.
Source: Reprinted by permission from Carl P. Gabbard, Lifelong Motor Development, 3rd ed. Copyright © 2000 Allyn & Bacon Publishers, Needham Heights.

and 9.4). Increases in strength are influenced by a variety of factors, of which the most important are serum testosterone concentrations in male adolescents—the point at which specific adult hormonal profiles start to emerge—and neural adaptations (Falk & Tenenbaum, 1996; Kraemer & Fleck, 1993). Motor unit activation is also essential to developing force within the muscle, and some of the increases in strength observed in children, especially in prepubescents and postpubescent girls, are attributed to this phenomenon. Blimkie (1989) states that "training-induced neural adaptation refers to increased ability to activate prime mover muscles and/or the improved coordination of synergists and antagonists" (p. 189). This results in an increased ability to apply a greater force in the intended direction of movement by way of increased motor unit activation. For some children with disabilities the ability to recruit motor units may be diminished and affect the ability to produce age-appropriate levels of strength. For example, children with mental retardation have demonstrated a reduced capacity in motor unit activation during controlled movement (Horvat, Ramsey, Amestoy & Croce, in review).

Muscular Endurance

Muscular endurance means the ability to persist and refers to a submaximal muscular effort repeated for a relatively long period of time. It is often defined and measured as the repetition of submaximal contractions or the holding of a submaximal contraction. Unlike strength activities, muscular endurance activities do not involve brief, all-out exertions. Rather, they require persistent, submaximal effort. Many activities in industry, workshops, domestic upkeep, and physical education require muscular endurance. Lifting medium-heavy weights or meeting medium-heavy resistance over an extended period involves muscular endurance. Insofar as repetition leads to skill, and repetition requires endurance, endurance is extremely important for skill and sport performance; hence, muscular endurance is often the key to success in sport.

Pure muscular endurance and pure muscular strength may be thought of as extremes on a continuum. Many activities that enhance strength can, with modest alteration, be used to enhance muscular endurance. Because of the intensity of a strength-developing activity, duration of that activity becomes limited by rapid onset of fatigue. The same activity could be used to develop muscular endurance by simultaneously reducing resistance, thereby increasing potential for duration. When muscles are fatigued gradually, as is the case in endurance exercise, they experience a training effect characterized by an increased muscular capacity to sustain a submaximal, protracted effort.

We would like to spend a moment comparing muscular strength and endurance. Endurance is achieved by many repetitive contractions of a portion of the available muscle fibers. These repetitive contractions require a continuous supply of energy; hence, the types of muscle fibers best suited for muscular endurance are those having aerobic characteristics: a good oxygen supply, numerous mitochondria, and sufficient amounts of aerobic enzymes needed to supply the cell's energy needs (i.e., adenosine triphosphate, or ATP). Strength, in contrast, requires a greater cross-sectional area or bulk of the muscle tissue, because a greater cross-sectional area contains more protein filaments within the tissue with which to produce force. One should keep these points in mind when designing muscular strength and endurance training programs.

To develop muscular endurance, three sets of 30-plus repetitions of any given exercise are recommended. Further, for a maximal training effect, the person should engage in such exercise approximately three times weekly. Such recommendations, though appearing frequently in the literature, are offered as rules of thumb only and in certain settings may need to be modified based on individual need or capacity.

Flexibility

Flexibility refers to the ability of body segments to move through typical ranges of motion. One must realize that the range of motion about various joints may differ; therefore, flexibility can be limited in some joints, while in other joints it may be well within normal ranges. For most joints, limitations in range of motion are due to one or more of the following factors: (1) bony structure anomalies, (2) muscle bulk, (3) tightness in the muscle and its fascial sheaths, and (4) tightness within the connective tissue proper (i.e., tightness within the tendons, ligaments, and joint capsule). For the most part, the more active an individual, the more flexible he or she will be. Second, flexibility is influenced by temperature: Local warming increases flexibility, whereas local cooling reduces flexibility. This factor becomes extremely important when conducting a stretching program for individuals with slight, spastic muscles.

Like strength, flexibility can be a major determinant of success in many physical and motor activities. Virtually all activities require a minimum degree of flexibility before the activity can be executed comfortably, correctly, and safely. Developmentally, Malina and Bouchard (1991) indicated that flexibility scores using the sit-and-reach test are stable from 5–8 years in boys, decline with age to approximately 12–13 years, and then increase up to 18 years of age; in girls, scores are stable from 5–11 years of age, increase up to 16 years, and then plateau (Gabbard, 2000; Malina & Bouchard, 1991). In contrast, Payne and Issacs (2002), citing data from the NCYFS (National Children and Youth Fitness Study) I and II studies, show an increase in flexibility for children 6–18 years of age, with girls demonstrating higher scores at all ages (Figure 9.5).

Unexpected muscle stretching beyond typical motion range may cause strain, ranging from mild strain to strain so severe that surgical repair is needed. The range of motion through which a body can move comfortably, even when disability affects flexibility (e.g., spastic cerebral palsy), is largely a function of the muscle stretching to which an individual is accustomed.

Maintaining flexibility is a lifelong need. Without flexibility, one's capacity to enjoy movement may become greatly diminished. For example, diminished flexibility in the shoulder may inhibit the individual's ability to push a wheelchair. Flexibility is also essential to maintaining fitness, preventing injury, and facilitating motor skill performance. Gabbard (2000) indicates that flexibility research has produced the following conclusions:

1. Flexibility is joint specific.
2. Flexibility is not related to limb length.
3. Strength development is compatible to range of motion.
4. Activity levels are better indicators of flexibility than age.
5. Females generally are more flexible than males.

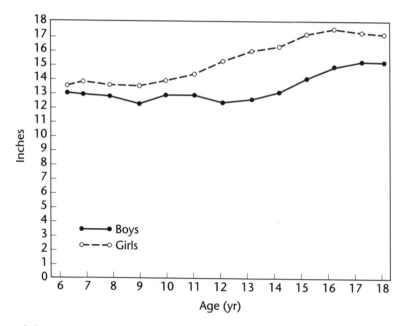

Figure 9.5 Average sit-and-reach scores for ages 6–18.
The zero point was located at 12 inches.
Source: Reprinted by permission from Carl P. Gabbard, Lifelong Motor Development, 3rd ed. Copyright © 2000 Allyn & Bacon Publishers, Needham Heights.

We commonly see a loss of flexibility as a function of disability as well as the aging process. Although some flexibility potential might be lost as a function of disability, a large part may be attributable to changes in activity patterns and use of the muscle. This is especially important for individuals with disabilities, who are often inactive and lose flexibility as a result of disuse rather than their disability. In other cases, such as muscular dystrophy, the resulting loss of muscle function is often accompanied by loss of flexibility, further complicating the ability to move.

Although some individuals may have more muscle flexibility potential than others, virtually everyone should strive to develop and maintain flexibility in accordance with her or his own potential. There may be exceptions to every rule, but it is doubtful that activity designed to develop flexibility would ever render one too flexible.

When developing flexibility, muscles must be stretched only to, but not through, the individual's threshold of discomfort. To be sure, stretching to the point of discomfort is essential to increasing a muscle's range of motion; however, it is equally true that stretching beyond that point risks injury. Should a muscle have been injured for any reason (i.e., strained), the general rule is to avoid stretching that muscle until it has healed. Stretching an already strained muscle will likely reinjure muscle fibers that have not yet fully healed.

Stretching for flexibility development should always be slow and deliberate. Rapid stretching, particularly bouncing (ballistic stretching) is undesirable, because it activates the muscle's myotatic (stretch) reflex. When this reflex is activated, the muscle actually resists the attempt to stretch by eliciting the reflex that actually causes the muscle to contract. As long as reflex contractions are being provoked, in this case due to ballistic-type stretching, flexibility exercise will be to no avail. In fact, stretching activity of this nature may actually cause muscle injury ranging from soreness to actual muscle strain (i.e., torn muscle fiber).

Typically, the person might stretch a given muscle or muscle group for a duration of between 15 seconds minimum and 45 seconds maximum. Fifteen seconds may be the point at which the muscle experiences sufficient stretch to become more pliable. Forty-five seconds may be the point past which the individual experiences diminished returns.

Body Composition

Body composition refers to the relative proportions of fat to lean body mass. Body composition data are valuable because weight alone does not reveal what sort of tissue comprises the weight showing on the scale. Two people who weigh the same can have remarkably different body compositions.

Placing priority on body composition, despite its potential contribution to fitness development, sometimes becomes the focus of controversy. Body composition, although it has been widely studied in adults, has yet to be widely studied in children and youth. For this reason, applying body composition norms taken from adults to children and youth is of questionable validity. Where body composition measures are applied to children and youth, results usually are reported in terms of percentiles derived from children and youth rather than in percentages of body fat derived from adult studies. Also, there is some concern that overconsciousness about being thin does not promote health and may provoke some children to eat improperly. There is additional concern that skinfold measures (i.e., telling a child he or she is fat), tell the child nothing she or he does not already know. Here, putting a number to the percentage of fatness with what one sees in the mirror may do little more than add insult to injury (Chapter 20).

Developmentally, adipose tissue plays a vital role in energy storage, insulation, and protection of the newborn (Malina & Bouchard, 1991). Essential fat makes up 3.5% of body weight in males and 8–12% in females and is used as energy for disposition of new tissue in children 3–10 years of age. Adipose tissue first appears in the fetus and at birth is generally well distributed, accounting for approximately 16% of body weight at birth, 24–30% during the first year, and 14% of body weight by 6 years of age. Some children will also experience a midgrowth increase at approximately 5½ to 7 years (Gabbard, 2000).

Body fat will increase during the first 6 months and then taper off from 1 to 7 years of age. During this period, no gender differences are evident. However, at age 7 the proportion of body fat increases and continues to increase in girls, whereas in boys it may continue to develop or actually decrease (Payne & Issacs, 2002). This difference may account for a body fat content that is 50% greater in females than in males of the same age (Rowland, 1996). For children with disabilities, an inordinate amount of body fat may be present, which restricts their overall functional performance. Inactivity and a high-fat diet will contribute to further difficulties in stimulating activity and motor performance (Figure 9.6).

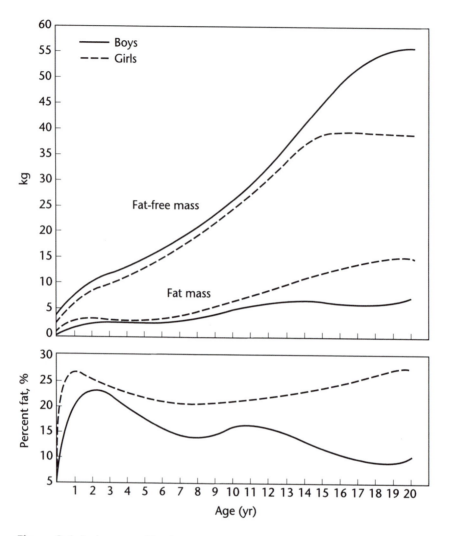

Figure 9.6 Body composition by age.

Effect of Training

As interest in developing resistance training programs for children increases, especially for prepubescent children, guidelines for such programs are needed. Aside from
the strength benefits of resistance training, a major goal of the program should be to
teach children about their bodies, to promote lifetime fitness, and to provide them
with a positive attitude about strength training and exercise in general. Also, teachers
must keep in mind that children are not only physiologically different from adults, but
also emotionally different. Therefore, children should not be treated as "little" adults,
but rather as uniquely distinct individuals. Rather than encouraging them to compete,
teachers should instead encourage children to feel good about themselves and their
performances and to concentrate on self-improvement (Faigenbaum, 1993). For chil-

dren with disabilities, performance should be related to improving functional skills needed for independence and the development of motor skills that will encourage an active lifestyle.

In addition, resistance training programs have been found not only to be relatively safe (Faigenbaum, et al., 1996; Williams, 1991), but also may prevent certain types of injuries in young athletes. It appears that the potential for injury during resistance training programs is no greater, and may even be less, than those risks associated with participation in organized sports and recreational activities (Faigenbaum, 1993). Both the National Strength and Conditioning Association (1985, 2000) and the American Academy of Pediatrics (1990) stress that children can benefit from properly supervised and properly prescribed resistance training programs. Major benefits cited were (1) increased muscular strength and muscular endurance, (2) decreased injuries during sport and recreational activities, and (3) improved skill performance.

Teachers should note that regular physical training is not necessarily the same as physical activity. Although physical activity involves some training, regular physical training refers to the habitual and orderly practice of physical activities, such as calisthenics, resistance exercises, running, and games/sports performed at specific intensities and for distinctive durations (Malina & Bouchard, 1991). Therefore, training programs vary in kind or type (e.g., endurance training, strength training, and skill training), and the effects of such programs are generally specific to the type of training stimulus (Saltin & Rowell, 1980).

Interpreting research on the effects of training during childhood on growth and maturation is exceptionally difficult because of problems associated with partitioning training-induced effects from changes associated with normal growth, maturation, and genetics. Also of importance is the fact that measures or estimates of "normal" activity are based primarily on surveys of adolescent sport participation, with little data for preadolescents (Malina & Bouchard, 1991). Even with these limitations, there is a consensus that regular physical activity is an important factor in regulating and maintaining body weight, increasing lean body mass, and improving cardiovascular functioning.

An important question for physical educators is that given the favorable impact of physical activity on fitness, how might a regular program of physical activity and exercise impact a child with disabilities? The answer to this question is not a simple one. Nevertheless, if we look at some of the research on exercise and disability over the last decade, the possibility that a combination of physical activity and prudent caloric intake throughout life may help to improve physical functioning in children with disabilities.

The implications for physical education are enormous: Early intervention may prevent obesity by way of promoting a sensible diet and substantial levels of physical activity. In addition, regular physical training is beneficial in preventing cardiovascular disease, respiratory disease, and certain metabolic disorders (Shephard, 1984). Sallis and Patrick (1994) have suggested that all adolescents be active daily and engage in physical activities that last for 20 minutes minimally per session and require moderate to vigorous exertion levels. Horvat and Franklin (2001) report that play at recess can promote greater heart rate and activity counts than sedentary settings. By controlling those risk factors specific to disease (e.g., coronary artery disease), exercise can protect against developing diseases in the future. Thus, given the sedentary lifestyle currently displayed by children and youth, all children—and in particular children with disabilities—require daily physical education that stresses a habitual and orderly practice of physical activities, such as calisthenics, resistance exercises, running, and games/sports performed at specific intensities and for distinctive durations.

CHAPTER SUMMARY

1. The degree to which children and youth respond to exercise depends on maturation and the exercise stimulus encountered during the activity program. In many ways, children respond to exercise in much the same way as their adult counterparts. Nevertheless, there are several age-dependent and gender differences in the response to exercise.

2. Maximal aerobic capacity, when using VO_2max per kilogram of body weight as the criterion, is not deficient in children; however, because of inefficient biomechanics during the performance of various activities, the metabolic cost of performing these activities is greater in children than in adults. Thus, when the total spectrum of exercise conditions are considered, children perform inferiorly to adults in aerobic activities. As the child grows, one sees a dramatic improvement in endurance fitness. Sufficient evidence suggests that children can adapt physiologically to endurance training.

3. Children perform inferiorly to adults in anaerobic activities (activities lasting between 10 and 60 seconds) and often display a lower tolerance for these types of activities than do adults. As the child matures, however, anaerobic capacity improves greatly with age. The primary reasons for this improvement appear to be the concentration and rate of utilization of muscle glycogen.

4. Recent research clearly demonstrates that following several weeks of resistance training, children with disabilities display increases in strength, increases in lean body mass, and improvement in skilled motor performance.

5. Childhood obesity and inactivity have increased substantially over the past decade. There is a consensus that regular physical activity is an important factor in regulating and maintaining body weight and generally results in an increase in lean body mass, with a corresponding decrease in body fat. A sensible diet and moderate to substantial levels of physical activity are the most efficacious way to mitigate the high levels of obesity found currently in our children and youth. Teachers should work in conjunction with medical professionals for advice on the dietary and exercise needs of the child participating in the physical education program.

REFERENCES

American Academy of Pediatrics. (1990). Strength training, weight and power lifting, and body building by children and adolescents. *Pediatrics, 86,* 801–802.

Bar-Or, O. (1983). *Pediatric sports medicine for the practitioner: From physiological principles to clinical applications.* New York: Springer-Verlag.

Bar-Or, O. (1989a). Trainability of the prepubescent child. *The Physician and Sports Medicine, 17*(5), 65–82.

Bar-Or, O. (1989b). Temperature regulation during exercise in children and adults. In C. V. Gisolfi & D. R. Lamb (Eds.), *Perspectives in exercise science and sports medicine: Volume 2: Youth, exercise, and sport* (pp. 335–367). Indianapolis: Benchmark Press.

Bar-Or, O. (1993). Importance of differences between children and adults for exercise testing and exercise prescription. In J. S. Skinner (Ed.), *Exercise testing and exercise prescription for special cases: Theoretical basis and scientific application* (pp. 57–74). Philadelphia: Lea & Febiger.

Beunen, G., & Thomis, M. (2000). Muscular strength development in children and adolescents. *Pediatric Exercise Science, 12,* 174–197.

Blimkie, C. J. R. (1989). Age- and sex-associated variation in strength during childhood: Anthropometric, morphologic, neurologic, biomechanical, endocrinologic, genetic, and physical correlates. In C. V. Gisolfi & D. R. Lamb (Eds.), *Perspectives in exercise and sports medicine: Volume 2: Youth, exercise and sport* (pp. 99–163). Indianapolis: Benchmark Press.

Faigenbaum, A. (1993). A prepubescent strength training: A guide for teachers and coaches. *National Strength and Conditioning Association Journal, 15*(5), 20–29.

Faigenbaum, A. D., Westcott, W. L., Micheli, L. J., Outerbridge, A. R., Long, C. J., LaRosa-Loud, R., & Zaichkowsky, L. D. (1996). The effects of a strength training and detraining on children. *Journal of Strength and Conditioning Research, 10*(2), 109–114.

Falk, B. (1998). Effects of thermal stress during rest and exercise in the pediatric population. *Sports Medicine, 25,* 221–240.

Falk, B., & Tenenbaum, G. (1996). The effectiveness of resistance training in children. *Sports Medicine, 22,* 176–186.

Gabbard, C. P. (2000). *Lifelong motor development* (3rd ed.). Needham Heights, MA: Allyn & Bacon.

Horvat, M., & Croce, R. (1995). Physical rehabilitation of individuals with mental retardation: Physical fitness and information processing. *Critical Reviews in Physical and Rehabilitation Medicine, 7*(3), 233–252.

Horvat, M., & Franklin, C. (2001). The effects of the environment on physical activity patterns of children with mental retardation. *Research Quarterly for Exercise and Sport, 72,* 189–195.

Horvat, M., Ramsey, V., Amestoy, R., & Croce, R. (in review). Movement response variability, distribution of fractioned response youth with and without mental retardation, in review. *Research Quarterly for Exercise and Sport.*

Kraemer, W. J., & Fleck, S. J. (1993). *Strength training for young athletes.* Champaign, IL: Human Kinetics.

Malina, R. M., & Bouchard, C. (1991). *Growth, maturation, and physical activity.* Champaign, IL: Human Kinetics.

National Strength and Conditioning Association. (1985). Position paper on prepubescent strength training. *National Strength and Conditioning Association Journal, 7,* 27–29.

National Strength and Conditioning Association. (2000). The National Strength and Conditioning Association's basic guidelines for the resistance training of athletes. *National Strength and Conditioning Association Journal, 22,* 14–27.

Payne, V. G, & Issacs, L. D. (2002). *Human movement development* (5th ed.). Mountain View, CA: Mayfield.

Pfitzinger, P., & Freedson, P. (1997). Blood lactate responses to exercise in children: Part 1, Peak lactate concentration. *Pediatric Exercise Science, 9,* 210–222.

Physical Fitness and Sports Research Digest (2000). Definitions: Health, fitness, and physical activity, Series 3 (9), 1–6.

Rowland, T. W. (1990). *Exercise and children's health.* Champaign, IL: Human Kinetics.

Rowland, T. W. (1996). *Developmental exercise physiology.* Champaign, IL: Human Kinetics.

Rowland, T. W. (1998). Oxygen uptake and endurance fitness in children: A developmental perspective. *Pediatric Exercise Science, 1,* 313–328.

Rowland, T. W. (1999). Adolescence: A risk factor for physical inactivity. *President's Council on Physical Fitness and Sports Research Digest, Series 3, No. 6,* 1–7.

Sallis, J. F., & Patrick, K. (1994). Physical activity guidelines for adolescents: Consensus statement. *Pediatric Exercise Science, 6,* 302–314.

Saltin, B., & Rowell, L. B. (1980). Functional adaptations to physical activity and inactivity. *Federation Proceedings, 39,* 1506–1513.

Seaman, J. (1999). Physical activity and fitness for persons with disabilities. *Research Digest, 3,* (5). Washington, DC: President Council on Physical Fitness and Sports.

Shephard, R. J. (1984). Physical activity and "wellness" of the child. In R. A. Boileau (Ed.), *Advances in pediatric sport sciences: Volume one: Biological issues* (pp. 1–27). Champaign, IL: Human Kinetics.

Williams, D. (1991). The effect of weight training performance in selected motor activities for preadolescents (abstract). *Journal of Applied Sport Sciences Research, 5*(3), 170.

Winnick, J. P., & Short, F. X. (2000). The Brockport physical fitness test. *PALAESTRA, 16,* 20–25, 46–47.

Teaching Individuals with Learning and Behavior Disabilities

Section II focuses on disabilities that affect learning or behavior and, in turn, performance. For children who have learning and/or behavioral difficulties, characteristics and teaching suggestions are provided to develop and implement the physical education program.

This section is designed to

1. provide information regarding the characteristics and physical/motor functioning of children with learning, attention, or behavior exceptionalities and/or autism or head injuries

2. provide instructional methods to develop and implement appropriate programs for the exceptionalities

3. provide teaching strategies and management systems that are appropriate to facilitate instruction in physical education

CHAPTER 10

Mental Retardation

The general public's conception of individuals with mental retardation is that they are incapable of learning or caring for themselves. Most of this sentiment probably stems from the medical definitions of mental retardation, which stress the pathology, disease, genetic orientations, and/or incurable aspects of the condition. Although the accomplishments of individuals with mental retardation and public awareness of those accomplishments, are increasing, it is still difficult to separate superstition and oversimplification from facts when it comes to children with mental retardation.

Clearly, the range of cognitive deficits found in individuals with mental retardation is indicative of functioning and potential. Individuals with less severe intellectual deficits are capable of independent functioning, employment in blue-collar jobs, and social relationships, including marriage and children. Most are capable of independent functioning with limited and less pervasive supports. In contrast, individuals with more severe cognitive deficits are limited not only by intelligence quotients (IQ) but also by the ability to relate socially to individuals in the community, to focus on goals, and to complete tasks. Individuals with less self-sufficiency or with accompanying motor deficits require more extensive supports on a continual basis. Contemporary thinking reflects the premise that the individual is capable of achieving basic functional skills, and it broadens preexisting definitions to encompass the individual's actual functioning in daily living and community settings. For this population, the ability to perform physically and process information adequately is essential to ensure independent functioning.

According to the classification and terminology from the American Association on Mental Retardation (AAMR) (1992), individuals with mental retardation will demonstrate primary cognitive deficits that are determined from an assessment of intellectual functioning and adaptive skills. *Mental retardation* refers to significantly subaverage intellectual functioning existing concurrently with deficits in adaptive skills and documented as occurring from birth to 18 years of age. Intellectual levels are based on an IQ score below 70 to 75 on a standardized intelligence scale. Because there is such variability in determining intelligence, a second component dealing with adaptive skills was added. Adaptive skills refers to the effectiveness or degree with which the individual meets standards of personal independence and social responsibility for age and cultural group. Pitetti and colleagues (1993) have indicated that these attributes fall under three categories: maturation, learning capacity, and social adjustment. In addition, the AAMR definition specifically requires documentation on a standardized test within the context of community environments that are typical of individuals in their peer group and indexed to the need for supports.

In this context, limitations in practical and social intelligence are addressed. Practical intelligence relates to managing activities of daily living and using physical abilities for personal independence that are crucial for adaptive functioning in such skills as self-care, safety, leisure, or work. Social intelligence is the ability to understand social expectations, including the behavior of others and acting in a socially acceptable manner. The interdependence of practical and social intelligence to adaptive skill functioning is closely linked and is a useful predictor of what the individual may actually accomplish within the community environment. Hence, the individual with a low IQ score may function appropriately in the community, while another person may record a greater IQ score yet not adjust to community living. In this definition, these dimensions are clearly intercorrelated and require standardized testing areas.

One should note that previous terminology of mild, moderate, severe, and profound mental retardation was directly linked to IQ testing and is no longer applicable. According to the AAMR definition, diagnosis may reflect a person with mental retardation who needs limited support in communication and social skills. The premise of needed supports relates to the ability to predict independence and integration into the community for the individual. Supports may be intermittent (short-term during periods of transition); limited (short-term, restricted basis, e.g., job training); extensive (long-term consistent involvement, in work or home support); and pervasive (long-term, constant, potentially life-sustaining). The system of supports links the concept of functional capabilities or limitations that are specific to each individual and his or her capabilities. Finally, the age of onset is documented as the condition occurring from birth to 18 years of age, or what was conceptualized as the developmental age, that is specifically related to cognitive growth and the level of cognitive functioning achieved.

Etiology and Incidence

The causes of mental retardation are not easily determined and are partly responsible for some of the misconceptions related to the disorder. Some causes may be organic, hereditary, or as in most cases, idiopathic; they may affect children at various stages of their development. Table 10.1 describes causes of retardation during different periods of development.

Prenatal Period

If infants do not have sufficient time in the womb (prematurity) or exceed the normal time by more than 7 days (postmaturity), mental retardation may occur. Likewise, infants with low birth weight (5^{1}/2 pounds or less) are at risk, as well as those who experience trauma, such as difficult deliveries from breech birth or cesarean section or unnecessary physical contact during the birth process.

Chromosome anomaly, or Down syndrome, is a common form of mental retardation in which an extra chromosome is present in each cell or the structure of chromosomes is affected. Other chromosomal abnormalities include fragile X syndrome, Klinefelter's syndrome, and Turner's syndrome.

Table 10.1 Mental Retardation Etiology by Periods of Development

Prenatal Period (Before Birth)	Perinatal Period (At Birth)	Postnatal Period (After Birth)	Combined Periods
1. Chromosomal anomaly, Down syndrome, Turner's syndrome, Klinefelter's syndrome	1. Prematurity; post-maturity	1. Disease (meningitis, encephalitis)	1. Trauma
2. Unknown prenatal influences (hydrocephalus; microcephaly)	2. Low birth weight	2. Environmental developmental retardation	2. Anoxia to the brain
3. Disorder of metabolism (phenylketonuria, PKU)	3. Difficult labor and delivery	3. Toxic substances (lead, mercury)	3. Tumors/lesions
4. Maternal disease (rubella)		4. Disorders of metabolism (galactosemia, endocrine or growth dysfunctions, diabetes)	4. Syphilis
5. Blood incompatibility (Rh factor)			5. Idiopathic conditions
6. Maternal care (nicotine, alcohol, drug addiction)			

Unknown prenatal influences may exist, resulting in abnormalities with no definite cause. Among those conditions with unknown influences are hydrocephalus, an accumulation of cerebrospinal fluid on the brain; microcephaly, a lack of development of the cranium; anencephaly, a malformation of the development or absence of the brain.

Disorders of metabolism may be present. An example is phenylketonuria (PKU), which is a condition caused by a lack of metabolic enzyme that prevents the building of protein and results in brain damage.

Maternal disease, such as rubella or German measles, can damage the developing embryo and subsequently damage the cerebral cortex, eyes, and ears.

Blood incompatibility between parents, in which the Rh factor is not contained in the mother's blood but is in the father's blood, will result in a high risk of blood incompatibility between mother and fetus.

Maternal care is also a primary consideration, especially in regard to the consumption of nicotine, alcohol, and drugs during pregnancy, which can damage the developing embryo.

Postnatal Period

Diseases that interfere with the development of the brain or infections of the cranium (meningitis) or the brain (encephalitis) contribute to mental retardation. Environmental influences that interfere with the development of the brain may result from deprivation of sensory experiences or stimulation.

Furthermore, any toxic substances, such as lead, mercury, arsenic, or manganese, or metabolic disorders, such as diabetes and malnutrition, adversely affect the developing brain cells. Other disorders of metabolism, such as digestive, endocrine, or growth dysfunctions, also affect development. Included in these are galactosemia (a digestion disorder of the mother's milk), and hypothyroidism, in which growth hormones are not sufficiently produced.

Combined Periods

Mental retardation is also caused by a variety of incidents that can occur before, during, and after birth. Trauma to the head, anoxia to the brain, tumors, lesions, syphilis or other sexually transmitted diseases, and psychological disorders are all possible causes of mental retardation. In addition, many forms of mental retardation are idiopathic (i.e., have no known causes) or may be due to environmental influences, sensory deprivation, abuse, or neglect.

Approximately 13% of the school population is classified as having mental retardation. The majority of children with mental retardation (90%) are mildly affected, require only limited supports, and are educated in regular classes. Approximately 5% are severely affected and require more extensive supports and assistance in their educational placement. Mental retardation will affect males and females in a similar manner, although some syndromes, such as Turner's syndrome (absence of X chromosome in females) and Klinefelter's syndrome (XXY sex chromosome in males) are sex linked.

Planning the Physical Activity Program

Most individuals will normally develop age-appropriate motor skills through maturation and observation of other children. Children with mental retardation progress through the same sequence of motor development as their peers, although they are deficient in some areas and may require more specific instructions, time to practice, and additional opportunities to facilitate maturation and learning of motor skills. Development of physical and motor skills is essential for improving functional skills, community integration, and appropriate leisure and work experiences. In this context, the term *functional* or *functional skills* relates to activities of daily living or self-care activities needed to function in home and community-based environments.

Generally, most children with mild to moderate involvement can be integrated into regular physical education classes and will closely resemble their peers in functional ability. In contrast, more severely involved children may function significantly lower in physical and motor development and possibly require more specific intervention and opportunities to facilitate development. Accordingly, teachers should match their instructional goals to the the individual child's developmental level in order to achieve program goals and objectives.

Assessing Level of Functioning

The level of physical and motor functioning should be ascertained before the IEP is developed and a physical education program implemented. Likewise, to facilitate learning and retention, teachers should strive to use the most efficient teaching techniques and appropriate cues (i.e., modeling) as well as needed supports for children to function in the educational environment. Norm- and criterion-referenced physical and motor assessments that are specifically designed for children with mental retardation may provide the appropriate information to adequately assess the level of functioning and entry point for instruction. Additional information should be solicited from the collaborative programming team to develop behavioral goals and objectives that lead to increasing functional skill development.

Functional Ability

A primary consideration in developing a program for children with mental retardation is their functional ability. Some children with mild involvement will function at a level that closely approximates their peers in physical fitness and motor development, although they may require more time or instruction to learn a skill. Clearly, the range of cognitive deficits found in individuals with mental retardation is indicative of functioning and potential (Horvat & Croce, 1995). The greater the severity of involvement, the less the individual is capable of independent functioning. Individuals with more severe cognitive deficits are limited not only by IQ but by the ability to relate socially to individuals in the community, to focus on goals, and to complete tasks. These individuals are less self-sufficient and may require more extensive supports on a continual basis to overcome deficits in physical functioning.

For children with more extensive involvement, deficiencies in motor development, as well as the social integration level, are more apparent. Younger children may require additional instruction and practice in focusing their attention to develop fundamental motor skills needed to facilitate movement, play, stability, and object control; older children may require instruction or observation of rules and strategies for group and team games, sports, and recreational activities that are common in their peer group and needed for community integration or work-specific skills. In addition, the overall growth and development may be affected by mental retardation, although environmental constraints, such as nutrition, can be addressed to facilitate growth (Cronk, Puelzl-Quinn & Pueschel, 1996; Lindgren & Kotoda, 1993). In contrast, individuals with minimal cognitive deficits are more capable of independent functioning, rely less on pervasive supports, and are more easily integrated into community and home activities.

Appropriate Management and Rewards

Many times children with mental retardation are prone to frustration, aggressive behaviors, or a lack of motivation, which can interfere with learning and achieving program goals. They may also demonstrate inappropriate behaviors when placed in stressful situations and when their instructional routine or environment is changed. Teachers and parents should try to facilitate an incentive system to eliminate inappropriate behavior and increase or maintain positive integrations and physical improvement. Controlling the environment may eliminate unnecessary and irrelevant stimuli that hinder the set routine for a particular activity. Teachers should provide children with opportunities for appropriate emotional outlets for play and physical activity, as well as reinforcing acceptable behaviors to provide incentives for children to participate in physical actives.

Community-Based Programs

At times teachers can become discouraged with the child's level of progress or lack of progress during physical activity classes. Often a skill taught on Friday is lost over a weekend or vacation period, requiring teachers to begin teaching the skill again. Most teachers would probably say that children with mental retardation require more opportunities to learn and practice their skill outside the classroom. In addition, the goal of any activity is to generalize the skill to community- or home-based settings, for example, developing play behaviors at home for young children. Several programs, such as Special Olympics or programs offered by recreational centers, provide opportunities for children to develop skills in sports and games as well as to gain exposure to the appropriate social development that is needed for optimal development. Although outside-the-school opportunities should not be substituted for physical education, it seems only logical that providing children with additional opportunities for participation will increase their physical and social functioning. Children should be encouraged to take advantage of organizations that provide sport or recreational experiences, and the development of strong parent-teacher teams should also be encouraged to facilitate community activities. Home-based programs developed by the teacher will allow parents to provide extra practice and instructional time needed to develop physical fitness, play skills, and social interaction. For older children, the development of physical fitness in community settings can be directly linked to increased work performance (Zetts, Horvat & Langone, 1995). For teachers, who are limited by time and the number of children in their class, community and home-based programs can enhance their instructional program and also encourage the generalization of these skills outside the school setting.

Implementing the Physical Activity Program

Teachers who strive to develop truly comprehensive and effective physical education programs for children with mental retardation should be mindful of those characteristics generally found to be unique to the population. The following analysis, and the outline of characteristics and instructional strategies in Table 10.2, can aid the instructor in tailoring a physical education program specifically to the needs of children.

Physical Fitness

Children with mental retardation have a tendency toward low levels of physical fitness (Pitetti, Rimmer & Fernhall, 1993). Research indicates that children with mental retardation lag behind their normal peers in static strength, dynamic strength, explosive strength, flexibility, cardiovascular endurance, and agility (Croce & Horvat, 1992; Pitetti & Fernhall, 1997; Fernhall, Tymeson, & Webster, 1988; Horvat, Croce & McGhee, 1993). Fernhall (1992) has indicated that individuals with mental retardation tend to have lower cardiovascular fitness, lower maximal heart rates, inferior muscular development, and greater body fat than nonretarded peers. In addition, these children may be obese because of poor dietary habits and the lack of opportunities to participate in physical activities. Further, the impact of environmental factors such as nutrition may affect the growth status of children with mental retardation (Cronk et al., 1996). The members of the collaborative programming team who can best develop a program of nutrition and physical activity include the nutritionist, parent, physician, and physical educator. These professionals should develop a broad base of physical fitness activities, behavior management, and appropriate dietary habits (Croce, 1990; Kelly, Rimmer & Ness, 1986; Rotatori & Fox, 1981).

Because of the variability of physical and functional skill development, fitness levels of children may be variable. Based on previous work, it is evident that changes in functional level can be initiated with activity programs. Horvat and Croce (1995)

Table 10.2 Characteristics and Instructional Strategies

Factor	Characteristics	Instructional Strategies	Physical Activity
Physical fitness	Tendency toward obesity; dynamic and explosive strength, flexibility, and cardiovascular endurance lag behind peers.	Provide a broad base of physical fitness activities based on the level of functioning and functional skill development. Gradually increase the duration and number of repetitions for each activity. Consult appropriate team members to develop diet and exercise program.	Aquatics, physical fitness and dance activities, aerobics, out side-the-school programs, walking, static stretching, yoga, parachute, jogging, and stationary cycling activities. Progressive resistance exercises (surgical tubing and weights).
Learning and memory functions	Limited vocabulary; trouble with abstractions and problem solving, short- and long-term memory, attention span, transfer of learning, and communication skills; unable to comprehend benefits of activity.	Use concrete examples and visual cues; provide opportunities to practice and demonstrate skill in a variety of settings; initiate activities that encourage verbalization; provide task-specific feedback.	Parachute, fundamental motor skills, activities coupled with modeling and visual cues, movement education activities, water exercises, stunts and games, swim skills, academic games and concepts, home and play activities.
Lack of opportunities	Sedentary lifestyle; restricted assess to activity; lack of spontaneous play and opportunities to participate. Lack of generalization to home and community settings.	Encourage activity; use outside-the-school, community, sports, and recreational centers. Facilitate play with family members and peers.	Play activities; Special Olympics activities, community recreation, sports and fitness activities, including swimming and walking, cycling, weight training.
Growth and motor development	Behind peers in balance, body perception, agility, locomotor skills, perception, and coordination; growth lags behind peers with insufficient nutrition.	Utilize a broad base of developmental motor skills based on functional skills, play behaviors.	Balance beam, board, line activities, gymnastics, tumbling stunts and routines, rhythms, movement education, homework activities, fundamental motor skill instruction, community recreation activities.
Social development	Poor self-image; tend to be imitators and followers. Lack of social interaction in play skills.	Provide appropriate social interaction activities with no failure concept; give praise for an accomplishment; utilize activities for appropriate level of functioning.	Social sequence activities, good behavior game, movement education, parachute, and play activities that require sharing and social interaction.
Inappropriate behavior and lack of motivation	Low frustration and poor performance under stress; aggressiveness; lack of motivation or ability to exert a sustained effort and comprehend benefits of activity.	Structure activities to ensure success; eliminate inappropriate responses and reinforce appropriate behaviors and any accomplishment; be an active model; utilize relaxation and activities that emphasize self-control and sustaining an activity.	Movement education activities, yoga, static stretching activities, community activities, recreation sports and fitness activities.
Play development	Inability to initiate play on an individual or group basis.	Provide numerous opportunities for solitary and structured play in school and after-school environment.	Manipulative toys, water play, balls in all variety of sizes and textures, sensory stimulation.

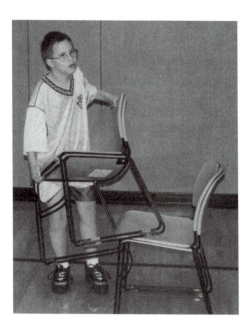

Figure 10.1 Work-related task.

consistently maintain that individuals with mental retardation will respond to training interventions in a manner similar to that of their nonretarded peers. A critical element of most exercise programs is the ability to maintain intervention and generalize the activity to home, community, and work settings (Figure 10.1). A progressive activity program that gradually increases the duration, repetition, or time involved in an activity should be used. If appropriate, additional opportunities should be provided at home or in community and recreation settings. Physical fitness activities, such as walking, jogging, aquatics, dance, aerobics, parachute activities, and stationary cycling, and progressive resistance exercises can be used with children with mental retardation in regular physical education classes. (A circuit training program, as depicted in Figure 10.2, is an excellent way to help children increase physical fitness.)

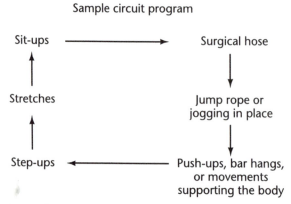

Figure 10.2 Sample curcuit program.

Learning-Memory Functions

Children with mental retardation often have problems with complex thoughts and encounter problems conceptualizing a rule and/or strategy needed in a game. Because they also may possess a limited attention span and disrupted memory functions, instruction should be repeated and demonstrated on successive days to promote learning. Transfer of learning, which is often utilized when children learn similar skills, such as soccer and kickball, is not well developed and will necessitate repetitions of teaching instructions for each new skill.

Teachers should use concrete examples and visual cues when teaching. A visual model of a person throwing a ball, as well as a poster depicting an appropriate throw, will reinforce the appropriate pattern in the early stages of learning. Once a throwing skill is learned, teachers should provide plenty of opportunities to practice. Throwing instructions can be followed by movement activities with balls, throwing at targets, or playing games that involve throwing, such as dodgeball. Teachers can also add a verbal response from the child during the activity to encourage appropriate verbalization and organization of movement information. As children learn about organizing relevant information, and they learn motor skills, they may become more efficient in retaining movement information (Horvat & Croce, 1995; Horgan, 1985). In addition, Croce, Horvat and Roswal (1994) have indicated that moderate levels of exercise increase the attention in children with mental retardation and can possibly facilitate learning. Other activities that improve fitness include parachute games, fundamental motor skills, water exercises, and swim skills; academic games and homework activities can be added for the purpose of organizing and retaining information as well as completing the skill.

Motor Development

Children with mental retardation are also deficient in their motor performance. Common development components of stability, body perception, gross agility, locomotor movement, and object control may be different because of motivation or difficulties in information processing (Horvat & Croce, 1995). It is apparent that developmental and learning impairments restrict motor performance. In a manner similar to developing physical fitness, children with mental retardation will learn and develop motor skills. In order to facilitate development, a broad base of developmental physical education activities should be used to overcome motor deficits.

For preschool-aged or low-functioning children, activities should be provided that involve stability, object control, and locomotor movements that can be used in home and community settings, especially with nonretarded peers (Figure 10.3). Developmental locomotor and object control skills that can be used in play settings should also be implemented outside the school to provide additional opportunities for practice and development.

Social Development

Children with mental retardation tend to possess a low self-concept and may feel inferior to their peers in integrated classes. These children may not demonstrate appropriate social interactions with others or hesitate to join in any physical activity. In some instances, the low social interactions may occur from a lack of motivation or

Figure 10.3 Improving motor performance.

from lack of opportunities to participate in play-based activities (Horvat, Malone & Deener, 1993).

Teachers should arrange activities that involve intratask variation so that the task may be completed without failure and will ensure success. For example, children may take as much time as possible to swim across the pool, or they may use a kickboard for assistance. Activities can be modified to reflect the normal social-sequence development from solitary play to activities that foster group interaction. Activities that provide opportunities to share turns, that alternate responsibilities, and involve waiting for their turn are appropriate for this population and level of social development. In addition, the development of skills that facilitate play behaviors should be encouraged and implemented in the home if possible.

Inappropriate Behaviors and Lack of Motivation

Inappropriate behaviors may be commonplace, especially when children are placed in stressful situations. To avoid completing a task, children may instead display inappropriate behavior. Children may also become frustrated because of their lack of understanding of a task, or they may display aggressive behavior when they cannot master a skill. Children with mental retardation may also be hard to motivate, often not seeing the importance of the task or need to practice or of the importance of participating with sufficient intensity to produce changes in functional ability (Croce, 1990; Croce & Horvat, 1992; Montgomery, Reid & Seidl, 1988).

Most times teachers can ignore inappropriate behaviors and, in conjunction, can positively reinforce appropriate behaviors or participation and completion of tasks. Behavior games and activities that do not involve failure can provide teachers with opportunities to praise children for success. In addition, teachers can use activities such as relaxation, stretching, and yoga that not only increase flexibility, but also aid in developing and regaining control. Outside recreational or play settings, such as the community pool or fitness center, also provide opportunities for children to display appropriate social behaviors when coping with stressful situations and possibly increase their motivation for physical activity. In addition, a behavior-prompting program should be used to increase exercise or play behavior. Deener and Horvat (1995) used self-recording and social praise program to successfully increase running duration in children with mental retardation. Others also have reported significant increases in participation with behavior management strategies (Eichstaedt & Lavay, 1994; Croce & Horvat, 1992; Pitetti & Tan, 1991).

Play Development

Many times the importance of play for children with mental retardation is overlooked. Participating in both solitary and cooperative play enhances the child's overall development and social, cognitive, and motor functioning, but such opportunities are not always available to children with mental retardation (Horvat, Malone & Deener, 1993). By participating in activities during and after school that involve the use of manipulative toys, stuffed animals, balls, sand, and different textures, children can develop appropriate play experiences. Activities that incorporate music will also allow children to move and play. In addition, water play, such as blowing bubbles, kicking on an inner tube, and splashing, can be used when teaching aquatics and as a method to develop leisure-time activities and community-integration skills. Play at recess and after school can provide still more opportunities for physical activity. It has been reported that children with mental retardation will display activity patterns similar to those of children without mental retardation during play at recess. In each case, heart rate and activity counts were elevated during recess, supporting our contention that children with mental retardation can benefit from play experiences (Horvat & Franklin, 2001; Lorenzi, Horvat & Pellegrini, 2000). Providing children with more opportunities to participate enables them to develop age-appropriate skills that will contribute to their overall development and integration into the school environment.

CHAPTER SUMMARY

1. Mental retardation refers to significantly subaverage intellectual functioning that exists concurrently with deficiencies in adaptive skills and that is evidenced during the developmental period.

2. Significantly subaverage intellectual functioning is specifically related to performance on a standardized intelligence test.

3. Adaptive behavior is generally related to maturation, learning, and socialization that are expected of the individual's peer group.

4. The development period refers to the time period from birth to 18 years of age.

5. The cause of mental retardation is not easily determined. In a majority of the cases, the cause is idiopathic, or unknown. However, some cases may be due to chromosomal abnormalities, trauma, metabolism disorders, and a variety of other causes that can be manifested in the prenatal, perinatal, postnatal, or combined periods.

6. Approximately 13% of the school population is classified as mentally retarded. Of these, approximately 95 percent are mildly affected with limited supports and are

in regular classes. Approximately 5% are more severely involved with more extensive supports.

7. Children with mental retardation progress through the same sequence of motor development as their nonretarded peers, only at a slower rate. These children require more specific instruction time, practice, and additional learning opportunities.

8. It is essential to assess the physical and motor functioning of these children before developing the IEP and implementing a physical education program. Appropriate norm- and criterion-referenced physical fitness and motor assessments should provide appropriate information to determine the child's functional ability.

9. Primary factors in developing the physical education program are the child's functional ability and level of functional skill development. Appropriate activities should be selected to enhance physical and motor functioning.

10. Opportunities outside of the school in community-based settings should be encouraged for additional practice, play, and socialization.

11. Children with mental retardation are prone to low levels of physical fitness and require a broad base of physical fitness activities and appropriate dietary habits that can be generalized to community and work settings.

12. Motor performance is also lacking and should reflect the development of balance, body perception, and locomotor and play skills that can be used in the home and community.

13. Appropriate social development and play should be included in the motor instructional program to facilitate appropriate behavior as well as developing skills.

14. Behavior management techniques eliminate inappropriate behavior and increase motivation and participation for children with mental retardation.

REFERENCES

American Association on Mental Retardation. (1992). Mental retardation: Definition. In *Classification and systems of supports* (9th ed.). Washington, DC: Author.

Croce, R. V. (1990). Effects of exercise and diet on body composition and cardiovascular fitness in adults with severe mental retardation. *Education and Training in Mental Retardation, 25,* 176–187.

Croce, R., & Horvat, M. (1992). Effects of reinforcement based exercise on fitness and work productivity in adults with mental retardation. *Adapted Physical Activities Quarterly, 9,* 148–178.

Croce, R., & Horvat, M. (1995). Exercise-induced activation and cognitive processing in individuals with mental retardation. In A. Vermeer (Ed.), *Medicine and sport science: Aspects of growth and sensorimotor development in mental retardation* (pp. 144–151). Basel, Switzerland: Karger.

Croce, R., Horvat, M., & Roswal, G. (1994). A preliminary investigation into the effects of exercise duration and fitness level on problem solving ability in individuals with mental retardation. *Clinical Kinesiology, 48,* 48–54.

Cronk, C. E., Puelzl-Quinn, H., & Pueschel, S. M. (1996). Growth standards in children with Down syndrome. *Developmental Brain Dysfunction, 9,* 59–71.

Deener, T., & Horvat, M. (1995). Effects of social reinforcement and self-recording on exercise duration in middle school students with moderate mental retardation. *Clinical Kinesiology, 49*(1), 28–33.

Dyer, S. M. (1994). Physiological effects of a 13-week physical fitness program on Down syndrome subjects. *Pediatric Exercise Science, 6*, 88–100.

Eichstaedt, C., & Lavay, B. (1994). *Physical activity for individuals with mental retardation.* Champaign, IL: Human Kinetics.

Fernhall, B. (1992). Physical fitness and exercise training of individuals with mental retardation. *Medicine and Science in Sports and Exercise, 25*(4), 442–450.

Fernhall, B., Tymesaon, G., Webster G. (1988). Cardiovascular fitness of mentally retarded individuals. *Adapted Physical Activity Quarterly, 5*, 12–28.

Horgan, J. S. (1983). Mnemonic strategy instruction in coding, processing, and recall of movement-related cues by mentally retarded children. *Perceptual and Motor Skills, 57*, 547–557.

Horgan, J. S. (1985). Issues in memory for movement with mentally retarded children. In J. Clark & J. H. Humphrey (Eds.), *Motor Development*. Princeton, NJ: Princeton Book Company.

Horvat, M., & Croce R. (1995). Physical rehabilitation of individuals with mental retardation: Physical fitness and information processing. *Critical Reviews in Physical and Rehabilitation Medicine, 7*(3), 233–252.

Horvat, M., Croce, R., & McGhee, T. (1993). Effects of a circuit training program on individuals with mental retardation. *Clinical Kinesiology, 47*(3), 71–77.

Horvat, M., & Franklin, C. (2001). The effect of the environment in physical activity patterns in children with mental retardation. *Research Quarterly for Exercise and Sport, 72*, 189–195.

Horvat, M., Malone, D. M., & Deener, T. (1993). Educational play: Preschool children with disabilities. In S. Grosse & D. Thompson (Eds.), *Play and recreation for individuals with disabilities: Practical pointers.* pp. 58–66. Reston, VA: American Alliance for Health, Physical Education, Recreation and Dance.

Kelly, L. E., Rimmer, J. H., & Ness, R. A. (1986). Obesity levels in institutionalized mentally retarded adults. *Adapted Physical Activity Quarterly, 3*, 167–176.

Lindgren, G. W., & Kotoda, H. (1993). Maturational rate of Tokyo children with and without mental retardation. *American Journal of Mental Retardation, 98*, 125–134.

Lorenzi, D., Horvat, M., & Pellegrini, A. D. (2000). Physical activity of children with and without mental retardation in inclusive recess settings. *Education and Training in Mental Retardation and Developmental Disabilities, 35*, 160–167.

Montgomery, D. L., Reid, G., & Seidl, C. (1988). The effects of two physical fitness programs designed for mentally retarded adults. *Canadian Journal of Sport Science, 13*, 73–78.

Pitetti, K. H., & Fernhall, B. (1997). Aerobic capacity as related to leg strength in youths with mental retardation. *Pediatric Exercise Science, 9*, 223–232.

Pitetti, K. H., Rimmer, J. H., & Fernhall, B. (1993). Physical fitness and adults with mental retardation. *Sports Medicine, 16*(1), 23–56.

Pitetti, K. H., & Tan, D. M. (1991). Effects of minimally supervised exercise program for mentally retarded adults. *Medicine and Science in Sports and Exercise, 23*(5), 594–601.

Rotatori, A. F., & Fox, R. (1981). *Behavioral weight reduction program for mentally handicapped persons.* Baltimore: University Park Press.

Zetts, R., Horvat, M., & Langone, J. (1995). The effects of a community-based resistance training program on the work productivity of adolescents with moderate to severe intellectual disabilities. *Education Training in Mental Retardation and Developmental Disabilities, 30*, 166–178.

CHAPTER 11

Learning Disabilities and Attention Deficit Disorders

Learning disabilities are one of the most recently recognized and controversial of all exceptionalities. Until the 1960s a scarcity of information was available about learning disabilities; most children with such disabilities were grouped in classes designed for the mentally retarded. To further complicate matters, a functional definition for identifying and placing learning-disabled students in special education was not available. There is no widespread agreement even today regarding terminology among academic disciplines. Psychology has used such terms as *perceptual disorders* and *hyperkinetic activity*, whereas the medical profession favors *brain injury* or *brain damage*, whereas language specialists prefer the terms *dyslexia* and *aphasia*.

In physical education, much of the work related to learning disabilities is based on the perceptual motor theories of Kephart, Barsch, and Cratty, the neurological development theories of Doman and Delacato, the sensory integration concept of Ayres, and the visual constructs of Getman and Frostig. Language disability theories concentrate on deficiencies in language and are generally based on the assumption that an intimate relationship exists between learning disabilities and deficits in language.

Recent attempts to define learning disabilities trace their origin to concepts of brain injury and minimal brain dysfunction. Children who were learning disabled originally were perceived as suffering from an infection or injury to the brain that caused deficiencies in perception, thinking, and emotional functioning. This idea was expanded with the concept of *minimal brain dysfunction* (MBD), which included children with deficiencies in language and motor development. In addition, the inclusion of minimal brain dysfunction in the definition of learning disabilities was an attempt to clearly differentiate learning disability from mental retardation by using the concept of near-average intelligence to define the population. The term *specific learning disabilities* then evolved to describe children with language, speech, and communication problems.

In order to consolidate these concepts into a unified definition, the federal government offered the following definition in the Individuals with Disabilities Education Act (IDEA) rules and regulations:

A disorder in one or more of the basic psychological processes involved in understanding or in using language, spoken or written, which may manifest itself in an imperfect ability to listen, think, speak, read, write, spell, or to do mathematical calculation. The term includes such conditions as perceptual handicaps, brain injury, minimal brain dysfunction, dyslexia, and development aphasia. The term does not include children who have learning problems which are the result of visual, hearing or motor handicaps, of mental retardation, or of environmental, cultural, or economic disadvantage.

In order to fully understand learning disabilities, one should note the differences in a child's capacity and actual achievement. Although the concept of discrepancy is not included in the IDEA definition, it can help us arrive at a more operational definition of learning disabilities. Discrepancy between capacity and achievement is assessed in one or more the following academic areas:

- oral expression
- listening comprehension
- written expression
- basic reading skills
- reading comprehension
- mathematical calculation
- mathematical reasoning

For teachers in physical education, a discrepancy is apparent if the child's performance level is one or two years behind the expected level of development. An individual who is functioning below the expected level of achievement will lag behind his or her peer group, and the discrepancy usually increases as the child gets older. Teachers must be aware, however, that discrepancies at various ages are not always comparable. Children who are deficient by one year in motor skill development at the age of 15 may not have as serious a problem as the 6-year-old who is deficient by one year in physical or motor development.

Recently, the terms attention deficit disorder (ADD) or attention deficit hyperactive disorder (ADHD) have been applied to children with learning problems. Childhood ADHD presents a significant educational problem in approximately 4% of the primary school population, of whom 80% are boys (Barkley, Dupaul & McMurrey, 1990). Children with attention deficit disorders demonstrate academic difficulties as well as social problems (such as difficulty in working cooperatively), are impulsive, and have difficulty at sedentary tasks (Cunningham & Siegal, 1987; Pellegrini & Horvat, 1995). Many children with attention deficit disorders also demonstrate learning disabilities as well as conduct disorders (Stanford & Hynd, 1994). The diversity of school-related problems associated with attention deficit disorders and its relationship to learning disabilities resulted in the 1991 policy mandate by the United States Department of Education to clarify funding categories to provide service to children with ADHD under the following disability categories: learning disability, emotional disturbance, or other health impairment. In this chapter we choose to include attention deficits with and without hyperactivity with learning disabilities.

More specifically, the American Psychiatric Association (2000) included diagnostic criteria for attention deficit disorders in their recent guide (DSM–IV–TR, pp. 92–93). See the box on page 160.

Etiology and Incidence

With such a broad interpretation of the definition of learning disabilities and attention deficit disorders, estimates of individuals who will qualify for special education services range from 1% to 40% of the entire school-aged population. It is interesting

Diagnostic Criteria for Attention Deficit Hyperactivity Disorder

A. Either (1) or (2):

   (1) Six (or more) of the following symptoms of *inattention* have persisted for at least 6 months to a degree that is maladaptive and inconsistent with developmental level:

INATTENTION

   (a) Often fails to give close attention to details or makes careless mistakes in school-work, work, or other activities.

   (b) Often has difficulty sustaining attention in tasks or play activities.

   (c) Often does not seem to listen when spoken to directly.

   (d) Often does not follow through on instructions and fails to finish schoolwork, chores, or duties in the workplace (not due to oppositional behavior or failure to understand instructions).

   (e) Often has difficulty organizing tasks and activities.

   (f) Often avoids, dislikes, or is reluctant to engage in tasks that require sustained mental effort (such as schoolwork or homework).

   (g) Often loses things necessary for tasks or activities (e.g., toys, school assignments, pencils, books, or tools).

   (h) Is often easily distracted by extraneous stimuli.

   (i) Is often forgetful in daily activities.

   (2) Six (or more) of the following symptoms of *hyperactivity-impulsivity* have persisted for at least 6 months to a degree that is maladaptive and inconsistent with developmental level:

HYPERACTIVITY

   (a) Often fidgets with hands or feet or squirms in seat.

   (b) Often leaves seat in classroom or in other situations in which remaining seated is expected.

   (c) Often runs about or climbs excessively in situations in which it is inappropriate (in adolescents or adults, may be limited to subjective feelings of restlessness).

   (d) Often has difficulty playing or engaging in leisure activities quietly.

   (e) Is often "on the go" or often acts as if "driven by a motor".

   (f) Often talks excessively.

IMPULSIVITY

   (g) Often blurts out answers before questions have been completed.

   (h) Often has difficulty awaiting turn.

   (i) Often interrupts or intrudes on others (e.g., butts into conversations or games).

B. Some hyperactive-impulsive or inattentive symptoms that caused impairment were present before age 7 years.

C. Some impairment from the symptoms is present in two or more settings (e.g., at school [or work] and home).

D. There must be clear evidence of clinically significant impairment in social, academic, or occupational functioning.

E. The symptoms do not occur exclusively during the course of a pervasive developmental disorder, schizophrenia, or other psychotic disorder and are not better accounted for by another mental disorder (e.g., mood disorder, anxiety disorder, dissociative disorder, or a personality disorder).

SOURCE: Adapted from the Diagnostic and Statistical Manual of Mental Disorders (4th ed.) (DSM–IV–TR), 2000, Washington, DC: Author.

to note that more boys than girls are identified as learning disabled, with a ratio of approximately 2:1 of boys to girls. We should use caution with these statistics, however, because boys are sometimes more obvious in exhibiting overt behavioral and learning problems than are girls, who may be overlooked because their problems do not attract as much attention.

More children in the primary grades than in the secondary grades are identified with learning or attention deficits. Although educators do excellent jobs in remediating or compensating for learning difficulties, we should not assume that learning disabilities disappear or that children grow out of problems as they enter high school, college, or the work environment. The continuous evaluation and identification of children with learning deficiencies and attention deficits are a concern for all teachers and are evident at all ages.

The causes of learning disabilities and attention deficits are generally unknown; rarely can the specific reason for a disorder be determined. One common speculation about learning disabilities is that they are *organically based,* and another is that they are *biochemically based.* The first theory holds that one of the primary reasons for learning disabilities is an injury to the brain that impedes the ability to receive and integrate sensory impulses. This is a widely accepted theory and is assessed by the administration of an electroencephalogram (EEG). The second theory posits that several biochemical factors, including a lack in amino acids, allergies, mineral and vitamin deficiencies, glandular disorders, hypoglycemia, and artificial foods and colors are related to learning difficulties. Theoretically, sensory input may be interrupted or stopped at synaptic junctions because of the breakdown of neurotransmitters, which interferes with the learning process. Finally, some researchers feel that the interaction between the biochemical and anatomical components of brain function disrupts the ability to receive, process, and retain sensory information.

Because learning disabilities have no visible physical dysfunction, and are often referred to as hidden disabilities, it may be more useful to observe the characteristics of learning difficulties. It should be noted that disorders of attention and impulsivity are part of these characteristics. Each characteristic may be difficult to determine, and teachers must remember that children may exhibit one or more of them at various levels of severity (Hallahan & Kauffman, 1997).

1. *hyperactivity*—aimless, constant motion around the room or rocking back and forth; tapping and/or shuffling while in a seated position

2. *perceptual-motor impairments*—inability to perceive or interpret sensory stimuli

3. *emotional lability*—low frustration tolerance and/or poor self-concept

4. *general gross motor deficits*—generally clumsy or awkward in relationship to gross motor skills; as reported by Bruininks (1978), a discrepancy of 2 years between gross motor skill levels and chronological age

5. *disorders of attention*—inability to stay on task (i.e., attending initially to an object), switch tasks, or stay with a particular task

6. *impulsivity*—inappropriate, sudden reaction to a variety of stimuli

7. *disorders of memory*—difficulty with short- or long-term memory

8. *specific learning disabilities*—difficulty in one or more academic areas

9. *disorders of language*—problems with plural formation, articulation, or expressive and receptive language

10. *equivocal neurological signs*—presence of learning disabilities due to brain damage or dysfunction

11. *behavior disparity*—a wide range of behaviors, with the capacity to excel in one area and the inability to comprehend another area

Impact on Functional Development

Children with learning disabilities and attention disorders are often characterized by decreased physical functioning. Alexander (1990) indicated that whereas many academic concerns are addressed in the education literature, a scarcity of information is available on the physical and motor concerns of children with attention deficits and learning problems. Several concerns relate to movement, such as balance and awkwardness; others to perception, such as a disrupted feedback mechanism and memory disorders; and still others to lower physical work capacity. Each of these concerns posit that many of the child's early experiences with activity are not positive and should be addressed before an instructional program is implemented. In addition, children may also be diagnosed as having a developmental coordination disorder. According to the APA (2000), this diagnosis is made for a motor impairment that interferes with academic achievement or activities of daily living. Problems of developmental coordination disorder included delays in motor and nonmotor (language, etc.) abilities in children 5–11 years of age and are not associated with medical conditions or personality disorders.

Planning the Physical Activity Program

Because of the lack of understanding among disciplines, children with learning disabilities are often misunderstood. Often teachers subscribe to the view that these children are LD (lazy and dumb). Because the exceptionality is not obvious (as is, for example, the disability of a child sitting in a wheelchair), teachers often neglect or do not understand the needs of children with learning disabilities. The exceptionality does not render children incapable of learning but does require teachers to develop the physical education program and proper instructional methods according to their unique needs and functioning level of learning. With this in mind, teachers should consider the environment, social-sequence level of development, incentives, medication, relaxation, and remediation or compensation in planning and developing a comprehensive physical activity program.

Environment

Many times stimuli within the environment are sufficient to confuse, distort, or disrupt child's ability to learn a motor skill. One preventive step for teachers is to control or adapt the teaching environment to best accommodate variations in learning. In rapidly changing environments beyond the control of teachers, teachers should take steps to prepare the child gradually to deal with distractions.

1. Physical educators can provide a highly structured program that establishes a routine for teaching procedures and arrangement of the physical education environment. Children should come to class in the same manner, at a specifically designated location, before receiving instructions for the activity. Classes should always follow the same routine, moving specifically from one station or group to another during the learning session. Equipment should always be distributed and collected in the same manner, large equipment always positioned in the same location. By structuring the environment in this way, children may develop a sense of security and confidence that allows them to participate and develop age-appropriate motor skills.

2. Reducing stimuli (or intensity of stimuli) can help an instructor deal effectively with small groups (Hallahan & Kauffman, 1997). Although it is often difficult to reduce space without disrupting the activity, it may be possible to divide a gymnasium or pool, or to condense the teaching area by using cones as boundaries, and still conduct the activity according to program goals. Thus the instructor may reduce a wide-open space, which often interferes with learning, and provide the secure environment needed for children. Teachers can also remove external stimuli or reduce their effect on the activity in progress. For example, many times teachers bring too much equipment to a softball activity; all that is needed is two bats (one light, one heavier) and two balls (one held by the teacher). Additional equipment may distract children and may not be needed for the activity. Similarly, it is difficult to teach a basketball class while cheerleaders are practicing, or to teach a motor skill while another group is bouncing on the trampoline. By reducing the outside stimuli (light, smell, sounds) during the activity, teachers can enhance children's ability to attend to teachers and/or class activities rather than to extraneous stimuli that disrupt the learning process.

3. Teachers should utilize an adequate number of teaching stations, audiovisual aids, and homework. Children may respond to such motivational devices as film loops, pictures, and posters, which may compensate for other deficiencies and which can reduce frustration by promoting an understanding of the activity. Teaching stations should be available to allow students appropriate time for instruction and practice, which is preferable to having the children wait in line, inadvertently attending to other stimuli. In addition, this procedure will provide concrete experiences and maximize the active learning time of all children in a class (Figure 11.1). Homework can also be effective for children with learning disabilities,

Figure 11.1 Heel-to-toe walking—a concrete experience.

providing additional practice and time to master a specific task. Horvat (1982) successfully used parents as tutors for static and dynamic balance development with elementary school-aged children with learning disabilities.

4. Educators can enhance the stimulus value of instructional materials by using such devices as brightly colored balls or targets, which help children differentiate equipment from the background, or whistles and shrill sounds, which are easily discernible and can also be differentiated easily from background noises. Although teachers may not be able to control the environment completely in the initial stages of learning, some reduction of outside distractions is essential to alleviate additional problems. Because physical education settings may include rapidly changing tasks or environments, teachers should gradually prepare children to deal with distractions as part of the learning process.

Social-Sequence Level of Development

Children with learning disabilities may be socially immature and often reluctant to engage in activities because of their learning problems. They tend to withdraw from social relationships and may become the person no one wants on the team. Concerned teachers can provide an opportunity for a successful physical education experience by selecting activities at the functioning social level of each individual. This can be accomplished by following the social-sequence level of development.

The social-sequence level is the degree of social interaction that is involved in a particular activity. For example, the solitary kicking of as a ball would be at the lowest level of a "ball-kicking sequence," whereas a kickball game would be at the highest level because more social interaction is required. The social-sequence levels are

1. playing alone
2. parallelling (two children playing with no interaction)
3. onlooker
4. two children in associative play, that is, informally playing together for brief periods
5. cooperative play, or playing together in small groups
6. cooperative play in which children play organized games in larger groups.

Teachers can use these levels to help select an appropriate and socially acceptable activity for any given child. If children can function successfully at one level, they can progress to the next level with a minimum of frustration and anxiety. In this manner teachers can facilitate social development by matching motor skills and provide appropriate learning experiences that encourage and develop social interaction.

Incentives and Rewards

Many times teachers can foster an appropriate behavior by utilizing an appropriate incentive and reward system. Social praise and incentives not only strengthen social acceptance but also reward children (who often are frustrated) for appropriate attempts or completion of a motor task. Teachers can also provide more tangible rewards in the form of stars, smiley faces, extra periods of activity, or free time on a piece of equipment initially for participation and later for task completion.

Finally, encouragement and goal setting can help children achieve their program goals. By actively participating and setting reachable goals, children can achieve success at their level of functioning and gradually move to more difficult tasks. As the children experience success, they become more motivated and can gradually take control of the pace for learning.

Medication

For children with learning disabilities, poor performance due to a short attention span may justify the use of medication. The physician and nurse will usually prescribe and dispense medication for such children; however, it is vital for teachers to recognize certain facts and reasons for using medication. Medication is used primarily to alter the neurological or biochemical makeup of children, rather than as a cure for a deficiency (e.g., short attention span). Teachers must be aware of each child's use of medication and of possible side effects that may contraindicate some activities, as well as periods of time the individual changes or is removed from medication (drug holiday). The two most commonly used medications for children and their side effects are listed below.

1. methylphenidate (Ritalin). Possible side effects include impaired coordination, loss of appetite, weight loss, insomnia, and nervousness.
2. dextroamphetamine (Dexedrine). Possible side effects include psychic dependence, insomnia, restlessness, nervousness, dizziness, tremor, and dystonic movements of the head, neck, and extremities.

Although teachers are not directly involved in dispensing medication, it is vital that they be aware of medication and its use to determine any detrimental effects on the individual's motor performance. Likewise, teachers should be aware of the possible benefits of medication and of any changes in dosage or termination of medication that might cause erratic behavior.

Relaxation

One method that is not often used by teachers, but that may be helpful, is relaxation training. The need for relaxation and stress reduction is common to most populations and perhaps should be used more frequently in all physical education classes. By incorporating relaxation activities, teachers can help children reduce anxiety and control tense muscles as well as improve concentration. Children can be taught to regain control especially after a period of highly excitable activities. In fact, relaxation exercises can be used to bring the class to a paced ending with a cool-down period and, more important, can help children regain their self-control. The following are examples of verbal instructions for several typical relaxation exercises.

> *Bend the feet upward. . . . Pull hard!*
> *Harder! And let go.*
> *Push the feet down as far as you can. . . .*
> *Push harder! And let go.*
> *Turn the feet farther, farther! And let them go.*
> *Straighten the knees as far as possible. . . . Now press your legs down into the mat, and let go.*

Straighten the knees again. . . . Press your legs together as tightly as you can . . . and let go.

Straighten the fingers and pull back the wrist joints . . . and let go.

Bend the fingers and wrist. . . . Now bend the joints of your elbows fully . . . more. And let go.

Straighten the fingers and elbows, farther. . . . Squeeze shoulders forward and together. And let go.

Close your eyes, and let your head fall to one side, return to middle, and fall to the other side. Repeat the movement again, and let go.

Lift your head off the floor . . . and now drop back again and let go.

Press your head back against the mat firmly, and then let go.

Tighten the jaw, cheeks, face, and let go.

Pull in the abdominal muscles, and let go.

Push the legs forward until your back touches the mat, and let go.

Sink into the mat, and breathe in and out as deeply as possible, and let go.

Tighten the muscles of the shoulder girdle, and let go.

Now tighten the fists, harder, and let go.

Other relaxation methods may be used, including the techniques of *Jacobson*, in which children learn to contract and relax muscles beginning with the extremities and proceeding to the head and neck and finally to the trunk. The child can tighten tense muscles and then concentrate on "letting go" and relaxing specific muscles or parts of the body. A similar technique developed by *Rathbone* uses static stretching for range of motion and breathing exercises to relax the diaphragm in conjunction with contracting and relaxing specific muscle groups. *Yoga* is a common activity that can aid in relaxation of muscles as well as control of breathing. Assuming specific postures—along with deep inhalation, retention of breath, and exhalation of breath—helps children develop flexibility and retain their emotional control and concentration. Other forms of exercise, such as *tai chi*, aid in increasing concentration and improving flexibility and balance for children and adults. Finally, an association set technique such as the *Yates relaxation technique* uses specific words to visualize a relaxed state. Words such as *melt* or *let go* are associated with relaxed or pleasant scenes that are anxiety free.

Remediation and Compensation

Many teachers mistakenly believe that children with motor deficiencies simply require practice in the motor skill in which they are having problems, and so they direct all their instructional time to teaching these skills. No single approach to teaching, however, will always eliminate the deficit. Teaching to a deficit may result in success with time and practice, but it may also result in failure for the individual who can tolerate only a minimum of stimulation. Teaching to the deficit also neglects the information available to the other sense modalities. Teaching *around* the deficits, however, assumes that intersensory learning is occurring and that the individual can integrate auditory, visual, tactile, and kinesthetic sensory information (French & Horvat, 1986).

The instructor should always remember that children will learn and respond to instruction differently. If the deficiency cannot be overcome, it should be compensated for by appropriate teaching strategies at the individual's tolerance level for learning and with the most effective modality or modalities. In some instances, the teacher can cue the child prior to the task to allow more time to process the correct response. Other prompts may use visual models or physical guidance to cue the response. The initial concern is that the child learn and that we allow the individual the opportunity to be successful. Specific learning styles may be determined in consultation with special educator, school psychologist, occupational therapist, and/or adapted physical educator.

In addition, the teacher or parent should be aware of the severity level of the learning difficulty. Mild to moderate learning disabilities may necessitate practice in school and at home on balance and coordination, whereas severe learning disabilities may require a more extensive perceptual-motor learning program as well as many of the other measures discussed earlier. The severity level of the specific learning disability *must* be determined by the appropriate assessment process before the teacher plans the physical education program.

Implementing the Physical Activity Program

Motor dysfunctions that are usually associated with children with learning disabilities include dysrhythmia and deficits in coordination, balance, body image, haptic awareness, and motor planning (Harvey & Reid, 1997; Wharry, Kirkpatrick & Stokes, 1987). For children who are unable to function adequately, a limited spectrum of movement has been developed. This is manifested in deficiencies in age-appropriate motor skills as well as poor social development and frustration that may be associated with the inability to perform motor activities.

It is especially important for teachers to plan the physical education program based on the individual learning characteristics. Most of the characteristics of children with learning disabilities have some effect on physical and motor performance. For example, although hyperactivity is not a specific motor problem, it will be difficult for children to attend appropriately to the teacher and/or movement. The child who is hyperactive will attend to nothing, whereas the child who is distractible attends to everything in the environment. Deficits in the auditory, visual, or haptic modalities may also interfere with how the children receives, interprets, or finally performs a particular activity, while receptive, expressive language problems may manifest themselves in the inability to follow directions or execute movements requiring a vocal response. In addition, children may require additional time to process information. For example, children may still be responding to a verbal request and have difficulty understanding the task while the teacher inadvertently moves to the next skill. Allowing extra time to process the information or cueing the response may allow the child the necessary time to process the appropriate information and complete the task.

It is essential that children develop a sound movement base to ensure the development of age-appropriate skills. If a skill cannot be learned because of a deficit, teachers should compensate for the activity by using other strategies (modalities that may be more functionally appropriate for the child). The following sections describe some common characteristics of children with learning disabilities, along with specific teaching strategies and activities that can be implemented in a physical activity program. See also Table 11.1.

Table 11.1 Characteristics and Instructional Strategies

Behavior	Characteristics	Teaching Strategies	Physical Activity
Hyperactivity	Constant motion or rocking back and forth, tapping and/or shuffling while in a seated position, inability to focus attention.	Conduct activity in an area free of outside stimuli; carefully structure the entire program; simplify rules and use brief instructions, medication, reduction of space; enhance instructional stimulus (e.g., colored balls), operant conditioning.	Structured program beginning with vigorous activities (parachute, aquatics, running, hopping, jumping skills) and ending with a quiet activity (relaxation training). Emphasis on how slowly an activity can be done. Dance and rhythms.
Perceptual-motor impairments			
Auditory Figure-ground discrimination Sound localization Temporal perception	Deficiencies in: • distinguishing sounds from background • differentiating between sounds • determining direction of sounds • differentiating pitch	Use percussion instruments that will distinguish the figure or sound from the background; spoons; bells that form distinct sounds.	Auditory games that stress locations of objects and sounds, such as scavenger hunts; moving to and away from sounds.
Visual Figure-ground discrimination Spatial relationships Perceptual constancy Discrimination Visual-motor match	Deficiencies in: • differentiating object from background • assessing varying sizes and distances • determining balls of various sizes • differentiating between large and small • matching visual cue with motor output	Put masking tape on wall and floors, basketball backdrop, and goals that stand out; use colored footprints, brightly colored balls or beanbags.	Ball games with brightly colored balls; footprints for rhythmic movements and gross motor skills; stunts, tumbling, and trampoline activities. Activities that incorporate seeing (visual), feeling (haptic), manipulation (visual and haptic), hearing (auditory), and moving (visual and auditory).
Haptic Body awareness Body image Tactual perception	Deficiencies in: • determining laterality and directionality • identifying body parts • differentiating between objects and sizes • crossing the midline	Utilize activities emphasizing body parts on self and others; touch-and-move activities; activities based on functioning level and concepts using directions and directionality.	Tunnels, tires, mazes to move in, out, around, under; balance beams, boards, trampoline; activities of laterality. Discrimination and crossing the midline all pertain to balance and cross lateral movement patterns. Mirror exploration with body parts.
General and gross motor deficits	Lack of balance, hand-eye, eye-foot coordination; awkwardness; dysrhythmia, poor motor planning.	Assess level of performance through direct observation. Use norm- and/or criterion-referenced tests. Provide program based on child's needs and most efficient modality for learning.	Utilize the part method or task analysis while teaching the skill. Introduce such activities as aquatics, rhythmic movements, balance progressions, parachute games, trampoline, group games, basic locomotor skills.

Behavior	Characteristics	Teaching Strategies	Physical Activity
Disorders of attention			
Distractibility	Short attention span; inability to concentrate on appropriate tasks.	Use concise terms and/or demonstrations; use a single-task approach; do not keep children passively waiting; repeat instruction and activities to ensure retention; eliminate irrelevant stimuli; enhance stimulus value (mirrors, colors, etc.); use behavior management.	A variety of gross motor skills and simple activities; also parachute, aquatic skills/games, and movement education activities.
Disinhibition	Random shifts in attention, daydreaming, lack of inhibitory control.	Introduce activities that can be set into a routine; stop and start activity at the same time; practice; structure behavior management to focus attention.	A variety of gross motor skills and simple activities; also parachute games, aquatic skills/games, and movement education activities.
Perseveration	Inability to shift attention to succeeding task or spending too much time on one task.	Guide the students to another task, utilize a variety of tasks, rewarding only when one is completed; change activities frequently, with each being distinctly different from one another, e.g., formation, starting position, skills, rules, and strategies.	Activities that are not highly sequenced: ball skills, rhythmic movements, simple games, movement education, gross motor skills, parachute, trampoline, physical fitness activities, stunts and tumbling, circuit games, stop-go, green light.
Impulsivity	Unplanned, meaningless, inappropriate reactions to a variety of stimuli; lack of inhibitory control.	Devise as a highly structured environment with no distractions; serve as an active model in all activities to increase attention.	Good-behavior game; structured progressions of gross motor activities including locomotion skills (running, jumping, hopping, balance progressions, stunts and tumbling).
Disorders of long- and short-term memory	Failure to recall information or in proper sequence.	Utilize simple tasks; reinforce and select activities that can be sequenced.	Dance activities and gymnastic routines, tumbling, parachute, low-instructional games; Aerobic fitness activities, trampoline.
Dissociation	Inability to see the auditory, visual, or social whole.	Use whole-part-whole method with little verbalization; use activities that demand integrated working of body rather than activities with part of the body.	Social-sequence activities; whole, part/whole locomotor activities; tumbling, balance activities.

Table 11.1 Characteristics and Instructional Strategies *(continued)*

Behavior	Characteristics	Teaching Strategies	Physical Activity
Specific learning disabilities	Disorders of mathematics, reading, writing.	Work with educational programming team to determine the level of functioning and most efficient modalities for learning. Enhance existing modality or compensate for deficiency.	Games and relays that reinforce academic concepts: number and letter grids; parachute activities stressing academic concepts; developmental physical education activities and games that involve counting or other responses.
Disorders of language	Problems with plural formation, articulation, expressive and receptive language.	Utilize visual cues with verbal instructions, demonstration, gestures, and haptic cues. Do not substitute words with similar meanings (*big/large*, etc.). Pair words with picture demonstration. Encourage verbal response before performing activity. Use concrete rather than abstract movement activities.	Academic games and relays that encourage verbal responses or response to visual cues; parachute activities and developmental physical education activities; games that involve counting.
Soft neurological signs	Neurological dysfunction, including brain damage.	Work with the educational programming team to determine the level of functioning and most efficient modality for learning. Enhance existing modality or compensate for deficiency.	Develop a sound developmental physical education program based on the needs and functioning of the individual. Utilize physical fitness, aquatics, dance, fundamental skills and patterns, sports, and games.
Behavior disparity	A wide range of behaviors, with the capacity to excel in one and the inability to comprehend another.	Work with the educational programming team to determine the level of functioning and most efficient modality for learning. Enhance existing modality or compensate for deficiency.	Develop a sound developmental physical education program based on the needs and functioning of the individual. Utilize physical fitness, aquatics, dance, fundamental skills and patterns, sports, and games.
Emotional lability	Antisocial behavior; lack of friends; being last one selected in games; inablity to cooperate with peers; low frustration tolerance; explosive behavior; passivity.	Use a gradual approach to participation, and allow time for practice before group participation. Praise any achievement or accomplishment (using successive approximations). Structure the program; ignore inappropriate behavior; be enthusiastic and consistent.	Implement social-sequence games and activities that require cooperation; movement education activities that require two people; parachute activities, stunts, and tumbling. Conduct the program in a small area; use a good-behavior game and movement education technique in which everyone is correct.

Hyperactivity

Children who are hyperactive are always in motion, constantly shuffling their feet, rocking, and manipulating objects. They attend to everything and often demonstrate the inability to sit or stand long enough to receive instructions for the activity. Physical activities should be aimed primarily at the problems caused by hyperactivity. Teachers should structure the environment by reducing the effect of outside stimuli to control the number of choices available and limit irrelevant stimuli to increase the chances for attending behavior. Medication may be used to promote attention and counter some of the symptoms of hyperactivity, but teachers should be aware of possible side effects, mood variations, or change in the dosage of or removal of medication that would result in changes in functioning. During the prekindergarten and kindergarten years, teachers are concerned primarily with social interactions and peer relationships, whereas primary grade children need to be taught to sit and attend to instructions. For the child who is hyperactive, this may signal the beginning of learning problems.

Teachers should also use methods that emphasize self-control, such as relaxation techniques or concentrating on how slowly an activity can be performed. Physical fitness skills that are structured, such as group exercises or training circuits, can be used successfully to counteract hyperactivity. Vigorous activities may be appropriate if they are followed by periods of relaxation that allow children an opportunity to regain control.

Perceptual-Motor Impairments

Perceptual-motor impairments can be auditory, visual, tactile, or kinesthetic (Chapter 8). Auditory perception refers to those functions that involve the ear's reception of sound and the integration of these signals. It involves discrimination of sound, locating the course or direction of sound, discriminating pitch and loudness, and selecting relevant from irrelevant auditory stimuli. This modality is very important in numerous physical activities, such as rhythmic movement and dance. Children with an auditory perceptual deficit may also have difficulty following the physical educator's verbal instructions. They may be unable to sequence the words correctly or to determine the direction of the voice because of the numerous noises within the environment. Likewise, children who are unable to distinguish verbal cues concerning the correct way to grip a baseball bat would also be unable to complete the correct procedure or form in hitting a baseball. Of course, the child who needs and is given additional time to process this information may respond more appropriately.

Visual perception refers to the brain functions that involve the eyes' reception of signals and the integration of these signals. It involves making spatial relationships, discriminating dominant features in different objects, discriminating an object from its background, and identifying a figure when it can be only partially seen. For example, children with a figure-ground deficit may have a problem catching a ball or throwing a ball to a specific location or a teammate.

Haptic perception refers to the brain functions that interpret information received through the tactile (touch) and kinesthetic (movement of the body and muscles) senses and is essential for development and control of movement (Figure 11.2). Tac-

Figure 11.2 Haptic instruction.

tile perception involves the discrimination of geometric shapes, textures, object consistency, pain, and pressure. Kinesthetic perception includes balance skills and sensitivity to direction or position. Children with a tactile deficit may have problems manipulating objects because of the lack of meaningful information provided by the sense of touch, whereas a kinesthetic deficit could include problems with body image, balance skills, and tension in the muscles.

Individual learning differences and learning styles should influence selection of instructional strategies or alterations in the program that may be beneficial to ensure success. By determining the extent of the deficiency in the learning process, teachers can maximize the achievement movement potential for children with perceptual problems.

Perceptual deficits that impede motor skill acquisition necessitate selecting meaningful teaching strategies to aid in distinguishing or enhancing auditory, visual, tactile, or kinesthetic cues. For example, a slight dysfunction in auditory perception may be overcome by using the hands, feet, sticks, or drums to create a rhythmic sequence used in dance activities and directing the child's attention to relevant input. Verbal cues, sounds made with implements (e.g., rattles), audio cassettes, records, or tape recorders can also produce a variety of sounds, melodies, and/or pitches that may provide the appropriate auditory cues or prompts that help children select a proper response.

Perceptual functioning in the visual modality may be enhanced by using posters, pictures, film loops, or slides to reinforce correct input information. Continually modeling the proper form or using distinguishable colors (such as optic orange) may help children match the correct visual information with a motor output. Visual input can be enhanced by providing a designated target or zone, such as a square on a basketball backboard, that cues the child to a specific or designated area. More important, the cues can be controlled by the child who has adequate time to process and use the information.

Kinesthetic perception may be enhanced by full or partial cues designed to increase awareness of proper position. For example, spotting belts allow the child to "feel" the correct location of his or her body in space. Lighter equipment, or a variety of textures and sizes of implements, can supplement input and decision-making data to ensure the proper position or the execution of the motor skill (output). In each use, the child is directed to the appropriate task specific information.

Gross Motor Deficits/Awkwardness

Often children with learning disabilities manifest awkwardness and are uncoordinated in their movements (Harvey and Reid, 1997). They may have problems running, throwing, catching, kicking, and balancing; as a result, they may stumble during games and activities. It is important to accurately assess the level of functioning through direct observation or appropriate assessment instruments. Many times physical educators will need to consult with the appropriate school personnel to determine whether the deficiency can be overcome through a program designed to develop maturational skills or activities designed to compensate for perceptual or sensory deficiencies. The program should be designed according to the child's level of development and effective style of learning. Activities such as fitness, fundamental motor skills, aquatics, dance, and group games and sports all may be appropriate.

Attention Disorders

Disorders of attention include distractibility, disinhibition, and perseveration. Many children with the problem of distractibility are unable to block out irrelevant stimuli and concentrate on a task. For these children, nonessential equipment, bright light or colors, and extraneous sounds interfere with the ability to concentrate on an appropriate task. A structured environment designed to eliminate inappropriate external stimuli or to gradually introduce children to the teaching setting can be effectively developed. For example, activities should be conducted in a softly colored room without pictures, posters, or obvious attractive visual stimuli. An activity perhaps should not be performed outdoors if, for example, someone is mowing a lawn nearby or if cars are rushing by the playground. Space should be limited to what is needed for the activity, while auditory distractions or background noises should be eliminated if possible in the early stages of learning. In addition, selected stimulus enhancement, such as the use of brightly colored balls that do not blend into the background, will allow children to concentrate more readily on the task.

Teachers should also remember not to overuse praise with destractible children. Too much positive reinforcement may actually complicate the problem further. A low-keyed positive reinforcer is more appropriate for children who find it hard to concentrate on the task at hand.

Another tactic is to increase gradually the stimuli that children can handle. For example, if children can follow only verbal directions, do not model the movement and issue verbal directions at the same time. Likewise do not select an activity that requires children to attend to several stimuli at once to be successful; instead, gradually integrate such activities with higher-level skills. This is as a common mistake of beginning teachers and may interfere with the child's ability to learn effectively.

Disinhibition, or random shifts in attention and daydreaming, will often manifest itself as an attention problem. Lazarus (1994) described this as a lack of inhibitory control and the presence of associated movement or movement overflow. A highly structured routine, including requiring specific clothing for class, locating equipment in the same position and dispensing it in the same manner, and beginning and ending the class in the same way, will at best relieve much of the anxiety leading to disinhibition. Parachute activities and gymnastic stunts, as well as fitness or circuit courses, are useful activities in structuring the environment and circumventing the problem.

Another attention disorder that may affect children is perseveration, or having difficulty shifting attention to a succeeding task or spending too much time on one task. By guiding children to another task and rewarding only the tasks that are completed, teachers can direct children to another skill. For example, if a child perseverates on bouncing a ball, the teacher can urge the child to stop and shoot by modeling and/or performing the activity simultaneously and rewarding the child only when both sequences are completed. Likewise, the teacher can have the parachute shaken vigorously and change the activity to hopping in a circle, thereby making it impossible for children to perseverate without being dragged around the circle. It may also be helpful for teachers to select distinctly different activities that are not highly sequenced, such as circuit games, relays, and/or physical fitness activities.

Impulsivity

Children may respond impulsively, or in an unplanned, meaningless, or inappropriate reaction, to a variety of stimuli. Impulsivity is one of the behaviors reported by Lazarus (1994) that reflect inhibitory control. Often these children respond to a stimulus without thought or fear of the outcome. For example, children may jump into the swimming pool without regard to the depth of the water or to their swimming ability. By serving as an active role model to increase attention and structuring all activities to provide discernible instructions, the educator may eliminate many impulsive responses. Many teachers also use structured games and progressions as well as fitness circuit activities to deal effectively with inhibiting unplanned responses and directing attention to completing the activity.

Disorders of Long-Term and Short-Term Memory

Children may be unable to recall information or to recall it in proper sequence. This is naturally disruptive and frustrating for children who are learning a motor skill. If they are given progressive tasks, children can link movements that can be processed more easily and successively built upon. Activities such as rhythmic movements, gymnastics skills, tumbling routines, parachute games, low-instructional games, trampoline, and aerobic fitness activities are all tasks that can be started simply, sequenced, and reinforced. For example, gymnastics skills can be taught separately and practiced in routines to enhance retention and to provide feedback on learning and additional opportunities for practicing motor skills. Likewise, modeling or guiding children through the response will help them remember the skill and/or sequence that is appropriate.

Dissociation

At times children will not be able to see the entire auditory or visual sequence. This is called *dissociation*. If something is missing that distorts the proper motion or sequence, it is apparent that children will not learn the motor skill. For example, not seeing all the movements in a swimming crawl stroke will prohibit the child from learning that particular swimming skill. By using activities that require little verbalization, and by using the whole-part-whole method of teaching a motor skill, teachers can integrate specific movements into a proper sequence of movement instead of just associating movements with parts of the body. Basic locomotor skills can be used to enable the child to see the visual whole. To create an auditory whole, the instructor should initiate activities that require little verbalization and that are paired with appropriate visual cues, such as a hand signal with the verbal command "Go." In addition, children who miss the point of a remark or the humor of a situation, should be involved in social-sequence and interaction activities appropriate for their own level of functioning.

Specific Learning Disabilities

Although physical educators are not directly concerned with specific learning disabilities, that is, disorders of math, reading, and writing, indirect benefits can be gained from a joint effort with academic instructors. By determining the most efficient method for learning, educators can enhance the existing functioning level or compensate for a deficiency. Academic games that reinforce number and letter concepts are appropriate for this joint effort. Physical education activities that involve counting or number and letter grids are useful to help children reinforce academic concepts, such as those in reading and mathematics. Instructors should not assume that academic learning is to be substituted for physical education; however, the joint effort of classroom and physical education teachers can enhance the overall development and self-concept of children with learning disabilities.

Disorders of Language

As in the case of specific learning disabilities, language disorders, such as difficulties in plural formation, articulation, and expressive and receptive languages, are not the primary responsibility of the physical educator. However, the physical educator can work with teachers on common concepts, such as integrating both sides of the body or tracking tasks that may facilitate academic behaviors. Teachers can also use appropriate visual and haptic cues to encourage movements. In general, teachers should use concrete rather than abstract activities and should avoid words with similar meanings.

Games that involve counting and that encourage verbal response are appropriate. Academic games, parachute activities, and developmental physical education activities are all appropriate for children with a language disorder (French & Horvat, 1983).

Soft Neurological Signs

The most important thing to remember about neurological dysfunction, or soft neurological signs, is that some damage has occurred to the brain. If teachers can address the specific problem area early in the child's development, other areas of the brain may take over impaired functions before the process of myelinization takes place. A joint effort with the collaborative team is essential to determine the child's level of functioning and the best ways for the teacher to present information. If children can learn through the existing modality, then enhancing their strengths with specific instructional methodology is essential. However, teachers may be forced to compensate for an existing deficiency by using other modalities, cueing children and presenting instruction in a way that aids in learning. However, teachers must ensure that they do not overestimate the capacities of children who can tolerate only a minimum amount of stimulation.

A sound developmental physical education program that is based on the child's needs and functional ability is essential for children with neurological dysfunctions. Older children, for instance, who fail miserably at games involving coordination and teamwork may do well in activities such as swimming and physical fitness. However, no aspect of physical education should be neglected in developing a comprehensive activity program.

Behavior Disparity

One of the unique characteristics of children with learning disabilities is the wide range of behaviors they display, such as the capacity to excel in one area and their inability to comprehend another. Children who are whizzes in mathematics but cannot read are often frustrating to teachers, to parents, and especially to themselves. In addition, these frustrations may hinder acceptance by peer attitudes. By not functioning well in physical activities that require coordination or perception, children may be placed at a disadvantage in making friends and interacting with others in peer group games (Alexander, 1990).

Nowhere is it more important to utilize the team concept for ascertaining the level of functioning and the most effective learning strategy for the child. Physical educators can provide the sound developmental program that is essential for children to gain peer group acceptance and social interaction, while regular classroom teachers and educational specialists can combine efforts to teach new concepts, provide practice, or reinforce learned concepts for these individuals (Zentall & Stormont-Spurgin, 1995).

CHAPTER SUMMARY

1. One operational definition for *learning disabilities* is a performance level of 1 or 2 years behind the expected level of achievement in one or more of the following academic areas: (a) oral expression; (b) listening comprehension; (c) written expression; (d) basic reading skills; (e) reading comprehension; (f) mathematical calculation; and (g) mathematical reasoning.

2. The causes of learning disabilities are unknown; however, speculations include an injury to the brain or possible biochemical factors, such as a lack in amino acids, vitamin and mineral deficiencies, and allergies.

3. Children with learning disabilities are often misunderstood and are considered lazy, mentally deficient, or behavior problems. Learning disabilities, however, do not render children incapable of learning but require the teacher to develop alternative instructional methods based on their specific learning characteristics.

4. Teachers can enhance the learning process by structuring the environment to limit outside distractions and external stimuli.

5. Teachers should provide appropriate activities at the functioning social level of each student.

6. Appropriate behavior management techniques should be utilized to strengthen the occurrence of appropriate behavior.

7. Teachers should also be aware of any medications being used, their side effects, and any contraindicated activities.

8. Relaxation techniques can be incorporated into the physical education program to help reduce hyperactivity, control and tense muscles, and improve concentration.

9. Deficiencies can sometimes be overcome with practice. If not, the deficiency should be compensated for by appropriate teaching strategies at the child's tolerance level for learning and with the most effective learning modality.

10. Many of the characteristics of children with learning disabilities will affect physical and motor performance. Children with learning disabilities are often deficient in coordination, balance, body image, haptic awareness, and motor planning. The physical education program should be based on the unique learning characteristics of each individual.

11. Teachers can deal with hyperactivity by structuring the environment and emphasizing self-control activities.

12. Teachers may also be required to select meaningful teaching strategies to aid in enhancing auditory, visual, or haptic cues.

13. Attention disorders are prevalent in this population, so distractions during the learning process should be kept to a minimum.

14. Children with learning disabilities display as a wide range of behaviors. They may excel in one area but be unable to comprehend another. Therefore, behavior disparity is a classic example of the importance of the team concept in assessing level of functioning and developing effective learning strategies. Physical educators can provide a sound base for peer group acceptance and social interaction, as well as incorporate academic games and concepts into the physical education program to assist in the total education of children with learning disabilities.

REFERENCES

Alexander, J. L. (1990). Hyperactive children: Which sports have the right stuff? *The Physician and Sports Medicine, 18,* 105–108.

American Psychiatric Association. (2000). *Diagnostic and statistical manual of mental disorders* (4th ed.) (DSM-IV-TR). Washington, DC: Author.

Barkley, R., DuPaul, G., & McMurray, M. (1990). Comprehensive evaluation of attention deficit disorder with and without hyperactivity as defined by research criteria. *Journal of Clinical and Counseling Psychology, 58,* 775–789.

Bruininks, R. (1978). Motor proficiency of learning disabled and disabled students. *Perceptual and Motor Skills, 35,* 131–137.

Cunningham, C., & Siegal, C. (1987). Peer interactions of normal and attention deficit disordered boys during free play, cooperative task, and simulated classroom situations. *Journal of Abnormal Child Psychology, 15,* 247–268.

French, R., & Horvat, M. (1983). *Parachute movement activities.* Bryon, CA: Front Row Experience.

French, R., & Horvat, M. (1986). The acquisition of perceptual skills by motorically awkward children. *Motor Skill Theory into Practice, 8,* 27–38.

Hallahan, D. P., & Kauffman, J. M. (1997). *Exceptional children: Introduction to special education,* (7th ed.). Boston: Allyn and Bacon.

Harvey, W. J., & Reid, G. (1997). Motor performance of children with attention-deficit/hyperactivity disorder: A preliminary investigation. *Adapted Physical Activity Quarterly, 14,* 189–202.

Horvat, M. (1982). Effects of a home learning program on learning disabled children's balance. *Perceptual and Motor Skills, 55,* 1158.

Individuals with Disabilities Act of 1997, Pub. L. No 105-17. (1997, June 4).

Lazarus, J. L. (1994). Evidence of disinhibition in learning disabilities: The associated movement phenomenon. *Adapted Physical Activity Quarterly, 11,* 57–70.

Pellegrini, A. D., & Horvat, M. (1995). A developmental contextualist critique of attention deficit hyperactivity disorder. *Educational Researcher, 24,* 13–19.

Stanford, L., & Hynd, G. (1994). Congruence of behavioral symptomology in children with ADD/H, ADD/ND, and learning disabilities. *Journal of Learning Disabilities, 27,* 243–253.

Wharry, R.; Kirkpatrick, S. W., & Stokes, K. (1987). Motor training and precision performance with learning disabled children. *Perceptual and Motor Skills, 65,* 973.

Zentall, S. S., & Stormont-Spurgin, M. (1995). Educator preference of accommodations for students with attention deficit disorder. *Teacher Education and Special Education, 18,* 115–123.

CHAPTER 12

Behavior Disorders, Autism, and Head Injuries

M any times during the school years, children encounter problems making friends, interacting with others, and learning. Their lives often appear to be in constant conflict with parents, teachers, and the peer group. These children are labeled as *behavior problems* or *behavior disordered*. In addition, there are many children with developmental disorders, such as autism, mental retardation, sensory disorders, attention deficits, and acquired disabilities, that involve inappropriate behaviors.

All teachers have been faced with children whose behavior falls outside the acceptable realm. These problems can include refusal to conform to the code of classroom behavior, excesses (acting out, aggression), behavior deficits (withdrawal), attendance problems (absenteeism), difficulties in interpersonal relationships (socialization skills, communication), motivation problems, and attention or learning dysfunctions. The number of different ways in which behavior problems are manifested, and the differences in terminology, make it difficult to determine whether a specific disorder is the cause of problem behaviors or whether children are initiating problems.

Because there is no common cause for behavior disorders, it is difficult to define and categorize them. The medical profession will often seek organic or neurological causes for behavior disturbances, while sociologists delve into social and cultural factors that influence behavior. Any description of behavior disorders must be considered in the context of the individual's educational placement. Placement in regular classes that disrupts the group or that places undue pressure on teachers or children is indicative of the educational concept of behavior disorders. Those involved in the educational placement should consider several factors that influence the severity of problem behaviors, including (1) tolerance level of teachers or parents, (2) impact on physical and motor performance, (3) frequency or persistence of behaviors, (4) effect on class behaviors and (5) effect on learning.

In addition, a review of the *Diagnostic and Statistical Manual of Mental Disorders*, or *DSM–IV–TR* (American Psychiatric Association, [APA] 2000), documents childhood conduct disorders of varying severity as well as many associated features, such as poor frustration tolerance, irritability, temper outbursts, and recklessness. Children with conduct disorders generally have difficulty in learning and may also include a diagnosis of a learning or communication disorder (APA, 2000). Additional aspects of conduct can be noted in children with attention deficit disorder, neurological disorders, or learning difficulties. Obviously, the term *behavior* is not related to one child or group of children but the overt characteristics of that child that interfere with the learning process.

Children may also exhibit behavior disorders in one setting and not another, or a particular behavior may be acceptable in one and not another. Talking, for instance, is inappropriate in a reading group but perfectly acceptable in the gymnasium or on the playground.

The definition of behavioral disorders included in the Individuals with Disabilities Education Act (IDEA) is closely aligned to functioning in the school environment and relies on the judgment of the school officials for placement. In order to be considered behavior disordered, a child must manifest one or more of the following characteristics to a significant degree over a period of time:

1. an inability to learn that cannot be explained by intellectual, sensory, or health factors

2. an inability to build or maintain satisfactory interpersonal relationships with peers and teachers

3. inappropriate types of behavior or feelings under normal conditions

4. a general pervasive mood of unhappiness or depression

5. a tendency to develop physical symptoms or fears associated with personal or school problems

Taken in total, it is necessary to describe the problem behavior and, if possible the origins of the behavior that can be addressed in the teaching/learning environment.

A more functional method to describe behavior disorders includes dimensions of their behavior—rate, duration, intensity, and context or type. Children with behavior disorders will display inappropriate behavior an undesirable amount of time or at a high rate, *rate* referring to how often the behavior occurs. Although all children will at times be unhappy, cry, or have conflicts with others, the rate that these things occur is more indicative of deviant behavior than an occasional tantrum or scuffle. *Duration* refers to how long children display behaviors. Children with behavior problems may display tantrums or crying for an hour or more as opposed to those who momentarily lose their temper during an activity. In addition, the *intensity* of the behavior may be indicative of a behavior disorder. Children who cry softly may not be considered behavior disordered, whereas children who scream loudly and violently and harm anything around them most certainly will be. Finally, the *context* or *type* of behavior should be determined. Some behavior, such as yelling and running, would be appropriate in a free play setting but not in a classroom.

Etiology

Behavior disturbances can be caused by organic, functional, or heredity problems. Organic imbalances include nutritional deficiencies, glandular imbalances, disease, drug use, neurological dysfunctions, trauma, brain injury, and chemical imbalances. Functional disorders are related to real or imaginary experiences associated with peers, parents, teachers, or the environment, and in physical education, perhaps the activity. Hereditary influences are difficult to determine but may be associated with abnormal behavior patterns of the family.

The incidence of behavior disorders may be as high as 42% of all school-aged children and often will include short-term and long-term behavior disturbances.

Because the percentage of children actually receiving special education services is closer to 2%, many teachers, and especially physical education teachers, often have children with or without disabilities who display inappropriate behaviors in their classes. An important element in effective teaching is to recognize inappropriate behavior, determine the nature of the problem, and implement behavior change strategies when necessary.

Characteristics

Because of the variability of what constitutes a behavior disorder, any of the following characteristics may be seen in many activity settings. Not every disorder approximates the seriousness of psychoses, neuroses, and personality disorders, but all are commonly seen in the instructional setting. Behaviors that often occur among all children in activity settings may include the following:

1. hyperactivity and attention disorders—constant motion, easy distractibility, and short attention span

2. poor interpersonal relations and conduct disorders—socially detached and shy, unable to form relationships, prone to temper outbursts and aggression

3. anxiety and frustration—excessive anxiety and fear of certain activities, low frustration tolerance, withdrawal from activity

4. learning and perceptual disorders—difficulty processing and interpreting sensory stimuli, learning problems, motivational problems

5. aggressive behavior—physical or verbal aggression, temper tantrums

Autism and Pervasive Developmental Disorders

Pervasive development disorders (PDD) and *autistic spectrum disorders (ASD)* are synonymous terms that refer to a continuum of related cognitive and neurobehavioral disorders, which have at their core impairments in reciprocal social interactions, impairments in verbal and nonverbal communication, and restricted and/or repetitive patterns of behavior (APA, 2000). Although most children with these disorders have average to below average intellectual capacity, there is marked variability in the symptomatology across individuals; the level of intellectual functioning can range from low to superior on conventional IQ tests (Bryson, 1996). Although many terms have been used to refer to these disorders, the most prevalent terms used include *autism, autistic,* and *autistic spectrum disorders* and fall under the broader umbrella of PDD. The terms *autism, PDD/autism,* and *PDD* are used interchangeably in this chapter.

Characteristics of Children with PDD/Autism

Kanner (1943) first described the syndrome of autism among individuals who shared unique and previously unreported patterns of behavior revolving around social remoteness, obsessiveness, stereotype, and echolalia. After its initial description by Kanner, autism was poorly understood and was often described as a "childhood psychosis." Recently, the umbrella term *pervasive developmental disorders* has been used to describe the problem, and autism is clearly differentiated from childhood schizophrenia for the first time. Currently, *DSM–IV–TR* (2000) includes five possible diagnoses under the PDD umbrella, including autistic disorder, Rett disorder, childhood disintegrative disorder, Asperger's syndrome, and pervasive developmental disorder not otherwise specified (PDD-NOS; including atypical autism).

The complexity and wide variability of symptoms within the autistic spectrum point to a multifaceted etiology (Filipek et al., 1999), with an incidence rate of 10–20 cases per 10,000 children, or one in 500–1,000 people (Bryson, 1996; Gillberg, 1999). Asperger's syndrome appears to be more prevalent than autistic disorder, whereas disintegrative disorder is much rarer (Gillberg, 1999). The current belief is that autism is a neurologically based disorder due to some sort of brain damage, yet the exact problem within the central nervous system is currently unknown. Hence, children and adults who experience autism appear to have aspects of their brains and nervous systems that respond differently than those of developing peers. Autism and the other PDDs are not the result of poor parenting and often are diagnosed not by medical examinations, but by observations of behavioral characteristics of the disorder.

PDD/autism is present across the life span. Although some of those with PDD/autism develop typically for the first several years of life (especially those children with childhood disintegrative disorder), most show signs of PDD within the infant or toddler years, continuing into adulthood. Autism/PDD is not merely a developmental delay. Rather, it represents a difference in development across several areas of functioning and learning, including

1. differences in social interactions, whereby the individual often resists changes in routines, forms inappropriate attachments to objects, and fails to form friendships or emotional bonds with others

2. restricted, repetitive, and/or ritualistic patterns of behavior, interests, and activities

3. decreased and delayed development of motor skills

4. abnormal responses to sensations (e.g., withdrawing from sight, sound, or touch)

5. involvement in self-stimulatory behaviors, such as rocking, hand flapping, or finger flicking

6. inappropriate communication skills

Almost 50% of autistic children do not acquire speech, and those who are verbal tend to speak in echolalia. Individuals with PDD/autism have difficulty with abstract or figurative language, inappropriate prosody (speech rhythm), comprehension difficulties, and pronoun reversals.

A child with PDD/autism also has difficulty relating to his or her environment and social interactions. Children with communication difficulties experience problems in learning, relating to others, playing with others, and coping with the emotional demands of everyday life. It is often difficult for the child with PDD/autism to make connections between facts, thoughts, and feelings, which may hinder transferring learning from one situation to another.

Most children with PDD/autism also demonstrate deficiencies in sensory motor development and motor proficiency (Reid, Collier & Morin, 1983). This deficiency may be related to difficulties in consciously managing sensory input and motor output of information: functions that most children perform automatically or specific to cognitive limitations (Morin & Reid, 1985). Because of challenges to communication, relatedness, and sensory motor development, children with PDD/autism have difficulty in self-regulation and often develop a variety of coping strategies to function within the given environmental constraints. Unfortunately, many of their attempts are ineffective, inefficient, and/or a social liability.

Because the behavior of children with PDD/autism is tied directly to their reaction to sensory input, many educators and medical specialists in the field of PDD espouse a sensory theory of autism. The basic tenet of this theory is that individuals with PDD/autism may protect themselves from the pain of overstimulation by withdrawal. Examples of this type of behavior include resisting hugs or any type of close physical contact, closing one's eyes, covering one's ears, and walking on tiptoes (Gilligham, 1998). Noises that are only mildly offensive to others are violating for them. Children with PDD/autism may also purposely overload their sensory systems in order to shut them down by, for example, staring directly into a bright light, screaming loudly, biting, banging the head (Gillingham, 1998). According to this theory, differences observed along the PDD spectrum can be attributed directly to the level of sensory involvement, the number of sensory modalities involved, and the different environment to which individuals are exposed.

Head Injuries

In contrast to autism, head injuries are characterized by an insult to the brain from an external source. In children these occur mainly from falls (42%) and motor vehicle accidents (34%) that contribute to severe head injuries (Molnar & Perrin, 1992). The resultant complications may affect cognitive or physical functioning as well as social and emotional capabilities. Severe head trauma occurs in pediatric populations at a rate of 3 in 1,000. A loss of consciousness or coma is often used as an indicator of severe head trauma and is generally associated with a higher mortality rate (Caldwell, Todaro & Gates, 1991). Medical treatment for postcoma children necessitates interventions that address any physical, cognitive, or accompanying deficits that are present. Primary physical concerns should emphasize muscle imbalances and skeletal and postural deformities that limit the child's functional development and self-sufficiency. Initial interventions may be hospital specific but should generalize to community and home-based functions. Recovery is based on the extent of injury, quality of medical services, and therapeutic intervention.

The prognosis and capabilities of the individual's functioning will require extensive intervention as the child returns to school and home-based activities. Movement and exercise interventions should be specific movement sequences that lead to self-sufficiency. Acceptable levels of muscular strength and endurance are required to overcome postural deficiencies, while mastery of movement control systems are needed to manipulate objects as well as to develop movements required for ambulation. Because the attention span and motivation of the child with a head injury may be affected, specific behavior management procedures may also be required to promote exercise and movement behavior. Any insult to the development or functioning of the central nervous system affects physical functioning and cognition, as well as social or emotional behaviors.

Only a fraction of children who survive severe head trauma recover completely and may be totally dependent on medical and family intervention. For other children, adequate participation, self-sufficiency, and integration into community and school environments will require intervention from medical, community, and educational services (Caldwell et al., 1991). Attention span, self-control, motivation, and short-term memory may be affected and require intervention strategies that may include behavior management, memory compensation, and functional skill development, as well as social and community-based participation skills (Caldwell et al., 1991).

Impact on Functional Development

Damage to the central nervous system may also contribute to a variety of physical problems associated with behavior. Depending on the severity of central nervous system dysfunction, individuals may have partial or little control of their extremities, or even total paralysis. Movement-related disorders complicate the efficiency of movement as well as disrupt the development of functional movement and physical fitness. Inherent in disorders of this nature in children is the rapid development of the central nervous system, which accounts for the difficulty in diagnosing movement problems in pediatric populations. Several factors can contribute to developmental or acquired central nervous system damage, including birth disorders, trauma, infections, fevers, severe illness, brain tumors, head trauma, or injury. In addition, the severity of involvement can affect treatment plans and functional capabilities. For example, the following classifications can affect the availability of physical and motor functioning in children with head injuries.

Mild to Moderate Involvement

- Head control
- Independence in self-help skills
- Perceptual deficits
- Muscle imbalance
- Postural deformities
- Delayed movement and fitness responses to intervention
- Deficits in feedback mechanism

Severe to Profound Involvement

- Lack of head control
- Skeletal and postural deformities that limit movement
- Contractures and muscle imbalance
- Perceptual and sensory deficits in processing and feedback mechanisms
- Dependence on self-help skills
- Compromised movement potential and retention of functioning

Planning the Physical Activity Program

Once a child has been formally diagnosed with a behavior problem that affects learning, specific evaluations in the major areas of service should be performed. These include the following:

1. a speech-language-communication evaluation by the speech and language pathologist to determine the level of receptive language and communication, expressive language and communication, and voice and speech production

2. a cognitive evaluation by either a clinical psychologist or a developmental pediatrician to determine the level of intellectual functioning

3. a neuropsychological and adaptive behavioral evaluation by a clinical psychologist or diagnostician to determine capability for self-sufficiency in activities of daily living and to establish a baseline of function in learning, performance, and socialization

4. a sensorimotor assessment by the adapted physical educator and/or occupational and physical therapist to detect potential deficiencies in physical and motor functioning.

Evaluation of sensorimotor performance is particularly important in situations where there is a question of motor delay or motor dysfunction, as well as to document areas of strengths and weakness for prognostic and intervention planning. Gross and fine motor functioning may be assessed through a variety of standardized assessment instruments appropriate for the developmental level of the child. Also, nonstandardized, more qualitative criterion-based observations of praxis (planning and sequencing of novel motor patterns and organization of goal-directed actions within the environment) are critical, because these capabilities are often deficient in the child with PDD/autism or other behavior-related disorders (Filipek et al., 1999).

Intervention (Table 12.1) should be aimed at developing functional skills and independence and requires extensive collaboration from various disciplines to foster behavioral, cognitive, communication, perceptual, physical, and social capabilities (Phillips, 1994). For young children, control of the head and trunk should be established to initiate sitting and standing or functional ambulation. Because postural control includes balance and the ability to change positions, the versatility of movement may be limited. Balance and motor control must be achieved to facilitate movement. If accompanying control is affected by the competing actions of reciprocal muscle groups, mechanical efficiency is limited, and correct movement sequences are disrupted. Specific care is required to inhibit inappropriate reflexes that interfere with motor control and to avoid movements that may overstimulate the child. Specific interventions should attempt to establish appropriate developmental sequences and control of movements that can be planned, replicated, and initiated independently (Diller & Ben-Yishay, 1989). After initial control is established, the coordination of specific movement patterns can be addressed to facilitate movement.

Traditional exercise programs can improve functioning in children that is conducive to mobility, movement development, perceptual development, and fitness development and that will generalize to overall functioning in tasks that are needed in home-based play, school, and social settings. Treatment should be based on a three-

Table 12.1 Physical Activity for Children with Autism, Head Injuries, and Behavior Problems

Behavior	Characteristics	Teaching Strategies	Physical Activity
Learning and perceptual disorders (motor control)	• Failure to retain information • Difficulty processing sensory stimuli • Impaired memory functions	Determine level of functioning and most efficient modalities for learning. Enhance existing modality or compensate for a deficiency. Emphasize short- and long-term memory by structuring task, providing physical guidance, and prompting.	Good behavior game and social-sequence activities; praise for any accomplishment; program of aquatic fitness, motor skill development based on child needs and activities that can be sequenced.
Physical impairments	Muscle imbalances, skeletal and postural deformities	Develop strength to overcome postural deficiencies based on functional ability; develop movement control to manipulate objects and to develop ambulation.	Aquatics, progressive resistance exercises (surgical tubing and weights), flexibility, stationary cycling, walking.
Hyperactivity and attention disorders	• Distractibility • Overactivity • Restlessness • Short attention span	Structure environment; use behavior strategies to strengthen or weaken behaviors.	Variety of gross motor skills, parachute, aquatics, dance, movement exploration activities that utilize simple terms, demonstrations, and concrete examples. Provide specific fedcdback. Demonstrate skills in a variety of settings.
Poor interpersonal relations and conduct disorders	• Social detachment • Extreme sensitivity • Shyness • Inability to form close relationships	Foster teacher-child communication to strengthen, enhance, maintain, weaken, or eliminate certain behaviors. Provide clear directions and age-appropriate activities.	Social-sequence games and activities that require cooperation; movement education; activities that require two or more people; parachute activities; aquatics; physical fitness, including running and dance.
Anxiety reactions and frustrations	• Overanxiousness • Excessive fears • Impaired motivation	Structure environment and appropriate activities; foster teacher-child communication; use behavior strategies to emphasize behavior prompts.	Good-behavior game and social-sequence activities initially in a highly structured environment, and activities in which everyone is correct.
Aggressive behavior	• Physical or verbal aggression • Temper tantrums • Lying • Stealing	Structure environment; use behavior strategies to weaken or eliminate problem behaviors. Reinforce appropriate behavior; examine curriculum to ensure age-appropriate activities.	Structured program with vigorous activities (parachute, running, jumping); movement exploration and dance therapy, acting out specific situations; relaxation training and activities emphasizing how slowly activity can be accomplished.

tiered approach that moves from dependent function to supported and independent function (Caldwell et al., 1991). An interdisciplinary approach should stress intervention in behavior management, cognition, and motor control focusing on the functional deficits that are reflective of the individual's behavior and cognition, as well as any accompanying physical dysfunctions (Phillips, 1994; Jaffe et al., 1992).

Behavior Management

Behavior management strategies should focus on appropriate behaviors at the child's stage of development including appropriate social interaction with peers in structured play settings. Strategies should aim to reduce manifestations of aggressive or passive behavior and impulsive responses to stimulation. Some behavior patterns may result from structural or neurological deficit and will be resistant to change. Careful management strategies must be maintained to ensure compliance with appropriate behaviors, such as active modeling and applying systematic consequences to eliminate inappropriate behaviors and to initiate and facilitate new behaviors. Physical activity responses generally respond well to behavior interventions and generalize to appropriate social interactions, such as play and activities of daily living.

Motivation is also an essential element of behavior that is important to restoration of functional capabilities. Children should not feel frustrated in their attempts to complete tasks, and in the early stages of learning they should receive appropriate rewards for initiating or attempting the task. Later, the criterion for the specific task can be altered to require a finer approximation of the task. Motivation is also essential for the child to exert sufficient effort to facilitate improvement in development and should be encouraged to ensure compliance. Rewarding appropriate behaviors will aid in developing new tasks and help eliminate unwanted behaviors. Likewise, the parent or teacher needs to structure the setting and behavior management system to ensure compliance for the treatment. Many children have a short attention span that is not conducive to a large number of trials or repetition of movements. Movement can be initiated and reinforced to gradually extend the time or number of trials the child can perform. Further, the environment can be structured to eliminate potential distractions in the early stages of learning and gradually reintroduce the child to situations where they must deal with multiple stimulation distinctions and vary their responses.

Implementing the Physical Activity Program

Learning Disorders

Primary cognitive deficits may be problems that require compensation if the behavior or development occurs at an age where neural plasticity does not allow for other parts of the brain to assume functions. Memory deficits are common concerns that may be related to speed of processing or complexity of the task. Information that is missing or not recorded interferes with the acquisition and recall of important elements of the task. Generally, slowing the amount of information to be processed makes the skill easier to remember and perform.

Because children often lose a great deal of task-relevant information in processing information, it is important to cue relevant parts of the task that are essential to performance and rehearse the task in a variety of settings (Croce, Horvat, & Roswal,

1995). When the child learns a new task, it may be more beneficial to block practice trials so that the child can be reinforced immediately to establish an appropriate motor program of the desired response. Random trials can be applied later to ensure retention and adaptability to a variety of settings. Reid, Collier, and Cauchon (1991) also indicated that a carefully designed system of visual, verbal, and physical prompting (often termed the *extrastimulus prompt morel*) greatly enhances skill acquisition in children with autism. Fatigue also effects memory functions and will degrade performance. Learning may still be occurring, but motivation and reinforcement may be delayed because the effects of fatigue are deleterious to performance.

Another aspect of memory and behavior is attention to the relevant components of the task. Children are normally less attentive to task-relevant information and crowd the system with irrelevant components of the task, resulting in faulty memory. Some attention may result from neurological deficits, whereas others can occur from a behavioral or motivational focus (Figure 12.1). The cause of the attention deficit should be determined in order to select the most appropriate method to present information. For example, the learning setting may not be conducive for focusing attention, requiring the teacher to minimize distractions within the environment or consistently employ their teaching and reinforcement strategies. Later, the child can gradually adjust to the environment by learning to deal with distractions or stimulation within the environment. The parent or teacher should also carefully structure their intervention to present instructions in a manner that the learner can assimilate and can appropriately and consistently apply behavior management strategies at the correct time (Martin, 1988). The greater the child's ability to maintain, increase, and focus the attention, the more likely the child will be able to process the information presented and improve memory and subsequent cognitive functioning. Uomoto (1990) referred to two basic approaches for intervention. The first is a curriculum-based model to train areas that are impaired, for example, providing visual information to cue a movement. The other approach is a functional/goal-directed model that focuses on compensatory strategies to use with other intact modalities. The success of either strategy will encompass ongoing dialogue between the school, home, and community setting in order to provide as many opportunities as possible to facilitate learning.

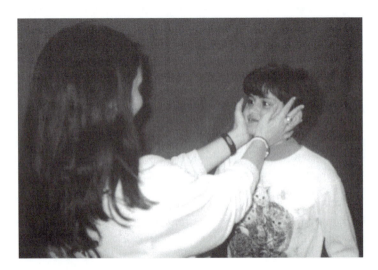

Figure 12.1 Establish eye contact to gain and maintain attention.

Perceptual Disorders

The basic conception that the child is "hard-wired" and will respond to maturational constructs will not always apply to children with behavior and cognitive difficulties. Whether the brain has not developed appropriately or has sustained an injury, there is a remarkable ability or potential in the brain for recovery that was not originally apparent. Instead of being fixed and rigid, the brain may respond to intervention by reorganizing its ability to process information. Cope (1990) implied that the rehabilitation process may facilitate reorganization and that recovery may depend on the amount of intervention. Reorganization may involve the development of new motor programs or schema that rely on a central mechanism and feedback to facilitate learning (Schmidt & Lee, 1999). This view would allow for retraining of previously learned skills or learning new skills that are developmentally appropriate. Tasks can be structured and reinforced at the child's level of functioning and gradually increased in complexity as the child develops cognitive and motivation skills.

Another approach to facilitate learning is the dynamical systems approach, in which control of coordinated movement deemphasizes the role of the brain and emphasizes the role of the environment and dynamic properties of the body and limbs (Magill, 2001). The coordinated structures of the muscles and joints will work in cooperative action to facilitate movement and will be developed through practice and experience. For children with autism or those with head injuries, the experience would be the rehabilitation process involving many disciplines. Muscles and joints can then act as a unit to achieve specific tasks, such as reaching for and grasping an object (Magill, 2001). Instead of a centrally stored mechanism that activates motor programs, commands are generated by a self-organized coordinative structure resulting from the child's intention to complete the action and environmental characteristics (Magill, 2001).

In contrast to closed-loop models of motor programming, commands are forwarded to the coordinative structures from the nervous system to initiate movement, not from a central mechanism but from internal and external sources. If available, feedback exists within components of the coordinative structures to compensate for nonfunctioning muscle units and does not need to be directed to a central mechanism.

One of the goals of intervention is to develop cognitive and motor functions through information processing. The child's brain is adaptable to learning new information, although learning strategies may be altered, requiring intervention, retraining, and behavior prompting. In some cases it may be neccessary to use information differently and to compensate to establish new behaviors (Cope, 1990).

As indicated earlier in the discussion on cognition, practice environments should be carefully structured to eliminate distractions and establish attention on the designated task. Physical guidance may be required to provide information relevant to positioning or feedback from the intended movement. As the child develops proficiency, augmented feedback concerning the consequences of a movement (KR) or the temporal, sequential, or force patterns of a movement (KP) can be utilized (Croce, Horvat & Roswal, 1995).

The goals of treatment and specific functional objectives should be consistent with those of other behavioral or neurological disorders. For some children, the ability to function in school, home, and community settings may depend more on cognitive and behavior deficits than on physical functioning (Cope, 1990). Long-term planning should rely on integrating children into similar peer group activities. Once the child enters school, services should clearly focus on transitional services for community and home-based environments. This may encompass the interdisciplinary team framework of school and community agencies, as well as home interventions involving parents or siblings. Lehr (1989) indicated that the effects of injury on higher problem solving and on behavior may not be apparent until the child reaches the period during which development normally occurs. These delayed effects should be addressed because medical treatment has probably ended. Teachers and parents need to be aware of emerging deficits as children progress through their developmental stages, because expectations will change as the child grows and matures (Martin, 1988).

Early movements should emphasize stability, positioning, and proprioceptive information in a relatively closed, consistent environment until the child can learn to deal with more open or changing situations that require versatility of practice, sufficient motivation, or reinforcement. Likewise, the control of movement may depend on persistent patterns of neuromuscular dysfunction, such as hemiparesis, bilateral spasticity, ataxia, or dystonia (Molnar & Perrin, 1992). Because the variability of functioning will be apparent, motor skill acquisition needs to be stimulated to develop functionally appropriate developmental skills required to explore the environment. If function or, more specifically, functional skills are the primary goals of intervention, priorities should be established in conjunction with academic goals and objectives. For example, in some children diminishing muscle tone may not prove to be functional in stabilizing a position that is essential to developing motor such skills as sitting at a computer and visually processing tasks from left to right. Initial activities can be selected that are functional for movement such as strengthening the trunk for independent posture and tracking an object such as a ball, which is consistent with classroom activities. Decision-making components can be prompted, guided, and overlearned, especially if the learning environments and behavior strategies are consistent. Walking, stair climbing, aquatics, and cycling are simple maneuvers that require little instruction and can be controlled by the learner and his or her rate of information processing. Children with lower levels of cognitive functioning and motivation can learn these tasks, which should then be generalized and prompted in home and community settings.

Long-term effects of cognition and learning should be viewed as essential. Early in development, physical or social limitations may preclude appropriate play interactions that contribute to exploring the environment and learning new tasks. The child, because of his or her limitations or lack of appropriate responses, may not establish the basis for cognition and social interactions. Play, solitary or with others, can provide the necessary stimulation to establish and reinforce ongoing development in home and community settings. Children learn through the medium of play to socially interact with others as well as developing stability, reaching/grasping movements, and cognitive tasks, such as sorting and stacking. If the opportunity to develop these skills is lacking or motor development is deficient, the child is more likely to demonstrate cognitive and social interaction deficits.

For children with autism, many of these skills are lacking and should be initiated as soon as possible. Ongoing stimulation from parents, peers, or others promotes the transition from school to home and community settings that are consistent with normal developmental principles. For some children, more active intervention by parents may be required to facilitate these sequences, especially in conjunction with the school intervention procedure. Further, tasks can be presented in a manner that is consistent and allows the child time to process information in a safe, secure environment that can be reinforced immediately. For school-aged children, the availability of services will vary according to states and school districts. Most schools and teachers probably will have minimal, if any, orientation to children with autism or head injuries. Because many children with mild dysfunctions will return to regular classroom settings (or, for more severely involved children, to special education classrooms), it is important to identify specific needs for successful school functioning. Although much of the school's function will focus on developing the child's cognition and behavior, it is vital to identify potential physical and motor needs that can aid in recovery and improve functioning (Fryer, 1989).

Activities that promote ambulation should be encouraged in schools, supplemented by community and home based programs that provide more opportunities for participation and aid in community integration. For example, a child who has overcome balance difficulties in school can progress to walking or riding bicycles with family or peers in community settings. Likewise, muscular strength and endurance can be developed in exercise programs, which enable the child to participate with peers in the neighborhood or community recreation settings. Further, processing and sequencing motor skills may generalize to activities of daily living (i.e., dressing) or may be used to promote the framework for developing cognition by encouraging attention and memory functions.

Older children should be encouraged to develop long-term regimens that foster mobility within the environment. Cardiovascular conditioning, muscular strength, and endurance will all contribute not only to overall physical functioning and fitness but also to the prerequisite skills for vocational training and to the physical skills needed in peer group interactions. It is apparent that most community-based and school-based programs are not sufficient to meet the diverse needs of children with head injuries, autism, or behavior difficulties. As a result, additional services (including those that address physical and motor functioning) are needed, in particular those that relate to transitional services, recreation, and vocational training (Mills, 1988). Long-term planning should address the physical and motor needs across the developmental life span and contribute to the total intervention program.

Hyperactivity and Attention Disorders

For children who have difficulty focusing on activities for a specific length of time, the first step is to structure the environment in an attempt to eliminate the cause of the problem. Minor distractions may cause the child to lose attention and focus on a different task. By structuring the environment and reducing external stimuli, the teacher can help the child focus on completing the task or on increasing their time on task. For many fitness and movement sequences, such as riding a bicycle, simple movements can be gradually extended. Moderate activity may also increase the attention and focus of children while they are performing motor and cognitive tasks (Croce & Horvat, 1995). Other strategies, such as token or point systems, prompts, and group consequences, can also be used to help children concentrate and focus on a task. Furthermore, teachers may use goal setting for individual children as a method to gradually build upon a task.

Teachers should avoid long strings of verbal instruction, because many children have problems remembering sequences of words. Activities should be selected that accommodate simple terms or demonstrations that make it easier for the child to maintain attention. Written direction or visual cues may also be more helpful. Children with autism/PDD are visual thinkers; that is, they tend to think in pictures and not language, so concrete visual concepts are essential. Gross motor skills, parachute activities, aquatics, dance, fitness, and relaxation activities can aid in maintaining attention and eliminating hyperactivity.

Poor Interpersonal Relationships and Conduct Disorders

Building interpersonal relationships is a goal of any activity setting and is evident in play activities in the preschool years. For children who shy away from an activity or from participating with others, teachers should establish specific causes for the problem. By structuring the environment and using social praise or point systems to involve the children gradually, the teacher usually can increase the probability of successful participation. Any activity that requires cooperation between two or more children can be used. For example, movement exploration activities can set the stage for social interaction by initially allowing children to perform in their own space and then gradually including others to complete a task. Likewise, parachute activities can be implemented to encourage movement initially at the child's pace and then be performed with others by having the children raise the parachute together or change places with other children. Play and recess activities also provide children the opportunity to participate alone or in small groups or games.

Many times, an unskilled child will shy away from activities until he or she can have some success. Fitness or movement activities can be provided initially until the child develops the necessary skill and confidence for group games. Some hyperactive children with autism are calmer if given a weighted vest to wear. For these children, the pressure from the vest aids in calming the nervous system. Other children respond to visual or tactile stimuli that aid in maintaining control. For the teacher, the key is to find the specific methods that open communication and responses within the child.

Anxiety and Frustration Reactions

Sometimes, children are anxious about school or physical education activities and exhibit excessive fears about the nature of the activity. These fears may be unfounded but are real for the child. A fear of water is very real and frightening until the child can have some positive experiences. Ideally, teachers can control their environments and eliminate any problems that can cause anxiety or frustration.

Activities that involve a minimal amount of competition and provide immediate success can be initially performed. For example, children who are anxious about swimming can gradually be encouraged into the pool by using a series of steps, starting with feet in the water, to being supported by teachers, and then to entering the pool by themselves. Likewise, children afraid of hard objects can participate successfully with soft Nerf balls and playground balls before proceeding to larger and harder balls. In addition, teachers can select activities at the appropriate social-sequence level of functioning (such as throwing the ball against a wall before throwing to a partner) to gradually involve participation and help overcome anxiety or fear of the activity.

If children do not have pleasant experiences in school, they may feel rejected or become frustrated, Likewise, if they have difficulty accomplishing a task they may become anxious or frustrated, especially if other children are successful. Children may also react suddenly to loud noises or sounds that are seemingly benign to others. Positive communication and interaction with children and eliminating the sounds can alleviate their concerns. In addition, we should provide opportunities for children to achieve successes, and we should reinforce their efforts.

Aggressive Behavior

Because aggressive behaviors may be harmful to other children, teachers should try to eliminate or weaken such behaviors as soon as possible. Punishment, contracting, and the Premack principle are behavior strategies that may eliminate inappropriate aggressive behavior. Teachers can also structure the environment to reduce stimuli or remove extraneous elements that may promote hostile behavior.

Consistent aggression may be an ongoing problem that requires communication, modeling, and contracting, whereas transient behavior problems can be overcome by structuring the environment, improving communication, and applying such techniques as modeling, contracting, punishment, prompting, and group consequences (see Chapter 22 on behavior management). Often, vigorous activities such as running or stationary cycling may be used at the beginning of class. In some instances, children can control their aggressiveness with physical activity.

Vigorous physical fitness, locomotor, and dance activities may be provided while the teacher or parents serve as active role models. In addition, other activities can be selected that emphasize control and incorporate relaxation training or visualization techniques. Dance activities may also be utilized for children to specific circumstances that may be troubling them or causing their problem behavior. Relaxation activities are especially beneficial in helping the child regain and practice self-control. They also are helpful for hyperactivity and attentional disorders.

CHAPTER SUMMARY

1. Behavior problems are difficult to define and characterize because there is no common cause for them. Any description of behavior disorders must be considered in context with the child's educational placement.

2. Children can be labeled behaviorally disordered in one setting yet not in another, depending on the teacher's tolerance, the frequency or persistence of the behavior, severity of the behavior, and effect on class performance.

3. The incidence of behavior disorders is as high as 42% and often includes short-term behavior disturbances. Only 2% of these children actually receive special education; therefore, many regular education teachers will have children who display inappropriate behaviors, such as anxiety, aggression, or acting out.

4. Autism represents a variation in development in social interactions, repetitive behaviors, delayed development, abnormal responses to sensations, self-stimulation, and inappropriate communication.

5. Some children with behavior problems may possess a high degree of physical and motor fitness; therefore, the teaching strategy may be more important than the activity.

6. Activities should be age appropriate, and vigorous activities can be provided with the teacher serving as an active role model. Activities should also be selected to emphasize control and to incorporate relaxation training methods. In this way, children can act out specific circumstances that may be the cause of their problem behavior.

7. Primary physical concerns in head injuries should emphasize postural deformities that limit functional development and self-sufficiency.

8. Movement and exercise interventions should be designed to improve self-sufficiency.

9. Behavior approaches should be implemented to facilitate appropriate social interactions, compliance, and motivation to complete a task.

10. Primary cognitive deficits may require compensation or feedback strategies to facilitate learning.

11. Reorganization of the neurological system may require building motor schema by prompting and guiding children through a task.

12. Intervention should incorporate a multidimensional team that calls on parents, peers, teachers, and clinicians to promote functional skills that can be used in school, community, and home environments.

REFERENCES

American Psychiatric Association. (2000). *Diagnostic and statistical manual of mental disorders* (4th ed.). (DSM–IV–TR). Washington, DC: Author.

Bryson, S. E. (1996). Epidemiology of autism. *Journal of Autism and Developmental Disorders, 26*(2), 165–167.

Caldwell, T. H., Todaro, A. W., & Gates, A. J. (1991). Special health care needs. In Bigge, J. L., (Ed.), *Teaching individuals with physical and multiple disabilities* (3rd ed.). Columbus, OH: Merrill.

Collier, D., & Reid, G. (1987). A comparison of two models designed to teach autistic children a motor task. *Adapted Physical Activity Quarterly, 4,* 226–236.

Cope, D. N. (1990). The rehabilitation of traumatic brain injury. In Kottke, F. J., & Lehmann, J. F. (Eds.), *Krusen's handbook of physical medicine and rehabilitation* (4th ed.) (pp. 1217–1251). Philadelphia: Saunders.

Croce, R., & Horvat, M. (1995). Exercise-induced activation and cognitive processing in individuals with mental retardation. In Vermeer, A. (Ed), *Medicine and sport science: Aspects of growth and development in mental retardation* 144–151. New York: Springer-Verla S.

Croce, R., Horvat, M., & Roswal, G. (1995). Coincident timing by nondisabled, mentally retarded, and traumatic brain-injured individuals under varying target exposure conditions. *Perceptual and Motor Skills, 80,* 487–496.

Diller, L., & Ben-Yishay, Y. (1989). Assessment in traumatic brain injury. In Bach-Y-Rita, P. (Ed.), *Traumatic brain injury* (pp. 161–174). New York: Demos Publications.

Filipek, P. A., Accardo, P. J., Baranek, G. T., et al. (1999). The screening and diagnosis of autistic spectrum disorders. *Journal of Autism and Developmental Disorders, 29*(6), 439–480.

Fryer, J. (1989). Adolescent community integration. In Bach-Y-Rita, P. (Ed.), *Traumatic brain injury.* (pp. 255–286). New York: Demos Publications.

Gillberg, C. (1999). Prevalence of disorders in the autism spectrum. *Infants and young children, 12*(2), 64–74.

Gillingham, G. (1998). *Autism: Handle with care* (3rd ed.). Edmonton, Alberta, Canada: Tacit Publishing.

Jaffe, K. M., Fay, G. C., Polissar, N., Martin, K. M., Shurtleff, H., Rivara, J., & Winn, H. R. (1992). Severity of pediatric traumatic brain injury and early neurobehavioral outcome: A cohort study. *Archives of Physical Medicine and Rehabilitation, 73,* 540–547.

Kanner, L. (1943). Autistic disturbances of affective contact. *Nervous Child, 2,* 217–250.

Lehr, E. (1989). Community integration after traumatic brain injury: Infants and children. In Bach-Y-Rita, P. (Ed.), *Traumatic brain injury* (pp. 233–254). New York: Demos Publications.

Magill, R. A. (2001). *Motor learning: Concepts and applications* (6th ed.). New York: McGraw-Hill.

Martin, D. A. (1988). Children and adolescents with traumatic brain injury: Impact on the family. *Journal of Learning Disabilities, 21,* 464–469.

Mills, V. M. (1988). Traumatic head injury. In O'Sullivan, S. B., & Schmitz, T. J. (Eds.), *Physical rehabilitation: Assessment and treatment* (2nd ed.) (pp. 495–513). Philadelphia: F. A. Davis.

Molnar, G. E., & Perrin, J. C. S. (1992). Head injury. In Molnar, G. E. *Pediatric Rehabilitation.* (2nd ed.) (pp. 254–292). Baltimore: Williams and Wilkins.

Morin, B., & Reid, G. (1985). A quantitative and qualitative assessment of autistic individuals on selected motor tasks. *Adapted Physical Activity Quarterly, 2,* 43–55.

Phillips, W. E. (1994). Brain tumors, traumatic head injuries, and near-drowning. In Campbell, S. (Ed.), *Physical therapy for children.* Philadelphia: Saunders.

Reid, G., Collier, D., & Cauchon, M. (1991). Skill acquisition by children with autism: Influence of prompts. *Adapted Physical Activity Quarterly, 8,* 357–666.

Reid, G., Collier, D., & Morin, B. (1983). Motor performance of outside individuals. In Eason, R. L., Smith, T. H., & Caron, F. (Eds.), *Adapted physical activity: From theory to application.* (pp. 201–218). Champaign, IL: Human Kinetics.

Schmidt, R. A., & Lee, T. D. (1999). *Motor control and learning: A behavioral emphasis* (3rd ed.). Champaign, IL: Human Kinetics.

Uomoto, J. M. (1990). Neuropsychological assessment and training in acute brain injury. In Kottke, F. J., & Lehmann, J. F. (Eds.), *Krusen's handbook of physical medicine and rehabilitation* (4th ed.). (pp. 1252–1272). Philadelphia: Saunders.

Section III

Teaching Individuals with Sensory Impairments

Section III focuses on children with auditory and visual exceptionalities. Children with sensory impairments may possess common characteristics that necessitate special considerations in order for them to participate in physical education.

This section is designed to

1. recognize the characteristics and physical/motor functioning of children with sensory impairments

2. provide instructional strategies that are beneficial in facilitating teaching

3. provide modifications, if necessary, for children with sensory impairments

4. provide examples of establishing communication to facilitate the instructional program

CHAPTER 13

Visual Impairments

In typical physical activity classes, most children rely primarily on vision to learn motor skills. They must be able to focus on different objects, such as balls and/or apparatus, determine the distance between near and far in changing situations, demonstrate eye-hand and eye-foot coordination, and discriminate between colors and background. In addition, children must remember what they see and be able to interpret visual sensations and react accordingly.

For children with visual impairments, proficiency in physical activity may depend on the amount of visual acuity they possess. Visual acuity is commonly measured with a Snellen test, which utilizes a chart of progressively smaller letters read at a distance of 20 feet. Normal, or 20/20, vision is the ability to read the selected criterion of symbols at a distance of 20 feet. As eyesight diminishes, the comparison with normal vision varies. For example, children with 20/100 vision will see at 20 feet what the normal eye can see at 100 feet. For children with visual impairment, the following classification system may be used for educational placement.

- *Legal blindness, 20/200.* The ability to see at 20 feet what the normal eye can see at 200 feet or a field of vision less than 20 degrees.

- *Travel vision, 5/200 to 10/200.* The ability to see at 5 to 10 feet what the normal eye can see at 200 feet, or enough sight to allow moving or walking without extreme difficulty.

- *Motion perception, 3/200 to 5/200.* The ability to see at 3 to 5 feet what the normal eye can see at 200 feet, or vision that can detect motion, but not a still object.

- *Light perception, less than 3/200.* The ability to distinguish a strong light at a distance of 3 feet that the normal eye can see at 200 feet, or to distinguish a bright light at 3 feet or less but no movement.

- *Total blindness.* The inability to recognize a strong light shone directly into the eye.

- *Tunnel vision.* A field of vision that is 20 degrees or less.

Besides the classification of vision, educational definitions based on the regulations of the Individuals with Disabilities Education Act (IDEA) define visual exceptionalities in the following manner: "Visually handicapped means a visual impairment which, even with correction, adversely affects a child's educational performance." The term includes both children who are partially seeing and children who are blind. The use of the terms *partially sighted* and *blind* is directly related to educational placement. For individuals who are legally blind, the visual acuity is 20/200 or less in the better eye after correction, or the field of vision is limited to an angle of 20 degrees or less out of the normal 180-degree field of vision. In this condition, vision is severely limited, with practically no peripheral vision even if the central vision is 20/200 or greater. With a severely restricted field of vision, physical activity and mobility may be limited.

Partially sighted children possess a visual acuity of at least 20/200 but not greater than 20/70 in the better eye after correction. This represents approximately 10–30% of normal vision and is sometimes referred to as functional blindness. In addition, most children who are blind have some residual vision that allows them to read large print and/or see some portion of a shape or implement.

Of specific interest for teachers is that in a survey of the activity limitations of visually impaired individuals, Kirchner (1985) indicated that 63% of these individuals have no major activity limitations, 20% have minor limitations depending on the nature of the activity, and only 17% have major restrictions on participation. Shepherd (1994) also indicated that the nature of the impairment and lack of residual vision is associated with developing motor skills as well as the incentive and ability to move proficiently.

Development and Structure of Vision

According to Holbrook (1996) one-tenth of 1% of all school-aged children are visually impaired, and approximately 85% of these children have some usable vision. The primary causes of visual impairment can be tracked to defects in development with the ocular mechanism, birth defects, disease, and injuries. Other causes cannot be traced and are classified as idiopathic. To understand the basic mechanism of vision, think of the eye as a camera that relays messages to the brain (Figure 13.1). Light

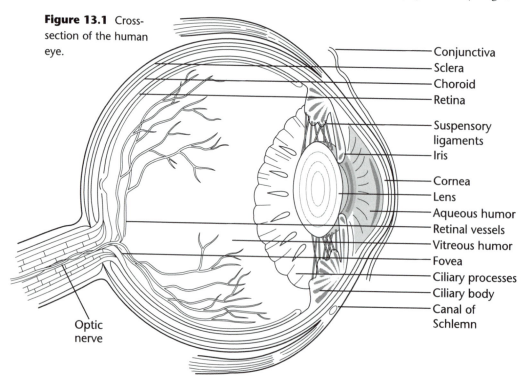

Figure 13.1 Cross-section of the human eye.

Conjunctiva
Sclera
Choroid
Retina
Suspensory ligaments
Iris
Cornea
Lens
Aqueous humor
Retinal vessels
Vitreous humor
Fovea
Ciliary processes
Ciliary body
Canal of Schlemn
Optic nerve

enters the eye through the "camera's" outer layer (cornea) and passes through the pupil. The eye is protected by the eyelids and bony socket of the skull, which is filled with fat to absorb shock and allow eye movement. Four rectus muscles allow motion of the eye upward, downward, inward, and outward, while the two oblique muscles add upward and downward movement.

The eyeball consists of three layers. The first layer consists of a protective covering made up of the cornea and sclera (white). As light enters, it passes through the middle layer (uvea), which is responsible for transporting blood to the (1) iris (which gives color to the eye), (2) ciliary body (which produces fluid for aqueous humor) and allows vision to be adjusted (accommodation), and (3) the choroid, or the blood supply for the retina.

As the iris opens and closes to regulate the amount of light admitted, light next passes through the lens, a transparent biconvex structure that focuses light rays on the back wall of the retina to bring objects into focus. The retina, which is the third layer of the eyeball, contains receptor cells (rods and cones), which collect color and light images to the rear of the eyeball, that becomes the optic nerve. The optic nerve then conveys visual impulses to the brain (occipital lobe), where the stimuli are processed and interpreted and which results in vision. Visual acuity is approximately 20/400 at birth, 20/50 by 1 year of age and 20/20 by the age of 4 (Blackman, 1997).

In addition to visual acuity, vision undergoes a developmental process that allows the child to use vision for reading as well as using visual information for learning. In the newborn, the muscles of the eye are weak, and vision is limited to focusing on near objects and responses to light. It could be said that we are born with sight but not vision. Vision will develop from several functions of the eye. For example, visual acuity is the ability to see objects clearly, as measured by performance on the Snellen test. In addition, the eyes must also demonstrate *visual fixation*, that is, the ability to gaze directly at an object; and *pursuant fixation*, by which they follow a moving object. Fixation of an object is pursuit at zero velocity, with the pursuit system correcting for small drifts off target. These movements are slower than the fast saccadic movements, (involuntary, abrupt, small movements, such as those made when the eye changes their point of fixation). The slower eye movements go by a variety of names but are most commonly called smooth pursuit or tracking movement. The brain must allow the ability to process information and slowly track the object.

After fixation, the eye can then learn to focus. *Accommodation* is the ability to adjust the focus of the eyes to changing distances and is usually learned one side at a time. Commonly we use accommodation in sports as we track an object and in the classroom as we shift attention from the blackboard to the desk by bringing near objects into focus. *Binocular fusion* occurs at approximately 4 to 6 months as the two optic nerves at the back of the eye receive information from each eye and form a unified image. If the eyes are not aligned, the brain may suppress vision in one eye to avoid double vision. This results in poorer visual acuity, as occurs in amblyopia.

As the ability to use images emerges, the eyes, in order to examine close objects, must then turn together to keep images on each eye focused on the fovea of the retina. This is known as *convergence*. Likewise, *stereopsis* is a function of binocular fusion that allows us to judge distances between two or more objects. The brain recognizes that objects at various distances have images in the two retinas that do not fall at exactly corresponding locations (i.e., the image has disparity), and the brain adjusts *accordingly. Visual perception* or visual motor skills coordinate both eyes and the action stimulated by the eyes. The child must receive, organize, and interpret visual images that can be used in the learning process and stored in memory functions for later use.

Identifying Visual Problems

Most school districts require a preliminary visual screening that may detect some visual problems. Teachers have a greater opportunity to observe daily progress and may refer students for further screening or more appropriate educational placement if they suspect a visual impairment. In order to screen children, teachers should be aware of the symptoms of potential eye disorders, such as an inability of the eyes to work together (i.e., impaired eye coordination). Improper eye coordination may result from a lack of adequate development for vision or lack of control of the eye muscles. In addition, injury, disease, or trauma can affect the coordination of the eyes. Symptoms such as double vision, headaches, fatigue, dizziness, reading difficulties, inattention, clumsiness, poor reading, or avoiding tasks that require close work all may be symptomatic of poor eye coordination (Table 13.1).

Table 13.1 Symptoms of Vision Disorders

Physical Appearance	Motor Behavior	Complaints
Styes	Walks tentatively	Dizziness
Variation in pupil size	Excessive blinking	Headaches
Eyes in constant motion	Trips or stumbles frequently	Eye pain
Crossed eyes	Is sensitive to light	Blurred objects or symbols
Bloodshot eyes	Frowns or closes eyes to see objects	Double vision
Crusted eyelids	Has poor color discrimination and problems seeing objects from the side or background	Burning or itching
Holds objects up close or far away	Squints	Headaches

The common visual abnormalities that may result in a deviation from this normal visual process include the following:

- *myopia*: nearsightedness, or the ability to see well up close; results when the eyeball is too long from front to back and light rays consequently fall in front of the retina

- *hyperopia*: farsightedness, or the ability to see well far away; results when the eyeball is too short from front to back and light rays consequently fall in back of the retina

- *astigmatism*: distorted, blurred vision due to an irregularity of the lens or corneal surface, which results in light rays not being focused sharply on the retina

- *cataracts*: clouding or opaque condition occurring on the lens, resulting in blurred vision

- *retinitis pigmentosa*: progressive retinal rod detachment, beginning with night blindness and producing a gradual loss of the field of vision

- *amblyopia*: deviation or wandering of the eye, in which the "lazy eye" does not focus on the same object as the nonaffected eye
- *albinism*: hereditary condition in which there is a lack of pigment in the choroid and irises, which is manifested in sensitivity to light and refractive errors
- *strabismus*: crossing of the eyes caused by shortened or imbalanced internal rotators, or outward separation caused by shortened or imbalanced external rotators
- *nystagmus*: involuntary condition in which the eyeball moves side to side, up and down, or in a rotary motion as though the ocular muscles were twitching
- *heterophoria*: condition in which the muscles of the eye do not function in a coordinated manner; affects the use of binocular vision
- *glaucoma*: increase in pressure of the fluid inside the eye, which causes the eyeball to expand, resulting in gradual or sudden loss of vision beginning with decreasing peripheral vision
- *retrolental fibroplasia*: visual abnormality resulting from pure oxygen given to premature babies, in which scar tissue forms behind the lens
- *conjunctivitis*: inflammatory disease that involves infection of the conjunctiva.
- *keratitis*: inflammatory disease affecting the cornea
- *accidents*: trauma to the eyes resulting in puncture, retinal detachment, or lens dislocation

Planning the Physical Activity Program

Because vision is critical for motor development and physical functioning, a clear understanding of children's functioning is useful before planning and implementing the program. The following issues should be considered when planning the physical activity program for the children with visual impairments.

Movement Skills

Fraiberg presents the most compelling evidence for movement difficulties in children with visual impairments (Adelson & Fraiberg, 1974; Fraiberg, 1977). Based on this work, we can see that children display inadequate movements during the developmental years. Movements are forced, repetitive, and stereotypical. Children are passive and not active in seeking information and responding to interactions in the environment. Fraiberg (1977) indicated that children display developmental arrests or roadblocks to developing movement sequences. Sighted children will reach, grasp, and manipulate objects that they see and are active information seekers. Children with visual impairments are more passive and constrained unless they adapt to their environments. Hatton, Bailey, Burchinal, and Ferrell (1997) indicated that some movement difficulties may be due to fear of movement, spatial disorientation, or parental overprotection.

Children with visual problems also demonstrate problems in extending basic reaching and grasping as a precursor to moving in the environment. Visual objects generally provide the lure to initiate movement in young children, whereas children with visual impairments must rely on sound to obtain directional and spatial information.

Figure 13.2 Teacher correcting form on throwing pattern of an individual with a visual impairment.

This results in delays of self-initiated movements, such as rolling. Rettig's (1994) observations of interactions among children with visual impairments reveal that these children are lacking in play skills and spend most of their time playing alone unlike sighted children: 56% of blind children played alone, whereas sighted children spent only 14% of their time playing alone.

Physical Fitness

Fitness is generally lower in individuals who are visually impaired. Any physical activity program should have as its aim the total development of children to encourage an active and productive lifestyle. Compared to their sighted peers, children are low in cardiovascular endurance, although performance on muscular strength and endurance tasks such as pull-ups, squat thrusts, flexed arm hangs, and standing high jumps is comparable to that of sighted children (Buell, 1983; Hopkins, Gaeta, Thomas & Hill, 1987). Most children with visual impairment will not meet age-expected norms for peers with normal vision in running and throwing events if they are limited in the opportunity to practice and develop these activities. There is no specific reason to believe that sensory impairment leads to lower physical functioning. In a study by Kobberling, Jankowski, and Leger (1991), comparisons of habitual physical activity and aerobic capacity between sighted adolescents and individuals who were blind indicated that the maximal oxygen consumption was higher among sighted subjects. The authors subsequently recommended that all adolescents, both the sighted and the blind, require a minimum of 30 minutes of daily activity to attain and maintain their age-predicated aerobic capacity. Shindo et al. (1987) reported that low physical work capacity in boys and young males with visual impairments is due to a lack of physical

(c)

activity and that mild training accentuates physical functioning and cardiovascular fitness. Blessing, McCrimmon, Stovall, and Williford (1993) also reported significant increases in cardiovascular fitness and decreases in body composition after training in children with visual impairments, while Ponchillia, Powell, Felski, and Nicklawski (1992) reported improved fitness in women who were blind after engaging in aerobic activities.

The overall lack of fitness seems to be related primarily to lack of physical activity and understanding of the capabilities of individuals with visual impairments. Skaggs and Hopper (1996) challenged teachers to provide opportunities to promote active lifestyle for children with visual impairments and indicated that specific strategies for improving motor skills are lacking. Sudgen and Keogh (1990) indicated that experience in physical activity among visually impaired children is limited by rhythmical stereotypes, such as body rocking and hand slapping, which are socially inappropriate and limit the opportunities for useful and functional movement experiences. Because many skills require externally paced movements, low scores among visually impaired children may not be so much an indication of physical capability as of the lack of opportunity to compensate for their inexperience.

Fundamental Movement Skills

The success of children with visual impairments in sport and games also depends on developing a sound movement base and providing opportunities to practice and refine skills (Richardson & Mastro, 1987). Because of the lack of visual feedback, self-corrections in form or movement patterns may not be as efficient as in sighted classmates. Children with visual impairments generally have more difficulty with postural control and greater instability after 10–12 years of age (Portfors-Yeomans & Riach, 1995). Ribadi, Rider, and Toole (1987) also recommended balance training in developing adaptations to the nonverbal environment. Nor is there any appropriate social interaction or response from sighted classmates. To compensate for the lack of vision, specific cues and prompts can be used by the teacher to augment feedback for the following locomotor movement skills (Figure 13.2):

1. *Walking-running.* Stress proper placement of form, emphasizing leg and arm movements, development of efficient patterns, sound perception, and changes of speed and direction.

2. *Jumping-hopping.* Stress movements of legs and arms to emphasize proper form and efficient patterns, determining when to jump, sound perception, anticipation, and form preparatory to landing.

3. *Galloping-skipping.* Stress movements to coordinate legs, proper form, and integration of both sides of the body.

4. *Throwing/striking.* Stress movements of arms and legs to develop efficient patterns, direction, gauging speeds, and accuracy.

5. *Catching.* Stress proper position of arms and hands in efficient patterns anticipating ball, with sound perception and gauging speed.

6. *Kicking.* Stress foot placement and follow-through to develop efficient patterns, direction, gauging speeds, and accuracy.

Orientation and Mobility

For successful integration, children will require the ability to move about the environment safely and will require familiarity with their surroundings. They will need to commit a new environment to memory in order to determine positions and relationships to other persons or objects in the environment. Initially, these children have difficulty moving or traveling in the environment. This may be an extension of their early movement difficulties. Sudgen & Keogh (1990) indicated that individuals who are blind solve problems as they occur rather than preparing for what is happening. In contrast, sighted children recognize an object visually, whereas children with visual impairments recognize an object by touch. Orientation must prepare the individuals to understand

1. common objects in the environment (e.g., mailbox, tree)

2. fixed objects, such as stairs or pools

3. movable or moving objects, such as a ball or rope

4. positions of objects in space

5. nature of the terrain, such as hilly or straight

6. directions and paths of stationary or moving objects, as well as sound localization (Hapeman, 1967)

Teachers should also strive to provide an awareness of the correct position or feel of an activity. By utilizing any remaining functional or residual vision, children can be taught to orient themselves to the instructional environment and make changes accordingly to enhance their movement efficiency. The following guidelines (Blasch, Wiener & Welsh, 1997) have been used to orient children to inside and outside activity settings:

1. Utilize shape changes in playground settings as well as changes in texture (grass, sand, asphalt) to foster independent movements.

2. Emphasize the use of sound, such as (a) voice clusters (swings, merry-go-round); (b) radio in a window; (c) sound echoes from buildings (although not all students are capable of using this effectively); (d) sound echoes from walls in a gymnasium (echoes may aid totally blind children through recognition of a "closed-in feeling").

3. Take advantage of small sound sources that can be made by local Bell Telephone Pioneer Clubs and implanted into Nerf or foam balls or attached to goals or targets. Portable goal locaters are also available from commercial sources.

4. Utilize the sun early or late in the day for orientation, although children seldom use it during activity.

5. Use high contrast in colors for court markings; use cloth or nylon strip to lay out different courts instead of many lines. Make sure there is a contrast between uniforms and court or field.

6. Utilize different aspects of lighting to include

   a. vision adaptation from daylight to indoor

   b. vision adaptation from day, to dusk, to dark

   c. adequate lighting indoors

   d. curtains to shield sun

   e. reduced light for electronic games

   f. black light for electronic games

   g. sun glare (avoid running into sun, if possible)

   h. brightness (shadow adaptation)

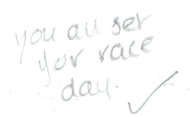

7. Utilize the following for additional sources of orientation or guidance:

   a. natural cues in the court or competition area—net, goals, goalball court

   b. various sounds, such as beepers, crickets, calling (with paper tubes), bells, radios, tape players (for dance and gymnastics), speakers (at roller rinks), walkie-talkies, remote control transmitters, voice commands

   c. guide ropes for high jumping, safety ropes to locate targets, guide rails for bowling or to designate swimming or running lanes, or linking runners hand to hand or hand to upper arm

   d. boundary marking, alternate textures outdoors (sand and grass, dirt and grass, tall grass and short grass) and indoors (carpets, rubber mats, nylon or cloth, straps)

   e. foot placement guides, as in archery, shot, or discus; or arm placement guides, as in archery.

Modifying Activities and Equipment

For most activities, instruction and equipment need not be modified or adapted in order for children with visual impairments to participate with their sighted peers. The use of residual vision, tactile, kinesthetic awareness, and auditory awareness is generally sufficient to provide minor modifications that aid in the learning process and participation. The following sections, however, describe some examples of minor modifications that may be needed in the initial stages of learning.

Physical Fitness

In cardiovascular endurance events, children may require a sighted guide to lightly touch the arm, grasp the arm, or maintain contact with a short cord (Sanka & Bina, 1978). Walking programs have proven beneficial to developing fitness (Weitzman, 1985). Harry Cordellos, one of the world's best blind athletes, utilizes a variety of positions to negotiate difficult terrains, such as hands on the sighted runner's hip, touch, and verbal commands to complete long-distance training. Because one technique may not be viable for all situations, all variations of residual vision, or all terrains, it is necessary to use the method that is most efficient and comfortable for runners. Generally, shorter races can be managed with a short cord tied to the sighted runner's belt. Specific lanes that are marked with the use of a guide wire or rope can be beneficial for sports. If physical guidance is not needed, verbal directions and safety hints can be provided for endurance races (Buell, 1983).

Cycling to develop strength and endurance can be performed with a stationary cycle, a tandem bicycle ridden with a sighted individual, or riding with a sighted partner. Skiing is accomplished with sighted partner, who gives verbal instructions concerning directions, changes in terrain, or the approach of other skiers.

Swimming is an excellent physical activity to develop cardiovascular fitness that requires few, if any, modifications. Depths are marked by raised letters on the side and deck of the pool, and swimming lanes can be separated with ropes and buoys to designate lanes, depths, and swimming areas. Auditory prompts, such as a metronome, can signal a swimmer's approach to the wall or can alert individuals to begin their turns. Diving boards usually contain a nonslip rough surface and hand rails that can provide tactile information for the diver. Finally, the use of residual vision will enable children to develop a mental plan of the swimming environment, enhancing their ability to locate ladders and ramps to enter and exit the pool.

Games and Sports

Most children enjoy playing games, especially if those games provide additional opportunities to develop gross motor and physical fitness skills. For children with visual impairments, balls that are bright orange or yellow can be helpful and can encourage additional usage of residual vision. Guide wires, cut base paths, or sighted partners can help children determine the correct direction to run or move in games (Figure 13.3). For some children a batting tee can be used; in kickball, a stationary kick can initiate action. In dodgeball, players can also use sighted children to avoid a thrown ball.

To play volleyball and basketball requires assistance from teammates and acute concentration on the sound of the ball. Training in auditory perception for responding to and differentiating between sounds allows children to move in the direction of

Figure 13.3 Technique used for running.

the ball or pass to the vocal cue of teammates. Many teachers will also use sound in the ball, or behind a goal, in soccer or basketball activities to provide continuous auditory cues.

Other Activities

Most children with visual impairments can participate in gymnastics, weight training, movement education, and hiking with minor modifications that help initiate the activity. In addition, sports such as wrestling, judo, and self-defense have been used with no modification in instruction or technique other than touching at the beginning and during the match (Mastro, 1985; Mastro, Montelione, and Hall, 1986). Other examples of activities that are suitable for children with visual impairments include throwing and jumping events in track and field that incorporate a minimum of verbal directions and positioning; bowling with a guide rail; archery with an audible goal locator; and relaxation and yoga activities (Krebs, 1979). Chin (1988) has used dance to initiate movements and develop spatial awareness in elementary school children with visual impairments. In addition, parachute activities that incorporate contact grasping of the parachute, and movement exploration and body image activities that incorporate verbal explanations can all provide movement cues and aid in positioning.

Competition for the Visually Impaired

Athletes are currently competing in events sponsored by the United States Association for Blind Athletes (USABA) organized in 1976. Opportunities are also available in track and field, swimming, wrestling, goalball, gymnastics, and downhill and cross-country skiing, according to the individual's functional classification (Table 13.2).

Table 13.2 Sports Classification for Individuals with Visual Impairments

Classification	Functional Ability
B_1	Ranging from no light perception in either eye to light perception, and inability to recognize objects directionally and at any distance
B_2	Ability to recognize objects or contours up to a visual acuity of 2/60 and/or limitation of field of vision to 5 degrees
B_3	2/60 to 6/60 vision and/or field of vision between 5 and 20 degrees

While many athletes are participating in the USABA, others are also competing, often with sighted peers, in clubs, schools, and universities. It is especially important for teachers to determine which opportunities may be available for children and direct them to the most suitable avenue for participation. As with sighted individuals, competition and sports may not be feasible. However, the opportunity to participate should be made available to everyone. In addition to events sponsored by the USABA, numerous opportunities may be available for children at every level of competition. One must only consider the many accomplishments by athletes with visual impairments to realize that individuals should be considered for competition strictly on their ability to participate in athletics. Some examples of athletes who are capable of outstanding performances include the following.

- In the 1984 International Games for the Disabled, Dr. Jim Mastro won a gold medal in wrestling and in shot put, and a silver in the discus. He is also an avid goalball player and former president of the American Beep Baseball Association, and he participated in the 2000 Paralympics.
- In 1981, five blind climbers were members of the Pelion Expedition, which climbed the 14,410-foot peak of Mount Rainier.
- Harry Cordellos has run over 70 marathons, many under 3 hours, and completed the Hawaiian Iron Man Triathlon in 16 hours (swimming 2.4 miles, tandem biking for 112 miles, and running a marathon).

Implementing the Physical Activity Program

Children with visual impairments will possess a wide variation in visual functioning and residual vision. Teachers should consider the loss of vision and other prominent characteristics of children (Table 13.3) when implementing the physical education program. In order to integrate children into physical education classes properly, teachers should consider incorporating the instructional strategies described in the following sections into the physical education program.

Cognition

The cognitive ability of children with visual impairments will vary as much as it does among their sighted classmates. A visual impairment does not imply a lack of mental capacity. However, it is essential to realize that abstracts are sometimes difficult for children to grasp because of the lack of visual cues. Children will adapt more easily to their surroundings if they are aware of the specifications of their environment or memorize dimensions of a facility.

Because there is no loss of mental functioning, teachers should not lower their expectations for children with visual impairments. By reinforcing their cognitive strengths and providing activity interventions at an early age, children should be able to participate in a comprehensive physical education program of physical fitness, dance, aquatics, sports, and games. Teachers should emphasize parts of the task before completing the entire task, and they should pair auditory and tactile/kinesthetic training to emphasize abstract concepts.

Haptic Perception

Because the primary sensory apparatus of vision may be restricted at varying degrees of functional ability, teachers should utilize other sensory apparatus to compensate for the lack of vision in learning a skill. For example, all movements contain tactile sensations, muscular and proprioceptive sensations, and a kinesthetic sense of the activity. When planning and implementing the instructional program for children with visual impairments, teachers should incorporate of an alternative modality to allow for compensation and, in turn, for learning to occur.

Children may observe a motor pattern or skill by placing their fingers on the performer's body during the activity. Likewise, dolls or mannequins can be used to demonstrate roles, stunts, and activities that may be difficult for children to compre-

Table 13.3 Physical Activity Suggestions for Children with Visual Impairments

Behavior	Characteristics	Instructional Strategies	Physical Education Considerations
Cognition	Intelligence varies as much as with sighted peers. Adaptation by memorizing. Difficulty with abstracts.	Do not lower expectations because of visual deficiency. Reinforce strengths in memory to increase mobility, and to learn rules and strategies. Utilize visual efficiency training.	Appropriate physical education activities emphasizing whole-part-whole method of instruction, and auditory and haptic senses; opportunities to pair auditory and haptic senses.
Sensory awareness	Wide variety of useful vision. Proprioceptive awareness frequently poor. Lack of sensory lures to initiate movement.	Compensate for loss of vision by utilizing other senses. Use auditory, tactile, and kinesthetic training and residual vision.	Orientation and mobility training to learn the environment; activities using bright colors and contrast, whistles, other sounds; body image with mannequins and/or models.
Growth and maturation	Physical development often delayed because of inadequate movement opportunities. Poor physical fitness. Fatigues easily. Tendency toward obesity.	Provide opportunities and practice in variety of settings; physical education class should be based on individual needs; supplement movement activities and fitness activities at home in weekly program.	Activities that emphasize spatial orientation, body image, balance, coordination. Basic motor skills that deal with locomotor and fitness activities, including swimming, cycling, and jogging.
Body image	Problems identifying body parts on self and others. Difficulty understanding the relationships and uses of body parts.	Assess functioning related to the ability of individuals.	Activities that enhance body parts, such as throwing, kicking, gymnastics, tumbling, and trampoline activities; static and dynamic balances.
Spontaneous play	Spontaneous play limited; difficulty with creative movement and social development. Anxiety initiating movements.	Provide numerous social opportunities for interaction in a variety of settings.	Social-sequence activities, parachute, dance, rhythms, movement exploration.
Emotional expression	Shows little facial expression. Often unresponsive to needs of others and to nonverbal cues, gestures, facial expressions.	Provide opportunities for a variety of emotions and settings; make individual aware of different facial expressions.	Movement games; creative dramatics that utilize different emotions, facial expressions, and nonverbal reactions, such as shrugging shoulders; movement exploration.
Self-confidence	Lacks self-confidence; professes more vision than actually has. Sensitive about modifications. Wants to be as normal as possible.	Determine and emphasize strengths in programming; compensate for limitations.	Program based on the physical motor and social functioning of the individual; many opportunities to interact with peers; communication to compensate for deficiencies.

Table 13.3 Physical Activity Suggestions for Children with Visual Impairments *(continued)*

Behavior	Characteristics	Instructional Strategies	Physical Education Considerations
Blindisms	Rocking back and forth; rubbing fingers into eyes, waving fingers in front of face; bending head forward; whirling around.	Encourage appropriate movements to replace blindisms; provide opportunities for movement; reinforce appropriate movement activity.	A menu of activities based on functioning that include fitness, motor development, dance, and aquatics.
Posture	Rigidity; forward bending and swaying.	Increase muscle tone and stretch tight muscles; actually inspect for appropriate postural cues; verbally reinforce correct posture.	Relaxation activities; yoga in static and dynamic position; postural exercises to develop inefficient areas and stretch tight muscles.

hend by touching only the performer. In addition, teachers may manipulate children to give them kinesthetic awareness of the activity. Ross, Lottes and Glenn (1998) used a five-phase approach to teaching golf: (1) a hands-on approach to putting, using sounds as cues; (2) swinging a weighted swing trainer; (3) practice with balls of various sizes; (4) community-based instruction; (5) participating in a school tournament. Teachers can also use tactile awareness or encourage explanation of the space or boundaries in which children are participating. During the initial stages of learning, it may be beneficial for teachers to allow children to touch them while the skill is being demonstrated. By breaking a skill into small components in a whole-part-whole method of teaching, smaller segments of the activity can be paired with a tactile cue. Buell (1983) described a method of teaching a complex skill (jumping rope) by having children stand behind the teacher with their hands on the teacher's hips. The teacher and child initially would jump together without the rope; later teachers would turn the rope; and finally the child jumped and turned the rope. To ensure successful learning, teachers should actively encourage movement that involves various concepts of up and down, space, and the environment, as well as activities that provide children an opportunity to organize and move within their environment.

Auditory Perception

Besides haptic perception, many teaching cues and/or instructions can use a verbal explanation to help teach a specific activity. Because it is difficult to imitate something that cannot be seen, teachers should use concrete examples in their instructional methodology instead of concepts or abstracts. By pairing verbal instructions with haptic cues, teachers can augment the child's understanding of activities, which will in turn promote skill acquisition and understanding. Teachers may also wish to determine the location of sounds in a gymnasium or playground. A continuous sound is more appropriate than intermittent sounds. The source of the sound should be in front of children as they are moving toward it, or immediately behind children so they can move away from the sound (Mastro, 1985). Likewise, it is important for children to recognize a wide variety of sounds. For example, picking out a teammate's voice may indicate the direction to throw or pass a ball, while tracking a sound aids in determining the direction of the oncoming ball. Distinguishing one sound from a background of sounds can help the child concentrate or judge the position of a target, as in archery, basketball, or bowling. Finally, auditory cues can be used to signal a boundary area, as when the child approaches the wall in a swimming pool, or to discriminate between rhythms, tempos, and fast and slow movements used in dance and sports skills.

Growth and Maturation

Children with visual impairments may be delayed in their physical development, may be overweight, and may fatigue easily because of the overprotective nature of those around them. As a result, these children may have restricted movement and fewer play opportunities as well as a lack of motivation. Because these children may not have adequate opportunities to move and to learn physical and motor skills, their physical development should be encouraged.

Teachers should provide opportunities, instruction, and practice in a variety of gross motor and physical fitness skills and should cultivate a positive attitude toward activity that is based on the child's interest. Additional opportunities can be provided with after-school homework and sports activities.

Body Image

Because of the lack of visual cues, children often encounter problems identifying body parts and understanding the uses of the body in relationship to its parts. By assessing the functional and developmental level of vision, teachers can emphasize appropriate body image activities that use various parts of the body and movements to stimulate development. For example, balancing on the left foot, or throwing with the right hand, can provide practice in identifying specific body parts and their movements.

Poor posture and balance may also result from a lack of visual feedback. Without visual cues, children are often rigid or may exhibit a forward bend and sway. When provided cues on correct positions and reinforcement of appropriate postures, children can become more aware of changes in their body positions. Activities such as relaxation training, yoga, and postural exercises designed to stretch tight muscles and/or increase muscle tone can be implemented to aid in overcoming posture problems. More important, proper balance and posture are required to initiate and control movement.

Sensory Awareness

Children with visual impairments also display poor proprioceptive awareness of their bodies. To compensate for their lack of visual information, other sensory modalities, as well as residual vision, should be used to develop body awareness and changes in position. Activities with bright colors and sounds may provide contrasts needed to maneuver in their environment and can enhance teaching strategies. In addition, orientation and mobility training can help develop appropriate landmarks necessary to provide ongoing information and cues within the environment.

Spontaneous Play

Most sighted children will initiate self-play and develop smoothly through their social-sequence level of development (Rettig, 1994). In contrast, children with visual impairments may not initiate purposeful play and thus may encounter difficulty with creative movement and social development. When given opportunities to play alone and with groups in activities that require sharing and taking turns, children with visual impairments can experience appropriate play and development of social interaction (Swallow & Huebner, 1987). Play and movement awareness may be the crucial components to stimulating activity and spatial awareness in children with visual impairments. Several activities, such as the parachute, movement exploration, and rhythmic movements, are excellent for encouraging social interaction and development.

Emotional Expression

Without visual feedback, children with visual impairments often will demonstrate little facial expression and will be unresponsive to others because they do not see gestures, nonverbal cues, or others' facial expressions. Teachers should promote an awareness of facial expressions and emotions by allowing children to experience nonverbal actions, such as shrugging shoulders, smiling, frowning, and movement exploration activities.

Self-Confidence

All children should be allowed normal risk-taking experiences. Children with a visual impairment are often sensitive about activity modifications but may lack self-confidence if they are restricted in their opportunities for participation. In order to build their self-confidence and help them develop a positive attitude, teachers should develop the strengths of these children and should compensate for their limitations with sensory training. Success in physical fitness, games, sports, and leisure activities will aid in physical and motor development as well as promote interaction and communication with peers that may lead to increased self-confidence and development of an appropriate social atmosphere.

Blindisms

To compensate for a lack of vision, many children will develop inappropriate movements (blindisms), such as rocking, rubbing fingers into eyes, waving fingers in front of the face, and whirling around. Much of the movement is inappropriate and often used to compensate for the lack of visual cues. Teachers should provide opportunities to replace these blindisms with more appropriate movements. The physical activity program consisting of physical fitness, dance, aquatics, and gross motor activities will allow children the opportunity for movement stimulation of the hands and bodies in an appropriate manner.

CHAPTER SUMMARY

1. In a typical physical education class, children rely primarily on vision to learn motor skills.

2. Children with visual impairments are individuals whose disability, even with correction, adversely affects their educational performance and ability to learn motor skills.

3. Instruction and teaching cues should be directed toward the haptic and auditory modalities of children to compensate for lack of vision.

4. Successful integration for some children with visual impairments depends on their ability to move efficiently and safely within the environment.

5. Orientation and mobility training may be helpful in acclimating children to outdoor and indoor settings.

6. Most activities, instruction, and equipment require few modifications for visually impaired students to participate successfully with sighted peers.

7. Athletes with visual impairments compete in events such as goalball, swimming, track and field, and downhill and cross-country skiing sponsored by the United States Association for Blind Athletes (USABA).

8. Children with visual impairments vary widely in visual functioning and residual vision. When selecting activities, the teacher should be aware of the child's cognition, sensory awareness, growth and maturation, body image, play level, emotional expression, self-confidence, blindisms, and posture.

References

Adelson, E., & Fraiberg, S. (1974). Gross motor development in infants blind from birth. *Child Development, 45,* 114–126.

Blackman, J. A. (1997). *Medical aspects of developmental disabilities in children birth to three.* Gaithersburg, MD: Aspen Publications.

Blasch, B., Weiner, W., & Welsh, R. (1997). *Foundations of orientation and mobility* (2nd ed.). American Foundation for the Blind.

Blessing, D. L., McCrimmon, D., Stovall, J., & Williford, H. N. (1993). The effects of regular exercise programs for visually impaired and sighted schoolchildren. *Journal of Visual Impairment and Blindness, 87,* 50–51.

Buell, C. (1983). *Physical education for blind children.* (2nd ed.). Springfield, IL: Charles C. Thomas.

Chin, D. L. (1988). Dance movement instruction: Effects on spatial awareness in visually impaired elementary students. *Journal of Visual Impairment and Blindness, 81,* 188–192.

Fraiberg, S. (1977). *Insights from the blind: Comparative studies of blind and sighted.* New York: Basic Books.

Hapeman, L. B. (1967). Developmental concepts of blind children between the ages of three and six as they relate to orientation and mobility. *The International Journal for the Education of the Blind, 27,* 41–48.

Hatton, D., Bailey, D., Burchinal, M., & Ferrell, K. (1997). Developmental growth curves of preschool children with visual impairments. *Child Development, 68,* 788–806.

Holbrook, M. C. (1996). *Children with visual impairments: A parents guide.* Bethesda, MD: Woodine House.

Hopkins, W. G., Gaeta, H., Thomas, A. C., & Hill, P. (1987). Physical fitness of blind and sighted children. *European Journal of Applied Physiology, 56,* 69–73.

Individuals with Disabilities Act of 1997, Pub. L. No 105–117. (1997, June 4).

Kirchner, C. (1985). *Data on blindness and visual impairments in the United States*. New York: American Foundation for the Blind.

Kobberling, G., Jankowski, L. W., & Leger, L. (1991). The relationship between aerobic capacity and physical activity in blind and sighted adolescents. *Journal of Visual Impairments and Blindness, 6*, 58–67.

Krebs, P. (1979). Hatha yoga for visually impaired students. *Journal of Visual Impairment and Blindness, 73*, 209–216.

Mastro, J. V. (1985). Diamonds of the visually impaired athlete. *Palaestra, 1*, 43–46.

Mastro, J. V., Montelione, T. J., & Hall, M. M. (1986). Wrestling a viable sport for the visually impaired. *Journal of Physical Education, Recreation and Dance, 11*, 61–64.

Ponchillia, S. V., Powell, L. L., Felski, K. A., & Nicklawski, M. T. (1992). The effectiveness of aerobic exercise intervention for totally blind women. *Journal of Visual Impairment and Blindness, 86*, 174–177.

Portfors-Yeomans, C., & Riach, C. L. (1995). Frequency characteristics of postural control of children with and without visual impairment. *Developmental Medicine and Child Neurology, 37*, 456–463.

Rettig, M. (1994). The play of young children with visual impairments: Characteristics and interventions. *Journal of Visual Impairment and Blindness, 88*, 410–420.

Ribadi, H., Rider, R. A., & Toole, T. (1987). A comparison of static and dynamic balance in congenitally blind, sighted and sighted blind folded adolescents. *Adapted Physical Activity Quarterly, 4*, 220–225.

Richardson, M. J., & Mastro, J. V. (1987). So I can't see . . . I can play and I can learn. *Palaestra, 3*, 23–26.

Ross, D. B., Lottes, C. R., & Glenn, B. (1998). An adaptive physical education program teaching golf to students with visual impairment. *Journal of Visual Impairment and Blindness, 92*, 684–687.

Sanka, J. V., & Bina, M. J. (1978). Coming out ahead in the long run. *Journal of Physical Education and Recreation, 49*, 24–25.

Shepherd, R. J. (1994). Physiological aspects of physical activity for children with disabilities. *Physical Education Review, 7*(1), 33–44.

Shindo, M., Kumagau, S., & Tanaka, H. (1987). Physical work capacity and effort of endurance training in visually handicapped boys and young adult males. *European Journal of Applied Physiology, 56*, 501–507.

Skaggs, S., & Hopper, C. (1996). Individuals with visual impairments: A review of psychomotor behavior. *Adapted Physical Activity Quarterly, 13*, 16–26.

Sudgen, D. A., & Keogh, J. F. (1990). *Problems in movement skill development*. Columbia, SC: University of South Carolina Press.

Swallow, R., & Huebner, K. (1987). *How to thrive, not just strive*. New York: American Foundation for the Blind.

Titlow, L. W., & Ishee, J. H. (1986). Cardiorespiratory testing of persons who are visually impaired. *Journal of Visual Impairment and Blindness, 80*, 726–728.

Weitzman, D. M. (1985). An aerobic walking program to physical fitness in older blind adults. *Journal of Visual Impairment and Blindness, 79*, 97–99.

Winnick, J. (1985). The performance of visually impaired youngsters in physical education activities: Implications for mainstreaming. *Adapted Physical Activity Quarterly, 2*, 292–299.

Winnick, J., & Short, F. X. (1987). *Physical fitness testing of the disabled: Project Unique*. Champaign, IL: Human Kinetics.

CHAPTER 14

Hearing Impairments

C hildren with hearing loss may be categorized as either *deaf* or *hearing impaired*. Deaf children possess varying degrees of residual hearing and encounter problems receiving auditory stimuli and understanding speech even with the aid of amplification. The more informal term hard of hearing refers to varying degrees of hearing loss. Individuals who are *hard of hearing* are able to understand speech and respond to auditory stimuli, usually with the assistance of a hearing aid. In this context, many individuals favor the terms *deaf* and *hard of hearing* to describe hearing losses.

However, the federal government defines hearing losses, both *deafness* and *hearing impairments*, in the Individuals with Disabilities Education Act (IDEA) rules and regulations. *Deafness* means "a hearing impairment that is so severe that the child is impaired in processing linguistic information through hearing with or without amplification, that adversely affects a child's educational performance." *Hearing impairment* means "an impairment in hearing, whether permanent or fluctuating, that adversely affects a child's educational performance, but that is not included under the definition of *deafness*."

Any child with a hearing loss is unable to hear the quality of a sound, either partially or totally. The term *hearing impaired* was previously used to identify children who are hard of hearing and is currently still identified in the 1997 revision of IDEA. In either case, it is essential not to group everyone with a hearing loss together because they vary in residual hearing and language development, which are essential for inclusion in regular education classes.

Sound waves are produced by the alternate compression and refining of particles of matter to make up a cycle that occurs per second and is measured in a unit to designate cycles per second, or hertz (Hz). The human ear is sensitive to frequencies between 20 Hz and 20,000 Hz. When the frequency of a vibration changes, we perceive a change in pitch; the higher the frequency, the higher the pitch. Although individuals are sensitive to a wide range of pitches, the range between 500 and 2,000 Hz is of primary importance because the energy of speech sounds is concentrated in this region. The intensity of sound is measured in units called decibels (db). An increase or decrease in the loudness or softness is an increase in intensity of sound.

The normally functioning ear will accept sound waves and transform them into neural impulses that are decoded in the temporal lobes of the brain. A breakdown in hearing may occur in one or more of the transmission processes. Hearing losses may occur from a restriction in the range of frequencies received by the ear, the intensity of the perceived sound, or both. Of critical importance to the educational placement are three factors that impact on the child's functional ability: (1) the site of the impairment, (2) age of onset, and (3) the extent of the hearing loss.

Site of The Impairment

The three types of hearing losses are conductive, sensorineural, and mixed. A conductive loss results from interference of sound impulses from the outer or middle ear to the inner ear (Figure 14.1). A dysfunction of the outer ear can prevent the transmission of sound impulses. The outer ear consists of the external ear (pinna) and the external acoustic meatus (auditory canal), a canal approximately one inch in length that extends from the external ear and ends at the eardrum (tympanic membrane). This is the separation point of the outer and middle ear.

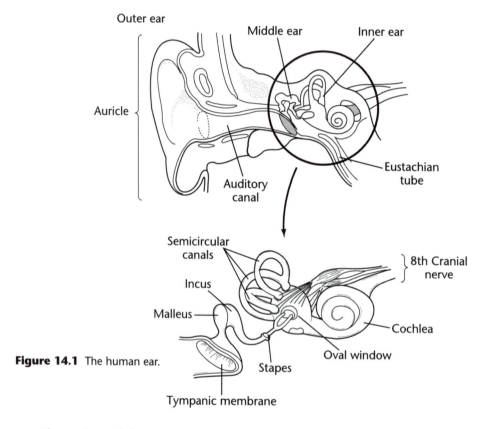

Figure 14.1 The human ear.

Obstructions of the outer ear include accumulation of wax, foreign particles, or inflammation, which may cause problems with conducting or transmitting sound vibrations and which may result in temporary losses of hearing. These conditions are generally corrected by medication and/or drainage and do not usually require placement in special education, although even temporary losses of hearing can hinder the child's ability to follow directions.

The middle ear is a cavity approximately one to two cubic centimeters in volume that is connected to the nasopharynx by the eustachian tube. A dysfunction of the eustachian tube will affect hearing as well as result in enlarged adenoids, allergic congestion, and colds. Most middle-ear infections begin in the eustachian tube, resulting in unequal pressure on either side of the tympanic membrane that interferes with the vibration of sound waves and results in a conductive hearing loss. The middle ear contains three bones (incus, malleus, and stapes) that connect the tympanic membrane to the entrance of the inner ear (oval window). The bones transmit sound waves across the ossicular chain, with the last bone (stapes) being implanted in the oval window.

The most common conductive hearing loss in the middle ear is otitis media, or an inflammation of the middle ear. Chronic inflammations result in adhesions between the tympanic membrane and ossicular chain that may restrict the mobility of the ossicular chain and inhibit normal transmission of sound impulses. Another conductive hearing disorder that is bone conducted instead of air conducted may occur when new bony growths surround the capsule in the middle ear and affect sound conduction. In most cases, this condition can be corrected surgically, whereas inflammation of the middle ear is treated by medication. If the condition remains chronic, the use of amplification and speech training allows children to remain in regular classes. However, teachers should be concerned that losses of 15 db can affect educational performance.

In the inner ear, the sound waves that have been transmitted are converted into neural impulses transported by the vestibular nerve and cochlear nerve and taken by the eighth cranial nerve to the temporal lobe of the brain for interpretation. Hearing losses in the inner ear are referred to as sensorineural. A large majority of children who possess sensorineural hearing losses have an impairment of the sensitive mechanisms of the inner ear or eighth cranial nerve. Unlike conductive hearing impairments, a sensorineural loss is resistant to amplification and generally cannot be corrected by surgery or medication. If a hearing loss results from an impairment of the neural mechanism, children may demonstrate a loss in the intensity of the sound, the sound may be distorted, or the sound may not reach the temporal lobe of the brain, a condition referred to as central deafness. Finally, hearing losses that occur in the outer, middle, and inner ear constitute mixed hearing losses and are part conductive and part neural. These hearing losses may involve variable amounts of residual hearing and range from difficulty understanding words to the inability to understand any speech sounds or language.

Age of Onset

The age at which a hearing impairment occurs is vitally important in establishing communication. Approximately 94% of all hearing losses occur before age 3 (Gallaudet Research Institute, 1991). Hearing losses that occur after children have acquired language (postlingual losses) have less severe implications for education than losses that occur before language had been acquired (prelingual losses). Because language development occurs in the first 5 years, children are at a severe disadvantage in responding to auditory stimuli if a problem occurs during this time. A postlingual loss may not interfere with educational development but may manifest itself in social and emotional frustrations because children miss portions of conversations or may not understand the actions of others, such as laughing at a humorous situation. Children may be deficient in motor functioning because they may not understand the rules and strategies of a particular game or sports activity.

Extent of Hearing Loss

Hearing losses can range in severity from slight to profound. Children with a 30 db loss are usually fitted with a hearing aid. Included in Table 14.1 are the general classifications of hearing loss (Hardman, Drew & Egan, 1999; Kannapell. 1984).

Table 14.1 Extent of Hearing Losses

Hearing Loss	Functioning and Educational Limitations
Slight, 0–25 db	Difficulty with faint or distant sounds but no significant difficulty with normal speech.
Mild, 25–40 db	Ability to interpret speech from a distance of 3–5 feet from the speaker, but approximately 50% of instruction may be distorted if the individual is not in the line of vision or distant from the speaker.
	Minor vocabulary and speech problems.
Moderate, 40–60 db	Faint conversations are misunderstood or distorted.
	Difficulty with group discussions and loud speech.
	Defective speech or tonal quality, receptive language problems.
Severe, 60–80 db	Limited vocabulary.
	Problems discriminating vowels and consonants; understanding speech.
	Defective speech that deteriorates or does not develop spontaneously if occurring before 1 year of age.
Profound, 80 db or more	May decipher loud noises and vibrations.
	Visual and haptic perception are methods for receiving communication; cannot understand amplified speech.
	Speech and language will be resistant to spontaneous development and deteriorate if loss is prelingual.

Etiology of Hearing Impairments

Of the 15 million reported individuals with hearing impairments in the United States, approximately 3–5% are school-aged. Most children with hearing impairments are educated in regular classrooms, with approximately 1 in 25 requiring extensive special education services. Among those individuals with hearing impairments, approximately 40% are classified as mild, 20% as moderate, 20% as severe, and 20% as profound (Kannapell, 1984; Gallaudet Research Institute, 1991). Although only a small number of children will require special services, it should be noted that even slight hearing losses place the child at a disadvantage and affect incidental learning (Craft, 1995). The causes of hearing impairments can often be determined from genetic or environmental factors. In the following list hearing impairments are grouped by etiology.

1. The *hereditary,* or *endogenous, group* includes all deafness related to genetic causes. More than 50 genetic syndromes are associated with hearing impairments, and approximately 50% of all profound hearing losses are genetically based. Deafness can be inherited as a dominant (14%), recessive (84%), or sex-linked (2%) disorder, whereas other hearing losses can be part of syndromes that produce other abnormalities (e.g., Treacher Collins syndrome).

2. The *prenatal group* includes those hearing impairments caused by prenatal infections or trauma. Rubella, or German measles, may affect the developing fetus by causing hearing loss or other disabilities. Other prenatal infections include mumps, influenza, and toxemias. Prolonged labor, premature birth, difficult or injurious deliveries, or breathing failures (apnea) can also cause hearing losses.

3. The *postnatal*, or *exogenous, group* includes all deafness that is a result of postnatal illness or injury, such as viral infections (mumps, measles, or meningitis), chronic inflammation of the middle ear (otitis media), or, less often, trauma, accidents, and high fevers.

4. Acoustical trauma or exposure to high-decibel noise over an extended period of time can cause serious hearing impairment. Acquired hearing loss is usually gradual, subtle, and cumulative. Exposure to the length and intensity of the sound can affect the sensory hair cells in the inner ear (Figure 14.2).

5. The remaining instances of hearing impairment are of *undetermined etiology.* No specific environmental or genetic cause can be blamed for the hearing impairment. Approximately 30% of all hearing impairments cannot be traced to a specific cause.

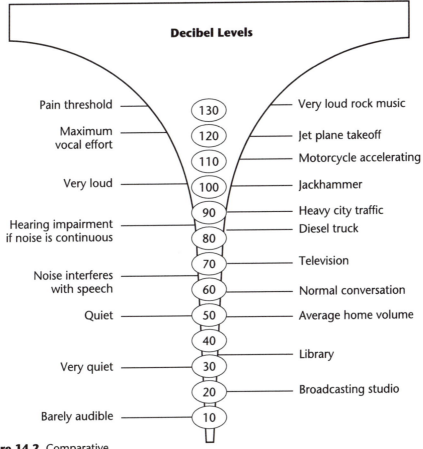

Decibel Levels

Pain threshold	130	Very loud rock music
Maximum vocal effort	120	Jet plane takeoff
	110	Motorcycle accelerating
Very loud	100	Jackhammer
	90	Heavy city traffic
Hearing impairment if noise is continuous	80	Diesel truck
	70	Television
Noise interferes with speech	60	Normal conversation
Quiet	50	Average home volume
	40	
Very quiet	30	Library
	20	Broadcasting studio
Barely audible	10	

Figure 14.2 Comparative decibel levels.

About 15–18 million individuals have hearing losses, of which 3 million individuals are school-aged; 5% of all school-aged children have a hearing loss, with fewer than 19% of these children requiring special education services.

Planning the Physical Activity Program

The development of communication is essential for integration into regular classes as well as for communicating in the deaf community (Stewart, 1987). Although many professionals may disagree on the methods for improving communication, several methods are viable for physical education teachers. These include signing, amplification, and auditory training.

Signing in Physical Education

Because communication is vital, sign language and fingerspelling are necessary instruction tools for physical education instruction. Eichstaedt and Lavay (1992) suggest that regular classroom teachers who deal with children with hearing impairments should be trained in signing and/or fingerspelling. Because signing is desirable, a workable composite of approximately 50 signs used commonly in physical education and athletics will assist the instructor of children who are hearing impaired (Figure 14.3).

Physical educators frequently use a single word or phrase to explain, encourage, correct, or control learning situations. Familiar expressions include: "Jump over, run to your left, come to me," "Good girl! Try again," "Crawl under. No, watch me," "Stop! Begin again," and "Sit down, stand up, run to boys." Such commonly used activity words are converted easily to signs, can be learned readily, and should become workable tools for every physical educator.

In many typical physical education situations, the child with a hearing impairment should be placed directly in front of the instructor so that directions and commands will be understood. Many children with hearing impairments can read lips, if the instructor is not too far away. When explaining new concepts, rules, stratagems, or skills, the instructor should use simple terms and avoid unusual or complex idiomatic statements. Children with hearing impairments will be unable to lip-read at far distances, such as from across the swimming pool or from the other end of the basketball floor. In such instances, the teacher may use signs and gestures that are consistent for all children.

The basic English alphabet can be learned in a short time. It is easier to fingerspell than to read fingerspelling. The dominant hand, held at shoulder level with palm out, spells the letters. Spelling slowly increases accuracy and eliminates confusion. If a letter is lost when the person is receiving the message, continue interpretation; the remaining letters may suggest the total word. Figure 14.3 shows the alphabet finger positions both as the receiver and the sender view them.

Most signs are for concept only—the idea, not the word, is stressed. The concept of *good* is signed in the following way: The left hand is open, palm up before the chest. The right hand, also open, touches the lips. The right hand is brought down so the back rests on the left palm (Figure 14.3).

Signing often requires shortening extraneous words or deleting word endings. "Go out to left field" is simply "Go"; the sender then points to left field. Common

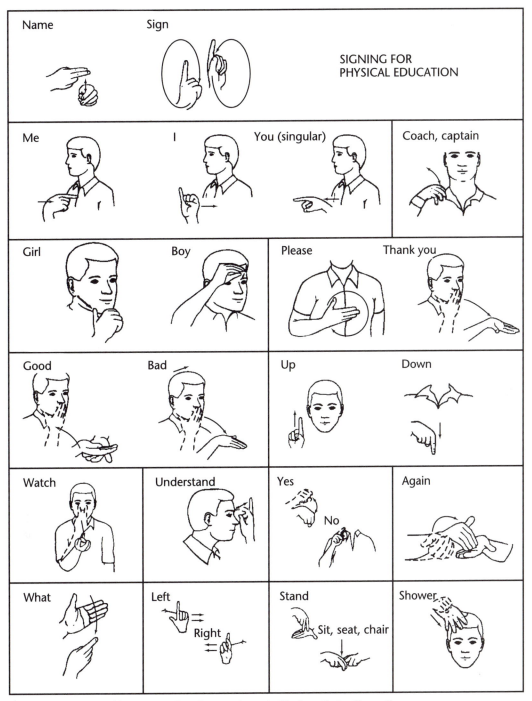

Figure 14.3 A working composite of approximately 50 signs that will greatly assist the instructor of children with hearing impairment.

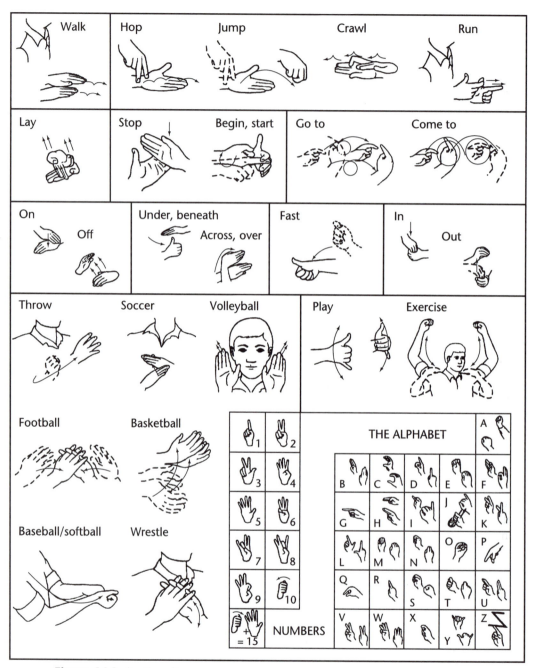

Figure 14.3 (continued)

everyday gestures, such as pointing, motioning, demonstrating, and signaling, are acceptable because most children with hearing impairments are familiar with them (Moores, 1987).

Many of our students use formal signing and fingerspelling, as set forth in a computer program titled Sign Finder produced by Pro-Ed Publications (1997) and the book *Functional Signs* by Bornstein and Jordan (1984).

Also, when initially meeting a child, ask "Can you read my lips?" If the child says yes, continue the conversation in a normal voice; without shouting. Speak distinctly, but do not overenunciate your words; face the person, and do not turn your head while speaking. Also, try not cover your mouth or speak with something in your mouth. People with a mustache are also more difficult to understand because visual input may be distorted. If you do not understand what a person who is hearing impaired is trying to say, ask them to repeat the statements. Pretending to understand when you do not only leads to confusion and frustration. If either party still does not understand, use a paper and pencil to converse. Also, it is apparent that beyond a 90 db hearing loss, vision becomes the primary modality for communication. Without the proper visual input, children are placed a disadvantage in social or learning settings that require communication (Nowell & Marshak, 1994).

Amplification and Auditory Training

Deafness does not always refer to a total lack of hearing. As previously indicated, hearing loss can vary in severity, and almost all children who are considered deaf have some residual hearing, especially those who have conductive disorders in the external or middle ear. Many children are also able to benefit from amplification, although it should be remembered that a hearing aid is not a panacea, and attempts to utilize residual hearing may be difficult. However, if amplification and auditory training enable children to learn a cognitive task, understand the strategies of a game, or interact socially, the use of such methods is more than justified.

Hearing aids are used to provide sound amplification within the residual hearing capacity of students. Ideally, the sound is magnified and can be distinguished from background noises or sounds. Amplification may enable the sound to become louder but does not necessarily mean the sound will be clearer. If the background sounds are confusing, children may not be able to discriminate or identify appropriate sounds in a noisy environment. The closer children are to the sound source, the more effective they will be in identifying sounds, although those with severe and profound losses must generally be within several feet to benefit from amplification.

Hearing aids are strapped to the body or behind the ear and can be worn on one ear (monaurally) or both (binaurally). For maximum effectiveness, children should wear the hearing aid throughout the day to effectively develop residual hearing. In this manner, children may learn to decipher and discriminate a variety of sounds necessary for communication. However, aids may be removed for physical reasons, such as earache, swimming, some contact sports, and excessive noise. At times, feedback in the amplified sound from the hearing aid is picked up by the aid microphone and goes through the system, creating a high-pitched sound that is extremely annoying. This generally occurs if the ear molds are not fitted properly and usually necessitates a new mold. It also occurs in closed in areas, such as a racquetball court.

The type of aid that is worn on the body consists of a small pocket unit containing a microphone, amplifier, volume control, and battery. The unit is connected to the ear by a cord, at the end of which is a loudspeaker. The body type contains all the basic components in a single unit set in an ear mold or eyeglass.

The hearing aid should be used in physical education, except during swimming or some contact sports, depending on the comfort level of the child. In addition, teachers should consider the following precautions in physical education for children with hearing aids:

1. Hearing aids should be securely fastened by means of a harness or tape.
2. Physical education teachers should have additional batteries if replacements are needed.
3. Clothing that causes annoying sounds to the wearer and distorts auditory discrimination and figure-ground should be avoided.
4. Perspiration should be wiped off the aid periodically.

Auditory training is another method to improve the use of residual hearing. Although the primary importance of auditory training may be for the classroom, physical education teachers must emphasize auditory training to aid in improving listening ability and communication. Awareness of a sound to start a race, signal a foul, or signal termination of play can be improved or taught. Teachers can also provide opportunities to help children distinguish a sound from a background, or they can set up games to help determine sound location or to discriminate between fast and slow tempos of music in dance activities. Many times sound distorations may confuse the child. Enclosed areas, such as a racquetball court or swimming pool, may initially confuse the child unless he or she can determine the location of the sound.

If children are able to recognize a sound, they should be able to match the sound with its meaning. In addition, information gathered from the visual and haptic senses will complement what children are able to hear and allow them to sort out information to distinguish and identify sounds.

Evaluation of Hearing Impairments

The extent of hearing is usually evaluated by a physician who specializes in disorders of the ear, called an otologist, or by an audiologist, who specializes in the science of hearing. Most children with severe and profound hearing losses are identified during the first 3 years, whereas other losses are not evident until school age.

Most schools utilize a sweep test, in which the child is presented with a tone of 25 db at frequencies of 500 Hz, 1,000 Hz, 2,000 Hz, and 6,000 Hz (Heward & Orlansky, 1992). Other informal evaluations use a watch tick or coin click to observe the pupil's response to various sounds or observe children who complain of earaches or have movement problems.

Based on these informal assessments, a decision may be made to refer children for a more precise measurement of hearing. According to Blackman (1997), formal tests establish the type of hearing loss by assessing middle-ear air pressure and eardrum compliance with acoustic emmittance measures, such as tympanometry. Abnormal results indicate a conductive hearing loss, whereas normal results indicate a sensorineural loss (Blackman, 1997).

Air conduction testing may also be implemented to assess the sound waves that pass through the outer and middle ear to the inner ear. The audiologist can bypass the outer and middle ear and assess the air conduction through the skull directly into the inner ear. With a conductive hearing loss, the bone conduction threshold will be normal, while the level of air conduction will be higher. A hearing loss in the neural mechanism is reflected by air and bone conduction of equal levels. Another technique called *impedance audiometry* can be used to determine the condition of the tympanic membrane and middle ear without a voluntary response from the individual. Blackman (1997) has reported that several newer techniques can be used for young children or those with physical or cognitive impairments. Electrophysiologic tests, such as auditory brain stem response or evoked response audiometry, measure change in brain function as the child's response to auditory stimuli. Octoacoustic emissions also can provide mechanical vibrations that begin in the chochlea and are transmitted to the outer ear via the middle ear (Blackman, 1997).

Typical assessments of performance in physical education classes can be used with a minimum of modification. Hand signals, gestures, flags, and movements can signal the individual to initiate a prescribed physical education movement.

Modification and Adaptations

Most children will be participating in regular physical education classes and will require only minor modifications or adaptations to participate. The biggest problem facing teachers is to establish a system of communication (Stewart, 1987). This must be developed through the school's preferred method of total communication and may include lipreading, amplification, auditory training, and/or signing. Teachers should be aware that instructions should be given at a moderate rate, at face level, and, if outdoors, with the sun at the hearing-impaired child's back. In addition, preferred seating and/or changing positions should be encouraged to facilitate lipreading or residual hearing. When activities take place in an open area, communication signals to stop and start, such as snapping the lights on and off or waving flags, can be utilized.

Visual aids can be employed in demonstration. Films, pictures, charts, and bulletin boards can take the place of detailed verbal explanations, and written instructions and rules can be provided to children prior to instruction (Schmidt, 1985).

In general, games or sports with a minimum of rules are easier to learn. Softball, volleyball, and kickball require little explanation, can be demonstrated easily, and proceed at a slower pace. Sports that are more intricate and that proceed at a faster pace over a large area, such as soccer and basketball, should begin with developmental drills and half-court or field games until children have mastered the fundamental motor skills. Once the game is spread out, appropriate signaling techniques can be used to move children into the proper position or sequence.

Teaching rhythmic activities requires some minor modifications. Auditory training and the use of vibrations can enable children to differentiate between sounds. Percussion instruments and/or blinking lights can also aid in establishing tempo or moving in conjunction with the beat.

Stunts and games that limit vision may be restricted. Because children have no visual feedback, the activity may be difficult and ultimately contraindicated. Lieberman and Cowart's (1996) book *Games for People with Sensory Impairments* should be consulted to aid in developing and modifying activities. Swimming is generally encouraged if water is not damaging to the ears; the teacher gives instructions when the child's head is out of the water or during a long drill. In other cases, a minor modification of the stroke (backstroke or breaststroke) that will not obscure vision may be helpful. With gymnastics routines and movements, children should be allowed to use their vision and develop the kinesthetic awareness necessary to perform the activity correctly.

Implementing the Physical Activity Program

Children with hearing impairments will display several characteristics that may hinder their motor performance, balance, and ability to interact with peers (Butterfield, 1988; Dummer, Haubenstricker & Stewart, 1996). However, it should be remembered that children will vary in ability levels as well as in their ability to hear. Some children may have very low motor function, while others may perform at a high degree of skill. With this in mind, teachers should implement the physical activity program based on the characteristics, strategies, and physical education activities presented in Table 14.2.

Socialization

One of the most important elements of the educational plan for children is developing opportunities for socialization. Because of their distorted and fluctuating tonal quality and guttural speaking, children with hearing impairments are often left out of play experiences. This may cause children to withdraw completely or to develop solitary play. In addition, their lack of social skills may restrict their interactions with other children and their ability to grasp team sports with complex rules.

Teachers should select activities that require the least amount of verbal communication and should integrate children with hearing peers. By utilizing individual sports and games, such as aquatics, tennis, badminton, and dance, teachers can create opportunities for success and acceptance that may promote feelings of self-worth and acceptance by the child's peers (Hopper, 1988). As children become more comfortable, they can progress to dual and team sports and games.

Language Development

Some children may experience difficulty expressing their thoughts and emotions as well as interpreting various expressions and gestures. To aid children in language skill development, teachers can present guided discovery and manual guidance activities—pairing movements with descriptions to allow them to interpret concepts. Additionally, appropriate nonverbal communication, hand signals, or cues will enable children to understand concepts in dance, swimming, and creative movement that encourage emotions, gestures, and ideas. It is essential to remember that a hearing loss of more than 90 db will require more use of the visual system in a manner that is conducive for children to understand (Nowell & Marshak, 1994).

Hyperactivity

Children with hearing losses frequently manifest restlessness, wiggling, and active movements, probably because they are unable to receive auditory cues. Given an opportunity to position themselves to maintain visual contact and to use activities to control tension, children may perform in a more appropriate manner. Yoga, relax-

Table 14.2 Characteristics of Children With Hearing Impairments

Behavior	Characteristics	Instructional Strategies	Physical Education Considerations
Socialization	Distorted tonal quality; guttural, highly fluctuating in pitch range; hard to understand; left out of spontaneous play and may withdraw and develop solitary play; difficulty grasping social situation, team games, and games with complex rules.	Use activities that require the least amount of verbal communication; socially integrate children on a hearing team, and create opportunities for success and acceptance by hearing peers; expand opportunities for deaf to interact with hearing peers (Dummer et al., 1996).	Individual sports and games, such as aquatics, tennis, badminton, dance; progression to dual and team sports.
Language	Expressive language difficulty; development of inner language delayed; difficulty expressing intense emotions; difficulty interpreting expressions and gestures.	Use guided discovery and manual guidance; pair movements with description of movement activities; stress nonverbal expression; establish appropriate communication system and visual stimuli (videos, posters).	Modern dance, aerobics, synchronized swimming, gymnastics, creative movement, movement exploration activities that encourage communicating emotions and ideas.
Cognition	Variable, based on ability to acquire language and read; decreased opportunities for incidental learning (Craft, 1995).	Present instruction in preferred method of communication, and use visual stimuli.	Emphasize active participation and exploratory activities that reinforce academic concepts.
Hyperactivity	Restlessness; frequent wiggling, shuffling, and other active movements.	Allow children to position themselves to maintain visual contact; give praise for appropriate speaking attempts and motor behavior; intervene to extinguish inappropriate responses; use activities to control tension and promote relaxation.	Yoga, relaxation techniques to regain control; parachute, active games, gross motor skills, dual sports and games emphasizing active, rather than passive, activity.
Posture	Abnormal tilts and rotation of the head; forward lean.	Model appropriate static and dynamic postures; reinforce appropriate posture responses.	A variety of fitness activities, such as walking, jogging, cycling, flexibility exercises, resistance exercises that impact on physical development, dance, and movement activities.
Balance	Static and dynamic balance deficits.	Use vision and haptic awareness to compensate for poor balance; establish a broad base of support and lower center of gravity.	Dance, martial arts, tumbling, gymnastics, trampoline, perceptual motor activities in a developmental physical education program (Butterfield, 1988).

Table 14.2 Characteristics of Children With Hearing Impairments *(continued)*

Behavior	Characteristics	Instructional Strategies	Physical Education Considerations
Motor speed	Distorted sense of time and temporalness; may be slow in accomplishing task.	Emphasize visual starting signals and activities that differentiate between fast and slow.	Dance, creative movement, and movement exploration; gymnastics and developmental locomotor skills.
Gait	Tendency to walk with a shuffling gait; dragging feet.	Reinforce and model correct walking pattern; utilize mirrors, visual and kinesthetic training.	Tap dance, rhythms, locomotor skills, and gymnastic activities.
Fitness and motor development	Overall motor development that lags behind peer group. Delays caused by environmental and experience factors (Butterfield, 1991).	Assess children and base program on individual functioning and capabilities. Provide quality instruction.	Sound developmental physical education program of physical and motor fitness, fundamental skills and patterns, aquatics, dance, sports, and games.

ation techniques, active games such as parachute play and relays, and dual sports and games can be incorporated to reduce hyperactivity.

Posture

At times children may lean forward and display abnormal tilts and rotation of the head to compensate for decreased hearing. Posture and balance should be encouraged to ensure stability for more intricate tasks. Teachers can model and reinforce appropriate postures that emphasize correct body alignment and movement positions. Activities that relate to overall development, such as cardiovascular fitness, flexibility, and muscular strength and endurance should be implemented to encourage appropriate body positions and development of key postural muscles.

Balance

Children who manifest static (stationary) or dynamic (moving) balance problems should compensate by using vision and haptic awareness. Because balance is an integral component of all physical education activities, it is essential to select activities that provide for the child's development. Activities such as dance, gymnastics, and trampoline are all conducive to promoting static and dynamic balance. However, if children have inner-ear impairments that affect their ability to balance, compensation activities can be used to help children establish a broad base of support and lower their center of gravity.

Motor Speed

Often the motor speed of children with hearing impairments is characterized by slow movements. Because children may manifest difficulties with the concepts of fast and slow, teachers should use signals or activities that emphasize differences in speed and time. Physical fitness, dance, and locomotor activities that contain temporal and speed elements should be implemented to differentiate between concepts of time and speed that are essential for optimal performance.

Gait

Children may also manifest a shuffling gait or a tendency to drag their feet. Because they may not receive auditory cues, teachers should reinforce and model correct motor patterns emphasizing form and precision. By using mirrors and visual and kinesthetic training, teachers can integrate rhythms, gross motor skills, and gymnastics to overcome gait-oriented problems.

Fitness and Motor Development

The overall motor development of children with hearing impairment will vary in comparison to their peer group. This is evident in terms of physical fitness (Butterfield, 1988; Winnick, 1986) as well as motor development abilities (Dummer et al., 1996). Because of the variability in physical and motor functioning among children with hearing impairments, it is especially important to assess the individual's level of functioning and provide a developmental physical education program. This program should emphasize physical and motor fitness, fundamental skills and patterns, aquatics, dance, sports, and games (Craft, 1995).

CHAPTER SUMMARY

1. Children with hearing impairments are classified as *deaf* or *hearing impaired*. Deaf children are restricted in hearing and understanding speech. There are varying degrees of hearing losses, and some hearing impaired children can understand speech with amplification.

2. Of critical importance to the teacher are three factors that describe the nature of a hearing impairment: the site of the impairment, the age of onset, and the extent of hearing loss.

3. Establishing communication is vital in developing the physical education program and socialization process, as is the use of vision for a loss of more than 90 db.

4. Total communication should be established based on school policies. Elementary signing and manual communication can be used to communicate with the hearing-impaired students. Amplification through the use of hearing devices and auditory training can also be effective tools in communication.

5. Most children with hearing impairments can participate in the regular physical education program with little or no adaptations.

6. In developing teaching strategies and instruction, the educator should be aware of several factors that will influence the learning process. These include socialization skills, language skills, hyperactivity, posture, balance, speed, and gait.

7. Children with hearing impairments will vary in physical fitness and motor development. It is important to assess the child's level of functioning and provide a developmental physical education program based on individual needs. Activities should be included that stress physical and motor fitness, fundamental skills and patterns, including aquatics, dance, sports, and games.

REFERENCES

Blackman, J. A. (1997). *Medical aspects of developmental disabilities in children birth to three* (3rd ed.). Gaithersburg, MD: Aspen Publications.

Bornstein, H., & Jordan, I. K. (1984). *Functional signs.* Austin, TX: Pro-Ed.

Butterfield, S. A. (1988). Deaf children in physical education. *Palaestra, 6,* 28–30, 52.

Butterfield, S. A. (1991). Physical and sport for the deaf: Rethinking the least restrictive environment. *Adapted Physical Activity Quarterly, 8,* 95–102.

Craft, D. (1995). Visual impairment and hearing losses. In Winnick, J. (Ed.) *Adapted physical education and sport,* (pp. 143–166). Champaign, IL: Human Kinetics.

Dummer, G. M., Haubenstricker, J. L. & Stewart, D. L. (1996). Motor skill performances of children who are deaf. *Adapted Physical Activity Quarterly, 13,* 400–414.

Eichstaedt, C. B. & Lavay, B. (1992). *Physical activity for individuals with mental retardation.* Champaign, IL: Human Kinetics.

Gallaudet Research Institute. (1991). *Today's hearing impaired children and youth: A demographic and academic profile.* Washington, DC: Center for Assessment and Demographic Studies.

Hardman, M. L., Drew, C., & Egan, M. W. (1999). *Human exceptionality* (6th ed.). Boston: Allyn & Bacon.

Heward, W. L., & Orlansky, M. D. (1992). *Exceptional children* (4th ed.). New York: Merrill/Macmillan.

Hopper, C. (1988). Self-concept and motor performance of hearing-impaired boys and girls. *Adapted Physical Activity Quarterly, 5,* 293–304.

Individuals with Disabilities Act of 1997, Pub. L. No 105–17. (1997, June 4).

Kannapell, B. (1984). *Orientation to deafness: A handbook and resource guide.* Washington, DC: Gallaudet University.

Lieberman, L. L. & Cowart, J. F. (1996). *Games for people with sensory impairments.* Champaign, IL: Human Kinetics.

Moores, D. F. (1987). *Educating the deaf* (3rd ed.). Boston: Houghton Mifflin.

National Information Center on Deafness. (1991). *Deafness: A fact sheet.* Washington, DC: Gallaudet University.

Nowell, R. C., & Marshak, L. E. (1994). *Understanding deafness and the rehabilitation process.* Boston: Allyn & Bacon.

Schmidt, S. (1985). Hearing impaired students in physical education. *Adapted Physical Activity Quarterly, 2,* 300–306.

Stewart, D. A. (1987). Social factors influencing participation in sport for the deaf. *Palaestra, 2,* 23–28.

Winnick, J. P. (1986). Physical fitness of adolescents with auditory impairments. *Adapted Physical Activity Quarterly, 3,* 58–66.

Section IV

Teaching Individuals with Congenital and Acquired Impairments

Section IV focuses on helping teachers incorporate into the physical education program children with posture and orthopedic impairments, neurological disorders, muscular dystrophy, and arthritis. Children with any of these impairments will benefit from physical education and require a thorough understanding of the condition.

This section is designed to help teachers

1. recognize the characteristics of children with impairments that affect movement or functional ability

2. understand the concerns and the appropriate treatment, first aid, and medication that may be essential for these children

3. to develop the expertise to design physical education programs based on the functional ability and needs of these children

4. to understand the interaction with various disciplines in the treatment of these impairments

5. to facilitate instruction in physical education for children with a breadth of impairments in the least restrictive environment.

CHAPTER 15

Posture and Orthopedic Impairments

The primary focus of physical education classes is the development of physical fitness and motor skills. Only a minimal amount of time is designated to improving proper body mechanics. Instructional time designated for children with posture problems is relatively rare. Such children may not receive appropriate strengthening or flexibility exercises for postural deviations that ultimately contribute to back and/or knee strains, poor muscular development, and a restriction in motor skill development. More important, poor body mechanics generally exists concurrently with a poor body image and lack of self-esteem.

Children with disabilities have is a greater incidence of postural defects than does the general school-aged population. For example, children with sensory impairments may exhibit faulty body mechanics or head tilts primarily due to the lack of feedback from the affected sensory apparatus that aids in maintaining and reinforcing appropriate postures. Likewise, nonambulatory children with amputations, spinal injuries, or neurological disorders may place undue pressure on their postural structure and must reassert their center of balance that was disrupted by injury or disability or compensate for remaining in a seated position. This chapter address the common posture and deviations that alter body mechanics, such as spinal injuries and amputations.

Posture

Posture is defined as the manner in which the body maintains alignment against gravity. Good posture involves the skeletal system, ligaments, muscles, fatigue, and the self-concept of the individual. Correct posture is achieved when all segments of the body are aligned properly over a base of support.

Posture encompasses more than maintaining a static position, because movement requires students to assume and change positions of the body constantly. A sitting position with the back against the seat, feet on the floor, and thighs and back supported by the seat permits students to sit in a relaxed position while the chair provides support of the body. Additionally, when positioned at elbow height, the arms rest on the chair supports and relax the postural muscles while conserving energy. Improper sitting is characterized by failure to align the body with the chair back, slumping of the back and shoulders, and concentrating the majority of weight on one side of the body. Children in a wheelchair are especially susceptible to seated postural faults and resulting complications, such as pressure sores or respiratory dysfunctions from pressure on the rib cage, because their disability may restrict appropriate physical development that is necessary to maintain proper sitting posture.

Standing posture is characterized by an erect position with an elevated head and chest, posterior-tilted pelvis, slightly curved abdomen and lower back, slightly flexed knees, and feet parallel and spaced a comfortable distance apart to allow for an even weight distribution. Various body builds will affect standing postures, necessitating an appropriate knowledge of each body type as well as an awareness of sensory or ortho-pedic impairments that may affect the standing posture. Common standing postural problems include slumping the shoulders, improper tilts of the head, protruding abdomen, and improper foot placement.

Walking is a natural extension of the standing posture and should encompass the basic elements of standing while adding movement and supporting the body by alternately losing and regaining balance. The head and chest remain erect, while the chin is tucked. Arms will swing in opposition to the legs while the shoulders are level, and the feet will move in a forward direction, alternately striking the walking surface first with the heel, then rolling onto the balls of the feet. Each walking stride will vary according to the length of the stride and pace maintained by individual children.

Common problems associated with walking postures include slumping the shoulders, tilting the head, toeing the feet in or out, striking flat-footed, and/or dragging the feet. Children with prosthetic devices may face further complications in walking, such as difficulties in shifting weight or regaining balance, a lack of proper feedback (in the case of individuals with sensory impairments), and fatigue (in the case of children in a wheelchair).

Individual Differences in Posture

When analyzing proper posture, teachers should be aware of individual differences that are associated with age, body type, and exceptionality. Children in the primary grades will exhibit a slightly protruding abdomen and curvature of the spine that are common at this age and do not constitute a posture defect. However, the same occurrence in young adults indicates a marked defect and requires corrective measures.

Specific body types are more apt to assume a particular posture because of their build. Children may possess a mesomorphic, endomorphic, or ectomorphic body type, or any combination of the three body types. The upper torso may be the predominant characteristic of one body type classification, whereas the lower extremities may characterize another specific body type. The mix of body type classifications may lead to improper posture development, such as a muscular chest and back coupled with a slender abdomen and lower limbs, which may appear as a rounded upper back. In conjunction, orthopedic problems such as spinal injuries or amputations may also contribute to improper body alignment or posture because the disabilities may affect the remaining muscle mass, mechanics, or stability of the body in maintaining appropriate posture.

Because children may demonstrate postural deficiencies, it is necessary to develop good posture habits and to correct improper body alignments before they inhibit the development of age-appropriate motor skills or possible injury. If postural deficits are the direct result of a specific condition, proper strengthening exercises or procedures should be implemented to correct problems related to structural body alignment.

Etiology of Postural Deviations

There is no single cause of posture deficits. Postural deviations can be either functional or structural. A functional condition can be overcome through corrective exercises or training in kinesthetic awareness of proper positions. Without proper maintenance of postural muscles and the use of corrective techniques, the deficiency may deteriorate, possibly become debilitating, and may either interfere with the physical performance capabilities of students or become a structural deviation. Structural deviations are due to abnormalities and/or deformities of the skeletal system resulting from disease or injury. Because of the severity of structural defects, most are treated by physicians with a combination of braces, casts, surgery, and prosthetic devices.

Teachers as well as the collaborative team members should constantly be aware of posture during the early school years, especially for those children whose condition may contribute to inappropriate posture. Reminders and reinforcement for proper sitting and standing posture may be the most effective way to eliminate postural defects. Posture deficiencies may also occur in a variety of positions and affect different areas of the body structure. In order for teachers to address posture problems effectively, appropriate exercises should be utilized for various parts of the body with consultation of the physician. Some of these exercises for specific body parts include the following (Daniels, 1977; Dunn, 1997; Kisner & Colby, 1990; Lasko & Knopf, 1992; Williams & Worthington, 1961):

Head and Neck Deviations

The head and neck may have a tendency to droop forward, and in more severe cases this deviation may result in a rounding of the shoulders and back. A forward head occurs when the neck is extended forward and downward. Torticollis is a tilting of the head to one side caused by a shortening of the sternocleidomastoid muscle that attaches behind the ear and inserts into the clavicle and sternum.

Neck extension and round shoulders are primarily caused by functional problems and can be aided by proper exercise. Round shoulders may also be the result of a habit, requiring a need to reeducate the child to proper positions. Additionally, a lack of overall muscular development may be apparent and can be corrected by utilizing appropriate exercises, including the following:

1. In a standing or sitting position, rotate chin and touch each shoulder; hold and return.

2. In a standing or sitting position, touch ear to shoulder; hold and return. Place one hand on top of the head, and gently apply a little more pressure to help stretch the neck.

3. In a standing or sitting position, lower the chin toward the chest and apply light pressure, using the hands to press the head forward. Lift the head up, tilt the chin at an angle, and bring the head straight down toward the chest, again applying gentle pressure; repeat on the other side.

4. In a standing or sitting position, rotate the head slowly in a circle clockwise, and repeat in a counterclockwise direction, being careful not to hyperextend the neck in backward rotation.

5. In a standing or sitting position, apply resistance to the back of the head and attempt to push the head backward, on its own strength, against the resistance.

6. In a standing or sitting position, interlock hands behind the neck and pull hands forward while pushing against the hands with the neck muscles.

7. In a standing position, place a beanbag on head while observing the proper posture in a mirror. Walk while balancing an object.

8. Lying supine, look up at the ceiling, bring the head and chin to the chest, and return (if lordosis is not present).

9. Lying prone, tuck chin, forehead against a mat, hold, and relax.

Trunk Deviations

Kyphosis is an abnormal increase in the flexion of the thoracic region of the spine and is sometimes called humpback. Kyphosis can also be structural and, if so, requires treatment by a physician. Functional kyphosis will commonly appear in conjunction with round shoulder and forward head. The more severe curvature or kyphosis is the result of weak back extensor muscles or fatigue as well as the shortening of the muscles of the chest and shoulder girdle. Stretching and strengthening the muscles involved in maintaining the spine, chest, and shoulder girdle allow more movement of the shoulders and rib cage and may correct kyphosis to some extent.

A lack of muscular development also contributes to a protrusion of the shoulder blades (winged scapula) from the spinal column. This occurs from the lack of shoulder girdle strength and may be corrected by stretching the muscles of the shoulder girdle while strengthening the muscle groups that align the scapula (trapezius and rhomboids).

Several exercises follow that may be used in overcoming trunk deviations.

1. In a standing position, use a bar or ladder and hang or climb for increasing periods of time.

2. In a standing or sitting position, pinch shoulders together while in front of a mirror and release. Bring shoulders up to the ears, contracting the muscles, and release the shoulders down.

3. In a standing position, clasp hands behind head and extend elbows forward, bringing elbows together in front of the face, and then extend elbows backward while straightening the spine erect.

4. In a standing or sitting position, raise elbows to shoulder level, clasp hands, and pull while providing resistance with each arm.

5. In a standing or sitting position, raise elbows to shoulder level in front of the body and cross one elbow over the other; then extend the elbows to sides.

6. In a standing or sitting position, raise elbows overhead, then touch elbows together behind the back.

7. In a standing position, grasp a towel or surgical tubing with hands spread, and

raise arms overhead. Move the towel back as far as possible while maintaining straight arms, being careful not to hyperextend the back and keeping the head straight.

8. Lying prone, extend arms overhead. Raise the upper body from the floor and return several times, keeping the lower back straight.

9. Lying supine, place the hands on the lower abdominal area and press the lower back flat to the floor, making sure the knees bend and the pelvis tilts downward.

10. In a standing or sitting position, bring the shoulders up toward the ears, and move in a circular fashion forward and backward. Alternate bringing one shoulder up toward the ear and then the other shoulder. Press both shoulders forward and backward.

11. In a standing position, simulate the back crawl swimming movement, extending arm overhead and reaching backward as far as possible.

12. In a standing position in a door frame, press the hands against the door frame and apply force overhead and slightly behind the head.

13. In a standing position, with the small of the back against the corner of a wall or door, place the fists together in front of the chest, and pull the arms back as far as possible.

14. In a standing position in front of a table, place the hands on edge of table and press the chest toward the floor between the extended arms. Ensure that the motion is performed with the head raised.

Scoliosis is a deviation that requires early screening to circumvent serious problems. Scoliosis causes the spine to deviate abnormally to the side and is present in approximately 20% of the school-aged population, ranging from mild to severe deviations and occurring mostly in females. The frequency of scoliosis detected in young girls is due to rapid maturation and hormonal changes during adolescence. Figure 15.1 illustrates four major types of scoliotic curves: thoracic, thoracolumbar, lumbar, and double major.

The *right thoracic* curve is most common and is indicated by a curve that deforms the ribs on the same side, causing a "rib hump" that will affect body alignment as well as the internal organs; the *thoracolumbar* curve is more gradual and less likely to cause a deformity, although it visibly affects the proper body alignment of the hips and is a primary cause of low back pain; the *lumbar* curve causes a deviation in the symmetry of the hips and is related to low back pain in the severe styles; and the *double major* curve includes two curves that are more balanced and less deforming, although the alignment of the ribs is primarily affected.

In scoliosis, the single curve will involve the entire spine and is commonly referred to as a "C" curve. Scoliosis with two or more curves is known as an "S" curve and results from the body's attempt to maintain balance. Functional scoliosis curves are approximately 90% genetic but may be accentuated by growth, abnormal posture, or overdevelopment of the back muscles.

Depending on the severity of the scoliotic condition and the physician's opinion concerning the effectiveness of exercise on scoliosis, the physician may prescribe exercises that may be conducted in a physical education or home setting to overcome

Figure 15.1 Scoliotic spinal curves: (a) thoracic, (b) thoracolumbar, (c) lumbar, and (d) double major.

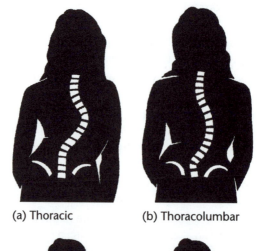

(a) Thoracic   (b) Thoracolumbar

(c) Lumbar   (d) Double major

functional scoliosis. Several exercises for a left curvature (which may also be reversed for a right curvature) include the following:

1. In a standing position, hang from a bar or ladder with the arms extended, and flex the trunk to the left, raising the left hip and moving the feet to the left.

2. In a standing or supine position, extend the arms overhead with palms turned upward; hold and return.

3. In a standing position, face a wall and move the hands up the wall on the side of the curve. Return on the opposite side.

4. In a standing position, with hands on hips, raise the right arm overhead and left arm sideward to shoulder height. Raise the body on the tiptoes, and move the right leg sideward on the ground, stretching the body; hold and return.

5. In a standing position, place the hands at hips; then stretch the left arm downward without bending the left side of the body.

6. In a standing position, place the hands on hips; then stretch the right arm overhead while pressing left hand against ribs.

7. In a standing position, place the right hand behind the neck and left hand against the ribs, twisting to the left while rotating the right arm.

8. In a standing position, place the hands on hips and bend slowly forward while holding the head upright.

9. In a standing position, flex the trunk to the left while sliding the left hand down the left leg and extending the right arm overhead, hands stretched out.

10. In a kneeling position, extend the left leg sideward on the ground, and extend the right arm overhead while pressing left hand against the ribs. Flex the trunk to the left while moving right arm in an arc overhead continuing pressure of left hand on the ribs.

If the cause of scoliosis is structural or a severe deformity of the vertebrae, corrective exercises will have minimal, if any, effect. Severe curvatures are treated by an orthopedic surgeon and include bracing, surgery, fusion, casting, or electrical stimulation. In either case, the program should be developed in consultation with the physician and implemented within a medical margin of safety.

For example, a bracing is used on curves of less than 40 degrees and supports the body from the neck to the pelvic region with two metal rods to align the spine. Most activities are appropriate and should be implemented in consultation with the physician, because movements that incorporate flexion, extension, rotation, and high impact are contraindicated. Another support treatment is a molded cast that can be used when curves are more than 50 degrees and that consists of plaster enveloping the entire upper body. Noncontact activities should be utilized, with particular emphasis on strengthening the upper body when the cast is removed.

Surgery is indicated in rapidly progressing curves of 40 degrees or more and may involve the implementation of a steel rod next to the spine. Additionally, a technique using electrical stimulation in curvatures of 40 degrees or less has also been utilized. Electrostimulation at the rib area near the spine is used to contract specific muscle groups, applying pressure from these muscles to straighten the curve over a gradual period. This procedure is generally implemented primarily at night, freeing students from cumbersome braces and cast and allowing them to participate in physical activity during the day.

Lordosis, or hollow back, is an increase in the lumbar curve that causes a forward tilt of the pelvic girdle. The primary causes of the forward tilt are muscle shortening of the lower back and hip flexors in conjunction with tight hamstrings and weak gluteal muscles that contribute to the forward movement of the pelvis. A common cause of lordosis is also weak abdominal muscles. Several exercises that may be utilized to correct lordosis include the following:

1. On hands and knees, alternate rounding and flattening the back while tightening the abdominals when exhaling air (cat back).

2. In a sitting position, reach slowly to the feet; hold and return.

3. Lying prone, contract the buttocks muscles; hold and release.

4. In a standing or lying position, contract the buttocks muscles; hold and release.

5. In a standing or lying position, contract the abdominal muscles, and push the back against the floor or wall.

6. Lying supine, bring one leg up slowly; hold and return. Repeat with the other leg.

7. Lying supine, bring both knees to the chest; hold and return.

8. In a standing position, spread the feet and bend forward to reach one foot while keeping a slight bend in the knees; hold and return. Repeat with other foot.

9. With bent knee, lying supine, place feet flat on the floor and fold arms across chest raising shoulders from the floor; hold and return (curl-ups).

A condition called *ptosis* is often associated with lordosis and is caused by a weakness, sagging, or total collapse of the abdominal muscles. Muscle groups in the abdominal region should be strengthened to counteract this condition and alleviate some aspects of lordosis, using the following exercises:

1. In a sitting position, with bent knees, fold hands across the chest and curl up toward knees; hold and return. If muscle groups are extremely weak, lift the head and shoulders, leaving the small of the back on the floor to prevent back strain.

2. In a hanging or sitting position, bring both knees up slowly as far as possible and return.

3. Lying supine, flutter-kick legs, or flutter-kick in an aquatic setting.

Hip Deviations

Hip deviations generally occur concurrently with back deformities. A downward tilt of the pelvis over 50 degrees will constitute an abnormality called *anterior pelvic tilt*. Shortening of lower back and hip flexor muscles, in conjunction with sagging abdominal and tight hamstring muscles, pushes the pelvis forward. A pelvic tilt may also occur from improper body mechanics and often accompanies ptosis, lumbar lordosis, and a protruding buttocks. In order to correct the pelvic tilting, exercises that stretch both muscle groups and strengthen weakened areas should be implemented. Several of these exercises follow.

1. Lying supine, bend the knees and place feet flat on the floor, contracting abdominal muscles and tightening buttocks region.

2. Lying supine, bend the knees and place feet flat on the floor, contracting abdominal muscles and raising the buttocks from the floor; hold and return (pelvic tilt).

3. In a standing or sitting position, contract the abdominal and buttock muscles; hold and relax.

Knee Postural Deviations

Knock-knees and bowlegs are two common orthopedic deviations of the lower extremities that may require exercises prescribed by physicians. Knock-knees occur when the knees overlap or touch medially and result from the stretching of the medial knee ligaments in combination with weak external rotators. This imbalance causes the knees to come in contact and should be corrected by assuming proper postures and developing a proper balance in the primary muscle groups of the thigh and knee. The outward rotators of the thigh can be strengthened in combination with stretching the muscles of the lateral side of the thigh by using the following exercises in a standing position or standing with the support of a chair or bar.

1. With the feet parallel, attempt to turn the knees out while simultaneously pulling calves inward.

2. Bend the knees slightly and turn in an outward motion.

3. With heels apart and toes together, rotate the knees outward.

4. With heels apart and toes together, rotate the knees forward.

Bowlegs occur when the feet are together and the knees do not touch. Bowlegs are attributed to injury, poor diet, disease, poor sleeping habits, or anything that places undue pressure on the inner parts of the legs. Some bowing is prevalent in young children but should disappear during maturation, when the peroneals counteract the pull of the tibia (Dunn, 1997). If the knees are 5 inches or more apart, medical attention is required, and exercise will not be effective. With slight bowing, gymnastic and swimming activities are strongly recommended to increase peroneal development, as well as the following exercises:

1. In a standing position, with the heels together, flex the knees slightly and rotate knees inward, attempting to touch the insides of the knee.

2. In a sitting position, with the legs extended while sitting on the floor against a wall, roll the legs inward and turn the feet outward.

3. Lying supine, place a pillow between the ankles, spread the straightened legs, and close on the pillow.

Ankle and Foot Deviations

Flat feet occur when the longitudinal arch is lower than normal, contributing to a poor functional posture development by changing the stability of the foot. Although flat feet are not necessarily weak feet and are a minor postural deviation that generally does not hamper physical development, proper stability is required to prevent injury to other portions of the foot. Because of this, corrective exercises such as the following (to be performed in a sitting position) are encouraged to strengthen the transverse arch of the foot and provide stability.

1. Pick up pencils with the toes and feet.

2. Roll a tennis ball back and forth under the arch of the foot.

3. Roll a towel with the toes and feet.

4. Flex and extend toes and feet.

5. With feet flat on floor, flex toes into the floor, and pull the heel in toward the toes in an inchworm-type fashion; then reverse the action.

Other common foot deviations that may affect body mechanics include toeing in and toeing out. Toeing in, or pigeon toes, results from an inward position of the feet, while toeing out involves the feet pointing out while standing or moving. Toeing out can also cause pronation, which can lead to more serious body mechanics problems. Specific activities, such a walking a balance beam, roller skating, and ice skating, will aid in strengthening weakened muscle groups and correction of foot problems. In addition, teachers may also use the following exercises, which are to be performed in a sitting position:

1. Rotate and extend the foot clockwise and counterclockwise.

2. In a chair, push the inside of the foot against a barrier (for toeing out), and press the outer side of the foot against the reserve (for toeing in).

3. Repeat exercise 2, kicking a ball with the outside and inside of the foot.

4. With the feet on the floor, 24 inches apart, move the feet inward and outward, fanlike, without moving the heels.

5. With one foot on a towel, cross the opposite foot over the foot on the towel and apply pressure to the ankle area.

6. Use the same position as in exercise 5, rotating the foot laterally to drag the towel back and forth.

7. Pick up objects, such as marbles or pencils, with the feet.

Orthopedic Disorders

Children with orthopedic disorders will manifest chronic conditions and make lifelong adjustments to their disability. These conditions generally indicate a lengthy process of the disease and/or treatment and are permanent, resulting in a loss of functioning. Approximately 2 million individuals under the age of 21 are orthopedically impaired in the United States and are included in IDEA under the categories of "orthopedically impaired" or "other health impaired." Most are integrated into the regular school setting. Children with more severe impairments are placed in special schools or hospitals.

Increasing the physical functioning and motor development of these children is the major concern for teachers. Children with orthopedic impairments will progress in a manner of development similar to that of their nondisabled peers. The disability should not be the focus of the educator's programming. Instead, a process of development and rehabilitation should be implemented to maximize the child's physical and functional skill development potential. When children are enrolled in regular physical education classes, teachers should strive to encourage peer acceptance through active integration into classes, as well as encourage additional opportunities for sport and recreation outside the school. Two types of orthopedic disorders that are commonly integrated into regular physical education classes with minor modifications or adaptions are spinal cord injuries and limb deficiencies.

Spinal Cord Injuries

The spinal cord is made up of nervous tissue extending from the brain to the lower back encased by the vertebrae. It is approximately 18 inches in length, cylindrical in shape with the same general circumference, except for an enlargement in the cervical and lumbar areas where the nerves innervating the upper and lower extremities exit. The spinal cord provides a pathway for neural impulses to and from the brain and the nerves and muscles of the trunk and extremities.

The spinal cord is protected by the vertebral column, which consists of 33 vertebrae (Figure 15.2). The 7 cervical vertebrae are the bones that occupy the neck; the 12 thoracic vertebrae are located in the upper back behind the chest cavity; the 5 lumbar vertebrae comprise the lower back; and the 5 sacral and 4 coccygeal vertebrae comprise the tailbone.

Functional activities

Functional activity for spinal cord injuries. Activity columns (left to right): Eating, Dressing, Grooming, Toileting, Homemaking, Driving, Public transportation, Wheelchair transfers, Ambulation, Communications, Bed transfer, Vocational, Sexual functioning.

Spinal cord segments		Eating	Dressing	Grooming	Toileting	Homemaking	Driving	Public transportation	Wheelchair transfers	Ambulation	Communications	Bed transfer	Vocational	Sexual functioning	
Cervical segments C1–T1 — Neck and arm muscles and diaphragm	C-1	*	*	*	*	*		*			*	*	**	**	**Q u a d r i p l e g i a**
	C-2	*	*	*	*	*		*			*	*	**	**	
	C-3	*	*	*	*	*		*			*	*	**	**	
	C-4	*	*	*	*	*		*			*	*	**	**	
	C-5	*	*	*	*	*	*	*	*		*	*	**	**	
	C-6	*	*	*	*	*	*	*	*		*	*	**	**	
	C-7	*	*	*	*	*	*	*	✓		*	✓	**	**	
	C-8	✓	✓	✓	✓	✓	*	*	✓		✓	✓	**	**	
	T-1	✓	✓	✓	✓	✓	*	*	✓		✓	✓	**	**	
Thoracic segments T2–T12 — Chest and abdominal muscles	T-2	✓	✓	✓	✓	✓	*	*	✓		✓	✓	✓	**	**P a r a p l e g i a**
	T-3	✓	✓	✓	✓	✓	*	*	✓		✓	✓	✓	**	
	T-4	✓	✓	✓	✓	✓	*	*	✓		✓	✓	✓	**	
	T-5	✓	✓	✓	✓	✓	*	*	✓		✓	✓	✓	**	
	T-6	✓	✓	✓	✓	✓	*	*	✓		✓	✓	✓	**	
	T-7	✓	✓	✓	✓	✓	*	*	✓	*	✓	✓	✓	**	
	T-8	✓	✓	✓	✓	✓	*	*	✓	*	✓	✓	✓	**	
	T-9	✓	✓	✓	✓	✓	*	*	✓	*	✓	✓	✓	**	
	T-10	✓	✓	✓	✓	✓	*	*	✓		✓	✓	✓	**	
	T-11	✓	✓	✓	✓	✓	*	*	✓		✓	✓	✓	**	
	T-12	✓	✓	✓	✓	✓	*	*	✓	*	✓	✓	✓	**	
Lumbar and Sacral segments — Hip and knee muscles	L-1	✓	✓	✓	✓	✓	*	*	✓	*	✓	✓	✓	**	
	L-2	✓	✓	✓	✓	✓	*	*	✓	*	✓	✓	✓	**	
	L-3	✓	✓	✓	✓	✓	*	*	✓	*	✓	✓	✓	**	
	L-4	✓	✓	✓	✓	✓	*	✓	✓	*	✓	✓	✓	**	
Hip, knee, ankle and foot muscles	L-5	✓	✓	✓	✓	✓	*	✓	✓	*	✓	✓	✓	**	
	S-1	✓	✓	✓	✓	✓	*	✓	✓	✓	✓	✓	✓	**	
Bowel, bladder, and reproduction organs	S-2	✓	✓	✓	✓	✓	✓	✓	✓	✓	✓	✓	✓	**	
	S-3	✓	✓	✓	✓	✓	✓	✓	✓	✓	✓	✓	✓	**	
	S-4	✓	✓	✓	✓	✓	✓	✓	✓	✓	✓	✓	✓	**	

✓ Normal or near normal function or performance

* Needs some type of personal and/or mechanical assistance

** It can be partially available but options need to be discussed on individual basis

☐ Not practical/probable

Figure 15.2 Functional activity for spinal cord injuries.
Source: Courtesy of the Health South Harmarville Rehabilitation Hospital.

Spinal nerves extend from the cord forming the peripheral nervous system and transmit messages from the brain and spinal cord to the working muscles. These spinal nerves include 8 cervical nerves (C_1–C_8), 12 thoracic nerves (T_1–T_{12}), 5 lumbar nerves (L_1–L_5), 5 sacral nerves (S_1–S_5), and one coccygeal nerve. The spinal cord itself is much shorter than the vertebral column and ends at the first or second lumbar vertebra. Spinal nerves of the lumbar and sacral regions comprise a group of long nerves referred to as the cauda equina.

Automobile, motorcycle, shooting, swimming, and diving accidents are responsible for a majority of spinal injuries, especially in the high school years. When the spinal cord is injured, the transmission of impulses to the extremities will be disrupted. The remaining functioning ability will be determined by the extent and level of the spinal cord injury.

A complete spinal cord lesion (injury) results in absence of sensation and motor function below the level of that injury. An incomplete lesion, in which the cord is not completely transacted, results in varying amounts of sensation and motor functioning below the injury. Injuries may involve several levels, such as T_2–T_4 (interfering with functioning from the second thoracic to fourth thoracic vertebra). This type of injury will also be characterized by the availability of more functioning ability on one side of the body.

The higher the level of the spinal lesion, the more restricted the movement, because the spinal cord can no longer innervate the muscle below the site of the injury. An injury above the third cervical vertebra generally will result in death because the muscles of the diaphragm will be paralyzed, and life will not be maintained unless manual respiration is implemented. Furthermore, the site of the lesion will directly affect the remaining functional ability if lesions occur in the regions described in the following sections (Bromley, 1981; Lockette & Keyes, 1994).

Fourth Cervical (C_4) Injuries at the fourth cervical vertebra generally will have control of the neck, including the sternocleidomastoid, trapezius, and upper paraspinal muscles and the diaphragm. The functioning of the upper limbs is impeded, and children have involvement of all four extremities, or quadriplegia. Assistance is required for transferring in and out of a wheelchair, and electrically powered assistive devices are used for upper limb functions.

Fifth Cervical (C_5) Injuries below the fifth cervical vertebra will allow functioning in the neck muscles, diaphragm, deltoid muscles of the shoulder, rhomboids, and biceps. Flexion of the elbow is possible as well as abduction of the shoulder, although shoulder extension relies on gravity to return to its original position. No functioning is available in the wrist and hand, necessitating manual supports on the wrist and arm as well as projections on the rims to maneuver a wheelchair.

Sixth Cervical (C_6) Injuries to children below the sixth cervical vertebra will allow the use of extensors of the wrist as well as more elbow flexion, shoulder flexion, and abduction. Children should be able to grasp lightweight and large objects, use an overhead bar for transfers, manipulate objects, and push a wheelchair.

Seventh Cervical (C_7) Injuries below the seventh cervical vertebra will allow functioning of the triceps, which permit extension of the elbow as well as flexion and extension of the fingers. Development of the triceps stabilizes the elbow and allows grasping and releasing activities. Children will be independent in maneuvering a wheelchair and transfers and can perform pull-ups, archery, and table-tennis–type activities.

Thoracic Level (T_1–T_5) Injuries to the first five thoracic vertebrae will allow movement in the upper extremities but not in the lower extremities (paraplegia). Children will be able to grasp and release and have total movement in the arms. Stability of the trunk will be lacking, necessitating a seat belt or brace for posture and body alignment. Transfers may be accomplished independently, and upper body strengthening and sport activities such as archery can be performed.

Thoracic Level (T$_6$–T$_9$)   Injuries at the level below the sixth thoracic vertebra will allow more trunk stability because the muscles of the upper back, abdominal muscles, and muscles of the ribs are functioning. Upper extremity strength is much more apparent, providing opportunities for weight lifting and activities that require a strong grasping technique, such as bowling. Children should be able to completely control a wheelchair, eat and groom themselves independently, and stand with the aid of braces and forearm crutches.

Thoracic Level (T$_{10}$–T$_{12}$)   Injuries at the level below the tenth thoracic vertebra will allow for complete abdominal control as well as use of the muscles of the upper back. Although the muscles of the lower back are weak, trunk control is available that allows participation in endurance activities such as swimming, propelling a wheelchair for moving, and weight training. Independent living can be achieved by children, and walking can be accomplished with the assistance of long leg braces.

Lumbar Levels (L$_1$–L$_5$)   Injuries to the upper lumbar vertebrae (L$_1$–L$_3$) allow functioning in the muscles of the hip joint that flex the thigh; the fourth lumbar vertebra will allow flexion of the hip and, together with the fifth lumbar vertebra, controls movement in the lower leg and extension of the hip. Ambulation and independent living are possible, and children should be able to participate in most endurance wheelchair activities, such as track, basketball, and tennis.

Sacral Levels (S$_1$–S$_5$)   Injuries in the sacral level will disrupt bladder and bowel control along with sexual functioning. The gastrocnemius and soleus muscles of the legs function if the injury occurs at S$_2$, whereas abduction and adduction of the lower leg is available if the injury occurs below sacral three (S$_3$). Maintenance of bladder and bowel control will involve a catheter until specific bowel and toilet training is implemented to regulate these functions. Sexual functioning will vary often, returning in lower spinal cord injuries after spinal shock is terminated. It is essential to remember that in a young individual with a spinal cord injury, sexual functioning may remain intact, with adequate potency and fertility available in both males and females. Children with sacral lesions have the highest level of motor functioning and can perform most endurance activities and sports that require intricate upper body movements.

Planning the Physical Activity Program

The most obvious aspect of a spinal cord injury is the loss of movement and physical functioning in the extremities. In addition, there are other complications that affect the functional capacity of children and should be considered in developing an appropriate program. Some of the complications include the following:

1. *Contractures,* or a shortening of the muscles due to remaining in a stationary position or central nervous system involvement for an extended period of time. Active and passive stretching exercises as well as positioning techniques can be used to stretch shortened muscles.

2. *Spinal deformities,* including scoliosis and/or pelvic distortion, can occur from a lengthy confinement or poor posture in bed, standing, or in the wheelchair. Effective prevention must involve strengthening the weaker muscle groups, pas-

sive stretching of shortened muscles, posture training, weight training (progressive resistance exercises), and corrective sports, such as archery.

3. *Edema,* or a swelling in the feet, ankles, and lower legs, is due to poor vasomotor control and loss of muscle tone. To stimulate the vasomotor system, the legs are elevated or encased in elastic stockings. In the hands, elevation or passive movements of the joints are encouraged. In addition, upper-body exercise may have beneficial effects in promoting circulation and preventing blood from pooling in the lower extremities.

4. *Osteoporosis,* or problems associated with the absorption of minerals, leaves the bones below the lesion susceptible to fractures. General treatments are passive movements to stimulate circulation and a high-protein diet with vitamin D supplements.

5. *Pain* can be either consistent or periodic above or below the area of injury. Generally, mobilization, medication, and/or diversionary activities are utilized in the treatment of pain. For some individuals, arm exercise or overuse syndromes from using the arms to propel a wheelchair may aggravate shoulder pain (Figoni, 1997).

6. *Ossification* of bone in the connective tissue, usually in the hips, knees, and elbows, limits range of motion and subsequent movement. Surgery is usually the only alternative to removing the bone after the disease recedes.

7. *Spasms* occur when the spinal cord resumes some autonomous function below the injury, resulting in reflex muscle activity. Spasms may be mild or involve an intense response of the muscle, such as an alternating flexion and extension of the knee. Spasms greatly inhibit effective movement in limbs where partial control is available and should be treated with passive stretching, relaxation, cryotherapy, and medication.

8. *Decubitus ulcers* are pressure sores that occur from remaining in one position for extended periods of time. To treat pressure sores, pads and change of position can relieve pressure, while the pliability of the skin is maintained through massage and application of lanolin.

9. *Obesity and poor physical fitness* can be due to the lack of physical activity and inadequate caloric expenditure. Pulmonary deficiency may be diminished due to a lack of musculature in the abdominal region. Proper dietary habits and planned physical activity programs should be used to overcome the sedentary lifestyle often associated with physical disabilities.

10. *Temperature regulation* is difficult in higher level injuries as the thermoregulatory system is deficient. The ability to dissipate heat by perspiring in warm environments or to conserve heat by shivering is not as efficient because the counterregulatory effects of the sympathetic and parasympathetic nervous system are not present above T_6 injuries.

11. *Sensory information* is deficient regarding feel or position senses. Information going from the brain to the spinal cord is affected, and the use of sensory and proprioception information from the limbs is deficient.

12. *Hypotension/hypertension* can affect resting blood pressure. Shifts in position from a supine to upright position may result in a decrease of blood pressure. Blood

pooling in the viscera and lower extremities may necessitate wearing support stockings or postural supports. In contrast, hypertension or autonomic dysreflexia from vasconstriction of the visceral arteries may lead to an increase in blood pressure. Figoni (1997) stresses proper bowel and bladder management and discourages "boosting," or inducing autonomic dysreflexia, in an attempt to enhance performance.

As the child adapts to the stress of exercise and rehabilitation, the following complications may also become apparent (Decker, 1990; Rimmer, 1994):

1. *Spasticity.* To allow the muscles to work functionally and to alternately relax and contract, it is necessary to inhibit antagonist spasticity.

2. *Incomplete innervation.* In muscles that are partially paralyzed, weakness may occur from disuse atrophy and where muscle innervation is intact. Training can restore functioning to a point where it is approximately intact. In cases of partial muscle degeneration, training will restore functioning in only a portion of muscle.

3. *Muscle substitution.* In order to compensate for muscle weakness, muscle substitution or movements are implemented to complete a task. However, if muscle cannot be retrained or if adequate musculature is not available for muscle substitution, a brace may be used for support.

4. *Medication interactions.* Alcohol and steroids may cause muscle weakness and necrosis and affect the process that elicits muscle excitation. Generally, muscle recovery occurs from withdrawal from alcohol. However, some spasticity-inhibiting medications, such as dantrolene sodium, act directly on the muscle. Other medications, such as baclofen and diazepam, act directly on the cord.

5. *Muscle length changes.* Immobilization, muscle imbalance, and posture malalignment may result from spinal cord injury and elicit changes in muscle length. Active intervention, including stretching and strength training, is necessary to prevent length-associated changes.

Implementing the Physical Activity Program

A primary concern in selecting and implementing appropriate physical activities is the individual's functional ability. Because functional movement will depend on the level of the injury and the extent (incomplete or complete) of the injury, teachers should attempt to maximize the remaining movement potential. In most instances, physical activity programs will improve tolerance for activity and the daily demands of independent living. This is especially helpful after an injury, when it is essential to establish independent functioning as soon as possible.

The primary goal is to exercise all spared musculature activity using assisted free-active or resistance exercise (Decker, 1990). Upper-body exercises, including weights, pulleys, and surgical tubing, may increase range of motion and strength that is needed to develop and maintain positive and independent functioning (Table 15.1). The neuromuscular system should be developed and adapted to the stress of exercise by following the basic principles of strength and conditioning (Decker, 1990):

1. *Overload.* The muscle should adapt to stress with resistance exercise designed to facilitate the frequency of muscle contraction.

2. *Progression.* For gains to occur, the muscle should be continually stressed by increasing the amount of weight, number of repetitions, or sets of exercises the individual accomplishes.

3. *Specificity.* Exercises should be selected according to the functional task. The exercise should duplicate the task to be performed by the muscle, including the movement pattern, range of the movement, and type or speed of contraction required. The exercise movement and strengthening activity should generalize to a specific movement or functional skill.

4. *Purpose.* The exercise should also be specific to the purpose of the movement. Exercises may be designed to promote endurance, increase resistance to fatigue, and increase oxidative capacity of the muscle fibers.

Table 15.1 Physical Activity Suggestions for Orthopedic Impairments

Complications	Physical Activity
Contractures	Active and passive stretching; surgical tubing and isometric or active resistance; water exercise and relaxation activities.
Sensory information	Body awareness and gait training. Emphasize postural stability and propriceptive and visual information to compensate for injury. Utilize body awareness and relaxation activities.
Spinal deformities	Upper-body strengthening with resistance exercises; water exercise, rowing, arm cycle, or archery. Strengthen weak muscles and emphasize postural training.
Temperature regulation	Caution in hot and humid environments; ensure child is hydrated, and closely monitor spinal injuries T_6 and above.
Fitness	Encourage active participation to restore function and involvement. Utilize sports and recreational activities to promote lifestyle changes.
Psychological functioning	Emphasize independent functioning and training interventions to promote fitness, activities of daily living (ADLs), and social interactions.

Many corrective activities, such as archery, can be used to develop the upper body as well as provide opportunities to actively participate. Fundamental skills such as running (rolling), throwing, catching, striking, and agility should be developed to ensure participation in team games and sports as well as outside-the-school competition. Parachute activities are also ideal to integrate young children with able-bodied peers as well as to develop upper-body functioning and posture and motor skill development (French & Horvat, 1983).

Lead-up games using targets, suspended balls, or rebound throwing may also aid in the development of fundamental skills for younger children and serve as the basis for more intricate sports and games, such as tennis, racquetball, basketball, and table tennis (Cratty, 1969).

Aquatic exercises and swimming are easily adaptable for individuals with spinal cord injuries. Because of buoyancy, children enjoy more freedom in the aquatic environment. Children should be able to assume a horizontal position and utilize swimming strokes with minor modifications, depending on the remaining muscle functioning. In this manner children can develop overall fitness, movement, and body awareness while being independent of their wheelchairs.

Dance is another activity that requires minor variations, such as expanding the formation to allow more room for movement. Movement sequence and tempos can be learned from performing dance activities, and skills and conditioning can be developed that may be useful in game, sports, and recreational activities.

Very little, if any, modification is needed for sports and games. At times the goal or standard may be lowered, if necessary, in volleyball or basketball. Court games may require allowing the ball to bounce more than once or picking up the dribble in basketball, while the large space required to play some games may be reduced to accommodate students with limited mobility. However, teachers should not disrupt a game to accommodate children in wheelchairs. Most individuals will desire to participate in a nonmodified atmosphere. For example, a child in a wheelchair may participate with his or her able-bodied classmates in basketball by following simple modifications:

1. Defender needs to guard child $1^1/2$ steps away to allow the opportunity to shoot and pass.

2. Children with disabilities are allowed to pick up the dribble and push the wheelchair, but only twice, before passing or shooting.

3. Children in a wheelchair are not allowed to rebound inside the lane lines; this allows able-bodied individuals to jump without fear of landing on the wheelchair.

Modifications should be used only when necessary for the benefit of all individuals in the class, and the safety of all children should be emphasized. Some activities that were once not available for children with spinal cord injuries may now be made possible through the use of more extensive equipment and/or technique modifications. Activities such as white-water kayaking, skiing, and mountaineering have been made possible through the use of special equipment designed to alleviate the disability. A kayak may be modified to allow positioning and stability by removing the hard cockpit and building a form insert and room for the individual's legs. The paddling technique may be altered by changing the paddle, stroke, or release mechanism, depending on the functional ability of the individual.

Functional Skill Development

A primary factor in developing functional activities of daily living are gross motor skills, transfer skills, and muscle strengthening for ambulation or gait training. Many of these skills should be initiated in the clinical and rehabilitation setting. The educator should build upon and expand these skills in order for the child to continue to develop and enhance these skills. Ultimately many of these skills will generalize to play and sport and recreational skills that can be incorporated in the individual's lifestyle. In this context, the teacher can view these activities as developmental and essential to independent functioning.

Gross motor skills should concentrate on the lying and seated positions. For example, rolling will require the child to use the arms, head, neck, and upper torso to initiate movement to front, back, or side-lying positions. Depending on the remaining muscle function available, strengthening should occur to facilitate the movement. The task may be accomplished in segments (i.e., side-lying movements initially) or in unison if sufficient strength is maintained.

Muscle strength and endurance exercises can be passive or active or used in conjunction with the medium of the water. Once the prone lying position is established, the child can do push-ups, upper and lower back extensions and scapular retraction, incorporating prone on elbows or prone lying as a starting position and gradually using the standard pushup position (Decker, 1990). Obviously, the lying positions should translate to a sitting position and necessitate establishing a level of balance using the upper torso to compensate for lack of lower extremity function. Exercises that use the upper body, such as stationary ergonmetry, activities using surgical tubing, or parachute activities, will assist in developing muscle function to maintain posture and can be supplemented with medicine ball activities, therabands, weighted ball throwing, weight shifting, and push-up activities as well as single or bilateral arm movements. Flexibility and range-of-motion exercises should be implemented on a daily basis to prevent contractures and facilitate functional movement (Lasko & Knopf, 1992; Lockette & Keyes, 1994; Rimmer, 1994). In order to sit, the child will also need to develop strength and stability to move the legs. This may necessitate developing upper-body strength to be used in conjunction with balance movements. For example, the child may balance on one arm supporting the weight while using the other arm to move the legs to a particular position. Strength and balance are required and essential for continued development and self-sufficiency.

Limb Deficiency

The absence of a limb may be either congenital or acquired. In congenital amputations, a limb or a portion of a limb is not present at birth or is malformed. Congenital amputations may include absence of an entire limb; absence of all or a portion of the distal half of a limb; absence of the proximal portion of a limb, with hands or feet remaining attached by that portion of the bone.

Acquired amputations refer to the loss of a limb resulting from trauma, injury, disease, or surgery, which is generally linked with a malignant condition such as diabetes, circulatory problems, or cancer. The point of the amputation and portion of the limb remaining (Figure 15.3) will determine the child's functioning level. For example, a below-the-knee amputation will require a leg prosthesis for ambulation. However, because the knee is intact, flexion and extension are still possible. Children will possess a developed quadriceps and some control of their lower extremities and the prosthetic device. Furthermore, the longer the stump, the easier it will be to fit a prosthesis while retaining as much original movement and strength in the extremity. When the amputation involves both legs, ambulation and functioning is significantly reduced; however, children should be able to manage a prosthetic device or use a wheelchair for movement. Comparisons of strength and flexibility of muscle and joints on both sides may reveal deficits in strength of as much as 50% on the affected side (Murray, Jacobs, Gore, Gardner & Mollinger, 1985). Flexibility is not as deficient but is typically lower in the affected side. These differences are more apparent in children than adults, making it more difficult to achieve muscle symmetry in muscle groups that move the prosthesis.

Upper-limb functioning is also affected by the site of the amputation. An above-the-elbow amputation will affect the movement of the arm because of lack of flexion

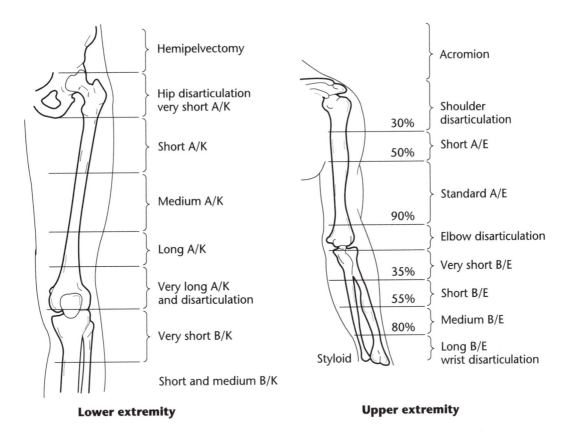

Figure 15.3 Classification of amputation.

Source: National Academy of Sciences, National Research Council, *Artificial Limbs,* 1963.

and extension at the elbow. Attaching the prosthesis will also present a problem if a small portion of the limb is remaining. It is difficult to develop a prosthesis to simulate the numerous small muscles in the hand, and these devices are not as beneficial as those used with the lower limbs. Most upper-arm prostheses can be modified to manipulate rackets or other physical education equipment. More recent devices more closely approximate the human hand and may be effective in eliminating the need for extensive equipment modifications. However, it should be noted that the hand will not only perform grasp-and-release functions but also provides sensory information that cannot be duplicated by a prosthetic device. In most cases, the physician will preserve as much of the hand and wrist as possible to maintain functional capabilities. For example, the loss of each digit of the hand is based on an assigned value in relation to impairment of the hand: thumb (40%), second digit (20%), third digit (20%), fourth digit (10%), and fifth digit (10%). Likewise, amputations through the forearm not only affect hand function but also rotation of the arm depending on the length of the stump (Figure 15.4).

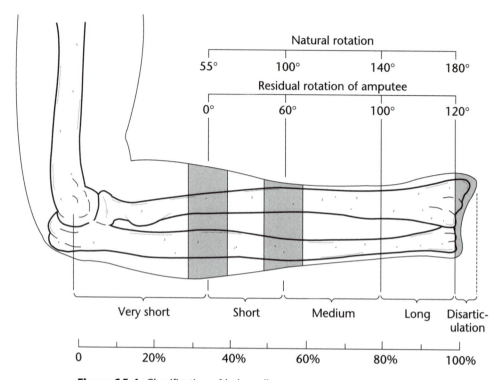

Figure 15.4 Classification of below-elbow stumps.
Source: National Academy of Sciences, National Research Council, *Artificial Limbs*, 1963.

Physical Limitations and Concerns

The loss of a limb is fairly obvious, but there are other limitations imposed by the amputation that may not be as obvious. First, standing and locomotion are affected. A lower leg amputation affects standing and locomotion without the assistance of an artificial limb or ambulatory device. Second, when an artificial limb is used, sensory information from the joints, propriceptors, or muscle is absent. This lack affects the ability to sense position or feel the movement or force generated. For example, a child in a physical conditioning class relied on his prosthesis with hooks. When asked why he didn't select a newer, lighter prosthesis that was cosmetically more pleasing, he answered that it could not provide any sensory feedback and that because he had worn his device for some years he felt comfortable with it. Obviously the loss of touch is important, especially in a child with an upper limb amputation.

Third, support of the body is also affected in addition to postural and locomotor movements. The muscles that are attached to bones contract with a neural impulse and produce force that move the bone about a joint. Because muscles produce tension and allow a contraction, an opposing muscle group is required to allow relaxation of the muscle and movement in the opposite direction and to provide stability for the joint. The force generated by the muscle depends on its length and cross-sectional area. A full range of motion is needed to manage the prosthetic device and avoid contractures.

In addition, the loss of a limb will affect the center of gravity and balance until children compensate or adjust to a prosthetic device. An above-the-joint amputation, especially in the lower extremities, will generally restrict movement and development of motor skills more severely because of the lack of stability provided by a knee and/or elbow. Because muscles may pass over a joint, their ability to transmit force to the bone may be effected.

A fourth concern for children is temperature regulation. With the amount of cooling surface on the body reduced by the missing limb, the amputee will encounter difficulty with thermoregulation. Because the body has less surface area to perspire, warm and/or humid days can cause overheating problems, thereby creating a need for monitoring to ensure safe participation.

A fifth concern is skin care, especially of the stump area, to eliminate irritation. The stump requires periodic ventilation to remove perspiration and body secretions, which may cause irritation or infections. A major concern for the surgeon is to avoid scar tissue and crevices that may preclude keeping the stump clean.

Another concern is that children may not acquire age-appropriate motor skills because of their amputation and/or attitude toward participation, or because of over-protection by parents and educators. Likewise, children may demonstrate a low degree of fitness and obesity because of their sedentary activity patterns. Although the loss of a limb may require compensation to learn a motor skill, teachers should encourage participation as well as alternative ways to move in the environment. Electrostimulation and exercise may also be used to strengthen the stump and corresponding muscles, to mobilize the joints, and to manage the prosthetic device properly.

Finally, children may possess a negative self-concept related to feelings of being different or inadequate. Many times children will avoid situations in which their condition is noticeable, such as the swimming pool. It is essential to educate other teachers and children about an amputee's condition and functioning of the prosthetic device to avoid any misconceptions about his or her condition and to facilitate as much active participation as possible.

Physical Activities

The most important concept in the physical activity program is the development of confidence for the individual with an amputation. Many times the limb deficiency causes a distortion of the individual's body image. By selecting goals that are easily attainable, the child can achieve a measure of success designed to encourage participation and increase self-confidence. Increasing the amount of skill required and participation time can aid in building confidence levels and acceptance by other classmates.

In addition, young children will be periodically experiencing spurts in growth that necessitate refitting of the prosthesis and adjusting to the new demands of the device, such as accommodating balance and changing gaits. More important, it is necessary to allow children to make their own adjustments in an activity. For example, activities that require throwing may be mastered by catching and then throwing with the same arm. Former major league pitcher Jim Abbott compensated for his loss of a right hand in this manner. Likewise, a lower-limb amputee may occupy a position in softball that does not require an excessive amount of running. Many times teachers will overadapt or modify an activity solely on the basis of a disability. A commonsense approach for including upper- and lower-limb amputees in physical education is to assess the functional capabilities remaining before making any modification or adaptation.

Most amputees can be successful in sports or recreational activities and can develop at a level similar to that of their able-bodied peers (Figure 15.5). Opportunities to participate in sporting events and to compete with able-bodied athletes may greatly enhance the psychological adjustment to disability (Horvat, French & Henschen, 1986). In addition, swimming activities are especially beneficial because of the lack of modifications and the overall benefits derived from the aquatic program.

Figure 15.5 Amputee athlete.
Source: Courtesy of OSSUR, USA.

Recreational activities may also be valuable for the physical development of the amputee. Kayaking or canoeing requires minor equipment or technique modifications to include amputees, such as substituting a prosthetic device to balance the nose weight in a kayak. Most sports and games should be actively encouraged and are not outside the capabilities of the amputee. Jogging, dance, golf, tennis, and weight training are examples of suitable activities for school-aged amputees that should be implemented to foster participation and functioning in an integrated environment (Table 15.1).

CHAPTER SUMMARY

1. Children with disabilities may be prone to a greater incidence of postural defects than the general school-aged population. Children with sensory impairments may exhibit poor postures and head tilts from lack of feedback; children who are non-ambulatory may place undue pressure on their postural structure and must reassert their center of balance, which was affected by injury.

2. Posture is defined as the manner in which body alignment is maintained against gravity. Correct posture is achieved when all body segments are properly aligned over the base of support.

3. Specific body types are more apt to assume a particular posture because of their build. In analyzing proper posture, teachers must be aware of individual differences that are associated with age, body type, and exceptionality.

4. Posture deficiencies may occur in a variety of positions and affect different areas of the body structure. In order to effectively correct posture problems, the teacher should utilize appropriate exercises for various parts of the body.

5. Children with orthopedic disorders will manifest a chronic condition and lifelong adjustment process to their disability. These conditions generally indicate a lengthy process of the disease and/or treatment and are permanent, resulting in a loss of functioning.

6. The major concerns for teachers of children with orthopedic impairments are physical functioning and motor development.

7. When children are mainstreamed into regular physical education, teachers should strive to encourage peer understanding and acceptance through integration and should provide additional outside opportunities for sport and recreation.

8. The most obvious aspect of a spinal cord injury is the loss of movement and physical functioning in the extremities. Other complications, such as spasms, contractures, decubitus ulcers, ossification, pain, edema, and temperature regulation also can affect functional ability. A primary concern in selecting and implementing appropriate physical activities is the functional ability of the individual.

9. Appropriate physical activity programs can aid in the improvement of day-to-day functioning and tolerance for activity.

10. Amputations will restrict the mobility and physical functioning of children. Some concerns include temperature regulation, center of gravity and balance, overprotection by parents, motor skill deficiencies, and a negative self-concept.

11. Goals should be selected that are based on improving functional ability and ensuring success as well as increasing the individual's level of self-confidence.

12. A commonsense approach for including upper- and lower-limb amputees in physical education is to assess the functional capabilities remaining before making any modification or adaptation.

References

Bromley, I. (1981). *Tetraplegia and paraplegia.* (2nd ed.). New York: Churchill Livingston.

Cratty, B. (1969). *Developmental games for physically handicapped children.* Palo Alto, CA: Peek Publications.

Daniels, L. (1977). *Therapeutic exercises for body alignment and function.* (2nd ed.). Philadelphia: Saunders.

Decker, M. (1990). Exercise for spinal cord injured patients. In Basmajan, J. V., & Wolf, S. A. (Eds.), (5th ed.). *Therapeutic exercise* (pp. 177–205). Baltimore: Williams & Wilkins.

Dunn, J. (1997). *Special physical education* (7th ed.). Dubuque, IA: Wm. C. Brown.

Engstrom, B., & Van de Ven, C. (1993). *Physiotherapy for amputees* (2nd ed.). New York: Churchill Livingstone.

Figoni, S. (1997). Spinal cord injury. In American College of Sports Medicine, *Exercise management for persons with chronic diseases and disabilities* Champaign, IL: Human Kinetics.

French, R., & Horvat, M. (1983). *Parachute movement activities.* Bryon, CA: Front Row Experience.

Horvat, M., French, R., & Henschen, K. (1986). A comparison of the psychological characteristics of male and female able-bodied and wheelchair athletes. *Paraplegia, 24,* 115–22.

Kisner, C., & Colby, L. A. (1990). *Therapeutic exercise: Foundations and techniques* (2nd ed.). Philadelphia: F. A. Davis.

Lasko, P., & Knopf, K. (1992). *Adapted and corrective exercise for the disabled adult* (3rd ed.). Dubuque, IA: Eddie Bowers.

Lockette, K. F., & Keyes A. M. (1994). *Conditioning with physical disabilities.* Champaign, IL: Human Kinetics.

Murray, P., Jacobs, P., Gore, D., Gardner, G., & Mollinger, L. (1985). Functional performance after tibial rationplasty. *The Journal of Bone and Joint Surgery, 67,* 392–399.

Rimmer, J. H. (1994). *Fitness and rehabilitation programs for special population.* Dubuque, IA: Brown and Benchmark.

Williams, M., & Worthington, C. (1961). *Therapeutic exercise for body alignment and function.* Philadelphia: Saunders.

CHAPTER 16

Neurological Disorders

C hildren with neurological disorders have their own unique characteristics that may complicate developing physical fitness and motor skills. These children are often prohibited from physical activity because of their disorder. Many teachers and administrators maintain inappropriate attitudes and misconceptions about neurological disorders as well as about the child's ability to achieve age-appropriate physical and motor skills. This chapter stresses the importance of physical functioning as it relates to children with disorders of the nervous systems.

The nervous system consists of the brain, spinal cord, ganglia, and nerves that transmit and receive information from the working muscles. If this system is disrupted or injured, the movement process will be affected. Because the degree of remaining function varies greatly depending on the site and extent of the injury to the nervous system, children should be treated individually and actively encouraged to participate in regular physical activity classes.

Cerebral Palsy

Cerebral palsy refers to a motor impairment that results from a lesion in or trauma to the developing brain. This impairment is not contagious, fatal, inherited, or a disease; rather it is a term that describes manifestations of observed motor characteristics and movement control problems.

Approximately 700,000 individuals in the United States have cerebral palsy. Of these, one-third are under 21 years of age, while 1,000 newborns and another 2,000 infants in their first year manifest cerebral palsy due to head injuries.

Cerebral palsy can be described as a group of conditions that originate in infancy and are characterized by weakness, paralysis, lack of coordination and motor functioning, and very poor muscle tone directly related to pathology of the motor control center of the brain. These conditions may also occur in different degrees of severity and extent of limb involvement (Mushett, Wyeth & Richter, 1995). Cerebral palsy is a nonprogressive disorder of the immature or developing brain. Although the disorder is nonprogressive, the neurological system typically develops so quickly that expectations are not consistent during development.

Abnormalities of motor tone or movement in the first several weeks or months after birth may gradually improve during the first year and eventually be "outgrown" as the child continues to develop. Conversely, children who possess relatively non-specific motor signs during the first weeks or months of life may develop severe cases of cerebral palsy. Therefore, the diagnosis of cerebral palsy should be very tentative; a definitive diagnosis should be made only after the child's second birthday. Although a definitive diagnosis is not recommended until after the second year, early intervention in the child with cerebral palsy can reduce the effects of the disability. With this in mind, all parents should be aware of important growth and development landmarks in the lives of their children. Some conditions that may indicate the presence of cerebral palsy are as follows (Schleichkorn, 1993):

- poor head control after 3 months of age
- stiff or rigid arms or legs
- pushing away or arching back
- floppy or limp posture
- inability to sit up without support by 8 months
- use of only one side of the body, or only the arms, to crawl
- extreme irritability
- failure to smile by 3 months
- feeding difficulties—persistent gagging or choking when fed; after 6 months of age, tongue pushes soft food out of the mouth

Children with cerebral palsy will encounter a lack of understanding related to their condition. Partial paralysis and facial or speech distortions may contribute to misconceptions that lead to social isolation. Although movement may be restricted in cerebral palsy, many children can function at levels that will meet the program goals of regular physical activity classes. It is the responsibility of teachers to adequately assess movement potential and provide movement experiences to promote independent functioning for children with cerebral palsy in a positive social environment. Children may also have other developmental problems, such as cognitive delays and perceptual difficulties, that will also limit skill development.

Etiology of Cerebral Palsy

Cerebral palsy results from a lesion in the brain that interferes with the development of the central nervous system. Although there are many possible causes, some of which cannot be traced, the major suggested cause during the prenatal period is anoxia in the fetus. Other suggested prenatal causes of cerebral palsy include maternal infection or disease, such as rubella; metabolic malfunctions; toxemia; and poor maternal care. Natal causes include premature birth, anoxia, trauma, breech birth, and prolonged labor. Postnatal complications include head injury or trauma, infections such as encephalitis (inflammation of the brain) or meningitis (inflammation of the brain and spinal cord), tumors, and toxic substances such as lead and arsenic.

Classifications and Types of Cerebral Palsy

It is sometimes difficult to determine the regions of the brain that are involved in cerebral palsy. The major areas of the brain that are affected are the cortex (pyramidal tracts), basal ganglia (extrapyramidal region), and the cerebellum (Figure 16.1).

The pyramidal tracts originate in the cerebral cortex and are responsible for voluntary control of the face, trunk, and limbs. Fibers from nerve cells that originate in

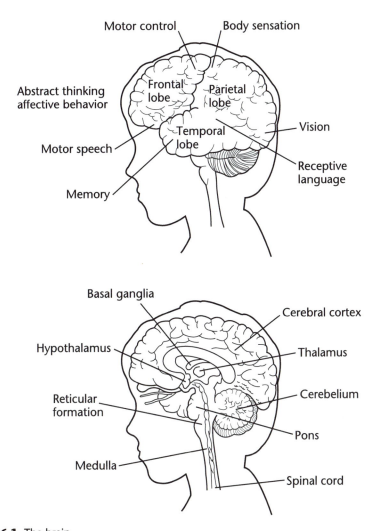

Motor control   Body sensation

Abstract thinking
affective behavior

Frontal
lobe   Parietal
lobe

Vision

Motor speech   Temporal
lobe

Receptive
language

Memory

Basal ganglia

Cerebral cortex

Hypothalamus   Thalamus

Reticular
formation   Cerebelium

Medulla   Pons

Spinal cord

Figure 16.1 The brain.

the cerebral cortex descend to the spinal cord through the basal ganglia, enter the midbrain and hindbrain, and cross in these areas through the corticospinal tract. Fibers from the nerve cells of the right side of the cerebral cortex innervate the left side of the body, whereas fibers from the left side of the cortex innervate the right side of the body. Typically, the neurons of the cortex via the pyramidal tract provide a desired channel from the brain to the spinal neurons that transmit impulses that cause the muscle to contract, relax, or initiate a movement. In addition, the corticospinal neurons also receive sensory information from the muscle that is essential for motor memory and control of movement. The cerebellum receives input from the motor areas of the cortex, brain stem, and sensory system, including the proprioceptors, consistently upgrades and monitors movement and feedback necessary for movement control. An injury to these nerve cells or fibers causes spasticity in the muscles innervated by these fibers in the right or left side of the body, depending on the location of the brain damage. In contrast, injuries in the basal ganglia or extrapyramidal system result in dyskinesia (uncoordinated or uncontrolled movement), as manifested by children with athetosis. This second motor pathway includes all motor axons not on the pyramidal systems. However these axons do not pass through the medullary pyramids and synapses in the basal ganglia, pons, medulla, and reticular formation. Rather, these axons descend through the internal capsule and laminate in subcortical structures to form a feedback loop. The function of the loop is to modify and adjust movements for postural and reflexive movements. Damage to the cerebellum area involves problems with coordination and balance generally seen in children with ataxia.

The complex pattern of these nerves and fibers makes it difficult to determine an exact classification of cerebral palsy. In fact, the traditional and prevalent classification is mixed cerebral palsy and reflects a combination of symptoms. The primary classifications of cerebral palsy are based on severity and movement characteristics.

One classification is based on the degree of motor involvement and includes children with the following:

Mild Involvement

1. Movement potential for self-help, physical fitness, and motor skills
2. Response to training and intervention
3. Loss of functional capabilities without intervention
4. Little or no activity limitations
5. Control of head and movement functions, ambulation

Moderate Involvement

1. Variations of independent functioning in self-help and functional skills
2. Functional head control
3. Perceptual and sensory deficits that affect learning and motor skills, regardless of the type and severity of cerebral palsy present; delayed skill acquisition
4. Loss of motor function that affects speech and motor control
5. Utilization of assistive devices for ambulation

Severe Involvement

1. Poor head and movement control
2. Dependence in self-help skills and functional capabilities; reliance on assistive devices
3. Skeletal and postural deformities; muscle imbalance and tightness
4. Perceptual and sensory deficits that affect motor skill acquisition and learning

Another classification is based on the type of motor disability that is prevalent. These include spasticity, athetosis, ataxia, tremor, and rigidity, while mixed cerebral palsy commonly displays symptoms of each. The first three are the most common in a regular physical education setting, and a discussion of each follows.

Spasticity   Spasticity is present in 50–66% of all cases of cerebral palsy resulting from damage to the motor cortex where voluntary motor responses originate. Muscle movements are poorly coordinated and hypertonic with permanently increased muscle tone. Spasticity affects the flexor muscle groups that contribute to the maintenance of posture. The muscles in the lower limbs are rotated inward and flexed at the hip; the knees are flexed and abducted, while the heels are raised. The result is a forced crossing of the legs at the midline that is referred to as a scissors-type gait. In the upper limbs, the forearms are pronated with flexion at the elbows, wrists, and fingers.

Some muscles may function normally or fluctuate because of response in static strength or length of the muscle (Mushett et al., 1995). In normal functioning, a slight stretching of the muscle stimulates the muscle spindle of the stretched muscle, causing the muscle to contract appropriately, and is essential for maintaining muscle tone and maintenance of posture. In spasticity, the stretch reflex is exaggerated and causes muscle tightness and abnormal postures. Spastic muscles may also demonstrate a clasp-knife response, in which a sudden passive movement creates an initial buildup in resistance, followed by a sudden release of tension accompanied by a positive stretch reflex, similar to the action of opening a knife. Additionally, voluntary movements of spastic muscles tend to be slow and uncoordinated as children experience difficulty breaking free of stereotyped movements from their reflexes. Inadequate control of force may be observed at the beginning, middle, or end of a movement (Sudgen & Keogh, 1990). As children mature and bones elongate, there is an increased amount of pull exerted by the muscles at the joint that exerts pressure on the muscles. This pressure causes tightening or contractures of muscles, such as the upward pull of the heel from a spastic gastrocnemius muscle. As a result, the child requires training programs to balance opposing muscle groups.

Children with mild spasticity will have a minimal loss of function caused by lack of coordination. Mild cases are usually characterized by hemiplegia. Most of these children should be able to walk and run but may have difficulty with refined tasks (Huberman, 1976). A child with moderate spasticity will have varying degrees of functioning on one side of the body or minimal involvement in four limbs. Most children possess functional ability on the nonaffected side of the body and exhibit more purposeful movement if they are not stressed, fatigued, or overstimulated. Moderate spasticity also requires stretching activities to overcome the impaired range of motion caused by contractures.

Children with severe spasticity will be extremely limited in movement and muscle tone in all limbs. Voluntary movements are minimal and are often accompanied by the retention of primitive reflexes that interfere with purposeful movement. As the severity increases, the child tends to demonstrate one-sided postural control. They generally tend to prefer the unaffected side and are positioned with the head, neck, and trunk aligned inappropriately. The arms are not used to counterbalance their movements and are initiated by the unaffected side in stepping, crawling, or reaching activities. Severe involvement will require a specialized program of special physical education and physical therapy aimed at inhibiting reflexes, initiating movement, and improving physical fitness.

Athetosis   Athetosis, or extrapyramidal cerebral palsy, results from a lesion in the basal ganglia that is located in the central portion of the cerebrum, which controls purposeful movement. Athetosis occurs in approximately 25–30% of all cases and is characterized by purposeless, involuntary, irregular movements in the extremities. Muscles of the head and upper limbs are mainly affected, with constant flexion in the upper limbs and extension of the fingers, wrists, and elbows while drawing the arms backward and palms downward.

Children with athetosis are constantly moving while demonstrating a lack of control and selectivity in movements. At times, movements are jerky and fast, while at other times movements may be slow and rhythmic. Contractures or increased muscle tension usually is not prevalent, because muscle tone is constantly changing. Generally, locomotion is uncoordinated, while protective and equilibrium reactions may still be present that interfere with development of purposeful movement. Children may also demonstrate a lack of head control, difficulty with speech, and facial contortions.

There are several forms of athetosis, the most common type of which is characterized by rotary movements. The amount of movement increases during periods of excitement or tension but can decline when children are in a calm and relaxed state. Mild to moderate athetosis includes movement in one or two limbs, whereas severe involvement entails three or four limbs. Another form of athetosis, called choreoathetosis, causes uncontrollable spasms that inhibit useful movement. Spasms in severe athetosis are more proximal and are characterized by flying arms and legs during movements. The distinguishing feature of athetosis is involuntary, uncontrollable movements of body parts. Although the reflexes are normal, performance of simple motor tasks may be difficult because of the uncontrollable, involuntary movements. It is also more noticeable during slow controlled movements, such as walking, as opposed to faster movements, such as running (Mushett et al., 1995).

Ataxia   Ataxia is the result of a lesion in the cerebellum. The cerebellum organizes information to coordinate movement and is the feedback mechanism in the brain for muscular functioning. Ataxia occurs in fewer than 10% of all cases of cerebral palsy and is usually not congenital but acquired.

With ataxia, the amount of useful functioning varies, especially in children with mild involvement. Children will demonstrate a poor sense of balance, kinesthetic awareness, and uncoordinated movement. Ataxia is generally not diagnosed until the child begins to walk and demonstrates a lack of coordination. The child's gait will be disrupted by a lack of postural control and by inconsistent foot placement. Additionally, spatial awareness and coordination are affected by the disrupted feedback mechanism that causes children to overshoot or undershoot when reaching for objects and interferes with the dexterity needed for dribbling or catching a ball.

Influence of Primitive Reflexes and Other Characteristics

Reflexes are automatic responses of the nervous system that are present at birth and controlled by the primitive regions of the nervous system, spinal cord, labyrinth of the inner ear, and brain stem. They are responsible for changes in muscle tone and movement and gradually become integrated into voluntary movements as the higher center of the brain develops. Reflexes also aid children in assuming postures and controlling movement. During infancy, reflexes will dominate movement until 6 months of age. In children with cerebral palsy, reflexes may be stronger, persist longer, and may reemerge, especially after injury or trauma to the brain.

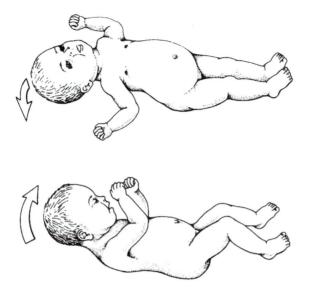

Figure 16.2 The tonic labyrinthine reflex.

There are many reflexes that are prevalent in normal development. Three primary reflexes that affect postures and movement are the asymmetrical tonic neck reflex (ATNR), the tonic labyrinthine reflex (TLR), and the positive support reflex (PSR). Each reflex is elicited by a stimulus, and all three reflexes will affect movement.

The ATNR is elicited by either active or passive rotation of the head. When the head is rotated, the ATNR increases the extension of the arm and leg on the same side as the chin, while the arm and leg in opposition increase in flexion. Children will remain in this position until the head turns and releases the reflex. The presence of the ATNR causes an increase in muscle tone and may affect changes in posture.

For the TLR, the position of the labyrinth in the inner ear provides the stimulus. Extending the neck or lying on the back tilts the labyrinth and elicits the reflex, extending the legs and retracting the shoulders (Figure 16.2). Flexing the neck or lying on the stomach causes the hips and knees to flex and shoulders to protract (roll forward). When the TLR is present but not strong, changes in muscle tone may occur without any accompanying changes in position (Olney & Wright, 1994).

The PSR is stimulated, causing extension of the legs, when the balls of the feet touch a firm surface (Figure 16.3). Normally this reflex contributes to supporting the child's weight while in the standing position. In cerebral palsy, this causes adduction and internal rotation of the hips, which interferes with standing and locomotion.

The persistence of undesirable reflexes and some developmental delay are characteristic of all types of cerebral palsy. For teachers it is important to understand the influence of these reflexes on normal motor development, muscle tone, and postures. For example, persistence of the TLR will interfere with postural control and mechanics, such as balance and tone needed for unsupported sitting or standing. The persistence of this reflex will not only disturb muscle tone and equilibrium in unsupported movements but also interfere with initiating purposeful movement. Many normal postural reactions may be totally lacking or incomplete. Movements that require con-

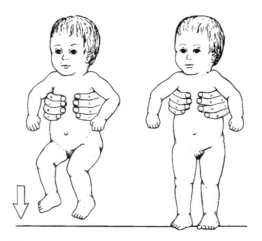

Figure 16.3 The positive support reflex.

stant changes in tone and equilibrium are then disrupted with the persistence of this primitive reflex. In addition, scissoring may occur because of the adduction and internal rotation of the hips (Figure 16.4) Toe walking may occur because of the tendency of a shortened gastrocnemius to lift the heel from the ground.

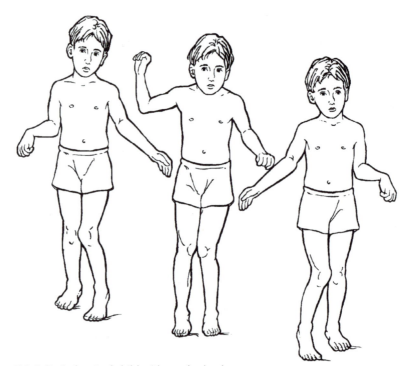

Figure 16.4 Typical gait of child with cerebral palsy, spastic diplegia, or paraplegia.

Effect on Functional Development

Growth Poor growth has been well documented in children with cerebral palsy. The main variables causing poor growth have been classified as nutritional factors and neurological, nor non-nutritional, factors. Stallings, Zemel, Davies, Cronk, and Charney (1996) stated that growth failure in individuals with cerebral palsy is often due to inadequate dietary intake. Non-nutritional factors causing poor growth have been classified as either direct, through a negative neurotrophic effect on linear growth; or indirect, through the endocrine system, immobility, or lack of weight bearing. Stevenson, Roberts, and Vogtle (1995) and Roberts, Vogtle, and Stevenson (1994) concluded that non-nutritional factors related to disease severity have a significant influence on the growth of children with cerebral palsy, even in the absence of malnutrition. Lin and Henderson (1996) supported these conclusions as they found that bone mineral content, bone mineral density, and lean muscle mass were all reduced in the affected versus the unaffected limb of hemiplegic individuals with cerebral palsy. They concluded that bone size and bone density both decrease with increasing severity of the disability, thereby causing reductions in growth and maturation.

Locomotion The development of locomotion or gait patterns is often affected in children with cerebral palsy. The primary focus in the generation and control of locomotion has been the role of higher brain centers, such as the sensorimotor cortex. The deficits in locomotion in children with cerebral palsy have been ascribed to damage to the basic circuitry serving pattern generation, to failed maturation of spinal reflexes and/or the descending systems that control them, and to changes in the mechanical properties of muscles (Leonard, Hirschfield & Forssberg, 1991). Leonard et al (1991) also found that normal features of adult gait did not develop in children with severe cerebral palsy. These problems were similar to those identified by Bar-Or (1983) and colleagues (Unnithan, Dowling, Frost & Bar-Or, 1996; Unnithan, Dowling, Frost, Volpe Ayub & Bar-Or, 1996). Bottos, Puato, Vianello, and Facchin (1995) also concluded that severe deformities, resulting from cerebral palsy affected the choice of locomotion pattern and indicated that locomotion pattern, age at onset, and even manner of execution all influenced prognosis for walking.

Planning the Physical Activity Program

Children with cerebral palsy have physical and motor limitations that are based on their predominant type of motor disability. Children with spasticity encounter difficulties in accomplishing activities that require muscular strength and/or endurance but are capable of more precise, fine motor movement than are children with athetosis. In contrast, children with athetosis are more proficient in performing locomotor activities than activities that require muscular strength.

A primary concern of teachers is the need to develop and maximize the movement potential of children. Early in the developmental process, the emphasis is on education, physical therapy, and surgery to enable children to function and develop appropriately. If the emphasis on movement is not continued, children will be at a disadvantage. The gains accrued from early emphasis on developing movement potential often dissipate without ongoing training. This will lead to a deterioration of movement and less ability to initiate movements, as well as increases in weight during the maturation process that are not accompanied by increases in strength and power (Bar-Or, 1983). Lack of physical training causes movement to become increasingly difficult, and children become less tolerant of the demands of activity as their cardiovascular functioning diminishes (Rose, Haskell & Gamble, 1993). Furthermore, the lack of training is complicated by the increased reliance on electronic wheelchairs and devices that reduce the need for physical development.

Increasing the overall physical functioning of children with cerebral palsy is essential in developing a physical education program. Teachers should consider several factors in this program, including the team approach, movement efficiency, and motivation.

The Team Approach

The treatment of children with cerebral palsy requires the concerted effort of the collaborative team. To provide a comprehensive program for overall development, the following may be necessary:

- surgery to stabilize muscular development and eliminate deformities
- identification of primitive reflexes
- therapy to achieve range of motion, and mastery of basic living skills
- educational instruction to overcome learning problems and establish communication

Physical activity is especially important as a contributor to the total program and should be used extensively with those children whose disability is in the mild-to-moderate range. Activity can contribute to the functional independence of children by providing the opportunity to learn motor skills, develop fitness, and participate in leisure activities that are essential to their overall development.

Movement (Mechanical Efficiency)

The movement of children with cerebral palsy is low, especially in children with spasticity performing arm or leg movements, because of wasteful contractions of the spastic, or dyskinetic, muscle (Bar-Or, 1983). For example, when children perform a rhythmic task such as walking, the agonist and antagonist muscles alternately contract and relax to permit efficient movement. In spasticity, these muscle groups may maintain increased tone in the arms and/or legs, leading to inefficient and wasteful motion. Furthermore, the amount of force exerted by the trunk muscles is difficult for children to overcome, which significantly contributes to a lower efficiency of the working muscles. When assessing performance capabilities, Bar-Or (1983) indicated that such inefficiency not only is less economical for movement but also varied from one trial to another. Inefficiency may also be due to the child's attempt to compensate for gait deficiencies, thus exaggerating the movement further and leading to more wasteful motions. Bar-Or's work has been expanded to demonstrate how cocontraction compromises gait patterns and produces higher energy costs in children with cerebral palsy (Unnithan, Dowling, Frost & Bar-Or, 1996; Unnithan, Dowling, Frost, et al., 1996).

Implementing the Physical Activity Program

The selection of physical education activities should be based on the obvious motor characteristics of children within their classification system or the combination of motor characteristics from a mixed classification (Table 16.1). All children with cerebral palsy should be provided with opportunities to develop strength, endurance, and flexibility according to individual needs. In addition, children with spasticity may require stretching of flexor groups and strengthening of extensors, whereas children with athetosis and ataxia require relaxation, muscle stabilization, and coordination activities.

Because of the individualized level of functioning, it is necessary to progressively increase the child's tolerance for activity. Resistance exercises using wall pulleys, weights, surgical tubing, handing activities, and medicine balls can promote the development of strength and encourage socialization (Horvat, 1987; McCubbin & Shasby, 1985). These activities also develop both sides of the body, which aids in developing proper and symmetrical body mechanics.

Table 16.1 Classifications,* Motor Characteristics, and Appropriate Activities for Children with Cerebral Palsy

Classification	Motor Characteristics	Physical Education Activities
Spasticity	Scissors gait resulting from the inward rotation of legs; hip flexion; knees and heels off the floor with toes pointing inward. Upper limb involves pronated forearms, which results in elbow, wrist, and finger flexion. Stereotypic movements from reflexes; increased muscle tone (hypertonicity) and possible clonus. Production of force is deficient with wasteful contractions. Lack of sensory information from muscle.	Aquatics, circuit and resistance training, weight lifting, hanging activities, slow stretching, flexibility exercises, yoga, relaxation activities, dance, rhythms, movement exploration activities to promote finger and wrist extension, body image and awareness using a mirror, jogging, track and field, and most ball sports (i.e., softball, volleyball, basketball), isometrics, pushing skills
Athetosis	Involuntary movements that are uncontrollable, unpredictable, and purposeless. Movements may be slow and rhythmic or jerky and fast. Also characterized by extra actions with voluntary movement. Unsteady and fluctuating muscle tone.	Aquatics, stretching and flexibility exercises, rhythms, dance, movement exploration and body imagery with a mirror, low-organized games, badminton, table tennis, softball, basketball, bowling, track and field, and volleyball
Ataxia	Poor sense of balance and position of body. Uncoordinated and unsteady movements in movements as child begins to sit, stand, and walk. Poor postural fixation with excessive righting reactions using arms to compensate.	Aquatics, balance activities, body awareness and movement exploration, flexibility and yoga exercises, stretching, rhythms, dance, bowling, golf, table tennis, most ball sports, and track and field

*Predominant classification. Often children will manifest mixed cerebral palsy, which includes motor characteristics from each classification.

Cardiovascular endurance can be improved by jogging, cycling, arm ergometry, aerobic dance, riding, wheelchair rolling, swimming, or water exercises. Teachers should implement these activities in a noncompetitive atmosphere and provide rest intervals to postpone undue fatigue.

Some children may be apprehensive about the aquatic environment because of splashing or anxiety that may elicit abnormal muscle spasm. However, swimming is ideal because of the buoyancy provided by the water, lack of gravity, and the suspension of the entire body. Training can easily be implemented to promote fundamental movements, range of motion, and cardiovascular conditioning through water exercises.

By using the medium of the water, teachers can also incorporate games and water exercises to progressively increase endurance. The emphasis in the aquatic program should be on the integration of body parts and free movements rather than on implementing a stroke precisely. Proper breath control and flotation devices are also encouraged to provide intermittent training and a progressive endurance program. Teachers should also provide warmer temperatures of water (85–88°) and air (85–90°) to protect children from undue cooling of the body. Aquatic activities in warm water may also aid in reducing tension, especially if the session does not exceed the child's comfort zone.

Dance activities can also promote fitness and are progressive in nature. Aerobics, line dances, folk dances, and other activities involve both sides of the body, use basic movements, and develop appropriate posture as well as provide an excellent social outlet for children.

Body image activities should be encouraged, such as body awareness and naming body parts. Movement exploration concepts are useful to stress movement of particular body parts as well as to improve balance and coordination. Laterality activities, especially in hemiplegia, can enable children to differentiate from the functional and affected side of the body.

Supplemental Activities

Children with cerebral palsy are generally less active than their peers and rely too much on mechanical devices for ambulation. Furthermore, the activity in regular physical education classes may not be rigorous enough to produce improvement in physical conditioning. The physical performance of children with cerebral palsy will decrease when an ongoing fitness program is not provided throughout the year (Lundberg, 1976; Sommer, 1971).

Obviously the motor functioning needs constant attention in order for the child to maintain overall functional ability. In providing an ongoing program, team members may consider the use of physical activity outside the school to provide an essential supplement to the physical education program. The potential benefits of physical activity in improving mobility have been well documented (Bar-Or, 1983; Rotzinger & Stoboy, 1974; Sommer, 1971). For example, a physical activity program outside the school led to improvements in walking speed, efficiency of movement, and some relief of spasms among severely involved individuals.

In order to avoid contraindicated activities, consultation with physicians and physical therapists is required. Children with spasticity should avoid activities that increase tension in already-tight muscles. For example, leg extensions may cause adduction in the lower extremities and would be contraindicated in some children. Likewise, children who experience grasping and releasing problems should not be evaluated for muscular strength using a hand-grip dynamometer.

For both spasticity and athetosis, relaxation and tension-reduction activities can be beneficial. In spasticity, relaxation may counteract tight muscle groups, whereas in athetosis the constant muscle contractions may be controlled or quieted with stress-reduction and relaxation techniques.

To appropriately supplement the school physical education program, teachers can use sports and assign homework to improve mobility and increase physical functioning. Most children can tolerate intense activity for 15 to 20 minutes twice weekly, while less intense activity can be tolerated for longer periods (Bar-Or, 1983). Therefore, home-based activities can easily be implemented to provide additional opportunities for developing motor skills and physical conditioning if supervised properly within a medical margin of safety. For example, exercises developed by therapists and teachers, such as progressive resistance exercises, can be used to strengthen muscles, while relaxation techniques can aid in maintaining muscle balance and stability as well as facilitate reaching (Fetters & Kluzik, 1996).

Sports and leisure activities should also be encouraged for children (Jones, 1988). Since 1978, sporting events have been held for individuals with cerebral palsy to provide competition and socialization opportunities. These events include bowling, billiards, table tennis, archery, weight lifting, swimming, track and field, softball, cycling, and wheelchair slalom. The National Disability Sports Alliance (NDSA) uses the following eight-level classification system. Category A is (NDSA 2002) based on the functional level for individuals with cerebral palsy and head injuries. Currently Category B is being developed for individuals with muscular dystrophy and other physical disabilities.

Class 1: Severe involvement in all four limbs. Limited trunk control. Unable to grasp a softball. Poor functional strength in upper extremities, often necessitating the use of an electric wheelchair for independence.

Class 2: Severe to moderate quadriplegic, normally able to propel wheelchair very slowly with arms or by pushing with feet. Poor functional strength and severe control problems in the upper extremities.

Class 3: Moderate quadriplegic, fair functional strength and moderate control problems in upper extremities and torso. Uses wheelchair.

Class 4: Lower limbs have moderate to severe involvement. Good functional strength and minimal control problem in upper extremities and torso. Uses wheelchair.

Class 5: Good functional strength and minimal control problems in upper extremities. May walk with or without assistive devices for ambulatory support.

Class 6: Moderate to severe quadriplegic. Ambulates without walking aids. Less coordination. Balance problems when running or throwing. Has greater upper extremity involvement.

Class 7: Moderate to minimal hemiplegic. Good functional ability in nonaffected side. Walk/runs with noted limp.

Class 8: Minimally affected. May have minimal coordination problems. Able to run and jump freely. Has good balance.

Most children are capable not only of participating in sports but also of training in ways comparable to those of their able-bodied peers (Jones, 1988). Modifications of activity should be based on the child's functional ability, and training should be progressive and intensive enough to develop overall functional ability and sport-specific skill. In this manner, sports can contribute to increasing the functional ability of children while providing avenues for competition and leisure that contribute to the socialization process. Teachers should consider children and their motivation levels before modifying or substituting activities. All individuals respond differently to competition and training and should not be confined to limited activities, such as bowling and shuffleboard; rather, children should be allowed to participate in sports advocated by the NDSA, such as basketball, softball, weight training, and track.

Motivation

One aspect of a physical activity program that is often neglected is the motivation required to continue with a training regimen. Because a child with cerebral palsy needs to expend more effort to maintain an adequate level of physical functioning, it is essential for teachers to enhance the motivational aspects of participation. Teachers can utilize charts, contracts, and self-testing activities to increase motivation, as well as continually praise children for their effort and participation. Additionally, teachers can intersperse enjoyable or reinforcing activities into the teaching and conditioning process that enable children to continue their participation at a level designed to increase their overall functioning ability.

Seizure (Epilepsy) and Convulsive Disorders

A seizure or convulsive disorder is a neurological condition initiated by abnormal discharges in the brain (Gates & Spiegel, 1993). There are no specific causes for seizures; seizures are symptoms of a period when consciousness is impaired, which may or may not be accompanied by convulsive movements. Recently, terminology concerning epilepsy, which comes from the Greek word for *seizure,* has expanded to include convulsive and/or seizure disorders. Seizures may be misunderstood by educators and/or other children, causing a social stigma or a connotation of disease.

Approximately 30% of convulsive disorders occur in the period from birth to 5 years from problems in pregnancy, birth disorders, trauma, infections, and/or fevers. In the early school years, 34% of these disorders are triggered by accidents and illness. Adolescent patterns include 13% of all cases and are due to severe illness, brain tumors, and head trauma, and 23% of the cases occur in adult years from brain injuries, brain tumors, and cardiovascular disease.

Heredity is usually not a direct cause of seizure disorders, although brain-wave patterns associated with seizures appear to run in families, and in males more than females. Also, there is a tendency for seizures to accompany other disorders that affect the neurological system, such as cerebral palsy, spina bifida, mental retardation, and learning disorders.

Susceptibility

Several factors may cause a seizure or contribute to lowering the child's seizure threshold. For children who are susceptible to seizures, this necessitates an awareness of the potential factors that may trigger a seizure. Some of these triggers include

- chronic and recurrent head trauma
- stressful conditions, including anger and fear
- hyperventilation
- alcoholic beverages
- changes in the alkalinity of the blood, with low levels increasing susceptibility to seizures
- the menstrual period
- changes in hormone levels
- fatigue

Types of Seizures

There are several types of seizures that teachers should be able to recognize that are generalized or partial and further subdivided into more specific categories. Although these classifications are widely accepted, classification is extremely difficult considering the diversity of opinion and classifications worldwide. As our knowledge about seizures expands, future classifications may be based more on specific biochemical defects, lack of neurotransmitters, or genetic base rather than on clinical observation and electrographic presentations. Included in Table 16.2 are characteristics of the more prevalent types of seizures and appropriate first-aid measures to be implemented by teachers (Epilepsy Foundation of America, 1998; Freeman, Vinning & Pillas, 1990; Lesser, 1991).

Partial Seizures (Focal, Local) There are several types of partial seizures. In one type of simple partial seizure, consciousness is not impaired; this type of seizure is also known as a sensory or motor seizure. The person may have a blank facial expression and experience psychic signs, such as the sensation of a smell or taste or unexplained emotions.

In another type of partial seizure, consciousness is not impaired but may be characterized by a jerking or twitching of the fingers or toes. This activity sometimes spreads throughout the body and becomes a convulsive seizure but sometimes remains localized to a certain part of the body. The person is awake and aware of his or her environment throughout the course of this type of seizure.

A complex partial seizure is the most common type of event and was formerly known as a temporal lobe or psychomotor seizure. This type of seizure involves an impairment of consciousness. The onset of this event is often preceded by an aura, and the abnormal activity is localized to a part of the brain. This type of seizure is characterized by loss of awareness of the environment and is very often associated with a blank facial expression and, possibly, semipurposeful movements. Seizures usually last from 1–5 minutes, and the person is often confused for a short period of time afterwards. Another type of partial seizure evolves to a secondary generalized seizure.

Table 16.2 First Aid for Seizure Disorders

Seizure Type	Characteristics	First Aid
Partial seizures A, Simple partial (consciousness not impaired)	Jerking begins in fingers or toes, and cannot be stopped by patient, but patient stays awake and aware. Jerking may proceed to involve hand, then arm, and sometimes spreads to whole body and becomes a convulsive seizure.	Provide reassurance and emotional support; provide first aid if seizure becomes convulsive.
	Preoccupied or blank expression. Child experiences a distorted environment. May see or hear things that are not there, may feel unexplained fear, sadness, anger, or joy. May have nausea, experience odd smells, and have a generally "funny" feeling in the stomach.	
B, Complex partial (impaired consciousness) C, Partial seizures evolving to secondary generalized seizures	Usually starts with blank stare, followed by chewing, followed by random activity. Children appear unaware of surroundings, may seem dazed and mumble. Unresponsive. Actions are clumsy and not directed. May pick at clothing, pick up objects, try to take clothes off. May run and appear afraid. May struggle or flail at restraint. Once pattern is established, some set of actions usually occurs with each seizure. Lasts a few minutes, but postseizure confusion can last substantially longer. No memory of what happened during seizure period	Speak calmly, and provide reassurance to child and others. Guide child gently away from obvious hazards, and stay with child until he or she is completely aware of environment. Provide assistance in getting home.
Generalized seizures (convulsive or nonconvulsive); absence seizures	A blank stare lasting only a few seconds; most common in young children. May be accompanied by rapid blinking or chewing movements of the mouth. Children may be unaware of what's going on during the seizure but quickly return to full awareness once it has stopped. May result in learning difficulties if not recognized and treated.	Medical evaluation is recommended; first aid is not generally needed.
Primary generalized seizures	Sudden cry, fall, and rigidity, followed by muscle jerks, frothy saliva on lips, shallow breathing or temporarily suspended breathing, blush skin, possible loss of bladder or bowel control. Usually lasts 2 to 5 minutes, followed by normal breathing. There may be fatigue, followed by a return to full consciousness. Often preceded by warning signal (aura) and characterized by tensing or static contraction (tonic phase) followed by spasmodic jerking (clonic phase).	Look for medical identification. Protect from nearby hazards. Loosen ties or shirt collars. Place folded jacket under head. Turn on side to keep airway clear. Reassure when consciousness returns. If seizure lasts more than 10 minutes or multiple seizures occur, obtain emergency medical care.
Atonic seizures (also called drop attacks)	The legs of children between 2 to 5 years of age suddenly collapse. After 10 seconds to 1 minute, child can recover, regain consciousness, and stand and walk again.	No first aid is generally needed.
Myoclonic seizures	Sudden, brief, massive muscle jerks that may involve the whole body or parts of the body. May cause children to spill what they are holding or fall off a chair.	A thorough medical evaluation should be performed; first aid is not generally needed.
Infantile spasms	Starts between 3 months and 2 years. If sitting up, the head will fall forward, and the arms will flex forward. If lying down, the knees will be drawn up, with arms and head flexed forward as if reaching for support.	Medical evaluation is required; first aid not generally required.

Generalized Seizures   Generalized seizures can be either convulsive or nonconvulsive. The type most people associate with epilepsy is the tonic-clonic seizure, formerly known as grand mal seizure. It involves the entire brain and is characterized by a sudden fall and rigid posture (tonic phase), which lasts approximately 10–20 seconds. This phase is followed by a rhythmic jerking of the limbs (clonic phase), or convulsing, and is often accompanied by frothy saliva on the lips and possible incontinence. Breathing is irregular during the seizure, and autonomic dysfunction is often prominent, resulting in cyanosis of the lips and fingers. The pH balance can be as low as 6.8, with a mixed metabolic and respiratory acidosis. The individual has no memory of the seizure itself. Afterwards the person is usually tired, may have a headache, and is confused (Gates & Spiegel, 1993). This type of seizure usually lasts about 2 minutes, although the person may still be unconscious after cessation of seizure activity.

Absence seizures, formerly known as petit mal seizures, are generally considered to be the second most common type of seizure. This type usually occurs during childhood and is "outgrown" by adulthood. Absences are characterized by a sudden interruption of activities accompanied by a blank stare and/or slurring of speech and, sometimes, eyelid flutter. Usually very brief, this type lasts an average of 3–10 seconds. The individual may not realize he or she has had a seizure or may be confused because of a perceived time lapse.

Atonic seizures, also called drop attacks, are another condition that is common during childhood, usually in children 2–5 years of age. The legs of these children suddenly collapse, causing them to fall to their knees, and recovery usually occurs after 10–60 seconds. Myoclonic seizures consist of sudden, powerful muscle jerks. They may occur in the whole body or only in certain body parts and are sometimes accompanied by a loss of consciousness.

Finally, infantile spasms, which can be caused by high fevers, usually begin between 3 months and 2 years of age. This type of activity is characterized by clusters of quick, sudden movements. The head falls forward, and the arms will flex forward if sitting. Legs will be drawn up if the child is lying down. Because variability is so great among children with seizure disorders, parents and teachers should be aware of the following warning signs:

- periods of blackout or confused memory
- odd sounds, distorted perceptions, or episodic feelings of fear or apprehension that cannot be explained
- "fainting spells" with incontinence or followed by excessive fatigue
- episodes of staring or unexplained periods of unresponsiveness
- episodes of blinking or chewing at inappropriate times
- involuntary movements of arms or legs
- any convulsion, with or without fever

Etiology

Epilepsy has a variable etiology, with concrete evidence to support some causes and mere speculation to sustain others; however, many seizures stem from still unknown causes. The relationship between epilepsy and previously sustained cranial trauma is extremely strong. This damage can occur in many different ways, including from external sources, such as hypoxia or hemorrhage at birth, or as a result of direct trauma to the brain. It can also arise from internal sources, such as infections, abscesses, strokes, toxic/metabolic entities, neoplasms, degenerative disorders, and developmental abnormalities.

There is much speculation throughout the medical and scientific communities around the possibility that a genetic factor could play a role in the development of epilepsy. This view stems from the discovery that there is sometimes a relatively high frequency of some specific types of epilepsy in one family and that the parents of a child with epilepsy often display abnormal electroencephalogram (EEG) readings. Nonetheless, a large portion of patients with epilepsy cannot attribute their condition to any identifiable cause.

Planning the Physical Activity Program

To develop an appropriate program for children with seizure disorders, teachers need a thorough understanding of medical considerations. Teachers can then develop the program based on relevant knowledge concerning fatigue, medication, diet, and physical activity in conjunction with the input from the educational programming team and can provide opportunities for social and physical development.

Fatigue

Fatigue is commonly identified as a trigger for seizures. However, most seizures seem to occur during rest periods or during sleep, not during periods of fatigue. Livingston (1971) indicated that more seizures occur while the individual is resting or idling and that physical and mental activity appear to inhibit seizures. Another misconception is that children with seizures require more sleep or rest than do their peers. But frequent rest periods are not needed beyond normal levels, and students should be encouraged to participate in the same manner as their peers. A regular sleep pattern is more advantageous than, for example, getting 6 hours one day and 12 the next.

The activity in physical education classes is seldom intense enough or of long enough duration to precipitate seizures. However, in cases where activities or the environment requires maximum physical exertion, periodic rest periods, based on the child's tolerance for activity, might be in order. As children adapt to these activity demands and increase their level of physical conditioning, fatigue can be delayed.

Medication

Anticonvulsant medication is effective in the treatment of 90% of all children with seizures. Children may receive medication throughout their lives or have their dosage reduced if seizures are controlled for 3 to 5 years (Bennett, 1995; Freeman et al., 1990; Chase, 1974). The common medications are anticonvulsants that counteract or stop the spread of abnormal electrical discharges in the brain. They are prescribed by the physician. Initially there may be a trial-and-error period in determining the type and dosage of medication required. At this time, teachers should be aware of conditions that should be avoided and provide feedback to physicians concerning the consequences of medication. Medication should be administered three to four times daily in individual doses. Most seizures occur only when the prescribed medication is not taken or the therapeutic range is not maintained.

Table 16.3 Common Medications Used in Seizure Disorders

Drug	Indications	Common Side Effects
Phenytoin (Dilantin)	Partial, tonic-clonic seizures	Fatigue, stomach upset, ataxia, drowsiness, nystagmus
Carbamazepine (Tegretol)	Partial, tonic-clonic seizures	Blurred vision, ataxia, low blood count
Phenobarbital (Luminal)	Partial, tonic-clonic seizures	Fatigue, skin rash, hyperactivity
Primidone (Mysoline)	Partial, tonic-clonic seizures	Drowsiness, hyperactivity, ataxia
Clorazepate (Tranxene)	Partial, absence, tonic-clonic	Ataxia, fatigue, nausea
Ethosuximide (Zarontin)	Absence seizures	Drowsiness, nausea, headache
Clonazepam (Klonopin)	Absence, myoclonic and akinetic seizures	Drowsiness, ataxia, drooling
Valproic acid (Depakene)	Partial, absence, and tonic-clonic seizures	Drowsiness, ataxia

It is also important for teachers to be informed of changes in dosage or type of medication to eliminate situations where the common side effects of medication could negatively influence performance. For example, children may not be able to participate in some gymnastic or bicycling activities if prescribed medications make them susceptible to dizziness and thus to injury. Several common medications used in the treatment of seizure disorders are included in Table 16.3, along with indications of specific seizures and common side effects (Bennett, 1995; Chusid, 1979; Jan, Ziegler & Erba, 1983; Freeman et al., 1990; Tettenborn & Kramer, 1992).

Diet

The physical health of children is directly related to their emotional health. Three nutritionally well-balanced meals should be consumed daily, especially when medication is administered three or four times daily. Fruit or other nutritious snacks can be used to enhance the student's energy level, although evenly spaced and well-balanced meals are the most important aspects of the diet. The diet becomes more important for children who are prone to seizures during periods of growth, when additional nutrients are needed, and during the teenage years, when children tend to skip meals or consume junk food.

A diet with high alkalinity or acidity may help to inhibit susceptibility to seizures. Acid-producing diets (ketogenic diets) with a high fat content, such as cream, butter, eggs, and meats, usually produce a quieting effect on electrical discharges and may be helpful in preventing seizures (Tettenborn & Kramer, 1992; Jan et al., 1983).

Physical Activity

In addition to rest and proper diet, regular physical activity should be encouraged. Most children with seizure disorders can participate in physical education and sports.

For those children whose seizures prevent regular participation, an exercise program designed within their abilities, such as walking or stationary cycling, should be encouraged until seizures are controlled. If children are multiply involved, regular activity is also important, especially manipulation of the limbs to prevent contractures and to increase functional capacity (Bauer, 1977).

Hyperventilation is generally thought to lower the threshold for seizures, and intense exertion usually is accompanied by hyperventilation. However, physical activity may have a suppressive effect on electrical wave abnormalities and seizures that may be induced by hyperventilation (Bar-Or, 1983). Activities that improve physical conditioning are important for all children with a history of seizures because of the possibility of reducing the number of seizures (Gates & Spiegel, 1993).

Currently, it is still not apparent why physical activity raises the seizure threshold. Emotional stress, hyperventilation, and an increase in body temperature are the results of activity, yet activity still seems to inhibit seizures. Possible speculations concerning why physical activity can reduce seizures include the metabolic acidosis of exercise, which counteracts the alkalotic effect of hyperventilation, or the release of catecholamines during activity, which may elevate the seizure threshold (Korczyn, 1979).

Social Acceptance

A primary concern for teachers is to help children with seizures achieve a normal status within the school setting. The social consequences are sometimes more damaging to students than the apparent physical problems. To dispel myths, pity, and negative reactions, teachers must inform others that seizures are not a disease or contagious and strive to eliminate any misconceptions about this disorder. When others are aware of seizures and their frequency, they will understand the condition and be able to provide first aid when required. Sometimes the attitude of the teacher toward the child who is subject to seizures is important to successful participation. Usually open discussions of the conditions will resolve any misunderstanding and dispel myths concerning seizures.

Additionally, a common problem is that most children feel embarrassed after a seizure. Since they may lose consciousness and not recall the incident, the stares of their peers lead to uneasiness. Parents and educators should also be supportive and understanding to remove the social stigma and help foster an appreciation of the medical nature of the disorder. Only through opportunities to participate and display their talents can children with seizures be supported and reinforced.

Implementing the Physical Activity Program
Developmental Physical Skills

Many children with seizure disorders can be delayed in academic progress. Moreover, other effects, such as deficits in memory, attention, and spatial abilities, may hinder the child's ability to perform physical activity. Although there are no direct effects on muscle function or cardiovascular development directly related to seizure disorders themselves, other than a sedentary lifestyle, seizure activity can impair gross motor control. Teachers should emphasize developing the large muscle groups and functional movement patterns as well as increasing muscular strength and endurance (Sillanpaa, 1995).

In early adolescence, seizure disorders may also impair a child's sense of self-esteem and physical competence. The combination of puberty and the unpredictable nature of seizures can made adolescence a very awkward and unstable time for these children. Development of physical skills and the body's hormonal adjustments at this time can be further impaired by a lack of activity due to parental overprotection (Shinnar, Amir & Branski, 1995).

Cognition and Motivation

The relationship between epilepsy and decreased cognitive function has been observed for years. The nature and the extent of the decline in cognition, however, have not been precisely classified. It is often unclear whether the decline is due directly to the epileptic condition or to the medication used in its treatment (Shinnar et al., 1995). It is also important to consider any behavior problems that may hinder a child's motivation or ability to function in group activities. Participation in physical activities and sports may foster the development of self-esteem and reduce any emotional problems that result from feelings of being different (Shinnar et al., 1995).

Community and Activities of Daily Living

Seizure disorders may disrupt daily living to the extent that some children may have difficulty in educational or work settings. In some cases, the disruption of the seizures themselves interferes with productivity or attending to school-related activities. Medication may also interfere with the child's ability to concentrate on physical functioning. Children may also feel self-conscious if others are present during a seizure. Any method that aids in reducing seizures or boosting self-esteem will improve the quality of life for these children. Physical and recreational activity should be emphasized to promote social interactions as well as to reduce seizure frequency and promote a healthy lifestyle.

Exercise and Activity

Activity should be encouraged for children with seizure disorders, especially during the early school years, by implementing programs similar to those of their peer groups. A statement from the United States Department of Health, Education, and Welfare's Commission for the Control of Epilepsy indicates that activity is important for children with seizures because evidence suggests that activity may reduce the likelihood of seizures (Bennett, 1995; Van Linschotten, Backx, Mulder & Meinardi, 1990).

Bennett (1995) has suggested that exercise programs progressively build stamina and help prevent children from reverting to a sedentary lifestyle. It is most important to promote endurance rather than necessarily strength or power. The primary goal is for the child to engage in physical activity, not only to reduce seizures but also to promote general health.

When preparing an activity program, the teacher must notify health care providers (such as physicians and school nurses) of the child's condition. The child must agree to report any seizure immediately.

A few suggested cautions to keep in mind include the safety of the environment. As previously stated, activities such as swimming and high-altitude sports are generally avoided because of the possible danger if a seizure were to occur. For the same reason, playing surfaces and equipment must be considered. An especially hard surface, such as concrete, could become a hazard if the child were to fall into a seizure. Wrestling or tumbling rooms are often utilized for early activity, especially in young children with uncontrolled seizure frequency. Although these special safety considerations must be made, the exercise program for the child with a seizure disorder should not differ than those of other children. A gradual progression to increase any noted weaknesses or to improve general fitness levels should be employed. This will entail a combination of strength and cardiovascular workouts, as well as sports and skill development to improve function and social interaction.

Children with seizures may be comparable to their peer group in physical and motor performance. Bar-Or (1983) related the example of a 13-year-old girl with psychomotor seizures who participated in long-distance running to overcome her disability and completed several ultramarathons. Other seizure-disordered athletes have demonstrated similar performance in physical functioning. The extent to which children participate depends on the control of seizures, their ambitions, and how well they comply with a particular training regimen.

Enforced inactivity due to overprotection is often more detrimental than the risk of a seizure during activity. Livingston (1971) indicated that 15,000 individuals over a 34-year period of clinical supervision did not demonstrate a single case of seizures from athletics-related head trauma. The American Medical Association (1974) does not currently exclude children with seizures from participation in contact sports.

Most children can participate in activities such as cycling, horseback riding, climbing, skin diving, swimming, or sports that involve throwing or shooting if proper safety precautions are taken to reduce accidents. Children whose seizures are not controlled by medication or who manifest consistent seizures should be temporarily removed from those sports until their condition is controlled. Swimming and water activities should be supervised closely because of the potential danger inherent in the water environment. Laidlaw and Richens (1976) reported that seizures will seldom occur while swimming, but if a seizure does occur, the child should be supported by the pool deck. Other precautions in swimming activities may include the wearing of a brightly colored cap or use of a buddy system to aid in identification.

Children whose seizures are not under control may manifest a low level of physical and motor functioning if they are excluded from all physical activity. Participation of these children may be limited but still should be encouraged after consultation with the physician. Their cardiovascular efficiency can be improved through a gradual and progressive program to postpone fatigue and possibly elevate the seizure threshold, while other motor skills may be achieved through a developmental physical education program. To select appropriate physical education activities for these children, teachers should employ the following guidelines (Bar-Or, 1983; Bower, 1969).

1. Encourage children to participate fully if their condition is under medical control.

2. Strenuous activity (e.g., long-distance running or a prolonged tennis match) is not contraindicated even if it causes marked fatigue.

3. Always supervise activities such as horseback riding, mountain climbing, swimming, or diving.

4. Limit bicycle riding if seizures are not well controlled by medication.

5. Collision sports (football, ice hockey, lacrosse, rugby) and contact sports (baseball,

basketball, soccer, wrestling) can be practiced by medically controlled children. As in any athletic event, participants should be coached in the prevention of trauma.

6. Boxing, because of repeated impact on the head, is contraindicated.

7. For unexplained reasons, some activities may trigger seizures. When they are identified, they should be avoided.

8. Activities that provide hazards to peers or spectators are not allowed for uncontrolled children.

9. Individualized participation should be determined with the cooperation of the collaborative team, parent, and child.

Spina Bifida

Spina bifida is a condition that refers to a developmental defect of the spinal column in which the arches of one or more of the spinal vertebrae fail to fuse. The disorder occurs in 3 per 1,000 live births. Normal development of the central nervous system (CNS) in the fetus begins when a single sheet of cells (that is, the neural plate), enlarges and forms a symmetrical longitudinal groove. This groove deepens, and the sides fuse to form a hollow cylinder that eventually differentiates into the brain and spinal cord. During development, supportive and protective tissues, such as the meninges, will line the cord and finally be covered by the bony structure of the vertebral column.

In spina bifida or any neural tube defect, part of the nerve cord may fail to close or fuse. The nerve cord at that point remains immature and improperly formed. If the nerve cord fails to form properly, then the supporting tissues and structures, including the vertebral column and/or cranium, will be abnormal. In very severe conditions, portions of the brain may not develop.

Interference with the normal growth and development of the neural tube and closure during the early weeks of pregnancy is complex and probably is caused by genetic and environmental factors. However, the exact nature of the neural tube disorder depends on the part of the tube that fails to develop and the extent of normal growth achieved. If there is a failure of closure in the midline or lower end of the neural tube, the result is spina bifida; failure of the upper end or head of the tube results in cranium bifidum or anencephaly (Tarby, 1991).

Clinically, most dysfunctions in development are due to an abnormal closure of the neural groove. If the neural groove does not close properly at the cranial end, the whole forebrain, skull, and scalp will be missing. The child is stillborn, or death usually occurs within hours. This condition is termed *anencephaly* ("no brain").

A corresponding condition at the caudal end of the CNS (i.e., in the spinal cord) is spina bifida and usually occurs a the L_2–L_4 region of the spinal cord. There are three major types of spina bifida: (1) occulta (in which the abnormality is confined to the vertebrae only and is due to an unclosed posterior vertebral arch) and two types of spina bifida cystica, (2) meningocele (where the meninges protrude through the defect), and (3) myelomeningocele (where elements of the cord also protrude through the defect, resulting in severe neural deficits) (Figure 16.5). Myelomeningocele is often associated with the condition *hydrocephalus*, which results in severe mental retardation.

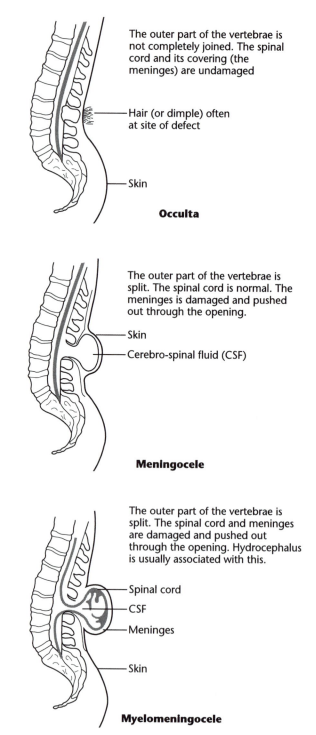

The outer part of the vertebrae is not completely joined. The spinal cord and its covering (the meninges) are undamaged

Hair (or dimple) often at site of defect

Skin

Occulta

The outer part of the vertebrae is split. The spinal cord is normal. The meninges is damaged and pushed out through the opening.

Skin

Cerebro-spinal fluid (CSF)

Meningocele

The outer part of the vertebrae is split. The spinal cord and meninges are damaged and pushed out through the opening. Hydrocephalus is usually associated with this.

Spinal cord

CSF

Meninges

Skin

Myelomeningocele

Figure 16.5 Abnormal development associated with spina bifida.

In spina bifida occulta, the malformation or lack of fusion usually is located in the lower spine of the vertebral arches. There is no distension or protrusion of the meninges, and the spinal cord and membranes are generally normal, with no accompanying loss of motor functioning. The site of the vertebral defect may be marked by slight swelling, dimple in the skin, or tuft of hair; or there may be no external evidence at all (Williamson, 1987).

In spina bifida cystica, some portion of the spinal cord or nerve roots are herniated through the vertebral arches into a sac-like cyst filled with cerebrospinal fluid (CSF). Of the two types of spina bifida cystica, meningocele is less debilitating and commonly affects 15–25% of all children with spina bifida cystica. In meningocele, the meninges protrude through the gap in the vertebral column to form a sac that is generally covered by the skin. Because the sac usually contains only the meninges and cerebrospinal fluid, the cord functions normally, and there is no significant loss of function. In many cases, surgery may remove the hernial protrusions.

In contrast, the other type of spina bifida cystica, myelomeningocele, results from the failure of the vertebral column to fuse. Distension of the meninges is accompanied by protrusion of the spinal cord into the sac. This results in permanent and irreversible neurological disability. Loss of function may not be confined to the lesion level and may affect normal functioning below the lesion and frequently several spinal segments above the lesion, with the possibility of autonomic abnormalities occurring at any point in the spine (Tarby, 1991). Many infants born with myelomeningocele have associated developmental abnormalities in the brain. The base of the brain (medulla) containing many of the cranial nerves and located within the skull may be present in the cervical vertebrae (in the neck region). This is commonly referred to as Arnold-Chiari malformation and affects up to 90% of children with myelomeningocele. It may obstruct the circulation of the CSF causing an accumulation of water in the cranial area (hydrocephalus).

Each child presents a unique set of clinical characteristics, with primary and secondary disabilities including the following

Primary Disabilities	**Secondary Complications**
muscle paralysis	low fitness
skeletal deformities	obesity
loss of sensation	poor functional strength
hydrocephalus	pressure sores
urinary and bowel incontinence	respiratory difficulties
	learning and perceptual difficulties
	motor functioning seizures

Planning the Physical Activity Program

Although multiple systems of the body may be involved in spina bifida, the leg muscles are most affected. The degree of muscular development and additional complications depend on the location of the lesion and the extent of the damage to the spinal cord.

Generally, individuals with spina bifida have bowel and bladder problems (incontinence), affected by the sacral nerves and level of the lesion. Difficulties with sensations result from dysfunction of the spinal cord. Paralysis in spina bifida occurs because of the lack of nerve innervation from the spinal cord to the working muscles (Tarby, 1991). However, some variation in functioning below the lesion is apparent. Spasticity and/or reflexive movement may be seen if the cord is not completely transected.

Hydrocephalus

Hydrocephalus refers to the buildup of CNS fluid inside the brain that occurs when normal circulation is obstructed because the open spine permits the lower portion of the brain to slip through the opening of the spinal cord (Tarby, 1991). Hydrocephalus occurs when there is an imbalance between the amount of CSF produced and the rate at which it is absorbed. If hydrocephalus is unrestricted, the nerve cells are damaged as the skull stretches to accommodate the fluid buildup. The condition is characterized by an oversized head. As the child grows and the skull bones become set, the fluid pressure buildup may damage the developing brain unless the pressure is released. A balance between the amount of fluid formed and the amount absorbed decreases the abnormal rate of skull growth and is referred to as *arrested hydrocephalus*. There are no adverse effects of arrested hydrocephalus.

Unarrested or severe hydrocephalus may damage the cognitive areas of the brain as well as the motor areas that control movement of the limbs. The condition may predispose the child to ambulation with a wheelchair. Eyesight will deteriorate, and control of the respiratory and cardiac centers may also be adversely affected, resulting in complications in cardiorespiratory functioning. Severe cases are treated with the use of a shunt to channel excess CNS fluid from the cerebral cavity into either the heart or the abdomen, where it is absorbed by the body. The shunt is a flexible tube that is placed in the ventricular system of the brain to drain the excess flow of CSF (Figure 16.6).

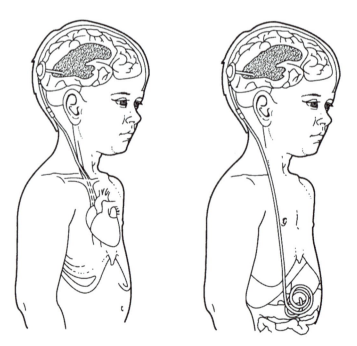

Figure 16.6 Ventriculoatrial shunt (left) and ventriculoperitoneal shunt (right).

Table 16.4 Motor Dysfunction and Suggested Physical Education Activities

Functional Levels	Physical and Motor Dysfunction	Impairment in Motor Function	Physical Education Activities
Thoracic (T_{12})	Lower limb paralysis; scoliosis; contractures	Standing brace and wheelchair required for ambulation	Develop body awareness and upper limb function in young children; emphasize strengthening postural muscles for stability and transfers; encourage range-of-motion exercises; strength and aquatics to encourage movement and develop independent functions.
High lumbar (L_1–L_3)	Hip flexion and adduction; knee extension; scoliosis; hip dislocation	Crutches; long braces with hip support required for home community ambulation	
Low lumbar (L_4–S_1)	Knee flexors; ankle extensors; hip flexion and hamstring tightness; foot deformity	Short braces and crutches for home and community ambulation	
Sacral level (S_1–S_3)	Ankle flexors; inner and outer peroneal foot muscles; foot deformity	Supports in shoes for home and community ambulation	

Motor Function

The loss of motor function depends on the location, extent, and severity of the lesion (Table 16.4). Cervical lesions usually do not involve the spinal cord and rarely result in a loss of functional ability, whereas sacral lesions may result in a slight dysfunction.

Most individuals with myelomeningocele are affected at the lumbar and sacral regions because this is the last section of the neural tube to close. Approximately 30–50% of individuals with myelomeningocele are totally "flaccid" paraplegics, whereas most others have significant secondary problems that impair locomotion, including scoliosis, kyphosis, rib cage abnormalities, dislocation of the hips, and ankle or knee deformities (Tarby, 1991). An affected limb may be held in an abnormal position (i.e., contraction) because the antagonistic muscle pair is affected, resulting in flexion or contraction without reciprocal innervation of the corresponding muscle group. Additionally the hips may dislocate, and knees or ankle may become rigid, requiring bracing or additional support for ambulation.

Intellectual Development

Children with spina bifida generally function within a range of normal intelligence, although this is not necessarily a fixed trait. These individuals are very verbal, which may give an initial impression of normal intelligence. Children with meningocele are likely to fall in the normal range of intelligence, whereas those with myelomeningocele demonstrate "low average" to reduced intellectual functioning (Dallyn & Garrison-Jones, 1991). Development depends largely on environmental factors and setbacks that may disrupt functioning, such as lengthy hospital stays, dependence, and poor self-esteem. Additionally, sensory and perceptual defects from damage to the areas of the brain involved in perception may also induce learning disorders and/or retardation in children (McLane, 1994).

Incontinence

Incontinence is another problem for children with spina bifida. Incontinence is the inability to control the function of the bladder and/or bowels. Ninety-five percent of children with myelomeningocele do not have functioning nerves between the bladder and bowels and brain and are unable to perceive a distended bladder or to control bowel function. Those without control of the bladder have either a hypo or hyperactive bladder that causes difficulty in voiding.

For those with incontinence, catherization is performed, in which a tube is inserted into the bladder in order to drain the urine (Spina Bifida Association of America, 1997). Clean intermittent catherization is necessary to avoid infections. For children with incontinence, a regular checkup by the physician is required to assess kidney function because the urine can back up into the kidneys and cause damage or infection. In addition, a carefully regulated diet is also necessary to aid in controlling bowel movements as well as obesity.

Implementing the Physical Activity Program

Motor Interventions

For young children, teachers should provide stimulation in the visual field and opportunities to fixate on and track objects and to manipulate objects. Eye-hand coordination can be improved by using toys of varying sizes and shapes so that they can be easily grasped and incorporated into activities that encourage movement. Teachers can promote tactile stimulation and eventually hand function by providing objects for the child to squeeze, grasp, wave, drop, and move. Teachers should also incorporate developmental tasks that stimulate upper and lower body movement.

Body awareness activities should include identifying body parts and encouraging movement within self-space of the environment. Group play activities should be encouraged to maximize movement experiences as well as to stimulate social interaction and behavioral skills. Group play should be conducted in order to introduce activities that can also be used in home-based and community recreation activities.

Movement in the lower limbs should be encouraged to facilitate functional movement and to prevent contractures. Children should engage in appropriate developmental tasks that maximize upper body development, such as parachute activities to develop upper body strength, functional movement, and perception. They should also participate in games and dance activities (French & Horvat, 1983). For some children, parachute and other play activities may require some prompting to initiate movements actively.

Exercise Interventions

A child with spina bifida needs a comprehensive program of physical activity to maintain a healthy life. Intervention should occur as early as possible to facilitate functional movement. Early in development, home-based programs should be designed to teach parents how to exercise their baby's feet and legs in order for the child to be able to walk with crutches or leg braces or, for those without lower body functioning, to use a wheelchair for ambulation.

An exercise program for a child with spina bifida should involve a wide range of activities and exercises. Flexibility training will help delay contractures that are due to muscle weakness, paralysis, and imbalance and should include stretching the hamstrings, heel cords, lower back, hip flexors, and shoulders.

Aerobic activity should be used to promote a healthy lifestyle and aid in weight management. During aerobic activity, the heart rate should be elevated gradually for 20 to 45 minutes. For children in wheelchairs, exercises such as arm ergometry, rapid wheelchair propulsion, wheelchair aerobics, and sports activities should be introduced to facilitate physical development and social outlets.

While aerobic training increases muscle endurance, resistance exercise increases functional strength. It is very important for children with spina bifida to strengthen all of their working muscles, particularly their triceps and shoulders. These are the major muscles that are used in transfers from wheelchairs and in walking with crutches (Figure 16.7). O'Connell, Barnhart, and Parks (1992) demonstrated that increased muscular endurance is highly correlated to wheelchair propulsion. Functional strength exercises include the overhead press, wheelchair pushups (grab arm rests and push body out of seat until elbows are straight), shoulder flies, tricep curls, and bicep curls (Lutkenhoff & Oppenheimer, 1997). Resistance training should begin at an appropriate age and concentrate on the muscles of the upper body to promote functional movements such as transfers and self-care activities. In conjunction with developing functional skill, a complete fitness program that includes stretching, aerobic exercise, and muscle strengthening may contribute to decreasing obesity, maintaining stronger bones, and better bowel function.

Special attention should be given to providing exercises to develop and maintain functional levels of physical fitness. Activities to strengthen the upper extremities that

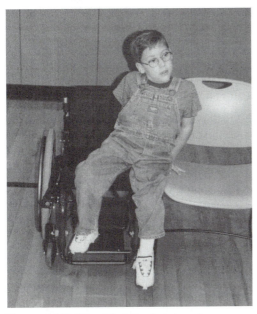 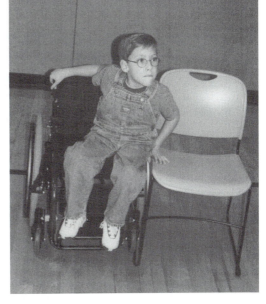

Figure 16.7 Wheelchair to chair transfer.

are used in transfers and propelling a wheelchair should be encouraged, as well as exercises designed to prevent contractures and increase range of motion. For example, the use of surgical hose, pulleys, hand weights, and dumbbells develops upper body strength that can be generalized to propelling a wheelchair (Shepherd, 1990). Additional resistance exercises, such as arm cranking, promote aerobic endurance and cardiovascular conditioning that are needed for ambulation in community and vocational environments. Further, aquatic exercises and swimming skills should be emphasized, because buoyancy in the water offsets the child's weakness in lower extremities and can be used to accentuate upper body and cardiovascular development. Each activity, and the extent of the exercise, should be based on the abilities of the child and functional goals that promote self-sufficiency. Home and community programs can provide activities for additional stimulation, opportunities to practice, and social integration (Freed, 1990; Hinderer, Hinderer & Shurtleff, 1994).

Obesity is common in this population if activity is compromised. If the child continues to be inactive, the resulting weight gain adds an additional complication to an already low level of functional ability (Dixon & Rekate, 1991). Excessive weight gain in infancy may also affect metabolism and the distribution of fat cells (Dixon & Rekate, 1991). For these children, dietary care in conjunction with physical activity that maximizes skills necessary for functioning in the school, home, and community should be emphasized (Cusick, 1991).

Exercise interventions and motor programming for a child with spina bifida depend on the child's functional ability and complications associated with the disorder. The teacher should ascertain movement potential to develop a program based on the child's functional ability and programmatic goals that emphasize community and home participation as well as future vocational training goals. The nature of the child's disability should be recognized to ensure safe participation in light of medical contraindications. Because the child may have impaired mobility, teachers should promote strengthening muscle groups to aid in ambulation and self-sufficiency for activities of daily living. Appropriate social interactions should be encouraged to aid in overall development and social integration. Major goals of intervention should include the following:

1. Teaching gross motor and spatial skills to facilitate coordination
2. Developing and maintaining fitness and flexibility (i.e., developing strength in the shoulders, trunk, and arms; also cardiorespiratory endurance) to emphasize self-sufficiency
3. Encouraging movement and fitness to overcome susceptibility to obesity
4. Developing physical skills that generalize to activities of daily living and vocational skills
5. Promoting social development in recreational and group play activities, such as aquatics
6. Providing appropriate social outlets for enjoyment and self-satisfaction on an individual basis as well as with family or peers within the community

Although spina bifida is a birth defect for which there is no known cure, it is very important for teachers and parents to understand the disability and intervene at the earliest time possible to aid in the child's development and self-esteem. The child will require assistance in learning how to care for himself or herself and become as independent as possible. Although some assistance may be required, most children with spina bifida can be independent and achieve functional skills necessary for a productive life.

Chapter Summary

1. Children with neurological disorders are generally integrated into the regular physical education classes. Each disorder has its own unique characteristics that interfere with the learning of physical and motor skills. Because functional capacity varies according to the site and extent of injury to the nervous system, students should be treated individually and actively encouraged to participate.

2. Cerebral palsy can be described as a group of conditions that are manifested during infancy and are characterized by weakness, paralysis, poor muscle tone, and lack of coordination and motor functioning.

3. Cerebral palsy can be classified by degree of motor involvement, limbs involved, and/or motor disability.

4. Children with cerebral palsy have physical and motor limitations that are based on their predominant type of motor disability. Increasing overall physical functioning is the primary thrust in developing the physical education program.

5. The selection of appropriate physical education activities should be based on the obvious motor characteristics of children with cerebral palsy. These children need to develop optimal levels of muscular efficiency and physical fitness.

6. A seizure or convulsive disorder is a neurological condition initiated by abnormal discharges in the brain.

7. To develop an appropriate program for children with seizure disorders, the teacher needs a thorough understanding of medical considerations. The considerations include fatigue, medication, diet, and physical activity. Opportunities for social and physical development should be provided in the physical education program.

8. In planning the instructional program, the teacher should understand the use of anticonvulsant medications and their common side effects.

9. Physical activity is beneficial in elevating the child's seizure threshold and should be encouraged. For children whose seizures are not controlled, consultation with physicians is required.

10. Spina bifida refers to a developmental defect of the spinal column.

11. Primary disabilities in spina bifida include muscle paralysis, skeletal deformities, loss of sensation, hydrocephalus, and urinary and bowel incontinence.

12. Motor functions depends on the location, extent, and severity of the lesion.

13. Intervention should include providing activities that promote muscle strengthening, flexibility, and aerobic fitness to facilitate a healthy lifestyle.

REFERENCES

American Medical Association, Committee on the Medical Aspects of Sports Epileptics and Contact Sports. (1974). Position statement. *Journal of American Medical Association, 229,* 820–821.

Bar-Or, O. (1983). *Pediatric sports medicine for the practitioner.* New York: Springer-Verlag.

Bauer, E. W. (1977). *Thoughts on parenting the child with epilepsy.* Landover, MD: Epilepsy Foundation of America.

Bennett, D. R. (1995). Epilepsy. In B. Goldberg (Ed.) *Sports and exercise for children with chronic health conditions* (pp. 89–108). Champaign, IL: Human Kinetics.

Bottos, P., Puato, M. L., Vianello, A., & Facchin, P. (1995). Locomotion patterns in cerebral palsy syndromes. *Developmental Medicine and Child Neurology, 37,* 883–899.

Bower, B. D. (1969). Epilepsy and school athletics. *Developmental Medicine and Child Neurology, 11,* 244–245.

Chase, D. (1974). With epilepsy they take the medicine and play. *The Physician and Sports Medicine, 2,* 61.

Chusid, J. G. (1979). *Correlative neuroanatomy and functional neurology* (17th ed.). Lange.

Cusick, B. (1991). Therapeutic management of sensorimotor and physical disabilities. In J. L. Bigge (Ed.), *Teaching individuals with physical and multiple disabilities* (3rd ed.). Columbus, OH: Merrill.

Dallyn, L., & Garrison-Jones, C. (1991). The long-term psychosocial adjustment of children with spina bifida. In H. L. Rekate (Ed.), *Comprehensive management of spina bifida.* (pp. 215–235). Boca Raton, FL: CRC Press.

Dixon, M. S., & Rekate, H. L. (1991). Pediatric management of children with myelodysplasia. In H. L. Rekate (Ed.), *Comprehensive management of spina bifida.* (pp. 49–66). Boca Raton, FL: CRC Press.

Epilepsy Foundation of America. (1994). *Epilepsy: Questions and answers.* Landover, MD: Author.

Epilepsy Foundation of America. (1998). *Seizure recognition and first aid.* Landover, MD: Author.

Fetters, L., & Kluzik, J. (1996). The effects of neurodevelopmental treatment versus practice on the reaching of children with spastic cerebral palsy. *Physical Therapy, 74,* (4), 346–358.

Freed, M. M. (1990). Traumatic and congenital lesions of the spinal cord. In J. Kottke & J. F. Lehmann, *Krusen's handbook of physical medicine and rehabilitation* (4th ed.). (pp. 732–733).Philadelphia: Saunders.

Freeman, J. M., Vining, E. P. G., & Pillas, D. J. (1990). *Seizures and epilepsy in childhood: A guide for parents.* Baltimore: Johns Hopkins University Press.

French, R., & Horvat, M. (1983). *Parachute movement activities.* Bryon, CA: Front Row Experience.

Gates, J. R., & Spiegel, R. H. (1993). Epilepsy, sports and exercise. *Sports Medicine, 15*(1), 1–5.

Hinderer, K. A., Hinderer, S. R., & Shurtleff, D. B. (1994). Myelodysplasia. In S. Campbell (Ed.), *Physical therapy for children* (pp. 571–619). Philadelphia: Saunders.

Horvat, M. (1987). Effects of a progressive resistance training program on an individual with spastic cerebral palsy. *American Corrective Therapy Journal, 41,* 7–11.

Huberman, G. (1976). Organized sport activities with cerebral palsied adolescents. *Rehabilitation Literature, 37,* 103–107.

Jan, J. E., Ziegler, R. G., & Erba, G. (1983). *Does your child have epilepsy?* Austin, TX: Pro-Ed.

Jones, J. A. (1988). *Training guide to cerebral palsy sports (*3d ed.). Champaign, IL: Human Kinetics.

Korczyn, A. D. (1979). Participation of epileptic patients in sports. *Journal of Sports Medicine, 19,* 195–198.

Laidlaw, J., & Richens, A. (Eds). (1976). *A textbook of epilepsy.* Edinburgh, Scotland: Churchill-Livingstone.

Leonard, C. T., Hirschfield, H., & Forssberg, H. (1991). The development of independent walking in children with cerebral palsy. *Developmental Medicine and Child Neurology, 33,* 567–577.

Lesser, R. P. (1991). *Diagnosis and management of seizure disorders.* New York: Demos Publications.

Lin, P. P., & Henderson, R. C. (1996). Bone mineralization in the affected extremities of children with spastic hemiplegia. *Developmental Medicine and Child Neurology, 38,* 782–786.

Livingston, S. (1971). Should physical activity of the epileptic child be restricted? *Clinical Pediatrics, 10,* 694–696.

Lundberg, A. (1976). Oxygen consumption in relation to work load in students with cerebral palsy. *Journal of Applied Physiology, 40,* 873–875.

Lutkenhoff, M., & Oppenheimer, S. (1997). *Spinabilities: A young persons guide to spina bifida.* Bethesda, MD: Woodbine House.

McCubbin, J., & Shasby, G. (1985). The effects of isokinetic exercise on adolescents with cerebral palsy. *Adapted Physical Activity Quarterly, 2,* 56–64.

McDonald, E. T. (1987). *Treating cerebral palsy: For clinicians by clinicians.* Austin, TX: Pro-Ed.

McLane, D. (1994). *An introduction to spina bifida.* Washington, DC: Spina Bifida Association of America.

Mushett, C. A., Wyeth, D. O., & Richter, K. J. (1995). Cerebral palsy. In B. Goldberg (Ed.), *Sports and exercise for children with chronic health conditions.* (pp. 123–133). Champaign, IL: Human Kinetics.

National Disability Sports Alliance. (2002). Kingston, RI.

O'Connell, D. G., Barnhart, R., & Parks, L. (1992). Muscular endurance and wheelchair propulsion in children with cerebral palsy or myelomeningocele. *Archives of Physical Medicine and Rehabilitation, 73,* 709–711.

Olney, S. J., & Wright, M. J. (1994). Cerebral palsy. In S. Campbell (Ed.), *Physical therapy for children* (pp. 489–523). Philadelphia: Saunders.

Roberts, C. D., Vogtle, L., & Stevenson, R. D. (1994). Effect of hemiplegia on skeletal maturation. *The Journal of Pediatrics, 125*(5), 824–828.

Rose, J., Haskell, W. L., & Gamble, J. G. (1993). A comparison of oxygen pulse and respiratory exchange ratio in cerebral palsied and nondisabled children. *Archives of Physical Medicine and Rehabilitation, 74,* 702–705.

Rotzinger, H., & Stoboy, H. (1974). Comparison between clinical judgement and electromyographic investigations of the effect of a special training program for CP children. *Acta Pediatric Belgian Supplement, 28,* 121–128.

Schleichkorn, J. (1993). *Coping with cerebral palsy* (2nd ed.). Austin, TX: Pro-Ed.

Shepherd, R. J. (1990). *Fitness in special populations.* Champaign, IL: Human Kinetics.

Shinnar, S., Amir, N., & Branski, D. (1995). *Childhood seizures.* New York: Karger.

Sillanpaa, M. (1995). Counseling and rehabilitation: The clinician point of view. In A. P. Aldenkamp, F. E. Dreifuss, W. O. Renier & T. Suurmeijer (Eds.), *Epilepsy in children and adolescents.* New York: CRC Press.

Sommer, M. (1971). Improvement of motor skills and adaptation of the circulatory system in wheelchair bound children with cerebral palsy. In U. Simiri (Ed.), *Sport as a means of rehabilitation.* Natanya: Wingate Institute.

Spina Bifida Association of America. (1997). *The teacher and child with spina bifida.* Rockville, MD: Author.

Stallings, V. A., Zemel, B. S., Davies, J. C., Cronk, C. E., & Charney, E. B. (1996). Energy expenditures of children and adolescents with severe disabilities: A cerebral palsy model. *American Journal of Clinical Nutrition, 64,* 627–634.

Stevenson, R. D., Roberts, C. D., & Vogtle, L. (1995). The effects of non-nutritional factors on growth in cerebral palsy. *Developmental Medicine and Child Neurology, 37,* 124–130.

Sudgen, D. A., & Keogh, J. F. (1990). *Problems in movement skill development.* Columbia, SC: USC Press.

Tarby, T. J. (1991). A clinical view of the embryology of myelomeningocele. In H. L. Rekate (Ed.), *Comprehensive management of spina bifida* (pp. 29–48). Boca Raton, FL: CRC Press.

Tettenborn, B., & Kramer, G. (1992). Total patient care in epilepsy. *Epilepsia, 33*(Suppl. 1), S28–S32.

Unnithan, V. B., Dowling, J. J., Frost, G., & Bar-Or, O. (1996). Role of concontraction in the oxygen cost of walking in children with cerebral palsy. *Medicine and Science in Sports and Exercise, 28*(12), 1498–1504.

Unnithan, V. B., Dowling, J. J., Frost, G., Volpe Ayub, B., & Bar-Or, O. (1996). Cocontraction and phasic activity during GAIT in children with cerebral palsy. *Electromyography in Clinical Neurophysiology, 36,* 487–494.

Van Linschotten, R., Backx, F. J. G., Mulder, O. G. M., & Meinardi, H. (1990). Epilepsy and sports. *Sports Medicine, 10*(1), 9–19.

Williamson, G. G. (1987). *Children with spina bifida: Early intervention and preschool programming.* Baltimore: Paul H. Brooks.

CHAPTER 17

Muscular Dystrophy and Arthritis

Skeletal neuromuscular disease is characterized by a persistent progressive deterioration of striated muscle tissue. Muscular dystrophy is distinguished from other neuromuscular diseases by four criteria: (1) a primary myopathy, (2) genetic base for the disorder, (3) progressive nature, and (4) degeneration of muscle fibers (Sarnac, 1992). In the disease, muscle cells degenerate, and fat and fibrous tissue emerge to replace the muscle tissue (Sarnac, 1992). Approximately 200,000 individuals in the United States have muscular dystrophy resulting from spontaneous changes in a gene (genetic mutations) or from idiopathic causes where there is no family history. Although the muscular degeneration is debilitating and results in decreased functional ability, the specific cause of death results from complications involving cardiac and/or pulmonary failure. Muscular dystrophies are a group of unrelated diseases transmitted by various genetic traits with varying clinical courses and characteristics (Sarnac, 1992).

The physical characteristics of the disease include muscular weakness, fatigue, and respiratory and/or heart complications. Individuals with muscular dystrophy commonly demonstrate low muscle endurance and fatigue quickly while walking and climbing stairs as the disease progresses. It is estimated that half of the individuals affected are children between the ages of 3 and 13. Major classifications (Table 17.1) that affect school age children include Duchenne, Becker, limb-girdle, facioscapulo-humeral, and myotonic muscular dystrophy (Blackman, 1997; Muscular Dystrophy Association, 2000; Sarnac, 1992).

Classification and Etiology

Duchenne Muscular Dystrophy

Duchenne muscular dystrophy (MD) is the most common childhood form of MD and is sometimes referred to as progressive or pseudohypertrophic muscular dystrophy. Duchenne is the most serious and debilitating of all the dystrophies. In approximately 90% of cases it can be traced to a sex-linked recessive trait characterized by the absence of the structural protein dystophin (Kilmer & MacDonald, 1995). This sex-linked genetic error occurs when a defective X (female) chromosome joins a normal Y (male) chromosome. The defective gene is carried by the mother and manifested in male offspring. The end result is a male with Duchenne MD (Kilmer & MacDonald, 1995) (Figure 17.1).

Table 17.1 Types and Characteristics of Muscular Dystrophy

Type	Hereditary	Sex	Onset	Characteristics	Life Expectancy	Other
Duchenne, or progressive, MD	Sex-linked	90% male	2–6 years	Progression upwards from calf muscles—false enlargement of muscle (psuedo-hypertrophic). Pelvis, upper arms, legs are first affected. Progression is slow, sometimes with rapid bursts.	18 years	Heart involvement; intellectual involvement early in 30% of cases and not proportional to the severity of the disease
Becker MD	Sex-linked	Male	2–16 years	Nonprogressive scoliosis. Progression from pelvis, upper arms, and legs—less severe contractures and slower progression than Duchenne.	Middle age	Same as Duchenne with less involvement.
Facio-scapulo-humeral MD	Autosomal dominant	Male or female	Teens to early adulthood	Develops from face to shoulders to arms and then spreads to pelvic girdle area. Progression slow, sometimes with sports.	Middle to late age	Usually no cardiac or intellectual impairment
Limb-girdle MD	Primarily autosomal recessive	Male or female	Teens or early adulthood	Develops from shoulders to pelvis first, then spreads. Progression usually slow.	Approximately 50 years but may vary	Usually no cardiac or intellectual impairment
Myotonic	Autosomal dominant	Male or female	Early childhood to adulthood; newborn period for congenital form	Abnormalities in muscle contraction; myotonia; facial features and speech affected by disease progression and severity. Slow progression.	Adolescence to approximately 50 years, but may vary	Mild to severe intellectual involvement

The remaining 10% of cases of Duchenne MD are *autosomal* (a chromosome other than sex chromosome) and not sex-linked. In these cases, both mother and father carry the recessive gene. A gene "mutation" may occasionally occur in conception, causing a dystrophic condition that may affect male and female offspring (Kilmer & MacDonald, 1995).

Early signs of MD include slow motor gains, low Apgar scores, and poor muscle tone. Changes in gait are evident during walking by 3 to 5 years of age, as well as evidence of clumsiness and frequent falls, wider base of support, waddling gait, and difficulty rising from the floor. Running and jumping are often effected by awkward movements and are characterized by lack of stability. Usually the disease progresses minimally until 7 years of age, when rapid decline in functioning is evident. A wheelchair is needed for ambulation by 10 to 13 years of age (Eng, 1992). Symptoms of both forms of Duchenne MD are similar. Slowness of gait, pseudohypertrophy of the calves (the calves appear muscular but in realty are weakening because the muscle tissue is replaced by fat, fibrous tissue), and Gowers' sign are the first noticeable characteristics of the disease. Gowers' sign is a characteristic of Duchenne MD that affects children while attempting to stand erect. While bending over, children place their

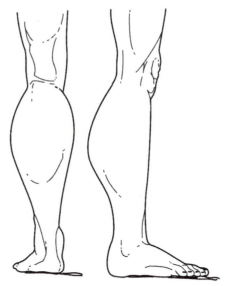

Figure 17.1 Calf manifesting pseudohypertrophy
in Duchenne muscular dystrophy.

hands on the knees and then move alternately up the thighs to achieve a standing
position (Figure 17.2). Weakness is often observed proximally, with subtle changes in
gait and initial difficulty in locomotor patterns and a tendency toward being clumsy.
In addition, the neck flexors are weak, and children may demonstrate difficulties in
lifting and controlling their head and neck.

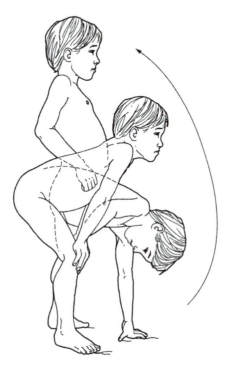

Figure 17.2 Gowers' sign.

The weaknesses of the hip flexor and extensors, as well as contractures, account for the deterioration of gait and difficulty in functional tasks, such as stair climbing, locomotor activities, and rising from the floor (Kilmer & MacDonald, 1995). As the disease progresses, the muscles of the abdomen, pelvis, and hips weaken, lordosis develops (due to weakness of the abdominal and gluteus maximus muscle), the gait becomes waddling (due to gluteus weakness of the medius) (Adams & McCubbin, 1990). By the age of 6, children may have difficulty keeping up with peers and start to lose strength in a relatively linear fashion (Aitkens, McCrory, Kilmer & Bernauer, 1993). Contractures are noticeable as early as 3–4 years at the ankles and hip flexor, causing difficulties in pushing the heels to the floor. Contractures may also be noticeable at the hips, knees, and elbows during periods of immobilization or inactivity. The decrease in functional activity may exacerbate these contractures and is a rationale for intervention. In the final stages of the disease, scoliosis, or lateral curvatures of the spine, is prevalent, resulting in severe postural and structural deformities and compromising pulmonary abilities. Kilmer and MacDonald (1995) have indicated that spinal curves can develop rapidly and may exceed 100 degrees, necessitating spinal fixation. In addition, pulmonary functions and cardiac sufficiency are compromised by the progressive muscular weakness and spinal difficulties. The respiratory muscles may also be weakened, resulting in complications such as pneumonia and/or cardiomyopathy. Cardiomyopathy leads to ineffective systolic contractions and congestive heart failure, which is a common cause of death in this population.

The progressive loss of ambulation, muscular strength, and functional ability results in the use of a wheelchair. At this stage, maintaining existing muscular strength and restricting further atrophy is vital to preserving the child's ability to propel a wheelchair. Obesity becomes a problem at this stage as the child requires more force to move the body, and fat does not contribute to generating force. In conjunction with deteriorating strength and contractures, body fat compromises the child's ability to perform functional tasks. In later stages, the fat weight is lost as the disease progresses. Intellectual capabilities may vary; some learning problems occur in approximately 30% of cases.

Becker Muscular Dystrophy

Becker muscular dystrophy is similar to Duchenne muscular dystrophy but progresses more slowly and has a later onset, generally around 10–15 years of age. A greater percentage of the children are males, and the disease is sex-linked from a recessive X-linked chromosome caused by reduced amounts of dystrophin (Kilmer & MacDonald, 1995). Symptoms are similar to those of Duchenne muscular dystrophy. Children demonstrate a prolonged ambulatory capacity until 16 years or later, less severe contractures of the ankle and foot, and nonprogressive scoliosis and skeletal deformities (Bar-Or, 1983). Intellectual impairment generally is not evident in Becker's muscular dystrophy, although children may demonstrate varying learning disabilities (Weisberg, Strub & Garcia, 1989).

Other characteristics include muscle weakness; wasting and contractures in the shoulder and pelvic muscles; pseudohypertrophy of the calves; loss of independent ambulation as disease progresses; and slow progressive weakness in the spine resulting in abnormal curvature of the spine that is not as severe as that seen in Duchenne muscular dystrophy. Respiratory failure is generally not significant, although heart abnormalities and cardiomyopathy may be present. Intervention should occur early in the course of the disease, when weakness and muscle fiber degeneration are minimal. Physical activity should be encouraged to maintain and maximize functional strength and range of motion for daily living skills and prolonging ambulation (Fowler & Taylor, 1982).

Facioscapulohumeral Muscular Dystrophy

Facioscapulohumeral MD is characterized by initial involvement of the face, shoulder, and upper extremities with moderate involvement of the pelvic girdle area that usually does not occur until adulthood. Pseudohypertrophy of the muscles is uncommon, and skeletal deformities and muscular contractures are rare. The disease can occur in either sex and is inherited by an autosomal dominant factor. Progression of the disease is slow, with ambulation remaining until middle age, and may be characterized by periods of remission.

The muscles most commonly involved are those that are associated with upper body function and object manipulation at the shoulders or above, including the trapezius, rhomboids, latissimi dorsi, and the pectoralis major, but not the deltoids. As the disease progresses, involvement and weakening occurs in the clavicular portions of the pectoralis, brachioradialis, biceps, wrist, and finger extensions. Involvement may also appear in the facial muscles, including the sphincter muscles of the mouth, buccinator muscles and the masseter muscles.

Limb-Girdle Muscular Dystrophy

Limb-girdle MD is the least distinctive of the dystrophies, with symptoms usually occurring in the late teens to the third decade of life. The disease involves an autosomal recessive factor and is generally benign with great variations even within family members. Initial weakness occurs primarily in either the shoulder or pelvic girdle area but may extend to other muscle groups, such as the biceps, portions of the pectorals, brachioradialis, and the wrist and finger extensions. Weakness begins in the hip, quadriceps, and hamstrings, with evidence of waddling gait and Gowers' sign affecting walking and locomotor activities. Some pseudohypertrophy may occur in the calves, but most appears in the upper extremities. Muscle contractures and skeletal deformities appear in the latter stages of the disease. Life expectancy is approximately 50 years of age. It is not uncommon for the disease to be asymmetrical, resulting in one limb being much weaker than the other. Early bicep involvement is evident as well as deltoid weakness affecting functional tasks of the upper extremities. The muscles of the neck are also affected, although the facial muscles are not involved.

The muscles involved in the pelvic girdle area include a weakening of the sacrospinalis, iliopsoas, quadriceps, gluteus maximus, anterior tibial, abductors, and the peroneal muscles. The muscles weakened in the shoulder and arm areas include the serrati, the trapezius, latissimi dorsi, rhomboids, and the sternal portion of the pectoralis major.

Myotonic Muscular Dystrophy

Myotonic muscular dystrophy (Steinert's disease) is the second most common adult form of muscular dystrophy. It is autosomal dominant and characterized by abnormalities in muscle contraction (Jones, 1985). Myotonia, the primary characteristic of this disease, is usually not clinically or electromyographically evident until 5 years of age, unless it is the congenital form that is diagnosed at birth and results in severe cognitive deficits (Sarnac, 1992). Myotonia is the delay or inability to relax muscles after repetitive discharge, or contraction of a single muscle fiber after activation induced by the stretch reflex or electrical stimulation (Sarnac, 1992). Myotonia is commonly demonstrated in the hands and distal muscles. Speech is often affected because of involvement of the muscles of the face, tongue, and pharynx. Cardiac involvement is manifested by blocks in the Purkinje system and arrhythmias instead of cardiomyopathy present in other dystrophic conditions (Sarnac, 1992). Facial features include masseter muscle atrophy and inability to close the lips. The eye muscles are weak, affecting the ability to close the eyelashes. Neck muscles atrophy and are weak mainly in flexion, causing some cervical lordosis (Weisberg et al., 1989). Weakness in the extremities is present in distal muscles, characterized by weak hand muscles and foot drop. As with other types of muscular dystrophy, learning difficulties may occur, and no specific medical treatment can counteract these symptoms.

Planning the Physical Activity Program

Children with muscular dystrophy battle several morphological constraints throughout the progression of the disease. The activity level of children should be encouraged to maintain the overall level of functioning. Depending on the progression of the disease, children progress through stages of functional ability (Bar-Or, 1995; Kilmer & McDonald, 1995):

1. low strength and endurance; normal ambulation with possible overwork weakness

2. reduction in activity; tendency to fatigue easily; reduced strength and endurance; mild contractures and possible overwork weakness; ambulation with assistance

3. poor strength and endurance; overwork weakness; contractures; limited ambulation and decrease in physical activity

4. ambulation significantly decreased; functional use of wheelchair; severe contractures and muscular weakness; pulmonary difficulties and cardiomyopathy

In order to postpone skeletal deformities and muscle deterioration, teachers should encourage increased activities at submaximals levels to promote ambulation. To promote physical activity, it is recommended that early intervention programs be implemented with the following guidelines:

1. *Medical Approval.* A physician's approval should be obtained prior to implementing a physical activity program. The physician will determine the type and stage of the disease and provide recommendations or contraindications to physical activities. Periodic evaluation will aid in determining progress or fluctuations in the child's functional ability.

2. *Assessment.* Initially, the individual's residual strength and endurance and flexibility in each affected area should be determined from medical reports, from parents, and from manual or quantitative strength tests by the clinician. The individual's overall ability to ambulate and the accompanying balance or gait disorders will determine the level and intensity of the training program. Strength,

flexibility, and functional capabilities should be periodically measured throughout the program to ensure proper daily management (Bar-Or, 1995).

3. *Intensity.* Submaximal isotonic or isokinetic exercises should be used in the program. Strenuous, "all-out" bouts of exercise contribute to overworking weakened muscles and should be avoided with MD individuals (Croce, 1987; Fowler & Taylor, 1982). Submaximal exercises should be used to avoid muscle overloading. Teachers should select exercises with a high repetition maximum and low resistance in a manner that is consistent with untrained individuals. Alternative resistance exercise, such as exercises with surgical tubing or hand weights and water exercises, can also be used in weakened muscle groups. A mutual set of 12 exercises should be selected before multiple sets are allowed and used. Duration should be individualized and determined by the type and progression of the disease.

4. *Warm-up and cool-down.* To prepare the muscles before exercise, it is necessary to increase blood flow and body temperature in preparation for the more vigorous exercise. A gentle warm-up segment consisting of slow, static stretches should last approximately 6 to 8 minutes. In contrast, a cool-down phase should consist of 6 to 8 minutes of gentle, rhythmic stretching exercises to gradually control stimulated muscles and prevent contractures. The cool-down phase will not only enhance flexibility, but also aid in preventing injury and minimizing muscle soreness.

Primary areas of emphasis in both warm-up and cool-down include the hamstrings, iliotibial bands (groin and leg), heelcords, hip and knee extensions, elbow flexor, and hand flexor. The warm-up and cool-down not only prepare the body for exercise but also aid in combating contractures (Croce, 1987; Eng, 1992).

Implementing the Physical Activity Program

Early recognition of muscular dystrophy is essential for early intervention and acceptance of the disorder. Medication is ineffective in the progress of the disease, but early intervention will help maintain muscular strength and functional ability. Physical activity designed to promote range of motion aids in preventing contractures and tight muscles. The shortening of muscle groups has been recognized as being preventable in children with muscular dystrophy (Eston et al., 1989). Teachers should encourage activities that require using the limbs and implement muscular activity on a regular basis that is of short duration and does not push the child to exhaustion. Although overly vigorous and intense exercise may be harmful, inactivity will contribute to the deterioration of the functional ability and to the development contractures, atrophy, and spinal deformities (Eston et al., 1989; Lewis & Haller, 1992). Exercise should be encouraged to maintain posture in sitting and standing positions. Range-of-motion exercises can aid in delaying muscle tightness, which first appears in the hip flexor, hamstrings, triceps, toe flexor, forearm pronators, and wrist and finger flexor (Croce, 1987). Although programs that emphasize stretching in these muscle groups can delay contractures, the response of dystrophic muscles to exercise is still under speculation (Croce, 1987).

Resistive exercise programs for muscular dystrophy may be controversial because of concern regarding the efficiency of the programs. Johnson and Braddom (1971) recommended that heavy resistive exercise be avoided for weakened muscle because lifting heavy weights results in a marked loss of strength in the affected area and fatigues the involved muscles. In contrast, Milner-Brown, Mellenthin, and Miller (1986) concluded that muscle strength will increase with no evidence of overworked muscle weakness in submaximal long-term programs. Further, Fowler and Taylor (1982) indicated that submaximal exercise does not appear to be deleterious if initiated before pronounced muscle weakness and degeneration occur. To put theoretical research into perspective, it is obvious that several concerns are evident in developing exercise programs for individuals with muscular dystrophy:

- the extent of muscle weakness
- progression of the disease
- degree and intensity of the exercise
- individual needs

The consensus of past research efforts seems to support the contention that unaffected muscle is trainable and can be strengthened, possibly aiding in slowing down the progression of the disease and deterioration of the muscles (Croce, 1987).

In addition, maximal aerobic power and muscular endurance is lower than in able-bodied individuals because of the smaller muscle mass and compromised cardiac and pulmonary functioning in individuals with muscular dystrophy. (Bar-Or, 1983, 1995). Decreases in exercise tolerance have been manifested by lower cardiopulmonary capacities and reduced endurance time. This decrease may be attributed to their decrease in leg strength as well as low aerobic power (Kilmer, Abresch & Fowler, 1993). Sockolov, Irwin, Dressendorfer, and Bernauer (1977) indicated that maximum heart rates in dystrophic children were 30% lower than in able-bodied children, and maximal cardiac output was nearly 100% lower in the dystrophic children. Cardiomyopathy is detected as early as 10–12 years of age, with accompanying restrictions in pulmonary functioning (Eng, 1992). It is essential in the total treatment program to assess pulmonary capabilities and functioning because this is the most common cause of death in this population.

Individualized Program Approach

The components of an exercise program for children with MD should include muscular endurance, muscular strength, and maximal aerobic power (Bar-Or, 1995). Muscular strength is essential for standing, walking, and performing other functional daily tasks (Bar-Or, 1995). It is apparent that healthy children will continue to increase their strength with age, whereas dystrophic children may display minimal increases or decreases in strength over a 10-year period beginning at 5 years of age. This nonprogression or deterioration in muscular strength has a definite effect on the child's functional ability and is a major concern in the development of the program. Other goals or concerns in developing programs include (1) self-help and ambulation, (2) anticipating prevention of complications, (3) recreational and vocational endeavors, and (4) counseling of children and family.

Factors to consider in the design of the program depend on the individual's age, the rate of progression, and the degree of muscular weakness (the extent of muscle fiber degeneration). A major consideration in establishing a program that contains submaximal strengthening exercises is the individual's tolerance level. Because the activity level of individuals with muscular dystrophy parallels the course of the disability, it is essential to facilitate development at their functional level. Bar-Or (1995) suggested that exercise programming follow these guidelines:

1. provide realistic short term goals for children and parents
2. focus on maintaining or reducing the rate of deterioration
3. focus on submaximal exercises and reducing intensity to avoid fatigue
4. prevent contractures and provide nutritional counseling in conjunction with training
5. provide activities in an enjoyable setting to facilitate compliance

The intent of the program should be to keep children at their highest functioning level. Decline in functioning is the result of a lack of residual muscle strength, especially in the knee and hip extensions; extent of contractures in the lower limbs; body weight and obesity; and psychological factors, such as fear of falling or withdrawal from social interactions (Bar-Or, 1983, 1995). As ambulation decreases, the exercise program can be altered to coincide with the functional ability of each ambulation stage. Adjustments in intensity or exercises may be needed to compensate for reduced functioning and are based on individual activity levels or periods of remission (Table 17.2).

Table 17.2 Physical Activity Suggestions for Muscular Dystrophy

Type	Characteristics	Instructional Strategies	Physical Activity Suggestions
Duchenne	Muscle weakness, clumsiness, Gowers' sign, contractures, scoliosis	Team approach to aid in ambulation and functional ability. Active participation and management of obesity and contractures. Cross-training applications for muscle strengthening.	Resistance exercises. Water exercises, stretching. Range of motion. Ambulation and stair climbing, parachute activities. Manipulative skills and recreational activities.
Becker	Same as Duchenne, with later onset and severity	Same as Duchenne.	Same as Duchenne.
Facioscapulo-humeral	Involvement of shoulder, chest, and face	Same as Duchenne, with emphasis on active participation and use of leisure skills.	Resistance exercises, parachute, aquatics and water exercises; manipulation activities that can be used in recreation, such as archery and bowling.
Limb-girdle	Involvements in shoulder or pelvic girdle; some pesudohyptropohy of calves but primary involvement in the upper extremities and pelvic girdle	Same as Duchenne, with emphasis on active participation and use of leisure skills.	Resistance exercises, parachute, water exercises, aquatics, lifetime sports and games.
Myotonic	Involvement in distal muscles; clumsy or slow in movement; inability to quickly relax muscle (myotonia)	Same as Duchenne, with activities that emphasize large muscle groups.	Resistance exercises; gentle flexibility and warm-up; aquatics, cycling.

Community and Home-Based Interventions

In order to facilitate the development of children with muscular dystrophy, teachers should encourage children to engage in alternate physical activities to maintain an active lifestyle (Table 17.2). Cross-training principles can provide physical activity in another mode to alleviate stress on dystrophic muscles and avoid overuse or fatiguing of muscles (Horvat & Aufsesser, 1991). Swimming seems to be the preferred activity for children with muscular dystrophy (Muscular Dystrophy Association, 2000). For example, water exercises can provide muscular strength, endurance, and cardiovascular development while maximizing the benefits of water. Swimming can aid in mobility and maintain range of motion, respiratory exchange, and general conditioning in a program that can be continued after the child can no longer ambulate (Eng, 1992). Conditioning can proceed in the same manner by incorporating repeated movement at a designated range of motion but using exercises and water as the resistance. In this manner, a total physical activity program may be utilized, as well as recreational activities that may be motivating to children to aid in retaining functional ability for as long as possible and generalize to community and home-based settings.

Used in conjunction with resistance exercises, cross-training can provide overall training benefits without undue fatigue in dystrophic muscles. Other activities that emphasize manipulation, object control, and stability should be encouraged to maintain functional ability, including ambulation. For example, activities such as parachuting, bowling, and archery can help keep the child active while emphasizing flexion and extension movements and can be used over the life span in home and community settings. Likewise, play activities in young children should emphasize active movements that can help maximize functional development. Early diagnosis and intervention can also facilitate designing and implementing programs while children are functioning at their highest level. Because the work output of individuals with muscular dystrophy is markedly reduced, obesity is a common problem associated with lack of mobility. As the amount of weight increases, the strength required for ambulation increases, putting an already compromised muscular structure at risk. Proper dietary management should be implemented and monitored. Daily activity can help children learn to control and use the muscles more efficiently, postpone some of the effects of a progressive disease, and allow them to participate with able-bodied peers and community and family-based activities. Psychologically there is considerable stress associated with the progressive nature of the diseases for the individual and family. Coping mechanisms may range from overprotection to denial of the disease (Eng, 1992). The frustrations associated with the disease, as well as social isolation and lack of self-concept and/or sexual expression, may result in attention and/or behavior problems. With proper medical supervision, trainable muscle should be maximized, and children should be encouraged to maintain their overall functioning physically as well as psychologically.

Juvenile Rheumatoid Arthritis

Juvenile arthritis is a general term for all types of arthritis and related conditions occurring in children (Arthritis Foundation, 2002). The primary pathology of the chronic disease is inflammation of the connective tissues (Scull & Athreya, 1995). Subtypes are distinguished by number of joints involved within the first 6 months of the disease's onset:

- systemic arthritis (Still's disease)
- polyarticular arthritis
- pauciarticular arthritis

Approximately 300,000 children have some form of arthritis, and 8.4 million young adults between 18 and 44 have arthritis. Approximately 50,000 have juvenile rheumatoid arthritis (JRA). Arthritis affects girls twice as often as boys and may occur anytime from birth to 16 years of age (Arthritis Foundation, 2002).

Juvenile arthritis is characterized by major changes in the joints, including inflammation, contractures, and joint damage, all of which can affect mobility, strength, and endurance. Children may come to school with varying degrees of pain and stiffness or miss school entirely (Arthritis Foundation, 2002). Nearly all children with arthritis experience periods when symptoms reduce in severity or disappear, although they may go from being symptom free to experiencing extreme pain and swelling quickly. When the child is symptom free, or even relatively symptom free, the child should be encouraged to participate in most, if not all, developmentally appropriate physical activities. Developmental appropriateness is emphasized because many children with serious and prolonged involvement are smaller and less physically mature than their typically developing chronological age (CA) peers. Splinting is occasionally the procedure of choice when the purpose is to rest tender joints or prevent or minimize contractures. Typically, removable casts may be used at nights or for periods during the day. For example, a wrist splint worn during the day may permit active finger use while protecting the painful and possibly malformed wrist from unnecessary trauma.

The psychological and social impact on a child with arthritis are multidimensional. Joint pain and stiffness may become an ongoing distraction for the child, which often mitigates against the child's ability to remain on task. To varying degrees, medication schedules can be disruptive and children may have side effects from the medication. Children may also feel embarrassed by the disease, isolated, inadequate, and angry about restriction resulting from the disease (Arthritis Foundation, 2002).

When children self-medicate, adults should take care to ensure that the children do, indeed, take their medications. Children sometimes simply forget to take their medications. Some children, however, may fail to take medications as a personal act of rebellion against the disease. Such children may perceive the disease as devaluing, and by opting not to medicate, the child demonstrates that he or she is no different from other children.

Children want to be perceived as being like other children. Taylor (1987) revealed several important differences of opinion regarding the consequences of JRA among children with the disease, their parents, and their teachers. The investigator found that both parents and teachers tended to focus on the physical symptoms of arthritis, whereas children reported that their major concerns centered on peer relationships and self-esteem. This finding suggests that from the child's perspective, the disease is secondary in importance to acceptance by others. In fact, children in the study were especially reluctant to allow teachers to inform classmates about the disease. Parents and teachers should try to foster an environment wherein the child is perceived by all as a person first. They should also encourage children to focus on strengths rather than limitations; encourage decision making and responsibility; promote physical activity and developing skills and peer relationships that emphasize similarities rather than differences; and promote social interaction and extracurricular activities (Arthritis Foundation, 2002).

Systemic Arthritis (Still's Disease)

Systemic arthritis often is referred to as Still's disease. The condition is so named, because its symptoms were first described in 1897 by British physician George Still. Systemic arthritis occurs in approximately equal rates in both boys and girls and occurs in approximately 20% of children with JRA (Kock, 1992).

This particular form of the disease is termed systemic because the entire body (i.e., system) is affected. Among earliest symptoms of systemic arthritis is a high spiking fever. Fevers commonly reach 103 degrees. Within a few hours, temperature may return to normal. Fever spikes and remissions may occur as often as once or twice daily. During periods of fever, the child may experiences chills and feel very sick. When fever is gone, the child often feels quite well. The spiking fever condition can last weeks and may persist into months. A rheumatoid rash manifesting as pale red spots and covering various body parts often accompanies the fever.

Other manifestations of systemic arthritis include inflammation of the lining of the heart (pericarditis), the heart proper, or the lungs. Other characteristics may include swelling of the lymph nodes and enlargement of the liver and spleen. The red blood cell count may be depressed (anemia), and the white blood cell count may be elevated.

At the onset of systemic arthritis, arthritis and concomitant joint discomfort are often relatively minor manifestations of the illness and may not appear until months after heretofore mentioned symptoms have come and gone. Because joint discomfort is not an initial manifestation of systemic arthritis, the disease often is difficult to diagnose. Episodes of this disease may persist for months, disappear, and reappear months or even years later. Children may require hospitalization and be restricted in early participation in activity because of the general aches, pains, fatigue, and stiffness (Scull & Athreya, 1995). In time, about half the children with systemic-onset arthritis recover nearly completely, whereas the remaining half show progressive involvement of more joints that includes moderate to severe disability (Arthritis Foundation, 2002).

Polyarticular Arthritis

The term *poly* means "many." By definition, polyarticular arthritis means having arthritis in five or more joints. This form of the disease occurs in approximately 35% of children with JRA and is subdivided into two categories: rheumatoid factor positive (RF+) and rheumatoid factor negative (RF-) (Koch, 1992). The child's major symptom is the severity of pain in affected joints, including the knees, ankles, wrists, neck, fingers (Figure 17.3), elbows, and shoulders. Children with polyarticular arthritis live in constant pain. When polyarticular arthritis occurs in the jaw, bone growth may be retarded, resulting in a receding chin.

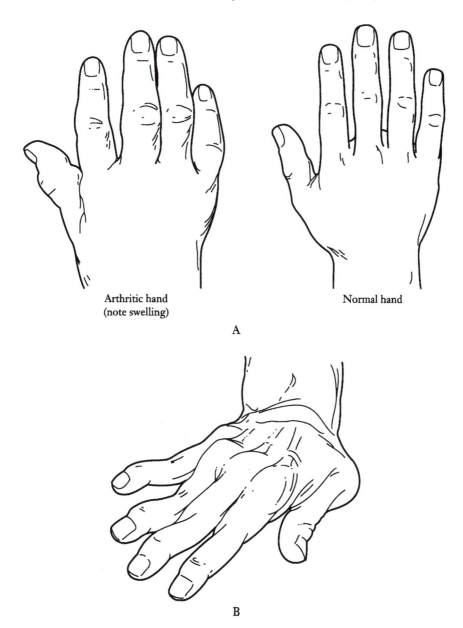

Arthritic hand
(note swelling)

Normal hand

A

B

Figure 17.3 (a) Arthritic hand compared with normal hand.
(b) "Swan neck" deformity caused by arthritis.

Given that pain is omnipresent in a child with polyarticular arthritis and that movement provokes pain, there is often a tendency for the child to avoid physical activity. The child's defense mechanism, in the face of pain, is often to sit motionless with joints flexed. Persistent flexion in affected joints, if not therapeutically managed, results in chronically disabling skeletal deformities and muscle contractures. The RF+

type will continue into adulthood, whereas the RF- may enter remission. The protracted nature of the disease typically results in the child's being small and sexually immature for chronological age.

Pauciarticular Arthritis

The term *pauci* means "few." By definition, pauciarticular arthritis means having arthritis in four or fewer joints within the first 6 months of the disease's onset. The large joints of the knee, ankle, elbow, or wrist are affected. This form of the disease most commonly occurs in young females but may affect either sex. Manifestations of this form of arthritis usually are limited to affected joints. Most commonly involved joints are the knee and ankle. Only one joint is involved in approximately 50% of cases. Joint pain and swelling often come on gradually when the child is between 2 and 4 years of age. The child with pauciarticular arthritis typically has no fever, does not have generalized symptoms, and does not appear sick. When compared with children who have polyarticular arthritis, children with pauciarticular arthritis seem quite well. The joint disease part of pauciarticular arthritis usually follows a benign course and may well resolve itself within a few years (Arthritis Foundation, 2002).

The most serious manifestation of pauciarticular arthritis often is not joint disease, but inflammation of the iris and muscles controlling the eye. This condition may develop unnoticed, because its onset and progression typically are insidious. Initial symptoms in such instances, because they are mild, may be dismissed as inconsequential. Children with red eyes, who rub their eyes often, and/or complain about bright lights should be referred to an ophthalmologist (a physician specializing in diseases of the eye). The condition develops in approximately one-fourth of children, mostly girls, who contract pauciarticular arthritis. Among children with the condition, approximately 60% recover completely, while approximately 25% may lose some vision. Early intervention eliminates or at least minimizes vision loss.

Planning the Physical Activity Program

Nonsteroidal anti-inflammatory drugs (NSAIDs) have become the preferred initial therapy in treating JRA. Within the NSAID family of medications, ibuprofen, naproxen (Naprosyn), and tolmetin sodium (Tolectin) have been approved for use in children 12 and under by the Food and Drug Administration (FDA). Six to 8 weeks often are required to fully determine NSAID efficacy, and laboratory tests should be administered to determine possible medication toxicity. Possible side effects of NSAID ingestion include stomach pain, nausea and vomiting, anemia, headache, blood in the urine, severe abdominal pain and peptic ulcer, fragility and scarring of the skin (especially with Naprosyn), and difficulty concentrating in school (Arthritis Foundation, 2002).

Aspirin may be prescribed for joint pain and inflammation and to reduce fever. Aspirin is often prescribed because of its effectiveness with relatively few side effects. Side effects do, however, occur. The child who takes aspirin in larger than typical doses may experience stomachaches, behavior changes, ringing in the ears, increased bruising following mild trauma, and a sensation of having "stuffed-up" ears. It should be noted that aspirin taken by children has been linked with Reye's (pronounced "rise") syndrome. Reye's syndrome is an acute and sometimes fatal condition involving brain inflammation and liver enlargement. The teacher should be familiar with Reye's syndrome symptoms, including persistent vomiting and unusual irritability in the student. Continued reliance on aspirin as a medication of choice is founded on the assumption that, on a case-by-case basis, benefits outweigh risks.

Glucocorticoid Drugs

Steroids, including cortisone and prednisone, are among the most potent anti-inflammatory agents prescribed to treat joint inflammation, pain, and swelling. Glucocorticoid drugs act as immunosupressants. They are administered to desensitize the body's immune system response that causes joint disease. This family of anti-inflammatory agents typically is prescribed to therapeutically manage only those cases of joint disease that are most resistant to treatment. Glucocorticoid drugs must be prescribed with particular caution because of the potential for varied and serious side effects. They must be prescribed in the lowest effective dose and for the shortest possible time. Side effects can include high blood pressure, osteoporosis (softening of bones), slowing of growth and maturation rates, heightened susceptibility to infection, weight gain resulting from increased appetite, and increased risk of ulcers.

Exercise Considerations

Physical activity and exercise are mainstays in treatment and management of arthritis (Table 17.3). Although affected joints do require rest and need to be protected from undue trauma, exercise and physical activity help prevent or control joint deformities and muscle contractures. For children with arthritis, therapeutic exercise and active participation in recreation and sports is needed to maintain an active lifestyle (Arthritis Foundation, 2002; Scull & Athreya, 1995), which leads to the following benefits:

- maintains joint flexibility
- maintains muscle strength
- regain lost motion or strength in a joint or muscle
- makes functional activities, such as walking or dressing, easier
- improves general fitness and endurance
- improves self-esteem
- prevents deconditioning of the cardiopulmonary system
- maintains bone density

Although children should be encouraged to actively participate, there are some potential adverse effects of exercise on arthritis. Therefore, input from members of the collaborative team is required. Special care should be taken to avoid exacerbating symptoms of the disease. For example, excessive swelling, pain, or fatigue may signal that the child has exceeded the safety threshold of the activity. Likewise, a child with low muscular strength may compromise joint integrity and be at risk for further injury. In addition, joints without an appropriate range of motion or underlying osteoporosis may present risks for fracture (Scull & Athreya, 1995).

Table 17.3 Physical Activity Suggestions for Arthritis

Site	Characteristics	Physical Activity Suggestions
Joints	Pain; inflammation; stiffness; loss in range of motion	Avoid high-impact and contact sports. Emphasize range of motion and stretching; hot compresses, yoga, relaxation, and aerobic exercise; water exercise with a mild warm-up and strength exercises to stabilize joint at the child's comfort level.
Muscles	Weakness; contractures	Range-of-motion exercises (active or passive); isometric exercises. Water exercises, swimming in conducive environment (88–92°) using flotation devices, swim fins, etc. Stationary cycling, yoga, and relaxation activities.
Psychological functioning	Fatigue; pain; self-esteem problems	Reduce activity if child is fatigued, but emphasize that deconditioning can cause fatigue. Encourage activity that is conducive to developing physical functioning and social interaction with peers.

Implementing the Physical Activity Program

In addition to the input from the collaborative team on maximum joint protection and on the child's functioning, high-impact activities and contact sports should be avoided. Children should develop confidence in their physical abilities and be encouraged to pick a sport or activity of interest, while stressing activities that exercise the joints without eliciting too much stress on them (Arthritis Foundation, 2002). In preparation for activity, affected joints can be readied for movement by warm baths or layered warm paraffin applications. These preparations help reduce discomfort associated with motion and thereby may encourage child to "stick with" an exercise regimen and activity program. Hicks (1990) has recommended that children progress from range-of-motion and stretching exercises to isometric exercises to aerobic exercises to recreational activities.

Pathways is a yoga-based program produced for the Arthritis Foundation that includes breathing, relaxation, stretching, strengthening routines, and aerobic exercises. Pool Exercise Program (PEP), People with Arthritis Can Exercise (PACE I & II), and Walk with Ease are all programs that are available from the Arthritis Foundation to help facilitate the exercise programs. Mild exercise (i.e., warm-up) should precede more vigorous exercise. Muscle strengthening and flexibility exercises will help control pain and minimize joint deformity. Pain perception, of course, is in part subjective and varies among individuals. A good rule of thumb is that the teacher should know that exercise is important and encourage the individual child to exercise to, but never though, his or her threshold of discomfort. The point at which discomfort is perceived as pain is the point where exercise exercise intensity and/or duration should peak.

Isometric exercises may be particularly valuable adjuncts to strength maintenance or development programs, because they require muscle contraction while causing little or no movement at the joint. Isometric contractions may be held for 6 seconds at near-maximum effort several times daily. Isometric exercises can be performed with light weights or surgical tubing to the point of fatigue.

Range-of-motion exercises may be active, assistive, or passive, depending on individual need. Stretching should be steady and deliberate, not bouncy (i.e., ballistic). Depending on the individual child's exercise tolerance, a given stretch may persist for at least 6 seconds. Limb movement activities to maintain or rehabilitate range of motion often can be done by the child. Care must be taken in such instances to ensure the child does, indeed, carry out prescribed exercises. Children often do not appreciate the long-range value of prescribed activities and may be reluctant to inflict discomfort on themselves. Any program designed to minimize effects of arthritis will result in some discomfort to the child. The teacher must be patient in working with the child, to prevent the exercise regimen or activity from turning into a battle of wills.

The use of the aquatic environment is one of the best and safest exercise regimens to use for children. The total body can be exercised with minimal joint stress, and the child can develop flexibility as well as muscular strength. Water exercise, in which the child moves against the resistance of the water, can also be used. In addition, the pool environment can be used to develop aerobic conditioning and to help promote ambulation. For some children, personal floatation devices, swim fins, or kickboards may be needed to initiate movements and build functional strength prior to developing swimming skills. It is essential that the water and air be warm enough (88–92 degrees for water, 95–98 degrees for air) to avoid joint stiffness and pain (McNeal, 1990).

During acute stages of arthritis, activities that jar or otherwise traumatize affected joints (e.g., jumping, wrestling, catching heavy objects) are contraindicated. Ideal activities are those that encourage exercise through reasonable ranges of motion that do not traumatize joints. In addition to aquatics, cycling is an ideal exercise to promote muscular strength and flexibility. Because cycling is a low-impact activity, it does not compromise joint integrity but does allow the child to reap the physical and emotional benefits of activity.

Children with arthritis may also experience mood swings. These occur, in part, because symptoms of the disease vary in intensity. After a good night's sleep or during the course of days when symptoms moderate, the child's disposition often shifts toward the positive. Bouts of discomfort from joint pain, in contrast, may result in the child's becoming fatigued or irritable.

Feelings of fatigue often accompany moderate and severe cases of arthritis. A response common among caregivers in such situations is to recommend reductions in activity, including rest. According to Ike, Lampman, and Castor (1989), fatigue results only in part from the disease. Unnecessary restriction of the child's activity plays a significant role in deconditioning, which in turn exacerbates the child's feelings of tiredness. Joint pain lasting longer than one hour after activity is an indication that the activity has been too strenuous. However, eliminating the child from participation may have adverse emotional effects. Activity should be encouraged that is beneficial to the child without triggering any of the side effects from their condition. Periodic assessment of physical functioning and constant monitoring of participation should provide the child with the opportunity to safely lead an active life.

CHAPTER SUMMARY

1. Muscular dystrophy is characterized by persistent deterioration of striated muscle tissue.

2. Primary characteristics of the disease are muscular weakness, fatigue, and respiratory and heart complications.

3. Major classifications include Duchenne, Becker, limb-girdle, Facioscapulohumeral, and myotonic muscular dystrophy.

4. Intervention activities should focus on maintaining muscular strength and functional ability.

5. Cross-training and home-based activities can be used to supplement the physical activity program.

6. Juvenile arthritis is characterized by joint inflammation, joint contracture, joint damage, and altered growth.

7. Three types of juvenile arthritis include systemic arthritis, polyarticular arthritis, and pauciarticular arthritis.

8. Activity is essential to develop strength, maintain flexibility and bone density, prevent deconditioning, and improve self-esteem.

9. Activity should be encouraged to support an active lifestyle, including isometric, isotonic, and flexibility exercises.

REFERENCES

Adams, R., & McCubbin, J. (1990). *Games sports, and exercises for the physically handicapped* (3rd ed.). Philadelphia: Lea and Febiger.

Aitkens, S. G., McCrory, M. M., Kilmer, D. L. & Bernauer, E. M. (1993). Moderate resistance exercise program: Its effect in slowly progressive neuromuscular disease. *Archives of Physical Medicine and Rehabilitation, 74,* 711–715.

Arthritis Foundation. (2002). *Arthritis answers: School success.* Atlanta: Author.

Bar-Or, O. (1983). *Pediatric sports medicine for the practitioner.* New York: Springer-Verlag.

Bar-Or, O. (1995). Muscular dystrophy. In American College of Sports Medicine, *Exercise Management for Persons with Chronic Diseases and Disabilities.* (pp. 180–188). Champaign, IL: Human Kinetics.

Blackman, J. A., (1997) *Medical aspects of developmental disabilities in children birth to three* (3rd ed.). Gaithersburg, MD: Aspen Publications.

Croce, R. (1987). Exercise and physical activity in managing progressive muscular dystrophy. *Palaestra, 1,* 9–15.

Eng, G. (1992). Diseases of the motor unit. In G. E. Molnar (Ed.), *Pediatric rehabilitation* (2nd ed.). (pp. 299–317). Baltimore: Williams & Wilkins.

Eston, R. G., et al. (1989). Metabolic cost of walking in boys with muscular dystrophy. In S. Oseid & K. Carlson (Eds.), *Children and exercise XIII* (pp. 405–414). Champaign, IL: Human Kinetics.

Fowler, W. M. (1982). Rehabilitation management of muscular dystrophy and related disorders. *Archives of Physical Medicine and Rehabilitation, 63,* 322–327.

Fowler, W. M., & Taylor, M. (1982). Rehabilitation management of muscular dystrophy and related disorders: The role of exercise. *Archives of Physical Medicine and Rehabilitation, 63,* 319–321.

Hicks, J. E. (1990). Exercises in patients with inflammatory arthritis. *Rheumatic Disease Clinics of North America, 16,* 845–870.

Horvat, M., & Aufsesser, P. (1991). The application of cross-training to the disabled. *Clinical Kinesiology, 45*(3), 18–23.

Ike, R. W., Lampman, R. M., & Castor, C. W. (1989). Arthritis and aerobic exercise: A review. *Physician and Sports Medicine, 9,* 51.

Johnson, E., & Braddom, R. (1971). Over-work weakness in facioscapulohumeral muscular dystrophy. *Archives of Physical Medicine and Rehabilitation, 5,* 333–336.

Jones, H. R. (1985). Diseases of the peripheral motor-sensory unit. *Clinical Symposia, 37*(2), 25–26.

Kilmer, D. D., & MacDonald, G. M. (1995). Childhood progressive neuromuscular disease. In B. Goldberg (Ed.), *Sports and exercise for children with chronic health conditions.* Champaign, IL: Human Kinetics.

Kilmer, D. D., Abresch, R. T., & Fowler, W. M. (1993). Serial manual muscle testing in Duchenne muscular dystrophy. *Archives of Physical Medicine and Rehabilitation, 74,* 1168–1171.

Kock, B. (1992). Rehabilitation of the child with joint disease. In G. E. Molnar (Ed.), *Pediatric rehabilitation* (2nd ed.) (pp. 293–333). Baltimore: Williams & Wilkins.

Lewis, S. F., & Haller, R. G. (1992). Skeletal muscle disorders and associated factors that limit exercise performance. In K. B. Pandolf (Ed.), *Exercise and sport sciences reviews.* (pp. 67–115). Baltimore: Williams & Wilkins.

McNeal, R. L. (1990). Aquatic therapy for patients with rheumatic disease. *Rheumatic Clinics of North America, 16,* 915–929.

Milner-Brown, H. S., Mellenthin, M., & Miller, R. G. (1986). Quantifying human muscle strength, endurance, and fatigue. *Archives of Physical Medicine and Rehabilitation, 67,* 530–535.

Muscular Dystrophy Association. (2000). *Facts about muscular dystrophy.* Tucson, AZ: Author.

Sarnac, H. B. (1992). Neuromuscular disorders. In R. E. Behrman et al. (Eds.), *Textbook of pediatrics* (14th ed.) (pp. 1539–1560). Philadelphia: Saunders.

Scull, S. A., & Athreya, B. H. (1995). Childhood arthritis. In B. Goldberg (Ed.), *Sport and exercise for children with chronic health conditions.* Champaign, IL: Human Kinetics.

Sockolov, R., Irwin, B., Dressendorfer, R., & Bernauer, E. (1977). Exercise performance in 6-to-11 year old boys with duchenne muscular dystrophy. *Archives of Physical Medicine and Rehabilitation, 58,* 195–201.

Taylor, J. (1987). School problems and teacher responsibilities in juvenile rheumatoic arthritis. *Journal of School Health, 57,* 186–190.

Weisberg, L., Strub, R. L., & Garcia, C. A. (1989). *Essentials of clinical neurology* (2nd ed.). Rockville, MD: Aspen Publishers.

Section V

Teaching Individuals with Health Impairments

Section V addresses the needs of children with disabilities that affect overall functioning. Respiratory disorders, diabetes, nutritional disorders, and cardio-vascular disorders are all health related and interfere with the child's functional capabilities.

This section is designed to help you

1. recognize the characteristics of children whose health and overall functioning is compromised by impairment

2. understand the concerns, appropriate treatment, and medication that may be essential for these children

3. develop the expertise to design intervention programs that facilitate functional ability

4. incorporate information from the collaborative team to facilitate instruction in physical education

5. facilitate instruction and participation in physical education classes within a margin of safety

CHAPTER 18

Respiratory Disorders

The most common respiratory disorders in children are asthma and cystic fibrosis. Respiratory disorders contribute to school absence, decreased tolerance to physical exertion characterized by shortness of breath, and a lifestyle that interferes with active participation in physical and recreational activities. Children with respiratory disorders have traditionally been given a blanket excuse from participation in physical activity. This prevailing attitude by teachers and administrators has denied children the opportunity to develop age-appropriate physical fitness and motor skills and has kept them as spectators at a time when motor patterns are learned and incorporated into future learning experiences.

Because most children with respiratory disorders can be integrated into regular classes, it is essential to develop a familiarity with the functioning of the respiratory system, etiology and characteristics of respiratory disorder(s), medication that may be prescribed, and the development of a progressive program of physical activities based on the child's functional ability.

The Respiratory System

The lungs perform the most basic function involved in respiration, which is the exchange of oxygen (O_2) and carbon dioxide (CO_2) between the body and the external environment. The respiratory system is separated into upper and lower tracts; the upper track consists of the nose, pharynx, larynx, and trachea; the lower tract includes the bronchi and lungs (Figure 18.1). Each lung occupies half of the chest cavity and is primarily responsible for respiration and exchange of oxygen and carbon dioxide within the lobes while providing oxygen to and removing carbon dioxide from the blood. The right lung consists of three lobes (upper, middle, and lower), whereas the left lung contains two lobes (upper and lower).

Air enters through the nasal cavity from the nose and/or mouth (which warms, filters, and humidifies the air) and then empties into the pharynx and trachea, or windpipe, before entering the lungs. The air enters the lungs through the primary bronchi, which branch into additional smaller passageways called bronchioles and finally into the alveoli, the tiny balloon-like air sacs in which oxygen and carbon dioxide are exchanged.

Ciliated mucous membranes line the nose, mouth, bronchi, and bronchioles and filter and warm the air in the lungs. If these inner membranes become irritated, mucus is secreted to protect the system and provide lubrication. In addition, the state of tension plays an important part in the diameter of the bronchioles (National Jewish

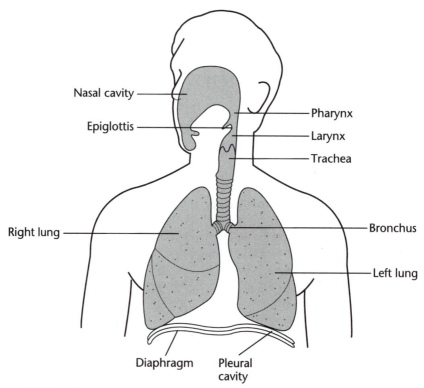

Figure 18.1 Respiratory system.

Center for Immunology and Respiratory Medicine [NJCIRM], 1995). The smooth muscles of the bronchioles expand and contract during the breathing process. If the smooth muscles contract and swell, respiration become narrow and decreases the flow of oxygen into and out of the lungs. If the muscles operate properly, they will relax and allow the bronchial tubes to expand. The inflammatory component of respiratory disorders may also irritate the membranes and damage the elasticity of the bronchiole tubes. A stimulus may cause cells in the lining to release chemical substance mediators that lead to inflammation (NJCIRM, 1995). The bronchiole tubes may also be predisposed to an increased sensitivity or hyperactivity that leads to muscle spasm and narrowing of the pulmonary pathways.

The diaphragm, a dome-shaped muscle separating the abdominal and chest cavities, is the primary muscle used in respiration. When the lungs expand, the diaphragm contracts, moving downward and increasing the chest cavity. When the diaphragm relaxes, it moves upward and decreases the chest cavity as air is being exhaled. Other muscles of the neck, chest, and abdomen (Figure 18.2) aid in the breathing process, although the diaphragm is primarily responsible for 65% of the respiration.

For children with respiratory disorders, the loss of elasticity in the pulmonary structures will ultimately weaken and depress the diaphragm, making it difficult to rise against the distended lungs. The other muscles used in respiration must then compensate for the diaphragm, resulting in shallow and labored breathing. When the breathing pattern is altered, the diaphragm may control only about 30% of the

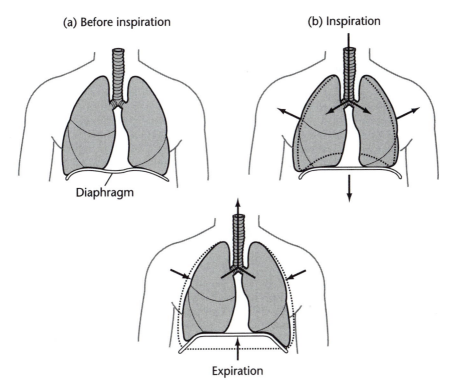

(a) Before inspiration

Diaphragm

(b) Inspiration

Expiration

Figure 18.2 Muscles of respiration.

breathing process, while the neck, chest, and abdominal muscles must assume the remaining 70% of the breathing process.

In addition, obstruction of the airways prohibits the efficient removal of the air in the lungs and causes an increase in lung volume, thereby exerting more pressure on the diaphragm and again causing the diaphragm to flatten. In time, the muscle fibers in the diaphragm shorten and become virtually useless, while the muscles of the neck, chest, and abdomen gradually assume more functioning in the breathing process. The prevalence of obesity also contributes to reduced respiration. The obese abdomen adds pressure on the diaphragm, decreasing the abdomen's ability to rise efficiently and interfering with expiration.

The very structure of the respiratory system presents problems that may hinder breathing. Inflammation and swelling of the passageways will restrict the airways, while mucus may clog the air channels or the walls of the alveoli, causing air to become trapped in the lungs. Although asthma and cystic fibrosis are not synonymous, each affects pulmonary capacity and physical tolerance. This chapter discusses their common characteristics and effects on functional ability.

Asthma

Asthma is characterized by swelling of the mucus membrane lining the bronchial tubes, or excessive secretion of mucus and spasms of the air channels. The major symptoms are a hacking cough, dyspnea (labored breathing or breathlessness) and wheezing, retraction, prolonged exhalation, rapid breathing, and constriction or tightness in the chest. In addition, an asthma attack may result in severe bronchiole obstruction with no passage of air.

The *hacking cough* constitutes the first indication of an impending asthma attack. Bronchiole tubes respond to irritants by secreting mucus, which in turn obstructs the flow of air into and out of the lungs. *Dyspnea* follows when the lining of the bronchiole tubes swells and constricts the airway further, diminishing the flow of air and causing difficulty in breathing. *Wheezing* occurs as a result of decreased air movement into and out of bronchiole tubes that have been constricted by the accumulated mucus. Because the air in the lungs is not completely expelled, the breathing pattern is altered. *Retraction* is evident as a sucking in of the chest or neck as the child exhales, while *prolonged exhalation* reflects a longer period to exhale than inhale because of the trapped air in the lungs. *Rapid breathing* may also be evident as the child tries to move the air into and out of their lungs.

Generally the reduction of breathing occurs during the expiration phase, when the airways are most restricted. The difficulty during expiration interferes with the entry of fresh air into the lungs as air passageways continue to swell and more mucus accumulates, further obstructing the breathing process. When the obstruction becomes severe, there is no wheezing or air movement. A *quiet chest* is symptomatic of a lack of air movement and is the most critical state of the attack.

Types of Asthma

Asthma is a chronic lung condition affecting approximately 6% of the school-aged population. Asthma is classified according to type (such as extrinsic, intrinsic, or mixed) or severity (mild to severe). Whatever the type, asthma causes breathing problems such as coughing, wheezing, chest tightness, and shortness of breath (National Heart, Lung and Blood Institute [NHLBI], 1995). Symptoms may occur from inflammation to the pulmonary pathways or exposure to triggers that exacerbate symptoms and cause an attack (NHLBI, 1995). See the accompanying box.

One type of extrinsic asthma, allergic asthma, is caused by the reaction or hypersensitivity of an individual to the introduction of a normally harmless substance. These substances are called allergens and usually affect the child during the early school years, boys more often than girls by a 2:1 ratio. Allergens include pollens, dust, molds, animal fur, fumes, and smoke. Nonallergic asthma is not as prevalent as allergic asthma but is nevertheless often encountered by physical education teachers. At one time, nonallergic, or intrinsic, asthma was thought to be caused by emotional stress and/or fatigue. Emotions may exacerbate symptoms, but the symptoms generally disappear when the cause of the emotional tension is removed. Asthma can also be precipitated by physical activity. This type of asthma is commonly referred to as exercise-induced asthma (EIA) or exercise-induced bronchospasm (EIB). Mixed asthma is a combination of both intrinsic and extrinsic asthma, generally occurring in late childhood or adolescence and exhibiting itself more often in females than males.

Allergic Asthma   The major causes of asthma are allergies to pollen, dust, molds, animal fur, smoke, dry cold air, and viral infections. Environmental allergies, such as grass, and unfavorable thermal conditions are more prevalent in outdoor settings.

Asthma Triggers

- Exercise—running or playing hard, especially in cold weather
- Upper respiratory infections—colds or flu
- Laughing or crying hard
- Allergens
  - Pollens from trees, plants, and grasses, including freshly cut grass
  - Animal dander from pets with fur or feathers
  - Dust and dust mites in carpeting, pillows, and upholstery
  - Cockroach droppings
  - Molds
- Irritants
  - Cold air
  - Strong smells and chemical sprays, including perfumes, paint and cleaning solutions, chalk dust, lawn and turf treatments
  - Weather changes
  - Cigarette and other tobacco smoke

Source: National Heart, Lung, and Blood Institute (1995).

Pollens from flowers, shrubs, trees, and grass in the spring and summer to early fall contribute to reducing forced expiratory capacity. In indoor settings, such as the gymnasium, dust can accumulate and affect the individual year-round. Molds are more prevalent in damp weather or in the cool part of the day, with seasonal peaks in the winter and fall. Animal fur and smog are the worst offenders because of continued exposure throughout the year.

Exercise-Induced Asthma   Another contributing cause of asthma is physical activity. Exercise may induce bronchospasm in children 6 to 8 minutes after maximal work of approximately 170–180 beats per minute, or in people of any age whose heart rate reaches about 50 beats per minute below the estimated maximum for at least 5 minutes—in other words, whenever exertion demands about 70% of the body's aerobic power. Exercise-induced asthma (EIA) may occur in approximately 75% of all individuals with asthma, beginning with the constriction of the muscles surrounding the bronchial tubes. The severity of EIA can be mild or intense and is characterized by dyspnea and wheezing. The airway increases in size during the initial stages of exercise (bronchodilation) and then contracts, restricting the passage of air. In addition, a late-phase or late-onset asthma can be noted hours later as a secondary response to the initial exercise and release of chemical mediators (Katz & Pierson, 1988; Gong, 1992).

Figure 18.3 illustrates the drop in expiration that occurs approximately 8 to 10 minutes after exercise. Recovery will generally occur 15 to 60 minutes after cessation of activity. Late-phase asthma occurs several hours after the initial exercise, although this period of bronchi constriction is not as severe as the original effects. The physio-

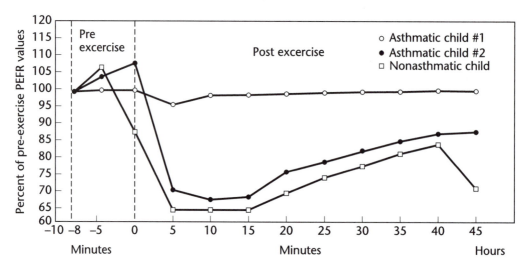

Figure 18.3 Exercise-induced asthma.

logical causes of EIA are relatively unclear (NHLBI, 1995). The activation of receptors in the cell membrane may result in the discharge of chemicals that tighten the bronchiole muscles and result in bronchospasm; defective metabolism of chemicals and psychological factors all may contribute to bronchospasm. Other theories relate to the loss of heat or water in the bronchiole pathways and the cooling of intrathoracic airways by incompletely conditioned air, which precipitates the liberation of bronchoconstrictive mediators (Cypear & Lemanske, 1995). In addition, it is apparent that a period of immunity from bronchospasm occurs if strenuous exercise is introduced within 40 minutes. If introduced within 40 minutes of initial exercise, additional exercise seems to diminish EIA with the same workload, although activity at 120 minutes reproduces EIA (Cypear & Lemanske, 1995; Katz & Pierson, 1988). This provides evidence that the introduction of medication may alleviate some of the symptoms that may be exacerbated by activity (NHLBI, 1995).

Psychosocial Considerations

Other causes of asthma involve psychosocial considerations. Excitement, fear, and stress can affect the production of adrenalin and the balance of the mechanisms required to maintain functional breathing. Although asthma is a medical and not a psychological malady, it may be a product of psychological factors accompanied by chemical changes in the body. More important, emotional problems and feelings of being different from one's peer group may develop because of the child's condition, exacerbating asthmatic symptoms.

Children with asthma often have difficulty coping with their illness and may experience feelings of fear and helplessness during attacks. Their overall ability is hampered by respiratory distress, which may contribute to depression and seclusion because of their activity limitations. Many children also possess a poor self-image or a negative attitude toward physical activity because they fear provoking an attack. The uncertainty of feeling tightness in their chest or shortness of breath may promote a negative concept toward activity. Parents and teachers often contribute to anxiety and a negative attitude by overprotecting children because they lack sufficient knowledge related to asthma and the benefits of physical activity (Butterfield, 1993).

Planning the Physical Activity Program

When planning the physical education program for children with asthma, the teacher must have a thorough knowledge of the child's needs, including medication needs. Proper training methods and the specific needs of the individual should be emphasized in the development of the asthma management plan. See the accompanying box.

Asthma Management Plan Contents

- Brief history of child's asthma
- Asthma symptoms
- Information on how to contact the child's health care provider and parent or guardian
- Signature from physician and parent or guardian
- List of factors that make the child's asthma worse
- The student's personal best peak flow reading, if the child uses peak flow monitoring
- List of the child's asthma medications
- A description of the child's treatment plan, based on symptoms or peak flow readings, including recommended actions for school personnel to help handle asthma episodes

Source: National Heart, Lung, and Blood Institute (1995).

Breathing is generally too shallow in children with asthma. Using the upper chest muscles inefficiently and contracting the abdomen while inhaling restrict the amount of air channeled to the lungs. Respiratory muscles may be developed through a proper training program as well as through teaching the proper use of these muscles during respiration. Ideally the diaphragm will be the major respiration muscle used in normal breathing and will help the child remove trapped air and breathe more efficiently. Children who use only the muscles of the shoulders and chest to breathe are not in a relaxed state and keep filling and emptying only the top part of their lungs.

If the diaphragm is relaxed, it will move downward and outward during inspiration, then proceed upward in expiration. The phrenic nerve, which innervates the diaphragm, is susceptible to tension and will restrict the movement of the diaphragm as well as the pectoral, intercostal, levatores costarum, serratus, transversus thoracis, abdominal, scalene, and erector spinae muscles.

To improve endurance and use respiratory muscles efficiently, breathing exercises may be introduced by teachers and practiced by children in school or at home. In this

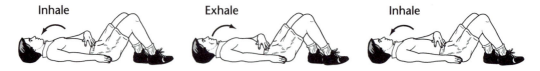

Figure 18.4 Diaphragmatic breathing exercises.

manner appropriate breathing techniques can be implemented to prevent the shortening of chest muscles used in respiration, increase the diameter of the chest, and strengthen the diaphragm. Before beginning a session of breathing exercises, teachers should emphasize proper breathing techniques, contracting the diaphragm downward and pushing the abdomen outward during inspiration. They should also demonstrate relaxed breathing with a short inspiration followed by a longer exhalation through pursued lips.

Children should then be placed in a relaxed position (lying, sitting, or standing). The easiest method to teach diaphragmatic breathing is to place children in a supine position with flexed legs and with hands on their abdomen to feel the motion of breathing (Figure 18.4). Children can focus on relaxed breathing and calmly inhale and exhale (Hogshead & Couzens, 1990). It is important for the children to feel they have control of their breathing. The teacher should emphasize slowly breathing in and out to regulate respiration. Children can also visualize emptying and filling their lungs and relaxing tight muscles as they seek to manage their breathing (Figure 18.4).

During an asthma attack, breathing and imagery should be utilized for 5 minutes or until wheezing has subsided. In addition, children can perform breathing exercises at home on a daily basis to promote deeper and more efficient inhalation and exhalation.

Diaphragmatic breathing can also be encouraged by vigorous games, such as raising a parachute, tumbling, or bouncing on a trampoline. Other activities that are appropriate for children with asthma (e.g., water exercises) also can be paired with diaphragmatic breathing techniques. Because swimming generally does not provoke symptoms in children with asthma, the natural inclusion of water exercises as a warm-up or conditioner will supplement a total conditioning program.

Medication

Medication is beneficial in preventing asthma attacks, relieving bronchospasm, and allowing children to train and lead a more normal lifestyle. It should be noted that medication can be taken daily to prevent symptoms or prior to exercise to alleviate EIA. Many symptoms of an impending attack are prevented through medication administered either orally or by aerosol. Each is effective, though aerosol medication may act more quickly with a reduced dosage. Most inhaled medications are available in metered-dose inhalers (RMDI or puffers) to ensure appropriate delivery of the prescribed medication (Fitch, 1986; NJCIRM, 1995). Table 18.1 includes common medications used in the treatment of individuals with asthma (Cypear & Lemanske, 1995; NHLBI, 1995).

Table 18.1 Asthma Medication and Treatment

Medication	Treatment
Theophylline	May inhibit EIA in oral dose at full therapeutic dosage. Short-acting is effective for 2–4 hours taken 30 minutes before exercise; long-acting is effective for 4–6 hours taken 60 minutes before exercise and is beneficial for night-time asthma.
Cromolyn/deodocromil	May be more effective as aerosol in providing protection against EIA for 1–2 hours when taken 20–30 minutes before exercise; stabilize cells that release inflammatory chemicals; both are preventive medications and need to be taken regularly to be effective.
Beta-2 agonists	May be valuable and effective bronchodilators to aid asthmatics before physical activity. Albuterol should be taken 20 minutes before exercise and is effective for 4–6 hours; terbutaline and metaproterenol are taken 10 minutes before exercise and are effective for 1–2 hours; fenoterol inhibits EIA and rapidly reverses acute symptoms and is taken 15 minutes before activity. Aerosols are preferred because of superior protection, rapid action after inhalation, and fewer side effects.
Anticholinergics	Bronchodilation that is slower-acting than beta-agonists and can be taken to achieve a longer-lasting effect.

Implementing the Physical Activity Program

Before children with asthma are exposed to a physical activity, teachers should accumulate information that will be useful in providing an appropriate program and that will contribute to awareness of the functioning, desire, activity, and history of the individual. In developing the asthma management plan, teachers should be aware of such factors as age, type of respiratory disorder, and the conditions that may trigger an attack. For example, cold air or allergic conditions from the environment may provide complications for the child. If physical education is carried out on a year-round basis, scheduling may be modified when pollen count is lowest or during the colder months, when sessions should be scheduled in the afternoon to take advantage of higher temperatures. Indoor participation may also be an alternative.

The degree of severity and the frequency of attacks are also important considerations. It is recommended that children with severe asthma not participate in sports that require activity for long duration, such as basketball and soccer, but instead in intermittent-duration sports, such as tennis and gymnastics. The biggest concern is to provide as few restrictions as possible for children based on their level of functioning and their desires.

Another consideration is the medication that is needed to alleviate symptoms of the respiratory disorder, especially in running sports and in cold weather (Hogshead & Couzens, 1990). Exercise is generally prescribed by physicians, and all medical information should be taken into account when the planning team considers possible contraindications and plans substitution of appropriate activities. Pulmonary efficiency can be measured by the physician through forced expiratory volume (FEV), which is the amount of air forcefully exhaled in 1 second after inhalation, or through the number of liters per minute children can move when asked to breathe as deeply

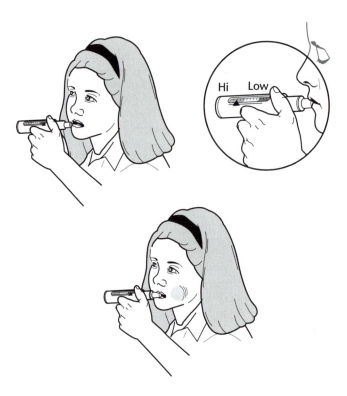

Figure 18.5 Peak flow meter.

as possible. A peak flow meter (Figure 18.5) can be used to measure the movement of air into and out of the lungs, aid in monitoring changes in asthma, and provide an indicator of potential problems, especially if the reading is below 80% of the child's normal reading (NHLBI, 1995).

Safety during respiratory distress must also be emphasized. Educators and children should be taught to recognize the warning signs of an attack and to administer appropriate self-care procedures. During coughing and wheezing spells, exercise should be stopped, and children should assume a relaxed position to concentrate on total relaxation of the entire body. If discomfort continues, children should practice relaxation exercises to remove trapped air from the lungs. For persistent wheezing, warm, moist air or warm water (e.g., tea, soup broth) should be administered, and relaxation and proper breathing stressed. Medication should then be provided if the preceding steps are not effective. As an attack subsides, children should return to class and proceed with the normal schedule of activities. This will enable them to assume self-control as well as allow other peers or teachers to understand that asthma is not a debilitating disease (NHLBI, 1991, 1995).

Although medication and breathing exercises help increase breathing capacity, physical education programs should also be designed to increase work tolerance by improving cardiovascular and musculoskeletal function, thus reducing the demands of physical exertion (Cypear & Lemanske, 1995; Bundgaard, 1985). It is extremely important for teachers to provide a well-rounded program, including physical fitness, motor skills, recreational skills, and relaxation activities, based on the asthma management plan. Teachers and coaches can follow the guidelines of the National Heart, Lung and Blood Institute (1995) included in the accompanying box. For example, a sprint in track or swimming will require a short burst of activity that commonly will not induce bronchospasm. However, if children do not adequately prepare for the demands of daily activity, their performance and condition may deteriorate if the activity is repeated over several days. This is also apparent in athletes who run or swim in several qualifying races before their final event.

In the past children with asthma have been restricted from participating in physical education. As a result, some children may possess extremely low cardiovascular efficiency. In some children the slightest exertion may cause heavy breathing, similar to that of individuals who are not physically fit, while strenuous exercise beyond 8 to 10 minutes usually elicits exercise-induced bronchospasm. It will be necessary for children, parents, and teachers to consult the asthma management plan, recognize the signs of an attack, and initiate proper safety procedures while the episode is still mild. When children become aware of an attack, they can slow their pace or stop the activity for a brief period. Additionally, with a well-controlled, progressive program, teachers may terminate exercise for the day, recording the child's performance as a goal to surpass the next day. For example, if children suffer distress while walking or jogging, teachers can record a distance ($3^1/_2$ laps) and time (3:15), which may become the next day's goal or even the next day's time for a rest interval.

Actions for the Physical Education Teacher/Coach

- Encourage exercise and participation in sports for children with asthma. When asthma is under good control, children with the disease are able to play most sports. A number of Olympic medalists have asthma.

- Appreciate that exercise can cause acute episodes for many children with asthma. Exercise in cold dry, air and activities that require extended running appear to trigger asthma more readily than other forms of exercise. However, medicines can be taken before exertion to help avoid an episode. This preventive medicine enables most children with exercise-induced asthma to participate in any sport they choose. Warm-up and cool-down activities appropriate for any exercise will also help the student with asthma.

- Support the child's treatment plan if it requires medication before exercise.

- Understand what to do if an asthma episode occurs during exercise. Have the child's asthma action plan available.

- Encourage children with asthma to participate actively in sports, but also recognize and respect their limits. Permit less strenuous activities if a recent illness precludes full participation.

- Refer your questions about a child's ability to fully participate in physical education to the parents and school nurse.

Source: National Heart, Lung, and Blood Institute (1991).

The potential for EIA is an obvious concern. If children become fatigued or dehydrated or are inadvertently pushed to exertion, some symptoms may develop. However, with medication, interval activity, and submaximal exercise, EIA will generally not be induced. Teachers should gradually increase the activity until mild exercise can be tolerated and sustained for 15 minutes, four times per week. One should remember that with severe asthma, this objective may take several years to reach and should be attempted only in consultation with the physician.

Generally, with proper medication and training, participation in physical education, sports, and recreational activities is within the realm of children with asthma. To provide a program for children with asthma, educators should use the following guidelines in selecting and implementing activities.

Warm-up and Cool-down Exercises

A gentle warm-up consisting of flexibility exercises and stretching, mild cardiovascular activity (walking), and muscular strength and endurance activities (push-ups and sit-ups) will aid in bronchodilation and the breathing process (Berman & Sutton, 1986; Hogshead & Couzens, 1990). Warm-up exercises should accompany each activity session for approximately 6 to 10 minutes, not raising the heart rate to more than 150 beats per minute (Bar-Or, 1983).

Progressive Exercise Activities

Initially, teachers should select activities that require the child to work for 5 minutes and then rest for 5 minutes, gradually increasing the duration and intensity (Katz, 1987; Gong, 1992). Swimming is probably the ideal activity for children with asthma. Fewer attacks occur during swimming, even in a competitive atmosphere. Also, children manifest fewer breathing problems in a horizontal position, although on land the horizontal position does not alleviate breathing difficulty. Forced and coordinated breathing in the front crawl also has positive benefits because of the proper diaphragmatic breathing techniques used in the stroke. Swimming is also ideal for a progressive endurance program, because children can stop when fatigued, rest at the end of a lap, and use kickboards and flotation devices to keep the activity submaximal. As muscular strength, cardiovascular conditioning, and swimming techniques improve, children will be more apt to increase endurance levels for the activity as well as postpone fatigue and possibly reduce their reliance on medication (Fitch, Morton, & Blanksby, 1976).

Traditionally, running has been contraindicated for children because of EIA, especially in cold weather. However, if running events are of short duration, they should not induce bronchospasm. Because most bronchospasm will subside in approximately 20 minutes, children may "run through" the condition after initially feeling some discomfort (Fitch, Blitvich, & Morton, 1986; Hogshead & Couzens, 1990). Generally, rather than run through periods of discomfort, it is more beneficial to utilize combinations of walk/jog/run and long and slow distances. In this manner exercise can be initiated at a submaximal level and increased based on the child's tolerance level for activity. Programs for children with asthma may vary, and activities can be modified or substituted to take into account atmospheric conditions and/or match the child's specific needs. For example, stationary cycling and walking are activities that are appropriate for developing a progressive exercise program. Hiking and cross-country skiing, even with thermal problems, may also contribute to increased functional ability.

Muscular Strength and Endurance

Resistance training may be utilized in a progressive strength program, especially if the exercises used to strengthen the respiratory muscles are implemented in a circuit training program (Bar-Or, 1983). By using low resistance with a progressive number of repetitions, children can stretch and increase the endurance of muscles in respiration. Teachers should also stress appropriate breathing and lifting techniques, because proper breathing while moving resistance is actually a form of diaphragmatic breathing and is required in a weight-training program. One precaution with progressive resistance exercises is that children should not move weights overhead because the increased stress of the overhead position may cause irritations of the lining of the lungs and bronchiole tubes.

Pre-exercise Medication

To stabilize the pulmonary structures, medication may be used prior to activity or in conjunction with the warm-up procedure. Especially in the case of EIA, medication should be taken approximately 30 minutes prior to activity. Medication, especially aerosols, may also be taken during activity to alleviate asthma symptoms.

Sports and Games

Most activities that are intermittent in nature are appropriate for the child with asthma. It is important for teachers to emphasize correct technique in tennis, golf, baseball, basketball, and skiing to minimize the amount of effort required to perform the activity. Teachers should have children perform at submaximal levels when learning the skill, gradually increasing the duration and intensity of the activity.

Adaptation may be necessary for individuals in some activities. For example, teachers may substitute more frequently in basketball, gradually increasing the playing time based on the student's tolerance. The child may not want to leave the activity, however, so it is essential to teach the warning signals of an impending attack and to stress increasing the tolerance and duration of activity. Additionally, activities such as the trampoline, gymnastics, and jump rope have been successful because they are intermittent-type activities and help dislodge mucus from the breathing pathways.

Relaxation

Relaxation activities should be used to stretch and relax the muscles of the diaphragm. In addition, relaxation is appropriate for relieving stress and controlling emotions that may precipitate an attack. Relaxation also promotes efficient breathing and can be used to forestall an attack once coughing has begun (Lehrer, Hochron, McCann, Swartzmann & Reba 1986). Progressive relaxation may help children control wheezing and relax the diaphragm, as may a cool-down exercise after strenuous activity (Freeberg, Hoffman, Light & Krebs 1987; Hogshead & Couzens, 1990). Another method of promoting relaxation and learning to recognize an impending attack is to develop home-based materials, including charts, activities, and motivational devices, for children and parents to learn about asthma and to take the appropriate steps when confronted with stressful situations or warm-up before activity. Many of these materials are available to teachers from the American Lung Association and the National Heart, Lung and Blood Institute.

Cystic Fibrosis

Cystic fibrosis is a genetic life-threatening disease with an incidence of 1 per 2,500 live births. The disease is inherited as a autosomal recessive trait carried by both parents and is primarily confined to Caucasians. Cystic fibrosis is assumed to be an abnormality or inadequacy of the hormones or enzymes of the body that involve the respiratory track, gastrointestinal tract, and sweat glands.

The child's physical appearance depends on the severity and clinical state of the disease. Because of hyperinflated lungs, the chest will have a large, rounded appearance, while the abdomen will be distended due to gas from poor digestion and frequent passage of a large quantity of stools. The limbs are thin, and children have a frail appearance. Puberty may be delayed as a consequence of chronic illness and motivation (Orenstein, 1995). The prognosis of the disease varies; approximately 60–75% of children die before 18 years of age. However, with an increase in early diagnosis and treatment intervention, life expectancy of individuals with cystic fibrosis may be increased to the third or fourth decade of life (Orenstein, 1995).

In cystic fibrosis, the membranes that line the organs produce an abnormally thick and sticky mucus that clogs the bronchiole tubes and interferes with the breathing process. Additionally, the pancreatic ducts are obstructed, preventing digestive enzymes from reaching the small intestine and resulting in malnutrition. Furthermore, the diseased pancreas contains cysts, and fibrous scarring can occur in advanced stages of the disease.

Although the lungs, pancreas, and intestinal mucus and sweat glands are affected, the clogging and obstruction of the bronchiole tubes and lower respiratory tract is the most serious problem of cystic fibrosis. More than 90% of all deaths result from progressive obstruction of the bronchiole tube resulting in infection (Nixon, 1997; Orenstein, Henks, & Cerney, 1983). The sputum that clogs these tubes allows for colonization of bacteria that cannot be eradicated, causing a low degree of pulmonary function. Because the mucus secreted by the bronchiole tubes is not easily expelled, the lungs are not cleared, the breathing passageways are obstructed, and the respiratory process is decreased. As in asthma, children with cystic fibrosis can inhale more easily because the bronchiole tubes will dilate, whereas clogged bronchiole tubes become smaller and more restricted during exhalation. Perhaps even more threatening to the progressive deterioration of the condition is the prevalence of infection in the bronchiole tubes, which is due to poor clearance of inhaled materials, inadequate removal of sputum, and damage to the tissues in the lungs. Infection and inflammation also may interfere with lung defenses. Tissue damage results from the release of toxins from inflammation and infection (Orenstein, 1995). According to Orenstein (1995), the rate and intensity of progressive deterioration varies; some younger children have several complications, whereas young adults may demonstrate only mild pulmonary problems.

Another concern for children with cystic fibrosis is the deficit in the reabsorption of sodium, which leads to an increased level of sodium and chloride concentrations in perspiration. Because of this, children may be at risk of injuries resulting from heat and/or humidity. In addition, the presence of cystic fibrosis is determined by analyzing perspiration for abnormal sodium and chloride concentrations.

The treatment of cystic fibrosis has developed to overcome some of the problems indicated by the disease. The pancreatic insufficiency necessitates synthetic pancreatic extracts to aid in the digestive process. Vitamin supplements (A, D, E, K) are utilized, because children may demonstrate malnutrition and have difficulty absorbing nutrients directly from food. Salt is given freely, especially after periods of physical activity, and fluid replacements are encouraged for children. The congestion in the lungs is treated primarily through the use of antibiotics, which work to decrease the production of sputum and the colonization of bacteria. Daily pulmonary therapy, including postural drainage, aerosol therapy, and mist tents to dilute the secretions in the lungs, is used outside school to aid in the ejection of mucus.

The primary responsibility of teachers should be to help children clear pulmonary secretions and to increase their tolerance for exercise. The use of activity as therapy for cystic fibrosis has only recently been advocated and includes the following beneficial effects (Bar-Or, 1983):

- improved clearance of mucus
- increased endurance of respiratory muscles
- reduced airway resistance
- improved exercise performance

Increased activity will aid in preventing the accumulation of sputum and possibly deter the progressive condition of the disease (Canny & Levison, 1987; Nixon, 1997). Because many individuals may be overprotected at home, it is necessary to encourage activity and allow participation with peers. Participation will not only increase tolerance to activity, but also promote the development of a positive body image and self-esteem (Edlund et al., 1986; Horvat & Carlile, 1991).

When selecting activities for children with cystic fibrosis, teachers should encourage individuals to cough freely and expel excess mucus and allow them to go to the bathroom often, take the appropriate medication, supplement salt, and base the program on their exercise tolerance to increase participation gradually. Activities should be selected to strengthen abdominal muscles, chest, and shoulders to overcome deformities associated with posture and the hyperinflation of the lungs. Activities such as tennis, canoeing, golf, skiing, horseback riding, and weight training utilize the respiratory muscles of the upper body and are ideal in helping to improve the exercise performance of students with cystic fibrosis (Horvat & Carlile, 1991; Keens et al., 1977; Strauss et al., 1987).

Active sports such as running, cycling, and swimming require short bursts of energy and help create coughing, expelling sputum and increasing endurance (Zach, Purrer & Oberwaldner, 1981). Individuals should be excused periodically to expel mucus, and any social stigma attached to this occurrence should be discouraged and, ideally, eliminated.

Orenstein and others (1981, 1995) have suggested a program consisting of warm-up, walking, jogging, cool-down, and games as appropriate for children with cystic fibrosis to increase their pulmonary function and exercise tolerance. Wilbourn (1978) has also advocated running to increase tolerance, while Schleichkorn (1977) has encouraged children with cystic fibrosis to participate in any form of exercise in which they feel capable, including football, basketball, skating, dancing, tennis, roller-skating, gymnastics, tumbling, and badminton. Orenstein (1995) has recommended games such as tennis, where skill is more essential than strength or endurance but encourages children to participate as fully as possible. Because the program and activities are similar to those of children with other pulmonary disorders, most activities may be used for either disorder. Of primary importance is to encourage active participation rather than exclusion from physical activity.

For children with cystic fibrosis, physical activity such as running, swimming, and upper body exercises may be used in conjunction with pulmonary therapy and may serve as an alternative to tedious chest therapy sessions. By working in conjunction with physicians, teachers can develop a program based on the child's needs that will increase his or her tolerance level, remove excess sputum, and consist of activities that are not injurious to the lungs (Edlund et al., 1986; Stanghelle, Hjeltnes, Michalsen, Bangstand & Skyberg, 1986; Stanghelle, Michalsen, & Skyberg, 1988).

CHAPTER SUMMARY

1. Two of the more common respiratory disorders in children are asthma and cystic fibrosis. Both contribute to school absenteeism and a decreased exercise tolerance, which may interfere with active participation in physical and recreational activities and with their quality of life.

2. Because most children with respiratory disorders are educated in a regular class setting, it is necessary that the teacher be familiar with the etiology and characteristics of respiratory disorders as well as the general functioning of the respiratory system.

3. The major symptoms of asthma are a hacking cough, wheezing, dyspnea, and a feeling of constriction in the chest. An asthma attack may result in severe bronchiole obstruction with no passage of air.

4. Asthma may be caused by allergies, exercise, the environment, or psychological factors.

5. Because breathing is affected by asthma, the muscles used in respiration need to be developed. Breathing exercises should constitute an integral part of the physical activity program for children with asthma.

6. Asthma is generally controlled through medication that aids in bronchodilation. The most common and fast-acting types of bronchodilators are the aerosols.

7. Activities should be selected that gradually increase work tolerance by improving cardiovascular and musculoskeletal functioning, thus reducing the demands for physical exertion.

8. Many activities need not be modified or adapted for children with mild cases of asthma; however, for those children who are more severely involved, activities that are intermittent in nature are advisable.

9. Cystic fibrosis is a life-threatening condition involving excessive secretion of mucus, saliva, and perspiration. Physical appearance depends on the severity and clinical state of the disease.

10. In cystic fibrosis the membranes that line the organs produce an abnormally thick and sticky mucus, which clogs the bronchiole tubes and interferes with the breathing process.

11. Physical activity has recently been advocated as therapy for children with cystic fibrosis and includes the following benefits: improved clearance of mucus, increased endurance of respiratory muscles, reduced airway resistance, and improved exercise performance.

REFERENCES

Bar-Or, O. (1983). *Pediatric sports medicine for the practitioner.* New York: Springer-Verlag.

Berman, L. B., & Sutton, J. R. (1986). Exercise for the pulmonary patient. *Journal of Cardiopulmonary Rehabilitation, 6,* 52–61.

Bundgaard, A. (1985). Exercise and the asthmatic. *Sports Medicine, 2,* 254–266.

Butterfield, S. A. (1993). Exercise-induced asthma—A manageable problem. *Journal of Physical Education, Recreation and Dance, 64,* 15–18.

Canny, G. J., & Levison, H. (1987). Exercise response and rehabilitation in cystic fibrosis. *Sports Medicine, 4,* 143–152.

Cypear, D., & Lemanske, R. F. (1995). Exercise-induced asthma. In B. Goldberg (Ed.), *Sports and exercise for children with chronic health conditions* (pp. 149–165). Champaign, IL: Human Kinetics.

Edlund, L., French, R., Herbts, T., Ruttenberg, H., Ruhling, R., & Adams, T. (1986). Effects of a swimming program on children with cystic fibrosis. *American Journal of Diseases in Children, 140,* 80–88.

Fitch, K. D. (1986). The use of anti-asthmatic drugs: Do they affect sports performance? *Sports Medicine, 3,* 136–150.

Fitch, K. D., Blitvich, J. D., & Morton, A. R. (1986). The effect of running training in exercise induced asthma. *Annals of Allergy, 57,* 90–94.

Fitch, K. D., Morton, A. R., & Blanksby, B. A. (1976). Effects of swimming training on children with asthma. *Archives of Disease in Childhood, 51,* 190–194.

Freeberg, P. D., Hoffman, L. A., Light, W., & Krebs, M. K. (1987). Effect of progressive muscle relaxation on the objective symptoms and subjective responses associated with asthma. *Heart and Lung, 16,* 24–30.

Gong, H. (1992). Breathing easy: Exercise despite asthma. *The Physician and Sports Medicine, 20,* 159–167.

Hogshead, N., & Couzens, G. S. (1990). *Asthma and exercise.* New York: Holt.

Horvat, M., & Carlile, J. R. (1991). Effects of progressive resistance exercise on physical functioning and self concept in cystic fibrosis. *Clinical Kinesiology, 45,* 18–23.

Katz, R. M. (1986). Prevention with and without the use of medications for exercise induced asthma. *Medicine and Science in Sports and Exercise, 18,* 331–333.

Katz, R. M. (1987). Coping with exercise-induced asthma in sports. *The Physician and Sports Medicine, 15,* 101–108.

Katz, R. M., and Pierson, W.E. (1988). *Exercise induced asthma: Current perspective.* In advances in sports medicine and fitness. W. A. Grana, J. A. Lombardo, B. J. Sharkey, & J. A. Stone (Eds.), Chicago: Year Book Medical Publishers.

Keens, T. G., Krastins, I., Wannamaker, E. M., Levison, H., Crozier, D. N., & Bryan, A. C. (1977). Ventilatory muscle endurance training in normal subjects and patients with cystic fibrosis. *American Review of Respiratory Disease, 116,* 853–860.

Lehrer, P., Hochron, S., McCann, B., Swartzman, L., & Reba, P. (1986). Relaxation decreases large airway but not small airway asthma. *Journal of Psychosomatic Research, 30,* 13–25.

National Heart, Lung and Blood Institute. (1991). *Managing asthma: A guide for schools.* Bethesda, MD: Author.

National Heart, Lung and Blood Institute. (1995). *Asthma and physical activity in the school.* Bethesda, MD: Author.

National Jewish Center for Immunology and Respiratory Medicine. (1995). *Understanding asthma.* Denver: Author.

Nixon, P. A. (1997). *Cystic fibrosis.* In American College of Sports Medicine, *Exercise management for persons with chronic diseases and disabilities.* (pp. 81–86). Champaign, IL: Human Kinetics.

Orenstein, D. M. (1995). Cystic fibrosis. In B. Goldberg (Ed.), *Sports and exercise for children with chronic health conditions.* (pp. 167–186). Champaign, IL: Human Kinetics.

Orenstein, D. M., Franklin, B. A., Doershuk, D. F., Hellerstein, H. K., German, K. J., Horowitz, J. C., & Stern, R. C. (1981). Exercise conditioning and cardiopulmonary fitness in cystic fibrosis. *Chest, 80,* 392–98.

Orenstein, D. M., Henks, K. G., & Cerney, F. C. (1983). Exercise and cystic fibrosis. *The Physician and Sports Medicine, 12,* 59–77.

Schleichkorn, J. (1977). Physical activity for the child with cystic fibrosis. *Journal of Physical Education and Recreation, 48,* 50.

Stanghelle, J. K., Hjeltnes, N., Michalsen, H., Bangstand, H. J., & Skyberg, D. (1986). Pulmonary function and oxygen uptake during exercise in 11-year-old patients with cystic fibrosis. *Acta Paediatricia Scandanavia, 75,* 651–61.

Stanghelle, J. K., Michalsen, H., & Skyberg, D. (1988). Five-year follow-up of pulmonary function and peak oxygen uptake in 16-year-old boys with cystic fibrosis with special regard to the influence of regular exercise. *International Journal of Sports Medicine, 8,* 19–24.

Strauss, G. D., Osher, A., Wang, C., Goodrich, E., Gold, F., Colman, W., Stabile, M., Dobrenchuk, A., & Keens, T. (1987). Variable weight training in cystic fibrosis. *Chest, 92,* 273–276.

Wilbourn, K. (1978). The lung distance runners. *Runner's World, 8,* 62–65.

Zach, M. S., Purrer, B., & Oberwaldner, B. (1981). Effect of swimming on expiration and sputum clearance in cystic fibrosis. *Lancet, 11,* 1201–1203.

CHAPTER 19

Diabetes

With proper planning, an appropriate physical activity program can be designed for children with diabetes. When the disorder is managed properly, individuals with diabetes are usually normal in appearance and not limited in motor functioning. In fact, some individuals with diabetes have had successful careers in professional sports. Many times the management aspects of their disorder prohibit individuals with diabetes from participating in physical activity programs. However, diabetes is not an excuse to avoid exercise but is in fact a reason to engage in activity. While diabetes may present management problems, an understanding of characteristics, safety procedures, treatment, diet, and appropriate exercise can facilitate active participation in physical activity programs.

Diabetes is a complex metabolic disorder that affects approximately 12 to 14 per each 100,000 children from birth to 16 years of age (Campaigne & Lampman 1994; National Institutes of Health, 1986). Peak incidence will occur around puberty, with males showing a later peak than females. The ability of the body in the person with diabetes to adequately produce and use insulin is affected, and the individual is unable to utilize sugar properly. There are two types of diabetes, both of which are characterized by metabolic disorders of carbohydrates, fats, and proteins. The current terms used to describe these two types of diabetes are Type I, or insulin-dependent, diabetes; and Type II, or non–insulin-dependent, diabetes. Type II diabetes is adult-onset diabetes and is usually treated with diet and/or medication to regulate blood sugar levels rather than with insulin injections. This chapter discusses Type I, or insulin-dependent diabetes, which affects school-aged individuals and is treated with insulin injections because of an inadequate production of insulin.

Characteristics of Diabetes

The majority of children with Type I, or insulin-dependent, diabetes are identified during the school years and constitute approximately 10–15% of all individuals with diabetes. The advent of diabetes will commonly occur during puberty, although it may develop earlier and sometimes develops in the 20s. When diabetes is controlled, the child's height and weight will be similar to those of others of his or her peer group. Type I diabetes is characterized by the sudden appearance of frequent urination, abnormal thirst, unusual hunger, weight loss, weakness and fatigue, blurred vision, skin disorders and infections, nausea, and vomiting. Diabetes also affects the production of hemoglobin and oxygen transport capabilities by the prolonged elevation of

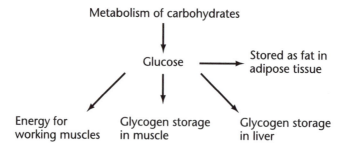

Figure 19.1 Metabolism of carbohydrates.

blood glucose levels and affects the endurance capabilities of the uncontrolled diabetic (Berg, 1986). There is also a failure to note increased capillary density with exercise in Type I diabetes (Horton, 1989). The onset of the disease may be recognized immediately or may become evident over a period of several months. Most people with Type I diabetes are not obese or overweight at the onset of the disease, in contrast to people with Type II diabetes (Horton, 1995).

Because children with Type I diabetes may be deficient in insulin production and in their ability to use insulin, it is necessary for teachers to understand the metabolic process involved in the disease. Diabetes involves the metabolism of carbohydrates, which are the main source of energy for the body. During this process the body breaks down consumed food and converts it into elements essential for sustaining life, enabling the cells to build and repair tissue (Figure 19.1). This substance produced by the body from the breakdown of carbohydrates is called *glucose*. Glucose is then transported to the working muscles and utilized for energy, while the remaining blood sugar is stored as glycogen in the liver, and as fat in adipose tissue, for future activity. In diabetes, the body is unable to use food and glucose properly because of deficient insulin production.

Insulin is a hormone produced by the beta cells in the islets of Langerhans in the pancreas. The pancreas is located adjacent to the stomach and spleen in the abdomen and involves both exocrine or nutritive functions (production of digestive enzymes) and endocrine functions (production of hormones). The body requires insulin in the digestive process to regulate the amount of glucose for use by the cells of the body. Through the action of insulin, the glucose derived from the digestive process will be utilized as energy for the cells as it is transported in the bloodstream and made available for use by body tissues.

This process can be explained by comparison with a lock-and-key scenario. In order to open a door, the key must fit a specific lock; for glucose to enter the cell, insulin must open the cell membrane to allow transport to occur. When insulin binds with the cell-receptor site, glucose can enter. When it is not used properly, too much glucose will remain in the bloodstream instead of being used by the cells to produce energy. This deprives the body of energy, while excess glucose builds up in the bloodstream and finally spills into the urine. If insulin is not available to transport the glucose, muscular functioning will be impaired.

Insulin is, then, responsible for making glucose available for muscular action during the consumption of food and making possible the storage of glucose as glycogen in the muscle and liver, and as fat in adipose tissue, for periods of fasting and/or future muscular activity. Insulin will also restrict the burning of body fat. People without diabetes have the innate capacity to regulate glucose levels via insulin, whereas people with diabetes must be cognizant of blood glucose and ingest insulin accordingly. For example, during the nondiabetic's sleep, insulin will circulate through the bloodstream, maintaining an adequate level of glucose in the blood and regulating the release of glucose from the storage deposits in the liver, fat, and muscle in a process called *gluconeogenesis*. In gluconeogenesis, when the body stores of carbohydrate are low (below normal), moderate quantities of glucose can be formed from amino acids and glycerol portion of fat (Horton, 1989). Approximately 60% of amino acids are converted to carbohydrates. Further, new glucose is formed and hepatic stores of glycogen are broken down to re-form glucose in cells by *glycogenolysis*. During this period of inactivity and lack of food, the blood sugar will remain in a relatively narrow range of approximately 60 mg/dl; when the person is awake and functioning, the blood sugar range is approximately 100 mg/dl, and 150 mg/dl following the consumption of calories. In the nondiabetic, amounts of insulin and glucose are regulated automatically, but in the diabetic the beta cells in the pancreas are not able to produce or secrete insulin. Because of the lack of production of insulin, the ability to make glucose available to the cells is affected, causing the blood glucose level to rise. This causes a stimulation of the pancreas to meet the need for insulin that it is unable to produce.

When the body is unable to control high glucose levels, the kidney releases glucose into the urine to decrease the level of sugar in the blood. This is a function of the kidney in terms of reabsorbing glucose. Glucose is spilled into the urine when the ability to reabsorb glucose is exceeded, at 175–200 mg/dl. When the capacity to reabsorb glucose is reached, glucose will be present in the urine. Unfortunately, the elimination of glucose is accompanied by large amounts of water to prevent the urine from becoming thick and resembling maple syrup, and the rapid water loss can lead to dehydration. In order to prevent dehydration, people with diabetes will exhibit excessive thirst.

In addition to excessive thirst (polydipsia) and excessive urination, excessive eating is also directly attributable to the lack of insulin. Children lose a large number of calories in the urine, often as much as three-fourths of the calories ingested, leaving only a small portion available in the blood that can be used to initiate muscular action. Additionally, glycogen cannot be transported to the bloodstream, thus depriving the cells of the glucose needed to produce energy. As a result, the person with diabetes consumes more calories to alleviate this deficiency. All of these are the "textbook" symptoms associated with diabetes and should be used strictly for identifying uncontrolled diabetics.

Children with Type I diabetes have poorly functioning beta cells to produce the amount of insulin that is required for controlling glucose metabolism. Low concentrations of insulin in the bloodstream then affect the regulation of the release of stored glycogen from the body to maintain an adequate blood sugar level. As a result, the large quantity of glucose produced by the body compounds the problem of already high blood sugar levels and the resulting failure of transporting glycogen to the cells. Insulin regulates glucose levels not only by entering muscle and fat cells but also by preventing stored glycogen from exiting muscle and liver cells by inhibitory responses. Glucose and fatty acids are the major metabolic fuels for muscle and are released into circulation by the liver and adipose tissue, and amino acids are available from the muscle (Horton, 1995).

The alpha cells produce and secrete a hormone called *glucagon*, which raises the blood sugar level by changing the stored glycogen in the liver to glucose, which is transported to the cells by insulin (Figure 19.2). Glucagon is a hormone secreted when the blood glucose concentration is low, primarily to convert liver glycogen into glucose to elevate blood glucose (Horton, 1989). In reality, glucagon actually helps increase the uptake of amino acids and stimulate gluconeogenesis. It also has glycogenolytic properties in the liver and, with epinephrine, is a major glucose counter-regulatory hormone during exercise (Horton, 1989). A balance is maintained, with the glucagon keeping the blood glucose from becoming too low while the insulin keeps it from becoming too high. If this does not occur and the balance is distorted, the body cannot use the available sugar to supply its own energy requirement and relies on the energy in fat stored in the body. This occurs in normal metabolism. Trained individuals performing at higher intensities (VO_2 max) will use less carbohydrate and more free fatty acids (FFA) than untrained individuals. In this context, the trained individual will have a slower rate of decline of muscle and liver glycogen stores, a trait commonly associated with greater endurance (Horton, 1989). The problem in diabetes is that instead of glucose metabolism, there is excessive fat metabolism and increased ketone production, which leads to ketoacidosis. Ketones form when the body cannot utilize glucose to supply energy. Although the presence of low levels of ketones is not dangerous when glucose levels are normal, when fewer calories are consumed the body breaks down excess stored fat. The production of ketones (ketosis) alters the acid base (pH) chemistry when the body cannot eliminate these by-products rapidly enough or when too many are produced, resulting in a high-acid state called *ketoacidosis*. Ketosis is the accumulation of ketones in the body from the incomplete metabolism of fatty acids. It is generally caused by carbohydrate deficiency or inadequate utilization and an abnormal state of acidity due to rapid and incomplete breakdown of fat (Campaigne & Lampman, 1994). The presence of ketones is a sign that diabetes is poorly controlled, requiring prompt attention. This is a life-threatening situation that calls for immediate medical attention and the administration of insulin to restore proper chemistry, regu-

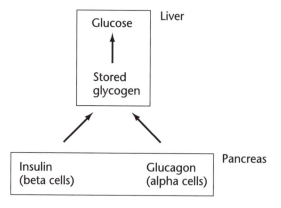

Figure 19.2 Regulation of insulin and glucose.

lating the amount of glucose and insulin in the blood. When the chemistry of the body is affected by the production of ketones, the blood sugar level is dangerously high, and dehydration occurs. A medical emergency called *hyperglycemia* occurs, which may lead to diabetic coma. Hyperglycemia, excess sugar in the blood, usually develops gradually over a longer period of time. A diabetic coma will occur when too much sugar remains in the blood because there is insufficient insulin to use it properly (Juvenile Diabetes Foundation International, 1996). The detection of hyperglycemia is quite difficult but is usually characterized by fatigue and lethargy. The most prevalent sign may be the "fruity" odor of the diabetic's breath. Individuals with diabetes are especially prone to hyperglycemia when insulin is omitted, during infections, in periods of stress, and when there is a minimal compliance to diet.

Immediate action is necessary to prevent diabetics from lapsing into a coma. Children should be taken to a physician or hospital for the injection of insulin. Physical education teachers do not administer insulin but must recognize these symptoms in order to circumvent emergency situations and provide prompt medical attention.

Hypoglycemia is the other reaction that results when insulin and glucose are not maintained in a proper balance. In hypoglycemia due to excess blood insulin, blood sugar is too low to sustain muscular action, and fainting occurs. Children and teachers should recognize that in strenuous physical activity extra sugar is required to balance what is burned during active participation. More energy is required for physical activity, illness, infection, periods of growth, fatigue, excitement, and anxiety that may adversely affect the balance between sugar and insulin (Juvenile Diabetes Foundation International, 1996). Individuals with diabetes must always be prepared to treat insulin reaction by taking quick-acting sugars to maintain this balance.

The hypoglycemic reaction (Table 19.1) is characterized by a confused mental state, lack of coordination, impaired movement, and finally a loss of consciousness. The onset of hypoglycemia varies in most individuals but is generally quite rapid. It is important, therefore, for teachers and children to recognize any warning signs or symptoms to prevent a life-threatening situation.

Table 19.1 Comparison of Hypoglycemia and Hyperglycemia

Symptom	Hypoglycemia (Insulin Reaction)	Hyperglycemia (Diabetic Coma)
Onset	Symptoms appear rapidly	Symptoms are gradual
Skin	Pale, moist	Dry, hot skin
Behavior	Confused, irritable	Drowsy, lethargic
Breath	Normal	Fruity odor (acetone)
Breathing	Normal to rapid	Heavy, labored breathing
Sugar in urine	Absent or slight	Large amounts
Hunger	Present	Absent
Thirst	Absent	Extreme thirst
Performance	Decreased	Decreased

*Symptoms may be present and vary according to degree of reaction and the individual's response.

Evaluation of Blood Sugar

In the past, urine tests have been implemented to record the sugar level in the diabetic's urine at periodic daily intervals to maintain essential blood sugar levels. These tests involved dipping treated paper into the urine. The color of the paper then indicated the amount of sugar present in the urine. Diabetics usually tested their urine three or four times a day with a tape corresponding to specific colors to determine the level of sugar in the urine. However, the accuracy of these tests in identifying blood glucose levels is poor, and the process is now obsolete.

Recently, several home tests have been developed to measure blood sugar by reading a single drop of blood. Self-monitoring devices can be used to measure more specific levels of blood sugar to determine how much sugar is needed to normalize the blood glucose level.

Former athletes have credited the monitoring of blood sugar as a precise method of monitoring insulin requirements and ability to improve performance. When the child's blood sugar is excessively high or dangerously low, he or she will tire easily and lack energy. By monitoring blood sugar levels with self-monitoring devices, the athlete can achieve more exact and quicker results than by using urine tests. The athlete will know immediately what remedy is required to reverse his or her current status—either eat more carbohydrates, or add more insulin to resolve their diabetic problem. Consistent monitoring will allow children to feel better and to postpone fatigue (Schechter, 1985).

Planning the Physical Activity Program

Children with diabetes will present unique problems for teachers. Although these children will require special assistance to manage their problems, teachers should not call attention to the disorder or cause children to feel different from their classmates. Children with diabetes may encounter difficulties in balancing their diet and partaking in physical activity but should function appropriately if communication is maintained among the educational programming team members to alleviate anxiety and confusion concerning diabetes. Shared knowledge and cooperation among parents, teachers, and medical and school personnel will contribute to accomplishing specific tasks in the management of diabetes (Table 19.2).

Initially it is helpful for teachers to gather information before the school year begins to determine the child's routine and specific needs. Teachers should be aware of the following guidelines when developing the physical activity program for children with diabetes (Juvenile Diabetes Foundation International, 1996):

- Do not assign vigorous physical exercise before lunch.
- Allow a midmorning or afternoon snack if this is part of the dietary plan.
- Allow children an inconspicuous place for snacking and urine/blood testing.
- Have sugar readily available.
- Encourage children to carry some form of sugar and to recognize their own reactions.
- Encourage children to consume extra calories prior to strenuous exercise.
- Be aware of symptoms of hyperglycemia and hypoglycemia, and inform teachers and coaches.

- Administer safety and treatment procedures consistent with school and medical policies.

Treatment for Hypoglycemia and Hyperglycemia

Although the proper management of diabetes should prevent any medical complications, teachers should be able to implement certain procedures that may be required in physical activity programs. Hypoglycemic reactions cause a rapid falling of blood sugar that necessitates immediate treatment and generally occurs before meals and during or after exercise. Mild symptoms include trembling, shaking, rapid heart rate, palpitations, increased sweating, and excessive hunger. Moderate symptoms may include irritability, and impaired concentration and attention. Severe reactions may result in unresponsiveness and convulsions (Gordon, 1993).

The following treatment for hypoglycemic reactions is recommended by the Juvenile Diabetes Foundation International (1996): *Provide sugar immediately.* This can take the form of a liquid fruit juice or one-half cup of carbonated soda pop (not diet), which can be absorbed more quickly than hard candies without the chance of choking. Children may need coaxing to eat. Within 10 minutes improvement should be evident, at which point additional food should be ingested with the resumption of a normal school routine. If improvement is not noted in 10 to 15 minutes, parents

Table 19.2 Guidelines for Children, Teachers, and Coaches

Behavior	Guidelines for Instruction and Participation
Communication	1. Let coaches, instructors, and teammates know you have diabetes and how to recognize and treat low blood sugar.
	2. Wear medical identification.
	3. Exercise with a partner.
Restriction of exercise	1. When your urine tests positive for ketones.
	2. When your diabetes is in poor control.
	3. When you have a cold, flu, infection, or other illness.
Adequate hydration	1. Avoid exercising in a hot, humid environment.
	2. Drink plenty of water.
	3. Restrict caffeine or alcohol.
Treatment	1. Stop immediately.
	2. Carry a quick sugar source always.
	3. Treat preferably with cool fluid (4 oz. fruit juice or 6 oz. regular soda).
	4. Rest at least 15 minutes so food can be absorbed.
	5. Don't continue exercising until blood sugar is at least 100.
	or
	Select proper injection site:
	6. Not an issue if exercising 1 hour after injecting.
	7. If exercising soon after injecting, use abdomen.

Courtesy of Diabetes Exercise and Sports Association, *Diabetes and Exercise, 2000,* Phoenix, AZ: Author.

and/or physicians should be notified. If children are unable to swallow, nothing should be given orally, and medical attention is required. Children should carry edibles with them for emergencies.

Teachers should also recognize the symptoms leading to hypoglycemic reaction to be aware of the balance between activity, diet, and/or insulin. If the balance has been altered or activity increased, proper management will include increasing food intake prior to exercise or decreasing the amount of insulin to maintain this balance. Included in Table 19.2 are specific instructional guidelines for children, teachers, and coaches for participating in physical activity and managing diabetes.

For hyperglycemia, immediate action is necessary to prevent children from lapsing into a diabetic coma. Children with diabetes should be taken to a physician or hospital immediately for an injection of insulin, though all parties involved should remember that the situation is not easily reversed and resolved with insulin. If symptoms approach a diabetic coma, there is a severe problem in management of this disease and in recognition of the condition.

Insulin is injected for absorption into the bloodstream because an oral dosage may be destroyed by the oral enzymes that digest or break down protein. Various insulins will be utilized for specific purposes. Short-term or rapid-acting insulin and intermediate-acting insulin work faster and last briefly but are useful in situations in which the quickest entry into the blood is required, whereas long-term insulin is used to provide insulin throughout the day. With monitoring and the use of multiple-dose insulin, children should be able to manage their own diabetes (Horton, 1995).

Insulin is commonly injected into the subcutaneous fat above the muscle and not directly into an exercising muscle. Care must be taken against injection into active muscles because of the rapid absorption into the bloodstream at the injection site and the subsequent drop in blood sugar level. Most injections should be in areas not heavily used, such as the abdomen, gluteal area, deltoid, or thigh area. The site of injection depends on the activity, that is, on the nonexercising muscles (e.g., in the arm when the child is running or in the leg when the child is swimming).

Insulin injections include a combination of the quick-acting insulin, peaking in 2 or 3 hours, and a long-lasting insulin, which peaks in 7 to 8 hours. Insulin pump therapy may also be used to provide short-acting insulin at a continuous rate or at times when blood sugar is too high or prior to a meal. The number, choice, or combination of insulins is selected by the physician and health care team and is based on the nature of the diabetes, age, size, diet, and activity patterns. Many children will require multiple injections or a split dose of approximately two-thirds the daily dosage in the morning and one-third prior to the evening meal or bedtime. Teachers must be cautioned that insulin in not a cure-all for the individuals with diabetes. Children should not rely primarily on insulin to manage diabetes but should stringently maintain a balance among insulin, diet, and exercise.

For insulin-dependent children, diet can contribute to the maintenance of daily living by lowering blood sugar and avoiding problems associated with insulin reactions. When used in conjunction with exercise, diet may aid in reducing dependence on insulin and avoiding complications associated with diabetes, such as blindness, kidney failure, and coronary disease.

Individuals with diabetes should strive for a balance of calories consumed and expended. Traditionally, the American Diabetes Association has recommended diabetic diets consisting of 60% carbohydrate, 30% protein, and 10% fat. Insulin secretion must be matched with dietary intake to maintain normal blood glucose levels, which should remain constant from day to day. When too many calories are consumed, the blood glucose will rise, so it is essential to keep and maintain this balance.

Children who exercise will find a greater demand for carbohydrates in their diets and should remember that exercise will decrease the level of blood sugar; therefore, it is necessary to plan accordingly to maintain this balance. Blood glucose will also continue to decrease after exercise, necessitating testing after exercise and an hour later to document a latent drop (Horton, 1988). The implementation of a diet is often restrictive and discouraging for individuals with diabetes. Each diet should be adapted for individual needs. For example, obese individuals with diabetes, who typically have Type II diabetes, will have an additional complication: Their beta cells are extinct and lose their sensitivity to insulin, and the body will require more insulin to absorb the glucose in the bloodstream and to maintain glycogen storage. This will require obese individuals to implement a weight-reduction program as well as plan a structured diet for their diabetes.

Most diets are planned according to the individual's size and energy expenditure and should be planned in conjunction with insulin usage to promote adherence. The following guidelines should be used in selection of foods for the individual with diabetes (Gordon, 1993):

1. To maintain stability, diets should be selected that do not vary in the types of food consumed and/or caloric content.

2. Concentrated carbohydrates, such as candies and soft drinks, should be avoided because they are readily absorbed when sufficient insulin is not available for metabolism. However, they may be used to counteract hypoglycemia.

3. Diets should be based on sound nutritional practices that can be incorporated into a family diet plan.

4. Motivation for compliance to the diet can be encouraged by allowing occasional deviations from the diet.

5. Diets should be selected in which six food groups (milk, vegetables, fruit, bread, meat, and fat) can allow for substitutions with other foods in the same group under the auspices of a physician.

6. When exercising, add food to the exchange.

During muscular activity or exercise, the primary fuel for the working muscles is glucose. To sustain exercise, more glucose is required, necessitating the release of glycogen from the liver and resulting in an increase of blood flow and glucose uptake to meet the increased energy demands. As exercise continues, the level of glucose falls, and body fat becomes the major source of energy. In a trained individual glucose sparing occurs with use of FFA as the major source of energy. Plasma glucagon also rises during exercise, stimulating glycogen breakdown in the liver and maintenance of blood glucose. The decline in insulin and increase in plasma glucagon function together to maintain a constant glucose supply (Horton, 1989). This will occur when glucose levels are near normal prior to exercise. If glucose is 250 mg/dl, glucose will either level out or increase due to increased production of glucose from the liver, with no corresponding increase in use by the muscles, resulting in poorly regulated diabetes. Most physicians recommend a blood glucose level between 100 and 250 mg/dl prior to exercise and caution participants to snack prior to exercise if blood sugar is below 100 mg/dl. In contrast, when the blood sugar level reaches about 250 mg/dl and ketones are present, exercise should be delayed. During activity, the uptake of glucose by the working muscles increases, while the level of insulin that is needed decreases. This is potentially significant for individuals with diabetes because these working muscles will not require increased levels of insulin during activity; thus, the person can rely less on insulin. In fact, activity may improve glucose tolerance as long as 24 to 48 hours after exercise (Landt, Campaigne, James & Sperling, 1985). At the completion of exercise, blood flow to the muscle decreases, although the uptake of glucose will remain three to four times higher than the resting level for approximately one hour in order to replenish the glucose level in the muscles (Berg, 1986; Campaigne & Lampman, 1994).

The lack of glucose output in diabetics may advance the onset of hypoglycemia unless individuals decrease the amount of insulin or increase the amount of carbohydrates consumed. Exercise allows for this reduction in insulin, while an increased consumption of carbohydrates allows for normal glucose metabolism and reduced insulin (Horton, 1995). A precisely managed exercise program will provide the benefits of reducing the blood sugar level by (1) enhancing the muscle glucose uptake, (2) increasing the sensitivity of the insulin receptors, and (3) increasing utilization of glucose, as well as free fatty acids, by the working muscles (Franz, 1984).

Because activity patterns among children with diabetes may vary according to growth, weather, time of year, and temperature, as well as intensity of exercise, it is essential to coordinate activity with diet and insulin. Previous experiences with activity in conjunction with diet and insulin can be helpful in selecting initial tolerance levels and intensity of physical activities. Most authorities suggest that individuals with diabetes eat before exercise and take a glucose supplement hourly to prevent hypoglycemia, to improve performance, and to maintain blood glucose levels (Horton, 1995). In this manner, individuals will not be required to increase their insulin and should be able to reduce their reliance on insulin by proper balance of insulin, diet, and exercise (Berg, 1986).

Implementing the Physical Activity Program

The benefits of physical activity have already been discussed as they relate to maintaining a balance between insulin and blood sugar. However, the physiological and social aspects of physical education and sport must not be neglected. By excluding children with diabetes from participation, teachers hinder the acceptance of their condition by their peers (Engerbretson, 1977). Bierman and Toohey (1977) have also indicated that activity should be practiced in conjunction with medication and diet, with emphasis on health and enjoyment.

No physical or recreational activity is outside the realm of children with diabetes if proper control is maintained (Gordon, 1993; Horton, 1995; Stratton, Wilson & Endres, 1988; Murphy, 1987). The activity should be selected on the basis of its ability to help maintain a proper balance between insulin and blood sugar. An evaluation of the child's functional capacity should give teachers an entry point for beginning a program (Fremion, Marrero & Golden, 1987). The level at which children are able to

Sample Exercise Session

Sugar Check	Warm-Up	Exercise Session	Cool-Down	Stretch (optional)	Sugar Check
2 min.	5 min.	20–45 min.	5 min.	5–10 min.	2 min.

Intensity Check   Intensity Check

Sugar check:	• Approximately 10 minutes before and after.
	• Record information: Discuss with your doctor and use to fine-tune insulin/medication and food.
Warm-up:	• Slow version of exercise.
	• Go through full range of motion.
Exercise:	• See safety precautions.
	• Evaluate intensity a few minutes after starting and a few minutes before stopping. Adjust speed if necessary.
Cool down:	• Gradually decrease intensity.
	• Bring heart rate down slowly.
Stretches:	• Focus on muscles used in exercise.
	• Hold 15–20 seconds, 3 times.
	• No bouncing; no pain.
	• Never stretch a cold muscle!

Courtesy of Diabetes Exercise and Sports Association, *Diabetes and Exercise, 2000,* Phoenix, AZ: Author.

swim or run should dictate the level of their participation and can be a measure for maintaining the balance between insulin and blood sugar. More intense participation or training for specific sports will require adjustments according to the child's potential and his or her management of diabetes (Blackett, 1988; Horton, 1995). The accompanying box includes a sample exercise session from the Diabetes Exercise and Sports Association (DESA, 2000).

In physical activity, teachers sometimes do not allow individuals with diabetes to participate because of possible reactions and because of their "delicate" condition. This practice not only is based on false assumptions but also may cause children to hide their condition from teachers and coaches. Clearly teachers must recognize the problems and considerations required to develop and implement an appropriate program; however, educators who take on too much responsibility may also provide a disservice for children with diabetes. Children must learn to manage their diabetes, and teachers should learn not to segregate children from their classmates.

The participation of children with diabetes should not extend beyond their limits or through periods of distress. Children should use these "down" times to sit, conserve energy, and take additional supplements. In addition, teachers must be aware that children with diabetes may use the disease to avoid activities. The best possible approach is for teachers to recognize the importance of activity, be prepared for reactions by keeping fast-acting sugars on hand, and encourage students to participate in as many physical education and sports activities as possible. By being knowledgeable, teachers will feel secure in classes, children will feel at ease with their classmates and with physical activity, and the benefits of physical activity are more likely to be achieved.

CHAPTER SUMMARY

1. Diabetes is a complex metabolic disorder that affects the body's ability to produce and/or use insulin.

2. Because diabetes may present a management problem for the teacher, several factors are essential in planning and implementing a physical activity program. These factors include the recognition of the characteristics of diabetes, safety procedures, treatment, diet, and exercise.

3. Type I, or juvenile-onset, diabetes is characterized by an insulin dependence due to inadequate production of insulin. Characteristics include frequent urination, abnormal thirst, unusual hunger, weight loss, weakness, fatigue, blurred vision, nausea, and skin disorders and infections.

4. Insulin is used to regulate the amount of glucose used by the working muscles. When insulin is not available to transport glucose, muscle functioning will be impaired.

5. Glucagon is a hormone produced by the alpha cells that raises the blood sugar level by changing stored glycogen in the liver to glucose, which is then transported to the cells by insulin.

6. Ketoacidosis is a high-acid and life-threatening state that calls for immediate insulin to regulate the balance of glucose and insulin in the body.

7. Hyperglycemia results when too much blood sugar remains in the blood or there is insufficient insulin to use it properly. Hyperglycemia can lead to diabetic coma.

8. Hypoglycemia is due to excess blood insulin and blood sugar that is too low to sustain muscular action. Quick-action sugar is required to maintain the balance.

9. Insulin injections may be quick-acting, peaking in 2 or 3 hours; intermediate, peaking in 6 hours; or long-lasting, peaking in 7 to 8 hours.

10. During activity, the uptake of glucose by the working muscle is increased, while the amount of insulin needed is decreased. Activity also improves the muscle's uptake of glucose after the termination of exercise.

11. Physical and recreational activities are appropriate for children with diabetes if proper control is maintained.

12. Management of diabetes should rest with diabetics, not teachers. However, educators must recognize management problems and program considerations of children with diabetes.

REFERENCES

Berg, K. E. (1986). *Diabetic's guide to health and fitness*. Champaign, IL: Human Kinetics.

Bierman, J., & Toohey, B. (1977). *The diabetic's sports and exercise book*. Philadelphia: Lippincott.

Blackett, P. R. (1988). Child and adolescent athletes with diabetes. *The Physician and Sports Medicine, 16*, 133–149.

Campaigne, B. N, & Lampman, R. M. (1994). *Exercise in the clinical management of diabetes*. Champaign, IL: Human Kinetics.

Diabetes Exercise and Sports Association (2000). *Diabetes and exercise*. Phoenix, AZ: Author.

Engerbretson, D. L. (1977). The diabetic in physical education recreation and athletics. *Journal of Physical Education and Recreation, 48*, 18–21.

Franz, M. J. (1984). *Diabetes and exercise: How to get started*. Minneapolis: International Diabetes Center.

Fremion, A. S.; Marrero, D. G.; & Golden, M. P. (1987). Maximum oxygen uptake determination in insulin dependent diabetes mellitus. *The Physician and Sports Medicine, 15*, 119–126.

Gordon, N. F. (1993). *Diabetes: Your complete exercise guide*. Champaign, IL: Human Kinetics.

Horton, E. S. (1989). Exercise and diabetes in youth. In C. V. Gisolfl & D. R. Lamb (Eds.), (vol. 2) *Youth, exercise and sports* (pp. 539–570). Dubuque, IA: Benchmark Press.

Horton, E. S. (1995). Diabetes mellitus. In B. Goldberg (Ed.), *Sports and exercise for children with chronic health conditions*. (pp. 355–373). Champaign, IL: Human Kinetics.

Horton, E. S. (1988). Role and management of exercise in diabetes mellitus. *Diabetes Care, 11*, 201–211.

Juvenile Diabetes Foundation International. (1996). *What you should know about diabetes*. New York: Author.

Landt, K., Campaigne, B., James, F., & Sperling, M. (1985). Effects of exercise training on insulin sensitivity in adolescents with type I diabetes. *Diabetes Care, 8*(5), 461–465.

Murphy, P. (1987). Children with medical conditions can go to summer camp. *The Physician and Sports Medicine, 15*(7), 177–183.

National Institutes of Health. (1986). *Diabetes in America*. Washington, DC: United States Department of Health and Human Services.

Schechter, A. (1985). The diabetic athlete: His toughest opponent is his own metabolism. *Sports Illustrated, 62*, 10–13.

Stratton, R., Wilson, D. P., & Endres, R. K. (1988). Acute glycemic effects of exercise in adolescents with insulin dependent diabetes. *The Physician and Sports Medicine, 16*(3), 150–157.

CHAPTER 20

Nutritional Disorders

Nutritional disorders most often encountered in the school setting are obesity, anorexia nervosa, and bulimia nervosa. Each disorder contributes to a decrease in functional ability and presents problems in maintaining a healthy lifestyle. To counteract these problems, teachers must understand the bases of these disorders and implement sound nutritional and exercise alternatives in an appropriate setting.

Obesity

Obesity is rapidly being recognized as a serious health problem for children and is commonly associated with individuals with disabilities because of their relatively non-active lifestyles. No longer is obesity confined to the adult population—it is presenting a genuine hazard for children. Even with variations in assessment procedures, the prevalence of obesity among children has increased approximately 50%. Since 1960, according to the National Health and Nutrition Examination Survey, rates of over-weight have increased to one in five children, which further increases the probability that these children will become obese in adulthood. An obese girl is 18 times more likely to become obese as an adult, while obese boys are six times as likely to be obese adults. Although individuals may lose weight, they cannot reduce the number of fat cells accumulated during the developmental years. Fat cells may shrink during weight reduction, but if the person gains weight they become bigger and often create more fat cells to store the additional calories.

Obesity also affects functional ability as individuals require more effort to initiate and sustain movement. Most children possess the ability to learn a motor skill; however, obesity may directly contribute to a lack of physical fitness and result in awkward movements. Children who are obese often encounter problems with a poor body image and self-concept and frequently become the target of jokes by their classmates. In addition, other health hazards, including high blood pressure, high cholesterol, heart problems, diabetes, and emotional problems, are commonly associated with obesity. Children may have problems from excessive fat accumulation that restrict their ability to bend and move the trunk and limbs; the insulating effect of fat will cause children to perspire more freely and increase their susceptibility to rapid increases in body temperature; sores and chafing will develop between the legs and under the arms, and the skin will become irritated and inflamed during activity. Finally, excessive weight contributes to postural faults, such as kyphosis, lordosis, flat feet, and general susceptibility to injury.

According to Ebbeling and Rodriguez (1997), assessment techniques such as weight for height (WH), body mass index (BMI) and triceps skinfold are available, although there is no consensus regarding the most accurate protocol for assessing obesity in children.

Obesity is generally defined in the educational setting in relation to the expected weight for a particular height and body type. Children who are *overweight* are 10–20% above their expected weight, whereas children 20–50% above their ideal weight are termed *obese*, and above 50%, *severely obese*. These definitions are complicated by what actually constitutes ideal body weight and methods for assessing body composition. Other factors, including body type, height, and the distribution of fat, all contribute to the determination of a judgmental ideal weight. Further complicating the determination of an ideal weight are changes reflected in the maturation process that affect the relationship of skinfold fat to body fat. For example, girls at 9 years of age may have a skinfold thickness of 24 millimeters, which may be normal at the 25th percentile for that age group, whereas the same percentage at 14 years of age may place them at the 50th percentile. Hence, the determination of body fat varies across age ranges as during development. In absence of what constitutes a standard for normal, Hubbard (1995) recommends using a body mass index (BMI) that is based on the 85th percentile values for age and gender from *Healthy People 2000: National Health Promotion and Disease Prevention Objectives* as an indicator of overweight in adolescents (U.S. Department of Health and Human Services [USDHHS], 1991). Overweight is defined as a BMI greater than or equal to the following (Hubbard, 1995):

23.0—males 12–14 years	23.4—females 12–14 years
24.3—males 15–17 years	24.8—females 15–17 years
25.8—males 18–19 years	25.7—females 18–19 years

Dietz (1995) indicated that the prevalence of obesity varies by age, sex, ethnicity, and regions of the country. More specifically, obesity increased in children 6 to 11 years by 54% and in adolescents 12 to 17 years by 39%, using the 85th percentile of the triceps skinfold as a reference point. Dietz (1995) also indicated that the largest increase in obesity occurred in African American children and in boys from 6 to 11 years of age of all races. Obesity is also more prevalent in the northeast, followed by the midwest, south, and west. It is more prevalent in winter and spring.

Biological, psychological, and sociological factors have also been attributed to obesity. Approximately 90% of children are overweight because they consume more calories than they are able to expend, with between-meal snacks accounting for 25–40% of daily caloric intake (Hoerr, 1984). The remaining 10% are obese because of conditions relating to improper functioning of the endocrine glands. However, the extra accumulation of calories does not always imply overeating and may result from a variety of factors (Clark, 1984). Some of the specific factors that contribute to an increase in the number of calories consumed and resultant obesity include the following:

1. *Overeating.* An excess of caloric intake over the normal expenditure will lead to an accumulation of fat. Overeating may mean extra portions at mealtime or eating between-meal snacks that are high in calories and low in vitamins and minerals. This problem may be the result of a physiological need but generally develops into a habit rather than hunger.

2. *Inactivity.* An imbalance may also be caused by not expending enough calories to balance the amount of consumed calories. Inactivity is probably the most prominent factor in obesity. Children who are inactive may become even more sedentary because of their obesity. Children with disabilities are generally inactive and overprotected because of their condition; limiting opportunities to participate greatly restricts their activity levels.

3. *Psychological problems.* When children are not able to cope with school, stress, social problems, and parents, they may overeat to cope with their problems or depression. Although there is no physiological need for food, the consumption of food initially fills the need caused by problem situations. This can lead to a vicious cycle if the child becomes more obese and insecure about his or her body image, thereby repeating the cycle by eating more (Clark, 1984).

4. *Genetic patterns.* It is interesting to note that fewer than 10% of children who are obese have parents who are not obese, whereas 40% have one parent who is obese, and 80% have two obese parents (Mayer, 1968). Genetic patterns also contribute to the accumulation of fat in certain areas of the body, such as the hips, thighs, abdomen, and chest. Specific body types are also determined by genetic background, and children should understand that weight loss may be evident in some areas of the body, while weight gain may accumulate in other areas.

5. *Family eating patterns.* Eating habits that are learned in infancy are passed down, as well as attitudes toward activity. For the family who snacks constantly and eats fast foods and desserts, the tendency to put on and retain weight is greater than for the family who plans sensible and nutritious meals.

6. *Endocrine disorders.* Disorders affecting one or more of the endocrine glands can contribute to obesity and generally include the following disorders:
   a. *Thyroid gland.* Malfunctioning results in puffiness and swelling of tissue, but not accumulation of fat.
   b. *Pituitary gland.* Malfunctioning is accompanied by excess hair growth, menstrual irregularities, deposits of fatty tissue around breasts, abdomen, face, and neck.
   c. *Hypothalamus.* Overreaction can cause a signal for hunger when calories are not required. Located in the brain, the hypothalamus regulates the neural input for hunger.
   d. *Adrenal cortex.* Overstimulation of the outer covering of adrenal glands embedded in perineal fat above each kidney is characterized by early development of secondary sex characterics.
   e. *Iatrogenic obesity.* This kind of obesity results from long-term administration of cortisone or adrenocortical steroids to control asthma, allergies, arthritis, kidney disorders, or leukemia.

Planning the Physical Activity Program

To develop an appropriate program for children who are overweight, it is essential to establish communication among the parent, health educator, nurse, classroom teacher, and the child. Classroom teachers should refer children who are overweight for a fitness and nutritional program while providing encouragement for adherence and monitoring the success of the program.

If children have little or no concern with their physical appearance or are resistant to weight-reduction programs, the likelihood of success will be marginal. Physical education teachers in conjunction with classroom teachers should attempt to create situations that develop an awareness of obesity and discuss factors that can contribute to a successful intervention program. These factors should include diet and nutrition education, self-confidence, parental involvement, modified lunch, behavior modification, attitude about physical activity, and the classroom teacher's availability for assistance in the program (Bar-Or, 1995; Sallis, Chen & Castro, 1995; Zakus, 1982).

Many times this communication can be established by a letter outlining the proposed program for classroom teachers and parents. In addition, physical education teachers can discuss the program at the parent-teacher meeting or parent education and training seminars. The cooperation of teachers and parents is necessary to ensure success of the program. The incorporation of every available resource will provide the support and monitoring that is required for effective intervention. In this manner all of those involved can best determine the activities and motivational procedures necessary to meet child's needs.

Evaluation of Obesity

To properly determine body weight, percentage of body fat, and the overall physical functioning of the child prior to a weight reduction program, the following characteristics should be assessed (Sallis et al., 1995).

1. *Height and weight.* A determination of the height and weight of children may be helpful for future comparison.

2. *Attitude and self-concept.* An appraisal of attitudes toward physical activity and self-concept can and should be conducted prior to an activity program to ensure the probability of success in the weight-reduction program. An informal observation by classroom teachers or by parents can provide useful information about the child's interest or lack of interest in physical activity. In addition, teachers or school psychologists can administer an attitude or self-concept inventory to determine interest, self-concept, and body image as an aid in determining the effectiveness of the program.

3. *Physical fitness.* Teachers should determine the physical fitness levels of children, including strength and perceived exertion for activity (Bar-Or, 1995). Body composition measurements or BMI can be determined to evaluate the child prior to activity and during the program. Using Lohman's equation for children, the calf and or subscapular skinfold can be used because of the relative ease of measurement and the high correlation to total body fat (Lohman, 1987, 1992).

The triceps skinfold can be measured over the right arm midway between the elbow and acromion process of the scapula, while keeping the skinfold parallel to the humerus in the upper arm (Figure 20.1). Measure the subscapular skinfold on the right side of the body approximately 1 centimeter ($^1/2$ inch) above the inferior angle of the scapula in line with the natural curve of the skin (Figure 20.2).

The following procedure is recommended for administering skinfold tests (Lohman, 1987; Rimmer, 1994):

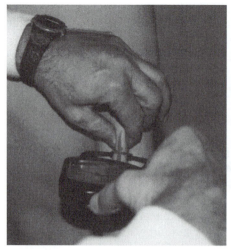

Figure 20.1 Triceps skinfold.

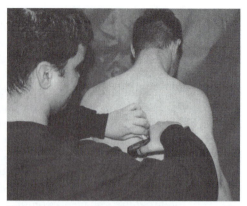

Figure 20.2 Subscapular skinfold.

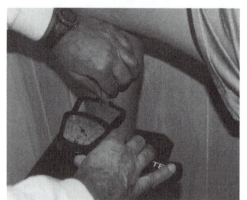

Figure 20.3 Calf skinfold.

1. Firmly grasp the skin between the thumb and forefinger, and lift the skinfold.

2. Place the contact surfaces of the caliper 1 centimeter, or $^1/_2$ inch, above or below the finger.

3. Slowly release the grip on the calipers, enabling them to exert tension of the skinfold.

4. Read the skinfold to the nearest 0.5 millimeter after the needle stops, 1 to 2 seconds after releasing the grip on the caliper.

5. Take the measurements three consecutive times, and record the middle score to the nearest millimeter.

In addition, it is useful to practice the testing procedure to become more experienced and accurate in the measurement. Furthermore, the subscapular skinfold should be administered to females while they are wearing a two-piece swimsuit or loose-fitting shirt. To determine percentage of body fat, the results of skinfold measurements can be compared to charts for boys and girls of all ages (Table 20.1). The specific skinfold measurements define risks of fatness for boys and girls (Lohman, 1992). For example, a boy whose sum of triceps plus subscapular skinfolds is 21 millimeters is located at optimal range or approximately 15–18% body fat. Measurement of skinfold thickness can determine the percentage of body fat and risk for fatness. The higher the skinfold, the higher the level of body fat.

Skinfold thickness between 10 and 25 mm in boys and between 15 and 25 mm in girls generally indicates an acceptable level of body fat. Scores in the high to very high range will indicate the necessity for a weight-reduction program, while children in the very low range probably have too little body fat. A scarcity of body fat may also be detrimental because it is indicative of a loss of lean muscle tissue that may contribute to health-related and growth problems. In addition, if medical supervision and evaluation are required, a more specific evaluation may be required before the teacher can develop reasonable training goals for child with weight problems.

Table 20.1 Percentage of Body Fat in Children

BOYS
Triceps plus calf skinfolds

Range	Skinfold Measurement (mm)	Percentage of Body Fat
Very low	0–5	0–6%
Low	5–10	6–10%
Optimal	10–20	10–20%
Moderately high	25–32	20–25%
High	32–40	25–30%
Very high	40 or above	30% or higher

Triceps plus subscapular skinfolds

Very low	0–9	0–6%
Low	5–13	6–10%
Optimal	13–22	10–20%
Moderately high	22–29	20–25%
High	29–39	25–30%
Very high	39 or above	30% or higher

GIRLS
Triceps plus calf skinfolds

Range	Skinfold Measurement (mm)	Percentage of Body Fat
Very low	0–11	0–12%
Low	11–17	12–15%
Optimal	17–30	15–25%
Moderately high	30–36	25–30%
High	36–45	30–36%
Very high	45 or above	36% or higher

Triceps plus subscapular skinfolds

Very low	0–11	0–11%
Low	11–15	11–15%
Optimal	15–27	15–25%
Moderately high	27–35	25–30%
High	35–45	30–35.5%
Very high	45 or above	35.5% or higher

Source: Data from *Measuring Body Fat Using Skinfolds* [videotape] by T. G. Lohman, 1987, Champaign, IL: Human Kinetics. Copyright 1987 by Human Kinetics Publishers. Used with permission.

Implementing the Physical Activity Program

Children require opportunities to lose weight. By incorporating opportunities for weight reduction into physical activity programs, teachers can help children lose weight and, more important, maintain the weight loss. Teachers should work within the auspices of the educational team for advice on dietary, emotional, and exercise needs while children are engaged in the program.

To implement a program, it is essential to recognize that calories are the specific amounts of energy that activity will require. Physical activities will burn various amounts of calories, and foods contain a specific caloric content.

For a clear picture of body weight and weight reduction, consideration should be given to caloric intake, caloric content of food, energy expenditure, and calorie cost of activities (Katch & McArdle, 1996). If children maintain a balance between the number of calories consumed and the number expended, they will acheive a constant body weight. By consuming more calories than expected, children will store extra calories in the fat cells, causing a change in body composition and increasing total body fat. If physical activity decreases while more calories are consumed, there is a tendency for the muscles to atrophy while the amount of body fat increases. If children consume more while they maintain the same level of physical activity, both body weight and fat will increase. However, if the amount of calories is reduced while exercise also is restricted, the gain of body fat is negated. Although weight loss is desirable, the decrease in physical activity may result in losing lean body tissue (Eisenman, Johnson, & Benson, 1990).

The best method for children to lose body fat is to reduce the number of consumed calories and increase the level of physical activity. This will ensure that weight loss will occur from the loss of body fat and not from loss of lean muscle tissue (Clark, 1984, 1990). A low consumption of calories also initiates metabolic changes, such as a drop in the blood sugar level, that aid in burning stored glycogen and fat and releasing glucose from the liver for activity. Many physiological factors contribute to a weight loss program besides simply caloric intake and the burning of calories. The teacher should consider exercise, nutrition, behavior management, emotional support, and the kind and amount of homework assigned when designing the physical education program.

Exercise

The activity levels of children with weight problems are often low, creating the imbalance of caloric intake that results in increased weight gain and a high percentage of body fat. Often this lack of activity is exacerbated by a fascination with television and video games (Hoerr, 1984).

Exercise expends a specific number of calories and may also help reduce the size of fat cells and prevent obesity (Brownell & Stunkard, 1980; Epstein, 1995; Oscai, 1974). However, exercise is a slow process, and it is difficult to maintain motivation. Often exercise alone is not effective for weight education (Snetselaar, 1997). Depending on body type and amount of excess weight, the child may not be proficient in moving. Teachers should consider the following approaches for an activity program that is recommended by Bar-Or (1995):

1. Emphasize large muscle groups.

2. Move the entire body over distance.

3. Deemphasize intensity and emphasize duration.

4. Raise daily energy expenditure by 10–15%.

5. Include muscle strength activities.

6. Use daily or near daily activity, and gradually increase the frequency and volume.

7. Select activities the child enjoys, and solicit parental and group involvement.

8. Provide reinforcement and token remuneration.

To select the appropriate exercises, teachers should develop reasonable exercise goals that are not overly strenuous or painful. As children lose weight and increase their physical proficiency, the program can be modified to accommodate increased performance levels. Selected activities should emphasize aerobic activities that start slowly and can be increased gradually in duration and intensity. Walking, jogging, cycling, swimming, water exercises, aerobic dance, and cross-country skiing are appropriate activities that can be used by children during and after school to aid in weight reduction (Hoerr, 1984).

Of particular importance is the acquisition of gross motor skill activities that are required for participation. If these fundamental skills are not mastered, obese children will be more likely to withdraw and avoid participation in any activity, because these skills are the basic component of games and sports. Although weight may restrict performance, the more successful children become in their performance, the more they will be reinforced for participation and will increase their activity levels.

Diet and Nutrition

Diet and nutrition are important factors, with an emphasis on reducing the number of calories consumed. In a school setting this may be accomplished by offering a nutritionally balanced diet that includes the four basic food groups. To lose one pound requires a deficit of 3,500 calories, so the selection of low-calorie foods may contribute to losing weight because it decreases the number of calories consumed. Teachers can assist with the development of a sound nutritional program without prescribing a diet and reducing dietary fat and excessive calories.

Epstein, Masek, and Marshall (1978) implemented a traffic-light program for children to reduce the amount of calories they consumed. By using a color-coded, calorie-based program, they increased the child's knowledge of the amount of calories in specific foods. Green-light foods, such as celery and carrots, contained less than 20 calories per serving and were encouraged. Yellow-light foods included staples such as meats and potatoes from the basic food groups, averaging about 20 calories per serving. Red-light foods, such as candy, cake, and soft drinks, had more than 20 calories per serving. These were the foods that children were encouraged to avoid. By learning the caloric content of specific foods and food groups and limiting themselves to only four red-light foods per week, these children clearly demonstrated the ability to avoid high-calorie foods, select nutritionally sound foods, and lose weight. The food groups were also helpful for parents in designing meal plans for children while they were in the program. *The Stop-Light Diet for Children* is now available for teachers, parents, and children (Epstein & Squires, 1988).

Table 20.2 Calorie Levels for Children

	Age	Number of Calories (kcal)
Boys	1–3	1,300
and	3–6	1,600
girls	6–9	2,100
Boys	9–12	2,400
	12–15	3,000
	15–18	3,400
Girls	9–12	2,200
	12–15	2,500
	15–18	2,300

The appropriate calorie limit will vary according to the child's age and activity level. In general, the guidelines in Table 20.2 can be used to help children meet the amount of calories required for healthful living and create an imbalance necessary for weight loss to occur (Eisenman et al., 1990). These guidelines adhere to the weight-loss provisions that are recommended by most experts, which advocate a nutritionally balanced diet in conjunction with exercise and behavior management as the proper method to lose and control weight.

Snetselaar (1997) also advocated mild calorie reduction (of 500 to 1,000 calories) resulting in a gradual weight loss without outstanding side effects. Because an energy deficit of 3,500 calories is needed to lose a pound of body fat, eliminating 500 calories a day (3,500 a week) will result in a loss of one pound without the side effects (dehydration; loss of electrolytes, minerals, and glucogen stores; and lean body tissue) that are prevalent in more extreme weight-loss programs. Children should not lose more than 1 or 2 lb a week and should avoid extreme diets that may disrupt the metabolism of waste materials and growth of muscles, organs, and bones. In addition, any limitation of fat or growth-restrictive diets should not be implemented for children under 2 years of age (Dietz, 1995).

Behavior Management

Although weight loss will occur with caloric restrictions and exercise, it is often difficult for children to initiate and maintain a weight reduction program. To achieve long-term weight loss and increase motivation, behavioral interventions are required. Several examples of appropriate weight loss and behavior management incentives follow.

1. *Self-monitoring.* Children or parents can chart and record the food consumed, caloric cost of the food, exercise, and weight on a daily basis. This information can be used as a personal recording to chart weight loss (Brown, 1997).

2. *Social reinforcements and prompts.* Another technique to provide incentives is the use of social reinforcement and prompts to praise appropriate behaviors. Teachers or parents can also provide additional praise for maintaining appropriate habits. In the traffic-light program, Epstein and Squires (1988) incorporated a lifestyle approach for the entire family to burn extra calories. For example, instead of riding to the store, children and parents might walk; instead of watch-

ing television after dinner, the family might ride bicycles or take a short walk to burn extra calories, thus promoting a generally more active lifestyle.

3. *Contracting.* Another method of encouraging weight loss is to develop a contract outlining a realistic program to help students lose weight and maintain weight reduction. Care must be taken to observe the rules of the contract and to select a reasonable weight loss time line (Brown, 1997).

4. *Activity reinforcers.* Activity can be a powerful reinforcer in a physical education class. By partaking in enjoyable activities, children can be encouraged to reduce their calorie intake and increase their activity. Dietz (1995) has recommended focusing on behaviors that reduce energy expenditure, such as limiting television viewing to increase time for more active participation. Reinforcement can also be provided for exercising 5 days a week or increasing level of performance and can easily be used during every class period or at home. Activity reinforcers also may enhance the child's attitude toward exercise and promote positive aspects of activity, much more so than using exercise as a punishment. The more children increase their activity, the greater the success of a weight reduction program.

Emotional Support

Many children suffer from a poor self-image and feel insecure about themselves. Losing weight is extremely difficult, and teachers or nurses can provide the emotional support that may be needed. Another supportive measure may be to establish a school health club, in which children meet periodically to create a learning environment for nutrition and a sounding board for problems. Teachers, parents, and school nurses can serve as consultants to the club and help arrange learning activities and provide guidance for children (Little, 1983). The club can also arrange an exercise and/or recreational outlets for children in order to change sedentary habits and encourage more active lifestyles.

Homework and School-Based Interventions

A homework program can also be devised to aid children in weight reduction and in increasing physical activity outside the school setting. Homework may involve a series of learning experiences about the body, diet, and nutrition that contain readings on a specific topic and a self-testing quiz. In addition, a home exercise program may be devised by the teacher to be used in conjunction with the school physical education program. Teachers can also allow children to accumulate points for a variety of additional activities performed outside the school or with the family.

The school provides the most important variable in the success of a weight reduction program. The Committed to Kids Pediatric Weight Management Program described by Brown (1997) incorporated lifestyle management exercise and behavioral intervention for children. Brownell (1992) also detailed strategies to support long-term weight loss that emphasized exercise, social support, and cognitive restructuring to understand overeating and adherence to a weight loss program. Sallis (1993) indicated that educational approaches to diet and exercise have short-term effects and instead recommended programs to teach children how to change their behaviors and create a supportive environment to facilitate exercise and a healthy diet. An ongoing project titled Child and Adolescent Trail for Cardiovascular Health

(CATCH) is a school-based program aimed at the health of children. The primary focus of this program is to promote the following:

- changes in food to lower fat content in school lunches
- changes in physical education to promote moderate to vigorous activity
- prevention of tobacco use
- promote healthful eating and activity choices

Over 5,000 children in California, Louisiana, Minnesota, and Texas have particapated in this program. It is a model intervention program that can be used successfully in schools.

Combining the Treatment Factors

A reasonable method of attaining calorie deficits, and thus weight loss, is to educate children at an early age in the benefits of nutrition and exercise. Because most parents will not be able to afford expensive clinical treatments, the school can effectively educate and treat factors related to obesity or coordinate programs between home and school (Sallis, 1993).

The team approach is the most effective and the safest way to lose weight and maintain the loss. A program emphasizing a weight loss of 1^1/2 pounds per week (one pound lost by dieting and a half pound by exercise) will result in a safe, gradual weight reduction primarily of body fat and very little of lean body tissue.

The combination of proper nutrition and exercise on a gradual basis is the safest method of conducting a weight reduction program. In addition, physical educators have an excellent opportunity to change attitudes and habits toward exercise. By offering emotional support, and sound nutritional and exercise programs as motivational techniques, teachers can safely implement and continue a weight reduction program for children with weight problems.

Eating Disorders

The eating disorders anorexia nervosa and bulimia nervosa have become increasingly important over the past two decades as their prevalence and the difficulties associated with their treatment have become focal points of educators and clinicians. Chronic forms of eating disorders develop in about 25% of patients, and between 5% and 20% of such patients are unresponsive to therapeutic interventions. Those individuals who are unresponsive to therapy die as a result of this disorder (Garfinkel, 1995).

Chronic forms of eating disorders are due, in part, to society's view of the ideal body (Barber, 1998; Williamson et al., 1995). In today's society, thinness is seen as a way of achieving acceptance. Teen magazines continually focus on women's figures, and dieting, and a majority of articles contained in these magazines emphasize ways of dieting and exercising for thinness instead of for health. Fitness videos offered in stores are routinely focused on appearance instead of health. Hence, individuals with either anorexia or bulimia nervosa are pathologically preoccupied with weight and body shape and have a very strong desire for a thinner physique. Unfortunately, for many adolescents, expectations for body shape and size are unrealistic, as are their approaches for attaining their desired body shapes. The ability to recognize when an individual's desire for improving body shape through exercise and diet is dangerous to health and what to do about it is a critical component of your job as a physical educator.

The two most common forms of eating disorders are anorexia nervosa and bulimia nervosa. Anorexia nervosa ("self-starvation disorder") is characterized by "a deliberate, self-imposed starvation owing to a relentless pursuit of thinness and fear of fatness" (Garfinkel, 1995, p. 1361). The most evident signs of anorexia nervosa include a distorted body image, rapid decrease in weight, preoccupation with food and its fat and calorie content, and the loss of hair from the head.

Bulimia nervosa ("binge and purge disorder") is characterized by "episodic patterns of binge eating accompanied by a sense of loss of control, and efforts to control body weight such as through self-induced vomiting or use of laxative" (Garfinkel, 1995, p. 1361). Individuals with bulimia are preoccupied with the fat and calorie content of foods. They have very unusual eating habits that consist of strict dieting, even fasting, followed by frequent episodes of binge eating. People with bulimia fear rejection and disapproval. They need the reassurance and approval; without it, their self-esteem drops.

In truth, individuals may exhibit symptoms associated with more than one type, and many individuals alternate between the features of both anorexia and bulimia nervosa. Hence, in addition to self-starvation, the person with anorexia may in some instances resort to purging when forced to eat; conversely, the person with bulimia may fast occasionally after a major binge episode to limit the amount of weight gained.

There are many misconceptions regarding what type of individual has an eating disorder. A major misconception is that eating disorders are found only in the young adult population, predominantly middle-class, Caucasian females. Contrary to this popular belief, eating disorders are usually first evident in infancy, childhood, or adolescence, and anyone—regardless of race, ethnicity, or social position—can suffer from an eating disorder. Although females constitute the majority of all people with eating disorders (Thompson & Sherman, 1993), over 10% are male, and the incidence of eating disorders in males has increased conspicuously over the past decade. Although the data on females and eating disorders are incomplete, even less is known regarding eating disorders in the male population. Based on the available data, experts believe that the reasons for disordered eating in males is similar to that found among females: that is, body dissatisfaction and attaining the "ideal body" (Keel, Klump, Leon & Fulkerson, 1998).

Recognizing the warning signs of eating disorders is the first step in helping the individual recover. Along with amenorrhea (lack of menstruation) in females, individuals with anorexia or bulimia may also suffer from the following (Wilmore, 1995; Williamson et al., 1995):

1. gastrointestinal problems, such as chronic stomach pain, bloating, constipation, diarrhea, and cramping

2. dental and gum disease

3. cardiac arrhythmias, hypotension, and hypothermia, which are related to dehydration and malnutrition, which in turn lead to decreased heart rate, decreased blood pressure, electrolyte abnormalities, and decreased cardiac output

4. mineral disturbances, which ultimately lead to a reduction in bone density and bone mineral content and, often, to osteoporosis later in life

It should be noted that excessive and compulsive exercising might also be considered a "red flag" of an eating disorder. What constitutes excessive exercising, however, is a gray area. As a general rule, motivation and attitude about exercise are what separate a compulsive exerciser from a normal exerciser. If the person does not view exercise as enjoyable and practices it only to burn calories and to relieve the guilt associated with eating too much, then that person may be a compulsive exerciser.

Excessive weight loss may lead to physical damage to the growth process and disturb the chemical balance of the body, contributing to depression, feelings of guilt, anxiety, and a sense of hopelessness. Frequently the child's emotional state is disturbed; she will appear scrawny or sickly and demonstrate a poor performance in school. Approximately 15% of all serious cases will manifest health conditions that result in death.

Individuals with anorexia are characterized as overachievers and perfectionists, and they generally manifest low personal esteem and a fear of not achieving parental expectations. They choose to lose weight through dieting as a method of achieving recognition, which leads to an obsession with losing weight. Compounding this cycle are parents who may become overprotective and less demanding, leaving the child to control things. The longer a person loses weight, the more recognition and reinforcement that person will receive for dieting.

Eating disorders are also on the rise in the athletic population, especially in the female athlete (Thompson & Sherman, 1993; Wilmore, 1995). Athletes are predisposed to eating disorders because of the pressures that surround them. Athletes strive for perfection. The goals of an athlete are strength, power, and endurance. Athletes feel that if they reduce their body fat percentage, they can improve not only their appearance, but also their performance. Athletes receive a lot of pressure from coaches, parents, and friends to strive for greatness, and the last thing that athletes want to do is to disappoint their coaches or families; consequently, they may go to extremes.

Specific sports are associated with a higher prevalence of eating disorders. In females, gymnastics, figure skating, cheerleading, and long-distance running have a high incidence of eating disorders. Competitors in these sports depend on and are judged by appearance as much as talent. Cheerleaders and figure skaters are lifted by partners, so it is imperative that they maintain a low body weight. Male athletes, especially in wrestling and distance running, are often susceptible to eating disorders because a low body weight is essential for performance. Other than starvation, wrestlers also engage in diuretic and laxative use, excessive exercise with the use of rubber suits, and saunas. Because of engaging in the aforementioned regimens, wrestlers often suffer from intense dehydration, which can result in death.

Options available to help these individuals are limited. Probably the most important advice for dealing with a child suspected of having an eating disorder is to proceed carefully and always be nonjudgmental in approach. Most important, these individuals need to be referred to competent professionals. For some children, the access to a teacher or coach can provide the essential information on appropriate weight gain and loss. Often a good first step is to call local hospital and mental health facilities for a referral to names of qualified professionals who deal with eating disorders. Another contact point is the American Dietetic Association, who can help you find a dietitian in your area who is expert in treating eating disorders. Having this information for parents of children with eating disorders can be a positive first step along the road to treatment (Salomon, 1999).

Some individuals recovering from an eating disorder may choose exercise as a compensatory behavior or replacement for restricting calories or purging behaviors. If this be the case, model healthy behaviors and avoid focusing on the child's weight and body shape. Emphasize instead that exercise is important for health and important for improving strength and stamina. Above all else, stress the importance of regular eating to maintain strength and stamina (Solomon, 1999).

Implementing the Physical Activity Program

The role of teachers who have children with anorexia or bulimia in their charge is dramatically different from the role they are expected to take on when developing a program for children who are obese. Focusing on reducing calories or increasing activity is not appropriate for a child with anorexia. Consequently, the collaborative programming team must work in unison to prevent severe problems. Physical educators, through the assessment of percentage of body fat, can ascertain the possible onset of the anorexic condition and can alert children, parents, and teachers to potential problems of excessive dieting and nutrition. For instance, children with too little body fat may lose too much lean body tissue or be at risk in the growth and development stage of life (Williams, 1993). Recognition of potential symptoms of anorexia nervosa should lead to appropriate consultation and treatment programs.

Teacher awareness and recognition of symptoms may also aid in providing the potential anorexic with information related to the hazards of dieting and dangers of losing weight rapidly. Teachers can also help provide the emotional support and reinforcement that are needed for these students. Anorexia nervosa will demand teacher awareness and a thorough understanding of the problem. Additionally, the role of educators working with children will include the following (Solomon, 1999):

- knowing their roles and limitations
- recognizing signs and symptoms of anorexia nervosa
- being supportive and avoiding judgments
- being understanding of parents
- acknowledging the psychologist's role as primary in the treatment process

Most of the treatment procedures for the child with anorexia revolve around the family and individual therapy, as well as appropriate behavior management techniques that can be developed with the support of the educational programming team. Teachers can provide expertise in the area of growth and development, exercise, relaxation training, body image activities, and appropriate behavior management strategies. In this manner teachers can provide an important link with the physician, psychologist, parents, clinician, and school personnel to aid in the treatment of eating disorders.

CHAPTER SUMMARY

1. Nutritional disorders that are often encountered in the school setting are obesity, anorexia nervosa, and bulinia nervosa. All contribute to a decrease in functional ability and present problems in maintaining a healthy lifestyle.

2. Obesity is a common problem for children with disabilities because of their rela-

tively nonactive lifestyles. Other health problems associated with obesity include high blood pressure, high cholesterol, cardiovascular problems, and diabetes.

3. Intervention for children should incorporate every available resource that can provide support and monitoring. The teacher should work within the auspices of the educational programming team for advice on dietary, emotional, and physical activity needs while students are engaged in the program.

4. Whether or not children lose weight depends on a simple energy balance concept. If more calories are consumed than expended, the child will gain weight. Conversely, if more calories are expended than consumed, the child will lose weight.

5. In selecting appropriate exercises, teachers should develop reasonable exercise goals that are not overly strenuous or painful. As children lose weight and increase their physical performance, the program can be modified to accommodate increased performance levels.

6. Activities selected should be aerobic in nature; duration and intensity can be increased as needed.

7. A combined approach that utilizes sound nutritional and exercise habits, as well as behavior management techniques, is the treatment of choice.

8. Anorexia nervosa is a common eating disorder affecting mostly females. It is characterized by loss of weight due to a reduction in food intake and loss of appetite.

9. Signs and symptoms of anorexia and bulimia include exaggerated interest in food, with refusal to eat; denial of hunger; excessive exercise; eating binges followed by vomiting; utilizing diet pills and laxatives to reduce weight; and distorted body image.

10. Excessive weight loss may lead to physical damage to the growth process and disturb the chemical balance of the body, contributing to depression, guilt, and anxiety.

11. Teacher awareness and recognition of symptoms may aid in providing the potential anorexic with information related to the potential hazards of dieting and dangers of losing weight rapidly.

12. Most treatment procedures revolve around the family and individual therapy as well as appropriate behavior management techniques developed by the multidisciplinary team. Physical education teachers can provide an important link with professionals to aid in the treatment of anorexia nervosa by providing information on growth and development, exercise, body image activities, and appropriate behavior management techniques.

REFERENCES

Barber, N. (1998). The slender ideal and eating disorders: An interdisciplinary "telescope" model. *International Journal of Eating Disorders, 23,* 295–307.

Bar-Or, O. (1995). Obesity. In B. Goldberg (Ed.), *Sports and exercise for children with chronic health conditions* (pp. 335–353). Champaign, IL: Human Kinetics.

Brown, D. K. (1997). Childhood and adolescence weight management. In S. Dalton (Ed.), *Overweight and weight management.* Gaithersburg, MD: Aspen Publications.

Brownell, K. D. (1992). *The Learn Program for weight control.* Dallas, TX: American Health Publication Company.

Brownell, K. D., & Stunkard, A. J. (1980). Physical activity in the development and control of obesity. In A. J. Stunkard (Ed.), *Obesity*. Philadelphia: Saunders College Publishing.

Clark, N. (1984). How I manage athletes' food obsessions. *The Physician and Sports Medicine, 12,* 96–103.

Clark, N. (1990). *Sports nutrition cookbook*. Champaign, IL: Leisure Press.

Dietz, W. H. (1995). Childhood Obesity. In L. W. Y. Cheung & J. B. Richmond (Eds.), *Child health, nutrition and physical activity* (pp. 155–169). Champaign, IL: Human Kinetics.

Dwyer, J. T., Stone E. J. & Yang E. N. (2000). Prevalence of marked overweight and obesity in multiethnic pediatric population: Findings from the Child and Adolescent Trial for Cardiovascular Health (CATCH) study. *Journal of American Diet Association. 100,* 1149–1154.

Ebbeling, C. B., & Rodriguez, N. R. (1997). Anthropometric techniques for identification of obese children: Perspectives for the practitioner. In S. Dalton (Ed.), *Overweight and weight management* (pp. 486–496). Gaithersburg, MD: Aspen Publishers.

Eisenman, P., Johnson, S, & Benson, J. E. (1990). *Coaches' guide to nutrition and weight control* (2nd ed.). Champaign, IL: Human Kinetics.

Epstein, L. H. (1995). Exercise in the treatment of childhood obesity. *International Journal of Obesity, 19,* 117–121.

Epstein, L. H., Masek, B., & Marshall, W. (1978). A nutritionally based school program for control of eating in obese children. *Behavior Therapy, 9,* 766–788.

Epstein, L. H., & Squires, S. (1988). *The stop-light diet for children: An eight-week program for parents and children*. Boston: Little, Brown.

Garfinkel, P. E. (1995). Eating disorders. In H. I. Kaplan & B. J. Sadock (Eds.), *Comprehensive textbook of psychiatry/VI* (vol. 2, 6th ed.). Baltimore: Williams & Wilkins.

Hoerr, S. L. (1984). Exercise: An alternative to fad diets for adolescent girls. *The Physician and Sports Medicine, 12,* 76–83.

Hubbard, V. S. (1995). Future directions in obesity research. In L. W. Y. Cheung & J. B. Richmond (Eds), *Child health, nutrition and physical activity.* (pp. 205–209). Champaign, IL: Human Kinetics.

Katch, F., & McArdle, W. (1996). *Nutrition, weight control and exercise* (4th ed.). Philadelphia: Lea and Febiger.

Keel, P. K., Klump, K. L., Leon, G. R., & Fulkerson, J. A. (1998). Disordered eating in adolescent males form a school-based sample. *International Journal of Eating Disorders, 23,* 125–132.

Little, J. (1983). Management of the obese child in the school. *Journal of School Health, 53,* 440–441.

Lohman, T. G. (1987). *Measuring body fat using skinfolds*. (Videotape). Champaign, IL: Human Kinetics.

Lohman, T. G. (1992). *Advances in body composition assessment*. Champaign, IL: Human Kinetics.

Mayer, J. (1968). *Overweight: Causes, cost, and control*. Englewood Cliffs, NJ: Prentice Hall.

Oscai, L. (1974). Exercise or food restriction: Effect on adipose tissue. *American Journal of Physiology, 27,* 902.

Rimmer, J. H. (1994). *Fitness and Rehabilitation Programs for Special Populations*. Dubuque, IA: Brown and Benchmark.

Sallis, J. F., Chen, A. H., & Castro, C. M. (1995). School-based intervention for childhood obesity. In L. W. Y. Cheung & J. B. Richmond (Eds.), *Child health, nutrition, and physical activity.* (pp. 179–204). Champaign, IL: Human Kinetics.

Sallis, J. F. (1993). Promoting healthful diet and physical activity. In Millstein, S. G., Peterson, A. C., & Nightingale, E. O. (Eds.), *Promoting the health of adolescents: New directions for the diversity-first century* (pp. 209–241). New York: Oxford University.

Salomon, S. (1999, May–June). Identify the eating disordered client. *Personal Fitness Professional,* 39–41.

Snetselaar, L. B. (1997). *Nutrition counseling skills.* Gaithersburg, MD: Aspen Publishers.

Thompson, R. A., & Sherman, R. T. (1993). *Helping athletes with eating disorders.* Champaign, IL: Human Kinetics.

U.S. Department of Health and Human Services. (1991). *Healthy people 2000: National health promotion and disease prevention objectives.* (DHHS Publication No. 91-50212). Washington, DC: U.S. Government Printing Office.

Williams M. W. (1993). *Nutrition for Fitness and Sport* (2nd ed). Dubuque, IA: William C. Brown

Williamson, D. A., Netemeyer, R. G., Jackman, L. P., Anderson, D. A., Funsch, C. L., & Rabalais, J. Y. (1995). Structural equation model of risk factors for the development of eating disorders in female athletes. *International Journal of Eating Disorders, 17,* 387–393.

Wilmore, J. H. (1995). Disordered eating in the young athletes. In C. J. R. Blimke & O. Bar-Or (Eds.), *New horizons in pediatric exercise science* (pp. 161–178). Champaign, IL: Human Kinetics.

Zakus, G. E. (1982). Obesity in children and adolescents: Understanding and treating the problem. *Social Work in Health Care, 8,* 11–29.

CHAPTER 21

Cardiovascular Disorders and Hypertension

O ver 25 million people in the United States are afflicted by cardiovascular disorders, and approximately 40,000 infants are born each year with heart problems. Cardiovascular problems are categorized as either congenital or acquired disorders that occur before or after birth and are the direct result of damage to the heart and/or blood vessels, septal defects, or valvular heart dysfunctions. Most causes of congenital defects are unknown, although some are genetically linked to or result from an injury to the fetus during pregnancy.

Because the severity of congenital defects usually requires surgery or medication to correct the defect, most children have received treatment by the time they enter school and therefore have few symptoms associated with their particular problem. Those children with severe congenital problems will require extensive medical supervision or treatment and may be confined to the hospital, home, or special school.

Primary concerns for teachers are acquired cardiovascular disorders among children in the school setting that may present a potential health hazard. Rheumatic heart disease, heart murmurs, arrhythmias, and hypertension are disorders that affect children and are the focus of this chapter. These conditions are often prevalent in the integrated setting or may be associated with other disabilities.

Children with existing cardiovascular disabilities and those who suddenly acquire a cardiovascular disability may manifest emotional frustrations because of their forced inactivity. They may withdraw from activity and feel inferior to peers in physical fitness and motor development because of their inability to fully participate in age-related activities. This may lead to social rejection that may be as damaging psychologically as it is physically.

For children with cardiac disorders, appropriate physical and motor fitness activities are needed. The cooperation of the collaborative programming team, including the physician, nurse, physical educator, health educator, and special educator, is needed to develop appropriate goals to initiate a comprehensive physical activity program. Teachers can also incorporate a well-rounded program of nutrition, exercise, and education for the elimination of cardiac risk factors to safely incorporate children into a physical activity program and contribute to a healthy lifestyle. Another concern for teachers is to determine the degree of participation in activities that will be needed to maintain physical fitness and promote total body development. Opportunities to relieve anxiety and depression through physical activity and relaxation training also can be implemented as a means of integrating children into regular physical education classes.

Rheumatic Heart Disease

Rheumatic heart disease occurs in children between 6 and 12 years of age who have had rheumatic fever. Rheumatic fever develops as a reaction to antibodies formed as a defense against streptococcal bacteria. Damage to the heart may often occur from inflammation, which causes scarring that most notably appears in the heart valves over a period of years. After children have contracted rheumatic fever, they are susceptible to repeated attacks, further increasing the probability of inflammation and scarring that may damage the heart. Although no existing cause is known, rheumatic fever may be identified by symptoms such as pain in joints and muscles, poor appetite, twitching of muscles, frequent nosebleeds, fever, streptococcal infection, sore throat, and difficulty in swallowing.

Because the buildup of scar tissue reduces the effectiveness of the heart and valves, the supply of blood is decreased throughout the body. Deterioration of the valves may result in the inability to open and close effectively. A leaky or constricted valve will affect the child's cardiac efficiency and ability to perform physical activities, because the blood supply to the working muscles is inadequate.

As a result of one or more attacks of rheumatic fever, the valves of the heart will suffer permanent damage. The mitral and aortic valves allow the blood to pass in one direction. Consequently, if the valves become inflamed, resulting in the development of scar tissue in the leaflets, the valve may become fused, restricting the movement and narrowing the opening of the valve. The result is a constricted, or *stenotic*, valve. Conversely, valves may atrophy and prohibit proper closure. This *regurgitant* valve allows the blood to flow back into the atrium or ventricle. Figure 21.1 depicts the fetal heart.

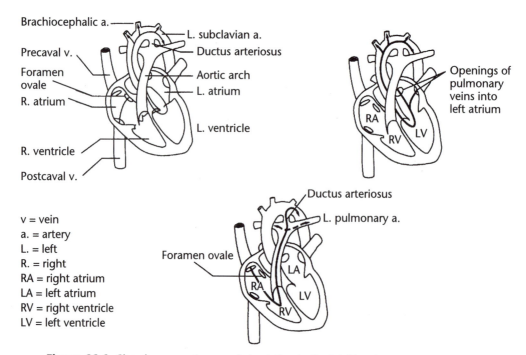

Brachiocephalic a.
L. subclavian a.
Precaval v.
Ductus arteriosus
Foramen ovale
Aortic arch
R. atrium
L. atrium
L. ventricle
R. ventricle
Postcaval v.
Openings of pulmonary veins into left atrium
RA
RV
LV

Ductus arteriosus
L. pulmonary a.
Foramen ovale
LA
RA
LV
RV

v = vein
a. = artery
L. = left
R. = right
RA = right atrium
LA = left atrium
RV = right ventricle
LV = left ventricle

Figure 21.1 Chambers, openings, and circulation in the fetal heart.

Recent medical advances have reduced some of the problems associated with rheumatic heart disease. Surgery can be performed to remove scar tissue, to repair damaged valves, or to implant artificial valves. Medication has also been used in rheumatic fever to treat symptoms and possibly prevent more serious heart damage or recurring attacks.

Heart Murmurs and Arrhythmias

A variation from the normal sounds of the heart may be audible during the school years. These sounds are referred to as *murmurs* and are not necessarily pathological. Shaffer and Rose (1974) indicated in their research on young athletes that approximately 85% possessed audible murmurs that were not pathological. In contrast, other murmurs may be indicative of a hemodynamic or structural abnormality that may not be evident to teachers.

A concern for teachers is the adaptability of children with a heart murmur to physical activity and sports programs. The Task Force on Blood Pressure Control in Children (1987) has recommended a thorough cardiac screening to eliminate suspected causes of heart murmur, including assessment of resting heart rate, respiration, and blood pressure, and palpation between the femoral and brachial arteries to determine extra sounds, clicks, or splitting of sounds. If a defect is suspected, children can then be referred for a more extensive evaluation, including an electrocardiogram. If no defect is evident, children will be able to participate in a physical activity program based on consultations with a cardiologist and the guidelines for participation presented later in this chapter.

Arrhythmias are changes in the regular beat of the heart and may occur from extra or ectopic beats of atrial, junctional, or ventricular origin (Task Force on Blood Pressure Control in Children, 1987). Most ectopic beats are benign and will not be dangerous to children and often disappear with low-intensity exercise. However, ectopic beats that persist require a more extensive evaluation to determine the specific cause of the defect and, more important, whether to curtail participation in physical activity and sports.

Teachers of children with cardiac disorders must be aware of how their performance may be affected. Active participation need not be eliminated and, as mentioned earlier, is an essential social and emotional outlet for children. With proper supervision, children should be able to engage in an activity program and eliminate or decrease cardiac risk factors that may impede physical functioning.

Hypertension

Another concern for parents and educators is hypertension in the school-aged population. Hypertension is also one kind of cardiovascular deficit that teachers and school personnel can help identify and incorporate into a treatment program. Because children with disabilities may be susceptible to high blood pressure, it is essential to remediate the problem before a more serious consequence, such as a stroke, might occur.

Hypertension, or high blood pressure, is a common threat to the health of many Americans. Essential or primary hypertension is usually prevalent in adults but is being discovered more frequently in school-aged children. Therefore, there is a need to understand the disease and to include blood pressure measurements as part of the school physical examination.

With high blood pressure, the risk of cardiovascular disease increases. Hypertension is a contributor to heart disease, kidney disease, stroke, and loss of vision. The major abnormality appears to be increased vascular resistance, which causes the heart and blood vessels to work harder to transport blood to the body (Jesse, 1982; Mitchell, Blount, Blumenthal, et al., 1975). Many cases of school-aged hypertension may be explained by an underlying disorder. Causes of this type of hypertension, called secondary hypertension, include kidney disease, coarctation of the aorta, and neurological or hormonal disorders. However, numerous authorities have reported an alarming increase in cases of primary hypertension being diagnosed during the school years (Levin, 1983; Loggie, 1975, 1992; Lieberman, 1978).

It is important to identify children with hypertension and begin treatment as soon as possible. Children with primary hypertension may be asymptomatic or may complain of frontal headaches, dizziness, fatigue, nosebleeds, anorexia, and nervousness. Causes of hypertension may include inactivity, genetic predisposition, stress, and diet. Any or all of the following risk factors may contribute to primary hypertension, which is no longer considered an adult problem and has been reported in individuals as early as 3 years of age (Londe, 1983):

- *Genetic predisposition.* Inheritance, or genetic predisposition, is an indicator of similar blood pressure levels in parents and children, but it has not been demonstrated to be a true predictor of future hypertension. Early reports indicated that about 28% of children with one hypertensive parent were also hypertensive, while the incidence increased to 65% if both parents were hypertensive. Current information indicates that the incidence of hypertension among students with one hypertensive parent is 51%. A family history of complications is usually apparent in 50% of all school-aged children with hypertension. A strong relationship in blood pressure levels exists between twins and siblings, while a weaker relationship is apparent in half siblings and in parents and offspring. Blood pressure in both females and males is the same until adolescence; after 14 years of age, males demonstrate higher normal standards of measurement (McCrory, 1982).

- *Obesity.* Obesity occurs concurrently in 50% of all school-aged children with hypertension. Londe (1983) reported that 55% of the hypertensive children in his study were obese, and after the children underwent a weight reduction program, subsequent blood pressure readings were decreased.

- *Race.* As a group, African American children usually demonstrate a higher blood pressure reading. Berenson (1983) also indicated that hypertensive African American children exhibited a high sodium excretion and a tendency for obesity, which may contribute to increased levels of hypertension. Hohn, Dwyer & Dwyer (1994) also reported increased blood pressure levels in African American and Asian children in comparison to white children.

- *Sodium.* There is a general agreement that increased levels of sodium contribute to hypertension. For example, primitive tribes in various parts of the world manifest no primary hypertension because their diet is low in sodium, whereas in northeastern Japan, where salt intake is high, hypertension is 40–50% higher than in other parts of the world. In a clinical setting, the reduction of salt has been shown to lower the blood pressure of hypertensive individuals, whereas increased consumption of salt increased the blood pressure readings (Langford, 1983).

- *Salt sensitivity.* Some individuals may also possess a genetically determined sensitivity to salt. Blood pressure in these individuals will increase when sodium consumption increases, whereas non–salt-sensitive individuals who increase their sodium intake will excrete more sodium and demonstrate less weight gain (Londe, 1983). The American Heart Association (1999) recommended a low salt intake for children at risk for hypertension as a preventive measure. Keeping a balance of sodium and potassium may also contribute to the absence of hypertension.

- *Stress.* Temporary stress may result in an increased blood pressure reading. Children who are predisposed to stress or who live in a stressful home environment may be susceptible to higher blood pressure levels (Loggie et al., 1984). Additionally, children with disabilities often encounter frustrations from their conditions that evoke stress and may contribute to hypertension.

Implications of High Blood Pressure

To adequately diagnose and prevent hypertension in school-aged children, blood pressure measurements should be incorporated into the pediatric physical examination for early detection. A primary source of information for screening children is available from the medical history and a limited number of laboratory studies, including a physical examination, urinalysis, and chemical analysis of renal function.

Secondary causes of hypertension can also be detected from the medical history and routine laboratory information. The previous history should be examined to determine the presence of hypertension and any contributing factors: the use of hormones (i.e., oral contraceptives, corticosteroids); indications of cardiac, vascular, or renal disease; diabetes; excessive dieting; and excessive sodium intake. The development of blood pressure distributions by age and sex have now made it possible to compare blood pressure values.

The Task Force on Blood Pressure Control in Children (1987) suggested that three elevated readings on separate occasions be obtained before diagnosing hypertension in an individual. The initial reading should be plotted on a measurement grid, and if that value exceeds the 95th percentile for systolic and diastolic blood pressure, the measurement should be repeated. Consistently elevated readings would then be indicative of high blood pressure, whereas a transitory high reading may be attributed to illness or environmental factors that influence blood pressure. In addition, the National Heart, Lung and Blood Institute (NHLBI, 1996) recently updated the 1987 Task Force report to develop new blood pressure standards for children 1–17 years of age that are adjusted for height. According to the NHLBI (1996), the upper limits for normal blood pressure (that is, the 90th and 95th percentiles for blood pressure readings) are lower for shorter children than are blood pressure standards based on age and gender alone. In contrast, the upper limites for normal blood pressure are greater for taller children (NHLBI, 1996). Table 21.1 and Table 21.2 contain condensed versions of the standards for boys and girls 6–14 years of age (NHLBI, 1996).

Some children may also demonstrate "tracking" or consistently high blood pressure throughout their school career. It is not known whether the "tracking" pattern

Table 21.1 Blood Pressure Levels for the 90th and 95th Percentiles of Blood Pressure for Boys by Percentages of Height

Age	BP† Percentiles	SYSTOLIC BP (MM HG) BY HEIGHT PERCENTILES*							DIASTOLIC BP (MM HG) BY HEIGHT PERCENTILES*						
		5th	10th	25th	50th	75th	90th	95th	5th	10th	25th	50th	75th	90th	95th
6	90th	105	106	108	110	111	113	114	67	68	69	70	70	71	72
	95th	109	110	112	114	115	117	117	72	72	73	74	75	76	76
7	90th	106	107	109	111	113	114	115	69	70	71	72	72	73	74
	95th	110	111	113	115	116	118	119	74	74	75	76	77	78	78
8	90th	107	108	110	112	114	115	116	71	71	72	73	74	75	75
	95th	111	112	114	116	118	119	120	75	76	76	77	78	79	80
9	90th	109	110	112	113	115	117	117	72	73	73	74	75	76	77
	95th	113	114	116	117	119	120	121	76	77	78	79	80	80	81
10	90th	110	112	113	115	117	118	119	73	74	74	75	76	77	78
	95th	114	115	117	119	121	122	123	77	78	79	80	80	81	82
11	90th	112	113	115	117	119	120	121	74	74	75	76	77	78	78
	95th	116	117	119	121	123	124	125	78	79	79	80	81	82	83
12	90th	115	116	117	119	121	123	123	75	75	76	77	788	78	79
	95th	119	120	121	123	125	126	127	79	79	80	81	82	83	83
13	90th	117	118	120	122	124	125	126	75	76	76	77	78	79	79
	95th	121	122	124	126	128	129	130	79	80	81	82	83	83	84
14	90th	120	121	123	125	126	128	128	76	76	77	78	79	80	80
	95th	124	125	127	128	130	132	132	80	81	81	82	83	84	85

*Height percentile determined by standard growth curves.
†Blood pressure percentile determined by a single measurement.

Adapted from the National High Blood Pressure Education Program—Courtesy of the National Heart, Lung and Blood Institute (NHLBI, 1996).

Table 21.2 Blood Pressure Levels for the 90th and 95th Percentiles of Blood Pressure for Girls by Percentages of Height

Age	BP[†] Percentiles	SYSTOLIC BP (MM HG) BY HEIGHT PERCENTILES*							DIASTOLIC BP (MM HG) BY HEIGHT PERCENTILES*						
		5th	10th	25th	50th	75th	90th	95th	5th	10th	25th	50th	75th	90th	95th
6	90th	104	105	106	107	109	110	111	67	67	68	69	69	70	71
	95th	108	109	110	111	112	114	114	71	71	72	73	73	74	75
7	90th	106	107	108	109	110	112	112	69	69	69	70	71	72	72
	95th	110	110	112	113	114	115	116	73	73	73	74	75	76	76
8	90th	108	109	110	111	112	113	114	70	70	71	71	72	73	74
	95th	112	112	113	115	116	117	118	74	74	75	75	76	77	78
9	90th	100	110	112	113	114	115	116	71	72	72	73	74	74	75
	95th	114	114	115	117	118	119	120	75	76	76	77	78	78	79
10	90th	112	112	114	115	116	117	118	73	73	73	74	75	76	76
	95th	116	116	117	119	120	121	122	77	77	77	78	79	80	80
11	90th	114	114	116	117	118	119	120	74	74	75	75	76	77	77
	95th	118	118	119	121	122	123	124	78	78	79	79	80	81	81
12	90th	116	116	118	119	120	121	122	75	75	75	76	77	78	78
	95th	119	120	121	123	125	126	127	79	79	80	81	82	83	83
13	90th	118	118	119	121	122	123	124	76	76	77	78	78	79	80
	95th	121	122	123	125	126	127	128	80	80	81	82	82	83	84
14	90th	1119	120	121	122	124	125	126	77	77	78	79	79	80	81
	95th	123	124	125	126	128	129	130	81	81	82	83	83	84	85

*Height percentile determined by standard growth curves.
†Blood pressure percentile determined by a single measurement.

Adapted from the National High Blood Pressure Education Program—Courtesy of the National Heart, Lung and Blood Institute (NHLBI, 1996).

will continue into adulthood or whether that value at or above the 95th percentile is predictive of future problems. More research is needed to determine specific levels of blood pressure in children, because values for adolescents may vary. Although information is needed on hypertension in children and a blood pressure examination is recommended, it is necessary to be aware that blood pressure varies and not wrongly classify children as hypertensive and thus subject them to needless medical treatment.

The Task Force recommended that children who exhibit sustained elevations in blood pressure be evaluated in the following areas before classifying them as hypertensive: (1) family history; (2) blood pressure of parents and siblings; (3) medical history citing complications or symptoms such as headaches, nosebleeds, dizziness, blurred vision; and (4) a physical examination. After the diagnosis of hypertension is confirmed, steps can be implemented to circumvent the potentially dangerous effects of hypertension. Lieberman (1978) has recommended counseling children and families concerning weight reduction, avoidance of salt, eliminating stress, not smoking, and participating in a physical activity program as essential for treating school-aged children with hypertension.

Monitoring Blood Pressure

Blood pressure may be monitored with a pressure cuff placed around the biceps of the arms. Pressure is applied to the brachial artery until the pressure inside the cuff approximates the blood pressure. Then the pressure on the arm is released, allowing the blood to flow. Measurements of the systolic and diastolic pressure are made by auscultation with a stethoscope (Figure 21.2). The more difficult it is for the blood to flow through the body, the higher the values that will be recorded.

Blood pressure is recorded in two numbers (e.g., 140/90). The upper pressure, or the systolic blood pressure, is the force generated within the arteries during contraction of the heart. When the heart fills with blood, it contracts, pushing the blood through the arteries; the systolic blood pressure is represented as the force exerted against the arteries by the blood as it is pumped through the vessels (Figure 21.3). The lower number, or diastolic blood pressure, is the pressure that occurs after contrac-

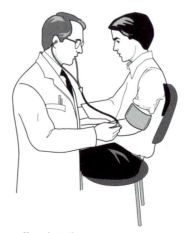

Figure 21.2 Blood pressure cuff and stethoscope.

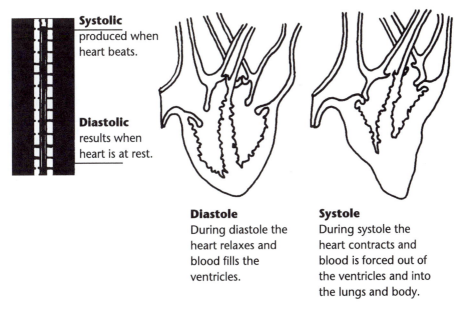

Systolic
produced when
heart beats.

Diastolic
results when
heart is at rest.

Diastole
During diastole the
heart relaxes and
blood fills the
ventricles.

Systole
During systole the
heart contracts and
blood is forced out of
the ventricles and into
the lungs and body.

Figure 21.3 Diastole and systole.

tion, when the heart is recovering and is beginning to refill before the next contraction (Boyer & Burns, 1984; NHLBI, 1999).

An elevated diastolic reading should be more cause for concern because the heart is between contractions and should be in a relaxed state. Consistently high diastolic readings may be indicative of serious heart disease, such as a narrowing, or constriction, of the arteries. Readings for a normal blood pressure are usually 120/80, with 140/90 considered an elevated reading in adults. However, blood pressure continuously rises from birth to adolescence and after age 14 may be higher in males than in females.

The difficulty is to determine normal limits of blood pressure in children. The Task Force on Blood Pressure Control in Children (1987) considered blood pressure exceeding two standard deviations above the mean by age group as indicative of hypertension. By these older standards, the upper limits for blood pressure in boys 9 years old were approximately 121/81, and 140/89 for boys 15 years old. Persistent supine readings of above the 95th percentile for systolic or diastolic pressure were used to define school-aged hypertension, with readings between the 90th and 95th percentiles considered high-normal (NHLBI, 1996). Although various values are used in determining blood pressure in children, it is now recommended that blood pressure values be compared to the percentile indicated not only by age and gender but also by height (NHLBI, 1996). Consistent readings at the 95th percentile are cause for further examination and possible treatment of the problem.

Planning the Physical Activity Program

The identification of cardiovascular problems and hypertension should focus on educating parents and children concerning the effects of the disorder. Teachers, either at a parent education meeting or with appropriate medical personnel, can discuss blood pressure, its fluctuations, complications, readings, and possible abnormalities in the heart. Several materials are available from the American Heart Association (AHA) that can be used in this education program, such as *Abnormal Heart Rhythms: What Parents Should Know, Congenital Heart Disease; Physiological and Functional Heart Mummers,* and *Children and Heart Defects.* Another source of educational material is the American Alliance for Health, Physical Education, Recreation and Dance, which offers *Heart Power* (a school program from preschool to grade 8), *Jump Rope for Heart, Hoops for Heart,* and *Heart Partners.* In addition, most physicians recognize the benefits of physical activity and adhere to the AHA (1999) guidelines, which cite physical inactivity as a risk factor for coronary artery disease, obesity, high blood pressure, and cholesterol. The AHA (1999) scientific position statement includes the following guidelines:

- regular walking, bicycling and outdoor play; use of playground and social interaction
- spending less than 2 hours per day watching television
- weekly participation in games and sports
- daily physical education of at least 20 minutes
- access to community facilities and schools to promote activity
- extracurricular activities in schools and communities
- regular family participation in physical activity
- active role modeling by parents, teachers, and physicians

To develop a program for individuals with cardiovascular problems, the teacher should, at the least, be able to identify and provide education in specific factors that contribute to the abnormality. To effectively plan and implement an appropriate program for children, the educator should also consider the effects of weight reduction, sodium intake, the kidneys, potassium and magnesium intake, medication, and exercise.

Weight Reduction

Obesity, especially in individuals who are more than 20 pounds over the ideal body weight and who possess a high percentage of body fat, is a major cardiovascular risk factor. Decreasing the amount of body fat not only is important in itself, but also usually entails other behaviors that help reduce cardiovascular risk factors: reducing fat, sodium, and total calorie intake in the diet, and increasing physical activity.

Dietary guidelines recommended by the National Heart Lung and Blood Institute (1999) to be used for weight reduction include the following:

1. Eat a nutritionally sound diet encompassing all food groups.
2. Base caloric intake on growth rate, activity level, and percentage of body fat.
3. Keep total fat intake to approximately 30% of calories: 10% or less from saturated fat, 10% from monosaturated fat, and less than 10% from polyunsaturated fat. Emphasize reducing total fat and saturated fat.
4. Keep daily cholesterol intake to approximately 100 milligrams of cholesterol per 1,000 calories, not to exceed 300 milligrams (to allow for differences in caloric intake per age group).

5. Eat protein from a variety of sources, keeping total protein intake to about 15% of all calories.

6. Consume carbohydrates from complex carbohydrate sources that are high in starch and fiber and provide necessary vitamins and minerals. Carbohydrate intake should total about 55% of caloric intake.

7. Limit consumption of foods with excessive amounts of salt, especially processed meats and condiments with a high sodium content.

8. Limit serving sizes, and increase physical activity.

Sodium

Sodium intake for Americans is ten times the needed daily requirement. The reason for restricting sodium is to reduce the excess fluid in the vascular system, which contributes to high blood pressure. An individual's capacity to excrete salt, rather than the amount of salt he or she consumes, is what contributes to hypertension (Morgan, 1983). This is demonstrated in older individuals, in whom impaired excretion of salt is often accompanied by a decrease in kidney function and, in turn, by hypertension.

The Kidneys

Some children may have a genetic sensitivity to salt and be unable to handle salt effectively. The retention of salt leads to increased fluid and pressure as well as an increase in the volume of blood flowing through the vascular system (Boyer & Burns, 1984). When excess fluid is eliminated, blood pressure is lowered because of improved runoff of the blood from the smaller vessels to the tissues.

Table salt is 40% sodium. Salt intake should be limited to 5 grams per day, or 2 grams of sodium per day. Canned foods, baby formula, pretzels, pickles, bacon, and any other foods that contain a large amount of sodium should be avoided. Loggie (1977) has also indicated that many dairy products and processed foods contain sodium. Because many parents and children may be unaware of the sodium content of foods, they must be taught how to restrict salt intake. Students who are salt sensitive and accustomed to eating foods high in salt must eliminate these foods gradually, which will necessitate a change in individual and family eating habits.

Potassium and Magnesium

A deficiency in potassium may also contribute to hypertension, whereas high intake of potassium may counteract the effects of high blood pressure and aid the kidneys in excreting sodium (Londe, 1983). In addition, an increased potassium intake may also protect against the onset of hypertension. Foods with a high content of potassium include fat-free milk, bananas, apricots, grapefruit, orange juice, carrots, cauliflower, corn, oranges, brussels sprouts, potatoes, mushrooms, and spinach.

Magnesium may also contribute to the control of high blood pressure by regulating heartbeat as well as helping the muscles of the arteries relax and contract. The correct magnesium intake may be met by a well-balanced diet including almonds, beans, peanuts, walnuts, whole-rye flour, whole-wheat flour, oats, bran, rice, and lentils.

Medication

Medication can also be effective in controlling hypertension but should be used only for severe cases. Most authorities contend that medication is dispensed too easily, especially in students with borderline hypertension (Boyer & Burns, 1984; Jesse, 1982). Because hypertension is a physical symptom of a possible serious future disease, physicians must balance the risks of medication and any possible side effects against mild elevations of blood pressure, which may be effectively reduced by dietary or exercise prescriptions implemented early in the treatment phase.

Lieberman (1974) recommended medication if the condition is severe or resistant to other preventive measures, with a periodic evaluation of the effectiveness of these prescribed drugs. Common medications include diuretics, such as cholorothiazide, hydrochlorothiazide, and furosemide; vasodilators, such as hydralazine; and agents that affect the actions of the autonomic nervous system, such as methyldopa and propranolol. The teacher should be aware of the potential side effects of medication on the exercising child. Gordon (1997) indicated that Beta blockers and calcium antagonists (diltiazem and verapamil) will decrease heart rate to both submaximal and maximal exercise, while dihydropyridine-derivative calcium antagonists and direct vasodilators may increase heart rate responses to submaximal exercise. Further, anti-hypertensive medications may predispose the exercising child to postexercise hypotension (Gordon, 1997).

Exercise

Often overlooked by the medical community is the value of physical activity in controlling hypertension. The American Heart Association (AHA, 1999) supports physical activity as a means of increasing overall physical fitness and lowering the risk factors of coronary artery disease. Gilliam, MacConnie, Geenen, Pels & Freedson (1982) also advocate exercise as means of controlling coronary heart disease, while Gordon (1997) recommends exercise as a primary factor in lowering blood pressure.

Choquette and Ferguson (1973) have further indicated that physical activity is essential in lowering diastolic blood pressure, and Jesse (1982) has recommended regular physical activity for children, emphasizing dynamic exercises such as cycling, jogging, and competitive sports as opposed to isometric or static exercises. Bar-Or (1983) has also advocated endurance-type conditioning activities to improve resting blood pressure values and overall physical functioning. In addition, McMahon and Palmer (1985) have indicated that aerobic conditioning may decrease resting peripheral resistance, submaximal systolic arterial pressure, heart rate, and pulmonary functions.

The Task Force on Blood Pressure Control in Children (1987) has recommended intense exertion in adolescents with hypertension for improving cardiovascular fitness, suggesting such activities as swimming, running, baseball, and basketball, as opposed to static exercises such as isometrics and weight training. More recently, the American Heart Association (1999) has endorsed exercise to overcome heart disease and has implemented *Jump Rope for Heart* and other programs designed to enhance cardiovascular conditioning in the school. The AHA also has provided funding for the state heart associations and the American Alliance for Health, Physical Education, Recreation and Dance to implement and expand this program to encourage all children to participate (American Heart Association, 1999).

Implementing the Physical Activity Program

Physical activity programs that address cardiac impairments or hypertension should be implemented for children recovering from temporary defects, rheumatic heart disease, and hypertension who may be participating in regular physical education classes. Most medical and support personnel agree that eliminating an individual from participation will be more harmful than helpful. Specific tolerance for activity is based on the child's functional ability and desire to participate. For example, at the University of Georgia, a member of the golf team originally learned golf to remain active after extensive heart surgery as a child. From his initial participation to promote activity, he developed his skill sufficiently to compete in college, along with enhancing his physical functioning.

Initially, when children return to school after rheumatic fever, they may be limited in their activity levels. Most children, after a three-month recuperation period, should gradually increase their participation in fitness activities and avoid contact sports, activities requiring maximal effort, or isometric activities. If valvular involvement is present, exercise may be contraindicated, and the physical activities should not focus on cardiovascular conditioning but on increasing tolerance for lifetime sports. Examples of these activities include leisurely hikes, golf, stationary cycling, and archery.

Teachers must use their professional judgment and work closely with physicians and appropriate school personnel in recommending guidelines for cardiac patients. Activities should be based on the AHA (1999) guidelines and include activities with mild, moderate, and marked restrictions. These activities should be used as guidelines for the teacher and be implemented in conjunction with the recommendation of the educational programming team.

Mild Restrictions

Most individuals with mild restrictions will have little, if any, activity limitations. Activities appropriate for children with mild restrictions include: swimming, aerobics, jogging, softball, cycling, walking, dance, and stationary cycling. Competitive sports may be included unless the atmosphere is highly competitive. However, isometric-type activities and activities involving maximal effort should be avoided.

Moderate Restrictions

Activities can be adapted for children with moderate restrictions by eliminating competition, reducing boundaries or height (e.g., lowering a volleyball net), or focusing on relaxation and progressive reconditioning activities, such as golf, bowling, volleyball, archery, walking, stationary cycling, flexibility exercises, relaxation exercises, table tennis, lead-up games, aerobic dance, and social dance.

Severe Restrictions

For children who are just returning to school and need severe restrictions, the teacher should include activities that involve a low expenditure of energy and that increase tolerance to activity. These activities include leisurely hikes, walking, bicycling, shuffleboard, archery, bowling, horseshoes, social dancing, and fly casting.

Graded Exercise Program

A graded exercise program should be based on the tolerance of an individual for physical activity. By gradually increasing the workload on the heart, physicians can determine the heart's functional capacity and reaction to work by the number of beats per minute.

To determine functionally the energy cost of an activity, METS, or metabolic equivalents, can be used. One MET is equivalent to the resting oxygen consumption per kilogram of body weight and can be used to measure the intensity of the activity. Most activities have a determined MET value and will allow teachers and physicians to control the intensity of the activity program. For example, individuals who are limited to a MET energy cost of 7 would participate in walking, social dancing, and other recreational activities below the intensity of 7 METS. This will then allow teachers and physicians to set a target heart rate and control the intensity of the program while providing for safe and active participation.

It is also critical to specify the duration and frequency of the activity. Most children will have little or no exercise restrictions. For exercise to be beneficial, it is recommended that it be conducted three times weekly for 15 to 20 minutes under the guidance of appropriate medical personnel (Gilliam et al., 1982; Pollock, 1979). In this manner children can participate safely, and the amount of future activity can be determined within a medical margin of safety.

Participation may be guided by several other factors that will be useful for teachers in implementing the program, including the following:

1. Develop diversified program by seeking input from the collaborative programming team, including parents, children, physical educators, and appropriate medical personnel. Base the program goals on the child's functional level and interest.

2. Implement relaxation exercises as a warm-up and cool-down after every activity session.

3. Examine children periodically for stress by checking pulse rate or blood pressure before or after exercise to determine tolerance and adaptability to activity.

4. Encourage children to follow an appropriate weight control and dietary program (eliminating salt, reducing caloric intake, and encouraging potassium intake).

5. Be aware that if adverse environmental factors, such as cold, heat, improper ventilation, humidity, or smog, are present, activities may need to be modified or decreased.

6. Reduce strain on the cardiovascular system by eliminating isometric exercises and teaching appropriate breathing techniques, such as exhaling in the effort phase of weight lifting or swimming.

7. Alternate periods of rest and activity, starting with a low number of repetitions and short time periods and gradually increasing the duration of the activity.

8. Avoid competitive or stressful situations by using relaxation or stress-reduction techniques.

9. If children have just returned to school, have them perform exercises in a back-lying position; have them gradually change positions to allow the cardiovascular system to adjust to a new position.

CHAPTER SUMMARY

1. Cardiovascular disorders are categorized as congenital or acquired. Congenital heart problems develop at birth, and the causes are generally unknown. Acquired heart problems include rheumatic heart disease, heart murmurs, arrhythmias, and hypertension.

2. Appropriate physical and motor fitness activities should be an integral part of the physical education program, as should appropriate nutrition and exercise habits. These program goals are to be developed with input from the educational programming team.

3. Rheumatic heart disease results from rheumatic fever. Damage to the heart occurs from inflammation, causing scarring to the heart.

4. Heart murmurs and arrhythmias are common disorders in the school-aged population. A child's participation in physical education should be determined in consultation with a cardiologist.

5. Hypertension, or high blood pressure, is increasing among school-aged children. Other health problems are associated with hypertension, and children should be monitored regularly.

6. Physicians often recommend regular monitoring, a detailed medical history, decreased salt intake, weight reduction, medication, and increased exercise for the management of hypertension.

7. Specific recommendations and activities that are appropriate for the implementation of an activity program should be based on a graded response to the student's tolerance for activity. The frequency, intensity, and duration of activities are of particular importance in designing and implementing an appropriate physical education program for the child with cardiovascular problems.

REFERENCES

American Heart Association. (1999). *Exercise (physical activity) and children: Health facts.* Dallas, TX: Author.

Bar-Or, O. (1983). *Pediatric sports medicine for the practitioner.* New York: Springer-Verlag.

Berenson, G. S. (1983). Racial differences in hypertension. In S. Blumenthal (Ed.), *Hypertension: Prevention, diet, and treatment in infancy and childhood symposium proceedings,* New York: Biomedical Information Corporation.

Boyer, J., & Burns, B. (1984, May). Eating away at hypertension. *Runner's World,* 77–82.

Gilliam, T. B., MacConnie, S. E., Geenen, D. L., Pels, A. E., & Freedson, P. S. (1982). Exercise programs for children: A way to prevent heart disease. *The Physician and Sports Medicine, 10,* 96–108.

Gordon, N. F. (1997). Hypertension In *ACSM's exercise management for chronic diseases and disabilities.* Champaign, IL: Human Kinetics.

Hohn, A.R., Dwyer, K.M., & Dwyer, J.H. (1994). Blood pressure in youth from four ethnic groups: the Pasadena Prevention Project. *Journal of Pediatrics, 125,* 368–373.

Jesse, M. J. (1982). Essential hypertension in children. *Hospital Practice, 11,* 81–88.

Langford, H. G. (1983). The role of sodium in hypertension. In S. Blumenthal (Ed.), *Hypertension: Prevention, diet, and treatment in infancy and childhood symposium proceedings*, New York: Biomedical Information Corporation.

Levin, S. E. (1983). Significance of hypertension in children. *Clinical Cardiology, 6*, 373–376.

Lieberman, E. (1974). Essential hypertension in children and youth: A pediatric perspective. *Journal of Pediatrics, 85*, 1–11.

Lieberman, E. (1978). Hypertension in childhood and adolescence. *Clinical Symposia, 30*, 1–43.

Loggie, J. (1975). Hypertension in children and adolescents. *Hospital Practice, 6*, 81–92.

Loggie, J. (1977). Systemic hypertension. In A. J. Moss, F. H. Adams, & C. C. Emmanouilides (Eds.), *Heart disease in infants, children and adolescents.* Baltimore: Williams and Wilkins.

Loggie, J. (1992). *Pediatric Hypertension.* Boston: Blackwell Scientific Publications.

Loggie, J., Horan, M. J., Hohn, A. R., Gruskin, A. B., Dunbar, J. B., & Havlik, R. J. (1984). Juvenile hypertension: Highlights of a workshop. *Journal of Pediatrics, 104*, 657–663.

Londe, S. (1983). Epidemiology of essential hypertension in children. In S. Blumenthal (Ed.), *Hypertension: Prevention, diet, and treatment in infancy and childhood symposium proceedings.* New York: Biomedical Information Corporation.

McCrory, W. W. (1982). What should blood pressure be in healthy children? *Pediatrics, 70*, 143–145.

McMahon, M., & Palmer, R. M. (1985). Exercise and hypertension. *Medical Clinics of North America, 69*, 57–70.

Mitchell, S. C., Blount, S. G., Blumenthal, S., et al. (1975). The pediatrician and hypertension. *Pediatrics, 56*, 3–5.

Morgan, B. (1983). Sodium intake and hypertension in the population. In S. Blumenthal (Ed.), *Hypertension: Prevention, diet, and treatment in infancy and childhood symposium proceedings.* New York: Biomedical Information Corporation.

National Heart, Lung and Blood Institute. (1996). *Update on the Task Force (1987) on High Blood Pressure in Children a Adolescents: A working group report from the National High Blood Pressure Education Program.* Bethesda, MD: National Institute of Health.

National Heart, Lung and Blood Institute (1999). *How to prevent high blood pressure: Cardiovascular information for the general public.* Bethesda, MD: Author.

Pollock, M. L. (1979). How much exercise is enough? In D. Cunliff. (Ed.), *Implementation of aerobic programs*, Reston, VA: American Alliance for Health, Physical Education, Recreation and Dance.

Shaffer, T. E., & Rose, K. (1974). Cardiac evaluation for participation in school sports. *Journal of American Medical Association, 228*, 398.

Task Force on Blood Pressure Control in Children. (1987). Bethesda, MD: National Institute of Health.

Section VI

Developing and Implementing the Physical Activity Program

Section VI describes the components of a physical education curriculum and provides teaching guidelines and strategies that are consistent with the best practices of teaching physical education.

The reader should be able to apply these guidelines and strategies in writing performance goals and objectives for developing the physical education program. In addition, specific techniques for behavior management are presented as they relate to environmental constructs and initialing or decreasing problem behaviors.

Instructional strategies in this section can be used to help the instructor write appropriate goals and objectives. Additional information from the collaborative programming team can further help to develop and implement a sound developmental physical fitness and motor development program based on the child's functional ability. Other exercises, play activities, games, or sports that are generally included in the physical education classes can also be used to develop the instructional program.

CHAPTER 22

Behavior Management

For learning to occur, the teacher must first manage or control inappropriate behaviors—in special classes as well as in regular physical education classes. Often educators develop their own strategies for managing behavior, which may or may not be appropriate. In physical education classes, teachers sometimes use physical activity or, alternatively, removal from the class or team as a punishment. Teachers should remain aware that not all misbehavior originates with the child. Other factors, such as the environment or actions of teachers, can initiate an inappropriate response. Many teaching strategies to overcome problem behaviors have already been developed. Table 22.1 includes examples of strategies that can be used to facilitate behavior change.

Environment

Behaviors manifested by children may be attributable to problems in the immediate environment. These problems may involve such variables as temperature, humidity, wind, lighting, background, auditory and visual distractions, water temperature, architectural barriers, and the amount of space and time. Because the environment is an antecedent event, occurring before the behavior, it is preventable. By carefully structuring or anticipating consequences of the environment, teachers can prevent many inappropriate behaviors. For example, eliminating excessive equipment that is not needed in the game eliminates distractions and safety hazards. In another example, the referee immediately steps between two basketball players, one who believes she was intentionally fouled and an opposing player. By separating the players, the teacher offers each child the time to regain self-control and avoid fighting or aggressive behaviors. Cowart (2000) has also referred to the activities/skills in the curriculum that may cause problem behaviors. Care should be taken to ensure that the

Table 22.1 Strategies to Improve Behavior

Component	Types of Strategies
Environment	Alteration of the structure of settings, activity, or equipment
Teacher/parent/child interaction	Teacher effectiveness in communicating, positive and assertive approach
Misbehavior of child	Establishment of new behaviors, development and maintenance of appropriate behaviors, decrease in or elimination of inappropriate behaviors

curriculum is age appropriate, and consistent with the child's needs and that the environment is conducive to learning.

The key is that behavior problems due to environmental factors can be prevented. Teachers may structure the environment to eliminate safety hazards or extraneous factors that serve as antecedent events to inappropriate behaviors. In other instances teachers or coaches may serve as intermediaries or buffers to help prevent or eliminate problem behaviors before they occur (Jansma, French & Horvat, 1984).

Interaction Between Teacher or Parent and Child

Another way to prevent problem behavior is to establish communication between teachers or parents and children. At times, teachers or parents may serve as the antecedent for a misbehavior. For example, providing children with a task that is unattainable, such as lifting weights that are too heavy, can lead to failure or criticism and possibly a problem behavior. Instead of ridiculing the child, the teacher or parent should provide lighter weights that are suitable for the child's ability while simultaneously praising accomplishments in order to establish positive interactions. In another example, the teacher can stand in front of a child before calling on the child in class and only when the child raises his hand. The teacher thus eliminates a potentially embarrassing situation by cueing the child that he will be called on and then responding to his raised hand. As a result, it is hoped, the child can answer the question and be confident in his response. In contrast, a teacher who calls on a child who does not know the answer may set the child up for criticism or ridicule from others in the class.

Communication between the teacher or parent and children can also be established by using a "talking bench" or provision for children to voice their concerns. In Figure 22.1 a child is explaining her reasons for pushing and shoving while the teacher serves as monitor. By hearing both sides and recognizing an appropriate solution, teachers or parents may eliminate many problems and establish communication before resorting to punishment or removing children from an activity. Cowart (2000) has also emphasized that teachers should provide effective demonstrations, assistance, and feedback as well as clear directions to facilitate learning. If the instructional strategy is not working, perhaps children do not understand what is expected of them, or, in some situations, the amount of stimulation may be affecting the child's behavior and ability to learn.

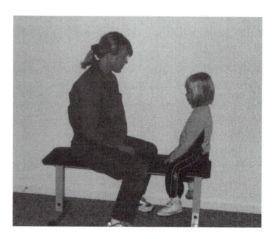

Figure 22.1 Talking bench.

Misbehavior

At times structuring the environment or establishing communication (controlling the antecedents) will not be effective. This may require specific strategies or consequences designed to develop or eliminate problem behaviors. Children who are not attentive in class may require prompting or shaping techniques. Likewise, to increase participation or to overcome fears, teachers may develop a written agreement to help children accomplish specific class goals. Strategies that develop or accelerate appropriate behaviors, as well as techniques that decelerate or eliminate inappropriate behaviors, should be used by teachers and parents to effectively manage genuine problem behaviors.

Accelerating or Developing Appropriate Behaviors

Reinforcement can be either positive or negative. *Positive reinforcement* is a response that is designed to increase or strengthen a desired behavior. For example, a child actively participates in swimming after several sessions of encouragement. The teacher can encourage the child to continue their participation by actively providing social and verbal reinforcement, for example, "You did really well in swimming." In this manner, the teacher is likely to increase and strengthen the participation behavior in swimming.

Teachers and parents also frequently use *social praise* to successfully manage behavior. In physical education, teachers can use pats on the back, gestures such as thumbs-up, a smile, looks of pleasure, or words such as "good job" or "well done," as social praise. Social reinforcers are especially effective if children are aware of why they are being praised. For example, "Ian, I really like the way you share your toys with Kala," will help Ian realize his sharing behavior is being reinforced. In addition, when the teacher is specific, the child is aware of the behavior that is being praised.

The most sophisticated type of positive reinforcement is when the child completes a task or maintains a behavior for the intrinsic feeling of self-satisfaction. For children with disabilities, this is a difficult level to attain. Initially, teachers should provide reinforcement after every response and later fade to an intermittent level to maintain a specific behavior. Ideally, any technique should be directed toward helping children reach a level of behavior in which they complete a task without outside reinforcement.

Tangible reinforcement involves the use of food, objects, and/or activities as reinforcers for performing certain behaviors. For example, children may be allowed to shoot baskets for 5 minutes after class for taking turns during the basketball drills. Teachers can use a variety of objects as reinforcers, such as patches, baseball cards, certificates, or physical activity, such as bouncing on the trampoline or leading a play group.

Some teachers may prefer not to use tangible reinforcement, particularly edibles, to establish appropriate behaviors. However, if a behavior interferes with the learning process, teachers must develop some kind of system to establish the instructional environment. If providing popcorn or a sport drink is appropriate, teachers should consider using whatever is essential for developing appropriate behaviors. As behavior improves, teachers can rely less on edibles and focus more on object or activity reinforcers. The goal of any behavior management program should be to allow children to manage their own behavior, using the natural medium of physical activity and play.

Accelerating or strengthening behaviors may also occur from *negative reinforcement.* Negative reinforcers are stimuli that, when removed or postponed as a consequence of an inappropriate response, result in an increase or maintenance of an appropriate response (Walker & Shea, 1995). For example, requiring children to swim with their faces in the water to avoid repeating a lap across the pool is negative reinforcement. Avoiding the aversive stimulus (having to repeat a lap) will reinforce the appropriate behavior of swimming with one's face in the water (Horvat & Forbus, 1989).

Negative reinforcement should not be confused with punishment. Punishment results in decreasing the frequency of an inappropriate response, whereas negative reinforcement strengthens an appropriate response by motivating children to avoid aversive consequences. Unfortunately, many teachers may misuse negative reinforcement and cause undue tension and anxiety in children.

Prompting is another method of strengthening or developing appropriate behaviors. The use of signals or cues can aid in managing behavior as well as in learning or completing physical tasks. Prompts can involve visual, verbal, or physical guidance. The most natural prompt is a verbal cue for the child to complete or initiate a desired task. A visual cue, such as modeling an appropriate skill, can also be used to prompt a behavior. Finally, physically guiding the child through a movement can provide a cue for a specific position, such as a swimming stroke, or a desired behavior, such as standing in line. As a way of using physical prompting in initial levels of learning, Cowart (1998) described a teacher physically assisting a child executing a leg kick until the child was able to demonstrate some independence.

Most educators would agree that visual and verbal prompts are the least intrusive and most natural prompts, whereas physical guidance should be used only when other prompts are not appropriate. Physical prompts are helpful to provide correct positioning or facilitate an appropriate motion, as in a tennis stroke; holding a child's hand while he or she is walking the balance beam; or placing a hand on a child's back to help stabilize his or her posture. However, teachers or parents should remember to avoid excessive pressure, so that the child will not perceive the physical prompt as punishment.

Nonverbal auditory prompts may also cue children that a consequence will occur if an inappropriate behavior continues. Blowing a whistle or signaling the class may serve as a warning that their behaviors are starting to become inappropriate and need to be controlled before a consequence is implemented. For instance, the teacher can call out a number that the class recognizes as a stimulus to modify their appropriate behavior. A verbal prompt can also cue children to initiate an appropriate response, such as entering the pool without assistance.

Teachers may also use visual stimuli such as posters, to serve as reminders for class rules and prompt the correct behavior. We commonly see the rules for the weight room or swimming pool posted as cues for participation. Other types of visual prompts include circles on the floor, cones, or boundaries, or a picture of one person on the diving board to depict correct usage of the board. Visual prompts have proven especially useful for children with autism, who require concrete visual examples in contrast to verbal instructions to initiate behaviors. Posters of athletes also can provide visual models of desired behaviors, such as staying drug free or remaining in school. For children with disabilities, the success of athletes in racing wheelchairs or skiing can provide role models and encourage active participation in physical activity.

Schedules of Reinforcement

Learning also depends on the different methods of scheduling reinforcement. The two methods to reinforce behavior are the continuous (immediate) method and the intermittent (delayed) method (Walker & Shea, 1995). If the pattern of reinforcement involves one reinforcement for every behavior, the pattern is a continuous one. Continuous patterns generally produce a high rate of appropriate behaviors but are difficult to implement because praising or rewarding children after every response is often impractical. By extending the pattern to one-to-two or greater, the teacher employs an intermittent reinforcement pattern, promoting a high response rate that is more easily maintained when reinforcement is removed and is easier for teachers to implement. For example, children can initially be rewarded every time they perform appropriately, then, gradually, every two or three times to develop an intermittent schedule of reinforcement.

Teachers should also be aware of the time between the response and the consequence. Many children can delay the need for reinforcement over long periods of time, for example, in trying to obtain first place in a fitness test. Children may not receive reinforcement for several weeks while conditioning themselves for the test; once the test is performed, recognition is finally given in the form of a patch or certificate.

Although most children can function with delayed or intermittent reinforcement, others, because of the severity of their condition or existence of problem behaviors, need more immediate reinforcement to change a behavior. Any delay between the response and reward will diminish the probability that the inappropriate behavior will occur or be maintained. Immediate reinforcement is more effective when teachers are developing a new behavior, because children can easily be motivated to emit a specific response (behavior) that is being reinforced frequently. However, teachers should strive to eventually use intermittent reinforcement in order to sustain the behavior and to approximate more closely the conditions needed for effective instruction. Likewise, by the increasing the reward lag time, teachers can gradually switch to delayed or intermittent reinforcement, which more closely approximates real-world conditions.

Techniques to Decelerate or Eliminate Inappropriate Behaviors

There are also techniques that can be used to decelerate, weaken, or eliminate inappropriate behaviors. These include punishment, time-out, and extinction. Punishment involves either the direct presentation of an aversive stimulus or nonpresentation or withdrawing of positive reinforcement. Some educators point out that punishment, by itself, will not teach the desired behavior (Daniels, 1998). Punishment should not be used alone but in conjunction with more positive approaches or paired with more positive approaches. Although effective in decreasing inappropriate behaviors, punishment should not be used until more positive approaches have been systematically tried or until a dangerous situation occurs that warrants immediate action (Coleman, 1986). Common examples of punishment techniques may include the following:

1. *Angry expression.* An angry expression or look without a verbalization can be effec-

tive in cueing a child to behave. Because the stare or angry expression is unemotional and brief, other children may not be aware that the child is being punished.

2. *Reprimands.* A reprimand is a brief and unemotional verbalization that is directed privately to the child and should address the inappropriate behavior without embarrassing the child.

3. *Response cost.* Rewards that have been earned can be withdrawn or lost if children demonstrate inappropriate behaviors. For example, arguing during a game may result in losing free time or losing use of a video game.

4. *Overcorrection.* A physical prompt to gently turn a child's chin or position in line may help the child establish a proper behavior. The teacher should take care not to exert excessive pressure but calmly aid the child correct the behavior.

Time-out (TO) can also be used to decelerate or eliminate a behavior. In time-out, children are withdrawn from the situation that is causing the inappropriate behavior. By placing children in a nonreinforcing or neutral environment, the teacher can help decrease or even eliminate the behavior. Because time-out is temporary and is used before more dramatic measures, children may self-correct or eliminate the behavior.

Many times teachers use time-out inappropriately by eliminating the opportunity for positive reinforcement. If the approach or situation is not a neutral environment, then time-out does not occur, and teachers have turned the situation into a punishment by eliminating the opportunity for reinforcement and making the situation aversive. Because time-out can be used successfully to encourage active participation, teachers should be sensitive to the proper application of this technique.

A mild application of time-out is simply to ignore all behaviors for a short period or until an appropriate response is evident, resulting in a temporary social (not physical) removal from a negatively reinforcing situation. This approach, too, is temporary, and children may self-correct before more dramatic measures are taken. Lavay, French, & Henderson (1997) have also referred to this technique as observational time-out, in which the child watches others but cannot actively participate.

Relegating children to a corner in the activity area, a technique known as contingent observation, is slightly more aversive and places them outside the activity but within sight of the group activity. Children may also be removed completely from the instructional setting. In both situations, inappropriate behavior is not reinforced because the children are not actively participating and because they are in a neutral environment. Lavay et al. (1997) have also referred to exclusion time-out and seclusion time-out as other ways to use this technique.

Other Techniques

There are several other techniques that can be used by physical educators to accelerate or decelerate a behavior. Four of these are token systems, contracting, group contingencies, and the Premack principle (French, Henderson & Horvat, 1992; Lavay et al., 1997).

Rushall and Siedentop (1972) have suggested that a point or token system is appropriate in physical education classes for recording appropriate behaviors. In this system, a point is allocated or subtracted for each behavior. The teacher uses check marks, stars, happy faces, or stickers to represent points. We commonly see football helmets adorned with stickers for appropriate performance among many college football teams. Whatever the form of token chosen, it should require a minimal amount of effort to record and be valuable to the child.

Data collection on a tally of points is important for teachers. If behaviors are not recorded, teachers will not be able to determine progress. By using tally sheets, data can be generated on specific behaviors to determine the effectiveness of the intervention. If behaviors are not being learned, an immediate change in the targeted behavior, specific consequences of the behavior, and/or environmental features should be evaluated to determine the effectiveness of the behavior change strategy (O'Neill, Horner, Albin, Storey & Sprague, 1990).

Depending on the rate of rewards, a variety of tally sheets is available. For instance, if reinforcement occurs every 10 minutes or fewer, children can use an index card and give it to teachers during the reinforcement period. At times, the teacher may use specific procedures for recording points that eliminate any temptation to add extra points or checks that were not earned. Responsible children can self-record their own progress and require only intermittent monitoring by teachers. This procedure was used effectively in increasing the running duration of children with mental retardation (Deener & Horvat, 1995).

When the time period is longer, teachers can employ individual or group tally sheets to provide reinforcement. These sheets are designed to give points (tokens) after children participate in specific activities, after engaging in target behavior during a total class period, or after emitting a target behavior over a longer period of time (e.g., day or week). A system can be utilized with these long-term tally sheets in which either an earned check (or other symbol) is recorded, or a cumulative number of earned points are placed under each heading.

Group tally sheets (Figure 22.2) can also be developed for squads to earn points for developing new behaviors or eliminating unwanted behaviors. A group program must be designed to allow everyone a chance of winning, the competition being focused within groups and not between groups. In this manner children may remain motivated to complete the task and earn reinforcement.

When the child is able to monitor his or her own progress, that benchmark is the most natural and highest form of positive reinforcement. Teachers should strive for children to self-manage their behavior so that teachers can become actively involved in teaching rather than behavior management.

Teachers can also use a written agreement with children to designate what each person is going to accomplish for a specific time period. These agreements may be developed by the parent or teacher alone or in concert with their child or other members of the family. These agreements may be specific to decelerate a behavior or to develop an understanding of what is expected for the child to receive rewards. The hope is that the written agreement will encourage children to attain their goals and assume responsibility for their own behaviors.

Some techniques may also involve using other children or peers to manage behavior. In physical education, children are often grouped in teams, whose members may exert pressure on other children in order to achieve a group reward. This approach has been used successfully in classroom settings and in certain instances was superior to individual reinforcement in managing behaviors. Vogler and French (1983) used group consequences in a game setting to strengthen appropriate behav-

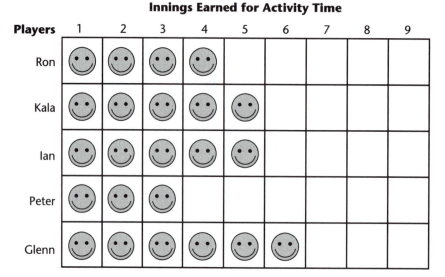

Figure 22.2 Sample tally sheet.

iors. With this approach it is hoped that children will work together to eliminate problem behaviors, such as ignoring the rules of the game or aggressive behavior.

Physical activity also has the potential to be a very powerful reinforcer. If children enjoy playing basketball, and teachers are interested in teaching alternating turns during basketball drills, then allowing the children to play basketball can be made contingent upon their doing the drills appropriately. This is an illustration of the Premack principle, often referred to as "Grandma's rule": Eat your vegetables before dessert. Target behaviors are reinforced by the opportunity to engage in other behaviors: "Practice your stroke, then you can jump off the diving board." Any behavior that children enjoy can serve as a positive reinforcer.

This principle, obviously, has natural applications in the field of physical education. The Premack Principle is activity based, so by offering activities that are enjoyable, teachers can reinforce positive behavior in children by allowing them to participate in such activities only if they also perform less enjoyable activities. Table 22.2 includes some traditionally low- and high-enjoyment activities that are commonly used in physical education.

Table 22.2 Low- and High-Enjoyment Activities

Low Enjoyment	High Enjoyment
Cardiovascular fitness	Five minutes shooting basketball
Drills	Game-related activity
Being dressed and on time	Participating first in an activity
Warm-up exercises	Selection of activity
Exercises	Using parachute
Swim laps	Diving

Behavior Intervention Strategies

When developing physical education programs for children with behavior disorders, teachers should be cognizant of all aspects of the environment, teacher-child communication, and specific behavior management techniques. Teachers need to use a variety of strategies that are appropriate for their situation and ensure that these strategies are developmentally appropriate for children in their classroom (Horvat, 1990). Table 22.3 provides a summary of behavior management strategies.

Table 22.3 Behavior Management Strategies

Behavior	Instructional Strategies
Curriculum strategy	Ensure curriculum is age appropriate and conducive to the needs of the child. Consider the size and composition of the group as well as equipment needs. Structure tasks for children to achieve success; use stations and peers to facilitate task completion. If inappropriate behavior occurs, redirect and restructure curriculum or teaching strategy to meet the needs of children. *Praise* appropriate behavior, and *ignore* inappropriate behaviors.
Lack of understanding	Ensure that tasks move toward achievement at the child's level of functioning. If the task is too difficult, use part-whole method to ensure task completion. Emphasize prerequisite skills and abilities needed to acquire concepts and reinforce understanding. Use *interest boosting* on particular topics, and use *active* assistance to overcome hurdles.
Biochemical factors	Clarify the underlying courses of the behavior that may result from medication, nutrition, or neurological dysfunction to determine causes of behavior. Use nonverbal techniques, such as *signal interference, prompts* or *cues* to initiate behavior. Temporary removal from the setting or proximity to another child may be used along with *relaxation* activities.
Environmental factors	Remove *distractions* not related to the teaching situation such as extra equipment, noise-makers and/or visual stimuli. Develop a daily schedule, and structure the class routine, especially in the beginning stages of the learning experience.
Feedback	Provide *feedback* that is specific to teaching and understanding the task as well as the demonstrated behavior. Use positive *verbalization,* such as "good job," "well done," "keep working"; *physical expressions,* such as "thumbs-up" or "high fives"; *proximity control,* such as interacting with the class and walking close to all children; and *incentives,* such as naming designated helpers and group leaders or providing free time and activity reinforcers.
Learning ecology	Consistently assess teaching strategies, prompts, and reinforcement techniques as well as the learning environment. Be aware of teacher behaviors that are verbal or nonverbal, and strive to be an active positive role model. Be consistent and specific with behavior management techniques.
Self-management	Teach children to manage their behavior with task *cards, contracts* or *self-recording.* Encourage social interaction and cooperative activities, and *praise* children for their accomplishments.

CHAPTER SUMMARY

1. For learning to occur, it is essential that inappropriate behaviors be under control. Teachers should develop a repertoire of strategies for managing behavior.

2. Behavior problems may be manifested as a result of environmental situations or in response to actions of teachers and other children.

3. Reinforcemnt can be either positive or negative. Positive reinforcement is the consequence of a response that will increase or strengthen the desired behavior. Negative reinforcement takes place when children respond in a manner that results in the removal or avoidance of an aversive stimulus.

4. Punishment should not be confused with reinforcement. Punishment is the administration of an aversive consequence, or the withdrawing of positive reinforcement, in order to reduce the probability of recurrence of the behavior.

5. Other techniques that can be used to modify behavior include point or token systems, behavioral contracts, group consequences, and the Premack principle.

6. When developing a physical education program, teachers should be aware of the effects of the environment, teacher-child communicatioon, and the various behavior management techniques.

7. Some children with behavior problems may possess a hifgh degree of physical and motor fitness; therefore, the teaching strategy may be more important than the activity.

8. Activities should be age appropriate, and vigorous activities can be provided with the teacher serving as an active role model. Activities should also be selected to emphasize control and to incorporate relaxation training methods. In this way children can act out specific circumstances that may be the cause of their problem behavior.

9. Behavior may be influenced by a variety of factors including the curriculum, biochemical factors, learning styles, feedback, and the learning ecologies.

REFERENCES

Coleman, M. C. (1986). *Behavior disorders: Theory and practice.* Englewood Cliffs, N.J.: Prentice-Hall.

Cowart, J. (1998). Teaching swim skills to the hard to reach student. *Palaestra, 14,* 32–38.

Cowart, J. (2000). Managing misbehavior in adapted physical education by good teaching practices. *Palaestra, 16,* 40–45.

Daniels, V. I. (1998, March/April). How to manage disruptive behavior in inclusive classrooms. *Teaching Exceptional Children,* 26–30.

Deener, T., & Horvat, M. (1995). Effects of social reinforcement and self-recording on exercise duration in middle school students with moderate intellectual impairments. *Clinical Kinesiology, 49,* 28–33.

French, R., Henderson, H., & Horvat, M. (1992). *Creative approaches to managing student behavior.* Park City, UT: Family Development Resources.

Horvat, M. (1990). *Physical education and sports for exceptional students* (Student Workbook). Dubuque, IA: Wm. C. Brown.

Horvat, M. A., & Forbus, W. R. (1989). Using the Adequate Environment for Teaching Handicapped Children (2nd ed). Kearney, NE: Educational Systems Associates.

Jansma, P., French, R., & Horvat, M. (1984). Behavioral engineering in physical education. *Journal of Physical Education, Recreation and Dance, 54,* 80–81.

Lavay, B. W., French, R., & Henderson, H. L. (1997). *Positive behavior management strategies for physical educators.* Champaign, IL: Human Kinetics.

O'Neill, R., Horner, R. H., Albin, R. W., Storey, K., & Sprague, J. R. (1990). *Functional analysis of problem behavior.* Sycamore, IL: Sycamore Publishing Company.

Rushall, B. S., & Siedentop, D. (1972). *The development and control of behavior and sport in physical education.* Philadelphia, PA: Lea and Febiger.

Vogler, E. W., & French, R. (1983). The effects of a group contingency strategy in behaviorally disordered students in physical education. *Research Quarterly for Exercise and Sport, 54,* 273–277.

Walker, J. E., & Shea, T. M. (1995). *Behavior management: A practical approach for educators* (6th ed.). New York: MacMilian.

CHAPTER 23

Teaching Physical Fitness

The efficiency of the heart and lungs constitutes cardiorespiratory endurance and is a primary and/or essential component of physical fitness. Cardiorespiratory endurance is generally achieved by exercising large muscle groups through aerobic activities such as walking, jogging, cycling, dance, or swimming. In addition to promoting cardiorespiratory endurance, aerobic activities may also contribute to developing muscular strength and endurance as well as burning body fat for the maintenance of appropriate body composition.

The ability to move the body through a range of motion and the suppleness of the muscles and joints is termed *flexibility*. This component of fitness is important for children with disabilities to prevent contractures and undue strain on the muscles and joints, as well as to provide the suppleness needed for sport- and movement-specific activities.

The amount of force that a muscle or group of muscles can exert in one maximum effort is termed *muscular strength*, whereas *muscular endurance* is defined as the ability to work against resistance for a prolonged period. The development of muscular strength also aids in reducing body fat and in functional and work- related tasks (Horvat & Croce, 1995).

Improvements in strength are usually made by the use of the overload principle, which states that the body increases in strength by doing more work than it is accustomed to doing. Any strength program should begin with very light resistance and increase resistance as the individual can accommodate it.

A general definition of endurance is the body's ability to sustain effort over a period of time. Endurance is usually classified as muscular or cardiovascular. In order to emphasize muscular endurance, the resistance should be decreased and the number of repetitions increased. A possible way to increase muscular endurance is to modify any task requiring muscular strength by decreasing the resistance in the task and increasing the duration of the task. The individual will be doing more repetitions at a lighter resistance. Developing physical fitness requires a level of exercise of sufficient duration and intensity to ensure improvement in each of these components.

Health-related fitness, which is the primary fitness objective of this book, can be defined as a condition whereby an individual has sufficient energy to avoid fatigue and injury and to enjoy life. It is directly related to the capacity of the heart, lungs, and muscles to function at optimal efficiency. The content area of health-related fitness includes learning experiences related to achieving optimal health and wellness through the components of cardiovascular and muscular endurance, muscular strength, flexibility, and body composition. One must remember that developing appropriate levels of fitness requires a level of exercise of sufficient frequency, duration, and intensity to ensure improvement in each of the components of health-related fitness.

All individuals have the same rights to the health-related benefits of physical activity programs. When you, the teacher, explain the benefits of fitness to children, you must explain the concepts in an age-appropriate way. For school children, this may include the following types of statements. Physical activity will

1. make your heart pump more strongly

2. help lower your blood pressure

3. reduce your risk of diseases

4. strengthen your bones and muscles

5. give you more energy to play and do your schoolwork

6. help you maintain a good body weight

7. help you deal with stress at home, play, and school.

According to *Physical Best Activity Guide* (1999) developed by the American Alliance for Health, Physical Education, Recreation and Dance (AAHPERD), the goal of teaching fitness to children should be to enable them to acquire skills, knowledge, and attitudes that lead to a lifetime of wholesome physical activity. Teaching physical fitness should be viewed as a long-term process of educating children not only about the types of activities required to develop health-related fitness, but also about the importance of regular physical activity in achieving appropriate levels of fitness and functional ability.

Based on the concepts of AAHPERD's *Physical Best Activity Guide*, optimum fitness is best attained through a series of objectives, which lead children from a level of dependence to one of independence. This hierarchical view of achieving fitness involves five steps (AAHPERD, 1999):

1. *Doing regular exercise.* At this stage, the teacher is most concerned that the children have fun and learn to enjoy exercise and physical activity. The main objective here is that children will develop personal habits of performing physical activity regularly, a component that is often deficient in children with disability.

2. *Achieving fitness.* Children will not achieve fitness goals without the motivation necessary to maintain fitness for life. Children must derive an intrinsic enjoyment of physical activity and have fun being active.

3. *Personal exercise patterns.* Children should select activities they personally enjoy performing and make the appropriate decisions regarding those exercise patterns that are best suited for them. At this stage in the hierarchy, the teacher begins to shift the decision-making process to the children, while the teacher becomes a facilitator for encouraging activity for the child and family.

4. *Self-evaluation.* By this stage, we hope that children can begin to appreciate which activities they enjoy most and to establish personal exercise habits. At this stage, children should also be able to make informed decisions regarding their lifetime fitness goals. By developing the ability to perform self-evaluations of their fitness programs, they essentially become able to revise their fitness goals and adapt their exercise and activity program to accommodate these newly acquired goals.

5. *Problem solving.* At this stage, children should be aware of the benefits of activity to promote fitness, independence, and work-related skills and be aware of various opportunities for participation in the community.

Guidelines for Exercise Programs

Whatever exercise program is employed, one must follow the basic physiological principles of overload and adaptation, progression, and specificity and apply these principles in an exercise program (McArdle, Katch, & Katch, 2000; Wilmore & Costill, 1999). The following guidelines can be used in teaching physical activity in children with disabilities.

Overload and Adaptation Principle

The body's cardiovascular, pulmonary, and muscular systems tend to adapt to exercise by becoming conditioned to meet the demands imposed on them and no more. To push beyond the status quo condition, one must make the systems exercised (e.g., heart, lungs, and muscles) work beyond the routine demands imposed on them. When the child adapts to a new work level, we must increase the load until the child reaches a new, higher working level. The overload (load beyond normal requirements) can be in the form of increased resistance, more repetitions, longer work periods, a higher percentage of VO_2 max, or a greater ROM, depending on program goals. (Figure 23.1 depicts, for example, a way to add resistance in a leg-strengthening exercise). Overload generally refers to doing a greater amount of work or exercise (increased duration), doing the exercise at a greater intensity than one did in prior exercise sessions, or doing the exercise more often (frequency of exercise). Generally speaking, the greater the duration, intensity, and frequency of training, the greater will be the physiological benefits.

Progression Principle

A second major precept for exercise is the progression principle. In spite of the fact that changes in fitness are primarily attributed to the overload and adaptation principle, the child must start with a light workload based on current fitness levels and gradually progress to a heavier or lower workload. This gradual and systematic approach to increasing exercise difficulty avoids exacerbating the condition, minimizes muscle soreness and injuries, and facilitates active participation. The progression principle is based on the need to overload the system being trained on a regular basis to achieve higher levels of functioning. To maintain the appropriate exercise overload, one must increase the amount of work performed (Figure 23.2).

Figure 23.1 Adding resistance to leg strengthening exercises.

Figure 23.2 Progression of leg strengthening.

Specificity of Exercise

A third major precept for exercise is the specificity of exercise principle (Figure 23.3). This principle stipulates that a particular exercise will bring about changes in one component of fitness (e.g., strength) and will have very little, or no, influence on other fitness components (e.g., endurance). Hence, resistance exercises are not designed to improve flexibility, nor is jogging designed to improve arm strength. The teacher must select the most appropriate exercises that not only involve specific areas but also will bring about the desired change. In other words, if one wishes to improve strength, one must perform heavy resistance exercise; if one wants to improve cardiovascular endurance, one must perform activities that involve large muscle groups and that tax the heart and lungs for extended periods of time. Table 23.1 on pages 397–399 provides program development suggestions for teaching fitness to children with disabilities.

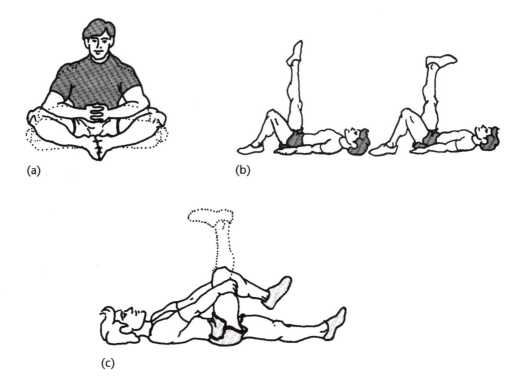

(a)

(b)

(c)

Figure 23.3 Flexibility exercises.

Teaching Strategies

The following teaching strategies should be included in any fitness program for individuals with disabilities:

1. Select the exercises based on the child's tolerance for activity. The exercise program should be stressful enough to induce changes in physical functioning without undue stress, discomfort, or fatigue.

2. Structure the exercise program so that it is progressive in nature; that is, increase the stressfulness of the exercise in small increments to ensure that improvements in functioning will occur.

3. Base the frequency of exercise on the individual's tolerance and functional capacity. Unfit children experience fewer exercise-induced injuries or complications when the frequency of exercise is established at three times per week. The frequency needed for conditioning should be at least three times per week to develop and maintain physical fitness.

4. Vary the duration of exercise according to the individual's level of functioning and type of fitness activity. For cardiorespiratory conditioning, the duration of exercise should be between 20 and 30 minutes to develop and maintain functioning. For other components of physical fitness, such as flexibility, the duration of activity may depend on the number of exercises selected and subsequent number of repetitions for each exercise. In this case, the number selected is more important than the time for the activity.

5. Vary the intensity of the exercise program according to the individual's tolerance level and component of fitness. Most cardiorespiratory exercises are recommended at 60% of the individual's maximum heart rate for minimum improvements. Some conditions, such as asthma and heart conditions, may require exercises of less intensity until the child's exercise tolerance improves. Muscular strength, endurance, and flexibility exercises should be of sufficient intensity to produce changes but should be selected individually within a medical margin of safety.

6. Vary the type of activity according to the component of physical fitness. Activities with high energy costs, such as jogging, cycling, and swimming, will help improve cardiorespiratory endurance and reduce body fat, thus improving the child's body composition. Muscular strength and endurance require a progressive resistance program incorporating free weights, surgical tubing, training machines, hand or wrist weights, or supporting one's body (Figure 23.4) that encourage repetition of movements. Heavy resistance and a minimal amount of repetitions will develop strength, whereas lighter weights or resistance and more repetitions will develop endurance. Flexibility exercises should utilize static stretches held for a given amount of time (at least for 15 seconds). These exercises should be included both in warm-up and cool-down procedures to eliminate injuries, develop range of motion, and prevent contractures, as well as prepare the muscles for vigorous activity.

7. Keep in mind that the psychological limits of activity should be extended for children with disabilities. Children unaccustomed to exercise will reach their psychological limit before they reach their physiological limit. Likewise, the psychological adjustment of some children should be developed to eliminate overprotection and encourage active participation and risk taking.

Figure 23.4 Developing muscular strength.

Program Development Guidelines

Table 23.1 provides program development guidelines that combine all aspects of teaching physical fitness to children with various disabilities.

Table 23.1 Teaching Physical Fitness

Dysfunction	Characteristics	Behavioral Strategies	Physical Activity	Instructional Strategies
COGNITIVE/ BEHAVIORAL Strength/ endurance ROM	Lack of motivation Problems with understanding directions, exerting effort, and completing tasks Aggressive behavior	Token systems Establish communication Peer modeling Self-recording Activity reinforcement Verbal encouragement Visual prompts Buddy system Restructuring task Good behavior game HR monitor	Swimming Cycling Water exercise Dumbbells Isokinetic training Surgical tubing Parachute games Pushups and situps Relaxation training Play and recess Swim training with fins/kickboards Walk/run	Progressive resistance program based on level of functioning and social interaction level; gradually increase from 5–10 reps to several sets of 10 at escalating weight. Emphasize extending task through range of motion in slow, controlled motion; incorporate tension reduction exercises and visual imagery. Pair behavioral prompts with physical activities. Gradually move to activities that can generalize to play, recess, and home environment.
Cardiovascular endurance/ body composition				Aerobic activity, such as walk/ run, stationary cycle, and swimming, paired with reinforcement strategies to gradually extend duration to 20 min. 3 times per week. Emphasize activity that can be used in play and community settings.

Continues.

Table 23.1 Teaching Physical Fitness *(continued)*

Dysfunction	Characteristics	Behavioral Strategies	Physical Activity	Instructional Strategies
HEALTH/ NUTRITIONAL Strength/ endurance ROM Cardiovascular endurance/ body composition	Obesity, low physical functioning	Verbal encouragement Activity reinforcement HR monitor Self-recording Token system Weight reduction program	Surgical tubing Dumbbells Isokinetic training Static strength exercises Flexibility exercises Play-leisure activity Swim training Water exercise Walk/run Stationary cycling Cycling	Emphasize dietary management and consistent level of physical activity. Encourage maintenance of activity level to maintain functional ability and increase strength and tolerance for activity. Establish baseline level of functioning and gradually increase duration to 20–30 minutes. Pair with dietary management and strength program to eliminate body fat and ability to meet demands of physical activity.
MUSCULAR/ ORTHOPEDIC Strength/ endurance ROM Cardiovascular endurance/ body composition	Reduced force output Contractures Muscle imbalance Reduced sensory input and balance Depression/anger	Physical guidance Verbal encouragement Communication Goal setting Dietary counseling Leisure counseling	Progressive resistance Exercise and gait training Surgical tubing Static strength Flexibility exercises Medicine ball Swim training Water exercise Stationary or arm ergometry Therapy ball Sports participation Activities of daily living (ADLs) Swim training Endurance sports	Encourage active movements at the individual's level of functioning. Strengthen remaining and intact muscle in a progressive program to increase functional ability. Encourage activities of daily living to promote independent functioning. If a prosthesis is required, strengthen surrounding muscle group to facilitate movement. Incorporate balance and strength training along with flexibility exercises to restore movement and ambulatory patterns. Implement strength and flexibility training to promote independent functioning for the use of wheelchairs and/or prosthetic devices. Direct sports training and leisure counseling to emphasize active lifestyles and to strengthen the unaffected or remaining functional ability. Encouragement and goal setting should strive to facilitate the child's psychological adjustments to disability.

Table 23.1 Teaching Physical Fitness *(continued)*

Dysfunction	Characteristics	Behavioral Strategies	Physical Activity	Instructional Strategies
NEUROLOGICAL Strength/ endurance ROM	Spastic muscle Contractures Increased sensory input Co-contraction Reduced muscular functioning	Verbal encouragement Activity reinforcement Social interactions Token system	Static flexibility exercises Surgical tubing Relaxation training Water exercises Active and passive movements Therapy ball Swim training to promote movement	Emphasize maintaining ROM and muscle strengthening to prevent contractures. Actively encourage muscle movement in functional skill related to pushing a wheelchair, using a computer, or independent functions. Intact muscle can be strengthened with active and passive movement through the range of motion to develop initial levels of strength. Wasteful motions and contractions may be eliminated with static stretches. Reflexes can be inhibited to initiate purposeful movement.
Cardiovascular endurance/ body composition				Cardiovascular functioning is not a critical goal but can be promoted in aquatic activities or resistance training to increase the level of functioning.
SENSORY Strength/ endurance ROM	Reduced muscular functioning and overall fitness	Physical guidance Establish communication Provide opportunities for participation and play	Strength and endurance exercises Swimming Cycling Play activities	Emphasize participation and opportunities to develop age-appropriate skills. Physical functioning should not be affected by sensory dysfunction.
Cardiovascular endurance/ body composition	Excess body fat			

CHAPTER SUMMARY

1. Physical fitness includes cardiorespiratory endurance, flexibility, muscular strength, endurance, and body composition.

2. According to the AAHPERD's *Physical Best Activity Guide,* the goal of teaching fitness to children should be to help them aquire skills and knowledge to facilitate physical activity.

3. The hierarchical view if achieving fitness involves the following:
   - doing regular exercise
   - acheiving fitness
   - personal exercise patterns
   - self-evaluation
   - problem solving

4. Guidelines for teaching fitness include the folowing:
   - Overload and adaptation principle
   - Progression principle
   - Specificity of exercise principle

5. Exercise should be progressive and based on the individual's tolerance for activity.

6. The frequency of exercise should be three times per week, and the duration 20–30 minutes to develop and maintain functioning.

7. The type and intensity of activity will vary according to the individual's tolerance and level of fitness. Because many individuals with disabilities are inactive it is essential to promote and sustain physical fitness.

REFERENCES

American Alliance for Health, Physical Education, Recreation and Dance (AAHPERD). (1999). *Physical Best Activity Guide*. Champaign, IL: Human Kinetics.

Horvat, M., & Croce, R. (1995). Physical rehabilitation of individuals with mental retardation: Physical fitness and information processing. *Critical Reviews in Physical and Rehabilitation Medicine, 1*(3), 233-252.

McArdle, W. D., Katch, F. I., & Katch, V. L. (2000). *Essentials of exercise physiology* (2nd ed.). Philadelphia: Lippencott Williams & Wilkins.

Wilmore, J. H., & Costill, D. L. (1999). *Physiology of sport and exercise* (2nd Ed.), Champaign, IL: Human Kinetics.

CHAPTER 24

Teaching Motor, Sport, and Play Skills

The ability to move, and move efficiently, is a goal for children as they progress in motor development from clumsiness to mastery. It is evident that this progression is ongoing and can be affected by numerous factors, such as maturation and the environment. For children with disabilities, the ability to acquire efficient motor skills and patterns is directly related to the quality and quantity of opportunity, practice, and instructional experiences afforded the child. Although a specific disability may impede or alter the developmental process, most children can achieve age-level skills with proper instruction, repetition, and practice. To develop these skills, children will require sufficient instruction and opportunity to ensure that learning occurs, the pattern is retained, and control of the movement is achieved and replicated when needed. (See for example, the balance activities shown in Figure 24.1). With the proper amount of instruction and practice, many children will develop specific abilities that can be used in competition.

Initially basic motor abilities may emerge on their own or require some instruction to achieve. Later the inclusion or combination of these skills into patterns will allow children flexibility of movement required for longer or more intricate sequences. Fundamental locomotor and nonlocomotor skills, dance, and perceptual-motor skills directly influence the child's motor ability and skill acquisition. Practice and feedback will allow the child to develop sports skills that can also be used in lifetime and recreational sports.

(a)

(b)

Figure 24.1 Balance activities.

Teaching Guidelines and Strategies

There are several basic principle in teaching movement skills. The following guidelines are examples that can be used to teach movement skills to children with disabilities (Kluka, 1999; Sudgen & Keogh, 1990).

Cognitive Processes and Sensory Integration

1. Intervention programs should reflect the sensory integrative, cognitive, conceptual, and motor components of movement. It is of the utmost importance that teachers distinguish perceptual difficulties from motor organizational problems. If the movement problems are caused by a severe perceptual deficit such as an impairment in vision, then remediation should encompass appropriate verbal instructions and accentuate body awareness and body-in-space exercises; conversely, if the problems arises from developing patterns of motor memories, intervention should emphasize practice and simplifying the task into its component parts.

2. When working with novice performers, instructors should allow the performer time to select a correct response, especially if several possible responses are presented. Consequently, the performer may initially be slow in selecting the correct response if it takes too long to process the information. This movement problem can be alleviated by minimizing the number of possible choices and eliminating distractions during the early stages of learning.

3. Some children do not cope well with vast amounts of sensory input. It is important to limit the number of stimuli presented at one time, thus allowing the child to attend to a smaller amount of information initially that can be gradually extended, processed, and integrated more efficiently. Many times we present children with too much information and ultimately confuse them.

Apply the Concepts of Practice and Knowledge of Results

1. Teachers must distinguish practice performance (temporary effects) from retention performance (permanent effects). Learning involves relatively permanent changes in performance and must be evaluated after temporary effects have dissipated, possibly a week or so after concluding the teaching of the skill (retention performance). The child should have opportunities to apply the learned skill in school and community environments. The teacher can also modify the task for alternative environments by altering the speed with which the skill is performed or by changing the size of objects used in skill execution.

2. Learning is frequently related directly to the amount of practice time. Children should receive the opportunity to practice tasks in a variety of environments and situations. Varying the environment fosters cognition during motor skill acquisition and enhances the ability to retain and transfer skills. Unpredictable schedules of reinforcement and feedback and limited knowledge of results will force children to problem solve and to develop learning strategies during practice sessions as seen in the body management movement sequence in Figure 24.2.

For example, the teacher can increase task difficulty by teaching the task in an open environment by first throwing bean bags at target and then making it more

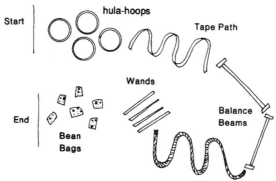

Figure 24.2 Varying the context to promote skill aquisition.

unpredictable by moving the target or the performer (Figure 24.3). During practice sessions, teachers should strive to present the skills not only in open environments, but also to organize sessions so that more than one task is learned under variable and random contexts. For example, practice sessions could involve asking the child to throw a bean bag or a ball from different angles or using different speeds, or at several different targets at varying distances away. The teacher can also vary the task during practice sessions rather than monotonously performing the same skill over and over again under the same, predictable environmental contexts; this will also increase motivation. Although random presentation of skills may be detrimental to practice performance, it is beneficial for retention and transfer of the acquired task (actual learning).

3. Frequent, immediate feedback may enhance performance during initial states of learning but may be ineffective for long-term skill retention. The preponderance of the research suggests that practice conditions with extrinsic feedback withheld on some trials, or delayed even for seconds after a trial, are more effective for learning than practice conditions using frequent feedback or using feedback presented instantaneously after an action.

4. Many functional tasks such as throwing use multiple criterion speeds. During class, children should practice these skills at multiple speeds (Figure 24.4). When accuracy and speed are both critical components of a task, which they often are, both speed and accuracy should be emphasized early in practice. Overall, docu-

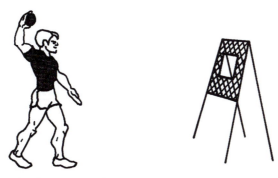

Figure 24.3 Throwing for accuracy: balls and targets of various sizes.

Figure 24.4 Varying throwing practice.

mentation of an individual's performance should include performance at multiple speeds with multiple strategies and should include multiple or changing task environments.

Understand the Task and the Environmental Context

1. Skill is the ability to solve context-dependent problems with a degree of consistency and economy of motion. Economy of motion implies that skillful persons use the optimal biomechanical and physiological solution for a problem. Teachers must provide individuals with opportunities to find the optimal solutions to meet their movement goals. To accomplish this task, certain characteristics of the individual (e.g., strength, endurance, range of motion, manual dexterity) may need to be maximized, and/or the environment within which the skill takes place may need to be adapted.

2. A concept known as degrees of freedom (dfs) is important for teachers. Degrees of freedom refers to the limited number of independent parts of the human body that can be used within the environment to produce a particular movement. A particular movement, narrowed from a wide range of potential movements, becomes skilled motor performance when and only when the body is directed into appropriate performance. For example, the golf swing contains numerous degrees of freedom. The potential movements possible at the joints in the foot (dorsiflexion–plantarflexion, inversion–eversion), knee (flexion–extension, internal rotation–external rotation, hip (flexion–extension, abduction–adduction, internal rotation–external rotation), trunk (lateral flexion, flexion–extension, rotation), shoulder (flexion–extension, abduction–adduction, internal rotation–external rotation), scapula (upward rotation–downward rotation, protraction–retraction, elevation–depression), elbow and forearm (flexion–extension, pronation–supination), wrist and fingers (flexion–extension, abduction–adduction), as well as the particular muscles involved to perform these actions, constitute alternatives of movement or degrees of freedom. They provide the many alternatives that must be constrained to produce the most efficient and effective movement. In certain situations, one might need to restrict the number of dfs used by the individual during the early stages of movement and then "unlock" more and more dfs as the individual becomes more highly skilled. A skill with several dfs may require several movements to efficiently coordinate the task.

Ordinarily, individuals with motor problems have a greater problem in controlling the many dfs available. In the golf swing, for example, children need to concentrate on certain elements of the swing initially. Instruction might, therefore, involve teaching these individuals how to initially control these such as the take-away and follow through dfs and slowly unlocking these dfs as skill efficiency and coordination as the skill is attained. This will allow for a greater degree of success during the early stages of movement which, in turn, would motivate the individual to proceed further into the learning process.

3. The concept of phase shifts is important in the transition from an inefficient to efficient movement pattern. It is often during this period of phase shifts when teachers may have their greatest impact on children by identifying and manipulating parameters that help control the movement, as in throwing a ball harder or softer depending on the task requirement.

Training of Rehearsal Strategies

Programs may also use memory strategies, especially for individuals with mental retardation or individuals with developmental disabilities. Motor memory involves stored sensory information that is associated with a motor activity that reminds an individual what specific movements feel like or how movements are visual represented. Performance can be altered or changed through visualization and mental training to meet information processing requirements. For example, individuals with capacity or cognitive limitations can practice small components of a task and gradually extend their participation. Also, individuals can select from several strategies such as visualization or prompting (visual or verbal) when required to remember bits of information, which can improve the efficiency of information processing.

Task Analysis

1. A skill may be acquired by breaking it into meaningful components than can be learned and practiced as separate tasks. If children have attention difficulties or problems completing the assigned task, a skill can be separated into subtasks that can be combined into more progressive units and, finally, the complete skill. For example, teaching a child to hit may involve holding the bat, stepping, hip rotation and follow-through, and contact with the ball (Figure 24.5).

2. Closely aligned to analyzing a task is the concept of part-whole method. For some children, using the entire skill may be easier than breaking the skill into subskills.

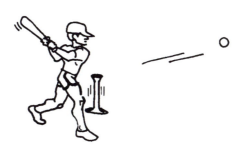

Figure 24.5 Task analysis of hitting.

In other cases, the task can be broken into meaningful parts that also take into account any environmental constraints.

3. An activity can also be modified to fit the ability levels of children. For children who have difficulties understanding rules or working together, a smaller area with fewer participants may be needed for learning to occur. Gradually we can expand the area or add specific rules as children learn more about the task. As teachers we commonly use this approach in games such as basketball, that require a different set of skills for a full-court 5-on-5 game as opposed to 2-on-2 in a restricted area. Likewise, in resistance training we use variable types of resistance or equipment to accommodate individual differences. Table 24.1 provides additional instructional strategies for children.

Teaching Strategies

Movement in the form of motor skills, sports, and play should be actively encouraged to facilitate functioning and dependence in children with disabilities. The following teaching strategies can be used to develop movement, play and sport skills for children with disabilities.

1. Select skills based on the child's developmental level.

2. Select skills that are functional for the child, such as developing balance by walking up and down steps or curbs as opposed to walking only a balance beam.

3. Develop movement concepts such as "up" and "down" as a basis for pattern and skill development.

4. Encourage distributed practice and additional opportunities, such as homework or outside-the-school activities, to promote repetition of movement and retention. Distributed practice contains rest components between attempts. This is in contrast to massed practice, which involves little or no rest between attempts and can directly impact on the level of fatigue in the learner. In general, the higher the level of fatigue, the more detrimental is the performance outcome: Physiological fatigue tends to hamper speed, while cognitive or central processing fatigue tends to hamper accuracy.

5. Emphasize the child's abilities, not his or her disabilities.

6. Develop and emphasize concepts and patterns before requiring skill or precision from the child.

7. Emphasize functional skill development that allows children to participate in playground, neighborhood, and/or recreational activities.

8. Once the pattern is learned, provide children with opportunities to retain their level of proficiency.

9. Development of physical fitness should occur concurrently to assist in the development of movement patterns.

10. Children should develop closed tasks before open tasks and/or environmental or temporal influences are introduced.

11. Prompting and reinforcement should accompany initial efforts at learning a task.

Program Development Guidelines

Table 24.1 provides program development guidelines that combine all aspects of teaching play, sports, and motor skills to children with various disabilities.

Table 24.1 Teaching Motor, Sport and Play Skills

Dysfunction	Characteristics	Behavioral Strategies	Instructional Strategies
Cognitive/ behavioral	Difficulty in maintaining attention Difficulty in understanding task Problems with task completion Impulsive behaviors	Prompt or cue instruction Provide specific feedback Task analysis Part-whole methods Eliminate distractions Behavioral prompting Reward system	Structure the environments and teaching instructions. Utilize a part method or task analysis while teaching the skill. Begin with individual and small group activities, and encourage motor skills required for play.
Muscular/ orthopedic	Low muscular functioning Muscle imbalance Reduced sensory input	Physical guidance and prompting Task analysis Part-whole method Goal setting Rehearsal and specific feedback	Promote large muscle activities and remaining functional ability. Modify activities or equipment to initiate skill development. Use feedback to encourage body awareness and feel of movements.
Neurological	Spastic muscle contractures Increased sensory input Co-contraction	Physical prompting Positioning and handling Inhibit reflexes Strengthen intact muscle	Promote relaxation activities and control of movement to facilitate mechanical efficiency. Concentrate on functional tasks related to ADLs and self-sufficiency.
Sensory	Reduced or no sensory input Hyperactivity Lack of understanding	Physical guidance and verbal/visual prompts Establish communication Orientation and mobility	Encourage body awareness and identifying body parts and relationships. Encourage participation and functioning to build self-confidence, and utilize communication systems and prompts to facilitate instruction.
Health/nutritional	Low physical functioning Obesity	Verbal encouragement Activity reinforcement Self-recording Prompting	Encourage physical activity as a means of managing disease or illness. Encourage activities and skill that can be used for recreational and play skills that allow for periods of rest.

Chapter Summary

1. Movement proficiency is directly related to the quality of opportunity, practice, and instruction. Many children with disabilities do not have opportunities to participate in play activities.

2. Guidelines to teach movement skills including the following:

   • Provide intervention programs that reflect sensory integration, cognition and conceptual components of movement.

   • Avoid overstimulating children with vast amounts of sensory stimuli, and provide time to process information.

   • Utilize practice to learn the skill, and provide opportunities for retention and generalization to the community environment. Practice should be carried out in a variety of environments and situations. Feedback also should be used to promote learning and correction of errors in performance.

   • Analyze the task and environment so that they can be presented to the child at a level to meet movement goals. Tasks may be restructured to find components that allow the child to attain success before moving to more difficult components.

   • Prompt memory functions and specific feedback by practicing small components of a task and extending a child's participation. Prompting or teaching aids can also aid in providing information for skill acquisition.

3. Teaching strategies should focus on the child's:

   • development level

   • ability, not disability

   • functional skill development

   • practice and outside-the-school opportunities

   • opportunities for generalizations

   • prompting and reinforcement strategies

4. The concepts of movement and play should be actively encouraged. Children with disabilities often are restricted in their opportunites to move and learn. The lack of participation is a major component in the lower levels of fitness and motor development displayed by some children.

References

Kluka, D. A. (1999). *Motor behavior: From learning to performance.* Englewood, CO: Morton Publishing Company.

Sudgen, D. A., & Keogh, J. F. (1990). *Problems in movement skill development.* Columbia, SC: USC Press.

CHAPTER 25

Teaching Aquatic Skills

The aquatic environment is especially appropriate for the development of physical and motor functioning. Swimming can contribute to the individual's total development and can be therapeutic in nature. The water may minimize the effects of the individual's limitations. In the water, the individual can move freely without being encumbered by a wheelchair, braces, or the land environment. Balance is not as great a factor, and more movements may be performed in the water. Furthermore, the individual's attention span may be improved, behavior problems are not as prevalent, and the water is naturally reinforcing to most individuals.

As this environment may produce some anxiety, the teacher has the opportunity to assist the individual in developing self-confidence. In turn, the individual may develop a positive self-concept through successful aquatic activities. Additionally, aquatics may provide an opportunity for the family to participate together and enjoy the water. Many families who have a child with disabilities do not engage in family-oriented activities; however, if the child is safe in the water and enjoys the activity, aquatics is perfect to promote family togetherness and leisure-time activities.

The water environment is also a superior place to develop and maintain physical fitness. Through the different activities, the child can strengthen muscles, make joints more flexible, experience various sensory stimulations, and increase muscular and cardiorespiratory endurance. Also, many activities that are not possible on land can be performed in the water.

In the same respect, the water environment allows the teacher to establish beginning movement patterns that allow an individual to explore movement possibilities. This enables children to move body parts they would not be able to move on land as a start toward establishing movement patterns. For some children, for example, the water environment enables them to sit unsupported (Figure 25.1).

Figure 25.1 Sitting unsupported.

If one is using the aquatic environment for exercise purposes, it is important to understand some basic principles regarding buoyancy. Archimedes' principle states that when a body is immersed in a fluid, it experiences an upward thrust equal to the weight of the fluid displaced. This upward thrust is buoyancy. Therefore, a body in water is subjected to two opposing forces: gravity and buoyancy. Buoyancy is an upward thrust and opposes the downward thrust of gravity. Three concepts regarding buoyancy will affect instructors in aquatic exercise programming. These concepts are buoyancy assisted, buoyancy resisted, and buoyancy supported.

1. Buoyancy assisted describes a movement that is assisted by buoyancy forces. This occurs when the movement is in the same direction as the force of buoyancy. Hence, when a child lifts his or her arm or leg up to the water surface, the force of buoyancy assists that movement.

2. Buoyancy supported describes a movement that is perpendicular to the force of buoyancy. In this case, the water simply supports the body or the extremity.

3. Buoyancy resisted describes a movement that opposes the force of buoyancy. For example, when a person moves a limb toward the water surface, the movement is being assisted because it is moving in the same direction as the buoyancy force. When the limb is returned to the beginning position, the muscles must work much harder because the movement is working against the force of buoyancy; in other words, it is a buoyancy-resisted movement. Anything moving up toward the surface of the water will be buoyancy assisted, and anything moving down through the water away from the surface will be buoyancy resisted.

4. Finally, resistance may be increased by increasing the drag force acting on the moving body part. This can be accomplished by having the individual increase the surface area being moved. For example, when performing arm exercises, one can use paddles to increase the surface area and, hence, increase the drag force acting against the limb. This will add additional resistance to the movement.

Teaching Guidelines

The success of an instructional program in aquatics is achieved by adhering to specific instructional procedures, guidelines, and strategies. However, although these guidelines are basically similar for all individuals, modifications and adaptations are often needed to meet each individual's unique needs.

The teacher should be flexible in planning for each individual. For instance, it may be desirable to teach one child to swim on his or her back, but another may learn faster in a prone position. By maintaining flexibility in the teaching program, the teacher can individualize skills according to the child's abilities or fitness levels and modify the program. Furthermore, the teacher should not hesitate to modify a skill to accommodate an individual's particular deficiency. For example, a flotation device that stabilizes the head and neck can help someone with poor head control to assume a back-lying position in the water. Another child, with limited or no controlled movement of the lower extremities, may utilize a shortened version of the elementary backstroke or a dog paddle to propel through the water. This kind of flexibility allows each child to progress at an individual rate and to perform successful movements in the water.

Teachers should be aware of swimming progressions, that is, the progression from simple to advanced swimming skills. After a progression has been established, the teacher can identify subskills, reinforcement procedures, and instructional cues (Horvat & Forbus, 1989).

Subskills

The progression of swimming skills is, in effect, a task analysis; that is, skills are broken down into subskills. When the individual completes a small step, the next subskill may be attempted. After continuous repetition, another subskill may be incorporated in conjunction with the first subskill. In this manner, the teacher can teach a new skill while providing the repetition necessary to maintain the first subskill. For example, once a kicking technique is established, the teacher may have the child practice this skill while learning basic arm movements (Figure 25.2). The repetition is necessary to add more skills progressively to the individual's repertoire and ensure retention of these skills.

Reinforcement

A reinforcer is presented following a response that the clinician wishes to occur with greater frequency. Some individuals prefer praise, hugs, and smiles, whereas others may require tangible rewards, such as stars, stickers, patches, and edibles. In addition, a favorite activity can also be used as a reinforcer. For example, water play using the following items may serve as reinforcement:

- inner tubes
- balls
- plastic toys
- squirt guns
- slides
- diving rings
- balloons
- swim fins
- diving board

If tangible or activity reinforcers are used, reward the individual if the skill or subskill was performed to the criteria established to gain the reinforcer (i.e., number of kicks, quality of arm pull, distance covered, time of floating, and so on). An individual may be praised for attempting a specific skill but should also be praised when the complete skill is accomplished. It is important that the reinforcer be appropriate for the response elicited.

Cues

Many children will require a prompt or a manually assistive approach to swimming. In this manner, the teacher can guide the individual through the intended movement.

Figure 25.2 Initiating kicking pattern.

Figure 25.3 Water entry.

As the individual becomes more proficient, the teacher may partially prompt or fade out this procedure entirely. Finally, simple verbal cues may be utilized as well as physical prompts. For example, the word "kick" can be repeated while the instructor moves the individual's legs in a kicking motion. In a similar manner, "arms" can cue the individual to move the arms with the instructor's guidance. As a result, teachers can fade out the prompting procedure when the individual performs the intended motion with only the verbal cue.

Avoidance

Fear is a factor that will affect the efforts of children to learn new skills. Trembling and muscular tension are physical conditions that the teacher must deal with often. By using behavioral techniques, the teacher can help the child relax and overcome anxiety associated with the water. The child's first experiences should be pleasurable, and it is important to give continual praise for any accomplishment. By including the following, the child may more easily adjust to the water and eliminate fear.

1. *Water adjustment.* The individual should be provided with several pleasurable experiences prior to entering the pool. Water play, splashing, plastic wading pools, and wet sponges can promote a child's feelings of comfort about the environment before water entry (Figure 25.3).

2. *Gradual participation.* The individual may be encouraged to participate gradually by first putting the feet in the water, watching another child in the water, and then entering the water with the clinician.

3. *Flotation.* The individual should be initially supported by a mat or flotation device or by the teacher or parent (Figure 25.4). In this manner he or she may enjoy the

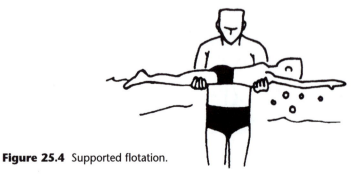

Figure 25.4 Supported flotation.

water while being supported. As the child increases functioning and reliance on supports, less assistance will be required.

4. *Building trust.* The individual should not be expected to do a skill without knowledge. If you want to take the child underwater, announce you are going to blow bubbles and go underwater yourself. In this manner, the child will feel more secure and will perform new maneuvers with more trust. Many times children will be more compliant if they know what is expected.

5. *Praise.* The child should be continually praised for any attempt at the skill. Fearful children need more praise and reassurance and will begin to learn only once the fear is overcome.

6. *Transfer or generalization.* The teacher can "transfer" or "generalize" behavior, that is, take behavior performed in one setting and use it in another. For example, water play or placing someone's face in the water or in a plastic pool can be transferred to the swimming pool.

Additional Teaching Guidelines

The following guidelines can be used to teach aquatic skills for children with disabilities (Horvat & Forbus, 1989; Lepore, Gayle & Stevens, 1998).

1. Keep in mind that many individuals may be uncomfortable or fearful of the water. A variety of different sensations and environments are needed as they experience the water.

2. Constant repetition of the same skill is not motivating. A variety of activities and games, or variations of practice, can enhance not only the enjoyment of the activity, but also retention and generalization.

3. A demonstration by another child may be more helpful than a demonstration by the teacher.

4. Ensure that the individual is safe during all phases of the lesson. Plan for emergencies, such as seizures, and ensure safety while having fun.

5. Allow the individual to be as independent as possible while in the water. Do not overcompensate for disabilities if the skill is within their own range of capability.

6. Fatigue, illness, cold water, and uncomfortable surroundings will affect the individual's performance and ability to learn. If the individual is tired or cold, allow opportunities for other activities, or discontinue the lesson.

7. Movement that is prohibited on land can often be performed in the water. Encourage attempts to stand, walk, and move in a variety of ways.

8. Manual support for severely involved swimmers during balancing, moving, and floating activities will help reduce the individual's anxieties. Use the best working body position to provide support, but not lifting the swimmer over the water, to stimulate a floating position.

9. Entry into the water is usually easier by sitting on the side, rolling over onto the stomach, and then sliding into the pool. This is the desired progression for individuals with sufficient body control. As the individual progresses and becomes more comfortable with this new environment, use different methods for entry

(e.g., wading, jumping, diving from the kneeling position, and so on). For an individual without sufficient body control, manual support should be utilized.

10. Select equipment with a specific purpose. For example, sponges can be used for water adjustment, Ping-Pong balls for bubble blowing, and so on. Suggested equipment includes hoops, foam or plastic balls, beach balls, cups, spoons, bubble blowers, plastic bottles, plastic flowers, pots, pans, washcloths, sinkable rings, plastic tubs, and small wading pools.

11. If you are using water for therapeutic purposes, you should ensure that the water temperature is from 88 to 92 degrees Fahrenheit. A water temperature within this range will minimize muscle tightening and spasticity. In addition, to ensure that the pool is accessible to persons with disabilities, make sure that chair lifts, ramps, steps with railings, and hoists are available.

Teaching Strategies

Teaching strategies that should be included in any aquatic program for individuals with disabilities include the following. (Additional program development guidelines have been designed specifically for various disabilities; see Table 25.1 on pages 415–416).

1. Find the individual's level of attention. If the attention span is quite short, the teacher will need to have several activities that work toward a certain objective. For example, if the objective is working on breath control skills, the individual can blow air into the instructor's hand or own hand; blow air at a Ping-Pong ball, toy boat, or balloon; blow bubbles; and, to initiate the head-turn with breathing, "talk to the fish, listen to the fish" (Figure 25.5).

2. Make sure that a measure of success is built into each and every activity or experience in which the individual participates. This will provide positive reinforcement and give a sense of accomplishment. Positive verbal and physical reinforcement should be provided to the child when a job is well done or attempted. Tangible reinforcers (i.e., food and candy) should not be given unless cleared with the parent.

3. Plan lessons in a progression from simple to complex. Take into account the individual's present levels of performance.

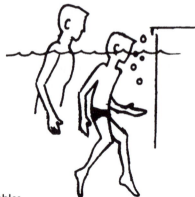

Figure 25.5 Blowing bubbles.

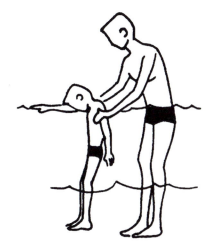

Figure 25.6 Physical prompt.

4. When explaining skills to the individual, use words that will be understood. Keep the words simple and at a minimum when giving instruction.

5. Skills should be based on individualized task analysis, including the child's developmental level, needs, and learning characteristics.

6. Skills should be based on developmental age; however, the teacher should also be aware of the chronological age-appropriate tasks and social/recreational outlets for the individual.

7. Instruction should follow a continuum that incorporates the following:

   a. sensory stimulation and development—from reaction to stimuli to learning a basic motor skill

   b. passive assistance (Figure 25.6) to independent responses (Figure 25.7)

   c. cephalocaudal to proximodistal development

   d. simple to complex tasks

   e. gross to fine motor movements

8. Equipment should be modified and adapted when necessary. Swimming assists, such as kickboards and pull-buoys or fins, should be used to support the child.

9. Reflex actions need to be inhibited as purposeful movement is initiated.

10. Appropriate behavior management techniques should be used to initiate, maintain, or eliminate responses.

Figure 25.7 Independent response.

Figure 25.8 Combining skills.

11. Skills that are used in the home and school environments should be learned.

12. Experiences in a variety of settings are suggested to incorporate multiple movements and generalization of movements.

13. Rest periods should be provided periodically. This will help overcome premature fatigue and the individual's low frustration tolerance.

14. Brief directions should be used, as well as tactile, kinesthetic, visual, and auditory cues.

15. Opportunities to practice newly learned skills should be plentiful. Each lesson should not only introduce new tasks, but also review previously learned tasks.

16. Activities and skills may best be taught by using the part-whole teaching approach. This approach accomodates lower levels of comprehension; also, it builds on previously learned and practiced skills and ultimately enables the child to combine skills (Figure 25.8).

17. Competitive games and competition must be used carefully. Excessive emphasis on competition may result in the child becoming withdrawn, aggressive, or uninterested in the activity.

18. Consider the use of an exploratory movement teaching approach. Movement exploration requires no one correct response from the individual. Thus it increases the potential for the child to experience success.

Table 25.1 Teaching Aquatic Skills

Dysfunction	Characteristics	Behavioral Strategies	Instructional Strategies
Cognitive/ behavioral	Instability of cervical vertebrae Difficulty in maintaining attention Problems with task completion Impulse behaviors	Prohibit flexion, hypertension of neck Provide specific feedback Prompt or cue instruction Restructure tasks Use a reward system Eliminate distractions Use personal floatation devices	Provide instruction based on entry level and simple direct instructions. Pair physical prompts and verbal cues to initiate responses, gradually fading prompts. Reinforce all attempts at task completion and appropriate behavior. Gradually extend the task and add components as skill level increases. Utilize flotation devices and physical prompting until child can initiate movement. Feedback should be specific and tasks repeated to ensure learning and generalization to other skills and play activities.

Table 25.1 Teaching Aquatic Skills *(continued)*

Dysfunction	Characteristics	Behavioral Strategies	Instructional Strategies
Muscular/ orthopedic	Contractures Low muscle force Muscle imbalance Reduced sensory input Depression/anger	Physical guidance Verbal encouragement Goal setting Dietary counseling Play Positioning and handling	Injury prevention is essential. Emphasize positioning and handling to ensure safe transfers. Water should be warmer to aid muscle movements and prevent stiffness in joints. Set goals to improve strength and flexibility needed for independent functioning. Personal flotation devices can aid in supporting the body until physical functioning is developed. Encourage passive and active movement to facilitate self-control and ambulation. Major goal is to achieve independent functioning, which may require stroke modification and enjoyment. If joints or flexibility are restricted, use isometric or water exercises.
Neurological	Spastic muscle Contractures Increased sensory input Reduced muscular functioning	Physical prompting Positioning and handling Flotation devices Inhibition of reflexes Maintenance of water temperature at minimum of 86°F	Stabilize the head to inhibit reflex movement, and strengthen neck area to achieve stability. Use physical prompts by the instructor or floating mat to stabilize body parts. Encourage swimming on back to allow breath control, and provide physical prompts, and cue movements. Gradually increase movements as muscles are strengthened and flexibility is improved. Keep child warm after exiting the pool.
Sensory	Reduced or no sensory input Hyperactivity	Establish communication Physical guidance and verbal/visual prompts	Adapt visual or verbal directions to the level of residual vision or hearing. For hearing impairments, incorporate a system of communication and physical guidance to facilitate instruction. However, too much sound in the pool can disrupt the use of residual hearing. Hand signals can start and stop an activity while visual aids can complement instruction. When sight is diminished, auditory signals can indicate different ends of the pool. Lane lines will also be useful while the swimmer can count the number of strokes needed to cross the pool. For all children, active participation should be encouraged to promote physical functioning.

Continues.

Table 25.1 Teaching Aquatic Skills *(continued)*

Dysfunction	Characteristics	Behavioral Strategies	Instructional Strategies
Health/nutritional	Low physical functioning Obesity	Verbal encouragement Activity reinforcement Self-recording Prompting	Establish a baseline level of functioning, and gradually increase level of activity. Refine strokes for more efficient movements, and provide rest periods and intervals as needed. Use kickboard, fins and pull-buoys to build endurance.

CHAPTER SUMMARY

1. Skills should be selected according to the child's functional ability.

2. Children should develop their physical fitness as well as swimming skills.

3. Instruction should be based on progressions from water orientation to advanced swimming skills.

4. Swimming techniques should be emphasized to alleviate undue stress and increase tolerance for exercise.

5. Swimming assists, such as kickboards and pull-buoys, should be used to increase participation and to support children in the water.

6. Teachers should not hesitate to modify a skill to accomodate the child.

7. Manual support and prompting will aid in increasing confidence and functioning.

8. Instruction should include sensory stimulation and cues, rest periods, games, and multiple movement experiences.

9. Skills that can be used at home or in the community are desirable.

REFERENCES

Horvat, M. A., & Forbus, W. R. (1989). *Using the aquatic environment for teaching handicapped children* (2nd ed.). Kearney, NE: Educational Systems Associates.

Lepore, M., Gayle, G. W., & Stevens, S. (1998). *Adapted aquatics programming: A professional guide*. Champaign, IL: Human Kinetics.

Index